Without memory there is no culture,
and without culture there is no future.

Anonymous

CAVORTING ═ *with* ═ STRANGERS

Great Ideas and their Champions

PARIS

F. Patrick Butler

CAVORTING WITH STRANGERS
Great Ideas and their Champions — Volume I: Paris
Copyright © 2007 by F. Patrick Butler

Cypress House
155 Cypress Street
Fort Bragg, CA 95437
(800) 773-7782
www.cypresshouse.com

Cover and book design: Michael Brechner / Cypress House
Author's photograph: Erin Frances Butler

PERMISSIONS / CREDITS

Front cover photograph by Brassaï (Gyula Halasz), "Bijou at La Lune bar, Montmartre," circa 1930-1932; Paris, Musée National d'Art Moderne, Centre Georges Pompidou; © ESTATE BRASSAÏ – RMN; CNAC/MNAM / Dist. Réunion des musées nationaux / Art Resource, New York. Used with permission.

Excerpt from Voltaire's letter on page 30 is from *The Story of Civilization X: Rousseau and Revolution*, by Will and Ariel Durant. Copyright © 1967 by Will and Ariel Durant. Reprinted with the permission of Simon and Schuster Adult Publishing Group.

Quotations on pp. 201 and 262 are from *Monet*, by Sophie Fourny-Dargere, English translation: Rosetta Translation, Konecky & Konecky. Reprinted with the permission of W.S. Konecky Associates.

LIBRARY OF CONGRESS CATALOGING-IN-PUBLICATION DATA

Butler, F. Patrick.
  Cavorting with strangers : great ideas and their champions-Paris / by F. Patrick Butler. -- 1st ed.
    p. cm.
  Includes bibliographical references.
  ISBN-13: 978-1-879384-71-2 (pbk. : alk. paper)
  I. Title.
  PS3602.U87C38 2006
  813'.6--dc22

                    2006018262

PRINTED IN THE UNITED STATES OF AMERICA
1 2 3 4 5 6 7 8 9

To Vice President Albert A. Gore
in recognition of his service to our country
and his energetic contributions to saving our
environment through the medium of culture

I started writing this book ten years ago in Monterrey, Mexico, with my partner, Ines Gassner. It began as one project among others. Ines made chess sets for sale and I taught at Monterrey Institute of Technology. When the time came to move on, we did, leaving behind our friends while gathering up two street dogs—Peanuts and Wags—who joined us for the ride.

We went where the jobs took us, happily surviving, but rarely prospering: Boca Raton, Kufstein, Innsbruck, Lugano. The project grew, more the threat of German and Italian TV than any unusual work ethic. Since I was never "given" time from my teaching to do it, I simply took it. Ines redirected her interests toward teaching and getting a master's. I spent many nights with Peanuts or Wags at my feet. My family encouraged me, but MaryLane, my eldest sister, said things that even an ocean away gave me inspiration for the developing manuscript; things that if not deserved were readily accepted while I rolled like the dogs in the fragrance.

Writing, as any author knows, is a lonely business, and as Ines pointed out on many occasions, patently antisocial. After a while, nothing stood in my way. I nurtured the manuscript like the proverbial demanding child. During evening dinners at McDonald's I started to read the *Financial Times Weekend Edition* religiously. The journalists were remarkable in their insight into our worldly culture, and their professional talents unparalleled. I am indebted to them all, in short, God bless the *Financial Times*.

Finally, the manuscript was finished, sent to a few agents and publishers—and ignored. Point of fact, I didn't think much of *them* either. In the striving, however, one gentleman's name came up from a respected source in the business, Joe Shaw, an editor at Cypress House. He read the manuscript and was complimentary. He was also, remarkably erudite (as a university teacher with thirty years under my belt, I know the meaning of erudite), and an honest friend. He was kind, smart, and critical; in my opinion a requisite set of talents for an editor. So we joined forces, which, with Cynthia Frank's sure eye for success, Michael Brechner, whose superb artistic skill creating the book cover and typesetting brought the book to life, and others on the Cypress House staff, helped to bring this book to you.

$\equiv$ CONTENTS $\equiv$

CONTENTS

Volume I: Paris

Therefore, as painters in their portraits labor the likeness in the face, and particularly about the eyes, and run over the rest with a more careless hand; so we must be permitted to strike on the features of the soul to give a real likeness to these great men.

Plutarch, *Life of Alexander*

Please Note: The historical facts related in this book were collected on the basis of research material provided in published sources written for the most part by established experts or professional journalists and are, therefore, accurate or "nonfiction" to that extent. The fictional characters and episodes are not meant to resemble any particular persons or events, and their lives as depicted in this book are entirely fictitious.

A LETTER ABOUT STRANGERS

Dear Reader,

It is claimed that the art of being boring consists in leaving nothing out. This book, I am happy to say, should leave one startled by its simplicity. Ironically, it is about ideas, which are plentiful, and, as René Descartes offered regarding common sense, an attribute in which few feel deficient. Nonetheless, I have tried to capture only those thoughts that are appealing, that are found successful if not enduring, and notable if not profound. And these, whether philosophical, political, artistic, or literary, have a distinctly French flavor; you get the picture. But it is also about the people, known by some, but strangers to many, who championed these ideas, each in his or her own way, by struggling toward humanity's horizons, and how we feel about them today. Finally, it embodies controversy, since contradictions in human character are one of its most consistent notes.[1]

Few have described the French character as either meek or humble. Toynbee pointed out long ago the Frenchman's habit of preaching repose while lauding martial qualities: "a lullaby performed on a trombone," he was heard to chuckle. In recognition of this disposition, there is one small incident from the 17th century, related by W. H. Lewis, that, for this author, captures the moment of the modern French national persona. On the morning of September 5, 1638, a son was born to Louis XIII and his Spanish queen, Anne of Austria, in the château of St. Germain. He was the first child of parents who hated each other, and who had been married for twenty-three years. The birth was hailed by all as a miracle, and the little dauphin was given the name Dieudonné, gift of God. The wine ran free and even the hungry were fed.[2]

From his cold-blooded, shifty, suspicious father the child seemed to have inherited nothing but a love of music and an interest in the minutiae of army administration, while to his mother he owed, among other things, a magnificent constitution and indomitable pride.

From the first, Louis was remembered as a solemn child, very well aware of who he was and what he was to be. His earliest recorded utterance is characteristic: on April 21, 1643, being then not five years old, he was taken to the bedside of his dying father. "Who is it?" asked the king. "Louis XIV," replied his son.[3]

So the French lean toward the imperious—nice story, not much new. But it could just be that we all secretly envy the French people, since they personify to many of us that matchless hubris that we attribute to dictators and the other strong-willed who tightly grasp the reins of their own destinies and literally make a world of difference. Just ask the likes of a Napoleon, Chanel, or de Gaulle.

Hopefully, you will find, despite some interesting lessons in arrogance, conviction, and culture, that the book's intent is to be entertaining. Without, however, looking for too-great portents in such a small vessel, you might also discover something you have lost, lost without realizing, or if realizing did not expect: your destiny.

Whoa! Destiny? That is a serious word, one too vital for the likes of this text and its author. Nonetheless, (with the reader's permission) discovering your destiny—some might call it your vision—is a lifelong project, more revealed than found.

How is it, then, one could ask, that the individuals in this book discovered and met their destinies, which changed the course of human progress? They were unique, but certainly not all celebrated; some died rich and at the pinnacle of their success, while others expired sick, hunted, penniless, and alone. They all began as an unimpressive lot: one copied music for a living, another made hats, yet another was a provincial teacher whose only exploits in WW II were as a theater director in a German prison camp. Nonetheless, for those like you, perhaps, who seek lessons, their lives and fortune are instructive enough.

The book's title, *Cavorting With Strangers: Great Ideas and Their Champions,* means to make merry with, well—unfamiliar people. These famous men and women, usually French and whose names many know, but only vaguely so, have egos that were uniquely altered and are now acclaimed revolutionaries of the human spirit. It could be then, like Pinocchio's shabby friends, that they will whisper of adventure, coaxing you to run off with them to do crazy things like painting nudes in Tahiti, opening a dress shop in Paris, espousing the destruction of sitting governments, or falling prey to some other nefarious end.

And, they were a sleazy lot. Consider this: despite fathering the ideals behind the French and American Revolutions, bringing down some of the great monarchies of Europe, Jean-Jacques Rousseau's youthful indiscretions included dropping his pants and exposing himself from the darkened corners of the village square to titillate the girls and faking insanity when he was caught. While none other than Victor Hugo, it was rumored, deflowered his daughter's first communion companion after Mass. Or Napoleon, deserting his men to die in the Russian snow while he hastily returned to Paris to save his throne; or Chanel collaborating with the Nazis to keep her suite at the Ritz Hotel; or Sartre sleeping with his lover's students and adopting one.

It all makes interesting reading, but make no mistake, despite their vaunted reputations, these citizens were just as sick as the best of us, so you won't have to bend over far to see the underbelly of fame. Therefore, put those pompous testaments of their superlative qualities away, their disembodied quotes hung out on the line to impress us. This book isn't about their fresh linens, but the personal lives of the people who soiled them.

The French Revolution seemed a likely place to start, or as close as one could strive for a time to be called "relevant." Louis XIV, the Sun King, had set the stage, and Versailles stood in his place, a symbol of more than royal housing. His successors, Louis XV and XVI, paid brief visits to history, but were more famous for their women: Madame De Pompadour and Marie Antoinette. Louis XVI, lacking any unusual talents except as a locksmith, was beheaded—by Robespierre and his lackeys—mourning the theft of his slippers, which, he lamented, had taken the shape of his feet. In Europe, the curtain was rising on Paris, the City of Light, the Capital of the 19th Century.[4]

To start with the French Revolution is debatable, of course. It was a terrible idea to many, supposedly dreamed up by disgruntled aristocrats, egged on by what Simon Schama in *Citizens*[5] calls the "polemical incontinence" of hack writers and bad actors. Individuals, he said, who had read too much Rousseau and so succumbed to Romanticism, with its addiction to the Absolute and the Ideal, its obsession with the heart, its preference for passion over reason, and virtue over peace.

In Schama's opinion, despite a corrupt court, an absentee king, incompetent ministries, suspended parliaments, huge foreign debts, a domestic recession distilled into bread riots and a tax system of unimaginable inequity, Louis XVI's *ancien régime* was well on its way to becoming a modern capitalist state. All it needed was better middle management. What it got instead was a revolutionary calendar with a month for wine and a month for mist, weeks for hazelnuts and roses, festival days for heroic deeds, and hearts of martyrs in agate urns.[6] Could a book on France start with anything else?

I would like to believe what John Leonard said in "Brilliant Together in Paris": that the reader needs only to be reminded that he or she was not one of those prurient souls who are incapable of imagining backwards except to finger sores, and seem never with a shiver to appreciate nobility of sentiment, heroic action, or genuine regret.[7] So ours, like theirs, despite our faults, is a mission: to seek the best in ourselves and perhaps change the course of history, or, failing that, at least keep our guests amused at dinner.

Finally, my task was to give a convincing life to the book's fictional characters in order to make their existence and their feelings resonate with the lives of the historical figures. The two main characters, Jean-Michel Levasseur, a French American professor who drinks far too much, and his client, Charlene Brooks, a travel-guide trainee recently given the boot from her position as editor at a textbook company in New York, have as their job to cover the culture of Paris in ten days; an enviable but impossible task.

From the book's perspective, their job was to highlight some of the important cultural and contemporary issues of today. But they and their friends, scalawags all, often get caught up in their own lives and foibles — seemingly real but modest reflections of their idols. Nonetheless, the questions remain: What, for example, made the famous creations enduring? And what was the source of these great ideas? Simply the curds and whey of a swirling gene pool, or the mysterious power of our Creator, obliquely exploring the landscapes of His own creations?

Perhaps there are no heroes left. Man, once elevated by Descartes to the "master and proprietor of nature," is now seen by many as a mere thing to the forces of technology, politics, and even history that surpass him and possess him. To paraphrase Milan Kundera, it seems the more man advances in scientific knowledge, the less clearly can he see or be seen.[8] It's time to take a hard look at this creature, man, through the prism of his culture. And who better than the French?

Please join me on an unusual trip to Paris, with our companion James Joyce...[9]

> *Welcome, O life! I go to encounter for the millionth time the reality of experience and to forge in the smithy of my soul the uncreated conscience of my race.*

Good reading. Bon voyage...
See you at the Vinoy.
fpb

I

New York

When a true genius appears in the world, you may know him by this sign, that the dunces are all in confederacy against him.

Jonathan Swift

CHAPTER I

=== TEXAS ===

The affection of young girls for stallions is well known and rarely in dispute. The reverse is suspect and debatable. This situation was present in a small town in Texas some years ago when a spiteful black stallion, the pride of his mistress, leaned close to her one hot summer day and unpredictably bit her. The bite went through her T-shirt and for all practical purposes severed her right nipple. Cosmetic surgery was only able to close the wound, not replace the nipple. She was, thereafter, destined, like Rousseau's mutilated whore, to destroy the ardor of sensitive men.

CHAPTER 2

━━ NEW YORK ━━

"Wow!"

"What?"

"Paris lost its bid for the Olympics," Roland said excitedly. The cubicle wall didn't conceal the fact that he was surfing the Net instead of working.

"Do you care?" she asked absentmindedly.

He hesitated. "Well, the Brits got it. French must be shocked."

"And?" She looked up at the little stuffed porcupine perched on the top ledge of the divider, and spoke to its owner on the other side, "Roland, it's a two-week track meet six years from now. Like, the future of one of the world's most beautiful cities is supposed to hang on the deliberations of a bunch of bureaucrats from some village in Switzerland?"

"Everyone thought Chirac had a lock on the games," he replied.

"Gee. Chirac. Go figure. Roland?" she called from her cubicle.

"Yes?"

"You speak German, right?"

A muffled "*Ja, naturlich*" sounded through her wall.

"What does '*Ich weiss nicht, was soll es bedeuten*' mean?"

A pause. "What?"

Her tongue clambered back over the words, fracturing them worse than before.

"*Ja*, well, it's, okay." Another pause, then, "I don't know what it means."

"Roland, you're German."

"*Ich bin* (I am)."

"And?"

"And what?" he said irritably.

"What's it *stand for*, Roland?"

"Jesus, Charly, it means, 'I don't know,' like, 'I know not what it means, this thought so full of woe,'" he replied. "It's the first line from Heine's famous poem *Die Lorelei*."

"Oh, yeah, Heine … 'woe' … terrific." She rolled her eyes. "*Die Lorelei*," she muttered and went back to her monitor. "Roland," she purred, "are you busy after work?"

A leer masquerading as a smile appeared around the divider, tousled hair neatly gelled. "Busy? No."

He was ten years her junior, but like most German males in the New York office, he prized the sophistication and sexuality of "older" American women versus their own thick-ankled counterparts from the villages of Bavaria. Since a large publishing house had purchased Charly's company, and Roland was a junior editor recently transferred to New York from its Munich headquarters, she was intelligence gathering. Downsizing was inevitable, if not already underway, and the German employees had the best contacts back home.

She turned and smiled at him, "Aquarius at six?"

"Sure." He ducked his head back into the cubicle, savoring his good luck, a fist pump, then hesitating, popped it back out again: "You're serious, right? You are going to be there?" His voice was an octave higher. He tried to cover his insecurities by faking a meeting with their boss, "Silverstein and I are…."

"Six, Roland," she said dryly.

"Right." And he retreated back into his shell.

A moment later, the senior VP's secretary, a short, thin woman with leathery tan and gaudy gold, came from the hallway and peered around Charly's divider. "Silverstein wants to see you," she said coldly.

"It's already eleven, editors' meeting is at two o'clock, can't it wait?" Charly said wearily, staring ahead at her screen.

"Uh … I don't *think* so," came the surly response. Silverstein's girl Friday, not a favorite in the office, had the disconcerting habit of confidentiality and cynicism, a predilection acquired through untold hours of personal phone calls steeped in banality.

"That important?"

"Yeah. That important."

Charly, a senior editor, swiveled in her chair, poised to confront the insolence, but the passageway was empty. Only cheap perfume and the receding click of heels in the half-finished corridor gave evidence of their messenger.

The publishing company was located in one of the newest skyscrapers in New York, befitting a large textbook enterprise of the third millennium. Unfortunately, the move-in had required considerable shifting around, and Charly's Higher Education division ended up four floors below Silverstein's, in temporary quarters, which meant an aggravating trip to the executive suite on busy elevators. "When?" Charly called after her.

"Now," echoed from somewhere down the hall.

An involuntary shiver went through her, as though hearing rats in the wall, late at night, above her head.

———

The reality of one's firing has been described by survivors as similar to being shot: first shock and disbelief, then numbness, then escalating pain, hopelessness, and, finally, smoldering rage. Charly had met with Aaron Silverstein, her senior operating VP, who made patronizing statements about her years with the company, advised her of the reduction in force, followed by a briefing of the company's termination policies, and divested her of keys and security card. She wanted to cry, but held back. Yet it was always those who have the power who insisted that being emotional was being weak. She was unceremoniously escorted from his suite by a black security officer, first to her office, then down to the lobby and out to the street, company policy in all such matters. Personal effects would be mailed home—employee reprisals were taken seriously. The guard offered a shy salute and left her standing on the sidewalk amidst the flow of pedestrians, his "Sorry, ma'am" still ringing in her ears. Charly hesitated, staring vacantly at the building, her quarters only this morning, at once a home and refuge from the city's relentless hustle. Dazed, she turned away, now dispossessed of a coterie of friends, memories, and status.

Teary-eyed and aimless, she wandered the avenue toward the municipal library, still disoriented from the wound. Her mind was collapsing in

12

a confusion of clutter, cacophonic debris of sharp worries and bitter anger churning within; yet, like hundreds of others sharing that busy street and passing around her, Charlene Brooks' dissolute presence appeared, to any urbanite who cared to notice, normal.

It was May in Manhattan, when thousands of lunching minions left their cubicles for short walks in the sun before scurrying back to fulfill countless duties of mundane matters from desks and counters. She sat high up on the front steps of the library, anonymous in a crowd of sunglasses, looking wistfully at the passing strangers below who had jobs...nursing one aching thought—well, two, actually: the end of financial security, Americans' ultimate peace of mind, and swift, certain revenge.

Some sage once said that timing was everything; the firing couldn't have come at a worse time. Charly had envisioned a promotion by December, and the first Christmas in her soon-to-be new apartment. Also, despite venturing onto the thin ice of working motherhood, if all went well in court, Charly was prepared to assume full-time responsibility for her daughter, Jodie, pleading to be rescued from Ernestville, Texas, away from the Billy-Bob who'd helped produce her. The confident anticipation of their summer vacation in New Hampshire and Jodie's autumn enrollment at Exeter evaporated that morning like meaningless puddles from a shower sometime between bagels and lunch. She had lacked the presence of mind, as with the untimely death of a loved one, to note the final moments of her publishing career.

One other old saw, not so readily apparent to Charlene "Charly" Brooks on that fateful morning, was "If you want to see God laugh, tell Him your plans."

Silverstein had given Charly a couple of weeks at a job-search organization to "reposition herself," as he so adroitly put it, a subtle reference to the utility of his recent MBA. And perhaps she could; New York was, after all, the publishing capital of America. On the other hand, the industry was extremely competitive, and contemplating any future "repositioning" phenomena from the Connecticut Mafia—those who had their lawns manicured in Greenwich and nails filed in Manhattan—was out of the question. She glanced at the newspaper recently pillowing the svelte cheeks of the ingénue beside her. The horoscopes caught her eye:

Taurus (April 20–May 20).
Your communication skills are superb today
You could negotiate your way into or out of anything.
This is a great time to express your feelings
to that special someone.

She flipped over the pages and began something she hadn't done since college: scan the classifieds. Help wanted: daycare, dental assistants, she read farther down, tailors … no; teachers … good God, no; travel agents. She put the paper down. It was gut-wrenching. Those skanky bastards! Already, the news would be all over the office that Silverstein had canned her, probably along with enough other employees to cover payments for top management's new benefits package, and certainly enough to pay for that little weasel's SUV and hideaway in the Catskills. She picked up the newspaper again, and her eye was drawn to one ad.

Travel Guide. Immediate opening.
Bilingual English–French speaker.
French–European experience necessary.
Classics-oriented person, familiarity
with European Union a plus, Call …

CHAPTER 3

═══ AT THE CAFETERIA ═══

"You can't be serious!?" Allen, Charly's significant other, and Channel 4's weather lead, had, to his credit, dropped everything, including his taping session, to meet Charly at their favorite cafeteria near the library. A small table by the window provided what refuge was to be had. Allen was determined and intense, Charly morose and expressionless, tearing off pieces of paper napkin and rolling them into little balls.

"I thought you were in line for a promotion," he ventured. She rolled her eyes.

"So, whatever. I've met Silverstein. I mean, he seemed nice enough at the parties; maybe he's approachable," Allen urged. She grimaced. He tried again, "Look, I know how you must feel, but in this city you have to fight for what you want." He waited for a reaction, but there was none. "Maybe he could get you something else in the company?" Still nothing. "But ... my God, Charly, you're not cut out to be a *travel guide.*" He sent the words zinging at her like two arrows marked "Sears ... trainee." Thud ... thud.

"I took literature courses at Aix, you remember that," she said defensively.

"Charly, that was six or seven years ago," he whined.

"Eight."

"That's what I mean." He took her hand, more to arrest the ball rolling than endearing. "You can't take people to France ... I mean, you know." He looked earnestly into her eyes. "Charly, you're just moving into a new apartment, you have no money, you don't speak French"—she eyed him—"you don't speak *enough* French, and, I love you, but what do you know about French classics? As much as I do, which probably means you saw 'Gigi'"

Charly was getting fed up. "Allen, I'm not a slug, for Christ's sake! I can

15

be a travel guide as well as the next person, maybe better. I like people. I'm good with people, and I've lived for a semester in France, maybe not Paris, but at least France."

Allen, exasperated: "Charrrlllyy, these aren't people, they're tourists," he hissed. "You are a New York editor, with all the savoir faire of a cattle rustler."

"Thanks. Obviously, I suck as a human being."

"You know what I mean. Why don't you wait a little, relax, you need the rest, something will come up later, wait and see. You were good at that job."

"Hey, *Allen!*" Being thought of prematurely in the past tense made her angry. She leaned across the table to make her point. "Sweetheart, I need a job! Silverstein wouldn't let me mow his fucking lawn, and I'm fed up with the publishing crowd anyway. All those smug bastards on the fortieth floor and their smarmy wives hanging out at "the club" in Rye, cutting each other up; it's enough to make cannibals queasy. Remember the Fourth of July party on the Sound, listening to those rich Republicans brag about "our nation" and "our trust"? They sounded like a bunch of herrings calling the ocean their lake and whales their sidekicks."

"So?"

"So there isn't one of them whose political philosophy could fill the back of a napkin."

He shook his head in resignation. "Charly—"

"Do you know how long it could take to find another editing job? Listen," she leaned forward again, nose to nose, "I've been out of a job two whole hours and the anxiety is already killing me. It'll take a week just to get an interview. My last paycheck's in two weeks, and unless I find a job, I'm screwed. If it's photocopying manuscripts at a printing shop or being morphed into a donut maker at you-know-where, there ain't no choice. Why stumble around waiting for the inevitable? Travel guide sounds a lot more satisfying than those do. I'm going to call. Maybe I'll like it. At least it'll get me out of this city." She began to clench her fists nervously, "I've got to get some air, let's go." She got up and looked down at him painfully. "You know I wouldn't ask," she hesitated, "but if I don't get this job, could you spot me a loan for a month or two?"

He looked at her with his own pained but perplexed expression. "I thought your aunt had some money."

CHAPTER 4

═══ VOYAGES CLASSIQUES ═══

The offices of Voyages Classiques, Inc. were in SoHo, which was a good sign; however, the shabbiness of the building, hallway, and front office would have intimidated all but the resolute. Nonetheless, Charly felt good, challenged; shabby rugs were no excuse for not landing a paycheck. Besides, if it went bad, Kee's Chocolates was only two blocks away.

The weekend was over, and the blood from Friday's assassination was cold. She was proceeding through the Personnel Termination stages nicely. She had received a form letter from the company, which was signed by the executive vice president himself, saying how much the organization would miss her, enclosing a small separation check, wishing her well, and concluding with a veiled threat not to keep the company laptop or cell phone or harbor any classified company information. The Associate Editor for Higher Education was no longer in shock, simply triaged to one of the walking wounded.

An unusual phenomenon is reported to take place when one no longer has work to go to, an ironic and narcotic feeling of well-being, likened by some to the prophylactic high attributed to swimmers—just prior to drowning. If you fooled yourself skillfully enough, you could banish thoughts of failure by retaining a liberating sense of urgency, just skip the damn bills and go hiking in Tibet. And if you didn't, there was a fraternity of jobless people at coffee shops, sipping on tepid cups of boredom, to remind you. Like junkies occupying vacant benches, they traveled effortlessly beyond their stools, staring complacently across Formica counters into distant dreams.

Her previous existence had been randomly swallowed up in the machinery of rapacious capitalism. In the larger scope of things it was nothing personal, simply one of those at the herd's edge who went down for whatever reason, to be feasted on by bill collectors and early morning anxiety attacks. She would never demean herself by going back to the office, a comfort to her executioners, since—being bullies without balls—they disliked confrontation.

Now, as the old saying went, one door had closed behind her while another was opening, every corner of her future life to be unforeseen, to smell of fresh paint. Revenge could wait…a while.

Charly had been promised an interview with the managing director for Voyages Classiques. Now it was time, and in a manner of speaking, she was ready. Led into the inner sanctum by a fiftyish woman more intent on leaving early than staying late, Charly was introduced to the boss's middle-aged nephew, a modestly educated man ensconced, through nepotism, in a position beyond his abilities; a Louie clone from the TV sitcom. A miniature man, gimpy and balding, he was brash as a trucker and thoroughly Brooklyn. He dispensed with the formalities right up front. "Have a seat, Ms Brooks," and struggled to side-saddle the desk with his shorter leg. "We're lookin' for a person…uh," he glanced down at the résumé, "Charly? Is that what people call you? Charly!" He grunted and paused to ponder the situation. "If this works out we may have to change that. We're lookin', ya know, for sophisticated employees. Do you speak British?"

"Pardon me?"

"You know, British. We like people with British accents, they sound classy."

"Sorry."

"Youse gotta take a bunch of our clients through Paris in five days—France in ten—and make 'em think they just completed a college course in French Humanities." He looked steadfastly at her, eyes dancing with the thought. Then, as one steeped in the responsibility and techniques of modern management, he backtracked, "Youse're not of the lesbian persuasion, are youse?" His eyes fondled her professional attire, but slipped into her cleavage. "Ya know, we're not supposed to ask, equal opportunity and all that, but youse can understand, it could cause trouble on our trips."

Charly's first reaction was to answer in the affirmative, "Only around men like youse," but when one's job is at stake, discretion was the better part of valor. "No," she replied demurely. "I'm surprised you asked."

"Well, it's obvious we're not speakin' dykes here."

"I'll take that as a compliment." A new thought struck her. "Is there someone else I have to interview with when you're finished?"

"Someone else?" he said, surprised.

"You know," she smiled coyly, "the big boss?"

"That was my uncle. He had a heart attack. *I'm* the big boss," he said, gruffly.

"Of course, I see." She couldn't help a disparaging look.

"See?" he asked caustically.

"You know—I understand. Just asking."

"Right. Listen, Charlene, we don't hire people right up front, I mean they have what youse call a probationary period. Ya know, to see if youse can make da team. So we can't pay a salary just yet, but, uh, we can send youse to Paris for a couple weeks to work wit' one of our consultants to get the lay of the land, if youse get my meanin'. Assumin' it all works out, youse take a test and if youse pass it, then, well, youse're one of us."

"I don't know," she hesitated. "I don't want to offend, but to paraphrase the old Clinton campaign, the issue's about money, stupid."

He squinted at her malevolently. "Youse callin' me 'stupid,' sweetheart?"

"No. But I need a salary."

"Yeah. Youse can understand we don't know wit' whom we're dealin', right?"

"You have my résumé. It's pretty strong."

"That's true, but travel guides is hard work. And," he held up his hand, "youse aren't just editin' other people's stuff, youse gotta be smart."

"I understand that, but you can see I've spent a semester at Aix-en-Provence in a master's program. I've studied Rousseau, Voltaire, Victor Hugo—"

He held up his hand again. "What do youse know about Rousseau?" he smiled confidently.

She hesitated momentarily. "Well, there's a lot to say, but Thomas Jefferson called him the Father of Liberalism and his writings the philosophical foundation of the American and French Revolutions. I think *Emile*—"

"Hey, Miss…uh, Charlene, youse gotta understand somethin': Our clients are different. They already read Rousseau, or they don't care; they're rich old alkys, retired teachers and like that. We sketch out the heavy material for 'em, but they want the inside story; they want to get up front and personal with the great ones, a little dirt and gossip, some anecdotes they can impress their friends wit' at the dinner party, like table talk back in Cincinnati."

He knotted his pudgy fingers together, leaned forward, and offered his perspective in a manner of intimacy: "Ya wanna know who Rousseau really was? He was an exhibitionist who wacked off in front of girls at the local well and acted insane when their boyfriends caught him. He played foot-sy with a Jewish fag in Turin, and at sixteen was boinkin' his guardian, a woman almost twice his age, and probably her boyfriend too! He stole and lied about it. He won an essay contest by tellin' everyone that they ought to burn all the libraries in France. Hell, he'd be a leader of the Crips if he lived in L.A.!" He crowed, leaning back to survey his results.

Charly was, in a word, stunned. Her pretensions at reviewing Rousseau's *Du Contrat Social ou Principes du Droit Politique* in French over the weekend had fallen considerably short of arguing the fine points of Rousseau's sexuality with a guy off the corner of Delancey Street. "I knew that, sort of—"

"Listen, Charlene, time's a little short. I like youse. Dat means *we* like youse. Check wit' Emma out front; get some tickets and per diem money. She'll help youse get together wit' our guy in Paris; Jean-Michel's his name. Cool guy...you'll like 'im. Spend a couple weeks and learn the ropes, know what I mean? Come on back and we talk some more. Meanwhile, read up on your classics," he admonished her, opening the door. "Youse're a little rusty, sweetheart, and youse gotta pass the test."

Twenty years from now you will be more disappointed by the things you didn't do than by the ones you did. So throw off the bowlines, Sail away from the safe harbor, Catch the trade winds in your sails. Explore. Dream.

Mark Twain

=== II ===

Rousseau

I am so disgusted with the society of my fellow men, and my dealings with them, that honor alone keeps me here; should I ever achieve my dearest wish and be free from debt, I would not be seen in Paris for more than twenty-four hours afterwards.

Jean-Jacques Rousseau

CHAPTER I

═══ THE TRAIN TO PARIS ═══

During a dreary night of drizzle and fog in May 1814, the famous Panthéon mausoleum (Cathedral of St. Genevieve) was broken into by determined grave robbers. Two coffins of France's most cherished philosophers were pried open and robbed of their hallowed remains. The musty, decaying bodies of Jean-Jacques Rousseau and Voltaire were roughly removed, shoved into coarse bags by political terrorists, and unceremoniously dumped into the sewers of Paris, or perhaps buried somewhere near the River Seine.[1] According to the confidential files of the Sûreté (the special investigations division of the Paris police), members of the ultraconservative Monarchist Party were responsible for this heinous political act, but no one knows for sure. What is known is that their pathetic attempt to expunge the public memory of these famous spokesmen for the rights of man was a complete failure. Democracy was already born, and burning brightly on two continents.

Today, the magnificently carved sarcophagi of Rousseau and Voltaire are still in the Panthéon's crypt, visited each year by thousands of reverent tourists. The French civil authorities will make no comment as to their contents.[2]

These two great men, their sarcophagi as diametrically opposed in the mausoleum's crypt as in their outlook, had died as enemies. Possibly only the heart and brain of Voltaire remain as the physical testament of that tumultuous period. The heart, removed at Voltaire's death, was passed down through his family and is kept in a golden capsule, safe in the Bibliothèque Nationale…or the family home at Ferney-Voltaire (on the outskirts of Geneva), depending on whom one wishes to believe, pretensions serving both accounts. Somewhere, perhaps on a dusty back shelf in the laboratory of an inconsequential mortuary, may also rest an old beaker preserving

23

the unusually large brain of Voltaire, taken during the official autopsy by a surgeon intent on preserving a special part of history. But lacking labels, and passed down through the centuries, it has been lost to posterity. Rousseau, on the other hand, left no organs for safekeeping.

The ultraconservative Monarchists had their reasons. In July 1793, the new revolutionary government of the first French Republic ordered that the tombs and mausoleums of former kings be destroyed to celebrate the anniversary of the monarchy's overthrow.

The Royal Basilica of St. Denis, just north of Paris, was a special target, since it was the largest repository and during its history had been closely associated with the French royal house. St. Denis, the martyrd first bishop of Paris and patron saint of France, was decapitated on the highest hill over looking Paris, which was subsequently named Montmartre, hill of martyrs. According to the *Golden Legend*, after his head was chopped off, Saint Denis picked it up and walked several miles, all the time preaching a sermon. The site where he stopped preaching and actually died was made into a small shrine that developed into the basilica.

As workers dismantled the monuments, the municipal government of St. Denis took charge of the graves, sending lead coffins and metal artifacts to be recast as arms against the Royalist insurgents within France. Bodily remains were to be transferred to "a common trench dug for that purpose of sufficient depth and width."

The exhumations that year were special in that they transformed the long-since dead into the trial, sentencing, and in many cases symbolically executing (dishonoring the corpse of) a convicted elite. The physical condition of the bodies exhumed at St. Denis in 1793 provided crucial evidence for their moral defense or prosecution. According to the exhumation reports, the most ancient were at best bone; a few later kings were relatively well preserved, and most others, despite embalming, were badly decomposed. The journal noted the problems surrounding the exhumation of the Bourbons, that there was nothing remarkable about the extraction of the coffins on Tuesday, 15 October 1793. Most of the bodies were putrified; however, they emitted a thick black vapor with an intense odor, which was checked with vinegar and burnt saltpeter, but not before workers succumbed to diarrhea and mild fever.[3]

The royal corpses were desecrated for political and moral reasons. The politics were easily understood. Not so often known, however, was the belief at the time that those whose bodies did not succumb to putrification were protected by God. There were degrees, of course, but Henry IV, Turenne, Louis XIV, and later Napoleon, all seemed blessed by God because of the unique preservation of their earthly remains. Nonetheless, only a few (such as Turenne, Louis XIV's most victorious general) who had the public's deep respect at the time, escaped the heave ho into the trenches.

Indignities against the corpses were rampant; the great line of French kings, for example, were laid out on the ground while some citizens marched in front of them in contempt. One gravedigger delighted in cutting hair from Henry's beard and making a moustache (where is the camera when you really need one?). Some tried to sell the teeth, and others cut off fingers, but the ultimate shame was dragging the royals, men, women and children, from their hallowed monuments and casting them helter-skelter into muddy trenches.[4]

When the corpses were finally retrieved from the trenches by the last of the Bourbon kings and returned to St. Denis, precious little could be identifed and, therefore, they were simply consigned to two large receptacles. Chateaubriand, for example, said farcically that Marie Antonette was only able to be recognized by her smile.

Concerning the sarcophagi and bodies of Voltaire and Rousseau, one could surmise it was simply payback time by the Monarchists.

Today, these presumably obscure facts are of little consequence to most people in their daily lives. Nonetheless, for a few academicians, and particularly one, Professor Jean-Michel Levasseur, a fellow of the Institute of Philosophy and Cultural Antiquity (IPCA)[5] in Paris, the hunt for the remains of Rousseau and Voltaire, his dissertation topic, had been a driving personal quest. His research and adventures, from the archives of the British Museum to the catacombs of Paris, if not the stuff of legends, were at least the basis of a remarkable study of wandering mummies.

Professor Levasseur, a man of acute intellectual curiosity from Lyon, born of a French father and an American mother, pursued his academic interests in the US and received his Ph.D. at St. Peter's College under the tutelage of the Jesuit fathers. Offered a teaching position in Paris at Saint Louis de Just

University, a cousin to the Sorbonne, shortly after graduation he returned to France and served for many years with some distinction, an uncommon tenure in so portable a profession. Fast approaching fifty, he gave up teaching for a fellowship appointment at the IPCA. There he was permitted to exercise his keen mind and intuition in the pursuit of knowledge, delving into the private lives of famous French artisans, philosophers, and explorers, while dedicating his life to research and writing. Or at least that was the official story in his old department at Saint Louis de Just University, before his sudden departure; there was another, less inspiring, story.

Earlier that year, an intriguing bit of evidence with regard to one of the institute's research projects had come his way. It concerned the theater donated to the citizens of Geneva by Voltaire. During recent renovation, an aged and yellowing political pamphlet of the Monarchist Party was found wedged in the walls of the old hall, and Jean-Michel was anxious for permission to bring the evidence of these fanatics back to his office in Paris.

On the morning Jean-Michel was to leave Geneva for Paris he was tired and grumpy. Previous appointments with officious Swiss functionaries had overly preoccupied him. Adding to his irritation, Voyages Classiques, an infrequent client, had sent a fax to the hotel requesting that he set up an orientation program in Paris for a new trainee. The money was good; unfortunately, this particular job was poorly timed. He knew little about the person except that her name was Charlene Brooks, a supposedly bright but naive American woman. They were to meet that morning at the Geneva station and catch the train to Paris.

Jean-Michel was not a morning person. Departing on early trains or planes was always an aggravation. Now his time was to be spent in a close cabin with this Brooks woman, versus reading *Le Matin* and a quiet nap. He had to prepare her for a ten-day introduction to the culture of Paris, a ludicrous but lucrative task, akin to completing the official tour du musèe du Louvre in a day.

His hotel room near the Geneva train station, stuffy and cheap, smelled of old farts and stale breath. Tired from the previous evening's libations, with masticated herring and a souring cheese odor emanating from some orifice or other, it meant time for his morning ablutions would be spent in Herculean efforts to cleanse acid breath and cropping his fertile nose hair, which grew insidiously like crabgrass around the deepening fissures of his nostrils. Jean-Michel was diligent and educated like many French professionals, but had their tendency to overlook life's smaller considerations, forgetting, for example, to rake in the sprinkling of his clipped nose hair deposited on bathroom appliances, which, similar to his cheese rinds, were left lying wherever they happened to fall, and despite parochial school training, frequently mixing his socks.

When he arrived at the station, the Brooks woman wasn't at the ticket counter. He waited until it was no longer prudent, then hurried off to the train, pulling his overnight bag behind him, and began composing a few carefully worded accusations designed to reduce his trainee to repentance or at least confusion. Years of teaching had demonstrated that it was best if people knew their place. He boarded the train hoping to find the compartment empty, but found her seated in the cabin next to the window dressed in Nikes, jeans, and UT sweatshirt.

"Mam'selle Brooks?"

"The same," she stood up. "And you are Professor Levasseur?" They shook hands while he went about placing his bag on the rack above the seat, adjusted his suit, gestured for her to sit, and positioned himself opposite.

"Can we speak English?" she apologized. "My French is rusty."

"French? A little rusty? Of course," he intoned cynically, "isn't everyone's?" Ready to chastise her, he drew up short. She had remarkably handsome features and a pleasing smell—Fendi, perhaps. With a chuckle, he reversed his strategy and assuaged his delivery, "But we can." More sensitive to her charms than her merits, he listened attentively, after all, one never knew what the evening might bring. "I understand you do know French," he said hesitantly.

"Oh, well," she giggled, "I can read a French novel when it is indecent."

"So, how was your flight over?" he asked politely, smiling under a large red mustache, bushy eyebrows arched inquisitively above half-lens glasses, the frames of which clung precariously to the end of his nose. He was, by and large, a friendly man with mischievous blue eyes, and accustomed—when it suited him—to waiting for answers, patient and expecting. But it was simply a question of courtesy, and she saw it as such. The French, and particularly males, were to be fawned over.

27

"The usual, I guess you could say. By the way, your English is perfect. Are you French or American? I assumed —"

He waved his hand modestly. "Perfect it is not, but you have before you the personification of a true post-World War II alliance, only in this case an American army nurse and a French sergeant. My parents were divorced when I was eleven, so I chose to be French and grew up in Lyon, but I spent summers on the Jersey..." he stopped himself, "that is, the American Jersey shore with my mother's family."

Their conversation progressed over the usual subjects, and especially that of Voyages Classiques, until the steward arrived. They were getting to know each other better, two cultures doing their best not to collide. The waiter served aromatic coffee and fine Swiss chocolates to both from his cart in the aisle, and then closed the glass door to their compartment. It was a sunny morning befitting late spring, and the countryside sweeping past the window was maturing into hazy green pastures framed at the horizon by snow-capped mountains. Seated across from each other on comfortable old velour, they had completed the formalities of work and had begun discussing the play *Les Misérables* to the heavy hum of steel wheels quietly clacking along the rails to Paris.

"Yes it was a wonderful musical, I saw it in New York a couple of years ago," he said.

"Do you think the play was supposed to have taken place in any particular section in Paris? I mean, were the characters students from the Sorbonne, or...?" Charly had also seen the play, and enjoyed the theater.

"I don't know, really. I live near the Latin Quarter myself and perhaps would have heard reference to what you say. I know Hugo's book, of course, but not the intentions of the playwright. By the way, do you mind if I smoke?" he said, searching for his pipe.

"Actually, I would prefer you didn't; my father did for forty years. She smiled so as not offend. "The Latin Quarter?"

"Oh, sorry." He ceased exploring his pockets with itchy regret, and reluctantly began doing his job. "The Latin Quarter? Well, we're talking about the Rive Gauche, the Left Bank, of course, which you probably already know. It is the oldest section of Paris. In earlier times, students of the Sorbonne took their courses in Latin and used Latin as their academic language, which no doubt drifted into the marketplace, thus 'Latin Quarter.'"

Rummaging through her bag, Charly produced a notebook and pencil. "I hope you don't mind." She saw her chance to add something useful. "All I remember about the Left Bank was the intersection of St. Germain and St. Michel, where Sartre supposedly hung out with Simone, and flocks of people in black turtlenecks sat around discussing the utter pointlessness of everything and smoking a lot of pot."

"Um-hm, about right. There are still a few around. As long as you are taking notes, Jean-Jacques Rousseau, though not a student, lived in the Latin Quarter at Hotel Saint-Quentin, but only a year or so. Rousseau said '…it was an ugly room in an ugly house on an ugly street.' The building's gone, but the French Ministry of Tourism probably stuck a plaque up to mark the spot. I doubt you'll ever take a tour group there."

Encouraged by Jean-Michel's friendly demeanor, Charly fished for intelligence about the job. "Will it be hard to get a position with Voyages Classiques?"

"I am sorry, it's not for me to say. I am simply a consultant for the company. They pay well for their size, as I said before; however, like many American corporations, their expectations are high and they don't tolerate problems well. I suppose I should also tell you," he hesitated, "that there may be other candidates who could be over in a few weeks." Charly's heart sank. The job didn't look too tough, she loved traveling, and believed most requirements were pro forma. Hearing the job was competitive unsettled her. Nonetheless, taught early in life to meet competition head-on, she was determined not to lose.

"Is Rousseau a hero of yours?" she asked. "According to my instructions, he's in my to-do-zone."

"To-do-zone?" He peered over his glasses.

"It's just something they told me I have to do," she said, absentmindedly burrowing into her pocketbook. "I usually try to avoid to-do zones on vacations—you know, like, 'What do you want to do?' But this time it's different…really different."

"I see. Well, it's true he is on our list. I don't think 'hero' is the word, though," he mused. "On the other hand, Tolstoy says that when he was fifteen, 'I carried around my neck, instead of the usual cross, a medallion with

Rousseau's portrait.'⁶ But sure, he is an individual whom I like and enjoy reading and teaching about. He was a very influential thinker in the eighteenth century, which, of course, you know?"

She was bent on asking questions, not answering them, and scrambled for a diversionary tactic. "Would you like a mint? They're American. Actually, I guess you've had an American mint. Probably all generic anyway." Embarrassed, she began tripping over each thought. "They are a little squished and, uh, the chocolate's sort of melted." She extended the box toward him and he bent forward to survey the lumpy contents, like a hound curiously sniffing a tidbit.

"Maybe after lunch, thanks." His voice lowered and he leaned toward her. "Did you read the material on Voltaire?" As though a chastising schoolmaster.

"Sort of skimmed it … you know."

"I think you will need to do more than just 'skim it.' I have some notes. Would you care to look at them while I take a turn with my pipe in the passageway?" He handed her a notebook from his briefcase. "Start with Voltaire's letter to Rousseau, that 'sort of' sets the tone." He got up to leave. She was very pretty in a Celtic way—black hair, white skin—and he smiled at her. She smiled back, opened the notebook, and began to read.

> To Jean-Jacques Rousseau.
> Les Délices, near Geneva. August 30, 1755.
> I have received your new book against the human race. I thank you for it. You will please mankind to whom you tell a few homely truths but you will not correct it. You depict with very true colors the horrors of human society, which out of ignorance and weakness sets its hopes on so many comforts. Never has so much wit been used in an attempt to make us like animals.
> The desire to walk on all fours seizes one when one reads your work. However, as I lost that habit more than sixty years ago, I unfortunately sense the impossibility of going back to it, and I abandon that natural gait to those who are worthier of it than you and I….
>
> *Voltaire*

Charly put down the book and looked out at the countryside. It was beautiful. The last few weeks had been a struggle, but at least she was airborne.

Jean-Michel returned to the compartment and settled back in. "What do you think of our friend Voltaire?"

"Well," she said returning his book, "I am a romantic when it comes to the Romantics. I studied for a semester—maybe 'hung out' is the correct French phrase," she smiled—"in Aix-en-Provence six or, uh…a number of years ago, tryin' to shake the Longhorn image." She gave the "hook 'em horns" hand gesture, leaving Jean-Michel mystified.

"Long Horn?"

"It's one word. You know, *Longhorn*. University of Texas, national football champs. I will just bet you thought I was from Deetroit!" she chortled in her best Dollyism. "I used to be a textbook editor, but things have changed recently and I'm lookin' to mend my evil ways and get to know some of the late and great in France, or at least Paris, a little better. Voltaire and Rousseau are included, I guess you know all that. They sent me to Geneva to check out his birthplace."[7]

"Rousseau? Good idea."

"Oh, you think so!" She was gratified. "Probably best to start at the beginning."

"True. Did you find Geneva enjoyable?" he asked, sipping the hot coffee.

"Very. Particularly the old section and the house on Grande Rue where he was born. Unfortunately, time was short. I was in Geneva before, but had to mix business with pleasure and didn't see much, except the inside of boardrooms and bars."

Charly was easily as tall as Jean-Michel, who could have stood eye to eye with Napoleon. He was a pleasant man, polite and intelligent, in a rumpled linen suit. Not bad-looking, chubby with matronly pectorals, but interesting. She wondered when he would make his move.

Charly had curly Cher hair and a penchant for adventure. Her confident manner, serious green eyes, and squint wrinkles established the demeanor of one raised among dusty horses and brawny men. Jean-Michel liked what he saw, and wondered what she would be like in bed.

CHAPTER 2

═══ ROUSSEAU AND TERRORISM ═══

Governments are betraying their promises on human rights.
A new agenda is in the making with the language of freedom
and justice being used to pursue policies of fear and insecurity.

Secretary General Irene Khan,
at the launch of Amnesty International's annual report, 2005

"May I call you Jean-Michel?" she asked. "We're not too formal where I come from, and the director said 'youse' was a 'cool guy.'"

He smirked and raised his cup. "Cheers, Charlene."

"Charly. 'Charlene' is not one of my favorites."

"Charly? Sort of masculine, don't you think?" he said shyly.

"Yeah, probably offends the French. Americans are comfortable with it. Do you often work in Geneva?"

"Not so much lately, though I did a number of years ago while doing research on Voltaire's theater. You know, some very creative Frenchmen and -women preferred Geneva to Paris. Voltaire, for example, spent the last twenty-six of his eighty-four years just outside this city, though his last days happened to be in Paris."

The theater being one of Charly's favorite avocations, she warmed quickly to the subject. "Voltaire had a theater?"

"In a manner of speaking. Later on it was a gift to the people of Geneva. It is still there, you know; if you'd like to see it. The theater has been very difficult to arrange for visits until recently, but I doubt they will ask about it. Nonetheless, it did serve as the catalyst for a clash between two of Geneva's most prominent residents, Rousseau and Voltaire."

She put down her pen. "I'm having trouble focusing on the target here. Honestly, I'm not sure where to start; the company mailed me stuff on Rousseau, Voltaire and a bunch of others. Is the director more interested that we know the creative works of these people, or their private lives? He gave me a rather vivid description of Rousseau's sex life," she said, rolling her eyes.

"True, it is easy to underestimate the director. But I wouldn't. He is," he paused...one to had be prudent, "he is a bit, shall we say, special. He expects both, but emphasize the private lives, they're more fun anyway. Since you are looking for suggestions, try thinking of it as making soup: you need the hearty ingredients; that is, a combination of the great ones' private lives, their creations, and probably most interesting, the contemporary issues that evolve from their creations. On the other hand, you have to add the spices, which are the anecdotes. Just be careful not to lose the interest of your group. Stick with the private lives; if you get too far into the complexities of their art you will bore them. What did you—"

"Did you like school?" she said, a good feint.

"Um-hm. I suppose. As the pudgiest kid in the class and slowest on the soccer field, there was not much left to grab on to, except being the class nerd. I didn't have any musical talent at the time, and my art was limited to amateur tattoos. But I had a great history teacher, and she gave me a life-long passion for literature," he mused. "Taught me a valuable lesson in the geometry of critical thought."

She gave him a puzzled look.

"All issues have more than one side, and differing angles of perspective," he said, fondling his pipe. "All of us need education, which certainly includes you."

She couldn't help herself. "Is that what the French consider flattery?"

Startled, he focused on his new trainee. "I was just saying that you, that is *we*, should be studying the lives of the famous ones first, then reading their literature or analyzing their politics or studying their art, and, well, you..." she was leaning toward him, exposing her ample cleavage, which his eyes settled on. "Uh...you understand. Internalizing their creations takes time."

"It certainly does, which I don't and nobody in America seems to have."

"So I hear. But, you know the cliché: education is like aging wine; of course, we also need some modest kibitzing from the teachers, or let's say, learned friends."

"Learned friends? Do you actually have 'learned friends'? God, Europe is so great!" She laughed. "My crowd mostly keeps track of the Dow, ball scores, and the Nielsen ratings."

"You never talk about the issues?"

"Hardly. Well Wolf and Larry do, I guess. Most people I run with are ignorant of the circumstances anyway, and just mouth a couple of sound bites to impress you. I don't want to suggest busting your bubble, but lots of people, and certainly Americans, could care less about the issues."

"Every society is confronted by issues of some kind," he muttered. "God knows, the Americans have a bag full. What do 'Wolf' and 'Larry' argue about? Politics? Economics? Crime?"

"Been away a while? Anyway, it is not cool to argue in public these days; people might think you have a gun collection."

Jean-Michel was genuinely perplexed. "Then what do you do?!"

"Work a lot. Watch "Seinfeld" reruns and walk the dog, I suppose. In my case, there are probably about five years left on both. Workouts are always in, of course. You see," she continued, "my friends come from those towns where people cruise about in SUVs filled with kids, play a lot of golf or tennis, have dinner clubs, and swap tips about hotels and museums in faraway places. That's what they *do*. What are you *supposed* to do?"

"Well, we find a comfortable café with tolerable coffee, and argue."

"About?"

"It's easy. The French are always being abused by something or other."

"Usually the baseness of Americans, I suspect."

"Good guess! The world's ultimate consumers. Although it would truly be a sea change if that were their only gripe."

"What's their problem? Afraid Americans will steal their truffles?" she said.

"That's not a welcome joke. Somebody is, you know."

"Stealing your truffles?"

"Stealing our truffles! Only this time it is the Chinese, substituting their poor-quality stuff for our homegrown variety."

"Don't look now, but I think they're also stealing your bistros. But, jeez, that's rough. Imagine that, truffle-less; however, we are talkin' about a little black ball of fungus, right?"

"Um-hm," he nodded, "one that's worth $570 per pound, and if you like the best of the crop at boutiques, like La Maison de la Truffe, a kilo will run you around $3,000."

"Sounds like the asking price for a binge on Botox."

"Botox?" He offered a pained expression. "But it's not true that the French are just picking on the Americans, which is the stereotype. The French see themselves as the cultural if not philosophical curators of the world; Americans, on the other hand, are perceived as world leaders in a materialist bazaar of action movies, military might, Nikes for every occasion, and Gucci whatever."

"And? You have something against Gucci?"

"Not particularly. Poor Aldo's gone, of course, but most of humanity is disenfranchised from those same social values that Americans take for granted."

"Which are?" she said, skeptically.

"To begin with, the pursuit of happiness, which according to your Declaration of Independence Americans obviously take seriously. You love the good things in life, mostly food, cars, and electronic toys. Unfortunately, whether we're talking about terrorists serving as cruise missiles or Third World robber barons, they are usually impoverished—either in mind or spirit—and feel powerless to stop the system, so they are ripping it up."

He thumbed his empty pipe pensively. "But even those aren't the scary ones," he said, gazing through the window.

"They're not!?" she exclaimed.

"Of course not!" He turned back, grimacing. "It is true these fanatics have killed thousands at the World Trade Center, Madrid, London, and other places; plus, done incalculable economic damage, but that is minuscule compared to the damage we are doing. We are the coercers. Communism is, or will be, gone. The dominant ideology is free-market capitalism in various forms. It's amazingly attractive, of course, and not surprisingly, the industrial countries have set up a world order that corresponds to their commercial interests—you know, globalization."

"Yeah...," she said, skeptically, waiting for the other shoe to drop.

He turned up the volume. "Look, what they're doing —"

"*We* are doing. I assume you have a car, TV, and leather couch."

He hesitated; she was good with a knife. "Right, what *we* are doing coincides with a rather vicious attack on the world. It is the developed world, led by the Americans, who perhaps regretfully, but no less determinedly, consume all they can before it's gone: clean air, energy, strategic minerals, and sweet water for your golf courses."

"Sweet water? It stinks. Besides, I thought you were the golfer. I ride horses for fun."

"Okay, but it is you and me and all our muddled middle-class neighbors in the so-called global village that the teeming masses have to worry about. This system is killing millions of them slowly and painfully."

She held up her hand as if to stop him, but he only became more cynical. "Of course, it's not that you actually want them to die, you just prefer their death to your discomfort."

"Wait a minute, just wait!" Charly was beginning to feel targeted. "What do you mean, '*you*'? It isn't my fault, and if you're trying to pin it all on America, we're doing our best, or at least as well as the rest." She didn't step back. It was that straight and level, unflinching gaze she directed at people like a sawed-off shotgun, which he was to experience often.

"Okay, look, the problem is," he held up a hand apologetically, "and I am not speaking of you personally, even if you cared, which perhaps you do in a benign sense, but Americans really don't know what the problems are, so how can you be at your best?"

"Tell me something I don't know," she volleyed back.

"The World Development Forum estimated that caring for an American baby does about 250 times as much damage to the environment as a Haitian baby, how's that?"

"Now there's a real twist!" she said churlishly. A card-carrying conservative republican and former "W" supporter; Charly was not about to step away from some liberal French demagoguery. "We happened to send an army down there, not all that long ago, to straighten things out, and we'll probably be expected to do it again. But in all deference, Professor, I enjoy my middle-class values. I particularly enjoy my Lexus and otherwise decadent lifestyle, or what's left of it," she murmured. "If the Third World is intent on riots and rebellion, and pumping out children sans Pampers at a prodigious rate, and can't educate or feed the results, that isn't our problem; we have enough things to fix at home in the good old USA." Years in conference rooms had made her a combative and agile adversary. "What's your solution? Somehow enfranchising the 'disenfranchised' and cutting down on consumption? That theory's already out there and it doesn't seem to be working," she said, her eyes hard and steady.

French professors are rarely intimidated. "My dear new American friend, please don't be so naive. Where do you think the threats to our world are coming from? Dubuque? Taking innocent lives by the hundreds and thousands through terrorism is among the most unscrupulous acts on earth, but a trickier question is whether anything justifies the fear that lies behind the terrorist actions."[8]

"This isn't 'tricky,' Professor; the answer is no. Absolutely not. I resent where it seems this conversation is going. Americans see themselves as a peace-loving people who don't threaten anyone else. Tell me, who was leading the charge against world terrorism, against the Taliban, Fascists, and communists? Was it Europeans? No. It was Americans. Who risked their lives working for peace in the Balkans, when it was the Europeans' responsibility in their own backyard? Americans. The little Dutch soldiers playing UN guards, protecting 7,500 Muslim men and boys who got machine-gunned by Ratko's Serbian thugs in the woods near Srebrenica, were all Europeans. If that had been a regiment of US Marines instead of UN soldiers, Ratko'd be dead."

"Charlene, all the important issues in the world don't center around America's fear of terrorism, despite what happened in New York and at the Pentagon. And not every war ends with a military parade down Fifth Avenue. Unless some political leadership is shown by the G-8 countries and others in creating economic viability in Third World countries, we are all in trouble."

"We give our share in foreign aid," she said hesitantly.

"Oh," he whined, "that's such damned poppycock. G-8 countries provide less than 0.7 percent of their national incomes for foreign aid. It's not enough!"

"It is! Why is it supposed to take *our* political leadership?" she demanded.

"Those so-called leaders in Africa and murdering jerks in Darfur that were or are happily slaughtering innocents got there all on their own. What would you suggest? Great conferences at the Paris Hilton, with profound proclamations and lots of foreign aid that always seems to get pissed away by the corrupt leaders of those countries?"

"If you're serious, repudiation of sovereign debt would probably work wonders."

"Oh, puh-leeze. The rich families of those countries are the ones who spent all the aid money or let their sons and daughters mismanage it, let *them* pay it back from their accounts in Switzerland. Joseph Mobutu, of merry old Zaire, died with six billion dollars in his bank account and left a poverty-stricken country. So while we're giving aid all over the world to free-wheeling dictators and their cronies, you suggest we also forfeit our profits? Great incentive for free trade. I can see why you're teaching philosophy."

Jean-Michel was getting angrier by the moment. "Giving aid to the poor in no way compensates for barriers against their exports."

Nor would Charly back down. "We offer lots of incenti—"

He cut her off, "I'm not talking about handicrafts and braziers from Honduras; the value of agricultural subsidies in rich countries is nearly six times that of overseas aid. Cows receive more aid than people. What do you think all those protest marches are about? *Fair* trade? Leaving things as they are is not a serious option."

She leaned forward. "Hey, Professor, things aren't that serious. You're just talking about a bunch of kids who demonstrate against the WTO and break some windows at Starbucks and McDonald's for their fifteen minutes of fame."

He looked at her in disbelief. "Do you read the newspapers? My God, woman, the Inuits are suing the United States for destroying the Arctic ice-cap by industrialized global warming and killing off their culture! That's globalization!"

It was obvious that they were of different tribes and times. He considered the moment, irritated by the situation, and attacked. "If the US poses no threat of any kind to other nations and communities, Mam'selle Brooks, how come it and its allies are so hated and the target of terrorist attacks in the first place?"

38

"Easy. Israel. If those reactionary Zionists would get off of all the Palestin- ian land and go back behind their walls to the UN's 1967 boundaries—"

"They are!" he exclaimed.

"And the West Bank? If they got out of there, most of this would go away," she said contemptuously. "And we'd have a honeymoon with the Arabs, and probably some dollars for the rainforests."

"Speaking of not liking where this conversation is going," he said, "let's put the Palestinian question aside. Americans should just get out of the Middle East."

"Why?" she said curtly.

"It's what the Arabs want! Look at it this way. One: Bin Laden and his lackeys like the Muslim Brotherhood want to overthrow the wealthy incom- petents who are running the countries in the Middle East and create Islam- ic states. Is that bad? What Westerner even cares? Churchill and the other European leaders carved up the Middle East to suit themselves way back when; now the Arabs are just reorganizing on their own. We created our revolutions and civil wars to establish what we wanted…let them be."

"Let them be!? So they can take out a few more American institutions like the World Trade Center and the Pentagon?"

"Let's keep to the subject, if you don't mind. Two," he held up his fin- gers, "the Muslims want all the nonbelievers and American military out of the Middle East. Is that hard to understand? What 'nonbeliever' wants to be there in the first place, unless he's a masochist? And how would you like a big Iranian or Iraqi military base outside Dallas or Philadelphia, driving armored vehicles around Washington uninvited because they didn't like your president? America's minutemen, a.k.a. 'insurgents', would be firing back in no time. And they would be our heroes."

She shrugged—he had a point.

"Three, the terrorists want to control the petroleum, first of all because it's theirs and they may take offense at watching us use it all while we make the Saudi royal family rich. Which makes sense, because you Americans are abusing it at a prodigious rate, causing pollution and global warming. Europeans pay twice what you pay, and are driving little 'smart cars,' and you are still complaining about the price and your special needs for SUVs. Where is the bigger threat?"

39

"You don't have any idea what you're talking about!" she said flatly.

"Maybe not, but one thing is for sure: they would sell the petroleum and, hopefully, spend the money on their people, like Hamas. They couldn't do worse than what is going on now. If you put both sets of men—terrorists and corporate oil barons—in a conference room, you couldn't tell the difference. And the terrorists wouldn't be beholden to your great petroleum companies. So—"

"So!" she demanded.

"So you'd all have to conserve and behave yourselves. Your sixteen-year-olds might even be reduced to riding bikes," he said contemptuously.

"So!" she retorted. "Afraid to take on a bunch of radical Jews? Is that why you left New York?"

"No. And it was Newark, which isn't Paris. Maybe you missed that, being from Texas. And I still like Woody Allen. That's beside the point. Many people the world over, particularly the Third World, see the US as an imperialist power that is gradually imposing its values and way of life on the rest of the planet. You see," he leaned forward intently, "it isn't just Israel, Ms Brooks. The US world conquest is being effected primarily by economic rather than military or diplomatic means. The generals who matter most in this case are found in the upper echelons of capitalist corporations, which have the scruples of Paris pimps, if that, which is why the attack on the World Trade Center had such symbolic importance for Muslim extremists."

"I guess you can see that, from my perspective," she said, "that amounts to arrant nonsense. Those attacks weren't motivated by poverty. It's like the man said, a clash of civilizations." The conversation was turning more rancorous; on the other hand, Silverstein always had reminded her of a pimp.

"Clash?" he said. "How about greed and total disregard for the culture of others? Please note, Ms Brooks, that as of 2003 the *Fortune* 500 CEOs earned 530 times the average employee's salary. In 1980 it was forty times as much. That's in your country, and those guys, like Bernie Ebbers, were out to take over the world. Saying that their services are unique in the twenty-first century is simply putting lipstick on a pig."

"Cute."

"Look, the Muslims are faced with a dilemma: either they can abandon their cherished traditions based on the Islamic faith, or they can remain forever in the rear of scientific progress. Neither alternative is very appealing; and the tension between their desire for power and success in the modern world on the one hand, and their desire not to abandon their religion and culture on the other, is resolvable for some, that is, the terrorists, only by exploding themselves as bombs."[9]

"They're rabid beasts."

"They *are* nuts, but it still takes balls. Do you have your MBA?"

"Working on it," she lied. "Is that supposed to make a difference?"

"It could. I'm in the business of education, and happen to know that generations of British, French, and US students, many of whom are in the financial markets, have been brought up on something called 'positive economics.' The word 'positive' signals the supposed cultural neutrality of Western economic thought. Market economics, the argument runs, is a purely technical discipline such as physics or engineering; it is factual, rather than what you might call normative or opinionated. It reveals, Ms Brooks, secrets of efficient wealth creation, but has nothing to say about how that wealth should be used or distributed. I suppose you've read about it."

"No, I haven't. Usually, I'm employed at making a living. And, incidentally, it seems like you just defeated your own argument," she said coolly. "Since your 'positive economics' has nothing to do with either politics or ethics, it's consistent with any value system, right? So the fact that Islam is a bloody religion that seems to relish stoning women, beheading prisoners, pounding their heads on the pavement every day, and wrapping up little girls in burkas, should have nothing to fear from the 'positive economics' of the West."

"True, but it is more complex than that."

"Yeah, like when a *Quran* or two got flushed down the toilet a few years ago, the Muslims got upset because it was done by positive economic infidels wearing army fatigues."

"That is not even true, and if it were, what is served? Holy books don't deserve that; it is not the books, it's the ideas that count. A spiteful contempt for their religion or culture, which was blossoming while Europe clambered about in the Dark Ages, doesn't serve anyone. No wonder the Muslims took to the streets."

"Really! How come they didn't 'take to the streets' when jihadist suicide bombers killed Muslim civilians shopping in the markets, walking in funeral processions, going to mosques, or volunteering to join the police in Iraq? Yet I noticed that these mass murders, this desecration and dismemberment of real Muslims and their kids, didn't prompt a single protest march anywhere in the Muslim world.[10] What's economics say about that? We ship them all sorts of products, with lots of choices, and the so-called insurgents want to kill us. And quit calling me Ms Brooks!"

This was not what he had in mind for a client, audacious and relishing a slugfest. She was supposed to be, according to the director, 'somewhat intelligent and naïve,' and, he hoped, at least benignly, subdued. It was obvious he was being confronted with an intelligent, belligerent, tough little Texan groomed in New York. "Excuse me, uh, what do you have in mind?" he said, his face pinched in irritation.

"You're abusing my name. I think they call it passive-aggressive."

"Okay. Charlene."

"Charly!"

"Charly. *Jesus!*"

"Jesus, yourself!"

"This is going nowhere. Let's drop it," he grumped, shifting uncomfortably in his seat.

"Give up? I need to know in case I'm supposed to move to another compartment and apply for another job."

"No."

"No, what? If you're trying to make a point, make it. I'm not trying to win friends or make enemies. If you have a point, Professor, I would like to hear it."

"Look who's being snotty now."

"So you admit that you were being 'snotty'?"

"Oh, mon Dieu!" he groaned.

"Professor?"

"Okay, okay! I suppose *you* would argue that if anyone in the world doubts that American institutions are culturally neutral—or in other words, have many different sets of beliefs and values—they need only examine your society. The strength of religious belief and the diversity of the faiths represented

42

in the US, including fundamentalist Islam, of course, surely must allay fears that globalization or the export of American-style capitalism, poses a threat for non-Western cultures and value systems. Am I right?"

"You keep subverting your own argument!" she cried.

"Look," he said, "unfortunately for you and the rest of America, this is not really the case. The remarkable thing about the US is that there are so many different forms of religions. It means that none can exercise significant influence over social institutions."

"And?"

"And this makes the American society in essence secular; in other words, it gives you the right to blaspheme without getting killed."

"Tell that to the staff in abortion clinics. But like I said, Professor, despite our moral majority, we all have choices."

"No, we *all* don't. The idea of choice in the Middle East is an illusory arrogance, fine if religion is viewed as purely a matter of conscience. But, Charly, it is not fine if it is viewed, as it is by many Muslims, as a set of traditional principles for organizing the communal or shared life of their nation. That's Sharia Law—their constitutional law. No choice, just genetics, history, and luck—God wills it, period. Islam itself is defined as supplication. Their definition of a human being extends beyond 'consumer.' A theocratic Muslim state has every reason to fear US-led globalization, because market institutions are the most unlikely to prove compatible with the kind of communal life that it favors. Remember, Charly, whatever else markets may be, they are not value-free. They promote one value above others: personal freedom, understood as a near-sacred "right to choose."[11]

Her face was hard. "Listen, fundamentalism is a curse on humanity; it is religion in its most perverted sense. It is dangerous because it's airtight. Just suppose you brought back someone from the fourteenth century and plunked him down in our society: he would be an idiot; his beliefs on just about everything would embarrass my dog—"

"Dog?"

"Jean-Michel, the man has never even seen a *cardboard box* for dog treats or a can for dog food, and my dog has serious expectations of both. *But,* our fourteenth-century man would know more or less everything about God; he'd be a dogmatist who would pretend to tell us something about the world, that is, *his* world. And if you didn't give him a wide berth, the bastard would find a text in his book that justified killing you. Would you listen to someone like that? Islam just happens to be a religion that's in love with death. Hard to see where consumerism would do much harm."

"He can be in love with whatever he wants, it isn't up to you or your fellow Texans to decide. He and his kind are still trying to live according to some sort of standard that befits their heritage."

"You skipped over that little part about killing the ones who didn't agree with him and his buddies. Not something you'd find in *The Social Contract*, right?"

"True, but Rousseau's point was that individual freedom, which is society's goal, still has its limits. The individual and his community negotiate a contract that allows for the maximization of freedoms and personal rights of each, *limited by the values of the community*. Americans seem to be wrestling with the problem all the time. But, the challenge that capitalism poses for mullahs is insidious: since it makes no effort to involve them or their community's values in any of this process, it is foreign, and just keeps exporting—the low-cut jeans, violent DVDs, porn sites, salacious movies, and subversive ideas."

"Oh, 'Finding Nemo' is subversive, yeah, I get'cha. And the mullahs," she sneered, "just what this world needs: changeless true believers with their noses buried in a book from the seventh century and dumb as tree stumps; whose unique fairy tales keep half the Moslem population covered from head to toe in black sheets."

"Well," he said, "they're fundamentalist, you know, and traditional societies aren't particularly aware that they are traditional; they're religious, not nationalist." He added, "The rise of Islamic terrorism is a reaction to the failure of Islam as a political movement. Their leaders have been dynastic, not democratic, which could have harnessed the economy."

"Oh, for God's sake," she whined.

He fondled his newspaper. "I think this is getting out of hand." He leaned back and sighed. "Look, you keep missing the point. I am not into xenophobic disputes; the only point I was trying to make was that Western corporate executives don't present a direct threat. They're only interested in commodities and profits, not in social ideas. Yet Western ideas flow into traditional societies along with the commodities. And as people learn to think of themselves as 'sovereign consumers,' they—and particularly their youth—become skeptical of authority, including theological authority. Capitalism corrodes that tradition and moral authority, including the very food their families eat, and it survives on change and innovation, but it is marginalizing those countries and cultures who don't hold those values."

"None of what you're saying justifies terrorism. And those charming traditional societies of friendly Imams you keep talking about are creating ignorant hellholes and economic disasters," she said.

"Listen," he said tiredly, "it is pointless to pretend there is, in this age of mass media, much difference between modernity and America. The global village is a system, one with a gargantuan advertising department, and Mr. America is leading it—perhaps driving it is a better word—pouring a gas-guzzling, flag-flying SUV over the road with the rapacious intent of a rustler, the CD player blasting the Star Spangled Banner, and a six-pack on the floor, while his wife, latte at her side, is counting 'carbs' and discussing beta carotene on her cell phone. And if you hate that *empire*? Tough. The balancing act for Islamic authority is holding down the envy of its young people sufficiently to keep them from revolting against their theocratic regimes."[12]

"Hey, Professor! If the issue is there're big threats out there, we already know that. I think we all want a better world, or at least a less disgusting one." Body language made it clear the debate was over; she stood up abruptly and excused herself to go the restroom.

CHAPTER 3

═══ 2,000 CALORIES ═══

Charly, returning from the restroom, decided on a change of venue. "How about a little lunch? The restaurant car is just two cars back," she said sweetly. She tried to look at ease; she could at least wait until the second hour of their first encounter before telling him to fuck off.

Jean-Michel had avoided her look, expecting perhaps tears or the freeze. She had neither. *Tough woman*, he thought. *The masculinity is there, and obviously suffering from penis envy.* He didn't understand women, never had, and learned early on to gauge American women carefully. He'd undershot in this case, but grabbed at the opportunity. "Lunch? Grand idea! Take your wallet and passport."

They walked back along the swaying corridor to the restaurant and found a table where he offered her a seat and then accommodated himself. She started by doing her best to apologize. "I don't want to offend, but I thought we were supposed to be discussing Rousseau and company. I doubt you're going to change your mind, so let's change the subject; you've probably noticed I'm not prepared to argue Armageddon with a Ph.D.," she said with amiable malice.

"Hm, can't remember when I was last marked as a fanatic," he said. She looked puzzled. He continued, "You know — someone who can't change his mind and won't change the subject. Perhaps I came on a bit too strong."

"A bit...? What's a lot? Listen, Jean-Michel, we've just met and I really don't want to argue with you. You seem like a nice guy. Maybe we should focus on monuments or something. I'm not even sure why we're debating!"

"We're debating because you have a responsibility to the people you're guiding."

"You mean to tell me that we're arguing over *tourists*?"

46

"I guess you could put it that way. It is what you are getting paid to do, you know, not just point at the Eiffel Tower and suggest a ride to the top. You are supposed to be talking about French culture, yet we all seem to be sitting around watching television and debating frivolous issues like anti-wrinkle creams and the mistresses of political personalities, while the Earth is imploding."

"So, according to you, if we're not debating the issues on our tour, we're living some kind of a fraud? Sorry, but that's not what I thought it was all about. Everyone I know seems to be looking to buy a house, planning a normal vacation, getting some electronic gadget or other, or going to the movies, all without complaint. It's the human condition."

"That is a little selfish, don't you think? And you certainly aren't talking about the 'human condition' of the Third World."

"Okay," she said, "how about this: give those poor folks you're pining for an excuse to take our quality of life and leave us on the curbside, they'd do it in a flash! Didn't Machiavelli, if I remember correctly, offer a few down-sides to the 'generality of men'? Besides, all this human rights stuff has a corollary, which would be that of a world police force and a world govern-ment, the ultimate aspirations of all totalitarians."

"Oh, please, too dramatic," he said. "And those folks you are speaking of have been sitting on the curb a long time. Rousseau may have been a screaming liberal in your mind, but he was one of Jefferson's favorites."

The waiter came, took their order, and returned along the aisle to the kitchen.

Jean-Michel began again, "Anyhow, those people living in poverty you were speaking of are probably a little closer to compassion than we are, since they have to rely on it so often. Common sense says we'd better get involved. We're going to be cheek by jowl with our worldly neighbors to the tune of over nine billion people by 2050. That's your daughter's generation, up five or so billion since 1950, and that's a lot of McDonald's, sewer plants, park-ing spaces, and potential terrorists."

"We *could* use a few more parking places," she countered, "but, I think we can handle that. What's your point?"

"My point, dear woman," he was becoming exasperated; his student wasn't taking notes, "is that we need to know, understand, feel, and wholeheartedly believe, that everyone on earth *needs and has a right to*, at the very least, approximately 2000 calories and 4.5 pounds of drinkable water per day. Shouldn't that be obvious? It is obvious enough that this is the time when our planet must be preserved against overwhelming plundering, ignorance, and neglect. That's our social responsibility, one I am sure both Rousseau and Cousteau would agree with, and until that problem is solved, we all need to be working toward the solution. If those humble folks in the slums from Cairo to New York don't get some small taste of progress, they will eventually attack us with suicide bombs, and our great weapons won't mean a hoot, or they'll simply pollute and destroy the planet as I said before."

"Look, Professor, I'm acutely aware that it probably takes 5,000 dead Ethiopians to furrow the brow of even one right-leaning white," she said, "but I don't agree with the 'Let's make everybody love us,' either. I still say that, given the chance, these people you're weeping about would gladly step over our bodies for our goodies."

"This isn't getting us anywhere," he said, shaking his head. "Look, as a friend of mine once said, we can't have infinite moral obligations, but I think we should be generous in where we draw the circle of our concerns. The concern of the US is its own security. Probably the biggest issue we all face is whether we are going to bring the developing world into the sunlight we enjoy. And in my opinion, education, not military prowess, is the answer."[13]

"Isn't that a little simplistic? It would take the resources of three Earths to satisfy the demands of those folks clamoring to get into the sunshine, as you say."

"'A little simplistic?' No."

"Don't equivocate for my sake."

"I won't."

"In my opinion," Jean-Michel offered, "education, like Balzac said, is the grand principle of life for all nations, the only means of diminishing the sum of evil and increasing the sum of good in all societies. Unfortunately, it is not sufficient to the task."

"I'll concede that, but education is education, some of it's right, some wrong, and some just fussy-headed, like those absurd fundamentalists and their religious brainwashing academies. But what's good education?" She looked bored.

The food came and they ate mostly in silence.

Jean-Michel was feeling out of sorts; he had offered a complex argument against a trainee barely three hours into the program. He retreated. "Charlene…Charly, listen, that's a very good question. A very tough question, let me suggest that you do your best to have fun, maybe educate yourself a bit, and it will show in your work, whether you get this job or not. He tore a page from his notebook and handed it to her.

"What's this?"

"A little quote from Rousseau's *Emile*, read it when you get a chance. She looked down and scanned it.

> All that we lack at birth, all that we need when we come to man's estate, is the gift of education. …This education comes from nature, from men or from things. The inner growth of our organs and faculties is the education of nature, the use we learn to make of our growth is the education of men, what we gain by our experience of our surroundings is the education of things. …I will say little of the importance of a good education; nor will I stop to prove that the current one is bad. Countless others have done so before me, and I do not like to fill a book with things everybody knows. I will note that for the longest time there has been nothing but a cry against the established practice without anyone taking it upon himself to propose a better one. The literature and the learning of our age tend much more to destruction than to edification.

Jean-Michel felt tired, he'd had these arguments before. "Perhaps I was too pessimistic, do your best to enjoy the moment," he said softly.

She was in no mood for compromises. "Shall we head back?"

They paid for the lunch and returned to the compartment, irritated from their recent friction, each wishing to be somewhere else.

CHAPTER 4

$\equiv$ THE ROLE OF GENIUS $\equiv$

The situation was strained. They were strangers, after all, and both tried to get comfortable in their seats, distracted by whatever was handy. Jean-Michel pulled out his newspaper. "Would you like the fashion section? Practice your French?" he said hopefully.

"Sports page," she said coolly.

"Why? You a soccer fan?" He had planned on reading it himself.

She hadn't thought about that. "No American sports? Editorial page."

Again his face fell. "Don't you like fashions? There's lots of photos, you know, in case your French…"

She gave him a sour look. "No."

They read for a while in the compartment, but Charly needed to quiet her anxieties.

"Jean-Michel?"

"Um-hm?" He concentrated on his newspaper.

"I appreciated what you said before, but I have a confession to make." He put down the paper. She hesitated to take him into her confidence, but was happy to change the circumstances. "I really need this job, that goes without saying. And I appreciate what you've been driving at, but I honestly don't see why studying these people helps. Look at this list they gave me!" And she waved a bundle of sheets. "Louie XIV, Voltaire, Rousseau, Napoleon, Victor Hugo, Monet, Debussy, et al., just for starters. When will I ever have time to read this stuff? The names are familiar, sort of, but I was under the impression you could help me learn how to get the tourists to the monuments and back. These famous individuals are hardly household names in America; do you think I'll really have to know them?"

Jean-Michel stiffened in his seat. "We need to get something straight

50

right up front, Charly: I'm not a tour guide for tour guides," he said firmly. "You'll have to get the bus schedules, and find the clean toilets and monuments on your own; you'll see the instructions in your package. I'm the 'why guy', not the 'how guy.'"

My God, she thought, *give me a break!* She tried again, "Look, I didn't mean it that way, it's just, well, these characters like Victor Hugo and the rest aren't candidates for *People Magazine,* if you know what I mean. I'm not sure I could convince some tourists from Hartford that Rousseau, for example, meant much to their lives."

Jean-Michel laid aside his newspaper, rotated his glasses back on his head, and leaned forward, placing his hands on his knees. "What I'm going to say, Charly, is what I would tell any person I know, whether a Ph.D. candidate from Harvard or your housewife from Hartford. These famous figures you're talking about are what held and holds us together from every dimension of our humanity. Without their search for the bottom and banks of our society, we surely wouldn't have the quality of life you spoke of and that most of us cherish.

"Think about it. This fellow Rousseau who, as you suggest, no one seems to know or care about. Ask yourself, Charly, how it transpired that such a man — born poor, losing his mother at birth, and soon deserted by his father, afflicted with a painful and humiliating disease,[14] left to wander for twelve years among alien cities and conflicting faiths, renounced by society and civilization, repudiating Voltaire and the Age of Reason, driven from place to place as a dangerous rebel, suspected of crime and insanity, and seeing, in his last months, the apotheosis of his greatest enemy have more effect upon posterity than any other writer or thinker of the eighteenth century. — You really have to wonder how it came about that this fellow, after his death, triumphed over Voltaire, revived religion, transformed education, elevated the morals of France, inspired the American and French Revolutions, not to mention Napoleon, influenced the philosophy of Kant and Schopenhauer, the plays of Schiller, the novels of Goethe, the poems of Wordsworth, Byron, and Shelley, the socialism of Marx, the ethics of Tolstoi, and perhaps had more influence on Western society than any philiosopher since the time of Christ."[15]

51

Charly became downcast and pensive, perhaps it was the jet lag, but she was beginning to lose hope. "You know, maybe I jumped into this without giving it enough thought." She shook her head dejectedly. "Maybe this isn't right for me…" her voice trailed off, and she stared out the window, seeking the comfort of the view.

"Look," he said, "I feel guilty. Forgive me for sounding so professorial. You've got what it takes, I'm sure. You're a good-looking, personable, intelligent woman, probably too good for this job. And I'm not trying to make things tough. Just let me finish because, well," he sought the words, "it's just important." She looked back at him. "In my opinion, Charly, your duty, and mine, for that matter," he patted his chest, "and every human being's to the limit of his or her ability, is to educate ourselves and others for the edification and survival of our species. There can be no question that a subtle and malicious havoc is gripping this planet even as we speak; your job, and I don't suggest demeaning it, is simply to feed and clothe yourself and your family. What your mission is, what you are going to attempt for your humble little tour group each time you take them out, is to explain the role of genius in history, our history, that which will help to save and improve our society. What they do with what you say is in God's hands." He hesitated, fearful of overpowering her. "And in that task, my new friend, I am most honored and pleased to assist you."

Jean-Michel folded the newspaper, put it in his briefcase, and settled back in the seat. Charly had made plans, approved by Voyages Classiques, to stop at Dijon to visit a university friend and also its famous academy. The train was coming to the station, and it was time to say their good-byes. "Looks like this is it," he said, peering out the window.

"So…we meet in Paris?" she said, as the train slowed to a stop.

"Of course."

"Thanks for the, shall we say, lessons." She said getting up, wondering whether a kiss on his cheek would be appropriate.

He stood and took the matter into his own hands, giving her a kiss on both cheeks and an affectionate squeeze on the arm. "Well," he grinned, "it is my nature. You have given me an opportunity to expound on my favorite subjects. Teaching is a wonderful profession; you can expect to speak without being interrupted. And you have been a gracious student. He leaned forward conspiratorially, raising his bushy eyebrows over wide, expressive eyes. "Do you know the three best reasons for teaching?" Charly shook her head. "June, July, and August!" He chuckled and, offering his card, said, "call me when you arrive, and let me know where you are staying," and reached to help with her bags.

CHAPTER 5

═══ THE COLONEL ═══

Dijon, a city Charly had visited only once before, was pleasant in its way, but remained foreign. Still, the get-together with her former roommate, Simone, had gone well; they'd talked a lot, shopped a lot, and made plans to meet in Paris. Although Charly had done a semester of her master's in French literature at a small college in Aix-en-Provence, she had only visited the capital a few times. Her French lacked fluency, but was sufficient and improving. Nonetheless, Paris was her path to a new career, and she looked forward to the challenge and her rendezvous with Jean-Michel, a man who, despite his professional responsibilities to her, had possibilities of being more than just a reliable friend.

They were to meet that evening at one of his favorite restaurants, Le Procope.[16] As her taxi approached the entrance to the Alma Tunnel, she noticed a large bunch of colorful flowers near a small monument cupping a flickering flame. The taxi driver spoke almost the instant she saw them. Pointing as they passed, he said, "They are left by sad people, where Princess Diana and Dodi were killed." At the eleventh pillar in the tunnel, more colorful bouquets stood, illegally, in stark contrast to the fluorescent lights, concrete, and road grime.

"Where can I let you off, mam'selle?" The taxi driver asked as he made his way through traffic down Rue de l'Ancienne-Comedie.

"Le Procope." The cab continued for another block and pulled over. Charly she paid, got out, and stood before perhaps one of the oldest restaurants in the world, established in 1686 and among the most popular bistros in Paris.

Stepping inside, she was immediately engulfed by the crowd's noise and smoke. Jean-Michel was sitting with his back to her at a table halfway down a long, narrow dining room decorated in red and gold, with inlaid tile floors and cut-glass chandeliers. It was filled with people at tables, smoking, talking loudly, eating, and gesturing, all to the cacophony of clanking dishes from the back.

Jean-Michel was in animated conversation with a man in his sixties. A number of customers seated along Charly's path halted their conversations to watch her pass. His voice became audible as she approached, "…the Northern League doesn't belong—"

"Professor Levasseur, I presume," she said from behind, touching him lightly on the shoulder.

Startled out of his conversation, Jean-Michel scrambled to his feet and gave Charly a quick kiss on each cheek. "You've come!" he said happily, then grandly gestured to his table mate. "This is my esteemed colleague, Colonel Maurice de Monteaux, a decorated officer of the French army!" Colonel de Monteaux rose to meet Charly and extended his hand. When Charly extended hers, he ceremoniously grasped it and, gently pulling it toward him, bowed and kissed it lightly.

She blushed. "That doesn't happen often in New York, and never in Texas!"

"It happens frequently in Paris, mam'selle," said Colonel Monteaux, an elderly man, yet tall and physically toned for his age, with a thickly accented and husky voice. "Gallantry is an art form perfected by aging Frenchmen to compensate for their youthful insouciance." He offered her a seat, which she slipped into gracefully, and the men sat down. Colonel de Monteaux was retired from the "regular army" as they say, and among other duties had served a number of years as a military attaché in the French embassy during the Indochina war. Oddly, his avocation was prisons, old dungeons, and he studied those of historical interest in great detail. He was known in a close and esoteric circle as a military scholar with few equals in this peculiar science, and his friendship with Jean-Michel, though personal, was also tied to his avocation.

"Charly, besides being an old friend, Colonel de Monteaux is an excellent asset for my work. I've been negotiating for his help, but he's a very busy man." He gestured toward some plates before them, "Would you like some hors d'oeuvres? The mussels are excellent with wine."

55

"Not yet. I hate to ask, but could we move to a nonsmoking section?"

The men looked at each other. "This *is* the nonsmoking section!" Jean-Michel said.

"Why is everyone smoking?"

"Nonsmoking means no smoking pipes and cigars."

"Like your pipe?"

He looked down at his pipe.

The three companions had dinner, then talked into the evening, sitting comfortably, sipping after-dinner espressos, and speaking of French and American politics, food, Rousseau, and Voltaire, including Voltaire's desk standing not far away. "I can see why Le Procope, with its literary motif, is one of Jean-Michel's favorites, but also one of yours, Colonel?"

"I have photos of my mother on my grandfather's knee at this very restaurant. You see, Mam'selle Brooks, for more than two centuries, everyone who was anyone, or hoped to become someone, in arts, letters, and politics, frequented this café. Look over there," he said, pointing to the paintings. "Voltaire came here, and Rousseau, Beaumarchais, Balzac, Verlaine, and Hugo. From La Fontaine to Anatole France, the list of the habitués of Le Procope is a list of the great names in French literature." He looked about the room, surveying it affectionately. "It was here in the eighteenth century that the new liberal philosophy was expounded; this was the café of the Encyclopedistes, of Diderot, d'Alembert, and even your Benjamin Franklin. The history of Procope is closely linked with eighteenth-century revolutionary ideas. Robespierre, Danton, and Marat used the cafe as a meeting place, and the young lieutenant, Napoleon Bonaparte, even left his hat here as a pledge."[17]

"And who might be next?"

"That's hard to say, but the Procope of today is still faithful to the memory of its distinguished past, like Voltaire's table over there. It's ready to accommodate new distinctions, let me assure you. The restaurant still attracts a mixed bag of writers and journalists, university professors like my friend here, and others of lesser account."

"Colonel," Charly said, "after all this talk of Paris, why do you immerse yourself in musty dungeons?"

"Mam'selle Brooks, it's a very good question."

56

"Call me Charly, please; all my friends do," she said.

"Well, Charly," the colonel said, "I am a student of history and human behavior, as I said earlier this evening."

"I thought it was prisons."

"It is, of course, but not solely; such things go together. In my experience it became apparent that many of the world's great leaders have been locked away in those depressing dungeons you speak of, and for me this has been a source of considerable interest. From Socrates to Bonaparte, and some years ago Nelson Mandela, these leaders have learned most about the nature of mankind while they were isolated in prison. Even Hitler wrote part of his *Mein Kampf*[18] while confined at Landsberg Am Lech Fortress Prison. He stayed only a short time, nine months, and in rather fine style for a jail; at one point he even complained to the jailer, to keep the visitors down."

Jean-Michel interrupted, "He likes old prisons, spends an inordinate amount of time in them." And added, "The colonel knows more about the ancient prison system than anyone in France. If he wanted to hide himself, or something special, no one would ever find him or it, right Colonel?"

"Ooh, something special, Colonel?" Charly said. "Some tasty bottles of rare wine, or a bunch of masterpieces overlooked by the Nazis?"

Uncomfortable with such banter, de Monteaux steered the conversation away. "Jean-Michel and I have been working on Diderot's imprisonment during the period when he was drafting his *L'Encyclopédie*."

"Wasn't he imprisoned at the Bastille?" she asked.

"In a word, no," the colonel replied.

"That's good. It must have been such a miserable place," she said.

"Nothing at the Place de la Bastille now except the traffic circle, Colonne de Juillet commemorating the overthrow of Charles X, and that..." he shook his head, "that modern monstrosity, Opéra de la Bastille."

Charly pulled her shawl around her shoulders and yawned. "Sorry, you two, but it's getting late. Maybe we could continue this another time?"

The colonel looked at Jean-Michel. "Vincennes?"

"Why not? Charly, we're headed out to Vincennes on Saturday morning to do some research on Diderot's prison cell. We could hike the path that Rousseau took. Would you like to go?"

"Sure. It's time I did something good for my body."

"Me too," Jean-Michel added, "besides burp it." He winked at Charly. "We'll help you get a taxi."

Once Jean-Michel and the colonel had put Charly in a cab to her hotel, they walked toward the subway. "Nice woman," the colonel mused.

"Um-hm," came the reply.

"Interested?" the colonel asked.

"Could be."

"Married?"

"Evidently not. When I asked, she said she had Googled her ex-husband a while ago and learned he was still in Texas, enjoyed fishing, had three dogs and a truck, liked eating fried jalapeños, and still couldn't spell properly."

CHAPTER 6

═══ VINCENNES ═══

Saturday morning, rainy and dismal. Charly sat gazing through the window of her hotel room. Do weather forecasters usually get it wrong, or do we only think so, since we're more conscious of the days when our plans are ruined? Allen suffered greatly at the hands of his friends and loyal audience on Channel 4 for not having better control of God's providence. When discussions of professional service seeped into conversations at neighborhood parties, innocent contempt for the prognostications of weathermen fed his paranoia. Charly realized early in their relationship that chiding Allen for his misses rarely served a higher purpose. He was, nonetheless, acknowledged by her group as a nice man, handsome despite a weak chin, and garrulous, but unless one took pleasure in discussing the nature of occluded fronts, boring.

As for her new adventure, the raindrops trickling down the windowpanes had changed Charly's mood to gray and filled her with worries. Now alone, living on croissants and coffee while exchanging witless comments with bellhops, she had been reduced to mailing sad postcards.

Simone, Charly's graduate-school friend from Aix-en-Provence, was one she could confide in—a surrogate sister with whom she needed to share the prospects of a relationship with this pudgy man—but it had been years since they had spent any quality time together. Her life was becoming aimless, contrived destinations made uncomfortable by the wanderings of fate's wobbly wheels. Her choice of career, mate, and home, like Jets football, impossible to predict and often disappointing, were going nowhere. This morning she clutched at one little straw, a picnic in Vincennes to help get to know both men. She felt fearful, yet desperately determined. Now, threatened by a discouraging rain, and possibly stuck for the weekend inside a

59

dreary, cheap hotel where even Hemingway in his youth would have hesitated to spend the night, she was more depressed than resolute.

The phone rang, startling her into the present. It was Jean-Michel calling to confirm their arrangements; the museum was closed for repairs, but he felt the weather stood a decent chance of changing to sunny and warm in the afternoon, allowing a walk. So the plan was to start out and hope for the best. A car and driver from the institute would stop by her hotel and take them to Vincennes, a Paris suburb and an easy ride in weekend traffic.

They arrived at the parking lot to find the weather improved and the forest of Bois de Vincennes rich with earthy scents unleashed by the recent showers. She was looking forward to the walk.

They began down the path, and Jean-Michel put his arm around Charly's shoulders, while the colonel limped along behind.

"Remember, Charly, what you said on the train last week, that you wanted to experience the surroundings of these famous people? Rousseau trod these very woods almost every week for a year to visit Diderot in prison. He was the creator of encyclopedias."[19]

"Yeah, but I'm only studying to be a tourist guide."

"Um-hm, and Einstein was only a patent clerk; still, I'm sure his transactions were correct. Look, I have to read this entire long passage on the Encyclopedists. With luck," he pointed to the left, across the park, "there might be some dry seats in that gazebo. It will be easier for you to take notes, the colonel to get off his leg, and me to sample the snacks."

"Snacks! I thought you guys promised a gourmet meal?" she pouted.

Jean-Michel looked sheepishly at her. "There was a little breakdown in communication between Maurice and me, so we just stopped off for some sandwiches."

"Did you also lie about the museum closing?" she asked suspiciously. "I was wondering if lunch might turn out to be strange smelly cheeses, stuffed olives, and bread." She tried to make light of the whole thing, but happened to hit precisely on the menu.

"We'll make it up to you," the colonel promised.

"Do that." And they ambled on ahead.

The gazebo floor was strewn with dry leaves, ice-cream wrappers, empty soft-drink cans, and cigarette butts, plus a fine netting of spider webs high among the beams. But the benches, dark green and dusty, were dry. They sat down while Jean-Michel lowered his shoulder bag and, situating himself comfortably, wiped down the area, spread out some napkins, and placed the sandwiches and small bottles of wine beside him and the others.

"Was Rousseau near here?" Charly asked.

"He was," Jean-Michel said, taking a sandwich in one hand and a book in the other while Charly uncorked the wine. "Remember" he cautioned, "Rousseau is going to see Diderot for the first time since he was jailed. Rousseau had walked from the center of Paris to Vincennes, where we are now. Shall I read?"

"Suggestion," she said. "Maybe we should cover the Encyclopedists later. How about we talk first? You know, like people do on picnics: How's your family, wife, and stuff like that?" She smiled over at the colonel for support.

"Family? They're fine." Jean-Michel saw it coming, a woman with a mission: find out the essentials — marriages, children, future, and fortune — all of which he wished to avoid.

"Oh, you don't want to miss this, Charly," the colonel said, coming to the rescue. "It's time for Jean-Michel's favorite part, and he loves it like a child his dessert!"

"Oh. Well. Good," she yawned, still a victim of jetlag. "What time is it?"

"Daytime." Jean-Michel grumbled. "Listen, on one of his walks to Vincennes to visit Diderot, Rousseau had what he called an illumination, which some compared to the St. Paul's vision on the road to Damascus. Rousseau thought that in order to moderate the pace of his walk, it would be a good idea to take something to read on the road.

> Once I took the *Mercure de France* with me, and reading it while I walked, I came across the subject proposed by the Academy of Dijon as a prize essay for the following year: "Has the progress of the arts and sciences done more for the purification or decay of morals?" The moment I read these words, I beheld another universe and became another man.

"What he claimed to have seen in this flash of inspiration was that progress had not purified morals at all, but corrupted them disastrously." Charly looked drowsy. "Now listen," Jean-Michel said, holding up his hand.

'If ever anything resembled a sudden inspiration, it is what that advertisement stimulated in me: all at once I felt my mind dazzled by a thousand lights, a crowd of splendid ideas presented themselves to me with such force and in such confusion, that I was thrown into a state of indescribable bewilderment. I felt my head seized by a dizziness that resembled intoxication. A violent palpitation constricted me and made my chest heave. Unable to breathe and walk at the same time, I sank down under one of the trees in the avenue and passed the next half hour in such a state of agitation that when I got up I found that the front of my jacket was wet with tears, although I had no memory of shedding any. Ah, Monsieur, if ever I had been able to write down what I saw and felt as I sat under that tree, with what clarity would I have exposed the contradictions of our social system, with what force would I have demonstrated all the abuses of our institutions, with what simplicity would I have demonstrated that man is naturally good, and has only become bad because of those institutions. All that blazed in my mind for a quarter of an hour under that tree has been thinly scattered in my three principle works — my first discourse on the arts and sciences; my second discourse on the origins of inequality and my treatise on education [*Émile*] — all three works are inseparable and form a single whole. Everything else is lost, and the only thing I wrote down there and then was the oration on Fabricius. So it was that, thinking least about it, I became an author, almost in spite of myself.'

There was a short silence, each waiting for the other to speak.
"Interesting. Think he was stoned?" she said with a smirk.
"No." Jean-Michel flinched. "It's a revelation; a young, impoverished man who copied music for a living brought democracy to the modern world," he said, offended by the inference. "Does everything have to be a *joke*?"

62

"Obviously he had more in common with St. Paul than with Machiavelli," the colonel offered.

Again silence.

"So what do you think, Charly?" Jean-Michel asked, helping himself to the wine. "De Monteaux is convinced this 'progress' of ours is going to kill us all in some disastrous way or another."

She was tired and tried to duck the question. "Come on, now, surely you jest: an American in Paris, in her thirties, sparring with two French intellectuals? Intuition tells me any eruptions of erudition on my part are bound to confirm suspicions either of you may have had concerning my titillating stories, but otherwise profound ignorance."

"Well, we would greatly appreciate your opinion." He had turned earnest.

"Progress. You mean like China's growing supremacy in stocking-stuffers? Or consumer behavior, like, why can't women put on their mascara with their mouths closed?"

Both men responded by staring at her with their mouths slightly open.

Ah, now it's show-and-tell time, she thought. *No more ducking behind one-liners.* "Okay," she shrugged, "so you're serious. At the risk of offending, and I'm not too sure how two French males will take this…" she hesitated, pushed her hair back behind her ears, "progress, for me at least, has to do with what Simone de Beauvoir said concerning the 'second sex.' You two probably see Rousseau's institutions from a masculine perspective, as I imagine most men would, a world constructed by and for men, and I grant that Rousseau enunciated the rights of man for all of us. A truly great thing, and I don't suggest diminishing it. But I am a female, looking at the institutions of *man,* not those created by woman, nor perhaps even about women." Jean-Michel and the colonel glanced at each other. "Look, the 'contradictions of our social system' are real enough, and Rousseau had good reason to challenge them, but he himself, dare I use the word, was a sexist. A very intelligent human being who knowingly, to my understanding at least, abused and relegated women to second-class status. As I recall, woman as second-class citizen is Aristotelian; Rousseau should have read the master, not the student."

The colonel emitted a small groan.

Charly was fully in gear. They had asked, and now she fixed de Monteaux with a hard look. "What women, or even woman, can either of you define as a major contributor to our sex?" she demanded. "Do you know who Margaret Sanger is?" Both men remained silent. "Of course not, but she established birth control as fundamental right of women and families. Her courage and ideas have affected billions of people, but few know anything about her or her sacrifices.

"I'm not prepared to say whether the world would have been better if it was a woman's world," she continued, "but I doubt it could be worse. If the potential for equality had arisen earlier in the concept of society, Rousseau's struggle for democracy might have paled by comparison. Since we are discussing brother Rousseau, as you enjoy calling him, we have ample evidence that his flaws of human nature were such that the queen of all philosophical questions can be debated."

"Queen?" Jean-Michel asked, fingering a small blade of grass.

"It's Sister Brooks' theory of philosophical nuances, according to revelations by my Aunt Ruth. I consider the *king* question to be: Why are we here and is that connected to where we're going? The *queen* question?" She leaned forward on the bench, hands on her thighs. "What is the relationship between the value of ideas and their source? For example, it's easy to follow Christ's teachings because we can see and appreciate his behavior, including his ultimate sacrifice. On the other hand, he didn't write a word. For that matter, neither did Socrates." She paused to collect her thoughts. "Look, I just came from the States, which is currently awash in an unpleasant surplus of conflicting, noisy certitudes. Probably that's why there is this bitterness going on, which, in my opinion at least, is ridiculously lopsided compared to our real differences,[20] even with the Europeans. There are people all over the world, from pygmies to Bedouins, who are no doubt convinced that they know who created the world and what the Creator wants them to do—at least that's their interpretation of the situation: make our little marble in the universe perfect, even if extreme measures, including violence, are required.

"For example?" Jean-Michel's curiosity showed. "You mean men as sources?"

"Mostly. But I'm saying it in a different way...not so much the sources, which are at the seat of the problem, but that men—Asian, American, European, African, and Arab—are doing all the *interpreting* and are ready to kill to prove their point. I just don't understand why there isn't an obvious, real, true, important relationship between the creator and the thing created, to reduce all this business of gender-based interpretation."

"In other words," Jean-Michel said, "however brilliant the work, it seems that the lives of our select, no matter what their calling, can be relied upon to exhibit an extraordinary incongruous behavior, from heroism to stupidity,"[21] and he nodded in agreement.

"Well...sort of. My point is, I really don't understand what the connection is between the created and the creator. I just think that the interpretations would be different based on being male or female."

The colonel interrupted, his face red with anger. "How on earth can you have creation without the superior creator, for God's sake? Leonardo da Vinci created, but who cares how he behaved? And he was hardly stupid. My supreme Creator was *male*. We're wasting our time."

"Alors, Maurice," Jean-Michel waved his hand, "Charly has a point: Balzac may have been boorish, Stendhal dull, and Baudelaire obsessive, but why should this color our approach to their creations, which suffer from none of the faults of their creators?"[22]

"What the hell are you talking about?!" de Monteaux growled. "They are the fathers of their creations."

"If you say so," Charly replied, "but I'm sure mothers had a little to do with it. More to the point, most feminists accuse Aristotle, Rousseau, and even the Catholic Church of having given short shrift to women's interests, which seems easy enough to understand when you read their stuff."

"It isn't 'easy enough!'" the colonel declared.

"Colonel," she said with strained reserve, "their lack of concern for the equality of women is obvious in prescribing allegedly feminine virtues such as obedience, silence, and faithfulness, that is, defining women by their relationship to men. Just take a look at the dogmatism of the bishops when they describe the Virgin Mary, the Catholic's ideal woman: celibate, motherly, and 'handmaiden to the Lord,' in short a questionable cover for *Cosmopolitan* magazine and virtually unattainable by any woman. And this new pope isn't going to be any different."

"Hm," Jean-Michel scratched his head. "Well—"

De Monteaux squinted malevolently at her. "You're a feminist. A disciple of that Steinem woman?"

"So?"

He became agitated. "How pathetic."

"Pathetic? Is that the French response to free speech? Steinem simply said that the most crucial question of democracy, feminism, and simple self-respect is not: What gets decided? That comes second. The first question is: Who decides? That's democracy. But tell me, Colonel," Charly asked, "if your mother told the story of your life, and then your father, would there be any difference?"

"Of course." But he had already stumbled into the trap. "I'm sure the … uh, structure would be the same, but the nuances—"

"That's Charly's point." Jean-Michel leaned over and grasped the colonel's arm. "She's got you, Maurice!" Jean-Michel chuckled, looking to lighten the atmosphere. "Why should women listen to the lives and traditions of great men and women—our Rousseau and the Holy Virgin for example—as they are written, narrated, and interpreted historically only by men? Charly is simply asking how we can get beyond the patriarchal prejudices in order to interpret these stories more objectively."

"Because all the women are out shopping, God damn it! Look, you two," the colonel tapped his cane on the ground, "if women were competent to do so, and God's will was there to guide them, then why didn't they damn well do it? Christ didn't trust a one to sit with him at the Last Supper. Women *served* Christ and his disciples, they followed the men, put up the tents, and made the fires." He stiffened his back. "Perhaps you should think of that! Furthermore, Rousseau's words created the spirit of the American and French Revolutions, not Thérèse's, for God's sake—his wife wasn't literate, couldn't even tell the time!"

"My point exactly!" Charly said. "You're quoting the Gospels, all written by male chauvinists, and Rousseau, who perceives women only as servants. Every time you quote someone supposedly famous, it's a male; it's the male reality! Why does this have to be repeated decade after decade, for heaven's sake? The anti-abortion issue is still alive and well, and Catholic countries like El Salvador are still putting women in jail for having abortions."

Jean-Michel stepped into the argument. "Please, enough."

"Well, if you must know," the colonel was getting beaten and tried to withdraw, "now that I'm so old as to be out of touch with your modern views on women, I for one mourn the extinction of household arts. Household conveniences like cold storage, deplorable as it is, have done far less harm to civilization than higher education for women."

Charly looked over at Jean-Michel. "He doesn't do frozen?" Jean-Michel closed his eyes and shook his head.

The colonel reacted. "We aren't limited to TV dinners for our cuisine, Ms Brooks. There are lots of fresh markets in Paris; but when you shop you have to know how to add," he said dismissively.

"Ooh, you old bastard!" Charly howled. "I think it's time to end this *picnic.*" With that she got up, grabbed her jacket, and stomped away from the men, who watched her stride off down the path they had recently come up and disappear around the bend.

"Now look what you've done!" Jean-Michel all but shouted. "God damn it, Maurice, every time we go somewhere together you upset the entire lot! Can't you just shut up once in a while? Mon Dieu!"

"Good riddance," the colonel replied.

"In case you've forgotten, that was my client's trainee you just tried to disembowel."

"Sorry."

"*Sorry?* What's that suppose to solve?" Jean-Michel said petulantly. "Go find her and make an apology."

"No."

"Do it!" He demanded.

"I'm not apologizing," the colonel said, eyes closed and head turned. "And that's final."

"Well, then, you can sit here as long as you like. I'm going to find her and apologize for both of us. This is an American only days away from home, and look at the way you treat her. You should be ashamed of yourself."

The colonel pawed the air with his hand. "Oh, stop. Go find her. I'll catch up."

"And?"

"Merde!" he exclaimed. "And express my regret."

"Comforting. Thank you."

Jean-Michel found Charly sitting on a bench a short way back toward Malmaison. She had been crying.

He approached quietly, and then said softly, "We owe you an apology, both of us, and ask you to forgive us." She just looked away. "He's not all bad, you know," he said, "just...well, just French."

"I don't usually cry." She continued looking away. "I've had a rough couple of weeks and things don't seem to be improving. I'd like to say I want to go home, but I have no idea where home is at the moment, particularly without a job."

Jean-Michel sat next to her and took her hand. "You have a home here for as long as you like, and we will work things out. That old codger will be along soon. I know him pretty well: he'll grumble and fuss and then ask your forgiveness." She shook her head. "Charly, believe me when I say that if you said you needed a place to stay he would be the first in line to help you. In this city, he can make things considerably easier, and believe it or not, he is a good man. I know from hard-won experience." He sighed. "Just ornery."

"Ornery? Men are a pain in the ass." She withdrew her hand, took her hankie, and blew her nose. "Sorry."

"Do you want to head back to the car? It is early but we might luck out and catch a taxi. We can wait at the parking lot."

"That should be fun," she said coldly and turned to look at him. "You are a sweet man. And I need a friend. I appreciate what you're trying to do, and I don't intend on being some weepy, temperamental woman, but...," her voice trailed off. They sat quietly for a while, relieved by the silence, until Charly finally spoke up again. "Tell me more about Rousseau. I have an exam to pass."

He smiled. "He was a success with women."

"Ah, a success with women." She hooked him with her eyes. "Are you?"

"Not really."

"Married?" she pried.

"Uh, no. Not any longer. She was killed." There was an embarrassing pause. "This isn't the time."

"Sorry."

"It's okay, perhaps we can share it sometime. But Rousseau?" He thought for a moment. "I guess I could use my relatives as an example, although it might simply be our culture; it took my uncle eleven years to make a marriage proposal to my aunt, which was always something of a family joke during our get-togethers. Rousseau, on the other hand, took twenty-three years to make up his mind to marry the girl with whom he formed an intimate attachment in spring 1745."

"Where are we?" Charly looked confused. "You know, like, what city?"

"City? Paris. At the Hôtel Saint Quentin, near the Jardin du Luxembourg. I told you about it before, remember? Ugly house on an ugly street? And this– this, uh, consummation lasted the rest of his life. Thérèse Levasseur was twenty-two." Charly raised her eyebrows and looked at Jean-Michel. "Yes, my name, and perhaps a distant cousin, nothing more," he grinned. "She was about nine years younger than Rousseau, and worked as an illiterate laundry maid at the hotel to help support her family. Her father had gone bankrupt in his business. She was a woman who had 'come down in the world' just as Rousseau had, which might help explain his sympathy for her. She was someone with whom he could identify in his life. They both dined at the same table as the landlady and her other guests.

"Let me read Rousseau's reaction to her." Jean-Michel took out his book, found the page, and began to read while Charly looked in her bag for a pencil and paper to take notes. "Rousseau describes the scene: 'The first time she appeared I was struck by her modest demeanor and even more by her lively and sweet expression; I had never seen anything like it.' He was lonely and shy as well as she was, but according to Rousseau, 'She believed that she saw in me an honorable man, and she was not mistaken; I believed I saw in her a sensitive girl, simple and without coquetry, and I was not mistaken either.' He recalls how the company at the table took pleasure in teasing the poor maid, while he claimed to have been her only defender. Rousseau offered that even if he hadn't found her attractive, pity alone would have drawn him to her. She could by no means be compared to Madame de Warens or any of those cultured upper-class young ladies to whom Rousseau professed himself attracted. She had none of the brains or the culture of his *maman*. Unfortunately, there are no pictures of her during her younger years, so we don't know whether she was indeed as pretty as Rousseau described her. By the way, are you interested in how Jean-Jacques looked?" He held Rousseau's portrait from the book before her.

"From his portraits he looks like a thirties movie star," she offered, "or a little like Shuhmacher; probably great in a Formula One, flaming red helmet under his arm."

"Formula One? Rousseau couldn't even ride in carriages, couldn't stand the vibrations on his bladder. I doubt he would do well with severe G-forces. Anyway, here we have it straight from Rousseau. Listen: 'I had a nice foot, a shapely leg, a free-and-easy air, a lively face and a pretty mouth despite ugly teeth; I had black hair and eyebrows, my eyes small and deep-set, but animated by an ardent soul.' Jean-Michel caught Charly's eye and winked. "Now, if I may be so bold, we'll come to the titillating part of his relationship with Thérèse. In his *Confessions* Jean-Jacques tells us about his first efforts to make love to her. She must have rejected him, and the first thoughts that came to his mind were that she had a venereal disease. Thérèse was evidentially very offended by this and began to cry softly, saying that she was a good girl, and her only fault was having been seduced as an adolescent. Rousseau's reaction was: '*Virginity, I exclaimed! Imagine looking for that in Paris, and in a girl of twenty! Ah, my Thérèse, I am only too happy to possess you as a good and healthy girl.*' Originally, Rousseau was only looking for sexual gratification in her, but the tenderness and compassionate attachment she could give him helped transform pleasure into happiness.

"And how did Thérèse feel about our young hero?" Jean-Michel exclaimed, stabbing his finger dramatically into the air. "According to Thérèse's testimony, Rousseau was an accomplished lover. When James Boswell went to bed with her — ten years after the romance between Rousseau and Sophie, which I'll get to later, Thérèse informed him that his youthful strength did not make him 'a better lover than Rousseau.' She told Boswell he had virility but lacked art, 'and of the two she preferred art.' She asked him as a man who had traveled much if he had not noticed how many things were achieved by men's hands, and instructed him in *arte amoris*, such as she had experienced as the mistress of Rousseau.[23]

"In the opinion of most of those who knew Thérèse, she was devoid of education. Rousseau admits that all his attempts to teach her reading and writing in order to improve her mind were wasted. She couldn't count or tell the time."

"Sounds like the colonel must think all women are the reincarnation of Thérèse."

He avoided the comment. "But," he said, "Rousseau was impressed with her common sense, which enabled her to give him advice in difficult moments and sometimes protected him from the dangers to which his own impulsive nature exposed him.[24]

"About the sexual aspects of his liaison with Thérèse, Rousseau says different things at different times. In the early years there must have been fairly regular sexual ... ah ... ah," he caught Charly smirking at him, "congress between them, since five children were born, which, oddly enough, didn't hinder several commentators from suggesting that he was impotent."

Jean-Michel hesitated, as before, not sure of the bounds of discretion. "Charly, tell me to stop if this offends," he said in tones usually reserved for doctors who insert cold steel devices in private places.

"You're serious, right? Are you going to say something dirty?" she asked.

"Well, you know." He became befuddled.

"Are you going to use the 'f' word?"

"No."

"The 's' word?"

"No."

"Okay, just no tits-and-ass words."

"Having fun?" he grunted, and began again. "Rousseau also obtained from her that form of gratification to which his habits of masturbation disposed him, manual stimulation such as he was ashamed to solicit from those women of higher social status to whom he paid court."

"So he liked to masturbate. Ho hum."

"Well, there was a little more to it than that. Listen," and he read from Rousseau's *Confessions*:

'My thoughts were incessantly occupied with girls and women, but in a manner peculiar to myself. These ideas kept my senses in a perpetual and disagreeable activity.... My agitation rose to the point where, unable to satisfy my desires, I inflamed them

71

with the most extravagant maneuvers. I went about seeking dark alleys, hidden retreats where I might expose myself at a distance to persons of the other sex in the state wherein I would have wished to be near them.'

"Exhibitionist. Strange behavior," she said. "Why do men do that?"

"I don't know. Why do women? The only difference is that women get paid handsomely for it in nightclubs, and men go to jail for masturbating publicly while thinking about women masturbating."

"Seriously," Charly said with furrowed brow, "would you feel comfortable taking a shower knowing that an unbalanced woman was standing outside your window masturbating?"

"Not unless certain conditions were met. But, seriously? Maybe males are trying to demonstrate to females that an aggressive parent, probably the father, had not successfully neutered them … you know, de-sexed them with the father's aggressive and repressive behavior against the son. Or maybe they are simply trying to atone for past sins by seeking humiliation. Who knows? On the face of it, they are simply resorting to juvenile behavior, which in the end is pathetic." He paused. "Do we continue?"

"We do."

He started again, "'I found in Thérèse the supplement which I needed.' You have to know, Charly…."

"Um-hm." She looked at him lasciviously.

She was sexy, no doubt about it, but hard to figure. "You understand that for Rousseau "supplement" was another word for masturbation, right? He used 'that dangerous supplement' not only in his *Confessions* but also in *Émile* in this context. Later in the *Confessions* he says of Thérèse: 'From the very first moment I saw her I never felt the least spark of love for her, and I had no more desire to possess her than I had to possess Mme de Warens; and the needs of the senses which I satisfied with her were solely those of sex, and had nothing to do with her as an individual.'"

"Doesn't say much for J. J., does it?" Charly said. "The man would be considered something of a heartless pig by today's standards."

Jean-Michel looked up from his book. "He is talking about 'the needs of the senses,' Charly."

"What's that supposed to mean?"

"These words rule out love, no doubt of that, but they don't rule out pity, companionship, dependence; and the older and more sickly Rousseau became, the more dependent he was on her care. The lost child in him may have recognized in Thérèse a kind of plebeian foster mother who would feed him and nurse him as well as occasionally give him *la petite branlette.*"[25]

"That's nice." Charly had an involuntary grin. "You're serious aren't you? You and that old fart who lives with his mother and who claims to know about women—you probably agree. Every woman's dream relationship: mother, maid, and jerk-off queen." Charly's grapes were rarely seedless. She was an honest and outspoken person by any standard, a virtue lauded by many, but practiced by few, and those few were usually looking for jobs.

"I hear you," he said, "but this wasn't yesterday on Avenue of the Americas."

"Can't you see how stilted that all sounds, for God's sake!" she demanded. "Being the handmaiden—literally—to an older man who professes no love for her except pity. Jesus!" She was angry and discouraged.

Embarrassment gripped the moment. Charly was a friend, but a new one, and Jean-Michel, at a loss for where to take the discussion, simply continued quietly. "Rousseau, a bachelor who tired of his own cooking and laundry, it seems—"

"Smelly socks and undies," she grumped.

"Maybe I should skip over some of this."

"Good idea."

"… it seems he decided that after a considerable time in two small apartments he would give up the single life in order to move in permanently with Thérèse. All of this happened during his 'reform,' having written his *Discours.* Still, it didn't change him enough to marry Thérèse." He kept his eyes buried in the book to avoid Charly's gaze. "But, he felt that he had to defend her more."

"I believe Guido's boys call it 'protection,'" she offered curtly. "Is that his take on sex?"

"He didn't cover it too well, but referred to it as a trivial thing in the state of nature."

"Trivial," she echoed.

"He was probably talking about animals."

"Care to step in front of a lion in heat?"

"No. He said it was used to bind human beings together in affection," he smiled amiably, "and...," he hesitated.

"And?"

"And divided them in bitter rivalry."

"Do you not just *love* this guy?!" She clapped her hands. "I mean, *Jesus.*"

"But, Charly, there's the other side. Rousseau and Thérèse were—apart from these problems—able to enjoy their new domestic life. In the *Confessions* he even writes:

> 'Our affection grew with our intimacy, and every day we felt more keenly how much we had been made for one another...our walks together in the country, when I would lavishly spend eight or ten sous at a tavern; our little suppers at our open window, sitting opposite one another. Who could describe, who could even imagine the charm of those meals, made out of nothing more than a loaf of coarse bread, a few cherries, a small piece of cheese and a half-bottle of wine, which we drank between us? Friendship, confidence, intimacy, peace of mind—what seasonings they are! Sometimes we stayed by the window until midnight, and would never have moved if Thérèse's old mother had not disturbed us.'

"Isn't that sweet?" Charly's irritation continued. "What does he say about love?"

"Love? That's what I was just talking about."

"No it isn't. He was talking about intimacy, like my father's hunting partner. Rousseau didn't say anything about *love.*"

"All right, so he 'loved' his share of women, but then we're talking France in the eighteenth century."

"Meaning?"

"Meaning, women were," he began to fumble around with his book. "Okay, 'love.' Here," he said defiantly, stabbing his finger at the book. "Love, Rousseau said, 'is extolled by women in order to establish their ascendancy and make dominant the sex that ought to obey.'" But then Jean-Michel began to backpedal, "I don't think we need to—"

"Yes, we do. After all, Professor, these are my *lessons*, and our philosopher friend here has something wise to say, no? So how does all this dominating, let's say, French art of seduction, come about? I mean, is there something here to be tucked between the glossy lipstick ads, cheap celebrities, and career-boosting horosopes of tawdry glamor magazines?"

He was trapped and sought escape, but there was none. "Well, as Rousseau said, since women were domesticated and dependent on men to an extent that men were not dependent on women, they have to use cunning to make men stay attached to them. Each must make some man, or men, love her enough to shelter and protect her, choose her as the significant other, as you say. For women to make men as dependent on them as they are dependent on men, they must dominate men, and dominate them by devious maneuvers and manipulations, since they cannot dominate them by force. Thus sexual relationships in human society are, according to Rousseau, from the beginning 'political'—that is to say, relationships of power."

"This is wonderful," she said. "I never realized he was so deep, so attuned to women's feelings." Her eyes danced. "So, from this great French philosopher—"

"Swiss."

"Okay, Swiss, which maybe explains part of it.. But I think you're fudging things. Let's see now, we have it on the best authority that the story of love is obedience, seduction is power politics, and sex is bitter rivalry. This is great—I can't imagine why we aren't all reading Rousseau. Obviously, the Muslims are." She sat straight up and held up her finger. "Oh, and I almost forgot, last but not least there are the children. I want to hear all about the loving father."

Jean-Michel began to shift uncomfortably in his seat. "We have to move on."

"No, we don't. I want to hear about his children."

"Children? He had five."

"Doctors, lawyers, and dentists, no doubt, a secure family, intelligent young citizens. Or wasn't there—uh, some strange rumor that he put all his children in an orphanage?"

"Charly, we are getting way off topic," he sighed.

"Are we?" she said demurely. "Indulge me."

"If you insist," he said, adopting his best professorial demeanor, "we think he did. But some people disagree, of course, because of his urinary problems. Anyway, Rousseau's first child from Thérèse was born in 1747 when he was still a young aspirant to fame and fortune. In the pleasure-loving society that Rousseau wanted to be part of, there was no use for children, and there was only one solution, the orphanage. Rousseau admits:

'I made up my mind cheerfully and without the least scruple. The only scruples I had to overcome were those of Thérèse; I had all the difficulty in the world in making her adopt this one means of saving her honor. Her mother, who had a different fear — that of another brat to feed — came to my aid and finally Thérèse gave in.'

"Brat? I assume someone translated that word correctly. The man is a pig, you know? I mean, how can any human being give away his children so ruthlessly?"

"The man was a genius in his own way, and geniuses are often obtuse," he said defensively.

"Obtuse? Is that another word for selfish, egotistical, and deranged?"

"Charly, please, I'm not condoning it, you know that; but even after he became famous, this child wasn't the only one — five kids, and he abandoned them all."

"Well, I'm sure he had his reasons. I mean, five kids, who could blame him? Surely he had more important things on his mind, like how to educate children, politics, encyclopedias, and prostitutes."

Jean-Michel shrugged his shoulders and again turned to his book to quote Rousseau. "Listen":

'I will content myself by saying that in handing over my children to be brought up to the public authorities, for lack of means to bring them up myself, and by making it their destiny to become workers or peasants rather than adventurers or fortune-hunters,

I believed myself to be acting as a citizen and a father would act, and I looked upon myself as a member of Plato's republic. More than once since that time my heart has told me I acted wrongly, but my reason, far from delivering the same judgment, has made me bless heaven for having saved my children from their father's fate.'

"In 1752 he had become a literary celebrity and his secret become known, so he had to justify his reasons, which led him to do this. One of the arguments he gives, other than that he couldn't provide a living for them, was 'And if I were compelled to resort to the trade of a writer, how could I find the peace of mind necessary to do profitable work in an attic disturbed by domestic cares and the noise of children.' He accuses the lifestyle of the rich, 'which robs my children of bread.'"

"So…what happened to the kids?"

"No one knows. The fate of his children remains a mystery."

"Are we done for today?" he said tiredly.

"Jean-Michel, I just have to say how much I appreciate the wisdom of the French, and that self-centered crank of a colonel, but let's bag it—I have a pain in my butt."

"Would you like my jacket to sit on?" Jean-Michel offered.

"Thanks," she said, and folded his sports coat for a cushion. A pained expression crossed her face. "Were you wearing sunglasses?"

"Oh, merde!"

"Gotcha," and produced his sunglasses, whole. "You deserved that."

"Charly, you know I didn't mean to offend you, and I'm sure the colonel didn't either."

She looked at him sourly.

"Charly, he's from a different generation."

"For centuries, Jean-Michel, women, like your mother and my mother and their mothers and theirs, have lived shut off from society, and, as Virginia Woolf wrote, guessing at what was outside, and inevitably magnifying what was within. We are just now experiencing some equality in our own right, and not being slapped about by the ruminations of some male chauvinist like Rousseau." She flicked a little pebble across the path. "Let's go."

She got up and he followed. "Will the car be here soon?" she said without looking back. They were uncomfortable, and the black limousine had not arrived at the parking lot. They waited for a while, but de Monteaux didn't show up, so they took the first taxi that arrived, and returned to the hotel.

———

Charly's cell phone rang as they drove along. She fussed with the phone, accompanied by the strains of "The Yellow Rose of Texas," then spoke quietly as Jean-Michel bantered with the taxi driver about the French soccer finals. Finally, she was finished, and Jean-Michel leaned close. "Everything all right?"

"Depends," she said. He waited. "My aunt. She has my daughter this summer."

Jean-Michel offered a polite smile. "Nice."

"My sixteen-year-old daughter, Jodie, just had her nipples pierced," she said dryly.

He hesitated, staring at his hands. "So?"

"So guess who's coming to dinner."

———

Rousseau's Death [27]

Rousseau was introverted, older looking in his early sixties, scared, and had isolated himself more and more from life in the city, which was expensive. He had hardly any friends left whom he hadn't alienated. One special friend, however, offered Rousseau and Thérèse some little rooms in a castle at Ermenonville, north of Paris, and they accepted gladly. Six weeks later, on 2 July, he went for his daily morning walk. Rousseau came back to Thérèse and sat down to have breakfast with her. They appreciated these quiet mornings before visitors might come. Suddenly he felt a terrible pain in his body and his head. He fell off the chair and was dead only four days after his sixty-sixth birthday. He had died of stroke and was buried shortly thereafter on the Isle of Poplars at Ermenonville.

But Rousseau's death did not put an end to the controversy created by his ideas and his personal idiosyncrasies, which are with us still today. He was an inspired and inspiring man.

In 1793 the official installation of Rousseau in the Panthéon of National Heroes occurred after Robespierre's fall from power. A report to the National Convention recommended that Rousseau's remains be removed from Ermenonville.

Rousseau's body was exhumed, and the self-styled simple citizen, the subject of official persecution during his life, was made in death the object of an opulent national ceremony stretching over the next three years. New decorations, sculptures, icons, and hymns were specially commissioned. A procession of government dignitaries, delegates, and musicians was organized. At stops along the way from Ermenonville to Paris, local ceremonies consecrated the occasion. Once in Paris, the coffin was placed on public view in the Tuileries gardens, where a replica of the Isle of Poplars at Ermenonville had been built. After a special service at the convention, the cortege wound through the streets of Paris toward the Panthéon. The procession was organized to include groups of standard-bearers representing various beneficiaries of the author's wisdom: artisans, mothers and children, Genevans, and even, for patriotic purposes, war orphans. Rousseau, a composer and musician, was serenaded by bands that played his most cherished compositions. A cart pulled by twelve horses exhibited a statue of the famous citizen. And a copy of *The Social Contract*, upheld as the "beacon of legislators," was carried in regal splendor on a cushion made of velvet. After the ceremony at the Pantheon, where the President of the convention laid a wreath and delivered a eulogy, the evening was given over to verious celebrations. At the Place de Panthéon, for example, there was dancing in the streets, while in theaters across Paris, playgoers attended revivals of their favorite spectacles by or about Rousseau. Not to be excluded, provincial capitals throughout France held similar ceremonies.

═══ III ═══

Napoleon In Love

Napoleon as host at a party:
"Madame, I do not like it when women mix in politics."
His attractive young guest: "You are right, General; but
in a country where they have their heads cut off,
it is natural that they should want to know why."

CHAPTER I

═══ FRIENDSHIP IS ONLY A WORD ═══

It may have been that Napoleon, a native of Corsica, was drawn to Rousseau because of Rousseau's unfinished work on what he called the Constitutional Project for Corsica in 1765, written four years before Napoleon was born. Whatever the reason, Napoleon favored Rousseau above all other authors, and his interest went so far, history records, that he even emulated Rousseau's penchant for entering essay contests (he attained the rank of fifteenth on one occasion). In 1778, the year of Rousseau's death, Napoleon was nine years old.

First Consul of France twenty-one years later, Napoleon visited the original site of Rousseau's grave outside Paris, on Stanislas Girardin's property in Ermenonville. According to Girardin, a biographer of sorts, the following conversation took place:

> When he reached the Isle of Poplars, Bonaparte stepped in front of Jean-Jacques' tomb and said, "It would have been better for the peace of France if this man had never lived."
>
> "And why, Citizen Consul?"
>
> "It was he who prepared the French Revolution."
>
> "I should have thought, Citizen Consul, that it was not for you to complain of the Revolution."
>
> "Well," he replied, "the future will tell us whether it would have been better if neither I nor Rousseau had ever lived." And he resumed his walk with a thoughtful air.[1]

Will historians tell us one day that it would have been better had Napoleon never lived?

There is no question that for centuries France has ruled Europe both culturally and politically, in part thanks to the Napoleonic period. And today it is not difficult to see that France continues to be caught between its desire to live with its neighbors and its desire to dominate them. The present leader of the Quai d'Orsay (France's foreign ministry) understands this, but he is a poet, or at least writes of poetry, and states the poet's duty to see beyond that which is today and prepare for that which is tomorrow. For the French, at the heart of this vibrant future described by their foreign minister, there is only one consideration, the centrality of France — no less a clear echo of its immortal leader, Charles de Gaulle, who said succinctly, "France cannot be France without greatness."

Spend some time with the minister's books[2] and Europe is oddly absent. Paris, he says, will never be satisfied with being just a partner along with others. So the presiding leadership of France has a mission in Europe if not the world, and it is this principle that drives the French, the eternal love affair of its people with greatness, and the enduring fame of their most legendary leader — Napoleon Bonaparte — and the romantic spirit of his reign.

There is in existence, according to an eminent biographer, Vincent Cronin, a large number of lives of Napoleon.[3] Needless to say, each perspective varies according to its author's inclinations. Cronin sought to find "the living, breathing man," and in this he found from any number of biographers and their dubious sources, glaring contradictions of character. To take one example of many, biographers often repeat Napoleon's phrase "Friendship is only a word. I love no man."

Napoleon supposedly acknowledged that he had no true friends. He claimed that he loved no man except his brother, Joseph, and that by force of habit, because Joseph was his elder brother. 'It takes time to make oneself loved,' he explained, 'and even when I had nothing to do I always vaguely felt that I had no time to waste.' Friendship and love were for women.

As for himself, 'No sentimentality! One must be firm, have a firm heart....
Otherwise one has no business mixing in war and government.'[4]

Cronin disputed this point by establishing that this friendship quote
occurs only in the Memoirs of Bourrienne,[5] Napoleon's former secretary,
who, as Cronin wrote, embezzled half a million francs from Napoleon,
had to be posted abroad, where he embezzled millions more, and finally
had to be released from the service. Bourrienne rallied to the Bourbons
after Napoleon's fall, but again had to be dismissed for dishonesty. Forever
in debt, he decided to publish his memoirs, but Bourrienne did not write
them; he only supplied notes, and these were then ghosted by a journalist favorable to the Bourbons. Eventually, Bourrienne was consigned to a
lunatic asylum.[6]

Some writers, convinced of their erudition and "objective" sympathies,
equate Hitler with Napoleon by virtue of certain parallels. One in particular
is offered by Napoleon himself: in France and throughout Europe, Napoleon
believed that he reigned only through the fear he inspired. He thought — no
doubt rightly so — that many of his generals would desert him if he ceased
to gain victories. He concluded, "My power is dependent on my glory, and
my glory on my victories. My power would fall if I did not base it on still
more glory and still more victories. Conquest made me what I am; conquest
alone can keep me there."[7] Hitler and his theorists notwithstanding, history has made Napoleon a legend and Hitler a goat. But it was not always
so; Hitler was revered before his fall. And it is forgotten, as Chateaubri-
and said in his *Mémoires d'Outre-Tombe*, that a great many people lamented those Napoleonic victories, "the sufferers, the victims' curses, their cries
of pain, their howls of anguish…, forgotten that the people, the court, the
generals, the intimates of Napoleon, were all weary of his oppression and
his conquests, that they had had enough of a game which, when won, had
to be played all over again, enough of that existence which, because there
was nowhere to stop, was put to the hazard each morning."[8]

Not long ago a horrifying event brought Napoleon's hazards boldly to
the fore at a construction site in a Vilnius housing complex in Lithuania.
The men were busily at work when the scoop of a backhoe began unearth-
ing skeletons. The workmen tried to count as the skulls and ribs, femurs and
tibias, appeared. "The bones wouldn't stop coming out of the ground," recalls

one. On closer inspection the bones seemed to be curled around each other as if trying to keep warm.

The shocked bystanders assumed they had uncovered a mass grave of Holocaust victims, or perhaps a site similar to those Polish soldiers murdered in the Katyn Forest by the brutal Soviet secret police. But these bones were far older. The investigators found brass buttons inscribed with a three-digit number, so the mystery wasn't long in solving — they knew that only one group had worn such items: Napoleon Bonaparte's Grande Armée.

According to the local media, the excavation conducted by Lithuanian and French teams unearthed 1,724 skeletons, almost 1,500 buttons, and a single five-franc piece emblazoned with a Napoleon bust and the number "13," to mark the thirteenth year of his reign. There were as many as forty regiments, including French, Spanish, Germans, and Austrians.

It is estimated that 45,000 men of this pan-European army are believed to have succumbed to the winter in Vilnius, then a bustling political and military center. Napoleon himself spent over two weeks there in June 1812, assembling his troops for the march to Moscow. They returned, thanks to General Nye's heroic rearguard action against a determined Russian army, around the first days of December, a half-dead rabble, exhausted and starving after marching to Moscow and back. Napoleon himself abandoned his army, not unlike his behavior in Egypt, and raced back to Paris in record time. Of the half million soldiers who crossed into that hostile barren landscape, barely 50,000 survived. Napoleon's Russia campaign — a mistake repeated by Adolph Hitler 130 years later — is considered one of the worst military blunders of all time.

So there has been a great deal written about Napoleon, reputedly more than any other figure in history. Over 80,000 books, according to one authority, and much of it questionable, including even a recent theory of his assassination at St. Helena by his close associate Montholon (also an embezzler, but a cuckold by Napoleon).[9] The reason for this veritable river of ink? For one thing, compared to previous conquerors, there is a literal treasure-trove of documents about him. He rose to prominence early in life, and much of that life was recorded in diaries by those around him. Nonetheless, there is still much that eludes the written record, so historians are left to guess at his character and charisma, having never heard his voice or looked into his eyes.

The question of Napoleon's character, then, his social contributions, conquests, and even his death, will serve for many years to come as good grist at a warm hearth and sips of a hearty port, or dorm-room debates and tequila coolers. In the annals of history, however, one thing is for certain: he cannot be ignored.[10]

CHAPTER 2

═══ THIS FELLOW DE MONTEAUX ═══

Charly and Jean-Michel had arrived by taxi at her hotel, tired, but relieved, from their visit to Vincennes. They remained seated in the taxi, their impromptu scheduling discussion irritating the driver, a thin, dark Magrebian impatiently massaging prayer beads in his right hand. Hearing English spoken, he muttered profanities in Arabic, secure in his contempt for their ignorance. Instantly, Jean-Michel paused in his conversation with Charly; he turned to the driver, placed his right hand over his heart, and bowed his head deferentially to murmur an Islamic prayer for his antagonist. Taken aback, the Arab returned the homily with great courtesy, leaped from the taxi, and scurried around to the curb to assist them out. Both men bowed, and the driver, refusing payment, stepped quickly into his car and sped into traffic.

"What was that?!" Charly exclaimed as they stood gazing after the receding taxi.

"A seriously surprised Algerian."

"You speak Arabic?"

"Some."

"Sounded like more than 'some.' Did you study in Egypt or something?"

"No. I roomed with a Moroccan cab driver in Newark for two years. He was a hafiz."

"Hafiz?"

"A man who has memorized the *Quran*. He gave me lessons in Arabic and introduced me to his family and friends."

"Oh." She continued looking down the avenue at the receding taxi. "Well, uh … listen, Simone is here for the week, and I think you and I are heading off to Malmaison either Tuesday or Wednesday." She turned to him. "Could she come?" Charley asked earnestly. "She's from Corsica."

"I wanted to call you about that. I have to be in Greece."

"Oh," she pouted. "I need you, I'll never survive that damn test without you!"

"I sincerely apologize, probably should come," he said distractedly, handing Charly her things, "but it is unavoidable. Just for the next few days," he said, then muttered darkly, "a family thing."

He obviously did not want to go into it. "Anything I can do?" she offered.

"Not really. You have your hands full with Jodie."

"Yeah, but at least it's next week."

"All the same. You could do me a favor. I have taken the liberty of asking Colonel de Monteaux if he —"

"Noooo way! Sorry."

"I know how you feel."

"Do you?"

"Well, not exactly, but he could help out. I told you before, he's a strange sort of…well, goose, but —"

"Goose?" She wrinkled her nose. "You mean duck?"

"Yes, whatever. Duck! As long as we are butchering metaphors."

"*We* are?"

"I am … butchering … mon Dieu," he groaned. "Anyway, he is a good man and means well. He feels that he trod a bit hard on your sensibilities last Saturday and suffers guilt that he no doubt deserves. But he is reliable, plus Simone could tag along." An experienced pedagogue, he read her face and spoke before she could say no. "De Monteaux's a retired old bachelor now, you know, at loose ends and all that. He would make an excellent guide at Malmaison, and Napoleon is his forte."

"Not that I care, but what happened to him at Vincennes?"

"He got a ride."

"Tough place to find a ride."

"He has his means."

"Look," she said, "I got the basket of fruit he had delivered to the hotel—he hadn't the guts to apologize in person, I presume. I'm not out to make enduring enemies my first week in Paris, but if we continue to be the three musketeers, I'd like to know a little history."

Jean-Michel groaned. "He goes back a ways; it could take some time."

"And last night?"

"Time to pay the piper?"

"Life's just unvarnished quid pro quos."

"What can I say? He's older—"

"And sharp as tacks!"

His head sagged. "Look, I wasn't knocking old age," he sighed. "It's just too short." He reached for her hand as though to depart, but she made no attempt to leave. "We're not saying goodbye, are we?" His face pinched in resignation. "Some other time?" he said hopefully.

She smiled, "A few minutes...please." The sidewalk in front of the hotel was crowded, and they sought refuge on a nearby shady bench already occupied by two stout, scarfed women of Islamic persuasion. Charly and Jean-Michel wedged themselves in at the end. She felt snug and warm next to him, and again he got a whiff of Fendi.

"Three musketeers?" he said, rotating his glasses from his nose to rest on his head, nestling into curly red hair. "Am I Depardieu's character in the movie, the fat one in the haystack, or perhaps the other movie and his role as Astérix the Gaul...you know, my mustache?"

"Isn't your dog named after Astérix?" She eyed him. "How often do you read the comics? They are both Vikings and they both have mustaches! We're talkin' Obelix, dear, the one who looked like he swallowed a watermelon. Anyway, the Musketeer with the two naked women in the haystack. Match Depardieu, though? Probably not, he has great cheeks. But, believe me, Herr Doctor Professor, you would look impossibly cute in boots, tights, and feathered hat," she grinned. "I didn't mean to hold you up, you probably have errands; but...de Monteaux?"

"Boots and a feathered hat? Hadn't thought of that...perhaps tomorrow night you could wear a headband, braid your hair, and wear nothing but a chastity belt."

She jumped in, "Should I send you shopping for some lingerie and..." her face turned sultry, "shall we say, *devices*?" she whispered.

"Not really—already been, just luminous rubber things," he said matter-of-factly. "They do have riding crops, though…and maybe this time without your T-shirt."

"It's cold."

"Charly, it's June," he complained, and struggled for more room, eliciting dark, condescending looks from his bench mates. He smiled deferentially and turned back to her. "De Monteaux, yes, he does take a little explaining. I wanted to do this later, but—"

"No buts—you're on the clock." She handed back her stuff.

"They're yours!" he protested.

"Were. I have my bag," she cooed.

"Comfy?"

"Quite," she smiled.

He leaned back, balancing the umbrella and coat on his lap. "De Monteaux? Well, what can I say? First, he is not one of those who give themselves away in small change. Very private fellow; has a mysterious brother, a monk, somewhere in Canada. He is away a lot and doesn't come back with a tan. Their father was a prominent Catholic, died years ago in a car accident with a younger woman at his side. De Monteaux's mother never got over it. She is very old, and ill, probably fatally. He is devoted to her. They still live in Faubourg and have an old family villa at Balbec, but the colonel usually stays in a small apartment here in the city. Comes and goes—fairly secretive, I must admit.

"Oddly enough, he was married to a Vietnamese woman by the name of Lan Than, against the family's wishes, as you could imagine, then divorced some twenty years ago. She has a successful boutique near the Dôme. He also has a son and granddaughter, Eurasians, of course, whom he visits on the required holidays, but I don't think he has much contact. Her whole family is a prominent part of the Vietnamese community here, but he can't bring himself to accept them. Too many memories of the French Indochina conflict, I guess."

"Foolish man."

"Perhaps, but he was in the thick of it for a while, even a prisoner of war—you've noticed his limp. That interest in dungeons he spoke of at Le Procope isn't just academic. He escaped from a nasty one where they relieved him of a kneecap. Unfortunately, he carries more than just leg wounds, and

91

gets aggressive when he sees a Vietnamese he thinks may have been in the Northern Regulars."

"Strange that he married a Vietnamese."

"He met her before being taken prisoner, but there is more to it than that. Monteaux speaks Vietnamese fluently, a northern dialect, which he is unwilling to demonstrate, but I overheard him conversing at length with a Vietnamese student a few years ago who later told me that the colonel speaks the language like a Hanoi street vendor. He had served as a military attaché at the embassy in Hanoi while the French were trying to bring the communists to heel. He met Lan at a resort in Cam Ranh Bay and immersed himself in the culture for a couple of years, which was strictly forbidden by the embassy for security reasons. He tried to be the French version of Lawrence of Arabia, rallying various factions of South Vietnamese against Uncle Ho and his communist cadres. But when the war broke out, he was captured with a French expeditionary force of Legionnaires and spent over a year as a POW until he escaped. He began to take the side of the South Vietnamese politicians on French strategic issues too eagerly and upset his superiors. The embassy thought he was going native on them, so they shipped him home. At least that's one story."

"There're others?"

"I don't feel comfortable discussing it," he said curtly.

"And I don't feel comfortable going with him to Malmaison."

Jean-Michel grunted with exasperation and reflected momentarily. "Look, you must never repeat this, the consequences would be difficult to imagine. You must swear."

"I swear," she said quickly, betraying a sense of insincerity.

He hesitated, then began, "In brief, back in those days de Monteaux's artistic tastes centered around painting, and a particular fondness for the Dutch painter Vermeer. During the communist takeover of Vietnam, one of the prominent French families in Hanoi entrusted their art collection, including some rare Vermeers, to a young French officer at the embassy. Some of the paintings were never recovered. In the confusion and anxiety that surrounded the turbulent battles and evacuations, that French officer was identified as Captain Maurice de Monteaux.

"He denied any wrongdoing, of course, but the whole episode made

92

him very bitter; he was a career army officer, and the reprimand crippled any hope of senior promotion. He's extremely intelligent and never naive, but," he wagged his head, "just so damnably aggressive, an angry man. One thing you'll learn about the French," he warned, "criticism is considered the supreme demonstration of intelligence. He's opinionated, and you'll have to treat him carefully."

"So, he's been around, maybe swiped the 'Girl with a Pearl Earring.'"

"Charly, I warned you," he murmured.

"And now I have to deal with his complexes."

He immediately regretted his indiscretion — she habitually shot from the hip. "Charly, don't you ever say anything about that. I consider de Monteaux a close friend, and if he gets any indication you have heard the story, he will know exactly where it came from, which, as far as I am concerned, is not even correct."

"Any other good news?" she asked. He gave her a distressed look. She pinched his arm. "And?"

"And I guess you could say he has, well...," he paused, "negative feelings about women."

"Really? You're kidding."

"Charly, *Charly*, probably not all women, just feminists. He hates feminists, as you no doubt gathered last Saturday. But he's okay, you can trust him. He likes you."

"So do mosquitoes," she snapped.

He began searching for his pipe. "He knows Napoleonic history far better than I. You'll be fine."

"Now, *there's* a little irony: he hates feminists; quite out of character for a male chauvinist legionnaire, wouldn't you say? Like an international soccer match without a riot." She shook her head in resignation. "Well, Simone is something of an expert in her own right. The colonel is difficult to get along with, but if the man needs a little female flagellation, so be it! Simone hasn't had a good joust since she dumped Roberto of Rimini."

"I am sorry, I know how you must feel. It is true, the colonel's a cantankerous old devil at times, but as soldiers say, I would share a foxhole with him anytime. He is tough and smart." He said, and resumed preparations to light his pipe.

"Haven't spent time in foxholes, and my priorities for men aren't 'tough and smart.' He probably fucks with his boots on, but if it's gotta be, then I suppose it's gotta be," she said, toying with the idea of threatening him with a phone call to Voyages Classiques.

He tried to ignored her remarks, which, when she chose, had all the subtlety of a gold tooth. "Let me just say he is more than just a *joust* with Roberto." Jean-Michel squeezed her arm affectionately and, dislodging himself from the bench, walked to the curb and hailed a cab. "I'll ring you when I get back," he said over his shoulder. "We should go over to Place des Vosges ... have lunch and visit the Victor Hugo museum!" A white Mercedes taxi pulled up. He jumped in, then, leaning from the window, called out her, "Jusqu'alors,[11] if you're still talking to me!" He grinned and waved as the cab left.

CHAPTER 3

——≡ AN ARGUMENT OVER SOUP ≡——

The restaurant, L'Avili,[12] where Charly and Simone were to meet Colonel de Monteaux, was the first stop for lunch and suggested by Simone for its Corsican-style cooking, then on to Malmaison, a short distance by train from the center of Paris. The day teetered on the brink of rain. Charly and the colonel had already arrived, and were sequestered in a corner table, making honest attempts at being amiable as they sipped Pietra beer.

De Monteaux had apologized and now tried to move on to more cordial things. "You have been with us a few days, Charly. Jean-Michel feels you are doing fine. I hope you're not homesick."

He seemed grandfatherly, but she had seen his raw side. "Well, you know, it's not easy to pick up and move when the culture is all McDonald's; plus, in the States you can't run up and down stairs in a building under an orange terrorist alert. So, I'm happy to be back in France, but it was tough to leave my old company," she said. "On the other hand, it was mostly a saga of weasels." He frowned. She felt uncomfortable with this Frenchman, like driving on ice, and lobbed the conversation over to him. "You must be proud of your home and family, I'll bet your walls are covered with history."

"Oh," he said modestly, "all that well-fed pompousness has been lost in black and white. My mother is quite ill, you know, but perhaps you can visit sometime; our shelves are heaving with photograph albums. Paris has been home to my family for centuries."

"It is beautiful," she said.

"Beautiful? Certainly, and it's a thoroughly modern, vibrant city, but as thoughtlessly vulgar as any other, I suppose. I prefer the countryside…" he tested her politics, "damned immigrants and their riots." She didn't react.

"Perhaps you have been to Longchamps racecourse near the Bois de Boulogne? It's—" Just then a commotion erupted at the entrance, and Charlie's friend, Simone, swept through the door, a tall gangly woman in her mid-thirties, with a swarthy complexion and jet-black hair worn pageboy style. Tossed by a gust of wind, her arms and umbrella askew, she was laughing, and gave a noisy salute to the bartender in Corsican dialect. Monteaux quickly rose to be introduced.

Charly stood to hug Simone and traded kisses. "So, Colonel," Charly said interlocking her arm in Simone's, "this raucous woman of questionable poise, is—or was—my roommate in our graduate days at Aix-en-Provence. As you can see, we have reverted to our old student habit of traumatizing strangers." Exchanging pleasantries, they sat down and, when the waiter came, ordered lunch, while Charly, curious as to Simone's lively demeanor, pressed for an answer. Simone at first declined in deference to the colonel, only to giggle again, struggling to regain her composure. "Well what *is* it?" Charly demanded.

"Do you remember that American student, William, who is staying with my brother? Well, Claude got a huge telephone bill this month. When he told William that he had to call his girlfriend less often, William said that the calls were to his uncle." Charly gave a quizzical look. "It seems that William's uncle lives on Long Island, but unlike William, speaks fluent French, or at least French Canadian. Anyway, when it came time for dinner, William would often call his uncle on Long Island and ask him to place a take-out order at the local pizza restaurant in Paris; felt he was being abused when he tried to order, I guess." She paused a moment only to erupt again. "God, you Americans are unique."

"I agree," said the colonel. "They are unique, of course, but he'd better learn to cook. And speaking of food, I think the waiter has come with ours." He chuckled, showing large ivory-colored teeth under a close-cropped mustache.

Charly looked over at the colonel and shrugged her shoulders. "He's creative … and lazy. I would like to hear, just once, that an American knew how to speak a foreign language."

"Well, William has his problems with French," Simone said. "He tried to explain to Claude—you know, my brother—that American food was filled with *préservatifs*." The colonel choked on his drink.

Charly was puzzled. "Preservatives?"

"No," Simone sniggered, "condoms."

"Condoms!"

"Um-hm, our little faux amis.[13] It sounds like English, but that's the trap. It took me at least two years to be comfortable with French."

"You should know, Colonel," Charly said proudly, "that Simone was born in Ajaccio[14] and has made Napoleon's life and work something of a career."

The colonel looked up from his soup with some surprise. "You have no accent yourself, mam'selle. Were you educated here, or..." he paused, "in Corsica?" His voice had the edge of irony to it.

Simone, knowing instinctively that there was a strong upper-class bias against *les émigrés*, immediately took offense. "I was, Colonel," she said coolly. "Like Napoleon himself, and for that matter Josephine, born on a small island, with a strange accent. We have a persecution complex born of French occupation. A man of your years and considerable experience knows, of course, that there are no universities[15] to speak of on our little island."

"Well, I have studied the Corsicans a bit, but never found the occasion to visit, you know. One of these days I must try some of your famous sausage[16] and go hunting in those rugged valleys, provided I am not at the pointy end of someone else's rifle." He grinned.

"Perhaps you should bring along one or two of your French divisions, like 200 years ago. I'm sure you will be safe from the peasants," she said stiffly.

"Isn't that rather ancient history, mam'selle? I was not inquiring into your politics," his face turned stern, "simply your lack of accent. It was meant as a compliment."

Simone, a Corsican nationalist, ignored decorum and pressed her point. "Forgive me, Colonel, it was not my intention to return to the disputes of the eighteenth century. I am indeed not French, but Corsican, a member of Dr. Simeoni's FLNC.[17] I am not a militant, simply one who energetically seeks peace through just relations with France. You see, we voted 'no' to unification in the election." His complexion reddened, but only nodded in response.

Charly tried to turn the conversation from confrontation, only to stumble deeper into the fray. "Simone spent a year in an exchange program at

Georgetown University. She has been studying public administration at the Sorbonne, and completing her master's thesis on the origins of nineteenth-century French civil administration and the Napoleonic Code."

The colonel offered a thin smile, finished his wine, and dabbed his mustache with a linen napkin. Carefully folding it in squares, he placed it neatly on the table. "Ah, Simeoni and that tribe," he sneered. "His idealistic and unemployed bombers. I trust you are not one," he smiled grimly at Simone. "And your dissertation, of course. At, what was it, Georgetown? Yes. Jesuits. There can be no doubt erudition is with us today. Tell me, mam'selle, what have you found our Buonaparte to be? A hero and martyr, or egotist and dictator?" Smiling malevolently, he leaned forward, his armature poised to parry a thrust or pierce her irksome self-assurance.

"The answer is quite simple, Colonel," Simone retorted, her gaze briefly scanning the room, then fixing on him. "Napoleon had one of Europe's most gifted minds and hearts. Without him, French society would still be powdering its face and wigs, still be strutting about shamelessly on its spindly economic legs, while their anemic military sipped pastis[18] in a lazy stupor. Napoleon, a Corsican, has made France what it is today. His code is still with us, the envy of the Continent, and thanks to his vision, the traditions of French industry and Force de Frappe are the best and most powerful in Europe. Perhaps France could return the favor with independence for Corsica, as De Gaulle provided Algeria in '62,"—she paused to measure her effect, then turned the blade slightly—"since we neither share your language nor, shall we say, your taste for elegance."

The colonel fixed her with an icy stare, his square chin and shoulders resembling an advancing tank. "You will forgive me, mam'selle, I don't cherish those ideals that you have recited so easily. As for Buonaparte, we are talking about an interloper who dropped the "u" from his Italian name. France meant little more to 'Buonaparte'"—the colonel continued pronouncing Napoleon's name in the Italian style, using the "u"—than a fiddle on which he could play a better tune than on any other instrument; except for a small twist of fate he would have attended military school in Britain."

"Then France should be thankful to have had him."

"Thankful?" he growled. "You are ignorant of your history. He was a despot!"

Simone tossed her hair. "You're rewriting history, Colonel," she said flippantly.

"Would you rely on Nostradamus? Is he historical enough for you?" She gave him sour look, but he continued. "Throughout Nostradamus' quatrains he speaks of three powerful and tyrannical leaders that he calls 'anti-Christs.' Perhaps they didn't teach that in your Theology 101. He said they would lead their people through reigns of terror after first seducing them with promises of greatness.[19] Your cherished Napoleon is thought to have been the first of these anti-Christs, mam'selle."

"Where do you get such—" she started to say, only to be interrupted by the colonel, whose anger was reaching the boiling point as he quoted Nostradamus:

"An Emperor shall be born near Italy
Who shall cost the Empire dear,
They shall say, with what people he keeps company
He shall be found less a Prince than a butcher."

"That's pure drivel," Simone said cynically.

He leaned across the table at her. "It's *history*, mam'selle!" He spoke in a deep, raspy voice. "Obviously, you don't know Latin. And if my recollection of history serves me well, the French legal historian, Esmein, says of Buonaparte's contribution to the civil code that he cannot be considered a serious collaborator in the great work, since it is the work of the professional jurists.[20] Napoleon's disdain for the clergy, and his Concordat,[21] speak for themselves. And as for your recitation of his so-called military traditions, we all know he departed France with over 500,000 men on his way to glory in Moscow, but was not even successful in meeting the Czar, much less conquering the country, and at a cost of 460,000 dead and wounded. His legacy is a highway of bleached bones and stolen national treasures. It is also true, mam'selle, that he was instrumental in unifying the Germans against us, the consequences of which perhaps you were too innocent, on your *little island*, to appreciate."

"So, to you, I suppose," she snarled, "Napoleon was just some little Corsican ragazzo[22] with an attitude!?"

99

"Which Napoleon, mam'selle?" He glared back menacingly. "Do you mean the destroyer, the despiser of men, the foreigner, the Corsican, especially scornful of Frenchmen, careless of French blood, devourer of generations of young Europeans, suppressor of all free opinion? Oh, no, mam'selle," he shot back, "his was no simple attitude — he was our consummate *tyrant*!"

The air became electrified, as during the instant after a flash of lightning and just before the nerve-shattering thunderclap. Charly clutched Simone's arm. "Oh, Jesus, let's drop it there. I mean, we have a lot to do, you know. Malmaison by two o'clock. We should go now and hope that the rain has stopped; taxis shouldn't be as hard to get," and jerked Simone from her seat. Making preparations to leave, the colonel limped forward to assist both women with their jackets. Simone, her face crimson with anger, ostentatiously donned her own. The small party left, much quieter than when they entered.

CHAPTER 4

═══ MALMAISON ═══

"Malmaison. Bad house?" Charly grimaced.

"Bad house." The colonel repeated after her as they strode three abreast down the carefully manicured lawns and gravel driveway toward the stately mansion in the distance, which had housed perhaps Europe's most famous couple: Napoleon Buonaparte and Josephine Beauharnais.

"Why in heaven's name would anyone call their home a 'bad house,' or for that matter call Milan's airport Malpensa, 'bad thought'?" Caught between the abrasive natures of these two strong-willed Europeans, Charly was showing strain and annoyance in her own right.

"Who knows?" he frowned. "At best, some records show that, back in the 800s, during the Norman wars, all that area was laid waste by plunderers and came to be known as Malport and Malmaison. According to legend, a Norman chief took refuge in the original Malmaison, perhaps a farm or, as some say, even a leper house, which could account for the name. Interestingly enough, no one, not even the Buonapartes, ever attempted to change it."

"But I think," Simone said, looking over at Charly and rolling her eyes, "the colonel would agree with me," extending the olive branch, "that despite the name, Malmaison, at least the eighteenth-century version, was the center of the relationship between Napoleon and Josephine."

"I do agree," he nodded at Simone, "but their marriage, like so many of the time, was more Josephine's attempt at social maneuvers than love and conception."

"Strange, I never gave much thought to Napoleon having a sex life. I thought he was all armies and brandy," Charly said.

"Oh, he had one, all right," Simone assured her, "but not much before Josephine. He had what amounted to a puppy love for a young woman named

Désirée from Marseille, and even wrote a love story, 'Clisson e Eugénie,' about their relationship. In his short story he posed the dilemma: either his career, or love in the wilds; and he chose to love in the wild. So it does help a little in understanding how he felt at that period of his life. His brother, Joseph, even married one of the sisters in the family, but when Napoleon made overtures toward Désirée, the mother was known to have said, 'One poor Buonaparte in the family is enough.' Désirée eventually married General Bernadotte, a hero at Austerlitz, who turned into an avowed enemy of Napoleon and was future King of Sweden.

"In any event, Napoleon definitely was not the kind of man women swooned over. On the other hand, he wasn't always that potbellied little man with the funny hat seen in the pictures, either. When he was an eighteen-year-old lieutenant, he had a certain panache: angular face, flowing hair, and piercing eyes, but in Paris he often walked the streets lonely and broke. Inflation was rampant back then, and army pay was poor. Napoleon recorded in his notebook that on the evening of Thursday, 22 November 1787, he went for a walk in the Palais Royal to cheer himself up. 'Taking long strides' as he said, he walked through the bright lights of the cafés, which offered English beer and ratafia. There was even a Café Mécanique, where the mocha was pumped to cups through the hollow central leg of each round cafe table. The biographies say he was vigorous by temperament and didn't mind the cold, but after a time it was beginning to bite." Simone stopped. "This part could be more interesting, Charly, if it was in his own words; would you like me to read it?"

"How long?"

"He has her panties down in less than a page. Colonel?"

He shrugged his shoulders. "I have no interest in Napoleon's carousing."

"Then perhaps you could find something *interesting* to do, Colonel," Simone said coldly.

"Perhaps I could. Excuse me," he said abruptly, and limped quickly on ahead.

"Good," Charly whispered, holding Simone back. "Besides, I haven't heard that many testimonials on males losing their virginity. Certainly *that* man will never have anything to contribute. I'd love to slip some Viagra into his beer and watch."

"Watch what? That old man? How perverted are you?"

Simone fished out a book from her voluminous shoulder bag, paused to find the right page, and read the following passage from Napoleon's diary:

> I turned into the arcades. I was on the point of entering a café when I noticed a woman. It was late, she had a good figure and was very young; she was clearly a prostitute. I looked at her, and she stopped. Instead of the disdainful manner such women usually affect, she seemed quite natural. I was struck by that. Her shyness gave me the courage to speak to her. Yes, I spoke to her, though more than most people I hate prostitution and have always felt sullied just by a look from women like that...But her pale cheeks, the impression she gave of weakness and her soft voice at once overcame my doubts. Either she will give me interesting information, I said to myself, or she's just a blockhead.

"You're going to catch cold," I said. "How can you bear to walk in the arcades?"

"Ah, sir, I keep on hoping. I have to finish my evening's work."

She spoke with a calm indifference which appealed to me and I began to walk beside her.

"You don't look very strong. I'm surprised you're not exhausted by a life like this."

"Heavens, sir, a woman has to do something."

"Maybe. But isn't there some other job better suited to your health?"

"No, sir, I've got to live."

I was enchanted. At least she answered my questions, something other women had declined to do.

"You must be from the north, to brave cold like this."

"I'm from Nantes in Brittany."

"That's a part I know...Mademoiselle, please tell me how you lost your maidenhood."

"It was an army officer."

"Are you angry?"

"Oh, yes, take my word for it." Her voice took on a pungency I hadn't noticed before. "Take my word for that. My sister is well set up. Why aren't I?"

"How did you come to Paris?"

"The officer who did me wrong walked out. I loathe him. My mother was furious with me and I had to get away. A second officer came along and took me to Paris. He deserted me too. Now there's a third; I've been living three years with him. He's French, but has business in London, and he's there now. Let's go to your place."

"What will we do there?"

"Come on, we'll get warm and you'll have your fill of pleasure."

I was far from feeling scruples. Indeed, I didn't want her to be frightened off by my questions, or to say she didn't sleep with strangers, when that was the whole point of my accosting her."[23]

"To the best of my knowledge, this is the first recorded time that Napoleon slept with a woman—at least he spent some quality time with his diary. I've been to Brittany, and she probably had the white skin and black hair typical of Bretons; perhaps also that dreamy quality that sets them off from the more matter-of-fact Parisians. What is certain is that she was slight and feminine, the type that appeals to most men—just my luck—and that Napoleon liked her soft voice. They say the first thing Napoleon noticed in a woman was her hands and feet. If her hands and feet were small, he was prepared to find her attractive, but not otherwise. The second quality he sought was femininity. Women with a giving, tender nature and a soft voice evoked his protective instinct. He looked for sincerity and depth of feeling. This was something more than a mere physical encounter; Napoleon tried to get to know her as a person, and felt sympathetic toward her situation."

"I was scanning the Josephine section in one of the files Voyages Classiques gave me."[24]

"And?"

Charly frowned. "Confused by the whole thing. Was Josephine somehow like a society prostitute? Did she love him or not? I feel like I've been here before. Remember that teacher at Aix-en-Provence who was always so coy with the handsome students in our class?

"I never noticed they had to be handsome," Simone said.

"True, the woman was a nymphomaniac. Remember how she would tell us in class that her door was open to everyone? The guys would come over to her office, she'd shut the door, and they would work on their grades. She was about as subtle as a spawning salmon. Devious woman, and it seems Josephine's running a close second."

"Oh, my!" Simone said, "Claws! I didn't know you were jealous of Deveraux's moves."

"That's her name! I forgot. God, how time flies. Good ol' Madame Deveraux. I wasn't jealous, really. Give any of those guys a glass of wine, a chance for a passing grade, and you would never get off your back."

"Didn't know you felt that way. But Josephine wasn't in Deveraux's class. On the other hand, she certainly was not the simple flower of nature Napoleon had imagined he would fall in love with; she was sophisticated, smartly dressed, and, above all, interested in his 'affairs.'[25] Despite her passion for parties and fashion, she had a more serious side. She was not necessarily good at politics, just good at people. In a way, he and Josephine were complete opposites, yet underneath they had a lot in common. They came from the same class, neither native French, they both believed in the Revolution, yet were both imprisoned by it, and they shared certain basic values — loyalty being a principal one, which survived both their marital indiscretions. But she was married before, of course; actually, her sister, Catherine, was supposed to marry the guy, but she died before they could tie the knot. Josephine's father needed the dowry, so he substituted Josephine for Catherine. It was a bad marriage despite two kids, Eugene and Hortense."

"What happened to him?"

"Alexander? Guillotined. He was a member of high society and a make-believe general."

"That'll teach 'im, no more makin' believe."

"You know what I mean. Josephine herself came within a day or two of getting her head chopped off, but lucky for her, Robespierre got it first."

"I thought he was assassinated."

"There was a good try; he was shot in the jaw, but it didn't kill him. His former lackeys guillotined him a day later. When they heard the news of his death, French high society had parties to celebrate the end of the terror. Out of respect for their families, the women wore a red ribbon around their necks, right where the blade would have hit if one of their members had been decapitated. Maybe it was at one of those parties that Josephine met Napoleon."

"So, Josephine had her red ribbon. Did Napoleon make much of an impression?"

"He didn't, but she couldn't make up her mind, and probably didn't love him. She found him strikingly attractive, which you can see in his younger portraits. He was different from the other men: he was cocky, and he liked her other name, Josephine. She was known as Rose at the time, but Napoleon didn't like it, so he convinced her to go with Josephine."

"Takes someone special to do that, unless your name is Ophelia or Gertrude. Maybe some handsome executive will sweep me off my feet at a socialite party down at the local chamber of commerce and rename me Madeline ...see, Josephine ... it rhymes."

"Um-hm. 'Charly' is a nice name for a donkey."

"Thanks."

"I'm sure it is a sign. Anyway, he did not give Josephine expensive presents, but he was sincere and had eyes only for her, which is nice. She, on the other hand, had to provide a living for her children and herself, and Napoleon was pressing.

"One fateful evening in January 1796, according to those who know, Napoleon made love with Josephine. For her this was doubtless a diversion, something she preferred to call *drolle*, a 'one-nighter.' But, for Napoleon, this was the first time he had possessed a woman he loved. He had a very passionate nature, which had been kept in check by his mother since adolescence. Next day he expressed his strong feelings for Josephine in a letter[26] that eventually became famous. Listen."

"You always carry that little book around with you?" Charly asked incredulously.

"You do when you don't get any letters of your own, and a certain friend, just like the old days, hasn't sent any." Simone opened the book to the appropriate page and read:
'Seven in the morning.

I have woken up full of you. Your portrait and the memory of yesterday's intoxicating evening have given my senses no rest. Sweet and incomparable Josephine, what an odd effect you

106

have on my heart! Are you displeased? Do I see you sad? Are you worried? Then my soul is grief-stricken, and your friend cannot rest.... But I cannot rest either when I yield to the deep feeling that overpowers me and I draw from your lips and heart a flame that burns me. Ah! Last night I clearly realized that the portrait I had of you is quite different from the real you! You are leaving at noon, and in three hours I shall see you. Until then, mio dolce amor, thousands of kisses; but don't kiss me, for your kisses sear my blood.'

"I love that man," Simone sighed wistfully, "and I only missed him by a couple of centuries. In Josephine's set, you see, it was considered poor taste to treat bed as more than a passing pleasure. She was undoubtedly very surprised by his reaction. It spoiled the fun of it all. She even tried to cool his ardor by telling him that she had been Barras' mistress."

"All that for a diminutive overachiever? I don't suppose it went over well?" Charly said.

"Don't know. Didn't deter Napoleon. First of all, he believed Barras was a homosexual and thought Josephine even more lovable for being 'experienced.' Dear Lord," she muttered, "just one man like that. He could have had her easily as his mistress, but he wanted something more regular and orderly, so he proposed to her. Napoleon knew that Josephine had no property in France, and that by marrying her he would have to adopt her children, both at expensive schools, and take over the full responsibility, at a time when he was already supporting two brothers and three sisters. He had only his general's pay on his side."

"General's?"

"I'll get to that. He was so deeply in love with her that he didn't mind. Whether his marriage would have an impact on his career didn't worry him. He believed that 'passion should be governed by reason', sort of like Roberto, remember? Except Roberto's passion had trouble discerning the 'reason part'."

"Ah, that great summer with Roberto and his sidekicks from Rimini. I told you, Simone, told you then, telling you now!" Charly exclaimed. "Never date guys who prefer creepshacks and live by beaches."

107

"May I continue, before we become engrossed in Roberto's beery-smell-ing charms again? As I said, Barras, Josephine's former lover, of sorts, and who had risen to power, approved of the marriage. If Napoleon's marriage provided stability, it would be to Barras' advantage to appoint him to the Army of the Alps, since any successes in that post would reflect credit on Barras, plus get the competition out of Paris. This would be his wedding present, you see, a little promotion slipped into the package. He also want-ed to be disentangled from 'Rose.' Napoleon was bound and determined to propose marriage to Josephine once he had assured himself that it would not harm his career and that he could afford it. Barras' offer was merely an added incentive. But Josephine didn't see it that way; the mingling of love and politics upset her. She made a scene and accused Napoleon of marrying her only in order to get the command in Italy. She looked into her heart, as they say, and asked herself what her feelings were for Napoleon. Josephine was able to be extraordinarily honest when she wrote to a friend," she dug into her bag again, "let me read you the letter.[27]

"'Do you love him?" is naturally your first question.

My answer is perhaps—No.

"Do you dislike him?"

No again—but the feelings I have for him are of that luke-warm kind which true devotees think worst in all matters of religion. Now, love being a sort of religion, my feelings ought to be very different from what they really are. This is the point on which I want your advice...to come to a decision has always been too much for my Créole inertness, and I find it easier to obey the wishes of others.

I admire the General's courage; the extent of his informa-tion on every subject on which he converses; his shrewd intelli-gence, which enables him to understand the thoughts of others before they are expressed; but I confess I am somewhat fearful of that control which he seems anxious to exercise on all about him. There is something in his penetrating gaze that cannot be described...He talks of his passionate love for me with a serious-ness that makes it impossible to doubt his sincerity, yet this...is precisely what has stopped me from giving the consent which I have often been on the point of giving....

My spring of life is past. Can I then hope to preserve for any length of time this ardent love, which in the General amounts almost to madness? If his love should cool, as it certainly will, after our marriage, will he not reproach me for having prevented him from making a better match?...

Barras assured me that if I marry the General he will get him appointed Commander-in-Chief of the army of Italy ... The General said 'Do they think I cannot get forward without their patronage? One of these days they will be all too happy if I grant them mine. I have a good sword by my side which will carry me on.' What do you think of this self-confidence? Does it not savor of excessive vanity? A General to talk of patronizing the chiefs of Government? It is very ridiculous. Yet I know not how it happens, his ambitious spirit sometimes impresses me so much that I am almost tempted to believe in the practicability of any project he takes into his head—and who can foresee what he may attempt?'

"She may not have been the best of women," Charly allowed, "but that woman was articulate."

"Had pretty good intuition, Simone added. So, for Josephine it was decision time, that nasty little dilemma we all seem to face. Thirty-two years old, still young and pretty—like us—but with no sure income, like us. Sure, she was not in love with Napoleon, and the prospects of a civil union could easily end in divorce, so not much security there. Still, Napoleon wanted the marriage ardently, and Barras wanted it too, so she finally said yes."

"Big wedding?"

"No. Her lawyer, a dwarfish-looking fellow, closeted himself in a room with Josephine the night of the marriage, but failed to shut the door tight. Napoleon heard him say through the partly open door, 'This is a very great mistake, and you're going to be sorry for it. You're doing something quite mad—marrying a man who has only his army cloak and sword.' To the best of my knowledge, two versions of history come out of this scene: one, Napoleon was deeply hurt and never forgot the incident; two, Napoleon was so impressed with the lawyer's honesty that he spoke to the man, congratulated him, and appointed him to a high post later in Napoleon's career. The second seems to me to have more truth. From the materialistic point of view, the marriage turned out to be extremely unfavorable for Napoleon. There was no community of goods, and Napoleon had to pay a considerable amount of money for the rest of his life."[28]

"Can you tell me what their marriage was like? Just in case I find my Napoleon." Charly said.

"And your faithful Allen, New York's celebrated weatherman?"

"I'm sending him postcards, and—"

"And?"

"A friend e-mailed me that he's been seen hanging out with his ex-wife. Besides, a Napoleon he ain't."

"Nice friend. Okay, so we need a little motivation here," she said, moving quickly to that subject on which all women have an opinion. "How about their wedding night?" The two, lagging behind the colonel, talked in the confidence of females. The colonel was left to survey the park as they walked toward the chateaux. "We can get to his and her affairs later," Simone whispered, and signaled with her eyes at the older man ahead as he limped along assisted by his cane.

"The marriage took place on the evening of 9 March 1796. She was older than him by six years."

"And the proud parents?" Charly asked.

"Dad was literally angelic by that time, and Mom is a story all her own, but none of Napoleon's family knew that he was to be married, which fueled their resentment of Josephine from the start. It was a small wedding. All the witnesses had gathered at 3 Rue d'Antin, the house of a nobleman, including Barras, Napoleon's pompous, money-grubbing boss and, as I said, one of the most powerful figures in Paris. Barras delighted in fine clothes, and at the wedding wore his ostentatious three-plumed velvet hat, which represented one of the five directors of government. Josephine, they say, wore a white high-waisted muslin dress decorated with red, white, and blue flowers. The last to arrive, two hours late, was the groom, in his gold-embroidered blue uniform, so small and thin in his big boots that the socialites called him 'Puss 'N Boots!'

"The acting registrar, an ex-soldier with a wooden leg, had dozed off beside the fire. Napoleon shook him awake. 'Come on,' he demanded, 'marry us quickly,'" Simone said in a gruff voice, mimicking Napoleon. "Then, after the brief ceremony of 'citizen' marrying 'citizen,' Napoleon and Josephine drove off through the cold March night to their pretty, unpaid-for house on Rue Chantereine.

"As a wedding present, Napoleon gave Josephine a simple necklace of hair-fine gold from which hung a little plaque of gold and enamel. On the plaque were inscribed two words: '*Au destin*,' meaning, loosely translated, that Providence had brought them together and would look after them."

"Didn't they have wedding rings then?" Charly asked.

"Good question. It was post-Revolution France, so maybe that was considered bourgeois. I don't know where the ring thing came from; I never thought to ask, particularly since no one ever offered me one," Simone said darkly.

Colonel de Monteaux had continued on ahead. Reaching the museum office, he occupied himself with purchasing the tickets, and waited for the two women to join him.

Simone continued, "The ground-floor bedroom was upholstered in blue, and hung with lots of looking glasses." Simone hesitated a moment. "Don't know why she hung the looking glasses, not something I'd do, but, well, maybe that was Josephine. Anyway, you're going to love this: Napoleon found that he was not to be alone with his bride. Josephine had a pug dog named Fortuné who was devoted to her. The pug had been with her in prison, and carried messages to her and her friends hidden in his collar. Since then, Fortuné had had the privilege of sleeping on Josephine's bed. When Napoleon sought to avail himself of the same privilege, Fortuné resented it. He barked, snapped, and finally bit his rival in the calf. Napoleon later told the writer Arnault that he, Napoleon, was given the choice of sleeping in another bed or sharing the one with Fortuné. The situation certainly annoyed him, he said, but it was a question of take it or leave it, so he resigned himself to a threesome."[29]

"I thought those things only happened in Woody Allen movies," Charly said. "Now I know where he got his material. Seriously, though, I thought France was such a fervent Catholic country—no priest at the wedding?"

"Well, not theirs at least. Napoleon had little use for Catholicism, and particularly the popes, except when it served his purposes; probably Josephine felt the same. I think there's some truth that he would have preferred Protestants in religious control, but they comprised only a percent or two of the population. That's also one of the reasons why Napoleon's mother, Letizia, a Corsican, of course, disliked Josephine from the beginning. Letizia was a very religious person—wenet to Mass every day of her life, I believe—and would never have agreed to a non-Catholic wedding; therefore, she wasn't even invited. On the other hand, Napoleon was in a rush to get married, like he was with everything, certainly more a consequence of his impatience than of any disrespect to his mother. She was a proud woman of strict principles, but later on, when Napoleon was married to Josephine, she could not overcome her dislike for her daughter-in-law." Simone leaned close to Charly. "How would you like to hear this from your mother-in-law?" And Simone quoted with a throaty Italian accent: 'This Creole says soft nothings to every man, and kisses every woman, instead of attending to her business and bearing children.'"[30]

"Sounds like my ex's mother."

"Wouldn't know, no marital bliss. Anyway, Letizia had given birth to thirteen children and helped raise the surviving eight to adulthood. She thought that Josephine's barrenness dishonored Napoleon and his family. She fancied that in the eyes of many of his adversaries she could read satisfaction and mockery because her son could not procreate. Coming from Corsica, these people were sober; I mean, they would have made the Godfather seem frivolous. Corsicans disliked Parisians in general for their highfalutin ways, and in this case their thrift was outraged by Josephine's new dresses, designed, they say, with a maximum of elegance and a minimum of material."

"Republicans," Charly said lamely.

"Absolutely. Oh, Texas! I forgot. Anyway, their conservatism was shocked by Josephine's hairstyles, and their sense of propriety by her Paris friends, one of whom, for example, had, for a wager, walked halfway across Paris bare-breasted in a flimsy dress."

As they approached the chateau, Colonel de Monteaux came up to them from a crowd of people buying tickets.

"Here he comes," Simone murmured.

"The tour starts in about fifteen minutes," he said, passing out the admission tickets.

"We were just talking about Josephine," Charly said.

"The family disliked Josephine," he said abruptly. "However, Charly, you should know that it was deserved: she was an adulterous woman with no scruples."

Simone groaned, but the colonel continued.

"I don't suppose Simone told you about Hippolyte Charles?" Charly shook her head. "Of course not," he said, scowling at Simone.

"There are many versions of Napoleon's life, Charly, and Simone has given you only one. As to Buonaparte's family, once they were all in Paris, they often saw what Buonaparte couldn't: the loving glances exchanged between Josephine and her new love, Hippolyte Charles. Buonaparte and Josephine were no sooner married, and he off to the Italian Campaign, than she was in an affair with this fagot!"

Simone held up her hand in protest. "Wait, wait! You'll never hear that part from me. I doubt, Colonel, you are referring to a homosexual here, particularly if he is bedding Josephine. I don't use that word, nor do I like people who do. Perhaps you could be more careful with your meaning." He was about to respond aggressively, but, caught in his bigotry, retreated, limping over to a nearby bench and taking out his cell phone.

Charly began to draw circles in the gravel with the toe of her shoe. "What was so alluring about this Hippolyte Charles that he could so easily win over Josephine against a man like Napoleon?"

"Well, it certainly wasn't noble birth. Josephine was never one to overlook aristocratic virtues. Hippolyte was, in fact, the ninth son of a draper and three years younger than Napoleon. He stood five feet six inches tall, about Napoleon's height, but had very brown skin, blue eyes, black hair, and sideburns...I would imagine an Antonio Banderas kind of guy. He was a good-enough soldier, but people, above all Josephine, were struck by 'his pretty face and the elegance of a hairdresser's assistant.'[31]

"That's it?"

"What else attracted Josephine?" Simone reflected. "Three things, I think, but remember he was nine years younger. First, like her and unlike Napoleon, Hippolyte was extremely interested in clothes. Just as many women do, he enjoyed the touch, cut, and color of clothing, and he supposedly took great pleasure cruising around Paris in his tasseled red leather boots and a silver-embroidered, red-fox-trimmed cape slung jauntily over the left shoulder.[32]

"The thing that Josephine liked about this man most, though, was that he made her laugh. Whereas Napoleon had a sense of humor, he seldom joked; Hippolyte, on the other hand, current with all the local color and banter from his friends, kept her entertained throughout the day.

"Another advantage over Napoleon was that Hippolyte made time for Josephine. Poor ol' Napoleon had only managed two days after the wedding before leaving for the war in Italy; Charles, it seemed, could always find occasions to get to Paris, and once there find reasons to stay.

"It's not too surprising that Josephine fell in love with him," she reflected. "This guy, a drawing-room officer, was not always glancing at the clock like Napoleon did, while he shared the latest gossip and the newest witticisms. Hippolyte admired Joesphine's latest wardrobe with a connoisseur's eye, and it takes a real man to do that. He was droll, she said, and beautifully turned out, and of course he had lots of time for her." Simone assumed an actress' pose and, in richly accented French, mimicked Josephine: "How fine he looked in his chasseur uniform, she was to say; and he tells such amusing stories, has an expert knowledge of the latest shawls and wigs, and his legs are so well formed![33] So, while the cat's away in Italy fighting for France, the mice were playing in Paris."

Simone looked around to see if the colonel was at a safe distance. He was, just out of hearing, intently on the phone. Simone leaned close and conspiratorially asked, "So, what's with this guy Jean-Michel?"

"I thought we went over that already."

"That was the train ride," Simone said exasperatedly. "What's gone on since?"

"Like I said, he's a hunk."

"A hunk? Really!" she said enviously.

"Really. About five feet nine and 200 pounds—obviously not susceptible to eating disorders."

"What 'disorders'?"

"Manorexia—you know, like Dennis Quaid admits to—but I like him. He's not fat-fat, and does have a good sense of humor. He's kind, it seems.

114

Smart, it also seems, and a typical academic."

"'Typical' how?"

"Pompous, with a reader's physique."

"Hm. So?" Simone dug for the information.

"So?"

"So, what's he like?" she whined. "Mon Dieu! Is he rich?"

"Poor. Can't afford brand-name toilet paper. But, he's typically French. When you ask him a question he shrugs, the shoulders lift, the corners of his mouth turn down, his eyebrows go up, his head tilts to the right. And he exhibits a certain facility with a corkscrew."

"Merde! Time is short, woman, you know what I mean. Has he tried to get you into bed?"

"Okay, we've spent time together, but he has something of a flawed comprehension of women. And he lingers on the toilet, reading Proust."

"Proust? Isn't this all a little *too* quick?"

"No lectures. I need friends."

"How old is he? Viagra?"

"Yeah, Viagra came up once. It's not a lifestyle. He's shy, says it prevents him rolling out of bed. Besides, he likes golf more than women."

"Golf?"

"Um-hm, men's passion. Swinging at things with all those sticks. Our dinner conversations eventually get around to shankin' his bogey."

"Yankin' his–?"

"I don't know either, skip it. You and Klaus?"

"Hey!" Simone said excitedly. "He's here, you know, living over on St. Jacques. But it's over. He is in love with his bicycle. I'm surprised they don't make a seat that feels like a muffin. We're getting together on Wednesday for a drink."

"Muffin?"

"You know...." She glanced down toward her crotch.

"You mean cunt, sweetheart, or pudendum, depending on the company you keep. God, good ol' Klaus," Charly said fondly. "So?"

"Remember, so many moons ago, just before you left Aix for the States, that Klaus and I went for the long weekend in Cannes?" Charly nodded. "And you know the story about skinny guys with big feet?"

"Yeah, I guess. I thought that was puppies and paws."

"Similar," Simone giggled. "Wow, has he got big feet! When I got back that weekend I couldn't walk, felt like I'd been," she hesitated, smiled, and whispered, "fucked by a Mack truck. He is here in Paris, you know, but Klaus can wait. More on Jean-Michel?"

Charly wrinkled her nose. "He doesn't stand close enough to the shower."

"What is it with Frenchmen?"

"You should know, but I seriously doubt it has to do with appearance anxieties. Could be their damn washing machines — the hotel's takes three hours to wash a bra and two panties. And he drinks. More than he should, but so do a lot of guys. As near as I can tell he holds it pretty well. He's a lot older than I am, and has hair growing out of most places, including his nose and ears."

"That's attractive. I wonder why they don't get their bodies waxed," Simone said.

"Why? To remove all traces of their primate origins? You think they really want to know what it feels like to have the most delicate skin on their bodies set on fire and then extinguished with Jack Daniel's, or perhaps be gored from behind by a rhinoceros?"

"Oh, my God, enough," she moaned. "Is he married?"

"That's what I thought at first, but…" Charly shrugged. "Men are good obscuring those things. I don't know him that well, at least not yet. He hangs out with the general there," she nodded her head disdainfully toward the colonel, "and some weasel named Pierre. He and the colonel are pretty tight. They work on dungeons and tombs. I get the feeling he's having trouble at his institute, though. He seems pretty cynical about his boss."

"Like?"

"Says his boss is a dork of the first order. 'A hawk-nosed little shit,' he called him, lives with his nose stuck up some rich guy's ass, his only claim to fame, except for screaming at his employees. In any event, doesn't have much respect for French administrators and all that, says they're tight-asses with a streak of vindictiveness a mile wide."

"Sounds like he has difficulty expressing himself."

"Um-hm, like me. It could cost him his job."

"Any future for Mr. and Mrs. Jean-Michel?"

"None."
Simone's eyes narrowed.
"Sure?"
"Nope."

CHAPTER 5

══ NAPOLEON: PARTY ANIMAL ══

"Ladies," the colonel called, "it's almost time."

The tour guide had begun to gather the people together.

"Do you think Napoleon and Josephine were well matched?" Charly asked hurriedly. "I mean, was Napoleon your typical Italian stallion with women?"

"Hm. Well, he was an Italian, sort of, or at least Corsican. Good question. Napoleon disliked bossy and meddlesome women, so that lets you out."

"Let's me out?"

"You know what I mean. Josephine, on the other hand, was a paragon of femininity. She wasn't into leather and cowboys. Napoleon loved her deeply, and no woman influenced him so much. But that's not to say he didn't have affairs with other women; seven, to be exact."

"I wonder how many women men average?" Charly asked.

"I know. Just read it. *Le Mond* says American men average sixteen. And French?"

"Hm, thirty-two?" Charly guessed.

"Nope, gotcha." Simone clapped her hands. "Thirteen!"

"Less!? I don't believe it."

"Well, according to the article, it is.[34] Anyway, if you were looking for an example, Napoleon's mistresses were young and smart. The article said that French men continue to see French women as staying sexy, even into their later years; Americans still want their women fast and young."

"Great! So we're natural Ferraris. What else?"

"We are? How about natural Volvos? Napoleon enjoyed socializing at parties, of course, where he met a lot of women, as you might imagine. And he invited the old nobility to his court, but being a commoner, there was coolness between him and them. Some funny exchanges took place, though."

"We gotta go," Charly cautioned. "Tour's almost ready. Tell me while we walk. Funny exchanges? Like?"

"Well, during one party, Napoleon brusquely addressed the Duchesse de Fleury, known to be fast with men: 'Well, Madame, still fond of men?' he asked. 'Oh, yes, Sire, when they are polite.'" Charly giggled. "On another occasion, Madame de Chevreuse came to the Tuileries in a blaze of diamonds. 'What a splendid array of jewels!' said Napoleon, then asked naively: 'Are they all real?' 'Oh, heavens, Sire, I really don't know. At any rate, they are good enough to wear here.'

"Napoleon was an entertaining man, and could give as well as take; you probably would have liked a date with him. He was fond of the arts, liked paintings of men achieving things, for example, with lots of color, movement, and historical exactitude. His favorite instrument, so to speak," she smirked, "was the human voice, and his favorite music that of Giovanni Paesiello. Of the aria 'Già il sol' in Paesiello's pastoral, *Nina,* he said that he could listen to it every evening of his life.[35] You'd have to like opera, though, because he was quite a fan, they say, attending around ten performances each year."

Charly wrinkled her nose. "No opera, thanks," then got that look in her eye. "What was that about his other instrument?"

"I didn't say—

"Get off it, did he have 'big feet' or…?" Charly insisted.

"He had very little feet, dear. I don't think you, coming from Texas, would have been happy."

"What's Texas got to do with it?"

"Don't be coy. By the way, what do you do in New York, anyway, still walking that damn schnauzer for fulfillment?"

"You knockin' my dog?"

"The one that pissed on your pillow? Seems the message was clear enough."

"Yeah. I had to give him away."

"Give away your dog?!" Simone exclaimed.

"Yeah, to a couple of Uzbekis. It's all right, we were neighbors for a while. They said they'd take good care of him. My aunt took the cat. So what was with the books?"

Simone shook her head. "Uzbekis? Why didn't you just say Klingons? Okay, books. Napoleon's favorite reading was narrative history, which, by the way, he believed was just for men. His library was full of such books: the *Iliad*, Voltaire's *History of Charles XII*, that sort of thing. He enjoyed plays, but tragic drama was his preference, even though he was known to have a good sense of humor."

Colonel de Monteaux called for them to join him and begin the tour. As the two women arrived, Simone spoke to him: "We missed you, Colonel. Charly had been asking about Napoleon's taste in women and the arts. She was interested to know if Napoleon was religious."

De Monteaux handed Charly a package. "I stepped into the museum shop to buy you a guidebook; there are some references to Malmaison and that, uh … Hippolyte Charles."

"Sweet of you, Colonel. Thanks," Charly said, examining the book, then stuffing it in her bag. "Can I make a suggestion? It's a little crowded … couldn't we do the tour on our own? You both know Malmaison well enough, and we could avoid all the people. Let's wait for them to move on a bit, then we can begin." The partners agreed and went back to the entrance area to wait for the group to move ahead. Charly gestured for them to sit beside her on the benches in the vestibule, a light, airy place where almost 200 years earlier the Buonapartes had received their guests.

"Buonaparte and religion? It's acutely boring," the colonel said, "since Buonaparte never cared a whit about religion, except where it served his need. He talked a good game, of course, philosophical and all that when he was courting a nation, appeasing his mother, or controlling his brothers and sisters.[36] Of the Gospels he said something to the effect that they are beautiful parables; excellent moral teaching, but few facts. He was always interested in facts. Jesus, he said, should have performed his miracles not in remote parts of Syria in front of a few whose good faith can be called into question, but in a city like Rome, in front of the whole population. To quote him, 'If I had to have a religion, I should worship the sun — the source of all life — the true God of earth.'[37]

"But there was in Buonaparte's Egyptian campaign an interesting story," the colonel continued, "in which he tried to win the support of the

Egyptian religious leaders. 'Napoleon,' after all, means 'desert lion' in Italian, and he took to the desert as most men do who love the sea. According to the biographers, he enjoyed racing his horse or camel across the sand, although some write that he rode poorly on each. The Spartan side of his character, however, responded to the Egyptians' simple life, where possessions seemed to count for little and character for much, and wished to emulate their trust in Providence.

"Napoleon told them he admired Muhammad, and once, in a euphoric mood, even declared that he would build a mosque half a league around, where he and his entire army could worship. He characterized the French as truly Muslims, and asked that all Egyptians take an oath of loyalty to the French government. The Muslims, it's said, were excited by the possibility of such a powerful leader joining their ranks, but responded that if Buonaparte and the army were truly Muslims, they must undergo circumcision and renounce wine." The colonel began to chuckle. "For Buonaparte, you see, this meant carrying adaptation a bit too far. It's well known, of course, that he had an unusually small penis, and any loss of mass, foreskin or not, would have been perceived by our hero as an extremely, shall we say, heh, heh, delicate matter." He snorted, reveling in his merriment at Napoleon's expense. "The compromise he eventually worked out was that he would continue to protect Islam, and the Muslims were to cite Buonaparte as one of God's messengers and a friend of the Prophet."[38]

"Hm," Charly said. "Must be tough negotiating over your foreskin; not exactly tantamount to recounting a mortar attack with the guys at the VFW."

CHAPTER 6

⸻ THE JOYS OF A TEENAGE WIFE ⸻

"I overheard you discussing Josephine's marriage. Did you cover Marie-Louise's wedding?" the colonel asked, then turned to Charly. "It's very important, Charly, because —" A cell phone rang and all three reached for their own, but it was the colonel's, chiming a stirring refrain from the Marseillaise, and he excused himself.

"Marie-Louise?" Charly asked.

"Didn't these Voyages Classiques people give you anything on this stuff?" Simone complained.

Charly shrugged. "I skipped this one. I thought the Napoleon stuff would be all trudging armies and dates."

"It's time to study," Simone said. "You're supposed to be doing this for your tourists shortly, and this isn't Aix, you know. You *are* doing this for money, right?"

"Right."

"Well, the wedding had some geopolitical consequences. Napoleon figured he needed an alliance with either Russia or Austria. He tried first with Alexander's fifteen-year-old sister, but the czar — the Czar and Napoleon got along pretty well — excused himself for a variety of reasons, mostly the Dowager Empress' disdain for Napoleon, who refused to be part of 'a pact with the devil.' Anyway, the family was having none of it, and the circumstances forced Napoleon to make a formal offer to the Austrian ambassador, which was immediately accepted, for the hand of the eighteen-year-old Archduchess Marie-Louise, eldest daughter of the Emperor Francis."

"Weren't the Austrians enemies of France?" Charly asked.

"Well, that's the point: Napoleon needed an alliance. He had set tongues wagging when he tried to marry up France with Russia; he knew attacks would eventually come from the north, but he needed allies, and being Europe's alpha male, he didn't care about his fans. He explained to a critic: 'This is ... a political action, and one to which I have given considerable thought. You don't like this marriage? I do. I regard it as a great success — a success on the level with the victory of Austerlitz.'"[39]

"And Josephine?"

"She was getting used to the idea. She'd had her beaux, and besides, Napoleon was experienced himself: a staff officer's wife in Egypt, and, of course, the Polish Countess Walewska."

"And what was she to him?" Charly asked.

"His whore," the colonel said, leaning over from his phone conversation.

"Colonel," Charly pleaded.

"To the contrary," Simone retorted. "Don't listen to him. Walewska was the second creature in the world who asked nothing from Napoleon, his mother being the first. He had never known another woman who did not expect him to shower her with jewels, money, palaces, and crowns. Marie wanted nothing from him except the freedom of Poland, and gave him everything that was hers: love, loyalty, and a son." De Monteaux stood facing them, smiling, cell phone to his ear, in what sounded like a discussion of the grounds of Malmaison.

Simone moved closer to Charly, blocking out the colonel. "Napoleon couldn't forget Marie; he met her before the Russian campaign. It seems Countess Walewska was the quiet and loving companion his soul had sought."

"Didn't Josephine's find out?"

"Of course," said Simone. "Since 1807 Napoleon had been trying to make up his mind about a divorce, painful though it would be to Josephine and to himself. Now, in the most graceful way in the world—"

"Simone, the guy was cheating on his wife."

"I know, but she had deceived him for years; maybe it was his turn. Anyway, he had his reasons: the intrigues during his absence from Paris had convinced him that the security of the empire demanded an heir, which Josephine couldn't give him."

"What about Eugène?" the colonel chided, finally off the phone and back with his companions.

"You know as well as I do that Eugène was a stepson," Simone said. "Besides, it would have been too great an affront to the Buonaparte family. It had to be their blood, Corsican blood."

"He had an illegitimate son, right?" Charly said.

"Um-hm." Simone paused and turned toward de Monteaux. "Ah, Colonel? I don't suppose they have bottled water in the museum shop?"

He saw it coming and tried to duck. "I don't think—"

"Would you be ever so kind, Colonel? Please?" she purred.

He got up heavily and limped away back toward the shop.

"Where were we?" Simone asked.

"Bastard."

"Right. In 1810 Marie bore him a bastard son, Alexander, and any doubts about his ability to beget children, arising from the sterility of his marriage with Josephine, were forgotten. The boy, later to be known as the Comte Walewski, was an intelligent kid, generous and upright, and was brought by his mother to Paris for visits with his father. By all accounts, Napoleon was delighted at last to be a father. Nonetheless, he was constantly preparing for war, though he continued to visit Marie when events took him near Warsaw.

"In the end, although Napoleon was still in love with Josephine, he decided he had to sacrifice his feelings for Josephine and hers for him. He felt the political situation was now so bad for France that a strategic marriage was the only way to a defensible peace. He needed allies, and either Russia or Austria was essential. He felt so strongly about ending his marriage that he even ordered the secret passageway between his apartment and Josephine's to be walled up. He had his staff appeal to the Diocesan Ecclesiastical Court of Paris for an annulment of their hasty religious marriage on the eve of the coronation."

"That must have been tricky," Charly said.

"Not so much, since the vows had been celebrated in the absence of the parish priest and of any witness. Needless to say, it was granted, and Josephine was informed that she must leave the Tuileries," Simone said.

"Was informed?! I wonder who brought those glad tidings. She couldn't have been queen for long."

"Well, for more than a decade, they had some very memorable lawn parties. The emperor himself broke the news to her. Napoleon needed a son;

124

she knew that, and he knew France needed an heir. All Europe knew that, for dynastic reasons, his son had to be the child of a princess of royal blood. The scene took place shortly after his return from Poland. Probably, he was feeling angry because he couldn't place his Polish love, who had borne his child, straightway upon the throne. "When the end came, it was a rough time for Josephine. Late that final night, according to Josephine, she crept into Napoleon's room and approached his bed, tears streaming down her face, and hair falling round her shoulders."

"Oh, God, it must have been painful."

"Um-hm, probably was. They clasped each other in an emotional crisis, two people who had spent so much of their lives together, soon to be torn apart by matters of state. Next day, 15 December, after fourteen years together, Josephine left, supported on Napoleon's arm. She was driven to Malmaison, her carriage filled with newborn Dalmatian puppies."

"Ah, the Disney version of Josephine and our little general," the colonel said, returning and handing each woman a bottle of water. "Perhaps, Simone, I might make a comment or two?"

"About?"

"Josephine, sans puppies, of course," he said snidely.

"If you have something to add."

"Oh, I do. Without question, Charly, making an empress of Josephine — a rapacious little immigrant from Martinique — was the height of Napoleon's folly." He smiled malevolently at Simone. "Josephine was a feather-brained, impulsive, little — literally — liar, who managed a number of adulterous affairs behind Napoleon's back while he was deeply in love with her, at war, and, at one point, wounded. She didn't love him; she lied to him about a false pregnancy to keep him at bay while she entertained the handsome young lover we spoke of, Hippolyte Charles — no deeper than herself. Charles, a joking, immature fop, whose main claim to life lay in being, to put it in Josephine's enduring words, 'a man better able to tie a cravat than any in the world.' And entertained, I might add, in a mansion, Malmaison, that Buonaparte paid for dearly, both literally and figuratively. A woman whose debts at one time amounted to almost 2 million francs, ordered dresses and shoes by the hundreds, owned 1,000 pairs of gloves, and bragged of never wearing the same stockings twice, with more clothes and arts of the toilet than the former queen of France. Her flagrant spending no doubt kept those strategic trades alive, while the technology of France collapsed behind the power and progress of England. Perhaps even Napoleon should have taken notice of his razor: only the quality ones came from England.

"Simone, do you disagree? He was fortunate to be rid of her, or perhaps I have misquoted my sources?"

"You made your point, Colonel. Are you satisfied?" Simone said.

"Quite." Addressing women on the frivolity of money misspent on fashion was an unconvincing argument and poorly understood by most men.

"Charly, join me in the ladies' room?" Simone said.

"Jesus, he irritates me," Charly groaned when they got to the restrooms.

"Think he will leave?"

"Who cares? If he keeps this up I'll call the old fart a taxi myself," she grumbled. "So how did Napoleon take it?"

"The separation from Josephine? Tough for about three days, then, like any male in heat, he was excited at the prospect of a new teenaged wife. He worked out an itinerary whereby Marie Louise was to arrive on the earliest possible date, and ordered a new suit from a fashionable tailor. He had stopped dancing the previous year — 'After all, forty is forty,' he was quoted as saying. Now, however, he took waltzing lessons in order to please his young bride. Napoleon's master of ceremonies drew up ten folio pages for the ceremonial of Her Highness's arrival, but they proved so much waste paper, for Napoleon, in his impatience to have a son, among other things, intercepted Marie Louise and carried her off to bed at Compiègne."[40]

"Was she as pretty as Josephine or Marie Walewska?" Charly asked. "I know it's in the eye of the beholder and all that."

"Well, Marie Louise was fair, with blue, slanting cat's eyes, a rosy complexion, and petite hands and feet. She liked rich foods, especially sour cream, lobster, and chocolate, and she was more sensual than Josephine. She even tempted Napoleon to richer and more plentiful food, and he began to put on weight. By 1812 he was quite a fat man by all accounts, with round cheeks and a rotund girth. On her wedding night, delighted with Napoleon's lovemaking, so it's said — obviously by him — she invited him 'to do it again.' But the main difference between the wives was one of character and education: Josephine and Marie Walewska had been brave and free; Marie Louise was fearful, having been brought up in a servile court by a strict father. She came to France full of fears. She even feared ghosts, and could not go to sleep without half a dozen candles burning. Napoleon supposedly liked total darkness, and after making love would stumble off to his own bedroom.[41]

"Historians seem to think that many at court judged her severely; Napoleon, however, concentrated on her good qualities, what he termed her rosebud freshness and her truthfulness. Knowing she was a foreigner and fearful in her new surroundings, he spent considerable time with her, and encouraged her taste for painting. By his reassurances and energy, which appealed to women, and his natural kindness, he won her over in a few weeks."

"Now, there's a man I could—" Charly sighed.

"Um-hm. Well, Marie Louise 'could' too, and she did—became pregnant. The gynecologists foresaw a difficult birth, and Napoleon told them if it was a question of the mother's life or the child's, he should save the mother's, an order Marie Louise was always to remember with gratitude. Forceps had to be used, but the child was born alive. Napoleon saw him and exulted: 'My son is plump and healthy.... He has my chest, my mouth and my eyes.... I am at the summit of my happiness.' This new Napoleon, his father believed, would reconcile the peoples and the kings. Napoleon II, decreed King of Rome by his father, had French—well, Corsican really—and Austrian blood in his veins; for the Buonapartes he was, in a new sense, a true European. He was a symbol of continuity for Napoleon, a future leader of his empire."

"Happy man."

"Um-hm. After the marriage with Marie Louise, everything in Napoleon changed, his physique as well as his character. His optimism increased; he tended even more than before to see the bright side of things."

"Was he usually depressed?" Charly asked.

"No, I don't think you could say that. He had his dark side, which the British helped along by trying to assassinate him on the way to one of his favorite operas, but maybe middle age had more to do with it. He was just beginning to enjoy himself, I think. Napoleon did have an interesting morning routine." Simone offered. "Want to hear it?"

127

"Sounds riveting; at least we're in an appropriate place," Charly said, looking around. Too bad the colonel isn't here, we could compare their morning ablutions."

"I don't. You know when you called me last week you caught me on the toilet."

"Are we going to get scatological?"

"Guess you're not interested. Like you, ranch hand that you, uh, were, Napoleon usually got up around six or seven a.m. He preferred his own bedroom, so that when he awoke he could sit before the fire, winter and summer. He drank a cup of tea or orange-flavored water, opened his letters, glanced at the newspapers, and chatted with his servant Constant. All before immersing himself in an hour-long steaming bath, which he claimed to be worth four hours' sleep. Too much l'amour, he used to say."

"Think it works?"

"Don't know, never tried."

"What else?"

"Well, like his mother, he was particular about personal cleanliness. He washed his hands with almond paste, and his face, neck, and ears with a sponge and soap, followed by cleaning his teeth. Not a flosser, of course, but he picked them with a toothpick of polished boxwood, then brushed them twice, first with toothpaste, then with finely powdered coral. From what I've read, Napoleon's teeth were naturally white and strong, and never required the attention of his dentist who, therefore, received 6,000 francs per year for doing nothing. Josephine, on the other hand, had bad teeth that looked like cloves, so she never smiled with lips apart, and laughed with a throaty gurgle. Finally, he rinsed his mouth with a mixture of water and brandy, and scraped his tongue, as the fashion then was, with a scraper of tortoise shell. Once a week, during Josephine's time, Napoleon had his hair cut by Josephine's hairdresser. His hair was fine and a light chestnut color; he had stopped powdering it at Josephine's request, but continued to wear it long until the end of the consulate. Napoleon completed his toilet by pouring eau-de-Cologne over his head, so that it trickled down his torso. He would then friction his chest and arms with a hard-bristled brush, while his servant did the same to his shoulders and back. Then he finally dressed and left at the stroke of nine."[42]

"In his Beemer."

"Beemer"?

"BMW: Boy–More–Women. We'd better get back."

———————

When they returned, the colonel was missing. Charly went looking, and found him sitting on a green wrought-iron bench, with his back to her, staring out at the gardens behind the mansion. "Colonel? I've been looking all over for you. Are you okay?"

He turned to look at her, and gestured for her to have a seat on the bench. "Please," he said softly.

She sat and began immediately to make amends. "I'm sorry we were late, there was a line at the toilet. Did we hurt your feelings?"

He patted her on her thigh. "We should talk a little, without your friend."

"She's on the phone."

"Good. Let's forget Napoleon and Josephine for a moment. Is that all right? There is something much more important to talk about than those two. That was Jean-Michel on the phone a while ago. He asked how you were doing."

"You mean for the job? Or, how was I doing?"

"Both. He's on consulting time, you know. They'll want to know your progress."

"Of course."

"Charly, all this talk of relationships brings me to an important question that has concerned me. It's about you and Jean-Michel. May I speak frankly?"

"Okay...." She hesitated. "I guess." Instantly, she felt like she was being confined in a dark room and forced into revealing confidences.

"I'll get right to the point. Are you and Jean-Michel having an affair?"

Not a tricky question. There was something going on in her life, but she was left to feel her way around this situation, with a man she did not really know or particularly like, concerning Jean-Michel, who was both instrumental in giving her a job, and perhaps a new life, in Paris.

"You're the second…" She dodged. "Why do you ask?" she said coldly. He looked out toward the garden. "I don't like doing this, but I have some special reasons."

"Can you be more specific?"

"Yes. First of all, he asked if I thought he needed cosmetic surgery on his nose."

"A nose job?" She giggled, relieved. "Are we talkin' about the same person? I don't think this is so difficult, you're just on the wrong part of his anatomy."

He gave her a puzzled look. "That's only part of the story. He thinks his face is too…well, full, and his nose too small, one of the reasons why he wears half-glasses. He wants a bigger nose for a more striking profile. And you're the reason. Excuse me." He succumbed to a nervous cough, and took out his handkerchief. "Charly, what's happening is good. He doesn't need a new nose, but he needs someone. Someone like you, in fact: you remind him of Cunegonde, Moliere's well-meaning naïf abroad in the world, learning that the diversity of custom and opinion of which she is utterly ignorant nonetheless influences her life decisively. You in Paris."

"Charly, he has been recovering from a bad situation over the past few years. Has he mentioned anything about it or our relationship?" She shook her head. "He's bitter about some things life has dealt him, except when he's had some drinks or is busy trying to survive one of his manias."

"Manias?" She looked blankly at the colonel. "I'm not sure, what are you —?"

He interrupted, "You see Charly, his wife and daughter were killed in an automobile accident some years ago. A tragedy. A tragedy for all involved, but he covers it up. Nothing's ever gone quite right for the man. Just a little luck mixed with a certain genius, however, and Levasseur, in my opinion, would be secure among French writers. Has he, uh," he became uncomfortable, "mentioned anything about his research?

"Research?" I don't think so. It's just whenever he seems harassed by things, he says he longs for the crypt."

"Um-hm." He looked at her suspiciously.

"Has he, you know, recovered?" she asked hesitantly, testing the waters.

"From the drinking? I'm not qualified to say. Not long after the accident, he was transferred over to our institute from a college associated with the Sorbonne, only for us to find that the school had slipped us a bad—or at least cracked—egg, so to speak. You are the first real positive thing that has happened to that man in the last couple of years. I took some responsibility for him, and ended up removing him, over a year ago, from a small apartment in the projects northeast of Paris that you could say was Spartan in simplicity and literally gothic in its squalor."

"Pretty bad, I guess?" she said, hoping for some good news.

He nodded. "It was bad for a while. Jean-Michel roomed with his son, Jean-Paul, and a lot of roaches that felt they owned the place. Nothing but bourbon, instant coffee, and cookies in the kitchen cupboards. You wouldn't have recognized him then. He is usually a friendly, humorous, intelligent man whom most people would like to rely on. He has come a long way back, living on my houseboat now."

"His son?"

"Jean-Paul? Long story. Calls himself Fausto, and has a history of suicidal tendencies. He's at a clinic in Greece; I think he'll be there a while. Jean-Michel has a few consulting assignments and works out of our institute—on probation—and it seems to be working. But you see, Charly, it is important that he not fail. He's useful to us...." Charly gave him an odd look and he corrected himself, "You know, he is a friend. Those at the institute who know say that for all the chaos in his life, Jean-Michel's prose is gifted and exceptionally disciplined. Despite this past self-destructive behavior, he could still survive as one of France's finest and have a life, perhaps become the man the muses meant him to be. I think you could play a significant role in that. He is enthusiastic about you, but reluctant to push himself into a relationship."

"I don't know what to say; sort of hard to react to a cupid that's a colonel."

"I understand," the colonel said, nodding his head. "I'm not comfortable in this role either, but he's a friend: overweight, older, and fighting this drinking problem. Honestly, Charly, I don't know what to say, except that you are without question the best medicine he has been given in" he hesitated and shook his head, "in I don't know how long." They sat for a moment in silence. He patted her knee, and with that pushed himself up on his cane and turned to assist her. "Let's stay in touch— you know, in case things go wrong, call me."

She stood up to go. "Is his son coming home?"

"After the accident, while Jean-Michel was recovering, I helped send his son to high school in the US on an exchange program. Fausto—Jean-Paul—left the States and came back to Europe, but…" the colonel shook his head. "Unfortunately, we don't know his prognosis; he's under the care of a Greek psychiatrist in Corfu. I have no doubt he'll show up eventually."

Charly and the colonel returned to the foyer and picked up Simone. Having been left alone, she was irritated and became reticent. Entering the building, they coincidentally met the small tour group coming down the hall, and joined them, facing the conference chamber room on the first floor of Malmaison. It was constructed to have the appearance of a campaign tent, resembling one of Napoleon's battlefield headquarters. Some of the visitors began to ask questions, and, while Simone was in a conversation with a woman from the tour, the colonel took Charly aside to quietly explain the significance of the room and those of Napoleon's personal traits that had made him perhaps one of the world's most famous generals.

Describing Napoleon to Charly, he said, "As a military officer, I have often pondered what possible trait it was that made this young lieutenant of no special birth or experience able to wrest control of the French government away from its politicians before he was thirty years old. I'm not a fan, which you know, but it's quite remarkable for someone without political experience. He was also an expert about the most technical division of the army, the artillery; he had a superb memory, and was a tireless worker. Consider that he organized and launched one of the largest armadas to Egypt, where Nelson got the best of him, of course. Add the fact that he was an acute observer of human nature and motivator of men and you have all the ingredients for an outstanding leader. He's been quoted as saying, 'I am a soldier, because that is the special faculty I was born with; that is my life, my habit.' But only one circumstance, as ironic and inconceivable as it seems, at least to me, provides the answer to his success: he was in love."

132

"In love!" she exclaimed.

"Yes. Even at St. Helena he retained a photographic memory of his army, and spoke of it in terms of love. When asked how he could remember the details of all the units engaged in one of his early battles, he replied, 'Madame, this is a lover's recollection of his former mistress.' And, also, his burning love for Josephine." He tapped his cane absentmindedly on the floor, eliciting unfriendly glances from the group. "Finally, his love or devotion to France."

"I never would have expected that from someone like yourself, Colonel," Charly said, startled. "I would have laid his genius for conquering nations or women to an overbearing egotism, aggression, cruelty, or at least some unique male or militaristic source."

"He was an admirable tactician, that I'll admit, but remember: at the beginning, Napoleon was not only a general in the service of the republic, but also a recently married young man deeply in love with an experienced older woman. Josephine's absence inspired Napoleon so much that she was, in a way, the heart of the Italian campaign, the beginning of his success. She was also the woman, despite his harangues, who was influential enough to make him forsake Egypt. He abandon his troops, which probably today would have had him court-martialed and perhaps shot. Then, in some masterful political ploys by his brothers, and a good bit of luck, he entered the political arena on the back of his military reputation and won a position of counsel, one of three."

"Then why did he always, or nearly always, emerge successful from whatever he did, politics or war?"

"Perhaps the simplest answer is the best: he was a consummate leader; he grasped the essentials. 'A leader' he once said 'is a dealer in hope.'"

Napoleon at War

Get your principles straight; the rest is a matter of detail, he said. Principles of military art shine in history like the Sun on the horizon, so much the worse for blind men incapable of seeing them.

The principles of warfare are those which guided the great captains whose high deeds history has transmitted to us—Alexander, Hannibal, Caesar, Gustavus Adolphus, Turenne, Eugène of Savoy, Frederick the Great.... The history of their eighty-three campaigns would constitute a complete treatise on the art of war; the principles that must be followed in defensive and offensive warfare would flow from it as from a common source.

All the great captains have done great things by conforming to the rules and natural principles of the art; that is to say, by the wisdom of their combinations, the reasoned balance of means with consequences, and efforts with obstacles. They have succeeded only by thus conforming, whatever may have been the audacity of their enterprises and the extent of their success. They have never ceased to make war a veritable science. It is only under this title that they are our great models, and it is only in imitating them that one can hope to approach them.

Tactics can be learned from treatises, somewhat like geometry, and so can the various military evolutions or the science of the engineers and the gunner; but knowledge of the grand principles of warfare can be acquired only through the study of military history and of the battles of the great captains and through experience.

There are no precise, determinate rules: everything depends on the character that nature has bestowed on the general, on his qualities and defects, on the troops, on the range of the weapons, on the season of the year, and on a thousand circumstances which are never twice the same.

These three things you must always keep in mind: concentration of strength, activity, and a firm resolve to perish gloriously. They are the three principles of the military art, which have disposed luck in my favor in all my operations.[43]

Charly and Simone finished the tour in Josephine's bedroom and went downstairs to meet up with the colonel, who, needless to say, had no interest in visiting the room where she died.

The three gathered in the foyer, the colonel intent on leaving. "As I said before, I have to go, but just for example, here is a little piece of history that our French government didn't bother to etch into the face of Napoleon's marble tomb. Three decades after the revolution, Victor Hugo learned from an English newspaper that shiploads of skeletons picked up on Napoleonic battlefields had arrived in Hull, an English port, to be crushed into fertilizer, 'the final byproduct' as he said, 'of Napoleon's victories: fattening up English cows.' Since the revolution, almost a million French and allied soldiers had died under Napoleon's care, half of them under the age of twenty-eight. And what did he buy with all that blood from so many nations? Nothing!"

"Napoleon was in the process of defending France against her enemies; those were not wasted lives," Simone said calmly.

"Then tell me, mam'selle, what did they accomplish? An empire created and lost in little over a decade. He should have quit—which he could have—while he was ahead. Since your preference for history seems tied to the bedrooms of the great men of Europe, let me offer you a final quote, my dear ladies, as best I can remember it, from our esteemed leader Napoleon, when challenged that Josephine was not qualified to be an empress: 'My wife is a good wife.... She is content to play the Empress a little, to have diamonds, beautiful clothes, and the deserts of her age.... If I make her Empress, it is through justice ... If I had been thrown into prison, instead of ascending a throne, she would have shared my lot.... Yes, she shall be crowned! She shall be crowned if it costs me 200,000 men.'"

De Monteaux allowed the figure to sink in. "How was that for conceit? Would you like it if your father, son, or brother were one of those 200,000 skeletons moldering away on European and Russian fields? Lives our Napoleon offers so easily for this little conniver's crown?"

Assuming that he was tired, and to expedite things, Simone set about calling for a taxi, which he tiredly refused and suggested that they should sit outside.

It was quiet, all in their own thoughts, then the colonel offered a final remark: "You should know, Charly, that by a convention signed in Paris on 2 August 1815, the four allies, England, Prussia, Russia, and Austria, declared your hero was their prisoner. Lord Liverpool wrote, 'We wish that the King of France would hang or shoot Buonaparte, as the best termination of the business.'"

"Someday when we have time, and despite the Colonel's calls for Napoleon's historical head," Simone said to Charly, "I will take you to see the museum at Bois-Préau; it's a large villa only fifteen minutes' walk to where Josephine's physician lived and where the collection of Napoleon's years at St. Helena were stored."

"Okay," Charly sighed. "Jean-Michel and I are headed over to visit Victor Hugo's place tomorrow—if I can walk." And she rubbed her feet.

De Monteaux nodded his head, and all three sat on the bench to wait silently, weary of each other and the day.

A droning sound arose from behind the mansion as they sat waiting for de Monteaux to say something or a taxi to arrive. But he sat quietly, lost in thought, simply looking out toward the large grassy field before them. The faint buzzing came closer and closer, until suddenly it sounded as though an airplane was about to crash into the roof above their very heads. Both women jumped to their feet as a WW I-vintage biplane roared directly over the old building, barely missing the roof, coasted silently downwind, then banked tightly to the left, and drifted down to a bumpy landing right before them, with a thump and rumble like distant thunder.

The colonel rose. "It's my ride," he said matter-of-factly. "I'd offer a seat, but…" he shrugged. "Goodbye." Getting up, he limped off toward the plane, which, coughing, vibrating, and trembling like an impatient Pegasus in battle colors, was taxiing to meet him. He stopped and turned, sheltering his voice with his hand. "Remember what I said about Jean-Michel."

Both women watched in wonder as the old man approached the plane, his hair blowing to and fro. He reached up to the cockpit to shake hands with the pilot and struggled into the forward cockpit. He put on a leather helmet and goggles, then turned and waved as the plane taxied away, the sound of the engine fading in and out. Finally, with enough field to take off, the pilot gunned the motor; the plane came rapidly toward them, then lifted into the air. The colonel saluted as they zoomed overhead.

"Well, in the saga of commuting and a lot of good-byes —" Charly started to say, only to have Simone finish, "that's definitely a first." Both women waved back at the small figure looking down at them.

"What does he want you to remember about Jean-Michel?" Simone asked as the plane flew off into the distance.

"He's thinking of getting a silicone operation."

"For his penis?"

"Nose."

Napoleon's Attempted Suicide

Early in 1814 Napoleon, retreating from Russia and finally losing the campaign, abdicated his title as Emperor of France, and laid down his arms against Russia, Austria and Prussia. It was agreed that he would be banished to Elba, but Napoleon demanded that his wife Marie Louise of Austria and his son Napoleon II would be allowed to join him. Metternich acting as the Allies foreign minister refused. He was told the Bourbons wanted change. When the comment was delivered to Napoleon, he replied that all the Bourbons would change were his sheets. Then Napoleon urged Marie Louise to ask her father Francis I of Austria to grant her Tuscany where she and her son would enjoy the warmth of Italy and culture of Florence while visiting Napoleon in Elba. This was also refused. The Allies, Napoleon concluded, would therefore seek to assassinate him. (Napoleon was wrong. He was later sent to Elba, but only remained for 100 days before sailing to Antibe and with a small band of his soldiers marched back to Paris and overthrew the King.)

At three o'clock in the morning on 13 April, an omen Napoleon certainly noticed, for he wrote the date at the head of a short letter to Marie Louise, he told her that he loved her more than anything else in the world. He signed it not 'Nap' like previous letters, but "Napoleon." He put the letter under the pillow of his bed, then went to his dressing-case and took out a screw of paper from a satchel. It contained a whitish mixture, which he had asked his surgeon, Yvan, to prepare during the Russian campaign. Its ingredients were opium, belladonna and white hellebore.

Napoleon had considered various ways of taking his life. He had fondled his pistols; he had thought of taking a pail full of burning coals into his canopied bath and asphyxiating himself. Finally he had settled for what seemed the clean method favored by the Greeks and Romans. Unscrewing the paper, he tipped the powder into a little water. He drank the mixture. Then he summoned his adjutant, Caulaincourt, and got into bed.

"Come here and sit down," said Napoleon when Caulaincourt entered. It was unprecedented to sit in the Emperor's bedroom, but Caulaincourt obeyed. "They are going to take the Empress and my son from me." His friend guessed what Napoleon had done and both men were in tears. Napoleon gave him some last instructions. Then he felt sharp pains in his stomach and began to hiccup violently.

Napoleon would not let Caulaincourt call a doctor. Napoleon's body became very cold, then burning hot. His limbs grew rigid; his chest and stomach heaved, but he clenched his teeth, trying not to vomit. During one such spasm, as Napoleon's grip on Caulaincourt relaxed for a moment, Caulaincourt dashed out and called for help. When he returned with the doctor, he found Napoleon vomiting spasmodically. What had happened was this. Napoleon had told Yvan to prepare him a strong dose, "more than enough to kill two men," as though he could not be felled by the usual means, and the violent dose he had swallowed proved to much for his body to assimilate. The bragging touch had saved him.[44]

The Death of Napoleon

On 3 May (1821) at Longwood, the doctors saw that their patient could not live much longer. It was out of the question for him to receive Holy Communion — he could barely swallow liquids — but the abbé Vignali administered Extreme Unction, anointing with chrism the eyelids, the ears, the nostrils, the mouth, the white hands and feet, that sins committed through each of the five senses might be forgiven, and reciting the age-old prayer: "Deliver, Lord, the soul of your servant, as you delivered Moses from the hands of Pharaoh, King of the Egyptians; deliver, Lord, the soul of your servant, as you delivered St Peter and St Paul from prison."

The fourth was a day of rain and wind, which uprooted the willow tree in the shade of which he used to enjoy sitting. Napoleon was bothered by the autumn flies that buzzed around his bed. But for most of the day he kept his hands crossed on his chest, fingers interlocked.

On the night of 4–5 May he suffered from hiccoughs and went into delirium. The end was plainly very near. Twice he asked, "What is the name of my son?" and Marchand replied, "Napoleon." Between three and four-thirty in the morning he uttered a number of unconnected words. Montholon, who sat beside him, twice thought he heard France — *armée* — *tête d'armée* — Josephine." Later he was seized by a convulsive movement and pitched sideways toward the floor. Montholon tried to hold him back, but was thrown on the carpet. There, as though wrestling with death itself, Napoleon pinned Montholon down with such strength that the younger man could not even cry for help. A servant next door heard the noise; Bertrand and Antommarchi the doctor were called, and they succeeded in putting the delirious patient back to bed.

Shortly before dawn on the fifth Napoleon became calm, and remained calm into the afternoon. His breathing came slow and faint. Antommarchi, seated at the head of his bed, watched the pulse beating in his patient's neck. Montholon occasionally pressed to his lips a sponge soaked in sugared water. The breathing became more and more difficult. Napoleon remained motionless, lying on his back, with his right hand out of bed, and his eyes fixed, without any appearance of suffering. At five forty-one the sun set and, far off, was heard the boom of a gun. Six minutes later Napoleon uttered a sigh. This was followed, at intervals of a minute, by two more sighs. Immediately after his third sigh, he stopped breathing. Antommarchi gently closed the eyes and stopped the clock. It was five forty-nine on the evening of 5 May 1821, and Napoleon was not quite fifty-two years old.

Although Napoleon had expressed the wish to be buried on the banks of the Seine, the English Government gave orders that his body must not leave St. Helena.

At ten o'clock on the morning of 9 May the abbé Vignali celebrated Requiem Mass. After Mass the coffin was placed on a carriage drawn by four horses and slowly taken to one of Napoleon's favorite places, called Torbett's Spring. Behind the carriage was led the last horse Napoleon had ridden, a gray called "Sheikh." The route was lined by English soldiers, muskets reversed, their bands playing a funeral march.

It was a beautiful clear day. When the cortège arrived a detachment of infantry presented arms. Bertrand removed Napoleon's sword from the coffin, Montholon the campaigning cloak, and the coffin was lower into the grave, in the shade of the willow trees.[45]

Eventually, Napoleon's will, when it was published, brought him back to France. Its second clause seemed to be the final command: "It is my wish that my ashes may repose on the banks of the Seine, in the midst of the French people, whom I have loved so well." (And others might have added, "and killed so many.")

An appeal was made by the French king to ask the British king for permission to bring Napoleon back to France. The British government responded at once and handsomely: "The government of her Britannic Majesty hopes that the promptness of its answer may be considered in France a proof of its desire to blot out the last trace of those national animosities which, during the lifetime of the Emperor, armed England and France against each other."

Napoleon's body was retrieved from St. Helena by the king's son. By steamer, barge, and coach it was eventually delivered to Paris down the Champs-Elysées lined on either side by applauding and rejoicing multitudes to the Arc de Triomphe. Later, on what was a bitter cold day, 15 December 1840, the corpse at last reached its destination at the magnificently domed church of the Hôtel des Invalides. Twenty seamen bore the heavy coffin to the altar, where the Prince de Joinville addressed his father the King: "Sire, I present to you the body of the Emperor of France." Bertrand laid Napoleon's sword upon the coffin; Gourgaud added the Emperor's hat; a requiem Mass was sung to Mozart's music; and the Emperor was at last where he had wished his remains to be — in the heart of Paris, on the banks of the Seine.[46]

Controversy to the End [47]

The five post-mortem reports produced at the time have been analyzed and summarized as follows:

1. The stomach was ulcerated, and there was perforation.
2. The perforation had been partially shut off by old adhesions to the liver and diaphragm.
3. The ulcer had a rolled, everted edge.
4. The liver was enlarged.
5. No lumps or nodules were found in the liver, although looked for.
6. Exudation was present in the abdominal cavity.
7. Partly digested blood was found in the stomach.
8. An abundance of body and abdominal fat was present.

In his report, Dr. Walter Henry noted that the body was feminized with hairless, white, delicate skin, well defined breasts, and a mons veneris (fat accumulating above the genitals). The genitalia were exceedingly small, suggesting testicular atrophy. Dr. Robinson suggests that these characteristics were as a result of an acquired primary hypogonadism (small testicles) resulting from an orchitis that led to testicular atrophy and impotence.

Based on the autopsy reports, Dr. Yarrow points out that if Napoleon had indeed died of cancer of the stomach, his corpse would have been wasted, shrunken, and devoid of body fat. Moreover, there would almost certainly have been secondary growths in the liver. That is not to say that there may not already have been early cancerous changes in the ulcer, as suggested by the rolled, everted edge, but the point is that this could not have been the cause of his death.

The controversy over Napoleon's death arises from the results of tests on Napoleon's hair, which revealed the presence of massive amounts of arsenic. On 28 August 1995, the FBI's department of Chemistry and Toxicology concluded, "The amount of arsenic present in the submitted hairs is consistent with arsenical poisoning." This was based on different, authenticated samples of Napoleon's hair taken between 1805 and 1821, all of which contained arsenic. This therefore poses two crucial questions: (1) What did Napoleon die of? (2) How did the arsenic get into his hair?

The latest speculation (there are others as credible) is that over-enthusiastic doctors killed Bonaparte. Researchers from the San Francisco Medical Examiner's Department, who studied records of his final weeks, say doctors gave him colonic irrigation each day and purges to relieve intestinal distress. That, they claim, would have triggered a plunge in potassium levels leading to heart malfunction. But, death by enema is hardly a demise fit for a hero.[48]

═══ *IV* ═══

Victor Hugo on the Wild Side

Imagination is intelligence with an erection.

Victor Hugo

CHAPTER I

≡ ROAD RAGE ≡
AT THE ARC DE TRIOMPHE

"Merde! Je déteste ce trafic horrible!" [1] Jean-Michel growled, wrestling with the steering wheel of his old Renault, a 4CV of uncertain vintage, sporting an urban texture of spotted rust on faded blue.

It was 8:45 a.m., and the little Renault, its frayed canvas top flapping, dodged and scurried among the sleek sedans cruising along the city's avenues on their way to work. The avenues led to boulevards, and the boulevards to a vortex of automobiles speeding round a great circle, one that sucked them irresistibly into the gigantic merry-go-round of morning commuters. Like a symphony of schooling fish, the cars swirled about the Arc de Triomphe and then out through the city streets, darting rapidly across perilous intersections, threatening all whose veniality included distraction. It was rush hour at what Parisians called the circle from hell.

Suddenly, the Renault sped ahead in a harrowing attempt to maintain its position, then lurching violently sideways, tires squealing, it tried to break free. Crouching as best she could in a cloth seat no more secure than a well-worn beach chair, Charly gripped the flimsy armrest and gasped, "Jeesus, Jean-Michel," then screamed, "Watch *out!*" as the Renault swerved to avoid a big silver Mercedes, Jean-Michel working his steering wheel like a harried astronaut dodging asteroids.

In the back, Astérix, a white Labrador with tan, floppy ears and large paws, struggled valiantly for balance against the centrifugal forces of his master's careening car, and whined urgently for escape.

Round and round the Étoile [2] they went, swept by the tide of automobiles, there a glimpse of the Champs-Elysées, moments later the Elysées again, then a third time, and always over their left shoulder the massive Arc de Triomphe. Jean-Michel struggled to guide the car out of the swirling forces, but by the third time around, he felt the rush of bona fide road rage, waving his arm from the window, shouting, "Ta gueule, salaud!"[3] The cursing incited nasty rebukes in kind. Then suddenly, as if ejected by a slingshot, they were off the racing carousel and into the safe haven of a vacant taxi stand. The old Renault coughed, bucked, and shuddered to a stop.

"Thank God!" Charly gushed, combing back curly hair with trembling fingers. "Now I know why the slowest traffic is called rush hour." Transfixed, she sat staring through the windshield, recovering from the maelstrom, not knowing whether to laugh or cry. "Sweet Jesus, Jean-Michel, I thought we were dead! Did you see," she said breathlessly, hand to heart, in halting voice, "the expression on that man's face?" He gave her a quizzical look. "You almost hit his Mercedes!" she blurted.

Sweat trickled down his cheeks and stained the armpits of his blue oxford in big circular patches. He was anything but trim; his belly touched the steering wheel, and his stout legs curled against the floorboards. Charly saw the phenomenon — usually attributed to pet owners — of a man and car grown seriously alike. "Close. Very close," he admitted. "Damned Parisians, worst drivers in the world," an irony not unlike the Plantagenets[4] condemning the crusaders. "I'm afraid we missed Avenue Victor Hugo." He gave her a questioning sideways look. "Want to make another go?" But even to the untrained eye his car appeared at the critical stages of meltdown.

Charly returned his bemused look: "You're serious! Don't you smell anything?!"

He sniffed. "Just a little rubber," he said, shrugging his shoulders.

"Well, if we're going somewhere it'd better be quick," she said sternly. Astérix himself, still pacing nervously from side to side, was determined to escape the little blue kamikaze through any aperture provided. Insistent horns of busy taxicabs decided the moment, and the old Renault departed in a trail of gray smoke, putting along to a side street off Avenue Victor Hugo until a convenient, albeit illegal, parking space was found.

"I've used this spot before," he said absentmindedly, swerved over the curb onto the sidewalk and coming to an abrupt, bumpy stop.

Escape dominated the thoughts of both passengers, woman and beast.

"Figures. How long ago was that?" she said, yanking on the flimsy door handle for freedom from the smoldering car. The door swung open and Astérix made a desperate lunge from behind her seat. "Hey, dog!" she cried, pushing him back.

"Problems?"

"Yeah, your dog's rude."

"Nah, just scared. He was in the last accident."

"Last accident?"

"My sister's car. I, er, totaled it." Ignoring their struggle, Jean-Michel clambered out from behind the steering wheel.

"How long ago was that?" she asked, heaving herself up from the little car.

"How long ago was what?"

"Jesus, Jean-Michel, how long ago was … actually, forget it!"

"Last here?"

"No!" she howled. "The accident! Jeesus."

"Hm, oh, mon Dieu, let's see." He scratched his head, pudgy fingers buried in curly hair, oblivious to the irony. "The accident?" He simply shook his head. "Doesn't matter. Last time I was here, a friend was living in an apartment behind the cathedral; about six or seven years ago," he said, coming around to her side of the car.

"You're serious, aren't you?" she said, squinting into his face. "Are you mixing medications?"

He gave her an uncertain look. "No."

"I don't suppose this was the car?" she said sarcastically.

He paused to calculate. "Why, damned if it wasn't!" he exclaimed. "Insightful, ma cherie! Lent it to a friend after I got married; sort of forgot about it. How did you know?"

"With or without the bark?"

"Hm?"

"Okay, without. Pigeon droppings," she said, looking at the car. "Petrified, top looks like the bottom of a birdcage, or just plain ol' intuition."

"Women are blessed with it, I guess."

"What?" she said, surveying their surroundings.

"Intuition!"

"Yeah, along with cellulite and paranoia." Charly stood and stretched, looking at the buildings around them. "I always wondered why we called them *apart*ments if they're all stuck together?" She took Astérix by the leash. "Shall we head back to the Arc de Triomphe?"

"Really?" he said with a start, then reached for the leash and unhooked the dog. "He doesn't like leashes."

"Walk and stop for an espresso. If this is supposed to be Victor Hugo day, shouldn't we begin at the arch?"

"Arc," he corrected her. "Why not? The walk will do us good."

"Um-hm." She glanced skeptically at his belly. "Yeah, you need to work on your abs. So, this is Avenue Victor Hugo; did he die around here?"

"Well, yes and no. Yes, he did die near here, but the house is gone. They built a replica of some of its rooms over at his place on Place des Vosges," he pointed vaguely in a forward direction and began to amble ahead, Astérix in close pursuit. "Come on, we can see it later," he said over his shoulder.

Jean-Michel loved the sidewalks of Paris. For centuries famous authors have tried to capture the ambiance created by the cacophony of city sounds, alluring avenues, and the rich aromas of baking baguettes, pungent cologne, strong fish, ripe cheese, cigarette smoke, and faint whiffs of sewer. None have succeeded, for as in great sex, descriptions don't suffice. Like many southern Europeans, Jean-Michel enjoyed walking arm in arm with friends, an endearing habit of warmth and conviviality unfortunately lost to Teutonic stiffness and Yankee homophobia. Also, like so many men of his culture, he had the disconcerting habit of stopping when he wished to talk. He would disengage, plant himself on the pavement—mindless of fellow pedestrians—place his hand gently on his companion's forearm, and intently converse until his gestures progressed to those of tapping on chests, hearty groans, and dramatic gestures.

A short, potbellied man with gold-framed half-glasses clinging precariously to the end of his nose, he loved to banter, and expected his partners to respond in kind. He never spoke in chapters of course, just a few pages, but at the end of some arbitrary paragraph, an inner clock signaled it was time to move on. Charly knew an afternoon stroll with Jean-Michel was predictably slow and deliberate, with the goal of discoursing, not arriving, the whole paradigm opposed, as it so happened, to his method of driving.

An experienced cab driver, his was an unnerving style that heaven itself could not restrain. Animated conversations were energetically pursued through his rearview mirror, or while half-turned to his passengers, one pudgy hand on the wheel as the other danced about with his words, offering terrified riders only transcendental hopes of safety.

CHAPTER 2

═ THE GOOD OL' DAYS ═

Jean-Michel had lingered in Newark for a couple of fruitless years, looking for a future after completing his graduate work at St. Peter's College back in the eighties. He lived in a stately but aged three-story Victorian house that exhibited a decaying front porch and a servant's side entrance leading to creaky stairs. The renters entered on the side, climbed to the second floor, and — in Jean-Michel's case — turned left down a short hall wallpapered in floral design, to a dingy room that smelled of an old man's clothes. A luxurious spot in its day, the house now shared a neighborhood where 24-hour gas stations and chain stores littered every significant corner and where a $1,000 fine for littering was not enforced.

He drove a taxi; worked sporadically at a manuscript on the deaths of 18th-century French philosophers, sent off innumerable résumés, took a turn as a substitute teacher, and dated Lulu, a young graduate student from Martinique. But little blossomed from any of his efforts, and he often found it far easier to take a bottle to bed than a woman. Eventually, fate intervened; a friend had mentioned his name to a search committee at L'Universite Saint Louis de Just during their annual recruiting period, and Jean-Michel was hired to teach in the Department of History and Culture as an assistant professor. There was little left for him in the United States, and he left it willingly.

He was happy to be back in France. The States, for all its energy and verve, lacked that indefinable quality of culture and panache of Old World cities, which nurtured most educated Europeans and remained oblivious to any but the most seriously touring Americans. He moved into an inexpensive flat at the corner of Rue Brochant and Avenue de Clichy, facing a noisy street above the Brasserie Le Soleil in Clichy, a poor ethnic neighborhood

150

consisting of immigrant Arabs, Africans, Asians, and poor white Parisians. The neighborhood teemed with activity, no less than one might expect from a bustling bazaar in Rome or Istanbul.

With its immigrant population, Clichy harbored a collection of cultures to entertain the most staid of its visitors. There was the ubiquitous McDonald's, of course, but the Magrebian fruit vendors with their infectious smiles, seductive-looking young women flashing alluring black eyes, and mustachioed Syrians in black suits, pacing in pairs like Damascus secret police, ruled the streets. Wandering into its bistros and bars, it was apparent from solemn stares that strangers were not easily tolerated.

Jean-Michel chose his haunts carefully. He joked with the shop owners about the issues of the day, the perennial headscarves debate, and like a true *flâneur*, hung out in the dependable bars.

Clichy also had another culture bubbling below the surface: that of whores and homosexuals. It included transvestites, those pseudo-women who added to the local color by their garish clothes and ostentatious makeup. He could hear them coming, stomping through the crowd in platform shoes, with the guttural voices of Klingons and shoulders like fullbacks. Theirs was pretension by nature, with a full portion of contempt for the milling crowds. But, there were families too: black women in tight bandannas pushing dilapidated baby carriages surrounded by skinny children yelling at each other in mysterious languages. And intermittently, young boys in soiled T-shirts sped through the crowds on plywood skateboards, neatly skirting each tree with its moat of cigarette butts and desiccated dog shit.

The Boulevard Victor Hugo bisected Clichy down the middle, its streets receding in different directions like shallow canyons. It was a colorful and comfortable place, not hostile like the infamous *banlieues* in the city's suburbs, which harbored the angry young immigrants and excluded them from the bourgeois city centers.

Jean-Michel enjoyed wandering Avenue de Clichy on restless nights, taking in the show. Into the evening the streets filled with cheap KIAs and Toyotas ferrying insolent-eyed young Arabs slouched in their seats, rap music blaring. They shared the busy lanes with delivery vans and enameled Jaguars impatiently driven by haughty foreigners dressed in Armani. To keep order, green-and-white police cars cruised slowly along curbs, with stern men in blue short-sleeved shirts, seeing more than the obvious, arms hanging casually out windows, fingers thoughtlessly caressing the stubs of smoldering cigarettes.

Periodically, a wealthy couple in silk and serge would glide by, refugees of Combray's caste, parading in the best of Proustian tradition. They sought what could not possibly be found in this neighborhood, but instead stood out like delicate tropical fish, pathetically vulnerable in the chaos among the street's bottom dwellers and predators. Unlike so many "special" parts of great European cities, this area was not pure: not pure white, nor pure black, nor pure yellow, but a heterogeneous mix of cultures, robust and yet sick; dark-skinned castaways working like clambering beetles cementing the formless foundations of their daily lives, creating crusty barnacles on one of the great flagships of the global village.

Routines were essential in Jean-Michel's life; they had given security from his loneliness while abroad, and helped to dispel periods of depression at home. He had quickly developed a pattern of coming and going that fit comfortably into the community, a quiet neighbor whom most ignored.

His job at Saint Louis de Just was an easy schedule of morning classes and a leisurely lunch at the cafeteria. Each workday began around 8 a.m.—at a 19-century university building, in décor more like that of a bag-lady than the grande dames' sophisticated architecture farther down the avenue—and ended around 4 p.m., when his dean routinely retired for home.

With the sound of the dean's steps receding down the hall, Jean-Michel would grab a few books, venture into the hallway from his office, and announce to anyone within hearing that he was going to the library, which he did. He rarely stopped there, however, except to drop off the books on a reserved shelf, to be retrieved the following morning; then brusquely moved on past students lounging around old desks, working on laptops and books, out the side door to the Metro, then down the stairs for a short ride, and eventually resurfacing near his apartment.

Jean-Michel was neither shallow nor seriously deceitful. He never laid claim to superlative moral merit, and socially was as unreliable and selfish

152

as any man could be, but his personal and academic commitments took the form of friendly benevolence. He was not austere, there was no hint of arrogance about him, and there was a softness in his eyes that students remembered. An intelligent man, he preferred a good museum to almost any other pastime, except those in his cherished bars and an occasional round of golf.

Having chanced upon a Swiss cultural grant to study the mystery of Voltaire's and Rousseau's missing bodies, which had fit neatly into his graduate work, he eventually earned a modest place for himself in the brotherhood of academia—"the maven of molder," they called him. But he lacked the political acumen to reach into the institutional elite, and despite his pretensions of serious scholarship to better hold his job, he did little of significance to promote his career. He was at heart a writer, working sporadically on a mysterious manuscript that no one took time to discuss or even notice. He didn't care, since the research and process of writing a book was for Jean-Michel sufficiently difficult and complex that it engaged a great deal of his intellect. He wrote wherever and whenever he had time, mostly with pen or pencil, and when queried by his students about the use of computers, he would tell them the story about Mr. Sam Goldwyn, who picked up a volume of *The Complete Works of Shakespeare* and said in admiration, "And to think he wrote it all with a feather."

During his years in America, Jean-Michel was tied to his taxi like Sisyphus to his rock. It was not an easy life. There was little that could liberate him, except his attendance at occasional hockey games, field trips, and writing. His Ph.D. dissertation had provided the foundation for his academic interests, which, like Mohammed's coffin, focused on empty graves.

It was ironic, since most of the populace took for granted that what lay in famous graves were the bones and artifacts of legendary people. As he learned, however, this was not always true. Certainly, the public had its fill of staggering, revengeful Egyptian mummies traipsing through their local cinemas. Nonetheless, he knew that certain famous bodies and their keepsakes were missing from their coffins: celebrated figures, even historical icons like Rousseau and Voltaire.

For obvious reasons, beginning with tourism, it was convenient for governments to promote the fact that famous people were in fact interred in their famous graves, and requests for proof, research or otherwise, were ignored. But like the children's riddle: "Who is buried in Grant's tomb?" it had a more provocative answer than most could imagine. It was not the business of ghouls; rather, the economics of rare relics.

But Jean-Michel knew it was far more: in all of us, deep in our past, crept a repulsive incubus whose calls from the forest of our ancient ancestors demanded scalps, ears, and breasts to serve the darkest shadow of our nature, and surfaced as far more than simply silken trophies, talismans, or tobacco pouches. It was visceral, primitive, and pagan. To have the fragments of another of our species for our use or abuse reached far deeper than the habits of affection most of us experience from saving wedding bouquets, pilfering the panties from the girl next door, or cherishing the collar of our dog-before-last.

In this morbid refuse Jean-Michel had become something of an expert, a dedicated explorer in the land of the dead. His was a vocation few would care to discuss in polite company; he longed to run his hands over the carcasses of famous people; it was a quest, like an extreme sport. The secrets that rested in the interstices of the Ice Man called Ötzi, for example, could unlock the pages of an entire era of man's history from the simplest seeds in his stomach to the arrowhead in his shoulder. And who, for example, would not wish to brag of kissing the actual cheek of a Voltaire, Lenin, Monet, or Monroe, with perhaps a tooth, ring, or brooch to prove it; the circumstances of which would make it all the more fascinating to the listener? And what magnate would not like to keep the ultimate symbols of fame in his possession: not a death mask or Napoleon's hat, but rather the master himself, the remains of a da Vinci or Peter the Great and, not incidentally, perhaps the ingredients for their recombinant DNA.

After graduate school Jean-Michel was liberated, to work, but his writing life was now at its most free, because he could select his materials, invent his tasks, and pace himself when passengers were not about. The counterpoint of this freedom was that his work was also meaningless. For himself alone, the manuscript rode along in the taxi, a voluminous three-ring binder on the seat beside him, worn leather cover, silent and waiting, worthless to the world, no one else caring whether he did it well, or at all.

Later on, after he returned to France, his freedom, if he was honest, was a byproduct of the triviality of teaching, like his assignments, which few students did except to copy from one another, and which he graded without reading. The manuscript, on which he lavished such care, had neither needs nor wishes; it was simply a thing of his thoughts, with all the empathy of a good solid table — unlike the companionship of a faithful dog. Dillard had taught him that. Admittedly, as she said, there were many manuscripts already; worthy ones, most edifying and moving ones, clever and powerful ones. If asked, however, it was this fact that bothered him the most. In those seminal moment of great doubt, staring at the bulging shelves of modern bookstores, often frustrated, he would think: Why not just burn it rather than finish one more excellent manuscript on which to gag the world?[5] It was, after all, a means to an end, not an end. Who reads Molière?

Generally liked by his colleagues, he drank with the best; but a standing joke among peers charged that he was noticeably slow to volunteer for departmental committees. He went out of his way to praise his colleagues' work, however, and learned early on that they eventually got around to condemning his. He preferred leaving academic duties to others, and instead looked forward to joining the crowds of students descending into the cool subway tunnel after classes, the results of which, like prescriptions, rapidly relieved his anxieties by half. Finally free of academic responsibilities until the following day, he would emerge at the Brochant Metro stop to begin his other life.

Climbing the subway stairs with its period green wrought-iron railings and ceramic tile decor, he resurfaced in the late afternoon's soft glow as though a free day had just begun. He would then cross the street to the Le Figaro newsstand, buy his daily copy of *Le Monde*, take a seat at one of his regular bars, and order wine or beer.

His craving for alcohol, nourished in the States, grew slowly at first, usually during mid-afternoons, after classes. Like a pent-up dog pestering for a walk, it persistently danced at his knees, begging to get out. It whined and whimpered in the corner of his thoughts, irritating like an obstinate itch until he could no longer ignore it. A few years later, no distractions survived the onslaught until he had had a drink: no reading, no conversation, no TV, no woman; by dinnertime the compulsion barked and howled such that his head rang, and the urge scratched so vigorously at his insides that it made him short of breath. Rationality drained out; nothing else mattered until two generous shots of warm whiskey slid down his throat from a bottle he hid in the bottom drawer of his desk at school. On the way home, at an off-campus bar near the subway, he leisurely took two more brim-full shots, which he balanced expertly between thumb and forefinger, flicking each into his mouth in one smooth motion. The hound succumbed drowsily and dropped at his feet. He held his liquor well, and once the craving was appeased, he led, it seemed, an ordinary existence, still safe from the raw edge of urban living.

If a stranger saw him sitting at a café, there would be little that told much; just another Frenchman who enjoyed his paper, wine, and supper while trading jokes or soccer scores with the locals. To those who might have noticed, they would have described him as a benign creature of habit, which inevitably centered on cuisine. Ask him and he would tell you cooking was as important as eating, and not simply that detached process, devised by the Americans, of quickly transforming food for vapid consumption, but rather a dialogue between nature and culture. It was an extension of the land itself, and therefore ancient, a series of value-adding steps whose end product was an extension of the dirt in which it had started. The French, he would say to his American friends, insisted on being reminded where their food came from. For example, he would quote a French politician famous for saying that the andouillette sausage wrapped in intestines, like politics, was better with a whiff of shit.[6]

It was a life. He had achieved gentile poverty as a professor, a position not unbecoming the son of a used-car salesman from Lyon; and truth be told, with the exception of writing his manuscript, sought little more.

CHAPTER 3

═══ ARLENE ═══

Not long after Jean-Michel started at Saint de Just University, he met Arlene, a former Georgia homecoming queen, or so she said, at a faculty brunch held in the stale environs of the student lounge for American students studying abroad. It was true she had the smile and the eyes, but not incidentally, had graduated to a size twelve. She was a typical young woman, yet yearned in an American way to be better: attentive to the French culture and sauces, the perfect scarf, red-wine glasses and white-wine glasses, and the use of the word "ennui," with hopes also of improving her tennis.

Jean-Michel was the best English speaker in his department, and had therefore been prompted by the dean to attend the brunch, while Arlene, a French-language major and lab instructor at Georgia Tech, was the trip chaperone to French-speaking cities. After introductions, the romance began quickly. Their late-night walks through the meadows of Luxembourg Park, and wistful lounging in dimly lighted cafes, broke down inhibitions, eventually encouraging furtive embraces, and finally episodes of urgent groping by shadowy walls, no less animated than those between a Bogart and Bacall.

It had all happened quickly, and she and her students were gone. After Arlene returned to the States, however, a long-distance affair developed, buoyed by Jean-Michel's witty e-mails and Arlene's affectionate words, carefully penned on grandmother's perfumed stationery sent in sepia-colored envelopes with stamps dedicated to Valentine. Love, according to some, is blind, and by Maurice Chevalier's estimate, many a man has fallen in love with a girl in a light so dim he would not have chosen a suit by it. Fortunately, the two lovers shared similar temperaments and bodies, in the manner of bookends, a state of affairs known to car dealers as "a seat for every ass." Each partner had something special in mind: Arlene's vision portrayed a designer home and romantic family life in the City of Light, while Jean-Michel envisioned a pretty au pair to administer to his comfort, cope with offspring, and tend to his periodic urges. The French word "affaire" can refer to both a love affair and a business deal, which the French, to the bewilderment of Americans, manage skillfully to combine.

Theirs was to be a truly mythological match made in Paris. Orville, Jean-Michel's new brother-in-law, said as much during his wedding toast hardly a year later, and noting the marriage's international flavor, pointed out that the happy couple was even blessed by the mythical gods in Athens. He had waited to give the moment its drama and then shouted, "*Georgia!*" Whereupon there were screams of "Go dawgs!" and the crowd broke into an enthusiastic rendition of the "Bulldog Marching Song," culminating in a tearful "Hail to Georgia."

The decision was made for Arlene to come to Paris to live. This was easy, since she didn't suffer from that syndrome of most new arrivals, who were always relieved to be able to avoid speaking French. Of course, there was great excitement and enthusiasm in Athens among Arlene's relatives and extended family, with stirring articles in the *Athens Chronicle* under "Local," plus promises by cousins and friends to visit Paris and send care packages of Georgia's treasured honey ham and shelled pecans. For his part, Jean-Michel vacated his old apartment and made other sacrifices, jettisoning his not insubstantial collection of rare pornographic magazines, and the notion of always being fond of people he had slept with. He recruited his sister to help Arlene set up house in the 6th arrondissement. Soon after, the lovers shared a renovated and, it must be said, cute, but small, two-bedroom apartment on the third floor. Arlene worked heroically on the place until it looked like a Vuillard painting, brimming over with details in Faubourg Shabby Chic and pretensions toward tranquillity. Then Mother Nature smiled on them, mirthlessly, and two children were produced, first a boy and then a golden-haired little girl.

Arlene taught at an upscale private school in Saint Germain and tutored when possible. Jean-Michel joined a local golf team, and even, to the surprise of his dean, volunteered for a modicum of committee work. The two children, Jean-Paul, the eldest, and Emmanuelle, Emma to her family and friends, flourished in their surroundings and grew to be gangly and rambunctious children mindful of their mother's household rules, where good manners came first and stuffed animals were separated into baskets of land and sea.[7] Jean-Michel and Arlene socialized, made couple-friends also blessed with children, and created a life of sorts, befitting the modest income accorded a junior philosophy professor at one of France's great small universities.

Things went well, all things considered, except for the parents' screaming arguments, threats of divorce, drinking bouts and broken china, their son's emergent rebellious nature, and Emma's touch of MS. For Jean-Michel it was more than he could endure alone, and his alcoholism grew, a quiet refuge—like a cozy nap—from most annoyances, especially his wife. He would usually retire early to his study to work on his manuscript.

Arlene fit his father's classic description of women: the old man saw females as tempting fruit from the Garden of Eden, whose fragrance, shapes, and colors excited men's strongest appetites. The men succumbed, like Adam took Eve, and ate their soft, pink flesh down to the core...Genesis never mentioned apples. Arriving at the womb, nothing was left except the women's true mission: reproduction, nourishment, and security. Genesis fulfilled; men were banished from the garden of delights; the pits.

Jean-Paul, pride of the family and pretender to the throne, grew tall and gawky, all but despising his mother, who had relapsed into an expat American and whose reality consisted of a large comfortable chair that she patronized with moans of delight. Magazines and newspapers from Georgia were stacked in neat rows along one of the living room walls, and organized by colorful IKEA plastic boxes coded by month to defended her against ennui, while CNN and TCM brought today's world affairs and America's classic entertainment into the very heart of Paris on cable. Visits to McDonald's, Burger King, and other fast-food restaurants leaned toward routine, with special days for special treats: Thursdays were always chicken, and she stealthily nibbled on more than her share from the children's Lucky Meals.

To manage a serious case of psoriasis, Arlene's frequent trips to her personal physician back in the States also helped to assuage a particularly virulent strain of recurrent homesickness. These trips relieved the household of a constant and terrible tension between husband and wife while she was gone. She was missed, of course, mostly by her daughter. The only sins by father and son were those of omission: forgetting to water her flowers and neglecting to vacuum once a week.

It was the stuff of which many family lives are made; however, a pathetic and serious turn of events occurred shortly after a faculty picnic. It was their son's sixteenth birthday, one of those summer days that everyone remarks about, sunny and fresh, when Jean-Paul decided to stay and swim with friends. Returning home, Jean-Michel, Arlene, and Emma experienced a tragic automobile accident, from which neither Arlene nor Emma walked away.

———

Not more than a few months after the appalling departure of the feminine side of the house, Jean-Michel and Jean-Paul moved from the suburbs of the 6th arrondissement to an area in the northeast of Paris, in the heartland of high-rises between Saint-Denis and Bobigny. These suburbs and their projects, home to the generations spawned from Algeria's war of independence, were often portrayed as trouble zones. But the rent was cheap, and Jean-Michel liked the ambiance, which sheltered his drinking, and his speaking a passable form of social Arabic marked him with a certain panache among those in the neighborhood. He attended a clinic for alcoholics, with modest results, but he frequently slipped over the edge. Jean-Paul learned quickly, as the children of alcoholics do, that the apartment was at its best when Jean-Michel was either out working, drinking with friends, or passed out at home, and the boy varied his routine accordingly.

After the accident, Jean-Michel had a public reason to drink and made little effort to conceal it. Therefore, it was understood, or perhaps tolerated, by friends and acquaintances, who saw him not as some sly, colorful rogue, but at his worst, a languid, quirky Nero.

Finally, based on the complaints of senior students about his inebriation in class, where his jokes were not funny, his unintended flatulence displeasing, and the irritation of influential faculty members unabridged, the university was forced to consider bringing an action against him. This was a tricky and distasteful business, since such publicity could do serious damage to the reputation of the school, and, by virtue of his alcoholism being considered a disease, contestable by his union. Also, Jean-Michel was genuinely liked and respected for his knowledge by the majority of his students, which could also cause trouble. Therefore, the decision was made to kick him upstairs, so to speak, into a respected position in an otherwise harmless organization. This adroit maneuver was performed by the dean, who, being a maestro at such strategies, executed it flawlessly.

Assistant Professor Doctor Jean-Michel Levasseur was promoted unexpectedly and quickly from the university to a new seat as a fellow at the Institute for Philosophy and Cultural Antiquity,[8] a highly respected organization, but surreptitiously employed by various and sundry successful French administrators as a dumping ground for aging, disgruntled, or otherwise dysfunctional individuals of education, stature, and risk, and all for the price of a modest endowment.

Professor Levasseur would have eventually sunk from view like many of the others, and died an anonymous death as an incurable alcoholic, had not a certain Colonel Maurice de Monteaux, son of one of the institute's founders and member of a prominent Parisian family, taken charge of the situation and, with courage and persistence, attempted to shepherd Professor Levasseur back toward sobriety. De Monteaux moved Jean-Michel from his shabby apartment in Tremblay-en-France to the colonel's houseboat on the Seine, away from the proximity of bars, while Jean-Paul was shipped off to a high school in the United States as part of a corporate-funded scholarship program.

Until the colonel had come along to help, few except Jean-Michel's sister and his friend, Pierre, cared or dared to interfere. Now the appearance of Charlene Brooks in his life offered perhaps the last prospects for a fulfilling relationship and a chance at a new life. She seemed strong and sure, some fifteen years his junior, bright, and energetic. But, as he lamented to his sister, this was probably a bridge too far: a fat man reaching for happiness with another American woman whose sense of expectancy and optimism was not likely to buoy up his old existence, clothed in its sad past, for long. No enduring relationship could tack well in such a crosswind, dragging her wayward daughter and his rebellious son in its wake.

CHAPTER 4

═══ ARC DE TRIOMPHE ═══

The Arc de Triomphe is not hard to find: simply look for the Place Charles de Gaulle at the end of the Champs-Elysées Boulevard. It's where twelve avenues converge in a star-like pattern, thus giving the location's former name, Étoile. Along with the Eiffel Tower, it is unquestionably the greatest symbol of France.

The Arc de Triomphe was commissioned by Napoleon in order to commemorate the Grande Armée and his victories; it was designed by French architect Jean-Francois-Thérèse Chalgrin and inaugurated in 1836. Yet the return of Napoleon's mortal remains in 1840 (nineteen years after his death) is considered to be the true inauguration of the monument. Its design was inspired by the ancient Arch of Constantine in Rome, but at fifty meters (164 ft.) high and forty-five meters (148 ft.) wide, it is twice as high and twice as wide as the original. Sculptural reliefs and panels on the Arc de Triomphe depict various Napoleonic, and subsequent French, military victories and treaties.

Today, the Arc de Triomphe with its eternal flame is considered the national war memorial of France; beneath it lays the tomb of the Unknown Soldier. It has also been the focus of some momentous historical occasions, such as the victory march of General Charles de Gaulle through Paris in 1944, after the liberation of the city by the Allies from the German army of occupation.

═══

As Charly, Jean-Michel, and Astérix walked from their car to the Arc de Triomphe, Jean-Michel offered his views on the great monument and its relation to Victor Hugo. "General Hugo's not there, inscribed on the Arc, I mean. I thought you knew. In fact, Victor was very upset by the whole thing, his father—a hero to his son, as one might suspect—being inadvertently excluded. The Arc de Triomphe, as I said earlier, had begun in 1806 under Napoleon's rule, then was inaugurated in 1836, fifteen years after his death, with the names of First Republic heroes inscribed on its walls—but not General Hugo's. Young Victor was wounded by this reckless slight, you understand, and determined to right the wrong by dedicating his *Les Voix Intérieurs*[9] to his father."

Charly and Astérix's pace ground to a halt as they waited impatiently for Jean-Michel to finish. "The dedication was something along these lines":

> 'Dedicated by his respectful son, To Joseph-Léopold-Sigisbert, Count Hugo.... Not Inscribed on the Arc de Triomphe: He offers his father this poor sheet of paper, which is all that he has, with the regret that he has no granite.... A nation is great, a family small. That which means nothing to one means everything to the other.'

"Um-hm, interesting," Charly said disinterestedly; longing for a cappuccino to soothe frazzled nerves, she gently prodded her companion toward a pleasant-looking corner café exposed to the sun. "Was General Hugo a genuine hero?" she asked, trying to keep him moving. "Maybe he wasn't simply overlooked, maybe Napoleon just didn't like him."

"Who knows?" he shrugged.

"Too bad Colonel de Monteaux didn't make it up there; he probably would have been a changed man."

"De Monteaux? Changed? I doubt it," he said, shaking his head. "You'd have to kill him to change him."

"He's just so—you know, what's his problem?" she asked. "I told you about his grand departure at Malmaison, didn't I? I mean, Jesus!"

"The biplane? Interesting hobby. His pilot can land practically anywhere. The police..." Jean-Michel stopped to respond, only to have Charly grasp his sleeve and pull him toward the café.

Once seated, drinks ordered, it was their first time to sit back and talk a bit without suffering interruption, inconvenience, death by traffic, or some other modern menace. When the waiter had brought their drinks, Jean-Michel took a sip of his beer, and asked, "Did de Monteaux behave himself?"

She looked displeased. "You have foam on your mustache," she said, and reached over to swab it off with her napkin. "Guess you like beer for breakfast?"

"Sometimes. Anyway, it's brunch, good for the digestion. Not a sweet beverage, you know."

"Yeah, so I hear, but aggravates pancakes. De Monteaux?" She pondered a moment. "Well, for most of the day he was egotistic, aggressive, pompous, overzealous, intelligent, proud, and pissy — probably just what you'd want in a French tour guide. Simone loved him, and they got along famously."

"So it was a disaster?"

"Well, we're having dinner Friday evening at, I understand, a very expensive restaurant, and —"

"La Tour d'Argent?" he said eagerly, having an instant vision of La Tour's famous duck, bred in the marshes of the Sologne region and served with its blood, in two courses: first the breast and then the legs; the very thought made him salivate.

"La Tour d'Argent? Doesn't ring a bell, probably someplace else. And my co-financier friend, Simone, bowed out."

"Oh, merde! So you lost the bet. I forgot to warn you that he loves to tease people with riddles as a contest for dinner."

"Tease? Cute little riddle. Don't worry, I wasn't planning on eating until my in-flight meals back."

Jean-Michel patted her on the arm. "He'll hold your feet to the fire for a while, then probably have it put on his monthly tab. Just don't panic and be unkind."

"Probably? What's 'probably'? Those dinners cost around 200 bucks. Each!" she groaned. "I'm going to be stuck living on two-course meals involving Tic-Tacs and water."

"Tic-Tacs?" He shook his head. "Lots of calories. Dinner price depends on the wine year, of course, but it is true, sometimes he is moody. Why the bet?"

"It was a sure thing: you know the riddle, four feet in the morning, two in the afternoon, etc. Anyway, how was...where did you say you went? Greece?" she asked.

"Um-hm, Greece. Also something short of a disaster," he sighed. "Rather talk about Vic's dad." There was little to be gained by complaining about a meeting with his son in Corfu, which didn't work out. Besides, he felt sorry for Charly, and de Monteaux had taken advantage. It was true the colonel was unpredictable: if he liked you, you'd eat like a king at his expense; if not, he'd eat, shake your hand, and leave you a very large bill. It was his personal test of character.

"And Jodie?" he asked.

"Due at De Gaulle Airport late Saturday morning. The big surprise may well be that her twenty-six-year-old boyfriend decided to come along and meet Mom."

"Waiting for Thursday's child. Excited?"

"Me or him?"

"Both."

"Yeah, my aunt says Jodie told her that the boyfriend has done a little time upstate, as they say, then found Jesus. Now they're both crusaders. I can't wait." She shook her head dejectedly. "Puh-leeze, God, don't let her be pregnant."

"Well, he'll be heading upstate again for statutory rape if she is."

"Is that supposed to be consolation?"

"No. Just sorry that—"

"Yeah."

They were losing time, and Jean-Michel figured the best thing to do would be to launch into his work. "Our Victor-Marie Hugo, according to his father, was conceived 'almost in midair,' by which he meant 'one of the highest peaks of the Vosges mountains.' One could speculate on what exactly Major Hugo and his young wife were doing in May 1801, 3,000 feet above sea level, but history is not quite clear." He winked at Charly.

Bored or perhaps bitchy, she seized the moment, "Not quite clear? What is it with you French?" she chided. "Seems clear enough to me: if his parents' epochal embrace took place overlooking the Rhineland, we know what they were doing. Certainly, if a man like Rousseau couldn't keep his cock in his pants for the benefit of admirers, why would that lusting bull be any different? The French seem so sexual, the world's preeminent lovers, but have this annoying habit of pretending they're too cool to care."

"And Americans? You're stereotyping. There's many an urge beyond our control, at least some of the time and perhaps most of the time." Jean-Michel wanted to slip in a little introduction about his drinking, but continued with sex. "Okay, take sex, for example. Sex indisputably energizes the attraction between males and females, without which, as we all know, there would be the collapse of our species and probably all others. Victor Hugo's father epitomizes the predatory nature of this sexual drive, but he's not an exception, he's the rule, and probably passed it on to his son, since Victor himself was a sexual athlete of the first order."

"That old monkey?"

"I think you have the wrong photos in mind. He wasn't always that old. He did his new wife eight times on their first night."

"Did what?"

"Mon Dieu," he bleated. "Can't you ever—"

"Can't I ever what?!" she demanded. "If you have something sexual to say, then say it!"

"All right!" he bellowed.

"Keep your voice down."

He got red in the face, "I– I…"

"Where were you conceived?" she asked, nonplused.

That gave him pause. "Conceived in bed, probably, or in the stands of a night game at the soccer stadium. What difference does it make?"

"It makes a difference; it's where the world began, at least for you; did you ever think about that?"

"No. And I wouldn't have liked to be there." He exhaled heavily and reached in his vest for his pipe.

She frowned at him. "Don't light that damn thing, please," she pleaded, "it stinks."

He quit searching. "Fine. You want some sexual examples?"

"It's better than being spoken to in a voice you'd use for your Labrador."

"Oh, my God," he whined. "May I continue?"

166

"Please." She smiled and lightly pinched his arm. "You're so cute."

He stared at her, not sure whether to melt or freeze. "Listen, please. These tidbits come from his diary and other records." Jean-Michel held up his hand and began matter-of-factly counting off Victor Hugo's more disturbing sexual conquests on each finger, taking what perverse pleasure he could from trying to make her squirm with every fact. "One," he held up his thumb: "Throughout his married life, Victor had sexual encounters with countless actresses, prostitutes, chambermaids, and various social acquaintances. He even recorded seven or eight sexual encounters the year he died, at eighty-four.

"Two: He managed, at one point, to have three wives in his extended family at the same time, one legally, and two mistresses, each unaware for a time of the other's role. Later, he initiated a liaison with his son Charles's mistress, and subsequently Charles's widow, and finally the wife of his hairdresser.

"Three: He loved live pornography by English 'actresses' who recreated famous works of art wearing transparent body stockings; and prostitutes who specialized in stripping.

"Four: His erotic and incestuous inclinations, portrayed in poetic yearnings for his daughters, seemed too blatant for most modest temperaments;

"And five: To keep it brief, the possible deflowering of his daughter Leopoldine's first communion companion." He finished with five fingers extended in the air.

Charly, chin in hand, elbow on the table, stared across the used plates and glasses at him. "Happy?" she said sardonically. "This is usually the part where your hormones take over and you invite me to your place to see some etchings."

"You asked, right? No etchings, and you've already holstered my hormones, for which I am eternally, and momentarily, I might add, grateful. I'm not an apologist, I'm simply trying to make a point."

"You did. Evidently, that old bastard was an incorrigible lech of the first order, like a few others I've met, and if he were here now he'd be doing hard time. Besides, I wasn't talking about what appears to be a serial pervert, I was talking about 'normal' people. It was just a simple comment: you French act like there is no 'down there.'"

"May I continue?" he earnestly petitioned.

"With what?"

"The old man, for God's sake."

"Oh, yeah. Lessons."

"Please," he implored. "Anyway, if you climb the 3,000-foot Donon Mountain today, you'll find the exact spot of Hugo's conception marked by a block of sandstone in section 99 of the Donon forest, just below the summit, near the ruins of a Celtic temple:

IN THIS PLACE
ON 5 FLOREAL, YEAR 9
VICTOR HUGO
WAS CONCEIVED

"Obviously we're into codes here," she said.

"It just means May 1801. Actually, why bother? I can assure you it has nothing to do with French sex, a topic with which you're obviously enthralled." He was resigned to give up the exercise.

"Hostility? Do I detect hostility?" she chided. "I assume you're being paid."

She hit a sensitive spot. "All right, no hostility. Here's the situation: our erstwhile French revolutionaries tried to remake the calendar, but their success was obviously short-lived. The National Convention of the French Revolution set up a committee on calendar reform, which produced a new calendar of, I think, rather charming rational symmetry. Look here," and he took out a pencil and made a diagram on his napkin. "In 1792 their decimal calendar replaced the seven-day week with a ten-day week called a *décade,* each day of which was given a Latin numerical name, three *décades* of which comprised a month. The day was divided into ten hours, each consisting of one hundred minutes, each minute of one hundred seconds. In addition to the 360 days of these twelve months, the extra five or six days were given edifying names: *Les Vertus, Le Génie, Le Travail, L'Opinion,* and *Les Récompenses,* with a leap day, called *Sans-culottide,* dedicated to holidays and sports."

"Sorry I asked," she said. Jean-Michel gave her a pained look. "Oh, I'm just kidding. But why? I mean, like my daddy used to say, 'If it ain't broke, don't fix it!'"

"I'm sure your daddy's right, of course, but this calendar was designed to loosen the grip of the Catholic Church on daily life and thought, and, as I said before, it didn't work—lasted only thirteen years, in fact. When Napoleon became ruler of France, he restored the Gregorian calendar, with its traditional saint's days and holidays, for which he received the Pope's blessing and probably every Frenchman's, too. I think it's a good indication, however, of the French keeping Catholicism at arm's length, unlike the Irish."

"Still, I wonder why we have a seven-day week?" she pondered.

"I thought you read the Bible. You know Genesis?"

"I do, but not literally."

"Who does? But the number seven has long had a special something: the Japanese found seven gods of happiness, Rome was set on seven hills, the ancients counted seven wonders of the world, and medieval Christians enumerated seven deadly sins—it's an attractive number, for some reason."

"And Elizabeth Taylor had seven marriages, I think. Maybe that was Mickey what's-his-name; there's *something* deep there. I don't suppose Victor had seven siblings?"

"No, but Napoleon did; and Victor no doubt would have enjoyed numerological comparisons with the emperor; but he only had two brothers, both older. Abel, the eldest, who attempted to promote Victor's fame, had trouble with his business and ran off to London for a few years. Eugène, the middle son, went quite mad and died in his thirties, confined to a mental institution. Talk had it that both Hugo and Eugène were in love with the next-door neighbor, Adèle; but Victor won out, as he did in most competitions with Eugène, who responded the only way he could—by initiating food fights."

"All the boys conceived up there on good ol' Donon Mountain?" she asked.

"What's this fixation on sex?!"

"Inquiring minds want to know."

He had pulled out his old Dunhill and stroked the worn bowl with his thumb. "Sure, but this mountain business is getting out of hand. It was a remarkable piece of detective work, though, the idea of Hans, a former head of Strasbourg Museums, an old associate, actually. He erected the memorial as a practical joke. I…"

"Is it still erect?" she purred.

"Charly, for Christ's sake!" he snorted, and ducked into his story. "Victor was born on 26 February 1802. A significantly insignificant event, you could say, which he did his best to imprint upon posterity. It goes something like:

> *This century was two years old. Rome was replacing Sparta;*
> *Already Napoleon was emerging from under Bonaparte,*
> *And already the First Consul's tight mask*
> *Had been split in several places by the Emperor's brow.*
> *It was then that in Besançon, that old Spanish town,*
> *Cast like a seed into the flying wind,*
> *A child was born of mixed blood — Breton and Lorraine —*
> *Pallid, blind and mute…*
> *That child, whom Life was scratching from its book.*
> *And who had not another day to live,*
> *Was me.*

"Um. Nice. Do you have anything, a little more, you know…"

He ignored her. "According to the opening poem of *Les Feuilles d'Automne*, one of the great verse autobiographies of the Romantic period, a double order was placed with the carpenter, for a cradle and a coffin."[10]

Charly became aware of a young man with a Vandyke beard and Trotsky-like sunglasses staring in her direction. He sat cross-legged at his table, writing postcards, and seemed to be deep in thought — at least until Charly would look in his direction, at which point he sought eye contact. "There's someone staring at us," she whispered to Jean-Michel. "Don't look now, but," at which point Jean-Michel turned to look directly at the young man. "I said don't — never mind!" she fretted. The stranger was casually dressed in black T-shirt and tan pants, his hair closely cropped. He waved hesitantly at Charly and Jean-Michel.

"Charly?" he called, then got up and started toward them.

"Klaus?" She hesitated. "Klaus Beck! Damn, what a surprise!" she exclaimed, charging from her chair to hug her shy friend. "My God, how long has it been? Where's all that hair of yours? And now a beard, well, sort of a beard. You look like Bruce Willis!"

"*Ja,* I guess I changed, a little," he allowed shyly.

"A little," she snorted. "Give me a break! You look twenty pounds lighter and two feet taller."

"It's probably the black T-shirt. The salesman convinced me it would make me look more professional." Klaus' voice was high, with a noticeable Bavarian accent: "er" endings reverted to "ah" and became lost in his throat.

"I can't get over it...." Realizing that Jean-Michel was still sitting, Astérix watching, she introduced them: "Klaus Beck, meet Professor Jean-Michel Levasseur. Klaus was one of my classmates from Aix-en-Provence, a sometimes beau of Simone, and otherwise smartest student in our class." Jean-Michel stood, and Klaus, tall and thin, extended his hand formally, smiled slightly, and bowed his head cordially, followed by a gentle pat on Astérix's head.

Jean-Michel returned the bow. "A pleasure, Charly's friends are my friends. Would you join us for an apéritif?" Klaus towered over Jean-Michel and Charly: gawky and pensive, a friendly, solicitous stork.

"It is kind of you to offah; I'm not intruding?"

"Get your stuff and get over here, you old giraffe," Charly quipped. "What's with all this formality? I heard you were living here." Klaus smiled in acknowledgment and left to gather his notebook and cards. He returned to the table, and they ordered drinks while the former classmates interrogated each other to catch up. Klaus was a good friend, and his reappearance gave Charly a strong sense of melancholia for her graduate days in Aix-en-Provence, where she, Klaus, Simone, and other friends had spent warm afternoons in cafés like this one, sipping San Bitter, snacking on olives and chips, and discussing every subject under the sun. They joked of classmates and briefly lamented the passage of time.

"Did you say you work for NanoNet?" Jean-Michel asked.

"Yes, Maestro. I have been here for three and a half years. I'm working as a programmah. I've got an apartment over on Rue St. Jacques." He paused. "Charly said you are a fellow at the Institute of Philosophy and Cultural Antiquity?"

"Yes, you've heard of it?"

"Of course, but I have never had the chance to actually meet any institute fellows. Some of your professors gave lectures at the Sorbonne, which I attended. I don't believe I've had the pleasure of one of your lectures."

"I'm fairly new."

"It would be an honor for me, Maestro," Klaus lied. He knew differently. The institute was well known for a variety of reasons, but mostly for sheltering old flacks, perhaps like the one sitting before him; the empty shells of some of France's greatest legends gone bad, intolerable misfits, or at least geriatric. The institute fellows were recruited to lecture when busy professors had better things to do. Despite living in Paris, Klaus had little respect for the French in any case, a defensive response to the French hatred of Germans. "So, Charly, you're still working as an editor?" he asked.

"No. Fired," she said.

"Um-hm," he nodded his head.

"Surprised?"

"No." Klaus shook his finger at her in admonishment. "Terry toiletmouth? Again?"

She grinned. "Not sure," she said, pausing to reflect. "It's hard to say. My secretary used to have this plaque over his desk with the basic rules of life: Never shoot pool with someone who brings his own cue; never party at an office party; and never install a new operating system with a low serial number.[11] I suppose I stubbed my toe somewhere there. Now I'm training as a travel guide, which should bring me to Paris quite often. Jean-Michel is educating me on the famous places of Paris, and today is Victor Hugo day. We're on our way to the Arc de Triomphe to see where his father's name wasn't inscribed, and on to Père Lechaise to find him," she said.

"Ah, Père Lechaise, where he isn't buried," Jean-Michel corrected. "His family is there, but Hugo's at the Pantheon, down in the basement, bunking with Zola. But we thought it would be nice to see the Arc de Triomphe, too."

"So, you aren't going to Père Lechaise?"

"Oh, we have to, I think," Jean-Michel nodded.

"Is his whole family there?" Charly asked.

"Almost. It turned out to be the place Victor could begin to reunite his family, even though the gravediggers had a tough time, literally, wedging them all in. Hugo despised the cemetery, you know. He was quoted as saying, 'it's a hideous place of rococo little buildings with their boxes and compartments where good Parisians tidy their fathers away, the ultimate bourgeois chest of drawers!' We're saving Père Lechaise for another day."

"But we still have to go back," Charly chimed in. "Cemeteries have an attraction for some people, and I'm the morbid one. Jim Morrison's buried there. I dropped by during graduate days to see his grave, even though my niece swore that he wasn't there; you know…alive and well, living in Ottawa."

"Did you find him?" asked Klaus. "It's a big cemetery."

"Yeah, big and no toilets; well, one shabby hut, but it was closed for a week, waiting for a wing nut. Morrison I couldn't miss: white paint splashed on various crypts spelled the word 'Jim,' and under the name, an arrow pointing the way to Hippie Heaven, hash and all. Had a little quiet time and sat by his grave, listening to his music on my 'Pod."

"Get a little misty-eyed?" Jean-Michel asked.

"I did, actually. Now the place is all cops and fences. It wasn't a big deal, but I was impressed. So many great people are buried there: Chopin, Oscar Wilde, Piaf, Gertrude Stein and Alice B. Toklas, Maria Callas—"

"And all quite dead," Jean-Michel mused, swirling the beer in his glass. "I'd love to look at Piaf now."

Charly blanched. "Thanks, J.M., I wasn't really hungry."

Jean-Michel ignored her. "Suppose one of the more philosophical of your tourists asks what made them great? Was it simply their art? Take Oscar Wilde, for example," he said, pointing his pipe in the direction of the cemetery. "A wondrously talented and intelligent man, who even met Hugo later in life at one of Victor's weekly receptions; nonetheless, a pederast, of course."

"Didn't he also meet Proust?" Klaus asked.

Jean-Michel chuckled. "Wilde? Well, you could say that, although Proust, speaking of pederasts, if you believe Gide, which I do; but Proust wasn't in the same league with Wilde. Proust was supposedly snubbed by, as he said, that 'powdered, perfumed, puffy Irish giant.'[12] But what a time in history: just imagine sitting in a circle of people including Victor Hugo, Proust, and Oscar

Wilde while they talked, and you trying to say something insightful!"

"Like, 'one small step for mankind,'" Charly ventured.

The two men looked at her. "Well, that was 'insightful,'" she countered.

Jean-Michel nodded his head, "insightful," and continued, "They say when Oscar met Hugo he sparkled as usual, but by then he literally couldn't keep the old master awake."

"Such a tragedy," Klaus said. He liked the Irish, and their neutrality in the war.

"Tragedy?" Charly asked.

"Um-hm," Jean-Michel said. "Wilde served two years in a British jail—you remember *The Ballad of Reading Gaol*— for his pederast behavior, and then was driven out of England to Paris.[13] Wilde, contrary to Proust, who was being catered to in his cork-walled room by his mother, suffered a great deal, a pathetic figure lost in Paris. He was usually seen sitting in an endless number of cafés not unlike this one, often unmindful of the rain, the brim of his hat drooping around his head, bumming drinks or cigarettes from strangers; friendless, often penniless, and horribly ill. But, the man was surely great."

"Possibly he got what he deserved," Charly added, spooning up the last of the cappuccino foam from her cup.

"That's harsh, don't you think?" Klaus said.

"Depends on how you feel about the boys who were his victims."

"'Boy' or 'victim' doesn't describe the Marquis of Queensbury's son, Alfred, and his faggot friends," Klaus retorted.

"Let's drop it, if you don't mind," Jean-Michel said. "Charly and I have a lot to cover, and pederasty with a pissant isn't on the list. My vote for greatness would be the first man on the moon, but will Neil Armstrong, although an immensely capable astronaut, ever attain the status of Christopher Columbus, or Victor Hugo, for that matter?"

"Fair enough, but perhaps you missed the part about not being French," Charly said.

"You don't have to be French to be great," he retorted.

"Well, well. You heard it, Klaus. The maestro here has come clean."

"Or an aging of the art?" asked Klaus. "Armstrong will be famous someday, but he probably has to die first so that fifth gradahs can hear his story and remembah the dates. Then again, maybe it takes someone like Van Gogh, whose reach for fame nevah succeeded until he was gone. And Victor Hugo? Was he great? *Mein Gott, ja,* his influence on French literature was second only to that of the Bible."

"No question," Jean-Michel seconded, "the crowd that followed his body to the tomb outnumbered the usual population of Paris. But is he great today? Only in France."

Klaus nodded. "All the Germans who have read his works could fit in Munich's Olympia Stadium and it would still be half empty. I've read most of his works. Am I any the bettah for it? I doubt it. Charly hasn't. Is she any the worse for it?"

"Well, I disagree," Jean-Michel said, elbows on the table, fingers interlocked, squinting into the intent faces of his two friends. "Christ, an unemployed carpenter; Muhammad, an outcast; Buddha, a beggar, and Einstein a patent clerk, are great. They have made a huge difference on the Earth, so it's ideas that make you famous.

"It's ironic that a man who had as huge a public following as Victor Hugo's in his day could sink so quickly into obscurity—a harmless Dr. Seuss, compared with his creations of *Les Misérables* and *Notre-Dame de Paris.*"[14] He is still revered here by the older generation, but the world's media, which cover soccer matches in excruciating detail, seem unwilling to take on the subject, much less communicate the author's genius with his creation. It's a sin to separate Monet from his paintings, or Chanel from her perfume, or Hugo from his novels, but that they are to creativity what simple bottles are to fine wines is indisputable. The source of inspiration that lies behind artistic creation is one of the intriguing secrets of the human mind, yet the great majority of people seem to have little interest in the creators."

"Maybe, but does that make any difference?" Charly asked.

"Then, what does that say about our future?" Jean-Michel replied.

"Nothing. Why should it? I don't care who invented foam rubber, I just enjoy sitting on it."

"She has a point, Maestro. In his dialogue, *Ion,* Socrates reaches the conclusion that the poets themselves are often the most ignorant of the meaning of their own works, and the very last who ought to be appealed to for an interpretation of them. So you think the poet is the instrument used by powahs highah than he realizes?"

"Listen, I agree: true criticism of art—far from being helped by the humble and sometimes actually sordid details of an author's personal history—is more likely to be hindered and distracted by them. I think that the contrast between what artists produce and what they themselves are is often so great that any attempt to connect them is like trying to bring heaven and earth together. Perhaps you'd also agree what cloddish men can do to their lives, and yet see the magnificence of what they have done. Some critics believe about authors, for example, that only by surrendering themselves completely to the power that inspires them can writers totally surpass themselves."[15]

"What 'power'?" Charly said. "Hash? You've been spending to much time talkin' to your soup, Professor. I happen to have some experience with writers, and all I learned about was grueling work, not surrendering to muses."

"You're referring to textbook authors," Jean-Michel said cynically. "We're talking about literature, gifted writers, but let's take it from the light that art throws upon the author's life, rather than the other way around, which is the usual approach. In the case of the real artist, it is art that is the more important part of the equation. Man lives in order to create, and without the creation, his life would most likely seem to be void and meaningless—you know, 'eat, sleep, shi– go to the toilet.' It's their reason to get up in the morning."

"Ain't mine, Professor," she said. "I got lots of reasons to get up in the morning, but most have to do with making a living; few have anything to do with my art."

"Okay, so we're excluding textbook editors too. Take Shakespeare, for example: I sometimes think it is a blessing that we know next to nothing about Shakespeare, the man, and are forced to concentrate almost entirely on the works, without getting involved in the difficult business of explaining the works by his life or deducing the life from the works. Of course, biographers will go on speculating endlessly about the Dark Lady and the 'second-best bed,' but we know before we read the biographies that they, and we, are indulging in fiction. Victor Hugo, on the other hand, has written about himself, and his biographers have so much history and personal data to go by that one gets turned every which way by the supposed historical details. In other words, we can 'peer' as often as we like and never find the true focus, only something different by which we can interpret his intentions."[16]

"I really don't see what difference it makes. I mean, really, who cares?" she sighed.

Charly had irritated him again, and he leaned forward in his chair — the period of polite conversations had drifted under the Pont de Neuf some days ago — and shot back, "God damn it, woman, Victor Hugo was not just some hack who wrote a couple of good stories or couplets. We're talking about the cultural heritage of one of the most sophisticated nations on Earth."

"Are we talking," she retorted, "about the same sophisticated nation that just scooped up, according to this morning's paper, 2.8 million copies of 'Astérix goes to La Traviata'?"[17]

Jean-Michel looked over his glasses, giving her his familiar blank look. "What's your point?"

"You don't detect a little irony here? After all, your dog's named for that cartoon character."

"We are talking about," he said exasperatedly, "Victor Hugo! He wasn't simply a poet or philosopher like Voltaire, Chateaubriand, or Sartre. Hugo was also a politician, an undisputed leader, and an immense cultural symbol to the French. More than just a writer, don't you see? It's obvious to anyone, I should think, that his audience extended far beyond the few who actually read his books."

"For example?" She was not impressed.

"For example, uh…" he pondered for a moment. "Take for example the centenary celebration of his birth in 1902."

"Silly me," she said, "how could one forget that?"

"Well, you asked for an example," he grumbled.

"So?"

"So, Hugo entered the fabric of French life with the force of– of, well, a multinational corporation. His face was seen on plates, table mats, pens, and pipe racks — I have one — and most cities in France named something after Hugo, usually a boulevard, like the one before us, or a main square. We have an obligation to cherish our culture and teach our young, too, whether you like it or not. The damage to Hugo's literary reputation, in my opinion, was incalculable."

"Because of pipe racks!?"

"He was a genius, his words were creatures with a life of their own."

"I don't see words as 'creatures,'" she countered.

"How about 'wiggle'?" he replied.

"How about it?"

"Look," he said, irritated, "for him to write a poem or a novel was not to go shopping for the best verbal approximation of a known reality, but rather to paint a verbal picture for the reader with a set of rhetorical paintbrushes that, like the impressionists, saw another reality. To see through into something that no others have seen before…to invent a new reality, his way with words, was driven by a set of image-producing devices; images like 'the shiver of the sky' showed, metaphorically, a painter's and author's ability to reproduce what he saw as the sky, his interpretation of clouds and an infinite number of colors." He held up a pudgy finger to emphasize his point. "Did you know that Hugo was once criticized for making up a word that wasn't in the French vocabulary? When his antagonist confronted him with the fact that there was no such word, his response was, 'Now there is.' The French language is the most beautiful, and, in my opinion, he is its unquestioned master; he communicated by painting with the words. Are you going to let just anyone debase it for a few dollars?

He turned up the volume. "Look, you give these promoters a chance to market his book any way they like, and you'll get the equivalent of non-alcoholic wine in a waxed box, like orange juice, and advertising its fiber content for bowel movements. Don't you see something wrong with that? We are experiencing a cultural Chernobyl in Europe today, thanks mostly to you Americans! Your young people seem to communicate with a vocabulary that's rich in 'fuck this, and fuck that' and—"

"Hold it right there," she demanded. "You love language, and since you do, you know you're going to meet up with an occasional expletive; let's just say it's the percussive side of our nature…and our language."

"I grant you that it's damned ridiculous to be tackling expletives while America's inalienable right to pack heavy ammo goes by. All the same, if we follow your lead, Europe's future leaders will be those best disposed toward pumping iron and professional wrestling."

"You're talking about culture," she said. "Okay, if it can hold its own; if it can't, there's no sense whatsoever supporting it. I'm talking about kids and people having fun, enjoying themselves thirty kilometers east of Paris, for example, at EuroDisney and Walt Disney Studios, where I've been and you conscientiously haven't. Everybody has profited. If Mickey Mouse and his gang have their own palace, which happens to be an American cultural icon, and to you, I suppose, a blatant form of cultural imperialism, then too bad, my august friend." She tapped her finger on the table. It became quiet. "Anybody for a San Bitter?" And she looked around for a waiter

CHAPTER 5

⸻ LES MISÉRABLES ⸻

"Oh, this is fun," she said, when their drinks arrived. "I feel like I'm back in class at Aix, where the professor was haranguing the students who ventured a comment on something they usually knew little about, to keep him going in some other direction, or just daydream while he blathered away. Then the shockmeister here would try to trip him up on assignments most of us hadn't read."

Klaus smiled bashfully, and Charly winked. "You're talking about why Victor's great? Or what?" she asked. "All I know about him I learned at the theater or the movies, and a few forgotten pages from *Hernani* that I read for my History of Romanticism class. I know it might sound dumb, but my father's 1950s collection of *Illustrated Classics* are the only books that taught me and other kids who cared about the classics—you know, *The Count of Monte Cristo* and stuff." The two men looked puzzled, and she hesitated. "Funny books to the uninitiated—that's you guys." They stared, perplexed, "Jeez! You know. Comic books! Graphic Novels! Spiderman! Jesus, where have you two been?" she exclaimed. Bemused glances from the boys. "Anyway, these musicals and Disney films gave most of us what we'd otherwise have missed: *Les Misérables* and the *Hunchback of Notre Dame*."

"You're talking about what's good for children, not adults," Jean-Michel said.

"Leave us not get too haughty; all we're talkin' about here is the desire to be entertained, nobody said educated."

"I do not think so," Klaus stated succinctly, sitting straight in his chair. "You could be right that everyone simply wants to be entertained, but our cultures should be more than the sum of our entertainment. These Hollywood filmmakahs are increasingly obsessed with creating the sort of titanic blockbustahs guaranteed to overflow theatah seats, DVD racks, and corporate coffahs; their distortion of reality misleads people. Don't you agree, Maestro?"

"I do, with a little reservation. There is great pressure to rework classic stories in order to improve their marketability, making them more and more palatable to an ever-broader demographic segment, of that there can be no question," he said. "On the other hand, I'm not sure what the alternative is for the common public. As soon as you pander to the 'common consumption,' however, I'm sure both of you can imagine that the rewrite will call for a little more sex and violence to spice up the plot for the teenagers, or just the opposite in the cartoon version, to please the kiddies. And just as much for the elimination of any controversial or political content, and almost always for some saccharine ending—just enough to make things come out a bit more upbeat. As a result we get a kitsch-book musical or Disney-fication of the classics, snappier and—how do you say— sappier, versions of what are in the end no longer the same traditional stories. Classic tales that I think raise our consciousness and probe the unsettling mysteries of the human heart—let alone teach how to read—are replaced by cotton-candy versions of passive entertainment."

"Well, wait a minute. I'm on your side, sort of," broke in Charly, "and I agree that the idea of reading the classics is great. But get this: Mark Twain, with whom I have at least passing familiarity, said that a classic is something everybody wants to have read and nobody wants to read. Isn't that true? If there weren't any movies, we probably wouldn't even be having this discussion, we'd be memorizing *Ulysses*; now at least we have a choice. But, who has time to read the classics? Didn't Proust write *Remembrance of Things Past* at 4,000 pages? I mean, let's get serious; did you read *Les Misérables* all the way through, Klaus? Actually, you probably did. But who else," she eyed Jean-Michel before he could speak, "is going to read even 1,200-odd pages of nineteenth-century French prose while they're snuggled in bed at night? Not you, J.M."

"Certainly me," he intoned.

"Well, maybe on the toilet," she countered.

He scowled. "Now listen, damn it, I know it's probably hard to imagine while you and your countrymen spend those innumerable inane nights glued to CNN or reruns of 'Baywatch,' but there are other things in life."

"Baywatch? You listen! The world is too busy for those books, and CNN at least shows you how life is changing, even if it doesn't change your life. The only way the classics change your life is that you spend so much time reading them, you have no time for anything else. The birthrate will drop by half; keep it up and you'll die mumbling. Maybe the story line and morals are abused a bit, but that's a small price to pay for the public's opportunity to be exposed to the work itself, even if the movie is only two hours long."

"I couldn't disagree with you more," Jean-Michel said tiredly, wagging his head. "Why is it that the intellectual faculties of mankind seem to crave entertainment of the crassest kind: foolish comedy, bloody violence, repetitious sports, and salacious sex—in other words, any night on TV? Everyone scatters when you have to use your intelligence. Have you heard of Bill Spohn?" She shook her head no. "Well, he was one of your own countrymen and a noted theologian, whom I heard on his lecture circuit some years ago. He said something like: 'A classic is a tale capturing something fundamental about the human experience,' It's a story capable of speaking a timeless and universal word to the human heart."

"For example?"

"Take for example Hugo's unforgettable description of the bloody barricades in *Les Misérables*, as the poor people of Paris fought shoulder to shoulder for their rights. It is unquestionably my favorite piece of all he has written, and only poetic in French, but you'll never hear it in the musical or movie; some Hollywood script editor would probably think it was too kitsch." Jean-Michel quoted Hugo's words in those tones born of a career before the podium:

> 'It was a collaboration of the paving-stone, the rubble-stone, the beam, the iron bar, the rag, the shattered window, the broken chair, the cabbage-stalk.... It was enormous and living, spitting thunder and lightning as if from the back of an electronic beast. The spirit of revolution covered that peak with its cloud in which the voice of the People rumbled like the voice of God.... It was a pile of rubbish and it was Mount Sinai.'

A man whose emotions rose easily to the surface, he paused, seeking refuge for a moment in his beer, and then wiped the foam from his mustache. "There's a voice that speaks to the heart, not the box office. *Les Misérables* is just pickle juice without the pickles until you've read it, but it is a story for the ages, in the best language imaginable; one that teaches each generation, in the finest traditions of its literature, when it is time to bring the revolution to the streets.

"This, in my opinion, is the touchstone of all adaptations of *Les Misérables*, musical or cinematic: to turn Javert, the tenacious respecter of authority, 'that savage in the service of civilization,' as he was called, into the villain of the piece."

"But he *was* a villain!" Charly exclaimed.

He turned on her, tired of her wisecracks and ignorance. "No! That deprives the novel of its dynamite, to point the finger at a single policeman instead of at the system he serves. Is it possible that a man who has fallen as low as this hardened prisoner could actually let go of past devastating punishment and crimes in a way that liberates and perhaps even reconciles him with others?"

Charly read the body language, tiring of his drinking, sweat, and bullshit. "Wait a second, Maestro!"

His face became contorted and he started to speak, "You—!"

She held up her hand. "Hey, isn't Javert, though I'll admit a little excessive in his prosecution of the law, correct in his belief that such people don't really change, that the mercy you're talking about is a pretty unsteady guide that would let loose anarchy in society? Doesn't it make more sense to seek punishment and restitution for all past offenses, to draw some sharp, unbending lines between the good and the bad? I mean, let's be real, Professor, there's bad, and then there's bad; snipers get the chair, no excuses. I'm not sure what terrible crimes Jean Valjean might have done, but the film doesn't show him raping someone's teenage daughter and slashing her parents' throats in cold blood—you know, your average Saturday night flick. Sure, the murdering rapist may be forgiven, but it's tough to say when he came to Jesus, before or after the jury's decision, and from my point of view, he would no longer be worth enough tax dollars to cover his expenses."

"Forgiveness is a universal concept, Charly," Klaus retorted. "It does not operate on degrees of sin, neh? When Jesus was asked how many times a sin could be forgiven, he didn't immediately ask for the gravity of the sin. And I don't believe your Texas Rangah justice has lowahd the murdah rate in Texas, although I admit I'm not sure. The unfortunate fact is that real forgiveness is not often practiced, because most of us don't have the stomach for it."

"Wait." We are getting off the track and our Ms. Brooks has an exam to take. … "Let's just drop it. Would you like to know what he thought of himself, at least physically? You know, that 'old monkey' you spoke of?"

"Ought to be worth a laugh."

"Hugo manages the unusual feat of describing himself seven times in *Les Misérables*, which shows the later Hugo's almost paternal affection for his younger self."

"You're kidding. Seven times? There's those numbers again."

"May I?" Jean-Michel held up his book.

"And if I said no?"

"I'll tell on you," and he reached into his well-worn bag for literary support, leafed through some pages, and then, with cold pipe in one hand and book in the other, quoted one of the world's most gifted authors, Victor Hugo, about himself:

> 'His manner was reserved, coldly courteous and unforthcoming; but as his mouth was charming, his lips exceptionally red and his teeth abnormally white, this air of severity was quite altered when he smiled…. His eyes were small but far seeing. In common with certain young men of the beginning of this century and the end of the last who became famous early in life, he had the extreme youth and fresh complexion of a girl but with moments of pallor. Already grown to manhood, he still appeared a child…. He was solemn and seemed to be aware that there existed on earth a creature called Woman.'[18]

"Ah, 'a creature called woman.' That says a lot, doesn't it?" Ever the iconoclast, Charly was moved only by cynicism. "That's a little too poetic for my taste; probably the best way to know Victor would be to see how he treated his wife and kids."

While she spoke, John-Michel was bent over, peering under the table, an awkward thing for someone of his girth to do, like folding a large bean-bag.

"What on Earth are you doing?" Charly demanded.

"Where's Astérix?" He scanned the area for his dog, who was directly behind him. "If you could ask Victor, he would swear by his love of wife and family," he grunted breathlessly, his chest compressed, "but he did not live for them. His...merde!" He struggled to get back up. "Oh, oh!" He looked distressed.

"What is it?! Are you okay?" Charly saw Jean-Michel bent backward, awkwardly reaching for Astérix, who was sniffing the backside of a patron in the chair directly behind him.

"We need the bill immediately!" Jean-Michel said urgently.

"What's the matter?" Charly said, concerned.

"It's Astérix—when his ears hang way down, he has to pee!"

Charly took the situation calmly in hand. "Just take him over to the curb, and..." She began to see the urgency of the situation. "I'll...oh, shit! Astérix! Astérrrrixx!" she hissed, and began pulling hard on the leash, but then with resignation, "Forget it, J.M." Astérix was relieving himself of a copious golden stream on the chair leg of a neighboring table, its occupants oblivious to the slight. Jean-Michel, a veteran of such dramas, quickly stood and dropped a few bills on the plate, while Charly and Klaus rapidly gathered their belongings.

"We'll talk about Adèle and her family on the way to the Arc de Triomphe," Jean-Michel whispered. "Come on, let's go!" They filed out nonchalantly through the tables to the sidewalk, Astérix happily trotting along behind under the adoring eyes and strokes of envious customers, ignorant of the growing commotion left in their wake.

CHAPTER 6

═══ ONE FOR THE ROAD ═══

"How much farther is the Arc?" Charly groaned.

"Arc?" Jean-Michel feigned surprise. "I thought you wanted to go to McDonald's."

"It's too damn hot to be cute," she whimpered.

"Less than ten minutes, Charly," Klaus said, taking pity on his friend. "How long have you had Astérix?" Klaus asked.

"About a year and a half. We've been friends a long time. He belonged to my father and came to live with me after Papa died."

"Sorry," she said.

"Long story." He began to hurry ahead. "I need the men's room myself. We had better stop off at the next café."

Klaus looked at Charly. "Okay, Maestro. We'll wait," he offered.

"No, come on. It's hot, we'll take a quick beer, get Charly off her feet, and be on our way."

"J.M., we've only walked five or six blocks!" Charly exclaimed. "Forget the feet."

They came to a small café, then followed Jean-Michel into the garden, and once again sat at a table on a vine-covered patio, while Jean-Michel excused himself for the men's room.

"I've had it," she groaned, "and we aren't even there yet."

Klaus fooled with the menu and looked about, tired of waiting. He had had his eyes on Charly back in Aix, but she was involved with a Spaniard and he was left with Simone. Old urges returned.

Klaus looked over toward the restaurant. "Does he always drink like that?" he ventured.

"Like what? He's only had a couple of beers," Charly replied.

"Well, he's over at the bar now," gesturing with his thumb toward the inside of the café.

She turned to see Jean-Michel through the window, tippling a shot of whisky in the bar. "I don't know, I've only known him a week, but my job depends a lot on the capacity of that man's help," she murmured.

Jean-Michel returned shortly, a beer in his hand, invigorated, and sat down in his chair. He started in by interrupting their conversation. "At heart, you know, I'm simply a curious man, given a wonderful gift by my society—a researcher paid to do what he loves: delve into the essence of things. Concerning those great people we were speaking of earlier, and certainly Victor Hugo was one, the only thing that could justify our curiosity is precisely — " he burped involuntarily—"excuse me, what must necessarily escape the biographer's analysis: the mystery of artistic creation. Don't you think?" And before Charly or Klaus could answer, he began to quote.

"Malraux summed up the issue quite pointedly when he said, he said, ah, yes:

'Our time is fond of unveiling secrets. First because we seldom forgive those whom we admire; secondly, because we vaguely hope that, amid these unveiled secrets, we may find the secret of genius. Under the artist, we wish to reach the man. But when you scrape a fresco, if you scrape it down to its shameful bottom layer, all you get in the end is mere plaster.'

"Even Hugo himself warned us," and with that Jean-Michel struggled to his feet and raised his glass to a small group at the café, "'All men of genius, however great, are inhabited by a beast which parodies their intelligence.'" They began to laugh.

Charly and Klaus looked up. "Sit down, sweetheart," Charly said, pulling at his sleeve, but he started again, "To kiss and chew and old tart's withered breast is all we can afford. Debauchery, our only pleasure, we take furtively...," he began to sway, then leaned on the table, "squeezing it like an orange to the last." And he slumped back into his chair.

"Jeez, don't be naughty," her face pallid, "we're drawing a crowd."

"Naughtier," he mumbled.

Klaus leaned over and whispered in her ear, "He must be real drunk 'cause he's quoting Baudelaire[19] and he thinks it's Hugo."

"'All men are inhabited by a beast which parodies their intelligence,'" Jean-Michel repeated.

"Yeah, you said that," she said disgustedly.

"…remarkable limits of his immodesty." His eyes were heavy.

"Oh, shit! Let's go," Charly implored.

"No!"

Klaus intervened, "Zola shares his tomb, Maestro, but I think Balzac and Hugo were comparable artists. Which do you think was bettah?" he asked, hoping to reach a sober site in his consciousness.

"Balzac? Good question. Balzac described Hugo as, uh, let me see now… ." His mind seemed to go blank; he took a sip of beer and wiped his mustache.

Charly stepped in, "I read that in my material. Balzac described Hugo as —"

Jean-Michel broke in rudely, "Of course, as an excessively witty man, as witty as he was poetic. His conversation, according to Balzac, was absolutely delightful, full of bourgeois ideas." He looked around distractedly. "Full of bourgeois ideas. All told, more good than bad in him, he said. Even though the good things were a continuation of pride, Balzac painted Hugo as very carefully calculated, but on the whole a likable man, quite apart from his being a great poet."[20]

"Good friends?" Charly asked, in a feeble attempt to keep him talking rather than drinking.

"Oh, they knew each other well enough, of course. In fact," he took a sip of his beer, "I think Hugo was one of the last to visit him before he died. He left some notes about Balzac's death: Balzac's face was purple, almost black, leaning to the right, unshaven, his grey hair cut short; his eye open and staring. Hugo saw him in profile and, seen like that, Balzac looked like Napoleon. Hugo recounted that an unbearable stench rose from the bed. He lifted the blanket and took Balzac's hand. It was covered with sweat. He pressed it, but Balzac didn't return the pressure.[21]

"I wonder," he went silent.

"Wonder?" Charly asked.

"Wonder what they'll have to say at my graveside."

"You're dead, why care? Anyway, I think it's time to go, don't you, Klaus?" Charly nudged Klaus under the table.

Klaus stood to help Charly get Jean-Michel up and on his feet, but he was heavy. "Whatcha doing?" he said cantankerously. "You wanted to know about Adèle?" Jean-Michel offered, swinging his head about to look for the waiter.

"That's okay. I mean, some other time," she replied, trying to prop him up.

"Well, we can't play all the damn time," he griped.

"All I meant was, to know the man, you have to meet his family," Charly said. "At least that's true in Texas; jury's still out on New York. Anyway, maybe we need to call it a day, no?" She heaved him up under one arm, disgusted by the sweaty shirt, while Klaus hauled on the other. "Jesus!" she grumbled. "He's really heavy."

"Alors! We've got work to do," Jean-Michel protested, wrestling his arm away and plopping back down in his chair. A half-filled beer bottle toppled over on the table, and, with a wet fizz, spilled onto the ground.

"Oh, Christ," she muttered.

"Merde!" Jean-Michel said sorrowfully and leaned over to gaze at the floor. "That's alcohol abuse right there." He shifted himself. "I need a rest," he said, and folded his arms on the table to cushion his head. "Family! Right, his amazing family," he murmured, his voice muffled.

"J.M.!" she demanded.

He lifted his head, "Anyway, that was since Madame Hugo considered Adèle a poor catch for her brilliant son. This encouraged the two lovers, as you could imagine, you could imagine that, couldn't you Charly? And almost 200 letters changed hands, secretly of cour...." He turned. "Sent any postcards, Charly?" He seemed serious.

"Uh, no, actually. At least none you'd be interested in," she said disconsolately. "Klaus, I think we need some help getting the coffee. Could you?" And she motioned him on his way.

"Right. Coffee! You both need an espresso!" Jean-Michel said loudly. "Around 1820 or thereabouts," he turned solicitously toward Charly, "that's before postcards, Adèle was discovered when one of Victor's letters fell from her bodice; you know, probably stuck between her tits. The secret was out.

Madame Hugo broke off all relations with the Foucher family, and Victor was forbidden to see Adèle. Poor Adèle," he whimpered, then took a sip of his beer and wiped his mouth on his sleeve. "Fortunately for his poems, it meant that he now had a focus for all his thoughts. The letters stopped, but Victor soon found a new outlet for his passion: Madame Hugo, it seems, had inadvertently helped revolutionize French Romanticism — isn't that great!" But Charly was studying him with hard eyes. "See," he said, "the poor bastard just needed a muse." He turned abruptly, rocking the table. "Where's that goddamn waiter? I want another beer," he growled, but Klaus had already told the man to stay away. "From then on, you see, whenever Adèle left her home, a passionate figure lurked in doorways or hid behind pillars, trying to catch her eye."

Jean-Michel's voice began to slow, and his gaze drifted off to the horizon. Charly and Astérix waited for the maestro to make his point.

"J.M.? You still with us, sweetheart?" Charly leaned forward and peered into his eyes.

"Hm? With you?" He turned his gaze toward Klaus' empty chair. "Where'd he go? I haven't finished my beer."

"Yes you have, honey. See? Klaus is coming with the coffee."

"Maybe it's time we headed home, Maestro." Klaus said, handing him the coffee.

"Home? No, noo. No!" He roughly pushed the coffee away, spilling some in the process.

"*Scheisse!*" Klaus looked at Charly for guidance, not knowing whether to add fuel to the fire by moving the conversation along or dragging Jean-Michel bodily to a taxi or simply abandoning him. She shrugged her shoulders.

The three sat motionless at the table as though searching for a leader. "Such a great man," Klaus said absentmindedly. "I love his verses, so full of life and sex." Wrong choice.

Charly gave him a murderous look. "Whaddya say we do 'verses' *next time*, Klaus?!" she snapped.

"Oh, distinct fondness for sex," Jean-Michel yawned, "and one could wonder if it sparked his creativity," — he gave another involuntary burp — "but I don't think at the begnegining."

"What was that?"

"Begnegining, and this is important. Victor had discovered the perfect medium for rebellion early in his school career: French versification!" He slapped the table, making the dishes and glasses jump. "Some say it seemed simply to sprout in his brain, and frankly I see no other evidence, except a penchant for Latin while he was very young. This was the disciplined revolt," he leaned forward and scowled at them, "that seemed to be the only answer to his father, that saved him from a more serious insanity, one that poor Eugène could only escape with fits of rage and, as I said, initiating food fights."[22] He nodded his head wearily to confirm his story. "Yes, my colleagues, food fights."

"Try a little more coffee," Charly encouraged.

"What the hell's all this goddamn coffee?"

"It's doing wonders for your temperament," she said. "Right, Klaus?"

"You know...," Jean-Michel whined, took another sip of the black coffee, and shook involuntarily, "Brrugh! Anyway, poor Eugene—"

"Poor Eugene?" Klaus asked.

"Klaus!" Charly warned.

"Um-hm. While Hugo was busy harvesting his wife's virginity, which he claimed to do eighteen times on his wedding night."

"Eighteen, Maestro?" Klaus said incredulously.

"Hm? Eight. Eight! There's a man for you. Eugene marked the occasion with a violent fit of madness and had to be restrained and sedated; eventually ended up in an asylum."

"Adèle must have been very beautiful," Klaus said, while Charly looked disconcertedly around the café.

"Oh, Adèle, she was loved by two of the best poets of the age: Hugo and her secret lover Sainte-Beuve. It seems a shame that she was not very fond of poetry. I love poetry." His head drooped.

"Adèle?" Klaus nurtured him along.

"Even Adèle's own father talks about her 'stultification,' and for every description of her 'Spanish majesty,' there is another that calls her 'stupid.' She often sat in the salon, according to some, interrupting conversations with dazzlingly trivial questions, only to be suddenly silenced by her glowering husband. One acquaintance was astounded by Victor's 'muse' after a visit. And *listen* to this," and he tapped the table:

'Hugo was very entertaining, very animated, and very friendly. But his wife! Ye Gods, what a disappointment! Is that the woman who inspired her husband and his friend Sainte-Beuve with such delectable poems? …I who was already half in love with her simply from having heard her celebrated in the works of my favorite poets, I was thrown into consternation by her coarse appearance, her rough voice, and her common tone.'

"Charles Dickens speaks of her in a different light, though, some years later. And I know you'll enjoy this," he chuckled, and with eyes closed began to quote again, color coming back into his face:

'I was much struck by Hugo himself, who looks a Genius, as he certainly is, and is very interesting from head to foot. His wife is a handsome woman with flashing black eyes, who looks as if she might poison his breakfast any morning when the humor seized her. There is also a ditto daughter of fifteen or sixteen, with ditto eyes, and hardly any drapery above the waist, whom I should suspect of carrying a sharp poignard in her stays, but for her not appearing to wear any. Sitting among old armor, and old tapestry, and old coffers, and grim old chairs and tables, and old Canopies of state from old palaces, and old golden lions going to play at skittles with ponderous old golden balls, they made a romantic show, and looked like a chapter out of one of his own books.'[23]

"Nice. Listen, sweetheart," Charly implored, "why don't we head on outta here and get to that ol' Arc, or better yet, grab a taxi and take you home." She got to her feet and prodded Jean-Michel, signaled the waiter it was time to go, and dropped some bills on the table.

"Well, I'm tired," he complained, struggling to get up. "Klaus?"

Klaus helped Jean-Michel to stand, only to have him grind to a halt five feet from their table. Charly rolled her eyes.

Jean-Michel put his hand on his forehead. "I don't feel well,"

"Are you going to be sick, Maestro?" Klaus asked.

192

Jean-Michel started to pant, "Playground...across the street...need to lie down."

"Oh, jeez," Charly whined. "You should just go home."

"Can't." And he lurched off toward the playground.

"This is nice," Charly said. "Just like my dad, a drunk in a playground, wrapped around a bottle of cheap wine, waiting for a visit from the local gendarmes."[24]

"I'm sorry, Charly," Klaus said. "Why don't we follow him and put him in a taxi when he wakes up?"

"Jesus! How the hell am supposed to learn all this stuff, with my teacher blotto in the grass?"

"I can help a little," offered Klaus as they crossed the street after Jean-Michel.

"Come on!" Jean-Michel shouted back, motioning to them as he lurched across the empty street into the playground, also fortunately empty, then wandered to a small patch of grass and laid down, his arm pillowing his head. Charly and Klaus sat on the child-sized, colorful metal stools nearby and stared at Jean-Michel. Lying on his side, he raised a hand weakly as if for them to wait a moment, then it fell of its own weight and he was instantly asleep.

"He's a nice guy, but Jesus, a couple of drinks," she said, shaking her head.

"A couple? He's sick. Maybe you need to give him a chance," Klaus said.

"My dad had chances; he's dead, but he did a good job of ruining our family." She looked around the playground, empty of children. "And their kids? Is there anything I should know about their kids?"

"Who? Adèle and Victor? They had five: three boys and two girls," Klaus said, then hesitated. "You don't speak German, right?"

"Sorry."

"Well, the first, Léopold, named for his grandfather, was sickly and sent to the general's wife; she was supposed to toughen him up, but the baby died. The second was Léopoldine, fat, pretty, healthy, and destined to be the subject of some of the saddest and most skillfully written love poems in the French language. The third child, François-Victor, a likable and industrious type, created a translation of Shakespeare during the family's exile in England,

and spent considerable effort thwarting his fathah's attempts at arranging his marriage to one of England's blue-blood families. His othah son, Charles, a talented but dependent and overindulgent offspring, died not on the Paris barricades, which he probably would have wished, but a gluttonous death, suffocating in his own vomit in a taxicab."

"Yuck!"

"*Ja*, choked. Well, the last child, Adèle II, a woman whom Balzac described as a dark-eyed beauty, was obsessed by an attraction to an English officah. It was really a sorry affair; she was a young woman whose feelings showed themselves as she played strangely beautiful songs on the piano, and had unexplained fevahs, delirium, constipation, and probably anorexia. She was the last witness of the whole adventure, and died in 1915, an old lady in a long-ribboned bonnet. A quiet funeral took place in the Chapel of the Virgin at Saint-Sulpice, where Victor had married Adèle years before. Sort of ironic: while Hugo's writings continued to grow into one of the great monuments in literature, the last survivor of his life was sitting in her room, shredding books and sheets of paper, stuffing the pieces carefully into her bag. Strange, no?"

"Doesn't really surprise me. Anyone else I should know about? Any favorites?"

"Favorites? Mine is Juliette Drouet, his loving, loyal, long-suffering mistress."

"More women."

"A wondahful woman. But she was his biographah in a very important way. It's estimated she wrote over 25,000 lettahs to him. She revealed, perhaps trying to show the real Hugo, the filthy state of his underwear, his habit of borrowing her toothbrush and leaving it in the washbasin, and giving her fleas. There are some, of course, who believe that her depiction of a shabby, middle-aged bourgeois dressed in 'an old dead dog,' his favorite overcoat, was an affectionate distortion, intended to isolate the Victor she loved from all the others. One can believe what best fits one's image of him, but I like to think it's true."

"Why?"

He thought for a moment. "I don't know. Maybe it's just the way I picture him."

194

"Is she your favorite?" Charly asked, as Astérix wandered the playground from one invisible attraction to another while his master slept.

"Would you like to see her?" Klaus offered.

"Not the way that comes to mind."

"She's sculpted in marble as 'The City of Strasbourg' in the Place de la Concorde. If you want we can take the subway over sometime and have a look."

"Old or young?"

"Nineteen. She was a model for a sculptah named James Pradier, who liked to think of himself as her guardian, friend, and lovah. Along with the advice—as you might suspect—he gave her a child, Claire, who then was sent off to live with her fathah."

Charly's stomach turned: it was exactly as she had done with Jodie, only the sculptor turned out to be the son of a Ford dealer in Ernestville.

"Times were tough, and to insure herself against poverty, Juliette made her lovahs overlap. It was probably she who taught Hugo the actresses' proverb: 'A woman who has one lovah is an angel, a woman who has two lovahs is a monstah, and a woman who has three lovahs is a woman.'"

"Surprise, surprise," Charly said. "On the other hand, actresses probably do make good lays—you know, good performers. At least that's what Simone said about Josephine."

"Simone?" He halted. "*Ja,* she told me you were here. What did she say?"

"That you were in love with your bicycle."

He hesitated. "Anything else?"

"Um-hm, that you had big feet."

He looked down at his feet, which were size 13 or so, and wiggled his toes. He had on white socks in sandals, like any German in summer. "Big feet?"

"Yeah, it goes with having, uh...big appetite."

"I nevah heard that."

"Speaking of appetites, shall we leave him here" she nodded to Jean-Michel sleeping soundly on the grass, "and let the police handle the situation, or..."

"I don't know. He could lose his job at the institute; let's give him ten more minutes, then get him up and into a taxi if we can."

"Okay, your French is better than mine, so if the police arrive it's all up to you." She was tired of drunks, having nurtured one for so long in her own family. "You know, if this was Turkey, they'd drive him ten miles out of the city and drop him off to walk back, which has its way of sobering up the person. Do you feel like talking anymore, or should we end the lesson for today?"

"I'm not the teachah, Charly."

"I know. Sorry. Sort of an unusual get-together."

"*Ja.*"

"Listen, let's finish up."

"Um, okay. I have to go soon anyway; the bicycle I'm supposed to love is sick and needs a chain doctah. If we leave the maestro here he probably won't go home."

"Sounds like my cat."

"Hm?"

"Both creatures of the night. So that carousing Casanova never married Jeanette after all those years?" Charly asked spitefully.

"Hugo? No, he nevah married her. It could be why I am so attracted to her. She was a tragic figure in a way: beautiful, dedicated, and unfulfilled. Particularly when you see this old 'couple' toward the end. Perhaps the saddest sight at the Hugo dinnah table in those final days was not the old, deaf poet already half absent, like someone about to leave on a long journey, but poor Juliette. They say she sat behind her plate in constant pain, concentrating on not throwing up, while Hugo urged her to eat and stay healthy."

"Cancer?"

"Of the stomach. Her only medicine was her 'domestic duties.' She survived a horribly long time on sheeah devotion. Every morning, she took Hugo his two eggs, opened his lettahs, read out the ordah of the day from the Senate, reminded him to wear his new overcoat, worried about his cough, and, when Hugo attended the Senate, waited outside.[25]

"Hugo, evah the deceivah, it seems, instructed his female acquaintances to address their lettahs to a friend. But even his official correspondence was stained with their doings: frivolous notes from women whom Juliette was forced to invite to dinner—having first made sure that their husbands

196

or lovahs had not been invited to the same soirée.

"Juliette died, still trying to convince her lovah that she felt no pain, in 1883, at age seventy-seven. A huge crowd followed her to Saint-Mandé, where she was buried with her daughtah. The names in the book of condolences included those of Georges Clemenceau, Alfred Nobel, and Auguste Rodin. Hugo stayed at home, overcome by her death; the doctahs had ordered him to rest.

"Two years before, Juliette had chosen a marble piece for her grave and discussed the epitaph with Hugo:

> *When I am nothing but cold ashes,*
> *When my weary eyes are closed to the light,*
> *Say to yourself, if my memory is engraved in your heart,*
> *The world has his thoughts*
> *But I had his love![26]*

"The gravestone remained blank."

"Why?"

"It wasn't engraved until long aftah Hugo's death — not until all the people who had known Juliette were dead — Juliette's devotion to Hugo."

"Remarkable. A sad lesson for all women. Thanks. You've been kind, but I've had enough of our hero. I'm leaving. What about him?" Charly said, getting up and pointing at Jean-Michel.

"I'll put him in a taxi." Klaus stared at Jean-Michel. "Would you like to come ovah and spend the night?" he asked shyly without looking up. "After I take care of —"

"The maestro?"

"Um-hm."

She looked at his feet. "What about your paws…er, pedals, for your bicycle?"

The Death of Victor Hugo

According to Graham Robb, one of Hugo's eminent biographers, on the evening of 27 June, after a hefty meal and a furious discussion of the relative merits of Rousseau and Voltaire, Hugo suddenly became confused. His speech was slurred, and it was feared that he had suffered a mild stroke, more serious than it first appeared. To his guests it seemed that the poem-writing part of his brain had been severely affected.

Hugo told the others it was as though he had been struck by lightning and gutted like an old tree. But the worst was kept from him, and he was moved to new quarters for easier care. In February 1881, Hugo's fame was recognized in Paris with one of the greatest public tributes ever paid to a living writer. It so happened that 26 February was his seventy-ninth birthday; therefore, the festivities began on the 25th with plays and presentations. Then, on the morning of the 27th, a Sunday, the longest procession seen in Paris since the days of Napoleon Bonaparte stretched from the Avenue d'Eylau, down the Champs-Élysées, all the way to the center of Paris. The marchers were forced to brave the bitter cold and the snow flurries that were blowing down Haussmann's wide avenues and into their faces as the procession set off at noon to give homage to one of their most cherished citizens. It was estimated that at the end of the day over half a million people had passed in front of Hugo while 5,000 musicians performed *"La Marseillaise."* He sat at the window with his grandchildren, Georges and Jeanne, urging them to engrave the sight in their memories. Occasionally, he was seen standing on the balcony. It was agreed by those present that he frequently had tears in his eyes.

Sad, deaf and old,
Thrice silent,
Close your eyes on earth,
Open them in heaven.

VICTOR HUGO

On 14 May 1885, after dinner, Hugo began his final show. In bed that night, he suddenly felt queasy, and during the next few days began to develop pneumonia. He lay in his four-poster bed, facing the mantelpiece with its old bronze clock, wondering how long it would take him to die. He was already finding it difficult to breathe, he said. The illness picked him up at times and shook him like a rag, coughing and sputtering.

The night of 19–20 May was dreadful. Hugo was intermittently spewing out phrases in French, instantly translating them into Latin and then into Spanish, as if for an international audience. At two in the morning, he suddenly leaped from his bed and had to be forced back in. Then he flung himself out the other side and stood on the floor for a few seconds, shouting, *"C'est ici le combat du jour et de la nuit"* ("This is the struggle of the day and night"). At dawn, he was still struggling, but overcome from the exertion of the night. "How hard it is to die," he said. "I was all ready." A constant stream of last words was transmitted to the crowd waiting outside, which included such luminaries as the lovely Sarah Bernhardt. The Catholic newspaper *L'Univers* found Hugo's last words 'heartbreaking by the absence of any religious thought', however, and showed its Christian piety by predicting an eternity of suffering. Hugo had rejected the prayers of all churches and asked only for a prayer from every soul.

That night, a noisy thunderstorm broke over Paris. In the morning a terrible struggle began at 7 a.m. Hugo raised his head, appeared to take a bow, and fell back onto the pillow. The clock was stopped at 1:27 on the afternoon of Friday, 22 May 1885. It was the unofficial end of the nineteenth century. The last words he ever wrote (19 May) were:

"To love is to act."

Thousands came to be part of the spectacle of Victor Hugo lying in state. The event turned into a carnival in which the Hippodrome circus nearby was doing a roaring, bizarre trade in Victor Hugo souvenirs being sold on the street by an army of peddlers. The crowd was entertained by a man claiming to have been Hugo's body-servant, who then shamelessly sold 400 pairs of trousers that had once "encased the legs of the greatest lyric poet of all time."

The city was celebrating one of its own, in its own special way: wine-shops stayed open all night and drunken bodies littered the Champs-Elysées. As the evening wore on, singing became merrier on the grassy avenues surrounding Hugo's sarcophagus, and the whores of Paris draped their pudenda in black crêpe as a mark of respect. Befitting the old poet, the whole scene was obscene and one in which he could be singularly proud (he had made love on eight different occasions the year he died at eighty-two).

It's estimated that over 2 million people, outnumbering the usual population of Paris, were there. As the procession poured into the Place de la Concorde, the whole of Paris seemed to come into view like a theater packed to the rafters. Every statue, fountain, advertising column, and chimney-stack had been occupied since early morning. Even the trees had been privatized by energetic entrepreneurs: 10 centimes for a leg up, 2 francs later on for a leg down.[26]

Hugo's coffin was eventually carried out of the sun into the torch-lit interior of the Panthéon, where it lay until the procession of admirers had filed past it. Several days later it was removed to the crypt, facing the tomb of Jean-Jacques Rousseau. Hugo now shares cell number XXIV with Emile Zola—oddly enough, since it was reported that on hearing of Hugo's death Zola rang his hands in glee. Now they are laid out in the wing dedicated to "Martyrs of the Revolution." It's very hard to see much, though: one can just peek through the grille in the locked door and see moldy flags over coffins, and a grime-covered window high up at the far end, which no doubt adds to the ambiance.[27]

V

Claude Monet: Impressionist

When you go out to paint, try to forget what objects you have before you, a tree, a house, a field or whatever. Merely think here is a little square of blue, here an oblong of pink, here a streak of yellow, and paint it just as it looks to you, the exact color and shape, until it gives you your own naïve impression of the scene before you.

Claude Monet

Anybody who paints and sees a sky green and pastures blue ought to be sterilized.

Adolph Hitler

CHAPTER I

—≡ PISSARRO'S PLAN ≡—

"You're late, Claude!" Camille scolded, fussing with her husband's jacket, brushing off stray dog hairs as she circled. He stood stiffly for his grooming, a broad-shouldered man, one who preferred tailored and close-fitting twill suits from England. The young artist had been working intently throughout the day on his sketches, and usually did so until interrupted at seven by two rings of the dinner bell. It was a familiar routine. After eating, he invariably went to bed early to catch the following dawn.

Tonight was different; there was no time for dinner. The gas lamps had already flickered on in the hallway of their snug home, and she hurried him through the door into the evening chill. He set out toward the station, striding briskly, glancing back only to wave perfunctorily in the twilight, anxious that he might miss the train to Paris. Despite December's icy moods, the path had no snow, but in fact smelled of sweet, wet grass, for 1873 had brought a mild winter to Argenteuil.

Pissarro, his old comrade, had called an urgent council of mutual friends from the Studio Suisse days. Renoir, Degas, Cézanne, and Sisley were expected to gather that evening at the Café Riche, a traditional hangout for drinking and debate.[1] Renoir had warned Monet that the agenda would be controversial and shouldn't be missed.

Pissarro was particularly keen to have Monet's support for a new idea creating a *société anonyme des peintres, sculpteurs, et graveurs*, as he had explained in a recent letter, sort of a commercial association of artisans. Paul Gauguin, Pissarro's new student, a former banker and entrepreneur, had suggested the idea, but that was only a rumor, of course; no one really knew for sure. Others, like Ernest Meisonnier, perhaps the most famous painter in France, simply attributed the idea to the critics' recent disdain for their efforts. Nonetheless,

Pissarro's desire to stage a sizable show of the group's own work without the involvement of the prestigious but conservative Salon was at its core. It would be the first time that artists in Paris exhibited their art to the public without the intermediary of a jury, but also without the expectation of prizes. Feelings were running high among the artists, and arguments at the Riche, though short-lived, often spilled into the boulevard, igniting shoving matches and cursing.

Monet slouched against the bench, his body swaying with the train's motion as it clacked along to Paris from Argenteuil. Fellow passengers would have seen a thirty-three-year-old man, handsome and bearded, in tweed suit and cap, lost in thought, staring through the window at the quiet villages drifting by in the night. What they couldn't see was a churlish man frequently possessed by anger, continually critical of himself and others, and often terrorizing his domestic staff. Monet invariably rejected compromise. He had his better moments: sending little presents to the family when he was abroad, worrying about the children's schooling and sickness and so on, but life was difficult. His career erratic, he was pestered by financial worries spurred by meager commissions, while struggling to support a large family and mounting Christmas bills.[2]

Now things were getting worse. He reached inside his jacket for a newspaper article and, unfolding it, reread *La Presse*'s harsh review of his group's recent projects: "The scribblings of a child have a naiveté and sincerity that make you smile; the debaucheries of this school are nauseating and revolting." His lips moved inaudibly, "Those bastards ... idiots!"

Originally contemptuous of Pissarro's plan, Monet's finances were becoming desperate and his mood had changed. Perhaps decent money could be made; after all, the public was hungry for new work. The idea seemed childish at first — Pissarro was always dreaming up some damned adventure or other. But it was also true, something had to be done about the Salon; the one in 1872 had been a disaster to artists and public alike. Good work, hard work, by both him and his fellows had been left stranded in their studios because committees of pompous, wintry men at the Académie des Beaux-Arts often barred their exhibition. The Salon required that contemporary paintings remain classic in technique, embodying virtue and civic dedication. But what did they know of contemporary art?

His mood darkened. These mucousy old connivers were neither interested in the livelihood of aspiring artists nor the new directions of the naturalist Barbizon painters. And certainly not in capturing on canvas the appearance of factories, railroads, and magnificent steamships from the new industrial era. As even the public knew, those imbeciles had rejected so many artists in the last exhibit that Napoleon III was forced to intercede and required the Salon to hold a separate Salon des Refusés[3] to help the artists market their paintings! But things were changing. France was a phoenix rising from the ashes of her Napoleonic wars…reborn, young, exciting, and progressive; and art, any artistic pleasure: poetry, literature, or music, he believed, should reflect it.

Passengers began to gather their bundles as the train pulled into the station. He removed an old crone's bag from the rack above and mumbled goodbye. Alfred Sisley, a fellow painter of seemingly modest talents, was to meet Monet at the Gare Saint-Lazare in the 8th arrondissement. As Monet stepped down from the train, Sisley, in bowler hat and large black coat, was already talking: "Did you hear?"

"No, what?" Monet recoiled instinctively, fearing yet another national tragedy was about to befall France.

"Victor Hugo's son, François-Victor, is dying, perhaps already dead."

Monet shook his head in resignation. "Poor old man, he's lost Georges, too."

"They say Hugo is fornicating with his son's nurse," Sisley added absent-mindedly.

"Pissants. How could they possibly know?" Monet growled. "Were they perched on his bedposts?" For he held Victor Hugo in high esteem. Sisley, a Chaplin-like figure in bowler and cane, had added to his irritation. "Where's Pissarro?"

"He couldn't make it. He's anxious that we get some things settled tonight. The Salon's exhibit committee met last week and the show is coming in four months." Sisley was an excitable man of British origin, whose energy involuntarily escaped through a high voice encumbered by a strong accent. "We need to compete, we've *got to* compete!"

"Compete, of course, but there's no damned hall to exhibit our work," Monet said, lighting one of his ever-present Caporal cigarettes.

"But we've got one!"

"Got one?" Monet eyed him suspiciously.

"Well, almost got one. One of Pissarro's friends, Nadar, is a photographer. He has a studio, a good studio, that we can use for an exhibit."

"I thought he was chasing that Bernhardt woman around."

"He is. Baudelaire and Delacroix, too; but he owes Pissarro."

"Where?"

"At 35 Boulevard des Capucines. It is a great location, I think. Don't you think?"

Monet receded back into his ruminations, ignoring Sisley and his annoying repetitious comments. Maybe Pissarro was right. The group could get admission fees, and any sales would be split among the partners with no commissions. He knew the idea of such an enterprise had arisen often in the past, particularly in the 1860s, when younger artists like him were having difficulty getting into the Salon. Now there appeared to be a climate of support for individual initiatives, proof of the country's creativity and the public's—

Sisley intruded on his thoughts. "You know how Pissarro is, he's a socialist and loves to organize people. He's good at it, I think. Don't you think, Monet?" Monet wanted to scream at him, "By Jesus, man can't you stop repeating yourself?!" But he continued walking intently along the dark cobblestone streets, head and shoulders bowed against the drizzle, cap secure about his head, and cigarette protruding profanely from pursed lips.

Pissarro wished to organize a stock-holding company, and Renoir would probably want some sort of trust run by one of his rich friends. Sisley would simply waver all night long, while Morisot, if she came at all, would insist on crossing every 't' and dotting every 'i.' She had been friends with Degas, but was nevertheless too independent for Monet's taste in women. Her affection for working outdoors brought her close to Monet and Renoir, but her insistence on leaving a number of her paintings apparently unfinished frustrated their feelings for symmetry and closure in composition.

The little group of painters was suspicious of Morisot, but unlike the others, Monet wasn't convinced Manet was secretly bedding the young fiancée of Manet's brother Eugene. She sat for Edouard, that's true, but the paintings lacked sensuality, and, contrary to complicity, she looked far more like a model than his muse. Manet was not to be underestimated, however; he was not simply some yellow-gloved, upper-class dandy either, which his "Le Déjeuner sur l'Herbe" proved.

As Sisley anticipated, Camille Pissarro took the lead that fateful night in guiding the group toward an agreeable resolution. Considerable time had been spent arguing over differences about who should be members and how the group should be governed. In the end, however, they agreed with Pissarro's proposal to form a joint stock-holding company, and a week or so later, in late December 1873, the group signed the founding charter together, including other acquaintances who had been invited to be part of the enterprise. With the Salon the obvious competition, it was decided to have their own show run simultaneously with the state's, but to upstage it—despite Renoir's refusal to participate—by opening their show two weeks before the competition's.

The group's efforts paid off on their opening day in April 1874. Surprisingly, considerable press coverage and a commendable number of visitors —approximately 3,000—were attracted, quite respectable for such a novel affair. None of them, perhaps least of all Monet, could have known the profound impact of his and his comrades' actions. A brilliant explosion of color was about to erupt in France and shortly thereafter the world. The impressionist era had begun.

The Impressionists

Art, like morality, consists in drawing a line somewhere.
Gilbert Chesterton

For most of us in this first decade of the 21st century, it is without question a fact of cultural life that the most popular form of high art in Western societies is that of the 19th-century French impressionist painters. This group, favored by museums, beloved by the public, adored by the critics, and an enduring subject of analysis, interpretation, and historical inquiry by scholars of every persuasion, Impressionism reigns without rival. It is perhaps the world's most accessible and least controversial source of aesthetic pleasure across the entire spectrum of society.

Impressionism remains so popular, first of all, because of the sheer painterly virtuosity of its principal masters and its range of subjects. No matter how many times one may have taken a hard look at a painting as familiar as Renoir's "Luncheon of the Boating Party," its creator's ambition and, one might even say, audacity, for covering such a mundane scene, still captivate the viewer. In both our cities and countryside, the impressionist eye seems to be on a perpetual holiday, enjoying leisurely pursuits and unthreatening pastimes. Its capacity to offer 21st-century sensibilities a sweet escape from the far more mundane realities of our own social environment should therefore not be underestimated in any account of Impressionism's current appeal.

A somewhat bland but accurate description of the impressionist style of painting is characterized chiefly by its concentration on the general impression produced by a scene or object, and the use of unmixed primary colors and small strokes to simulate reflected light.

The actual source for the term "impressionists," however, came up in an article by Louis Leroy in *Charivari*, 25 April 1874, between references to "Monet's Boulevard des Capucines" (1873), two paintings by Paul Cézanne, and a Boudin beach scene. It therefore should be seen as deriving from the group as a whole and not, as some have done, from one particular picture done by Monet named "Impression, Sunrise" (1872). In fact, the group was just as often referred to in the press as the "intransigents" as the "impressionists," the former name evolving from an anarchist wing of a Spanish political party whose radical political challenge was seen as parallel to the one the impressionists posed to painting. It should also be pointed out that the group avoided the term until their third exhibition, in 1877, when they agreed to place a sign above the entrance to the space they had rented for that show which read, "Exposition des impressionistes." They only adopted this technique that one particular time. In addition, the catalogue that accompanied that exhibition, like those for the seven other shows they staged, did not mention impressionists or Impressionism.

The group clearly did not want to be typecast or easily catego-
rized. And in many ways they were correct, as all the impressionist members of the core group had quite different styles. Degas
tried, with Pissarro, to maintain the unity of the group over the
years, but eventually failed. Pissarro was the only member of the
core group that exhibited in all eight exhibitions. Renoir dropped
out, calling Pissarro a "Jew" and a "revolutionary." Monet felt the
entire group had lost its integrity. "Our little temple has become
a dull schoolroom," he told a journalist in 1880, "whose doors
are open to any dauber." The seventh exhibition of independent
artists was to become the Salon des Indépendents two years later.
The movement, first experienced in painting, metamorphosed
later on into the water music of such French composers as Ravel and Debussy.

Perhaps the most penetrating remarks about the impressionists, however, came from Frédéric Chevalier, an art critic for
the conservative magazine *L'Artiste*. He liked many of Monet's
submissions, but he made the following generalization about
the impressionists' work as a whole, which had special relevance
to Monet's series of Gare Saint-Lazare paintings. With keen
insight, he cited the disturbing ensemble of contradictory qualities that had distinguish the impressionists — the crude application of paint, the down-to-earth subjects, the appearance of
spontaneity, the conscious incoherence, the bold colors, the contempt for form, the childish naiveté that they mix heedlessly
with exquisite refinements, all of this not without analogy to
the chaos of contradictory forces that trouble our era.

Musée d'Orsay is the 19th-century French arts museum known
worldwide for its famous impressionist collections. Built by archi-
tect Victor Laloux in 1900, the "Gare d'Orsay" was one of the
Paris railroad stations with trains to the southwest of France
(Orléans and Bordeaux). Located across from the Louvre on the
Seine's left bank, it has been beautifully renovated to house the
Orsay museum, whose architecture has often been praised as a
major success in industrial-building renovation.

CHAPTER 2

══ EVENING CLASS AT THE SORBONNE ══

Charly was in trouble and she knew it. Jean-Michel was in trouble and he knew it. He had demonstrated that he was still an alcoholic in a pathetic manner at the park, and she, a veteran of such behavior, understood that her future in a foreign land was perilously tied to an addict. He apologized with roses, and contritely — in resolute honesty — offered a pledge that it would never happen again. She accepted, coolly and with resignation, knowing that she had little choice, and that for certain it would happen again.

Nonetheless, theirs, like most quarrels between the sexes, with the immediacy of emotional jousting, eventually led the combatants to understand each other better and — for the lucky ones — to embark on some aggressive sex during the reconciliation as a rewarding consolation. Also, since real understanding doesn't come from the good times alone, it was a naturally good thing for relationships — if it didn't destroy them.

Two days later, with considerable care and deference, Jean-Michel toured the Arc de Triomphe and Victor Hugo Museum with Charly.

They had even done some shopping that afternoon, and Charly helped choose a new outfit for Jean-Michel. He objected, of course, only to be advised that his tastes were as far removed from fashion as a can of paint or a pair of pliers. Unlike most women, men have a stubborn affection for their most comfortable shoes, and convincing Jean-Michel to replace his espadrilles was tricky. It required patience — after all, the shoes were not for her — and diplomacy, which she used by explaining with strained reserve that his sneakers had the durability and smell of Velveeta cheese.

After their visit to the Victor Hugo Museum in Place de Vosges, Jean-Michel left Charly at the subway near the Bastille Opera House. He had given her instructions on how to get to De Gaulle airport to meet Jodie and her friend the next morning. He wanted to drop off Astérix at the river barge turned houseboat, gently rocking at its moorings on the Left Bank of the Seine, and do a little reading. Later he had planned an evening's get-together with his nephew Guy.

The afternoon sun had warmed the boat's interior. It made him tired, and the late lunch with Charly had included a tasty Saint-Julien, Château Beychevelle Bordeaux, cautiously shared, which, though light on the budget, laid heavily on his intentions, coaxing him into bed for a nap.

Jean-Michel had asked Guy to meet him at Café de la Paix, a local sidewalk café wedged among some well-patronized bookstores near the Sorbonne. Heavily frequented by students and faculty, the café was a comfortable old place that usually served tasty soups and Croque Monsieur — until the army of summer tourists arrived. Then, a parade of stiff and reticent Japanese or Germans — in manner and step like a gaggle of geese — took place. A cacophonous group of clueless Americans sometimes led the way, their conversations centering around monuments or fashion displays, "Oh, Marcia, look at those sandals. The French tastes are sooo refined ... and the prices! You won't find *those* in Boca."

Guy contemptuously likened the intruders to a herd of cows descending on the placid little tables, oblivious to whatever scholastic ambiance existed, bumping and mooing their way through the café's traditional patrons, ruining the food and service. The regulars, a clutch of avant-garde scholars, detested the tourists, like butchers flies. Jean-Michel took little notice, remembering earlier faux pas in foreign lands and the kindness of strangers. The locals, a group of so-called intellectuals purporting self-importance and voicing snide remarks that offended only the few who spoke the language, were never a serious concern, simply French.

Jean-Michel had taken Guy under his wing shortly after Guy's father committed suicide when Guy was fifteen. He was the only child of Jean-Michel's sister, who spent his young life regretting the lack of finances, essential to high society, that had prevented him from attending one of the more prestigious schools of Paris, leaving him instead to matriculate at a small college in Lyon. Guy grew into his teens defending himself against his father, who constantly pestered him with attention and advice. He became convinced that his father did not understand him, that people in general did not understand each other, and that, considering the foibles of even his uncle, Jean-Michel, it was Guy alone who understood the world properly; that indeed there was possibly even a plot, as he said, "to make me see things the way they were not, and I had to defend myself." He was convinced that he was unique — and in fact he was extraordinarily handsome—in a world where no one resembled him, and that he therefore had to "guarantee my integrity," not allowing himself to be tarnished by common stupidities.[4] The real mark of genius, he felt, was not to mistake oneself for anybody but oneself, and that applied to nations too, so he hated any Frenchmen whose pretensions included "behaving like Americans."

Guy fancied himself as a wit for those French people who disliked the French people, not unlike Charles de Gaulle, who loved France but not the French. Guy resolved the paradox by worshipping the past, thus allowing him to hate the present. He condemned all forms of modernity as the work of "electricians," and boasted among his limited coterie of friends, "I am not an electrician. I don't care a fig about the voyages to the moon: the smallest drawing by Delacroix, the least sketch by Manet, seems to me," he bragged "immeasurably more important."[5]

His idol was Jean Cocteau: poet, novelist, playwright, opera librettist, songwriter, artist, and movie director. Both young men shared suicidal fathers, and like Cocteau, Guy was a homosexual with a certain fetish for gray flannels and corduroys. Guy, also like Cocteau, wished to be the consummate Parisian exhibitionist, and rarely could abide another who strove at his expense for a place in his sun. He aspired to emulate Cocteau's famous comment "Too much is just enough for me."

Jean-Michel tried to understand Guy, his need for recognition, and teenage sensitivities. He had befriended him as though a favorite student. Shortly after Guy's father's death, Jean-Michel, doing his duty, invited Guy to Paris, but the youth was distant and difficult in the Levasseur household. A boy whose churlish intellect and emotional outbursts became an unwelcome distraction, he could not be tolerated even at summer camp. He tormented those around him until, eventually, he was sent home.

At the time, Jean-Michel was happy to see Guy go, since he himself was slowly backing out of life. He often had the sensation of peering at the figures in his life through a haze, as if seen on a bumpy road in a rearview mirror, his wife and children jiggling, receding, out of focus, and hard to keep looking at. His drinking was a compromise, making his life peaceful, but coincidentally running in reverse.

His youthful days were over; the demonstrations and cadence of the chanting marchers on the Champs-Elysées now bored rather than stirred him. He more readily lent his ideological books than quoted them. In short, he had ensconced himself not uncomfortably on the shelf, like one of his books, avoiding responsibility by wedging himself in among other conformists with a fondness for obscurity.

In the evenings Jean-Michel enjoyed sitting back in the dimly lighted parks or quiet bars, working on his manuscript, competing in games of chess, or listening and kibitzing a bit with the firebrands of the time, who argued the political issues of the day into the night. Occasionally, he egged them on, challenging and chastising—convinced it was their duty and right to wrestle with the problems of mankind—then pushed back and watched. His personal dharma, however, lay in celebrating pretty women, the taste of hot, meaty sandwiches, and the golden glow of frothy beers. His days ended when he eventually wandered off into the night and lurched home.

After the car accident, the pain of losing his wife and daughter had changed all that; he no longer bothered to lurch home, but simply slept where he fell. Police and other intercessions began, and with counseling, the pain had receded over time like a benign tumor, a knot that ached when stretched, but not malignant.

CHAPTER 3

═══ PARIS BABYLON ═══

At virtually the same moment as Jean-Michel's late-afternoon nap on *Chrysalis,* a dozen or so young men sprawled on sagging couches, stuffed chairs, and other vestiges of seemingly indestructible furniture in the classroom of a decrepit music hall opposite the Luxembourg Gardens, Guy among them. The teacher, a slim and athletic man in his early fifties, elegantly dressed in flamboyant Italian fashion, was conducting an evening seminar on the poetry of Arthur Rimbaud. The syllabus on the desk before him read: "Sorbonne: Humanities A602: Paris Babylon: (Seminar). Instructor: Licensié Monsieur Jerôme Dumas."

A student was asking, "I don't understand, are you saying that the poetry of Rimbaud in the 1870s, for example, was used by the impressionists for their work, and the paintings themselves inspired Ravel and Debussy?"

"No." The instructor sat motionless and patient, waiting while the student struggled to develop his point.

"Well, I wondered about it; I mean, it is hard to see the urban chaos that especially Rimbaud seems to reflect in his poetry culminating in the bu—the—"

"Bucolic?"

"Bucolic scenes of Monet's lily ponds or the tranquil music, say, of Debussy's 'Claire de Lune.'"

Dumas spoke: "Remember we are referring to the Symbolists, particularly Stéphane Mallarmé, who could be considered a strong influence. However—"

A student raised his hand.

"Yes."

"What's Symbolism?"

Dumas paused, irritated. "Your assignment was to study Emile Bernard,[6] who was steeped in the ideas of the Symbolist movement. How could you possibly have done it without knowing what Symbolism is?" The student looked down and studied his notes in embarrassment. Dumas, an adjunct professor, was a financier by profession, who taught for the enjoyment of it and, not incidentally, to fraternize with young men. The exercise of his vocation leaned far more toward a prurient nature than to building an academic reputation on his students' fear. "What's your name?"

"Pierre, sir."

"Obviously, Pierre, you had other priorities on your agenda this past week. I am not seeking to shame you, only to comment on your commitment." Pierre didn't answer. "Do you recall last class, Pierre, when we spoke of transforming the universal to the particular? Where the storms of Shakespeare's *King Lear* were also the storms raging in King Lear's head?"

Pierre shook his head. "No, sir."

Dumas looked disappointed. "You must study, son, or take up delivering newspapers. Let's get to today's lesson. We are talking about Mallarmé, who said that to name an object is to suppress three-fourths of the enjoyment of the poem, which consists of the pleasure of comprehending little by little. To suggest it, that is the dream, you see. It is the perfect utilization of this mystery that constitutes symbolism: to evoke an object bit by bit in order to show a mood or, conversely, to choose an object and extract a mood from it by a series of decipherings. The mastery with which the artist suggests is, of course, the key. Do you understand?" Pierre nodded his head meekly.

"All right, then, getting back to Rimbaud; in my opinion he was an exception, but let me offer a suggestion, how you could see the evolution of this magnificent creativity flowering in the Parisian avant-garde. Actually," he looked momentarily to the ceiling for inspiration, and absentmindedly parted his lips, sucking air through a small aperture between his front teeth, a short, juicy sound like a small burst of air from a wet balloon. "Pssst, Rimbaud is perhaps a good place to start, since he began his poetry right after Hugo's *L'Année Terrible*. Think of it this way: Rimbaud and his young contemporaries of the early 1870s were down in the dirt and shit of the Franco-Prussian War. They were the children of its consequences and the torturous crimes of the Paris Commune. These poets, the seeds of chaos, penniless and angry, gave root to a new poetic vision that shook the nation and inspired the impressionists, who in turn sought to forget the past by creating colorful new images for the pleasure of France." He mused, "It was a rare and special moment, my young friends, when—if you are moved by such things, as I am—the voice of God could be heard in the refrains of French poetry, His mysticism in its musical genius, and His face in the oils of our artists."

Another student raised his hand. "Rimbaud was a homosexual?" he asked, seeking to imply the sexual nature of France's new creative source and perhaps score one for class participation.

"Homosexual? I know some of you have idolized these nineteenth-century artisans as your models, but history, I'm sorry to say, pssst, doesn't support any renaissance of homosexual inspiration.

"I'm not sure how well you know Rimbaud; it is true he was a homosexual, but even the concept itself was misunderstood at the time." Dumas sat back in his chair and choreographed the scene with his hands. "Try to imagine yourself one sunny afternoon in the autumn of 1871, sitting in the drawing room of a prominent Parisian family. Suddenly, through the door, peremptory and unannounced, comes a beautiful, dirty boy of sixteen with long blond hair, his wrists and ankles protruding awkwardly out of an ill-fitting jacket and trousers. He has no luggage, his socks are an alarming electric green, and he comports himself like a monosyllabic lout; but in his pocket resides the manuscript of '*Le Bateau Ivre.*'[7] What would you think?" He looked expectantly at his mute audience, young faces twisted in puzzlement. "Is this one of France's greatest new poets? Perhaps. An astute observer of France's future? I doubt it, and, may I suggest, with good reason. But what about this 'creativity' thing?" The students, shy of the question, avoided his gaze. He scanned a few, musing whether to harass one or two into a response, but decided against it.

"Let's continue then; perhaps your creative juices, still locked in your loins, will venture out. Rimbaud's Parisian sponsors innocently showed him to a spare room in their apartment and immediately regretted it. Rimbaud thieved and sulked and showed no politesse, let alone gratitude. He smoked a pipe, stank of alcohol and sweat, and crawled with lice; after a week he was asked to leave." Monsieur Dumas leaned into his young audience. "Anyone have a brother like that?" Some chuckles and knowing glances and grins skittered across the musty room, perhaps more at his mannerisms than his jokes.

"Consider, gentlemen, that at this very time," wagging his index finger to make the point, "the great men of France: Victor Hugo, Claude Monet, Renoir, Rodin, Eiffel, and Clemenceau, to name a few, were all alive, wandering the very streets of Paris you will take home tonight. They were literally rubbing shoulders with rebellious young men like Rimbaud, and in some ways not unlike you. But," he smiled and growled, "he was a nasty boy, so gauche as to pointedly wipe his ass with pages torn from the expensive journal *L'Artiste*."

Dumas paused to scan his notes. "We can see that Rimbaud, like many of his generation, evinced the demeanor of a debauched child: insolent, drunken, foul-mouthed, and a hashish smoker. Although rumors of his genius spread round what remained of Paris' bohemian quarters, it was hard to see him as anything other than a nightmare adolescent with a chip on his shoulder. But!" Dumas held up his finger again and looked up, his eyes sparkling. "Despite his reputation as a brutish little vagrant who made himself at home in the murkiest parts of the human mind, Rimbaud, just like Monet and Rodin, was also creating. Not by our standards, perhaps, or even those of the absinthe-swilling symbolist poets Verlaine and Baudelaire; he was an antihero, a nihilist like that of the Creator Himself! There were no standards. Don't ever forget, my young colleagues, that our great Creator not only commissioned the magnificent sunsets and fragrant flowers, but with seemingly great gusto He also created—with the aid of *His* Children of Darkness—agonizing wars, poisonous insects, merciless pestilences piled high with rotting corpses, and the random, senseless destruction of nature's innocent.

"Unfortunately, talent and originality do not, as we know, always attend nobility of character. How can we, with our humble lot—egotistically, it seems—deem ourselves the Children of Light by simply assenting to His power through our feeble attempts to copy His pretty sunsets?"

A student raised his hand. "Do you think Earth is purgatory?"

"This is a poetry class!" he laughed. "But, perhaps. I have a colleague who envisions Earth as a gigantic penitentiary. No one is leaving until he's paid his debt." He turned earnest. "At the very least it's where most of us sinners aspire to land: hell undeserved and heaven too grand, no? Can you imagine it? Will you go home tonight and compose a poem about it? Perhaps give us an impression of what it is like to be here, swaggering and strutting among our cellmates occupying this peculiar little island, adrift on a desolate rim of a distant universe, serving our time amidst the muck and horror?"

Peering at them expectantly, he raised his hand theatrically toward the stars. "Can you see home from here, boys? Is it out there somewhere deep in the cosmos beyond our gaze, or simply in the damp fragrance of a rose? Ah," he sighed, "such perplexity on such a lovely night."

A student raised his hand.

"Yes."

"Will this be on the exam?"

Dumas winced, then reached into his shirt pocket for a pack of cigarettes to relieve his irritation, disappointed that no hearts seemed lifted. Yet, he knew there was hardly a one in the room who wouldn't end up as a common bureaucrat, bartender, or salesman. There were, with the exception of one, no poets. "Should it be?" he replied.

Unaccustomed to such challenges, the students moved uncomfortably in their seats, their minds scrambling to contribute some small blank to the mint. One shy young fellow raised his hand. "Was Rimbaud's poetry comparable to Baudelaire's?"

"No." And he paused to light his cigarette. "But Arthur's poetic adventure was finished when he was young; by the time he was in his twenties he had moved on to other pursuits, running guns and slaves in Africa. The work itself, however, showed that this prize-winning schoolboy had frequently trampled the flower beds of French poetry with an expert boot. It is true they were often slangy and obscene, even incomprehensible at times, but his poems had the smell of real experience. For poets like Baudelaire, many creations of humanity were scary and disgusting; our lives seemed to have that quality of puzzling monstrosity. But where, then, is God?" He paused and scanned his class. "Be assured, my boys, that our reality is not tame," he whispered. "Not tame, boys," he whispered again, sadly. The room filled with the students' embarrassment. He was overpowering. They sat silent.

He felt the evening heat and the weight of the task. "Okay, then, shall we take a break?" he said briskly. Relieved, the young men put their notebooks aside and gathered in little groups for cigarettes and drinks.

Guy, having gotten the older man a cola from the machine, asked, "To what extent, Professor, do you think the homosexuals of Paris were known … or at least understood?"

Dumas stood and moved around his desk to a chair, joining the intimacy of Guy's circle of friends, and set down his drink. As if managing a short skirt, he crossed his legs carefully so as not to crush the trousers' crease, then placing his Turkish cigarette to expectant lips, took a drag, and exhaled its spicy smoke, watching as it rose slowly like a totem for his young disciples. He glanced around the circle of students. "Listen," he said in a husky voice, "sophisticated literati gossiped knowingly about Paul Verlaine's relationship with 'Mam'selle Rimbaud,' but even the poet's wife and family remained astonishingly innocent of its homosexual nature. They seemed to have assumed that the dreadful youth was just a difficult poetic type. This should not surprise any of us," he counseled. "Homosexuality was, as we discussed last week, unarticulated in the bourgeois consciousness, except in the vaguest terms."

Dumas' blondish-colored hair, so carefully brilliantined, was coifed straight back, sparse, and poorly dyed. He had gray-blue eyes and a noble, albeit pockmarked, face, gaunt in the shadows, like that of a Polish count, tanned and worn from the sun. His voice carried the whiskey timbre of a female barfly speaking at the highest level of educated French, betraying the courtliness of his demeanor. "So, Guy," and he placed his hand lightly on the young man's thigh, "in my opinion they did not 'understand' homosexuality. It was accepted that men who dressed and behaved like women did so as a peculiar distraction, not a sexual compulsion." Dumas' gaze was penetrating; he was practiced at stepping through the adoring eyes of a young audience to search and seize upon the innocence of post-pubescent boys.

Holding an ashtray loosely in one hand and cigarette in the other, he listened and responded in the give-and-take, leaning attentively forward at times to show his interest, more genuine than in a lecture setting. He exhaled a final stream of smoke, then carefully, meticulously, even, extinguished his cigarette and returned to his desk.

"*Alors!* Consider the question, then: Rimbaud had leapfrogged, shall we say, the thunder of Victor Hugo and the bombast of imitators. His originality was to ignore the formal conventions of meter, grammar, and logical association, he preferred to chase the prompting of a mind intoxicated by an unedited tumble of words, impressions, and images. To make sense was very dull indeed, but that did not mean," he held up a cautionary hand and shook his head, "he was joking. Now," he looked at his charges, "who would like to analyze…?" Guy had gotten up silently from the group and made his way to the door at the back of the room. He gave a small salute to the seminar leader, his heart's companion and exciting new friend, who waved casually in return. Guy exited the building quickly; he had an engagement with Jean-Michel. And he was late.

CHAPTER 4

═══ A JOB FOR GUY ═══

Lights were coming on at the Café de la Paix. Alfresco tables and chairs choreographed daily by wandering tourists now accommodated lounging locals seeking to be cooled and comforted in the evening breeze. The sound of voices murmuring in the café's ambiance, lubricated by sips of strong coffee and the aroma of pungent cigarettes, merged with the periodic clinking of cups and saucers and tinkling spoons.

In the dwindling twilight, Guy found Jean-Michel seated at a table close to the entrance and eased himself into the opposite chair. "Smells good."

"It is," Jean-Michel gestured with his sandwich. "Would you like some?" Guy shook his head, holding up his cigarette. "So, how is the job search going?" Jean-Michel asked, between mouthfuls. "Anything from the people at *Le Monde*?"

"Nothing from *Le Monde*, but they've only had my application for a few weeks. It's very frustrating, you know; these media people treat you with such arrogance. I gave my résumé to everyone, by e-mail, hard copy, and visits. It's been two or three months in some cases, and nothing, the bastards." He flicked away his cigarette in disgust. Guy's voice had a quality of femininity that betrayed the low register of his masculinity, soft and sure, but evoking sensuality, not aggression. "Even a rejection is better than simply leaving me to hope day after day that I can finally have a job and a future that does more than simply pay off a few bills and a school loan. I tried at the beginning to be professional, then understanding, then philosophical, and now I'm just angry. Even an influential woman I thought an ally never returned my calls, and my so-called friends have no interest in bad news. What is it that possesses such people who must imagine themselves so sophisticated that their busy lives can so easily ignore sympathy? I hate them. One of their lackeys will probably call tomorrow offering some donkey job, programming new subscribers into a computer, for which they suppose I should be eternally grateful."

Jean-Michel finished his meal and massaged a linen napkin, giving his face a toweling in the process. "Let your old Unc give you some advice, Guy: don't hate people; it's not good for you or them. You have a master's, correct?" He searched for some reasonable strategy to overcome Guy's predicament.

Guy looked at his uncle coldly. "You don't remember? I was even nominated for membership to the Cultural Renaissance Society of Paris, which ought to mean something, but obviously doesn't." Guy's frustration and disappointment contorted his handsome face. He retreated. "If you hadn't given me the loan and contact at *Le Monde*, I would have returned to Lyon already."

"Give them a chance," Jean-Michel said, and paused to take a long draught of beer, followed by a gratuitous burp. "Mediocrity and media are cognates of the same Latin root. As you know, Guy, and have heard before, it takes time. Just be patient and a little persistent—"

"Pardon me, Unc, but I am persistent," Guy interrupted, petulantly toying with his spoon. "Those idiots are wearing me down. It isn't fair, it's depressing, and I'm seriously running out of money."

Jean-Michel finished his beer and signaled the waiter for another. "Look, I have an idea. A client company of mine from the States, Voyages Classiques, sent over a prospective employee to study French culture, and she needs some help. They want me to give her an orientation course for one of their tour programs; she's training to be a travel guide. I'm doing the best I can, but it does affect my schedule. She's trying to use her time constructively before she has to go back to New York for her test. Perhaps—and this is just a suggestion—you could be her guide." Guy gave Jean-Michel a suspicious look. "Guy, I know. I *know*, how you feel about tourists, and particularly Americans, but she's okay. You'd like her," he paused, "I think." He considered whether to offer a description of Charly and decided to let Guy work it out for himself. "There could be some quick money in it for you, maybe enough to pay the rent. Are you still staying in that youth hostel off Boulevard Saint-Michel?"

"No, I moved in with a friend," Guy said quietly.

"That's wonderful! Perhaps you can save some money. Who is he, or should I say she?" And he winked.

"It's a he, and you wouldn't know him," Guy said softly.

"Probably not. Where did you meet him? I mean, at school, or…?"

"At the Le marché aux puces."[8]

"Le marché? Is he into antiques?" Jean-Michel felt a twitch of nervousness in Guy's demeanor and let the subject—for which there are no closets big enough—drop.

"Look, Unc," Guy said, feigning interest, "the American idea does sound like something I could do and make some money at; they all seem to have money to throw around." He felt the blood rush to his face. Jean-Michel, although suspicious at times, knew nothing of Guy's homosexuality, and Guy led him away from his friend, like a mother bird leading a predator from her nest.

Hearing the uneasiness in Guy's voice, Jean-Michel determined to leave him to his own diversions. "Good. I would be interested in having, that is, paying, someone to help her get a professional introduction to the impressionists, particularly Monet, and that's a subject in the area of your master's, is it not?"

Guy nodded positively and added, "I'm taking a seminar at the Sorbonne called 'Paris Babylon,' which fits right into the late nineteenth-century, so there might even be some free material I could get for her, but it's all in French, of course."

"That's fine, she speaks French and is improving; plus, you can practice your English."

"You think my English is bad?" Guy said defensively.

"No, but, the French have little reason to criticize Americans; at least the Yanks usually own up to their ignorance."

"Pfft," Guy pouted. "But they seem incapable of anything except spewing English in the face of anyone they please, or practicing their Mickey Mouse French phrases from their cute little *Berlitz* books, as though we should be pleased. They'll never speak French."

Jean-Michel stopped him short. "Listen to your uncle, Guy. You are taking the wrong approach." His voice was quiet, but commanding. "Eighty percent of the world's computer languages are in English, two-thirds of the scientists use English, one-third of the globe's people speak it, and to well over a billion people it is their native tongue or at least their official language, as with India. You may not like it, certainly the French don't, but you will never succeed in your profession without it. You will be better off with English-speaking friends than enemies." Guy shifted uncomfortably in his seat. He was being outgunned by a man who spoke four languages fluently and whose worldly experiences were undisputed; to defy him was, as old sailors would say, pissing into the wind.

"I'll tell you what, why don't you meet her, and make up your own mind?" Jean-Michel tried to assure him: "She's interested in the Musée d'Orsay and Giverny. I'll make arrangements for you to meet. If all goes well, you'll make some good money."

Guy got up to leave. "I appreciate it, Unc. I owe you ... again." He smiled as he stood and reached down to put his arm around Jean-Michel's shoulders for an awkward hug.

Jean-Michel patted him on the arm. "I'm glad. Something will work out. Besides, you're helping me paint the boat this summer. My best to your mother if you happen to call, which, if you haven't, you should. Guy, you said the course was Paris Babylon at the Sorbonne? Who teaches it?"

"You wouldn't know him, he's an adjunct professor."

"Probably not, probably came after I left Saint de Just. What's his name?" he persisted.

"Dumas. Jerôme Dumas."

"Dumas?" Jean-Michel rolled the name around in his head, "Dumas, wasn't he...?," and let the topic drop.

CHAPTER 5

═══ THE FRANCO-AMERICAN WAR ═══

Charly was pleasantly surprised to find a handsome young man sporting brown wavy hair combed straight back, reminiscent of the '30s, casually but fashionably dressed in maroon sweater and tan slacks, standing near the entrance to the Musée d'Orsay where they had agreed to meet. He was thin, athletic, and carried a leather bag slung easily over his shoulder. She flushed momentarily as do those who anticipate a change in their lives. *Jesus,* she thought, *wait until Simone gets him in her sights.* Or...cradle robbing be damned, this could prove interesting.

"Mam'selle Brooks?" He walked up and removed his sunglasses, "Guy...Jean-Michel's nephew," offering a limp handshake and a cool smile. He took a moment to scrutinize. *Not bad,* he thought. *Pretty. Black curly hair, but a body difficult to visualize in her loose linen suit, size nine, probably, longing for a six, ancestrally French, perhaps. L'Air de Temps, or is it Fendi? Unc's unrivaled storytelling gifts obviously haven't deserted him.*

"Hello, Guy," she smiled easily. "Have you come like Lafayette to save an American's day?" *And for once,* she thought, *a Frenchman with fragrance instead of stale sweat.* Guy himself, the typical insouciant French male, showed no particular interest in Charly's efforts to be friendly.

"My uncle was very persuasive. I'm normally quite busy this time of year." He spoke quickly and in dialect.

"Oh, what do you do?"

"Consulting." Guy, like many social aspirants in their twenties, had not given much thought to establishing his professional image, except as it involved posturing.

"Ah. Consulting. Great opportunities, of course. What kind?" Albeit an innocent question, street-wise New Yorkers sized people up quickly; she was curious about a twenty-five-year-old whose schedule was filled with consulting in the summertime.

Caught immediately in his lie, Guy snatched at an answer, a trait that seemed to run in the family. "I do media consulting."

"Interesting." She acted impressed. "What sort of media?"

Guy was becoming tangled in his own web, and maneuvered awkward-ly for a way out. "Maybe we could talk about it later." And then, inspiredly, "Perhaps your publishing company could use my services."

"I thought Jean-Michel told you, I'm not in that line of work anymore. But I still have contacts."

He handed her his card, crisp and white, nondescript except for his name and number in gold.

"So some other time, then," she smiled. "Jean-Michel said that it would be necessary to get tutored in Impressionism and the impressionists; they're such a fascinating group."

"It's possible. I see you are working on the French language," he patron-ized, using a French colloquialism she would have to guess to understand.

"I'm doing the best I can, which probably isn't much." She began to feel the hostility in his manner. "Jean-Michel tells me your English is very good." French men were such easy victims of flattery.

"Yes, I also speak Italian. I may apply for an INSEAD scholarship next year." He looked nonchalantly away, but his arrogance snared him.

"Excellent," she said emphatically, catching his eye. "Then we'll speak English, as long as the company's paying you."

He hesitated momentarily, trying to decide if the money was worth it, and switched to English, becoming more awkward under the scrutiny of a native speaker. "Well, Miss Brooks, what were you looking exactly to edu-cate yourself for?"

"I'm looking exactly to educate myself for Monet," she mimicked his stilted English, fixing him with a steady gaze.

Guy's vanity created complications. He made the cardinal mistake of underestimating the opposition; if he wasn't careful the day could turn into a rout of the French. He tried to relax, focusing on his English, and said slowly and precisely, "The museum is having …an exhibit of Cézanne's works…loaned to it from the Cézanne Museum in Aix-en-Provence.

Would you like to see it?"

"That's why we're here, right? Please, lead the way." They joined the line waiting to enter the museum. Once inside they walked in silence toward the section dedicated to Cézanne's paintings.

"Were Monet and Cézanne good friends?" Charly asked to break the silence, more deafening with each step.

Relieved, Guy cooperated. "Friends? Of course. But I think Monet felt sorry for him more than anything else."

"How do you mean?" They finally stood in front of one of Cézanne's self-portraits, of which there were many.

Guy decided to handle the day by relying on what he knew best. His English improved with use, so if he were to be a paid guide, he would act like one. "I'll give you an example by way of a story, if that would meet your needs." She nodded her approval. "One day in November 1894, we're not sure quite when, really, a horse carriage drew up at Monet's home in Giverny and deposited this curious figure (Guy pointed to the colorful self-portrait of Cézanne) wearing a Cronstadt hat. It was Paul Cézanne, of course, and he had not seen Monet for a considerable time, no? A recluse by nature from Provençal, he, like others, wanted an opportunity to paint at Giverny. Monet invited him to reside in a small hotel near his home. The two men now saw one another regularly and exchanged canvases, which gave Cézanne encouragement and support.

"The story goes that Monet invited him to lunch often, but five minutes before the food was served one never knew whether the temperamental Master of Aix, as some called him, would appear or not."

"I lived in Aix," she ventured shyly.

He ignored her. "See, here is a picture of Monet's dining room," and he showed Charly a photo from his book taken at Monet's home in Giverny. "Magnificently colorful, no? Cézanne and Monet sat together at that very table."

"Um-hm, colorful."

"As you no doubt know, Cézanne was a peculiar man. He's described as generous and had a certain tenderness, but also was capable of unleashing an ugly nature. He was easily frightened at the prospect of meeting strangers, convinced that even polite praise directed at his work was in fact a poorly disguised form of mockery. Oddly enough, however, when introduced to Clemenceau, a powerful new figure in French politics and frequent visitor to Monet's home, Cézanne was not intimidated. In fact he took open delight in the wit and charm of the future prime minister's…" Guy paused searching for a word, "ah, lapidary turn of phrase."

"Nice shot." Charly commented.

"Nice shot?" Guy looked startled and confused.

"Lapidary—'gem-like' turn of phrase. You use English well."

"The word is French, Mam'selle Brooks, 'lapid' means stone. May I continue?" he said sarcastically

Jesus, here we go again, she thought. *Probably related to the colonel.* "At your convenience," and waved him on.

"As I was saying, one day when Cézanne felt particularly sociable, he was lucky to meet Gustave Geffroy at Monet's. It's said that he immediately warmed to the critic, Cézanne wrote informing him that he would like to do his portrait, and signed the note 'Paul Cézanne, painter by inclination.' Guy chuckled as if it were an 'in' joke. "He obviously had a severe ego problem, wouldn't you agree Mam'selle Brooks?" He continued, "Meanwhile, on the same day of the encounter with Geffroy, Monet also had as his guests Clemenceau, Mirbeau, and the sculptor Rodin, the latter of whom became the occasion for some of Cézanne's most bizarre behavior. A witness attests that the sight of Rodin's Legion of Honor rosette so impressed Cézanne that he drew Mirbeau and Geffroy aside and expressed surprise: 'M. Rodin isn't at all proud; he shook hands with me! A man who's been decorated!' After lunch, when everyone went for a stroll around the garden, it's said that Cézanne suddenly fell to his knees in front of Rodin and thanked him for shaking his hand.

"At the Hôtel Baudy, the hotel I was telling you about near Monet, Cézanne's presence did not go unnoticed either. As we know from Mary Cassatt, the American impressionist," he paused, "you know her, perhaps?"

"I'm afraid not."

Guy grimaced as if he had been speaking to a gymnasium student, and continued, "As she wrote to her friend, Madam Stillman, Cassatt was somewhat disconcerted by the French artist's odd ways. It is one of the few good representations of Cézanne's demeanor," he said to no one in particular.

228

'Monsieur Cézanne,' she said, 'was from Provence and is like the man from the Midi whom Daudet describes: "When first I saw him I thought he looked like a cut-throat with large red eyeballs standing out from his head in a most ferocious manner, a rather fierce looking pointed beard, quite grey, and an excited way of talking that positively made the dishes rattle."

Guy then quoted Cassatt by reading from the brochure: "'I found later that I had misjudged his appearance, for far from being fierce and cut throat he had the gentlest manner possible, comme un enfant, as he would say. His manners at first rather startled me. He scrapes his soup plate, then lifts it and pours the remaining drops in his spoon: he even takes his chop in his fingers and pulls the meat from the bone … Yet in spite of the total disregard of the dictionary of manners, he shows a politeness toward us which no other man here would have shown. He will not allow Louise to serve him before us in the usual order of succession at the table; he is even deferential to that stupid maid, and he pulls off the old tam-o'-shanter, which he wears to protect his bald head, when he enters the room. Cézanne is one of the most liberal artists I have ever seen. He prefaces every remark with: pour moi, it is so and so, but he grants that everybody may be as honest and as true to nature from their convictions; he doesn't believe that everyone should see alike.'"[9]

"I particularly enjoy the quote," Guy said.

"Another example of his bizarre behavior occurred one day while lunching at Monet's with Renoir and Sisley, who had been invited to Giverny in honor of Cézanne. The two visiting impressionists seized on the occasion to praise their difficult colleague's art. Overcome by their attention, Cézanne abruptly got up and left the table, his eyes filled with tears. After seeing no sign of him for several days, Monet went to ask for Cézanne at the Hôtel Baudy, only to learn that he had departed, leaving all his canvases at the auberge. Obviously, this troubled Monet, since he realized that Cézanne must have thought Renoir and Sisley were making fun of him. To his credit, Monet gathered up all the abandoned pictures and forwarded them to poor Cézanne, who subsequently sent a letter full of apologies, but rather obscure in its explanations of the sudden desertion.

"The next and last time that Monet saw Cézanne was along the Rue d'Amsterdam. Monet told a friend that it seemed as if Cézanne recognized him, too, but Cézanne simply pressed on down the street and disappeared. Unfortunately, the old friends, if friends they ever were, never met again after the Giverny visit."

"He does sound strange, but I guess Monet liked him. How would you describe Cézanne?" Charly asked. "I mean, what were his artistic attributes?"

"As I said before, Mam'selle Brooks, I don't think the word is 'like.' I think most analysts agree that Cézanne was difficult to like; most simply felt sorry for him," he said matter-of-factly. "Are you speaking of how I would characterize his art or his person?"

"It's the same old question." Charly struggled for a toehold in the conversation.

"What old question?"

"Whether the art itself is a true reflection of the artist, writer, whatever, or whether the human is simply the medium, so to speak, through which the creation is communicated." Guy rubbed his chin and turned pensive for the moment. "I really don't see your point."

She tried again. "Well, what drives artists to create?"

"What do they want to tell us?" he asked.

"Um-hm, I guess. You know, like how much artists suffered for their art. I read that Cézanne was the artist's artist, but that he was difficult, peculiar, and sometimes violent, right?" Charly was speculating, and hoped to avoid criticism from her tutor.

"Yes, but I already said that. He hasn't produced any school, if that's your meaning, but I think you could say he has given an impulse directly, or even indirectly, to almost every new movement of art since he died, not the least of which is Picasso and Matisse, of course, both beginning their adventures in primitivism."

"Ah, I saw the movie 'Picasso,'" she said triumphantly, "with Anthony Hopkins." Guy gave her a blank stare, which obviously ran in the family, and she tried to regain her momentum. "Picasso's museum is here, isn't it? I've seen some of his work." She tried to assume a serious persona and moved to stake out a small sense of belonging.

"Some? He was a compulsive creator."

"Well, like I said, only some."

"He made over 20,000 works, Mam'selle Brooks. Were there 'some' you particularly liked?"

Now Charlie stared, a petite rabbit mesmerized by a coiling cobra. "Well, the one where the couple was kissing, I think it was all in blue, that was nice."

"Yes, it was *nice; erotic art, then?*"

"I don't think it's really erotic."

Guy turned and began walking ahead like a Moslem lecturing to his wife. "When Picasso was questioned about the relationship between art and sexuality, he replied, 'It is the same thing.' It was a constant theme throughout his career. Probably from his experiences in the brothels of Barcelona and Paris, I suppose; however, I think by the 1930s, this early naturalism was sublimated into erotic symbolism."

"Why do males always see erotic sex in a plain ol' kiss?"

He turned to face her. "We *males*, Mam'selle Brooks, are simply describing what we see. Sexuality, as portrayed by Picasso, is aggressively male and… " He hesitated, then started in spitefully, "Females, Mam'selle Brooks, are dwarfed by huge phalluses, their faces sculpted from male genitalia. Perspective is subverted to present female bodies as rolling landscapes of breasts and orifices. It is something first-year art students seem to visualize immediately; perhaps you missed it, in the *movie*."

They passed a restroom, and Charly took refuge to assuage her anger, more of a mind to spit than piss. When she returned, Guy was detached and aloof, continuing as if nothing had happened.

"I think we were speaking of Cézanne. Some say he is the father of modern art, but I think that's a particularly American cliché. If you are really looking at the artist, I believe that his power comes from his ability to excite other artists, perhaps because he realized so many different sides of his art. It has often been true of leading modern painters that they developed a single idea with great force." Guy disliked playing proverbial tennis with a beginner who had no ability to even swing the racket, much less return the ball. "Some one element or expressive note, which has been worked out with striking effect, for example." Charly, not knowing exactly what to contribute, simply stood and listened.

"Are you hungry?" he asked.

"No. Why?"

"Hemingway observed that paintings were sharpened and clearer and beautiful if you were, as he said, 'belly-empty, hollow-hungry.' Hemingway learned to understand Cézanne much better, and to see truly how he made landscapes, when he was hungry."

Knowing little more about Hemingway than about Cézanne, Charly remained speechless and note-less.

Guy involuntarily let out a breath of exasperation and decided to try another approach: "In Cézanne, Mam'selle Brooks, one is struck rather by the comprehensive character of his art, even though you might suggest that later artists have successfully built on a particular element of his style. Drawing, structure, color, and expression — if any of these can be isolated from the others — are carried to new heights in his work. He is arresting, at least in my opinion, through his images, more evocative in content than has been supposed, and also through his uninterrupted strokes, which, as you can see," he waved his hand toward the picture, "can be qualities of greatness in little touches of paint. I don't know whether you have noticed, Mam'selle Brooks," he said pedantically, "in his paintings, single patches of the brush are divulged as an uncanny choice, deciding the unity of a complete expanse of forms. By this time, Gauguin had developed a renewed and deeper appreciation of Cézanne, and incorporated the technique into his own paintings; Cézanne even complained that Gauguin had stolen his 'petite sensation' in order to roam with it through the South Seas.'" He looked at her with mild contempt. "In case you're wondering, building a painting's surface with small strokes of color, Mam'selle Brooks." Charley had begun scribbling furiously in her notebook, more to avoid inquisition than record information. "See how they are placed here on the canvas," and he pointed to different painted lines in the artist's portrait. "Out of these emerges a touching semblance of a natural world with a deepened harmony that invites reflection, don't you think?"

Charly turned to look at the Cézanne portrait, then back to Guy. "You saw all that?"

He smiled confidently. "Cézanne's painting, as can readily be seen by the expert, is a balanced art, not in the sense that it is alleviated in its effects, but that opposed traits are joined in a scrupulously proscribed play. He is inventive in many different aspects of his art." Guy felt more influential and in control with each word.

Charly felt related to the Beverly Hillbillies 'in a scrupulously proscribed play' that left her mystified. "Perhaps we could take a look at some of his other paintings," she said.

As they walked, Guy began to expound, and Charly vigorously attempted notes. "In this striving for fullness, you know, Cézanne is an heir of the Renaissance and Baroque masters. It's easily observed," he said nonchalantly, with the sophistication of a Sorbonne don. "Like Delacroix, he preserves from Rubens and the Italians a concept of the grand—not in the size of the canvas, obviously," he laughed derisively as if including Charly in an audience of wide-eyed fish, "but in the influence and complexity of dissimilarity, no?" Warming to the subject, he postured by running his fingers through his luxuriant hair.

"Of course," she added as a foil, hoping to keep him from fencing with her and delivering a fatal blow. They walked on past some of Cézanne's finest.

Guy continued his attempt to impress, waving one hand or the other in the air and ignoring the paintings. "In my opinion, Cézanne's sumptuousness is without convention, and inheres in the spectacular power of large disparities and in the bluntness of his means," his hands continually gesturing in the empty air as he led Charly through the museum. "Cézanne's detached deliberation of his subjects arises from a zealous nature, which can be readily seen, that seeks to master its own inclination through an objective attitude—" Charly cut him off.

"What...the *fuck*...are you talking about!?"

CHAPTER 6

═══ THE UGLY AMERICAN ═══

"And then you know what that goddamn cow said to me!?" he shrieked. Guy was seething; his creamy cheeks splotchy-red with anger. He lay prostrate on their bed in the apartment's ornate bedroom, relating his tale to Jerôme, who sought only to console him. "That horsy bitch! My God, I can't believe the rudeness with which she treated me, in front of a Cézanne, for Christ's sake, in d'Orsay! In Paris! She asked me, 'What the *fuck* are you talking about!?'" Practically in tears, he buried his face in his pillow. Jerôme attempted to calm his mate, rubbing his back and shoulders soothingly.

"Guy, Guy, it is one of life's ugly lessons. Certainly she is ignorant, but she is ignorant of art; that's in fact why you were there. She needs help, someone like yourself, who has the wonderful ability to show her the beauty of art."

"She's a goddamn cow–cow– cow-woman from Texas," he stammered. "She wouldn't know a piece of art from a cheeseburger."

"I'll get you some tea," Jerôme offered nervously. "And maybe some aspirin," he said to himself, "and try relaxing for a while," he cautioned, appealing to the spirits of the house.

Guy did not hate *who* the Americans were. Historically, they were, after all, mostly refugee Europeans and peasant emigrants from around the planet; a people whose worldly contributions consisted of "All-you-can-eat" buffets and oblivious to anything sophisticated, except their obsession with big cars, pornography, and violent video games. Rather, he hated *what* they were—the very substance of their culture or lack of it—from that ugly little orphan, Huckleberry Finn, to Andy Warhol and Hip Hop music. He hated the brashness of their arrogance and ignorance, their brutal sports, and their insufferable action movies. He hated the consummate aggressiveness that seemed to color everything they did, from their infernal war machines molesting Third-World countries, to the stupid louts shouting "America #1" at the Olympics, and scrawling it on the toilet walls of Europe in English, far too stupid to know the words in another language. All of which made them, even to the average European, detestable. And now this foul-mouthed woman, who would confuse a Cézanne with a Monet and *never* recognize the difference, had revitalized and energized his hatred of Americans.

The shouting match between the two had ended when the guards asked both to leave the museum and summarily escorted them to the exit.

Late in the afternoon, Guy got a phone message from Jean-Michel asking if they could get together over a coffee in a nearby bistro that evening. As he said on the answering machine, there evidently was a problem.

Guy hated the idea as he left the apartment. He knew the reason only too well. After the museum guards had escorted that hysterical bitch and him from the museum for their rowdy altercation, Charly had threatened to take him on physically if he ever touched her again, referring to his inadvertent push while in the gallery. The whole world was turning to shit! No job, this fiasco, and now his uncle sticking his nose in Guy's business—all for a few Euros.

"Beer?" Jean-Michel held up his glass in salute as Guy arrived at the café and signaled for the waiter nearby.

"Pernod," Guy ordered quietly as he sat down.

"First, Guy, I would like to apologize," Jean-Michel offered, taking Guy by surprise and putting him off balance, since Guy had been thinking of various defenses to fend off his uncle. "Charly, that is, Miss Brooks, is a very direct person, and I didn't advise you of that. She has a very low tolerance for," he hesitated, "shall we say, ambiguity."

"She's detestable! An all-American bitch!" he snarled. "She's wasting her time in museums, she should be at the Bon Marché department store, pushing a trolley while eating macaroons."

"Control yourself, Guy," Jean-Michel said sternly. "I'm your uncle, and we're discussing a communication problem, not the agenda for an anti-American demonstration. Would you like to tell me what happened?"

Guy proceeded to outline the situation as he remembered it, turning various situations to his advantage, as one might suspect; but feeling, nonetheless, some of the heavy rancor drain from his body while Jean-Michel cajoled and counseled.

"My first reaction after hearing from Charly, who as you might imagine is also upset, was to drop the rest of the plan," Jean-Michel said. "That, however, is the easy way out. I know you both, and you are fine people. In the end, there should be every reason for you to understand each other, if you could just get the words right. You have an opportunity to learn something from one another."

"We learned we hate each other," Guy said peevishly.

"It isn't difficult to love one's friends, Guy, but nothing's learned or won."

"You're not suggesting that we continue this– this joke are you?" he pleaded.

CHAPTER 7

=== BACK AT D'ORSAY ===

The facts about Monet's early upbringing are surprisingly few given his renown. They are also unrevealing, which makes them frustrating but simple to review....

The heavy, scratchy, metallic-sounding voice with rich French accents was transmitted by Charly's museum Tour-pak, which she carried in her pocketbook, a small microphone attached to one ear. The cassette "Monet, His Life and Works" was playing as she walked the halls of the d'Orsay Museum. The previous day's encounter with Guy was truly a gut-wrenching experience that had her on the verge of quitting and heading back to the States early. He was a pompous, arrogant, French fool who had not quite reached the age of maturity, give or take a decade. If Guy symbolized what the French considered their educated elite, Charly wanted no part of its people or its culture, thank you. The Jean-Michels of life were the rare exceptions to a nation of supercilious snots. She tried to keep her mind on the Tour-pak voice as she walked.

Claude Monet came into the world in the 9th arrondissement of Paris on 14 November 1840 in a small apartment on the fifth floor of 45 Rue Lafitte, the year that the sculptor Auguste Rodin was also born. He was the second son of Claude-Adolphe, forty, and Louise-Justine Aubrée Monet, thirty-five, whose families had come to the capital in the late 18th century from the Dauphiné and the Essonne, respectively. He was named Oscar-Claude, and baptized as such in their local parish church, Notre-Dame-de-Lorette, just steps from their house. They apparently called him

"Oscar" and, like a good son, Monet obediently used that name to sign his paintings and drawings until his early twenties. He must not have found it terribly endearing, however, as he always signed his name "Claude." Sometime in 1862, he perfunctorily dropped the "Oscar" altogether and never used it again....

She thought about changing her name too: *"Charly"—too informal. Maybe that's why that faggy bastard thought he could trample on my feelings.* Charly had turned off the Tour-pak and sat disconsolately on the wooden bench. *Damn. Damn it!* she thought. *Why does everything have to be so ... so damn difficult?!* A dream trip to Paris was turning into a nightmare. Money was tight, the weather was turning prairie hot, and Jean-Michel's nephew, a bona fide jerk, was no doubt at this very moment filling his uncle's head full of derogatory notions about Charly's behavior. She began to walk again to relieve the stress, and turned the tape back on.

No records survive regarding Monet's performance in the school; we are not even certain when he left or whether he graduated. But we do know he took classes with Ochard, an earnest man whose keen interest in teaching his young students how to manipulate a pencil or piece of chalk more than compensated for his modest talents.

Monet's mother died just after his sixteenth birthday, and his uncle, who owned the chandler's business...

These soulless comments reminded Charly of her own mother's passing, depressing her even more, revitalizing her intentions to leave early for the States. She could still save part of her money, look for a job, and get some essentials for her apartment.

We know little about Monet's activities as a child, or what kinds of experiences he had as an adolescent....

The Tour-pak chatted away as she walked, considering whether to return to her hotel.

Later in life he claimed he never liked school, that he favored his drawing pad over his books, and that as soon as he could, he abandoned academe. He also said he drew spontaneously as a child, covering his schoolbooks with fantastic designs, but never indulging in mechanical renderings. However, the evidence suggests otherwise. Although none of his school texts has ever come to light, three sketchbooks from his high school days have survived. You will notice sketches on your right...

There was nothing on Charly's right but a very substantial wall, devoid of art. She was lost. Disgusted, dejected, she slumped onto a nearby bench and stared at her Nikes, bumping her toes.

Perhaps she needed to get out of the city. She would cancel the room reservations at her hotel, meet Jodie and her friend, and rent a car. If there was 'charm' to be had in France, they would be making a mistake by staying in its cities. Besides, after Jodie and her friend, Randy, spent a few days in the countryside, they could go back to Paris before returning to Texas. They would certainly appreciate French villagers, who couldn't be as bad as the likes of Guy and his ilk. Maybe drive down to Aix, where she knew the territory, that would be fun. Maybe J.M. would even consent to tag along. Spirits renewed, Charly began to walk again.

Monet's medium also suggests his traditional bent for pastel, which had been favored by many Barbizon artists. It emphasizes the fact that Monet followed the time-honored path of learning his craft from his predecessors, despite the claims he made later in his life to being an independent, self-made artist....

So, it's settled, she thought as she walked. *I'll give notice to the hotel, cancel both sets of reservations (Jodie will be rooming with me, of course) when I get back, talk to Jean-Michel, and then I can go wherever I want to. Freedom!* She was relieved.

At the age of sixteen, Monet was filling his notebooks with caricatures of his teachers. Although no sassy marginalia have survived, many independent drawings of this type have, including numerous portraits of Parisian notables...."

"Am I interrupting anything?" Jean-Michel said, touching her shoulder from behind, startling her. "I thought I might find you here."

Charly turned off the Tour-pak. "Yep, coolest place in Paris."

"Figuratively?"

"Literally." But Charly was having trouble smiling and Jean-Michel sensed it.

"See that painting over there?" Jean-Michel pointed across the room. "It's Monet's first, as far as anyone knows, and fairly famous for just that reason. It's the View of Rouelles 1858; meticulously rendered, I think. Monet submitted the painting to an exhibition in Le Havre where it was accepted and listed as, let's see," he pulled out his brochure, "yes, number 380," and took her by the arm. Reluctant, she hesitated, but he cajoled, "Come on, it isn't all that serious," and they walked closer.

"Not bad for a first try," Charly admitted as she gazed at the painting. "My mother hung one of mine upside down and I didn't catch it for a year." But the moment was heavy.

"You paint?" he said enthusiastically.

"Um-hm. It was Ernestville's first ninth grade exhibition, and if we didn't contribute, we had to clean the blackboards during study hall."

"Ah. Candidates for the Louvre."

"Hey, I read that some guy was smuggling his paintings into the famous art galleries of Europe; hung them up, and for days no one even noticed."

"To be honest, Monet might have been tempted to do the same. Anyway, we don't even know if it was his first. Even the critics say that this painting is too refined to have been his first try at placing pigments on canvas."

"Well, it's tough putting little piglets on canvas."

"Truly. Anyway, his touch is too sure, they said, the color scheme too subtle, and the light and atmosphere too tangible. It is a remarkable picture, though, don't you think?" He coaxed her. "Especially for someone who was barely seventeen."

"You're asking me? I left my crayons at McDonald's. But since you're asking," she leaned closer to the painting, "probably tenth, eleventh grade—you know, no ketchup or Coke spills, and a noted absence of little boogers. You should ask Guy." *That effeminate, cheese-eating surrender monkey,* she wanted to say, but deferred to civility, since Guy had already been on the receiving end of that particular tribute to the French at the museum.

Her hostility was palpable. "Look, Charly," Jean-Michel offered, "I am very sorry that situation occurred, particularly since I was its author. I hope you will forgive me. Of course, no harm was intended, and Guy is, uh, highstrung. Perhaps it's that way with young, highly educated people," he said lamely. "There still might be areas of common ground."

She was peeved, thinking how Guy had put his limp, boneless hand in her tough little paw. "Look, Jean-Michel, how your nephew behaves, which was abhorrent, by the way, is definitely not your fault. And he and I have nothing in common except being bipedal. He is perhaps the only person I've met who has instilled in me, possibly forever, the gratification of knowing that I'm ignorant of art." Her eyes brightened. "Did you see 'The Graduate'? You know, with Dustin Hoffman?"

"Yes. Old movie."

"Let me ask you some questions. You have my permission to pass them along to your nephew."

"Okay."

"What was Mrs. Robinson's major in college?"

"What?"

"In the movie, what was Mrs. Robinson's major in college?"

He shrugged his shoulders. "I don't know."

"Art! What was her illegitimate daughter's name, and where was she conceived?"

He shook his head again.

"Elaine! In the back of a Ford Coupe. What beer was Dustin drinking in bed with Mrs. Robinson?"

"How in heaven's name would I know?" He was getting irritated.

"The point, Professor, is what your nephew never learned; like Will Rogers said, 'We're all ignorant in something.'"

He nodded. "I understand how you feel, but I can make it up to you. I have spent a great deal of time in these museums. I would enjoy showing you what are, in my opinion, some of the best objects of art."

"Jean-Michel, there is no one's company I enjoy more—when you're not drinking—than yours, my august friend. Matter of fact, you're about the only person I know in Paris, but I realize you have a life here, a busy life, so I don't want you to be tied to my wagon. Unless..." her voice trailed off. There was that awkward silence. "You know, maybe we got intimate a little too early."

He had gotten laid, a lucky strike. Now he was hooked, but she had given him enough line that he hadn't felt the real jerk back toward the boat—until now. He was an overweight academician with a drinking problem, and no innate gifts when it came to wooing women. At a loss for words, he simply picked up her hand, held it against his cheek briefly, then kissed it.

"Let's take a spin," he said quietly, "down some of these venerable marble hallways to see what they've got. Then we can stop off at the café and have a croissant or the like." He reached over and gently removed her earphone still dangling from her ear.

"Let's see, where did we leave off? Ah! The first picture, which probably wasn't his first, 'View of Rouelles.' One of my favorites."

"Leave off? I thought we were talking about intramural pissing contests."

He looked at her perplexed. "What?"

"Never mind. Why? And plainly, please," Charly said coquettishly, wrapping her arm around his. Relationships are measured by intuition, an attribute far more refined in women than men. Nothing written, nothing pledged, but she had her man in Paris. What she had was still in question.

"At least that's easy," he said proudly, sporting his woman in public. "Because it shows the French countryside as it is, so idyllic. See," he pointed to a spot on the painting, "the young boy fishing, the blue sky; I feel like we could wander down that path through the field, sit alongside him, and listen to his stories about when he fell in the river or caught this really great fish. And look here," he pointed again up close to the canvas, "see how smooth the texture of the paint and how the colors are joined? He had a wonderful technique for his age. The painting strongly suggests to me Monet's ability to absorb the lessons not only of his Barbizon mentors, some of whose paintings you can see later, but also of a local Le Havre artist. These painters got out into the countryside and sunshine, away from

242

their studios, which in itself was a new technique. I'll show you some of their paintings in the next hall."

"Le Hav–? Is that how you pronounce it?"

"Um-hm. The Le Havre artist was Eugène Boudin. Monet would claim more than thirty years later that Boudin was his inspiration and true mentor along with Jongkind, a Dutchman, about whom Monet said, 'It is to him that I owe the definitive education of my eye.'

"It is sort of ironic in a way," he continued, "since Monet's first impressions of Boudin were bad. Boudin had prowled the Normandy coast since the late 1840s, painting and drawing its terrain under varying light and weather conditions. But, unlike his Barbizon peers, Boudin did not turn his back on contemporary developments in the area. Beginning in the early 1860s, he boldly—"

"Boldly, like, where no painter has gone before," she panned.

He missed it. "Yes, boldly rendered such modern aspects of the once unchanging coast as Parisian pleasure seekers on the beach, and new hotels that began to line these watering places to accommodate the influx of tourists and day-trippers. To see the analogy, I suppose you could imagine painting a new Holiday Inn just being built at, uh, the Jersey shore."

"Jeez, now that's enticing. Can we get serious a minute? We're talking about an eighteen-year-old here, are we not? I mean, how deep can this guy be at eighteen? I haven't heard the words 'child prodigy' yet."

"Like?"

"Well, like Elvis."

"Elvis. Elvis? Mozart, maybe?" He stroked his chin pensively. "Elvis didn't paint, did he?"

"Maybe. But what's all the excitement? It's a nice painting, terrific by an eighteen-year-old. Period. It wouldn't surprise me to find similar talents in a high school senior somewhere in Texas."

"Do I still note a little testiness in your voice?"

"A little."

"*Mais pourquoi, mon amie?*" he exclaimed. "Forget about yesterday if you can; today we are going to enjoy ourselves in a wonderful museum. Open yourself up to the experience."

"Last time I heard that was in the back seat of my girlfriend's boyfriend's

243

Chevy with a jug-eared football player." Then she stopped and faced him. "Okay, Guy got me going yesterday, it's true, but at the bottom of it all is this business about what we are even doing here, that is, trying to appreciate art. At least he had an opinion. I seem to be just seeing different-colored paints on canvas, when the rest of you are hovering inches from orgasm. Perhaps you know the secret, which I admittedly don't, like, what is 'good art'? I know it isn't something whose quality is determined by how closely it resembles a photograph, although in my opinion that's not a bad start."

"Good art?" He scratched himself unconsciously in his crotch. "Oh, God, that's a terribly difficult question. I don't know."

Charly lifted Jean-Michel's sacred pipe from his vest pocket. "Speak. I have needs." And thrust his pipe pistol-like into his chest.

"Ouch!"

"I'm still trying to figure out what it is I'm looking at. What, for example, is this huge appeal for the impressionists?"

"Hostility," he said, snatching back his pipe and jamming it into his vest pocket, "will get you a broken nose. In my opinion, dear colleague, a large part of Impressionism's appeal is that its vision of life is so modern, yet so down-to-earth and compatible with our notions of a bourgeois paradise, that—"

"Yo, hey, it's me, Charly! Does this stuff run in the family? I went through that yesterday with little Lord Fauntleroy."

"Sorry. The impressionists, you see, didn't bother to trouble the contemporary viewer with complex scenarios drawn from the Bible or classical mythology. You know, there are no Madonnas in this type of painting, with artists hoping for divine inspiration; no religious agonies, no battle scenes commemorating obscure victories. Charly, you can be as ignorant as a newborn babe of all matters concerning religion, politics, theology, and the triumphs and tragedies of history, and still find the masterworks of impressionist painting both completely accessible and deeply pleasurable, like a bird on a fence on a snowy day. But despite his technical erudition, it is a lesson Guy has yet to learn. For him it's a religion, and he doesn't take fools or heretics lightly."

"Thanks. Maybe we can start a new school: the newborn fool of art."

"*Alors,* look, he has to make his own apologies, but he's young—you know, new wine in old bottles and all that; he simply wanted to impress you and didn't know better, is my guess."

"Can't we just forget about him?"

"Superlative idea. What shall we talk about?"

"How about art."

He gave an exasperated sigh, then rubbed his chin. "Let me go back a bit. About the beginning of the twentieth century, desire for radical change was strong among artists in every medium. There was feeling that the forms of the European tradition were played out, their possibilities exhausted, that verse must get away from rhyme and meter, that music had to break the confines of the diatonic scale —"

"Now there's something I know about," she broke in brightly.

"What?"

"Scales. I'm an expert."

"We're talking about music."

"Yeah, I know. I was talking about calories."

"May I?" he said wearily.

"Please. I just need to say something proactive every once in a while, instead of 'oh really.'"

"Um-hm. As I was saying, diatonic scale, that painting must reject the concern with imitating natural appearances, which had been the mainspring of visual art in Europe since the Renaissance. It is interesting, at least to me, that this desire for a new start should have been common to artists in so many different media. The various arts do not necessarily move in step, you know."

"I know."

"Are you being proactive?"

"No."

"Good. The arts don't share the same ideal or the same crisis very often. I'm speaking of one of those times. It must have been exciting, you understand: rejection of the past was in the air, and certainly not only within the domain of the arts."

"Certainly not," she mocked.

"Listen, no twenty-five-year period in human history has created so many original aesthetic conceptions as the years 1890 to 1914. And it was a period

245

of unparalleled ferment in the sciences, the period that brought to birth the theory of relativity, quantum theory, psychoanalysis, symbolic logic, as well as radio, radium, the X-ray, and the airplane,"[10] he said, feeling pedantic.

"Is that so unusual? How about the alphabet, fire, and the wheel?"

The stare. "Okay, you've got a point, but not all in twenty-five years. Nevertheless, there's nothing unusual about this sort of coexistence of new and traditional idioms, nor is it unusual for violent hostility to exist between the exponents of the old and the new ways, right?"

"Um-hm."

"Well, today a gap has opened up between the art establishment and the public. Avant-garde art remains a minority taste, as you no doubt appreciate, but when it is claimed that such art is now 'fashionable,' all it means is that the minority that accepts it includes those who are wealthy or clever or have official status, not that it has become well liked. What can be said, though, is that the public's attitude toward it has changed from utter hostility to one of puzzlement—often a puzzlement that is pretty modest, since absurdly high prices are being paid for it."

"Yeah, I was puzzled, although it wasn't about the prices. It was the bullshit pouring forth from your nephew's, shall we say, panegyric, which, despite his obvious love of the subject, obscured some of the basics."

"Hm. Look, paintings speak to people."

She groaned.

"That 'art thinks' is pretty common stuff these days, Charly; so true that it's difficult to even imagine a professor of literature bothering to write a book to prove it." He put his hand on her arm. "You know what our Monet supposedly said?" She shook her head. "He said, 'I plunge back into the examination of my canvases, which is to say the continuation of my tortures.'"

"Gee."

"Be serious!" She was not the brightest he had bedded. "You asked about Impressionism. Impressionism, and practically every innovation in the visual arts you can think of, resonates with the important issues of its age, no matter what they are, from war to great discoveries. Therefore, putting paint on canvas, you know—your little piglets—with all the ability and, certainly, doubt that great artists bring to the task, is perhaps the greatest challenge to conveying one's vision of reality and, of course, helping to form other people's. I guess you could say that painting is philosophy that you can see. Unfortunately, there is also a bunch of crap out there passing itself off as art."

Still distressed from Guy's "lesson," she changed venue. "Your smarty-pants nephew didn't even say anything about Van Gogh," she said defiantly.

"Van Gogh?" He sighed. "Well, what would you like to know? Great painter—but the man was nuts."

"Something without an irrelevant string of adjectives."

"Charly, every once in a while one is compelled to use a few adjectives. I don't think there is a lot to say about Vincent in this case; maybe that's why Guy skipped over him."

"Tell me, how does one 'skip over' Van Gogh? His paintings are on the front of every menu in town, and he's not even French."

"He's not a true impressionist. Vincent had read about Impressionism, I'm sure, but imagined it to be simply the use of, may I say 'lighter' tones. Remember 'The Potato Eaters,' his first major figure painting? It was so dark that the five peasants seated at the table beneath the gaslight seemed almost black by comparison."

"Yep, somber."

"Van Gogh said that painting peasants was serious business, so he stuck with his palette covered with grey, black, and dark green, until he moved to Paris around 1886. By 1887, according to some art historians, he had undergone one of the greatest transformations in the history of art. He discovered the older painters, like our friends Monet and Pissarro, and met the young avant-garde of the day, like Toulouse-Lautrec, Seurat, and Gauguin."

"Must have been a shock."

"It was. His old palette went right out the window, and he wrote a friend, "Last year I painted almost nothing but flowers, so I could get used to the colors other than gray."

"So, then he was an impressionist?"

"No. I wouldn't say so." She moaned and shook her head. "It's not that bad," he said. "Understand, Van Gogh experimented with impressionist brushstrokes, and pointillist stippling, of course; he even copied some of the same scenes—like the nearly identical views of the Boulevard de Clichy by Signac and himself, for example.

"But," he held up his finger, "that's debatable and didn't make him an impressionist. You can get stuck in these definitions, which are really shades of gray at times. What is 'Impressionism'? And, of course, coming back to your original question, 'What is art'? It's all pretty difficult. I guess if you are one of those who reject or ignore traditional understandings, then you are willing to call almost anything 'art.' Picasso was once asked, "What is art?" He replied, 'What isn't?' Some critics even call a few minutes of absolute silence a work of art on a level with Mozart's compositions."

"I'd like to meet those 'critics,'" she said. "Actually, I wouldn't. All I can hear in silence is my ears ringing when I decide to listen. So, your point is, despite these deep thinkers, there is a lot of confusion about art. Have a seat and tell me something I didn't already know." She led him to a bench, sat, and patted the seat next to her. "I've got a little secret."

CHAPTER 8

═══ A LITTLE STUDY IN ═══
THE PHILOSOPHY OF ART

A letter to Pierre Mainguet, the editor of the arts magazine the *Revue Heb-domadaire*, in its contents:[11]

> I have just written a little study in the philosophy of art, if I
> may use that slightly pretentious phrase, in which I have tried
> to show how the great painters initiate us into a knowledge and
> love of the external world, how they are the ones 'by whom our
> eyes are opened, that is, on the world.' In this study, I use the
> work of Chardin as an example, and I try to show its influence
> on our life, the charm and wisdom with which it coats our most
> modest moments by initiating us into the life of still life. Do you
> think this sort of study would interest the readers of the *Revue
> Hebdomadaire?*
>
> Marcel Proust

Perhaps, as Alain de Botton explains in his book. But since the editor of
Revue Hebdomadaire was sure it wouldn't, the readers had no chance to find
out. Turning the piece down was an understandable oversight today, but this
was 1895, and Mainguet didn't know Proust would eventually be Proust.
What is more, the moral of the essay lay not too far from the ridiculous.
It was only a step away from suggesting that everything down to the last
lemon was beautiful, that there was no good reason to be envious of any
condition besides our own, that a hovel was as nice as a villa and an emer-
ald no better than a chipped plate.

According to de Botton, however, instead of urging us to place the same value on all things, Proust might more interestingly have been encouraging us to ascribe to them their correct value, and hence to revise certain notions of the good life, which risked inspiring an unfair neglect of some settings and a misguided enthusiasm for others. If it hadn't been for Pierre Mainguet's rejection, the readers of the *Revue Hebdomadaire* would have benefited from a chance to reappraise their concepts of beauty, and could have entered into a new and possibly more rewarding relationship with salt-cellars, crockery, and apples.

Why, he asks, would they previously have lacked such a relationship? Why wouldn't they have appreciated their tableware and fruit? At one level, such questions seem superfluous. It just appears natural to be struck by the beauty of some things and to left cold by others. There is no conscious rumination or decision behind our choice of what appeals to us visually; we simply know we are moved by palaces but not by kitchens, by porcelain but not by china, by guavas but not apples.

However, says de Botton, the immediacy with which aesthetic judgments arise should not fool us into assuming that their origins are entirely natural or their verdicts unalterable. Proust's letter to Monsieur Mainguet hinted as much. By saying that great painters were the ones by whom our eyes were opened, Proust was at the same time implying that our sense of beauty was not immobile.... Great painters possess such power to open our eyes because of the unusual receptivity of their own eyes to aspects of visual experience: to the play of light on the end of a spoon, the fibrous softness of a tablecloth, the velvety skin of a peach, or the pinkish tones of an old man' skin — qualities that can in turn inspire our impressions of beauty. We might caricature the history of art as a succession of geniuses engaged in pointing our different elements worthy of our attention, a succession of painters using their immense technical mastery to say ... to the world, and (in Chardin's case) some of the dissatisfied young men in it, 'Look not just at the Roman campagna, the pageantry of Venice, and the proud expression of Charles I astride his horse, but also have a look at the bowl on the sideboard, the dead fish in your kitchen, and the crusty bread loaves in the hall.'

The happiness that may emerge from taking a second look is central to Proust's therapeutic conception. It reveals the extent to which our dissatisfactions may be the result of failing to look properly at our lives rather than the result of anything inherently deficient about them. Appreciating the beauty of crusty loaves does not preclude our interest in a château, but failing to do so must call into question our overall capacity for appreciation. The gap between what the dissatisfied youth could see in his flat (as related by Proust) and what Chardin noticed in very similar interiors (which he painted) places the emphasis on a certain way of looking, as opposed to a mere process of acquiring or possessing.

———

"Secret? What 'secret'?"

"*You* know." She offered a lascivious grin.

"Jesus!" he exclaimed. "It hasn't even been thirty days yet!"

"Not that, silly. I made a little trip to Madame Durant's sex shop." Just then, a small group of students came to view the paintings Jean-Michel and Charly were standing next to. One of the girls was smirking.

Jean-Michel began to talk—fast. "Art is a function of the human being. Acts of God, nature, or the universe are not what most people would call art. I suppose André Gide would contradict me, though. He said, 'Art is collaboration between God and the artist, and the less the artist does, the better.'"

"I don't know Gide, of course," she said, toying with the idea of trying to embarrass him, "but I can see that, sure. All those black velvet paintings with Jesus' sad countenance on them, God must have had a hand in that. Along with his son, he probably also liked Elvis, gypsy queens, and stallions." Jean-Michel slowly wagged his head and stared at the floor, but she continued, "And, hey! We use the word 'art' every day." The students moved on.

"You know," he said, "you're not making this any easier."

"Neither are you. Is everyone suppose to know Gide? You know, household names, like Churchill, De Gaulle, Tony Bennett, and Gide?"

"Can I go home now?" he said.

"No. Teach me about art without making me feel more stupid than I already feel."

"This is getting, you know, a little tiresome. Maybe we should do it tomorrow. Let's head out."

"Actually, that sounds good. Perhaps you can find some grade-school books on art."

"Okay, I'll look. But it won't do any good. Definitions are complicated, and it can be very difficult to find a commonality among all the different usages of any word. Take, for example—

"Is this going to be *another* lecture?" Charly said tiredly.

"Well, you're the one who wanted to know about the definition of 'art'!"

"You win."

"I win? Where's the prize? Listen, definitions are difficult. Take, for example, the word 'game.' It may seem easy to define. Some might say that a game is something done for fun. This is clearly a bad definition, because some people cook for fun, but we don't call cooking a game. Others might say that a game is something one plays. This is not necessarily so; people play pianos and guitars also, but they're not games. We might even say that a game involves competition, unless you're playing a game of catch, which doesn't involve competition. Or how about this, a game is something that two people play. But, solitaire is a game and only one person plays it. In fact, some would say games are physical—"

"What in heaven's name is that?!" Charly and Jean-Michel had just entered a large exhibit room when they were confronted by a huge painting by Monet. Charly never could stand lectures.

"That, my friend, is what they, or at least Monet, called one of his 'machines.'"

"I never thought that Impressionism was necessarily meant to impress," and she walked closer to examine the huge painting.

"Um-hm. He liked to paint things the size of your average wall." They lingered a while and stared at the paintings. "it's Monet's idea of today's giant-screen CinemaVision."

"Speaking of walls," Charly stepped back and moved to the side of the room to lean against one, "I'm tired—you must be, too—and you said we were almost done. Can we stop off at the café for a Coke and rest my weary feet for a while?"

"Coke? Something wrong with your Nikes?" he mocked her.

"Yeah, there's too much weight on 'em. Wanna make something of it?"

"Surely you jest," he grunted, "and I need the restroom." And they wandered off to the café.

The museum café was a light and airy place filled with young and old art aficionados, tourists from various countries, and a small clan of disconsolate gymnasium students unashamed of their boredom. Charly and Jean-Michel sat at a small table near the window, comfortably sipping their drinks and munching pastries. Charly scanned her brochure, pausing as she reviewed the paintings. "Did we see this one?" she pointed out the painting as Jean-Michel leaned closer over his snack. "Camille: Woman in a Green Dress. 1866?"

'Um-hm. In the 'machine' room, remember?"

"Sort of," she mumbled.

"*Sort of,*" he grunted disparagingly.

She kept leafing through her brochure.

He attempted to capture her attention. "According to legend, Monet painted the picture in four days, delivering it to the Salon jury at the very last moment."

"Four days? He must have used a roller," she said distractedly, and continued leafing through the brochure, ignoring him.

"Probably," he continued in a low monotone voice. "Never before had any artists exposed themselves so defiantly as Gilbert and George did in their now infamous 1994 'Naked Shit Pictures,' baring their arseholes to the world and surrounding themselves with blown-up images of their own turds."

She looked up suddenly. "What? What did you just say?!"

He smiled. "You know, four days, but I think the story is probably false, since the painting is quite ambitious—Camille is life-sized—and has a very complex surface. And there is no question that drying time between working sessions alone would have required more than four days."

She gave him a disbelieving look. "What in God's name are you talking about? Were you just talking 'turds'?"

He ignored her. "It was also carefully planned. While painted in primarily darker tones to recall older, more traditional portraiture, it nonetheless depicts a woman who is clearly dressed in the latest fashion and who assumes the disdainful but quite popular pose."

"Some things never change. Models. Seen one frosty anorexic, seen 'em all," she said, looking at him suspiciously.

"Don't like models, either?"

Charly peered around the café, which had emptied. Their snacks gone, it was time to move on. Jean-Michel decided to repair the damage between Charly and Guy. "Guy is gay, isn't he?"

"I assumed you knew," she said.

"Suspected, perhaps. Avoided the subject, really; his mother, you see." His voice dropped off. "Didn't want to see is perhaps a better description. It is disconcerting, but not uncommon. The thing that surprises me is your reaction. Why hate gay men? What do you see that angers you so much?"

"What do I see?" She leaned back in her chair, one arm resting on the table, her hand tapping a staccato beat with a straw, and began in a hard, flat voice, "I see a ludicrous male preening over his appearance: a mustache, a pumped-up body in black jeans and a tank top, an eye-catching tattoo like barbed wire and roses around biceps — a mockery of manhood, swaggering around, pretending to be free. I see an over-exercised body of some forty-year-old clone with an aggressive stare and soft voice, if not offensive, at least unappetizing."[12] She stopped with the straw and leaned forward. "'They must be put to death.' Leviticus 20:13. How's that?"

"That's clear enough. But let's talk about Guy. I think that at a certain point in his young life Guy underwent a bewildering conversion into a new state, the unknown, which he then set about trying to figure out. I see everyone, in fact, at one time or another, experiencing his or her life as an artifact, as molten glass being twirled and pinched into a shape and set to cool, at once capacious and suspenseful; but no one is more a *Homo faber* than a homosexual, and that's the way I see Guy. It would be vain, of course, to suggest that this creativity is praiseworthy — I know you wouldn't put up with that — but it's not his ambition, it's his response."[13]

"Gay is gay," she replied.

"Look, Charly, sexuality's unruly force, roiling beneath those polite middle-class conventions of ours, is a recurrent theme we had all better get used to. We are all prisoners of our desires. No one can choose whom or what they desire, that should be pretty obvious. Otherwise, in the world that we live in, probably everyone would choose to be heterosexual and not have to deal with all the horrible things people do. I mean, why in heaven's name would anyone choose to be homosexual in a world where people are reviled and bullied for being so? It should be pretty clear Guy had no choice."[14]

"Listen, sweetheart, get used to this idea: I'm not out to indict humanity and say, 'Who are these awful people?' I'm saying we have to accept the truth of who we are. I can't stand him, and he can't stand me."

"So gays just irk you," he said, annoyed. "You just regard them as some rhinestone distractions in your peripheral life; in other words, of what earthly use are gays?"

"Rely on it, she said icily. They sat in silence, eyes wandering in opposite directions.

"You sound a little hostile, you know," he said quietly.

"I know. I have to tell you about it sometime." She changed the topic. "You know what they called me at the office in New York?" He shook his head.

"Cobra," she smirked.

"Cobra?"

"Yeah. I wasn't sure if it was an insult or a sign of respect, so thanks to Maureen Dowd, I figured I'd read up on cobra traits. 'The cobra, she wrote in one of her columns, 'lives near towns where mice and rats abound.' Well, that fit New York, of course. 'Cobras have extensive tissues that store fat.' Yep, that fit too, for me at least. 'The venom of cobras acts powerfully on the nerves of those it attacks.' Clearly."[15]

"I didn't know cobras preferred attacking gays," he said.

She snorted.

"Is that why they fired you?"

"Probably. I guess I was a major-league viper at times."

"So it's more than just Guy?"

"Yeah." The silence began again. She rolled little balls of paper from her napkin.

"Well, Guy is willing to show you Giverny. Tomorrow, if you like."

"Jesus! You're kidding."

"I'm sure he wants to make up, and he is well schooled in Monet."

"Well, well. That could be interesting. Why not? Looks like we're the sole survivors in here anyway, and I need a little sunshine." Jean-Michel began to rise when she reached for his arm. She looked at him painfully and quietly whispered, "I'm damn near broke, you know. I still don't have a job, my parents and dog are gone, I can't sleep, and I have an illegitimate daughter hanging out in Texas, arriving here shortly with her jailbird boyfriend. I'm wandering around a foreign city with one real pal, you, whose nephew I just about cold-cocked, and now I'm challenging you to a pissing contest. I'm just so goddamn depressed. How is it that some of my sweetest memories — my little daughter, good ol' Mom and Dad, the smell of the ranch, my dogs — all come back when I'm low and alone, and sting me so bad?" She sighed. "How did this all happen?"

"I don't know," he muttered, reaching across the table to take her hand. He squeezed it. "But I learned long ago that when such things happen, such things pass. Do me a favor: let's see what tomorrow will bring."

Charly sighed. "Skin-scorching ash from Mordor."

CHAPTER 9

$=$ GIVERNY $=$

The weather had been mostly rainy and gray for days, but the morning of Charly's trip to Giverny was sunny. When the train arrived she had fully expected to see Guy waiting at the Giverny station as she descended. He was nowhere in sight. The crowd of tourists poured out of the station—a modest, house-like building in white with French doors—and clambered aboard the bus for the twenty-minute ride to Giverny. The station quickly emptied except for a thin, older man dressed in a tan suit and straw hat, who stood staring in her direction.

"Ms Brooks?" he called politely.

"Yes?"

"Guy," he said approaching, "our mutual friend, has succumbed to an unfortunate bout with the flu. He asked if you would be kind enough to excuse him and allow me to serve as your guide today at Giverny. My name is Jerôme Dumas."

"Guy is ill?" she said, relieved. "Well, it's the time of year, I suppose. Paris is filled with strangers…and their diseases. I hope he feels better."

"Certainly," Dumas paused to study her face. "He is rather fragile, but a wonderfully intelligent young man," he said, guiding her to the taxi stand, evidently satisfied with her physiognomy.

"So I'm told," she said coolly. "It was kind of you to offer."

"You are very welcome, I am sure. Guy and I share a great deal of affection for the impressionists." He signaled for a taxi. "And what is it that you would like to explore, ah, Ms Brooks."

"You can call me Charly."

"Certainly. Charly, yes of course." He smiled congenially, displaying capped teeth, even and squarish, but did not reciprocate. "Is there anything in particular you are interested in seeing?"

By now Charly understood considerably more about her brief encounter with Guy: he had betrayed signs of his homosexuality, and this man was in all likelihood his lover. Jean-Michel, if he knew, had not bothered to mention Dumas. She had serious misgiving about her new guide to Giverny; it was like throwing over a date with Hitler to go bowling with Mussolini.

"Well, my plans were to get a small taste of Monet's life here at Giverny. That is not so unusual, I hope," she said, testing the waters. He nodded his head approvingly. "Even the most modest of art lovers, Ms Brooks, wish to imagine themselves standing near the lily ponds and walking over the famous Japanese bridge to experience what Monet saw."

A taxi soon pulled up. Dumas took Charly's arm, smiled, and gently helped her into the old Renault. "Unfortunately, it is midsummer and terribly crowded, unseemly so," he sighed. He gave directions to the driver in rapid French, then turned to her. "The irony is somehow lost on the French and other innocent pilgrims who believe the spirit of Monet can be found among the horde at this enchanting place during these sunny afternoons," he said in thickly accented English.

"Are there any Monet family members left in Giverny?"

"I don't know, actually," he confessed. "It's a quiet little place off season." He leaned forward and asked the driver to slow down.

"Is that the reason Monet chose Giverny?"

"Solitude? Perhaps. There wasn't much here," he said sitting back. "Well, poor man, he bequeathed us quite the contrary. I regret to say that now you will find his home a tumultuous activity of tour buses, taxies, lines, souvenir shops, ice cream, and all species of humanity in search of aesthetic perspicacity. But in all likelihood, I'm afraid to say, neither you nor they will find it."

She pursed her lips. "No better than the lines at Versailles, I guess. I just thought—"

He interrupted, "I didn't mean to create any despair, Ms Brooks, just a gentle reminder that the world has approximately three times more people in it than when Monet was industriously working in his garden. And in a manner of speaking, at least Monet got what he sought—money, lots

258

of it. His notoriously calculating manipulation of the art market—he created more than 2,500 paintings, you see—"

She interrupted again, "Significantly less than Picasso, of course."

"Significantly. I see you know the artists well, Ms Brooks."

"I wouldn't say well, but I've read quite a bit."

"Ah, certainly. Accomplished." He smiled.

"Have you had much experience with Americans?" she asked.

"Yes, I have business connections in New York."

"I live in New York. Did you like it? The people, I mean."

"Americans are like big friendly dogs," he smiled, "constantly looking for affection. Unfortunately, they also respond much too quickly to other basic instincts."

"Um-hm," she said, conjuring an image of herself as a St. Bernard in pumps. "We're all pretty much the sons and daughters of peasants who were mistreated elsewhere on Earth."

"Unfortunately, lacking the more cultured refinements of Europe, particularly in art."

"Professor Levasseur doesn't think so."

He grunted condescendingly, "Levasseur? I have heard of him. I wasn't aware art was his area."

"Probably not, but that was his opinion."

He grimaced. "No artist, Ms Brooks, to use Johnson's distinction, can possibly be made who is not born with inspiration. This, as you say, is not necessarily the product of peasants."

"I didn't realize you knew Professor Levasseur. I assume you mean he isn't 'inspired'? Or perhaps I should say half-inspired," she said coldly. "He is only half American." She loaded her shotgun.

"I was speaking of artists, and the extension is correct: he has no appreciation of art. Therefore, I don't lend much credence to anything he would have to say about art, particularly when he is drinking; in this case, however, he and I are in agreement.

"Do you know Colonel de Monteaux?" she asked.

"De Monteaux?" He hesitated. "Why do you ask?"

"He's a good friend of Professor Levasseur."

"Those two," he sighed. "De Monteaux comes from a very old and wealthy family in Paris, known to have fallen on hard times. He is now an art collector of dubious distinction in the Delft school, and is known to prowl around decrepit prisons for some strange reason."

"I guess you don't like them?"

"I have little reason not to, but I think you should be more circumspect about the company you keep." Both felt the tension rising and, considering the close confinement of the taxi, he tried to pull away. "Shouldn't we move on to a more enlightened topic? As I was saying, drawings and pastels set the precedent for what is now Monet's legacy, the second most visited site in France after Versailles."

"This car makes me tired," she said absentmindedly. "You know, tourism, lines, jet lag."

"I don't sleep well either. Age, I suppose. I've lost the sleep of innocents."

"You should get a goose-down pillow."

He pondered. "Do you think so? I never thought of that."

"I sleep on a mix of goose feather and down pillows. I've even been trying to save up for two more pure Hungarian goose-down versions, very soft and exotic."

"Modest aspirations."

"Yeah, they are, but in the absence of mugging baby geese, I am also being distracted by things like new Gucci dresses, poverty, and a bed that still lacks the requisite number of pillows."

Despite their close proximity, Charly found it more comfortable to gaze out the car window while speaking. He was direct; she would reply in kind. "It's strange in a way that people, someone like you, for example, loves art and seems so at home with the artists, and I—"

He put his hand lightly on her arm, and she turned back to look at him. "May I suggest a way of easing your dilemma, Ms Brooks, how you may look at the appreciation of the artist and his or her art?" She nodded agreement. "As you know about Monet, he was a difficult human being at times, cursing his staff, or all curled up in his blankets because he was frustrated with his work or it was a rainy day. Not someone you would deem a genius.

"But look at this way: If you wish to try to fathom the meaning of his skill, or a deeper understanding of the themes he chose, and the form, color, and perspective in his pictures, it would in my opinion be pointless for you to know in detail his life, to talk with him on the subject of art, of life and death, or to eat in that beautiful dining room with him every evening. You would be no closer to the solution of the inscrutability of their source and of their worth, since he himself, to tell you the truth, no longer knew them; they were all ceded to him with exact precision, like strange sea nymphs, you might say, muses on the tides of inspiration, which set about him. I'm sure what he should be able to tell you would bear no likeness to his creations, that is, the physical part of their construction. For example, such and such a landscape he had actually seen, such a cultivated plot of land he had once admired, and the like. But," he squeezed her arm gently, "his advice would contain few clues to the similarities that united them, the soul of which, though it must have been present once in his mind, since unaided he had chosen it and painted it, was, nevertheless, like you, Ms Brooks, probably nameless to him."

"You said you teach, right? Can I come to your classes? Could I learn things like that? It all just seems so far from my experience, and—"

He cut her off with a wave of his hand. "Like Descartes said, and Plato before him, few if any men think they lack common sense or in fact need more of it. Therefore, they believe, perhaps rightly, that art is simply a question of taste, *de gustibus*. Despite the criticism of my friends, but unlike them, I agree with Descartes. I have some faith in my own view of the universe. And if I did not so delight in the majestic scenes that are laid before us each day by that sovereign of all the old masters, Nature, I should come to believe that I had in me no appreciation of the beautiful whatsoever. So, Ms Brooks, you have some formidable allies in your common sense. Say what you think, it's your given right, just not out of ignorance," and he patted her gently on her arm.

"What do you think of Monet?" she asked.

"My perception of Monet is probably similar to the way I would describe you, Ms Brooks, keeping in mind our brief acquaintance: that is, a difficult nature, testy and moody, ceaselessly displeased with his, or in your case, her, work, although I confess I don't know what it is. Angry with intelligent but pretentious young men, or perhaps men in general, and probably an expert in the kitchen. My guess is that when either you or Monet are in such tempers, nobody dares or dared to speak a word or make a noise. And the tension would be broken only if and when you or he reappeared, beaming and full of fresh zeal for the day. But in the end, there is little question in my mind that both of you are blessed with courageous hearts."

Charly turned and stared silently at him. Dumas stared back with a slightly crooked grin.

Just then the taxi pulled into the parking lot. "Oh, my God," she moaned. "Look at the lines!"

Monet's Death

On 5 December 1926, in his bed overlooking his gardens, Monet died of pulmonary sclerosis. He was eighty-six. Blanche Hoschedé, his faithful stepdaughter, his younger son, Michel, and his old friend Clemenceau were at his side. Appropriately, it was Clemenceau who closed his eyelids and lingered to hold his hand.

Monet was buried in the Giverny cemetery alongside Alice Hoschedé, her first husband, Ernest, their two daughters, Suzanne and Marthe, and Monet's elder son Jean. Monet had insisted early on that the occasion be simple. Thus only about fifty people attended the ceremony, which was strictly non-religious, as Monet had requested. There were no eulogies or flowers, and nothing to mark the tomb but a single shaft of wheat, a reminder of his undying love for the land. France had lost one of its great citizens.

> *How difficult it is to paint...it really is torture. Last autumn I burned six paintings with the dead leaves from my garden. It is enough to make you lose all hope, yet I would not want to die without having said everything I have to say, or at least tried to say.*
>
> Claude Monet

VI

Maurice Ravel

CHAPTER I

═══ AT THE CRAZY HORSE ═══

Sex for sale can most readily be found along the congested sidewalks of Montmartre.[1] It is a chaotic place, noisy and crowded, where the fumes of idling cars fuse with summer's humidity and the night's bright lights. This concoction of milling crowds and their pheromones creates an ambiance along Rue Saint-Denis[2] that visitors describe as "having fun." The loud, brassy music mingling with the odor of stale beer wafting through the doors of erotic bars is the same routine as in most European cities, like Hamburg's Reeperbahn or Amsterdam's Red-light District. It is expected, akin to the mold gathering in the crevices of their famous cheeses, adding a pungent taste, rank smell, and a shiver of excitement to the lives of inhabitants of otherwise jaded cities.

Up and down Rue Saint-Denis, like a gauntlet of vice, muscular lotharios and black men in Gucci hustle gawking tourists into the bars, calling out to any eyes they can capture. Sidling up to shy victims, they whisper of prurient sex, champagne, and adventure inside. Embarrassed young honeymooners and grandparents alike giggle and timidly scurry away, while others, mostly prowling males and sauntering teens, loft leering glances promoting their own darker versions of chance and seduction.

Colonel de Monteaux stepped out of the crowd and walked lamely across Avenue George V through stalled traffic to a street-level lobby guarded by doormen dressed as Royal Canadian Mounted Police, and made his way downstairs into the modest, 420-seat theater decorated in sumptuous red with an Art Deco flavor. The stage, flanked by nude golden statues partially hidden behind a silver curtain, was barely adequate to the task. Signs everywhere proclaimed, THERE IS ONLY ONE REAL CRAZY HORSE.[3] The crowd was mixed: about three men to every woman. One could assume there were no families about; however, the colonel believed that the shows were necessary for any young man's education, and to their credit he saw a few parents shepherding excited teenage boys. He chose to stand by the bar with its veterans and locals, as it gave the best view. On his right a Swiss engineer whom he had seen on occasion, and on his left one of the most beautiful brunettes he had come across in Paris, accompanied by a gentleman even older and seemingly richer than himself. As he scanned the audience, a hand waved from a table across the smoky room. He picked his way among the crowd to Jean-Michel's side.

Jean-Michel took the colonel by the arm and pulled him down into an empty chair. "They are on any moment," he said impatiently. His glass empty, Jean-Michel signaled the waiter.

No sooner had they begun to talk than a siren went off, louder and louder. Then trumpets, martial drums, and the voice of a British sergeant barking commands. The glittering curtain pulled open, bright lights were lowered on the audience, and there they were, the famous line of eighteen proud-breasted girls in shiny boots, white gloves, great beefeater hats, and nothing else save tiny black triangular patches over hairless crotches. Lifting their knees high to military music, these soldiers marched, saluted, and about-faced, mesmerizing the crowd with jiggling alabaster breasts, rose-colored nipples, and heart-shaped derrieres.[4]

Jean-Michel whistled and clapped with the others, one of his occasional cigarettes dangling from the corner of his mouth, while the colonel, a man given to moneyed reserve, drank in the motion of nubile bodies in rhythm. When the sexual routine was complete and the music abated, Jean-Michel leaned close to the colonel's ear and said over the noise of an excited crowd, "There's someone I want you to meet." He teetered on the edge of drunkenness, stinking of smoke, beer, and sweat. The colonel nodded, and they left for the subterranean offices of one of the most invigorating music halls in France, the Crazy Horse Saloon.

The Crazy Horse isn't really a music hall at all. Cabaret-size, its brochure boasts the title of theater and "the most beautiful femmes fatales in the world." Since opening in 1951, the Crazy Horse has become an institution in Paris nightlife, and its lighting effects have been copied worldwide. Its origins lie partly in striptease, partly in a French talent for sensuality, but it has little in common with the Folies-Bergère or Moulin Rouge tradition with their great lines of tourists marching in and out and promotional drinks for tour guides and bus drivers.

Located on the swank Avenue George V, across from Yves Saint-Laurent, The Crazy Horse's high style is very much its own, continuously under the guidance of founder and owner Alain Bernard.[5]

As they entered his plush office, Bernard stepped around his desk to give Jean-Michel a warm hug. "You old pig, must you always be cajoled with little goodies to bring you back?" He held Jean-Michel at arm's length, scrutinizing him up and down, wrinkling his nose. "You've put on weight and smell like a keg. And still those damned sneakers!" Bernard himself was casually elegant, in a black shirt with streaks of an orange color like the lighting effects in his show, neatly pressed slacks, and soft leather shoes. He was a tall man with doubting eyes, close-cropped hair, and a long face. In his seventies, fit and calm, he looked a good twenty years younger, with the tanned health of an aging movie star. Since the beginning, it had been all his — his design, his property, and performers including his mistresses.[6]

"No excuses, Maestro. Time runs off for hours, amusing itself in the shadows, and never comes when I call," Jean-Michel offered sheepishly, struggling for sobriety. "But I would like you to meet an old friend," and clasping the colonel's arm under his own, Jean-Michel introduced him at length. De Monteaux grinned uncomfortably at Jean-Michel's familiar and expansive comments. He tried to act as formal as the occasion permitted, since naked dancers seemed to be everywhere in the hallways. De Monteaux explained, wryly at times, how much the Crazy Horse had meant to his lonely nights over the years, and the voluptuousness of Bernard's young women.

"You're no doubt familiar with artillery, Colonel, so you should know that to win my war with the competition, I'm looking for cannons," Bernard explained. "But my 'cannon' is an aggressive girl who doesn't have fear in her eyes: a sparkling, brilliant, bewitching sorceress. One in fifty, you might say; I can recognize her in a instant," he explained earnestly. "First, she must have marvelous breasts. Then she must have trained already as a dancer. And she must be a 'good girl.' And," he took the colonel's lapel between his fingers in camaraderie, "I don't find them, they find me! We have girls from all over Europe." One voluptuous young woman lingered in the hallway and eyed the men. "Those Czech girls," he signaled with a nod of his head, "are crazy, but they have strong temperament and personality. They're great onstage. Offstage, of course, they're gold diggers. She's just eighteen; the oldest is twenty-eight. You see, Colonel, I want to provoke the public by putting them in the path of these cannons. If we give them their cleaning woman, they won't come. They want a dream money can't buy, inaccessible because of me," he smiled, "Pygmalion. But I try not to fall in love with my Galateas!"[7]

The conversation fell momentarily silent. "So you called," Jean-Michel said. "What's this about a splendid recording of Boléro?"

Bernard turned to the colonel. "Perhaps Jean-Michel has told you, Colonel, that I am a dabbler in discography, but Pierre, a mutual friend of Jean-Michel's and mine, has collected music over thirty years and specializes in French artists, particularly Debussy, Ravel, or what some call the impressionists. He has found an extraordinarily rare recording of Ravel's *Boléro*." He hesitated. "Bolero is a generic name, of course. Perhaps you are interested in French music, Colonel?"

Jean-Michel broke in rudely, "De Monteaux is far more interested in Michele of the Magnificent Mammaries than Ravel, I assure you. Right, Colonel?" he quipped, a whiskey or so from slurring.

"Jean-Michel often drinks before he thinks," snapped the colonel, creating an awkward pause. "To my knowledge, Monsieur Bernard, Ravel isn't French, but Basque and Swiss. I prefer Debussy," he smiled aggressively, ever eager to wage unconditional war on anyone's opinion.

Bernard stood his ground. "Ravel's mother was French Basque, Colonel," he explained politely.

"I'm speaking of French blood," the colonel volleyed back, "'de Sanguine,' I believe the lawyers call it. Ravel was Basque, born in Saint Jean-de-Luz, not French, not Spanish—and his music shows it." Irritated by Bernard's assertion, he continued the charge, "Even his mother grew up in Madrid, barely literate in French!"

"Surely, Colonel, you don't mean to imply that a man who lived in this country, Paris, in fact, for over five decades, is not French, even with a Swiss father and Basque mother. I think most would agree, Colonel, that

268

Ravel is one of France's great national treasures," looking to Jean-Michel for affirmation.

"I don't agree, Bernard," the colonel replied. "If you doubt me, take it up with the Basque. And Stravinsky himself called Ravel 'the Swiss watchmaker.' To my mind he was simply a diminutive, cat-loving fag who stumbled into a single composition that itself would never have survived into this generation without the aid of that American movie '10'. Nothing he wrote could ever compare to Debussy's *L'Aprés-midi d'une faune* or *Clair de Lune*. Ravel's emotional life, if he had one, was spent adoring his mother."

"So," Bernard said incredulously, still trying to recover from the surprise attack, "if I understand you correctly, *Boléro* is a 'stumble' and its composer a 'common fag'?"

"A fortunate stumble, yes," de Monteaux said confidently. "Ravel's lifestyle speaks for itself. He was an artificial man."

"You and I are at odds, Colonel." Bernard was struggling to retain his composure. "Ravel, in my opinion, was one of Europe's most successful composers, and *Boléro* was not his only orchestral masterpiece; even you must admit that his music for the ballet *Daphnis et Chloé* had great charm, and there is no evidence he was a homosexual."

The colonel leaned forward on his cane. "Perhaps your opinion stems less from instruction than from music for your topless dancers?" he retorted. Bernard began to squint at the colonel as if to pierce him with his eyes, but de Monteaux took little notice. "I assume you don't recall that when a woman of advanced years was shouting 'Rubbish!' after a performance of *Boléro*, one thinks of Ravel commenting, 'That old lady got the message.'[8]

"And did you even know, Monsieur Bernard," he continued haughtily, "that a British study published recently[9] suggests that Ravel's *Boléro*, reputed to be the most often played composition in his repertoire, was the work of a sick mind? Of course you didn't," he gestured about the room condescendingly, "there are no books in the room. But for your edification, a Dr. Cybulska, the author of the study, claims that *Boléro*, repeated eighteen times without change during the course of the piece, if you can stand to count them, demonstrates that Ravel was quite possibly succumbing to Alzheimer's disease. She claims, legitimately, I believe, that perseveration—in case you don't know, an obsession with repeating words and

269

gestures — is one of the more notable symptoms of the pathology. In other words, Monsieur Bernard, the repetitive nature of the score's principal theme, which you and others no doubt worship as genius, is simply symptomatic of the degenerative condition beginning to overtake Ravel in his early fifties, a phenomenon not unlike the insane scientist making an unintended, but unique discovery."[10]

"You can't believe that– that!" Bernard stammered.

"Ravel died of a diseased brain, that's an irrefutable fact," the colonel replied.

Jean-Michel, embarrassed and anxious to escape the conflict, looked over toward Alain's desk for the recording. He wanted the subject changed before being summarily thrown out by what was rapidly becoming his former friend, "Is the recording here?" he mumbled.

"Unfortunately, no," Alain said, pursing his lips, not taking his eyes off the colonel. "Pierre brought it over last week but retrieved it yesterday. Perhaps," and he moved them firmly toward the door, "you should stop by."

The colonel abruptly limped away as if nothing had happened — the proverbial senior officer in command — and began scanning photographs on Alain's office wall. Suddenly he leaned closer to one of the photographs and peered intently at its figures. "My God, that's Salvador Dali with you!" he exclaimed.

Bernard eyed the colonel's back for a moment, determining his strategy. Simply kicking him was probably out of the question. Perhaps this pompous ass had crouched too close to the exploding shells of his past and should be pitied. Bernard was transfixed for a brief moment, then just as easily as the colonel, seemed to dismiss the altercation. "Of course, Colonel, I suppose you've never met him. Dali was a good friend of mine, must've come twenty times. Perhaps he enjoyed my *background* music," he practically shouted. The colonel turned and stared at him, but Alain returned to his subdued voice. "Dali used to say, 'The Crazy Horse girls are all virgins.' One evening he arrived and Andy Warhol was here — you've heard of him? Well, it's no matter. Dali said, 'Tonight the omens are not good.' He turned on his cane, not unlike yours, I might add, Colonel, and *left*. Elvis also came one night — I don't suppose you've met him either." The colonel tried to protest, but was ignored. "See, there he is in the picture," Bernard was saying. "He was an American singer, brought here by a mutual friend, you see. As I recall, Elvis asked for one of our dancers: 'I'll stay only if you give me a girl for the night.' I refused. So, the friend had to loan Elvis his fiancée." Bernard leered at him. "Perhaps I could locate an old whore or a young boy for you, Colonel, something to suit a military taste?" The colonel's face turned crimson. Jean-Michel stepped between them, but the onslaught continued. "Oh, and there's a photo of Gypsy Rose Lee," Bernard grinned menacingly at de Monteaux. "But some said she was senile, like most your age, Colonel."

Suddenly, a sloe-eyed brunette ripped in, naked except for her crotch patch, slippers, and orange-colored scarf tied loosely about her neck. She shot Bernard an intense look, abruptly turned, leaving a fragrance of lemons, and disappeared into the hallway. "A new girl, French," he said. He was about to continue his attack when the brunette peered around the door inquisitively. "Monsieur Bernard?"

Alain apologized, "Ah, gentlemen, my little chocolates call. And Colonel," he moved in close, eye to eye, again taking the colonel's lapel firmly between his fingers, "at times God speaks to all of us through music, even from the refrains of tormented little men like Ravel. Intelligent souls might surmise they were the most loved of His messengers, no matter what we might think of their habits." He turned and shook Jean-Michel's hand. "Sorry to see you leave," he said coldly.

The colonel looked at him. "Mephistopheles has his music too," he murmured dismissively, "like that filthy rap playing in your halls even now," and turned to depart, pushing Jean-Michel before him.

CHAPTER 2

═══ PIERRE ═══

Pierre's apartment, like a musty spinster, spoke silently of 19th-century origins, from its high-necked ceilings and lacy filigreed coping, to its mammoth cream-colored ceramic stove. It stood at attention like a tightly corseted woman, commanding the salon, a dusty, narrow dance hall. It was the kind of place where, in earlier days, the Hugos, Monets, and Ravels would have watched proudly from the security of their balcony doors the great events of Paris in the street below. Not much had changed except for the accumulating city grime, which in Pierre's case had settled so securely on his windowpanes that a crusty foundation sufficient for an urban reef had gathered.

The inner sanctum was occupied by obsolete furniture that seemed to set the stage, like shabby props for a defunct theater. From the wall in the living room, a moth-eaten lion's head peered savagely at a doleful-looking mannequin in the foyer, literally hung by her neck with a golden rope from the ceiling. Faded costumes and unusual hats—tricorne, bowler, top, and helmet, each reflecting the fashion of its period—lay casually about, as if their owners had been taken by surprise and beamed up to the mother ship of some tattered dimension of the Comédie Française. Pierre wore them about the apartment at times to fit his moods, which leaned more to the soundtrack of *Fame* than *Fanny*.

Yellowish newspapers were stacked throughout the apartment, those closest to seats serving as modest little tables, stained with bits and droppings of past meals. Other stacks sat lonesome—tall like mesas—and still others short with no apparent use. At the far end of the apartment, audio equipment braced the wall, black boxes and wires animated by dials and little blinking lights, sufficient to excite the envy of any electronics engineer intent on eavesdropping on the Elysées. When one scrutinized the room, however, the stacks of papers took on a more rigorous design, like that of a sound studio engineered to acoustic perfection.

Ferret-like in appearance and behavior, a heavy shock of black hair, clothed in Tide-less gray T-shirt and expired jeans, it was obvious that Pierre had never held a real job or loved an honest woman, but lived instead for his craft. Jean-Michel was one of Pierre's few friends since gymnasium days, the two having studied together in the States, and each shared the other's habitat like brothers.

"Jean-Michel, wait until you hear it!" Pierre gushed, ushering them from the hallway around the unfortunate mannequin into his inner sanctum, glancing suspiciously over his shoulder at the colonel. Pierre and Jean-Michel had spent untold hours listening and discussing the 20th century's greatest French composers. On their sophisticated equipment, the nuances of a recording, despite its age, sometimes allowed the trained ear to actually hear into the chamber of a recital more than a century in the past. They participated in moments of history, active imagination and closed eyes allowing them to sit in the presence of the greatest maestros. With luck, they heard one of the first renditions of an everlasting classic, or even a muffled cough of a duke or prince spanning the century.

Music, like literature, is often imperfectly transcribed, because of translation errors, dialects, or printing expediencies, to the point that great controversies exist over even a simple space between letters or notes. For example, the spaces between symbols or letters in ancient texts like the Bible were deleted to conserve paper. A phrase such as "heisnowhere" could be translated as "he is nowhere" or "he is now here"—a phrase that itself could give theologians anxiety for centuries. Similarly, music, so often written by hand, as Rousseau had done for his living, might have been transcribed by candlelight, perhaps mistaking a sixteenth note for a quarter note, based purely on the thickness of the point of a quill or the aging eyes of its transcriber, forever changing the intent of its composer.

Jean-Michel introduced the colonel, while Pierre, assuming the cordiality of a maître d'hôtel, responded with magnanimous gestures of hospitality toward a grimy-looking niche in the wall of his apartment, which served as a makeshift kitchen. Both visitors, caught off guard by this ludicrous proposal of refreshment, stumbled awkwardly through protestations of fullness to the moldering smells of Pierre's foul cupboards. The whole setting was more easily confused with a careless workbench, splotched with decomposing food of unpleasant fish-like odors, than a dinning area.

Pierre gestured to the lumpy, overstuffed furnishings at the rear of the apartment, enjoying the anticipation of his old friend and the audience of what appeared to be an educated aristocrat, anxious to play out his discovery in detail.

"Maid's day off?" Jean-Michel sighed, dislodging a cheese rind from his seat on the threadbare couch.

Selecting an oversized chair, the padding of which had receded over the years to reveal protruding springs, the colonel sat cautiously on its edge. Pierre's attempt at artistically arranging his suite according to a past burst of creative insight resulted in a stage-like presentation in which his intention was to place the furniture in a half circle as if facing an audience.

"Do you have experience with recording technology, Colonel?" Pierre said, sitting casually with one arm, stick-like, holding him in place on the protuberance of a tattered lounge chair, and fixing the colonel with an unnerving steady gaze. His black, deep-set eyes, large thin nose, and narrowly shaped head portrayed the confidence and poise of a Semitic surgeon in complete control of his profession—or through different eyes, a curious, ravenous bird.

The colonel, unsettled by the experience, surveyed this energetic little man before him, whose disturbing scent and fossil-like body made him involuntarily grimace. Yet there was something about Pierre: a question that possibly his intelligence was hidden by his demeanor, for it was not unusual that genius sought refuge in the discomfiture of others.

Jean-Michel moved to familiarize the two Parisians. "You'll find the colonel an avid student of anything truly worth studying."

The colonel raised his hand for him to stop. "Jean-Michel is too effusive...."

"He's a goddamn prince," Pierre shrugged. "Do you have knowledge of music?" he said, looking steadfastly at the colonel for an unequivocal answer.

"I confess, uh, Pierre, that I have had relatively little experience in the field of recording, but you'll find me attentive. However, I am ignorant of—"

"You mean no, correct?" Pierre interjected.

Expecting a blast from the colonel, Jean-Michel instinctively leaned back.

"I mean—" the colonel began petulantly, but once again Pierre interrupted.

"You mean that a man of your obvious intelligence and experience would find the engineering concepts very simple," Pierre offered, while de Monteaux retreated to a gratuitous smile. "Think of it this way, Colonel: recording editors are creating an illusion, essentially helping the composer bring his intentions to their absolute best. The interpreter, the musician, is a part in that chain. The whole recording process does not really help the musician much, but it creates an illusion for the listener, making him think that the piece was performed that way. Without editing, the whole piece could be in trouble; for example, every time you hear an imperfection on a recording, it is very distracting. It is frozen there, and after a few hearings you know it will happen before it does.[11] In short, the recording is documentary even when it comes to imperfections; it is history."

"Do you record?" the colonel asked innocently.

Jean-Michel could barely muffle a laugh. "He is one of the finest in Paris, Colonel."

"Thank you," Pierre said laconically. "Ironically, Colonel, even silence is an important part of music. Pauses in the piece, for example. For years when I listened the next morning to pauses I put in the previous evening, I wondered why I put in such short pauses. It took me a long time to figure it out."

"And?" The colonel sat forward transfixed by Pierre's expertise.

"And everything seemed the same. But what was different?

"The heartbeat is different, and so the whole sense of timing is different. In the evening my heartbeat is around one hundred fifteen, and in the morning it is around eighty. It's a biological clock, ticking inside. That clock guides the reaction to the pause length, and sometimes conflicts with or changes the subjective sense of timing. So, we have to correct these things and average them out before we ask the artist for approval of the edited master."

"Wonderful!" bellowed the colonel, for he was enjoying himself immensely, absorbing the nuances of this technology for his considerable databank, to be used as ammunition against unwitting souls.

"You have a collection?" the colonel wondered.

"Yes, but it's locked away. I have some interesting CDs over there, though," and signaled with his thumb toward the shelves, "that you would like to hear."

"You don't say!"

Pierre got up and went over to the electronics shelf, picked a CD from his collection, and waved it at the colonel. "Here is Tennyson, recorded in 1890, where he reads from 'The Charge of the Light Brigade' in a mournful drone, accompanied by pops on the soft wax cylinder that sound like hoof beats thundering down into the jaws of death." He smiled at the colonel's attentiveness. "And here is Robert Browning, recorded the year he died—"

"1889."

"Exactly. He sounds quite as mad and frenetic through the static of time as you might expect."

"You two seem to be getting on well enough," Jean-Michel interrupted, "so if you don't mind, Charly mentioned that she and her daughter would stop by Chrysalis to say hello. May I take the Aubort recording?"

"And the colonel?" Pierre asked defensively. "How about our guest?"

"I've got to give a lecture to a group of American tourists at Shakespeare and Company."[12] They looked at him blankly, as though earning a living was somehow superfluous to the moment. "Well, later," Jean-Michel grumped. Taking no interest in his farewell, Pierre and the colonel offered only perfunctory good-byes.

CHAPTER 3

═══ ON CHRYSALIS ═══

Meeting friends and relatives on incoming flights usually has its own rewards—if they show up. If they don't, however, disappointment turns to anxiety, which turns to a mixture of spoiled plans, fear, and bewilderment. Charly waited at the gate until it seemed all were off the plane, and then asked the flight crew if any more passengers were left. The answer was no. There were no more flights scheduled from New York that afternoon, and the counter agents refused to reveal the passenger list for that evening. She had no choice but to return to her hotel, worried and wondering.

There was a message waiting for her at her hotel: Jodie and Randy had missed the flight and would be arriving on Saturday, at the same scheduled flight time. The message also said: "Got held up," leaving Charly to guess whether it was traffic or Billy the Kid. She was pissed and disappointed, a common phenomenon among mothers of teenage daughters.

After Charly was fired, shifting vacations from New Hampshire to Paris was poorly received by Jodie. A trip to Europe was a dream for most, but a world away geographically and psychologically for Americans, and for teenagers it usually didn't include the company of man-friends. But Jodie had the pluck and ease of her grandfather, plus the constitution of Texas leather. Randy was coming. Period. She had paid her dues two summers ago by surviving a Caribbean cruise with her mother. It had turned out to be nothing but a lurching mall in drag, and a bad case of sore ankles.

The trip to Paris had caught Charly in the process of cleaning out Jodie's old room at her apartment. As with most moves, each forgotten little item uncovered from a shoebox or back shelf had become a poignant memory. There came that moment, she knew, when kids were somehow grown up. They were as tall as you, and their rooms still composed of teenage chaos.

Pooh and the dinosaur books, however, had been relegated to higher and higher shelves until finally they were jettisoned. A new page of family life had begun, and Jodie's battered trophies and paraphernalia, which had survived her mother's earlier purges, were dumped unceremoniously in with the trash of strangers.

Now Jodie was flying to Paris with a man-friend and a strong sense of entitlement. Charly called Jean-Michel for some promised company, and made a mental note to remind Jodie that she would be responsible for paying her own college tuition.

Charly and Jean-Michel were seated comfortably on the deck of his houseboat, warmed by the afternoon sun and enjoying cloudless skies. They were accompanied by the calls of noisy wheeling seagulls overhead, and cruising ducks along the river, quacking for a handout.

He was on the phone. "Yes, she can come too! I'm throwing myself a party on the boat next week…no, no, I don't want any presents…oh, Astérix always appreciates a good bone. And I have a surprise guest!" Jean-Michel hesitated. "No, we're not together anymore, um-hm…it's, ah, someone new. Right. No, I agree…." He smiled, giving a wary look at Charly, and then began drawing a map in the air to his caller. "Okay, yes, yes…exactly, you can't miss it. Black. The one with the palm tree and deck chairs on the stern, her name is *Chrysalis,* pier number seven, moored just after…right…nine o'clock sharp. I know that means ten or eleven to your Chilean friends, but try to come on time; it's difficult to get the drunks off the pier after two a.m., the security people lock up the gates. Of course…of course, you don't. Okay, see you then. *À bientôt.*" Jean-Michel pocketed his cell phone and returned to his conversation.

"As I was saying…" he looked perplexed. "What was I saying?"

"Previous girlfriend, I believe," she said snidely. "You know, that age-old problem of an ex-sweetheart moving on to someone popular."

He looked bemused. "History, my dear. Not worth relating. I thought—"

"It was barges, remember? Living in Europe," she prompted, averting any tiresome descriptions involving his former trysts.

278

"Come on," he said, getting up, "it's getting cool, and we need some more drinks; let's go below." They took their glasses and climbed down the passageway to the salon.

"I can't get over how nice this barge is. Beautiful!" she said, surveying the boat's rich interior. "You don't kid around," knowing that it belonged in some fashion to the colonel.

"Astérix and I love our boat." He was embarrassed to admit it was not his. He had, after all, the intention of offering to buy it if the money were somehow to materialize.

"How much?" she asked curiously.

"Oh, let's see, you can buy a seventy- to eighty-foot barge, already converted to living quarters, anywhere from $100,000 to $150,000."

"Like this?" she exclaimed. "Things are different back home."

"Different?"

"Yeah, imagine if Starbucks were allowed to set the prices on everything, and you've got daily life in New York."

"Well, it sort of came like this through a good friend; you get two bedrooms, at least one bathroom, a large stateroom or saloon, a galley, and a diesel engine. Most of the stuff," he yawned, "belongs to a friend who's out of town." They sat in the salon on tan leather couches arranged in a large conversation circle that Elsie de Wolfe [13] might have pronounced as sincere, with common sense, light, and simplicity.

There were no photographs, except one, in an elaborate silver frame, of a playful blonde girl posing with a beach ball.

Chrysalis was a testament to androgyny, a black steel barge with the lingering scent of charred wood from its coal-hauling days, while warm and sensuous in its décor. Jean-Michel longed to have pride of ownership and justly impress Charly, but his were only squatter's rights. The colonel paid little attention; it was only those with money who seem to treat such value with discreet disinterest.

Jean-Michel had gotten up to put on a CD of Ravel's music, remoting it to one of his favorite pieces, and continued to the small galley, well lighted, shiny and as functional as the space shuttle. She called to him, "What's the downside?'

"You can't sink a house. Watch the valves in the toilet. Have you tried listening to the French composers yet?"

She turned to look over her shoulder at him. "Was I just remoted?!"

"What?" he called.

"You! One minute you're acting like a barge captain, and the next you're discussing French composers." No response. "Did you watch the 'Eurovision Song Contest' last night?"

He stepped from the galley with drinks and hors d'oeuvres. "No. But in case you haven't noticed—and to do otherwise you would have to be stoned—I like, despite my years in the States, most things French, particularly food and music. Goes with the job, even the cheese that Americans claim smells like moldy socks" and handed her a plate of rank Boulette d'Avesnes.[14] She blanched.

"Stoned? Have you ever been stoned?" she asked, pushing the cheese back across the coffee table. "I thought you were supposed to 'just say no.'"

"You're kidding, right? Look what just saying no did for addicts."

"What?"

"Nothing. I mean, I was just trying to make a point—you know, like what 'have a nice day' did for mental health." He reached for the cheese. Astérix returned from the galley, circled once, and strategically positioned himself between the two. He assumed his most attentive position and gazed longingly at the balls of coagulated udder milk.

"Besides, I thought we'd already had this discussion, at my expense, I might add. Do you mean 'stoned' or 'smashed'? You already had your fun with my habits on Victor Hugo day." He reached down and fondled Astérix's ears.

"Pick your poison. You know what I mean," she said.

"You know there is no question that I drink a bit, particularly, usually . . ." and he stopped. She knew all she needed to know from the episode in the park with Klaus.

"I assume people drink too much for a reason," she said, "and you have something that hides in your shadows. It's disconcerting to someone like me who doesn't know you well, and likes you a lot."

"A lot?"

"Sorry, didn't mean to scare you, but it's hard to tell how intriguing—or even menacing?"

"Menacing? You mean like mutilated bodies of young women down in the hold?" Jean-Michel studied his glass. "Sorry. What can I say?" He nibbled a ball of cheese and looked up. "Do you know why I do what I do?"

"I know what you do, I think. But, no, I don't know why you do it, though you obviously do it very well, Professor." It was a compliment, in its way. She sipped her wine, leaning forward from the chair, chin in hand, and waited.

"That's deceiving. I think what we humans are is difficult to explain in any of us. For example, the lives of these famous French that we take such satisfaction in rummaging through, poking around their laundry to sniff at their vanity and debauchery, who, very much like us, nonetheless write, paint, or otherwise fascinate mankind with their talents. I need to know what happened, need to know how at odds with themselves they were, how they survived it, or didn't. Listen," and with an invisible baton, he began conducting the music surrounding them. "It is Debussy," he said, eyes closed, "mellifluous," his voice dropped off to a shrug; "but what in heaven's name did this ingenious man do that drove his beautiful young wife to point a pistol at her breast and shoot herself? How can a composer of such wonderful music be a beast that drives his wife to attempt suicide?"

"Maybe she was a royal bitch."

He reached over and poured himself another glass of wine. "Maybe. Don't we all qualify?"

"No."

"Well, I study them because it eases my disappointment with myself. How much like us they really are."

"Yeah? Well, not me."

He gave her a cynical look. "Have you read Proust?"

"Not yet. That's the third time you've asked me. Is there a message, or just another senior moment?" He stared. She added, "We're not talkin' Harry Potter, you know."

He sat with an amused look: "Again, sorry. May I?" He filled her glass. "Proust can be a little tough to follow, but he is still worth reading." She wrinkled her nose. "I'll assume that is a no," he said. "Anyway, the artists in Proust's work, for example, are the only characters who are built up in the reader's esteem instead of being broken down. Just thought you should know, in case you finish reading about Muggles World. The highest place in Proust's spiritual hierarchy belongs to the creative artists; below them come the interpreters of art and the aesthetes, or as Proust calls them 'the celibates of art' who are limited to the appreciation of the works of others. That's what I am..." he took a sip of his wine and paused.

"Which is? You certainly aren't celibate," she retorted.

"Just curious; a self-appointed provincial hack with few nourishing qualities. On the other hand, our society doesn't understand these creations and spends its time pursuing different forms of vanity."

"Vanity?"

"You know, a nifty Rolex or pearl-colored SUV. Like Proust said, 'striving after wind.'

"I'd be happy with a pearl anything."

"Um-hm. Listen," he shrugged, "don't get me wrong: everyone needs a stunning pair of socks at Christmas. Nonetheless, despite the great ones' tribulations, they rose from the greedy masses and created! Not some common backyard variety of creation, but the real, enduring essence of the perfect aspirations of our species that might prove us to be very distant cousins of the creators." He gestured toward the CD player, "Was Debussy or Ravel uniquely able to create sensuous harmony, or would any of us six billion brutes do?"

"Sorry, I'm not a brute. Perhaps you're drinking in the wrong places."

"Let me assure you, they are not the ones planning wars and pillaging the pockets of the poor." And he shook his head.

"Anyway, when those illustrious creators, the altered egos, are put to composing music, painting sunsets, designing fashion, writing poetry, leading people, what are they doing? Where does that uniqueness come from? At that supreme moment of true creation, are they as close to God as possible? Why did they produce humanity's finest art? Were they mere tools, or the source of pleasures released into our midst by God to placate our miseries and remind us of our genesis?"

"I doubt much divinity rubbed off," she said.

"All right, but I would like — no, love — to be one of these people. Inspired."

"Inspired? How about tortured?"

"Valid point, it is a different life. You know, Picasso once said something

282

to the effect that 'The cat eats the bird; Picasso eats the cat; painting eats Picasso.' It is the obsession, the compulsive behavior, that carries so many over the brink. I never will be one, of course," he said sadly. "I can only mess around in what they were and what they did, but I will never make the inner sanctum; I can only help preserve them for others. When I drink, or do a little hash, I get swept up in the magnificence of their creations." He paused again and clicked his remote. "Now listen...listen," he leaned back in his chair. "It's Ravel's *Pavane pour une Infante Défunte*.[15] Is it Ravel speaking to us through his music by telling us what he has heard mysteriously whispered into his mind?" He closed his eyes and soaked in the music, then spoke. "Some people thought he was writing about the death of a young princess, a Sleeping Beauty, perhaps. But, sadly, he said he was writing about the passing away of that kind of music."

"Maybe it's God speaking to us directly through Ravel, simply a call from heaven, and fate decides who will answer the phone?" she said.

"You know what Debussy believed?" She shook her head. "Well, something like 'One has to tell oneself that when it comes to art we are nothing, merely the instrument of some destiny, and we have to allow it to fulfill itself.'"

"So how do you know if you are one of the creative ones?" she asked.

"Debussy was making the point to Chausson, I think, whom he was actually criticizing, that you have to let yourself go, allow enough play to that mysterious force that guides us toward the true expression of a feeling."

"So," she said, "if I come up with singing cats or flying chandeliers, I can expect a good musical? Or do I have to wait for the force to be with me?"

"Probably do, but I think you already have to be called to the phone." He winked. "You know, if you are Andrew Lloyd Webber, you got it; if you don't, then dedicated, single-minded searching only weakens it, nothing left to do but just take in a good soccer game or tit show...sorry.

"But what is it that wells up inside us and makes us want to cry when we see or hear beautiful things—with or without the aid of drugs—as simple as a sweet song, the death of an innocent animal, or a setting sun? Are we the refugees from Eden having a glimpse of home?"

"Do you ever pray?" she asked.

He chuckled. "All French pray. We are Catholics and love all that pomp and sense of occasion, but really," he thought for a moment, "we just save it for emergencies."

"I know at lot of people who pray," she said defensively.

He sat up. "Not knocking prayer, my dear, and I don't believe it is just for the devout, but most of us use it as a form of bargaining, with saints or even God Himself, sort of a rough familiarity, in my opinion. The tone of voice, I mean the internal tone of voice."

"Like the voice that says it's time for a trip to Ben and Jerry's?" she said.

"Ah, no, it's the tone that we adopt like a stubborn child, our prayers should be granted on the face of it—you know, it's elementary logic: 'Mother isn't well; please make her better' or, 'I really need the promotion,' that sort of thing. Longing for ice cream doesn't qualify. It is what I would call 'a winning style,' and it demands an equally flexible attitude on the part of the saint or the Man Himself. Don't you think?"

"To tell the truth, I haven't had all that many prayers answered," she sighed. "We have the religion of healthy-mindedness in the States."

"Hm?"

"You know, Californians. They live the proverbial 'cheer up, the earthquake may never happen' routine. Seems God just has it out for the Pakistanis. In spite of all the evidence, we Americans keep trying to convince ourselves that happiness is the natural state of our race. I don't know about the French, but our kind was meant to conquer and work and laugh and spend, not sit around head in hand. But, when things get a little rough, and talking the talk doesn't seem to help, then…"

"Then?"

"It's time to jump off a cliff. More people kill themselves than are killed."

"An exciting few seconds in the air, then you're free. Doesn't sound so bad."

"Do you ever think of suicide?"

"A shortcut to the pearly gates?" He shrugged, "Or hell. Everybody does. But the sincere use weapons. Cowards alcohol," he slowly wagged his head, he was becoming bleary-eyed. "It is slow, but pleasant in its own way. Beats

284

having your brains splattered all over the wall by a bullet for some poor bucket to clean up and flush down the sewer."

"Yuck! How about a silver Cadillac with leather seats, a pitcher of margaritas, and some sweet music; then just press the remote on the garage doors?"

"Will a twelve-year-old rusty Renault and skipping Walkman do?"

"Yeah, I see what you mean: it could look pretty tacky in the papers."

"Well, I will most likely end up dying the traditional death of the French atheist: on the floor, like all those bourgeois scenes, screaming for a priest to come hear my act of contrition for all those sneaky sins, and save me from an eternity of ingenious torments. What about you?"

"Suicidal? Maybe, but I'm not at the weapons stage. I doubt I ever will be. I have a daughter to care for, and, with some luck, a grandchild or two to look after and love. But your life looks so full; maybe you won't be famous, but hardly something you'd kill yourself over, unless I've seriously misjudged. Obviously, there's something you don't want to tell me, and it also—obviously—hurts so much that you can't talk about it."

He put on a brave face. "I don't. Women love to, of course, but men aren't comfortable with show-and-tell. In my fantasies, I wish I could have gone down heroically in my flaming Spitfire over France, saving Europe from the Nazis, with tearful relatives weeping silently by my flower-strewn grave. But," he sighed, "not my gift to be a hero. Quite the opposite, actually. Don't misunderstand me: as I said, I want to be glorious too, Byronic style, maybe, die at Mussalonghi for a greater cause than tenure." He sat hunched over as though speaking to himself, "To eat the flowers, and sleep with the dancers, in a revolutionary month of mists." He looked tired and gray. "But suffice it to say," he hesitated, then reached for her hand, "suffice it to say, my dear friend, that if your daughter is a bit of challenge for a time, my little girl can be found at the Montmartre Cemetery, her angelic body burned beyond recognition, a charred face with a demonic grin showing chalky teeth." He looked beyond Charly, eyes brimming with tears. "Would you like some more wine? Of course you would." And, laboring to his feet, trundled into the galley, Astérix padding close behind.

The room was silent. Charly felt embarrassed and wanted to comfort him, but didn't know how. "Oh, I'm sorry," she blurted, but he didn't hear.

She called louder, "Shall I put on some more music?" No answer. "Do you like Debussy or Ravel best? They were rivals, right? Hello?" No answer. "Oh, Jesus, that was trivial," she mumbled to the empty stateroom, trying to soften the moment. Charly felt betrayed, like walking the decks of a charming old boat, caught up in its classic strength and grace, only to go below and see fatal cracks in its hull, dry rot in its frames. Her own life was filled with problems; her stormy waters needed steel and a sure course. How could she make a commitment to this old boat, despite his class and character? Perhaps it was best to simply walk away, just let him settle into the mud of his own discord.

He hadn't answered her, probably didn't hear, but returned to the stateroom moments later carrying a bottle of claret. He preferred dry reds from Bordeaux. The people there, his father used to say, were gentler, and you could taste it in their wines.

His eyes red-rimmed and glasses askew, he sat heavily into his chair, with no apologies. He picked up on the diversion. "Frankly, I don't think theirs was a rivalry," he said, doing his best to ease the moment, pouring both more wine. "I think people believed Ravel should also have won the Prix-de-Rome, which evolved into controversy. Ravel wanted it, but never got it. Debussy won it, but didn't want it; had little interest in leaving his girl-friend and going to Rome for three years. Both young composers were influenced by the Symbolist movement of the time, and debates often erupted over who might be copying whom. It is all pretty parochial stuff." He was losing interest and took a large gulp of wine. She had determined to leave, but worried that if she did, he might expire below or inadvertently topple into the Seine above.

"Simone says that they were impressionists, but I—"

"A lot of people say that, but it's a stupid generality." He was growing irritable. Her father, despite his otherwise gentle nature, was a mean drunk, and she had learned to either lean with the wind or exit gracefully.

"Well, she's no expert, but—"

"But, she read a book once, right," he remarked sarcastically. "People, who—"

"I guess you're not in the mood to talk."

"Sorry."

"Maybe I should go."

"Don't go. We can find something else to talk about."

She snatched the moment. "Do you believe in afterlife?"

"Do you?"

"Of course."

"I don't know about God, but religions?" He grunted mockingly. "I have no use for them, turning mystery into magic, and I wouldn't appreciate any lectures on Jesus' love, et cetera."

"Hey, the fact that something is hard to explain is no reason not to try, right? You're a smart man, but we obviously disagree, again."

He held up his hand in protest. "Our whole family believed in God as a matter of discretion. My father, who taught me his prejudices, was too much of a goalie not to need a Great Fan, but as I recall, he hardly ever thought about God, except in those defining moments. As Papa was sure of finding Him in the hour of his death, you could say he did his best to keep Him out of his life." He attempted to pour himself another glass and realized the glass was still half full. "And to the coarse gaiety of his anti-papist brothers, he never missed an opportunity after dinner to ridicule Catholicism."

"Yeah," she nodded, "what can you say about Catholics?"

"Um-hm. Papa's table talk resembled that of Luther. Honestly, at bottom the whole business bores me. Who knows," he said, disgruntled, "God probably resides in the cortex or other mysterious terrain of the brain, like some vestigial organ. He's a bunch of chemicals and electromagnetic signals resonating in your skull when you're in deep trouble or playing mind games with drugs or meditation. Meanwhile, the 'true believers' are busy explaining the inexplicable with their assorted holy books, and lonesome for an audience."

"You really believe that?" she looked at him sadly.

"Look, there are more than six billion of us down here in this godforsaken penal colony, I recollect that means about fifty-six million people are outward bound in an average year. Do you really think the heavenly host are busy processing all those souls?"

"J.M., get serious. For a large part of humanity the global village sucks. We need a change. Jesus' central message from God was to love one another totally and unconditionally. What's wrong with that?"

"I *am* serious! But, God? Well, I'll grant you that when someone like Matisse says, as best I can recall, 'Yes, I do'—he meant believe in God—'when I am working. When I am submissive and modest, I feel surrounded by someone who makes me do things of which I am not capable.' I like that answer. But, Jesus…?"

"Sure, but since the rest of us aren't up there with Matisse and God, there was probably meant to be another way."

He was becoming aggravated again. "Look, in my opinion, religion is to rationality what bullshit is to horsepower. And there isn't any hell! Unless it is here," and he jabbed his finger on the coffee table. "Jesus' love is fundamentally at odds with the impulses of those of us who have to live in this *village*. We're all suffering and probably already in hell."

"Well, who knows if there is a hell or where it's at; is hell your only reason?" she said.

"Hell? Personally I think it's near Newark, and I don't want to go there forever, and that's reason enough."

"Is that all? I thought it might be life without chocolate, or eternal shampoos with Ajax," she said, hoping to reduce the friction, and fed Astérix some cheese.

"He has terrible farts when you do that," he cautioned.

"So, you don't believe in anything?" She was frustrated.

"I believe in the soul, the warmth of a woman's smile," he said, and she smiled. He continued, "High fiber, good liquor, affectionate animals, and that the novels of Erica Jong are self-indulgent crap."

"Honestly," she exclaimed. "We all will have some explaining to do, but what you're saying really is this: does this particular person, guilty of that particular sin, deserve hell? Right?"

"Right!"

"Well, if he doesn't, he won't get it; that's certain. No just God is going to do that!"

"How about this?" He pointed his glass at her, his face contorted in grief. "How was God's justice served when an inebriated professor drove his young family into a concrete wall and was the only one who lived to tell about it?" He got up and rubbed his eyes. "Shit," he said.

She had feared he would eventually return to that subject, and this time both friends had tears in their eyes. Charly excused herself to the bathroom to escape, and returned in time to hear a voice from above.

CHAPTER 4

═══ THE NIGHT CALLER ═══

"Helllooo, down there!" A high-pitched call carried down the stairway of the barge.

"Oh, merde!" Jean-Michel moaned, returning to his chair. "It's Pierre."

"Jean-Michel, got someone down there? With her clothes off?"

"*Ferme ta bouche,*[16] you little weasel, I've got company," he roared back over his shoulder, not moving from the chair.

"Ah 'ave brought wine," Pierre enticed.

"I've got wine! Go home...it's late."

Charly was ready to welcome a visitor, any visitor. "I'm dressed," she called back. "Come on in."

Jean-Michel glared at her and hissed some inaudible French.

A skinny little man bounced down the stairs and, fixing Charly in his sights, paused to enjoy her bodice. "Ah! An American in Paris," he said in thickly accented English. "And you must be zees Texan Jean-Michelly talks so much about. May ah introduce myself? Ah'm Pierre."

"She was just leaving. So must you. I don't feel well."

"She will stay, ah will speak ze English. Ee's a goddamn prince, no?" Pierre winked at Charly. "Ah'm hungry," and before either could say anything Pierre had made for the galley.

"Ow can anyone be zo fat, and still 'ave no food in zees...zees 'ouse? Zees leaking bucket 'ee calls abode," he said to himself, loud enough for all to hear, rummaging through the cupboards. "Eez ze cheese all gone? Christ, Jean-Michel, you're a goddamn prince, just a goddamn prince. Mon Dieu! Ee fed you Boulette d'Avesnes!? Where eez all ze Bleu d'Auvergne!" he whined. "Did 'ee try and feed you Boulette? Eez just belly rot." He continued to rummage about the galley searching for food.

"Geez, your friend loves that phrase," she mused.

"What?" Jean-Michel sat with his shoulders hunched like a man waiting for a cold rain to stop.

"Goddamn prince...wasn't that—"

"Holden Caulfield."

"Right! *Catcher in the Rye.*"

"Yeah, Salinger is Pierre's hero. Pierre and I spent a year or so together in the States; he tried to be one of the angry young men ranting against what they perceived as phony."

Perplexity showed on Charly. "Then where's his hat?"

"He wore one for a while; too hot, I guess. He looked like a Disney rat wearing a red condom." She looked at him oddly. "On his head, dear." He smiled.

"'Ark, do Ah 'ear my name?" Pierre was back with some sardines, crackers, and a glass of wine. He lounged easily into one of the chairs, kicking off his Birkenstocks in the process, revealing feral feet. "By ze way, that colonel of yours eez a voyage."

"Trip!" Jean-Michel snorted.

"Voyage, trip, zo?" he said petulantly. "You know, Charly, Jean-Michel enjoys to bring home ze Boulette, especially when 'ee's expecting ze guests. Eet eez un test of character, ze perversity.'Ee loves de Gaulle, you know," he said, pouring himself some wine.

"She doesn't give a shit about de Gaulle!"

"Everyone gives ze sheet about de Gaulle!" Pierre retorted. "Zo, de Gaulle, 'ee wondered 'ow anyone could govern a country with ze two-hundred seventy different cheeses, zo 'ee eez Jean-Michel's 'ero. Do you like de Gaulle? I 'ate 'im. Fond of some sardines? I adore zem." He stretched to offer her an oily sardine glued to its cracker, dropping crumbs on the carpet. An experienced host would have spread newspapers around his chair.

"What in hells the matter with you! Your English is horrible. Are you on uppers?" Jean-Michel growled. "Where's de Monteaux?"

"Well, what's ze troubling you?" Pierre asked mockingly. "'Ee left, going back to ze Crazy 'Orse for—"

"Never mind. Did you bring the recording?"

"Enjoying you Paree?" Pierre asked, popping the last sardine into his mouth.

"Well, I'm learning," Charly replied tiredly.

"Learning!? Paree eez God's city!" Defiantly French, he was displeased by her answer.

It was getting late, and Charly, infected with Jean-Michel's irritability, felt no obligation to be courteous. "What has God got to say about the dog shit and snarling salespeople?"

"Simple: shoot zem!"

"That's a bad joke in the States."

"Of course eet eez, but we don' provide ze public wiz automatic weapons in France." He was speaking very quickly, from cocaine, perhaps.

"You just introduced yourself to me. A friend told me that French people don't share their names with strangers."

"Share ze name? Your friend must be a tourist. 'Ow would we meet people?"

"Okay," she offered, "one more question: why do Parisians do everything so fast?"

"Because zey are—we are—agitated. Voilà. Only a person from Texas could live 'ere for a few days and maintain your rhythm. Look," he pointed to Jean-Michel snoring peacefully in his chair. "You 'ave put my friend to ze sleep."

"It must have been the cheese."

"It eez ze wine! You may have notice Jean-Michelly likes eet; 'ee only refuse a drink when 'ee's asleep or doesn't understand ze question."

"He's a big boy. Maybe he drinks too much."

"True, but 'ee feels zat anyone who does not drink wine with 'is meals eez throwing 'eez friends out of work." Pierre took some cheese. "You must be careful: 'ee's very difficult to put in ze taxi."

"So I've heard. You know, I've noticed that Parisians make fun of a lot of things. How do you Parisians compare yourselves to other Frenchmen?"

"What ozzer Frenchmen?"

Chrysalis' stateroom, albeit well appointed, nevertheless had the ambiance of a distracted bachelor in all but one respect: the occupant's feeling for audio-visual; one wall was filled, perhaps crammed is the word, with what looked like a huge collection of art books, CDs, electronic equipment, sin-gle-sideband radio, screens, and speakers. "Do you know how to work all that stuff?" she gestured toward the audio equipment.

"Of course. 'Ave you such equipment?"

"I don't have anything that requires more maintenance than a Frisbee. Please put something else on, I'm being underwhelmed with Impressionism."

"You don'like eet?" Pierre seemed sincere enough, but so totally French you were never sure if you were being set up or being made the dupe for a colum-nist from *Le Monde* — headlines: AMERICAN IN PARIS: RELISHES BIG MAC, FORSAKES THE LOUVRE. "What would you like to 'ear? Eez Reznor okay?"

"Who?"

"Reznor."

"Sorry — she, he, or it?"

Pierre turned to look to see if she was teasing.

"You know, Trent Reznor. "*Ze Downward Spiral, Ze Fragile?*"

She stared at him blankly.

He stared back, waving a CD in his hand. "*Industrial Rock,* Marilyn Man-son? Oliver Stone?" No change in her expression. "Alienation, distress, Ah'm running out of ze words."

"I think I was away that weekend. Snoop Dogg?"

"No Snoop," he flipped the CD in the air, "'ow about Gershwin?"

"Actually, I like Norah Jones or even her dad, Shankar," she said hope-fully, but now Pierre returned her vacant look, "but, okay, Gershwin," she relented, "would be nice."

"Ah was just amusing," he said flatly.

"Amusing? You're not. Just joking? I wasn't."

Again that pregnant pause, a cultural standoff, which gave in to irritation. "Tell me something, Pierre, why do you think the French have a worldwide reputation for being quarrelsome and cantankerous?"

"Because we 'ate each ozzer." He slipped in the Gershwin CD, then stepped around her and flopped like a gangly teenager back on the couch, but closer. "Ozzer zan zat, ze language makes eet sound like ... like — how do you say — like we're bowling?"

"Bawling?"

"Yes, ze bauling, angry. Bauling one another out even when we aren't.

293

We are just 'aving fun."

"Oh."

"Alors, don't feel bad. We 'ate everybody. We 'ave been invaded by ze British, Russians, Austrians, Italians, Algerians, Germans, and now Disney; anyone who eez not French in zees city eez considered an invader, see, 'eet's all just . . . natural," he said, taking a sip of his wine. Swallowing made his Adam's apple bounce. "We are difficult to get to know, polite to ze foreigners and strangers, but less zan welcoming. Jean-Michel said you were 'ere to learn about ze French culture, no?

"Ahh, you know," she looked dejected.

"You 'ave learned so much! In less than ze week?"

"I'm certainly getting my lessons. See, I can barely carry on a conversation with you in English!"

"You 'ave been doing wonderfully. Conversation 'as been elevated to ze art form in France; eet's probably one of ze most difficult things to learn, and even if you speak ze French well or your 'osts speak fluent English, eet eez an area loaded wiz ze peetfalls."

"It's true, you know!" she said enthusiastically. "I used to sit in amazement and listen to dinner conversations; it sounded like an aviary, everybody all chirping at once. Why are they so superficial? Why doesn't anyone answer you seriously when you ask a question, or why don't they listen to your answer when you reply to the question?"[17]

"*Oui, mais oui,*[18] ze serious questions are out! You could bore ze entourage. As one of our authors, André Maurois, put eet, "Ze conversation-game eez a work of art, a passionate man always spoils ze conversation-game. 'Ee seriously refutes light arguments; 'ee follows themes which 'ave been abandoned. Ze rule eez to accept all ze movements of ze ball and follow eet weezout regret."[19]

"And the kissing?"

"Kissing? Ah, ze baisemain.[20] Well, zat's different. Eet's often about age. Then, rather more zan you might think, eet depends on ze social circle. Neverzeless, for my generation ze baisemain eez technically off limits in ze case of unmarried women, women wearing ze gloves, and women in public places. On ze uzzer 'and, ze bise[21] could intimidate most experienced foreigners. Some French give one, some two, ozzers even ze three and four bises. Eet's very 'ard to keep up wiz. 'Owever, don't worry about ze kisses; one of ze worst faux pas you can make in France eez to drop in unexpectedly on a friend, even a good one. We French don't like to 'ave unexpected visitors."

"Like you?"

"That's different — we are brothers."

"I've noticed, like Schwarzenegger and DeVito."

"De Vito?"

"Never mind, continue," she waved him on.

"Well, we don't like ze unexpected visitors; in fact, we don't like anything unexpected. Never forget zat unlike ze US, France eez a one-time-zone country, in which everyone eez doing everything at just about ze same time, 'ence a certain predictability in eating times, being 'ome times, and ze bedtimes. Neverzeless, ze rituals or codes of manners actually 'elp to make life simpler — if you know ze rules. Just like a graceful minuet, each dancer knows ze steps expected. Miss a step and ze rhythm eez broken. So it eez wiz ze decorum of French social life.[22] Should you place ze foot in ze mouth, or your giant lettuce leaf anywhere else, no one in France will embarrass you by 'owling wiz laughter. That most certainly eezn't done, at least not until you 'ave left ze room."[23]

"How easy you make it all seem," she said sardonically.

"Well, no foreigner should ever mock ze French language, first because 'ee does not understand eet properly, and secondly because eet 'as divine status in France."

Charly groaned.

"Every foreigner, 'owever," he held up his finger in admonishment, "needs to watch ze French mocking each uzzer on 'ow zey use zeir language zemselves." He smiled that knowing and superior smile, and feeling the effects of his wine, leaned back on the couch, fiddling with his recording of Boléro. "Don't you like ze impressionist music? Some consider eet very romantic."

"Not particularly. I suppose I'll have to explain French elevator music to my tourists, but even Jean-Michel says the name doesn't apply."

Pierre gestured toward Jean-Michel, who slumbered peacefully, chin on chest and glasses askew. "Zat old frog wouldn't know; all 'ee leestens to eez Bonnie Raitt and Pat Metheny."

"Well, does it!"

"Does what? Ze Impressionism? Of course! Do you think Impressionism eez just ze name fluttering out of ze sky and lasting a century?" he said petulantly. "Eet was ze time in both Debussy and Ravel's lives zat zey came into contact wiz ze progressive of French poetry and art by meeting and talking to ze artists: ze Symbolist poet Stéphane Mallarmé,[24] for example, and ze impressionist painters Monet and Renoir. During zat time, each Tuesday evening, not far from 'ere, zese men and zeir friends gathered to discuss ze aesthetics of new movements. Debussy was fourteen years Ravel's senior, you know, but both were influenced by zeir ideas — at different times, of course — and particularly by zeir conversations wiz Erik Satie.[25]

"Satie?"

"Oh, 'ee was an eccentric," Pierre put his head back and laughed. "Our most unique French musician."

"Was he that funny?"

"Not funny, but strange, ze eccentric, you know."

"Like?"

"Like, 'ee 'ad a one-room apartment[26] in which 'ee 'ad a collection of one hundred umbrellas. 'Ee also once bought twelve gray velvet suits at ze same time. He used one suit until eet was worn out, then 'ee put on ze new one. When 'ee died, zere were six suits still left een 'eez room, along wiz 'eez 'undred umbrellas. Wonderful composer, and 'ee knew all ze great ones: Picasso, Diaghilev, Ravel, Debussy, Cocteau —"[27]

"Debussy?" she asked. "I'm working on him."

"Good! 'Ee eez interesting. Debussy met Satie in 1891 and zey became close friends. Satie was earning 'eez living by playing ze piano in a Montmartre cabaret. But 'ee was also ze composer of strange, exotic pieces for ze piano, which had silly titles like *Desiccated Embryos*, and *Flabby Preludes for a Dog.*

"One wonders what substances brought on those revelations? Did he write something I can repeat to strangers?"

"Hm. *Ze Ogives* was probably 'eez first well-known work." He looked at her questioningly.

"No. Jesus. *Ogives!*" She tried to pronounce it and he winced.

"Ah," he snapped his fingers. "You must know Scott Joplin's ragtime flavor, no?"

"Yes."

"So, you must listen to *Le Piccadilly* and you will 'ear where, you know, Scott Joplin probably got 'eez ideas. Everyone knows zat, for decades, jazz has not succeeded in enlarging Debussy's stock of chords, no?"

She gave him a caustic look. "No."

"Satie's ideas complemented for 'eem ze principles set down by ze Symbolists and impressionists, giving 'eem still a clearer musical aesthetic. In ze end, Debussy was simply trying to approximate in music what ze Symbolists and ze impressionists were doing in ze poetry and art, wizout abandoning 'eez own style."

"Pierre," she said tiredly, "stick with Debussy. I've got to learn enough to take some people to his birthplace and maybe hum a few choruses of *Clair de Lune*. No American is interested in a man with an umbrella fetish who wrote *Dessicated Embryos*, but sure as hell, someone is going to confuse Debussy with an impressionist painter, and I have to explain the difference."

"*Clair de Lune?* Eet's from 'eez *Suite Bergamasque* for piano, 'eez best-known composition and ze only music of Debussy zat people ever remember."[28]

"Right," she held up her hand to emphasize her point. "That's good. Now tell me something about it."

He was confused by her interruptions and disliked being led. "You want to know ze piano music? Debussy's piano music eez ze most important creation by a French composer since Chopin, everyone knows eet." Pierre wiggled his fingers pretending to play the piano. "Debussy created a style zat made new demands on performing technique, and ze shifting, blurred sonorities of ze style were achieved by a new use of ze damper pedal. So you think tourists play ze piano?" he asked innocently.

She leaned forward and buried her head in her arms. "Jesus," she whimpered.

"Would you like some more wine?" he said, sensing he might have found a weakness.

"No! More about the goddamn *impressionist!*" she demanded loudly.

Pierre's eyes popped, and Jean-Michel grunted with a start. "What?" he said, startled.

297

"Impressionist musicians," she whispered.

"Impressionists? Some more wine?" he attempted to croon, but she waved him off. "Well, Debussy associated leetle wiz musicians, you know. He enjoyed ze company of ze leading impressionist poets and painters who gathered at ze 'ome of ze poet Stéphane Mallarmé, like I said. Zeir influence eez felt even in Debussy's first important orchestral work, *Prelude to the Afternoon of a Faun*, inspired by Mallarmé's poem *L'Apres-midi d'une faune*. Lasted nearly twenty years." He stared at her breasts. "I'm getting tired," he yawned. "He rarely appeared in ze pubic as a performer. Aren't you tired," he said hopefully.

"Pubic?"

"Alors, public! Can't we speak in French?"

"No, you offered!" she demanded. "And?"

Pierre was losing interest. He got up and moved to the pillow next to her. "*And*, I forgot my glasses. I can see you better 'ere," he said lamely. "More cheese?"

"No," and she quickly put her hand over her plate.

Pierre began to angle in on his prey, keeping up his prattle on the impressionists. "Impressionists, especially Debussy, you know, regarded chords as entities in zeir own right, intended to arouse a sensation apart from any context. Do you know you arouse a sensation in me?"

"Too bad."

"Eet's life! We need to be free." He waved his arm around his head, gesturing like a composer with his free hand. "Impressionism released ze chord from eets function in regard to ze movement and goal of ze music. Chords should be free, don't you think? We describe zees as ze 'emancipation of ze sound.' Harmonic patterns were free to move in nontraditional manners. We should be emancipated from our binding clothes, our inhibitions, no?"

He moved in closer. "Impressionist composers put colorful chords together, like your lips and eyes," he tried to sing his words, "and left eet to ze ear of ze listener to interpret ze whole. Our melodies are elusive. You are elusive," he crooned again. "Ze short brush strokes of an impressionist painter were similar to ze short melodic lines of narrow scope used by our composers." He reached over to stroke her hair. She moved her head away. "Zeir repeated melodic fragments were common." He stopped his attempt at singing, drew his knee up on the couch, and with his other foot shoved himself against her. "Especially in ze music of Debussy," he whispered, "unity of form was not demanded. You 'ave a wonderful form. Your breasts are beautiful and I can see ze form of your nipples through your blouse. Nor was eet desired, like I desire you. Ravel, you know, 'ee was classicist in form. We should not be so formal, no?"

He leaned close, breathing heavily, cupped his hand around her right breast, and began to squeeze. His thick eyebrows wobbled with each emotion, as though trying to avoid skidding down over his nose. He leaned forward to kiss her.

She sat up abruptly and looked at him coldly. Then, taking his bony wrist, she jerked his hand from her breast, holding it out as though to squeeze the neck of a snake. "You touch my breast again and I'll cut your dick off," she said. Casting his hand to the side, she moved to a chair.

She took a large gulp of wine, then, "Tell me, Pierre, is it true Debussy shot his wife?"

"Of course not. Ze crazy woman shot 'erself!" The hunt was over, and, unhappily, he knew it.

"I'm very good with guns," she said, looking directly at his crotch. "What do you think of that?"

His eyes narrowed suspiciously, and he looked around the room for her handbag. "Do you 'ave a gun?" His Adam's apple bobbed as he craned his neck to look.

"If Debussy's wife had one, why shouldn't I?"

"Lilly was crazy."

"Okay, so she shot herself. Everybody's a little weird. Care to elaborate?"

"Elaborate?" he said warily, eyes narrowing again.

"Uh, make things, you know, ze clear."

Pierre had fallen back to regroup. He took a sip of wine and placed his glass on the table. "Well, Lilly was, you know, ze devil and ze angel. She was violent," again quickly scanning the room for her purse. "Debussy said she was very quick to anger, even een front of 'er family." He tried to retreat behind his point. "Eet eez not good, you know, violence; violence with ze servants, *any* violence. Zey quarreled about money, she told lies of every

kind, and avenged herself on 'im by tyranny over 'eez thoughts and dealings."[29] He shrugged his shoulders. "You know ze women."

"Yeah, I 'know ze women.' What's the matter, did one steal your Froot
Loops?"

"She was crazy," he insisted. "And crazy about 'im, so she took ze pistol
and shot 'erself."

"So how do you know?"

"Eet's all recorded. Mary Garden, one of 'eez singers, wrote about eet in 'er
biography. She said zat after Lilly tried to commit suicide, zey took 'er to ze
hospital and she asked for Mary. Zey took Mary into a tiny room, and zere
lay Lilly, wiz ze bullet in 'er breast, wanting to die because 'er Claude had
not come back to 'er. You must understand zat zis young seamstress never
knew anything else in life but 'er love of Debussy." He looked at her, trying
to judge his prospects for a second chance. "We French are very emotional
when eet comes to love."

"Ain't love grand?" she said, avoiding his gaze. "So then what?"

"She took care of 'eem like ze child. Zey had worries and debts and dis-
appointments, but eet's true nobody ever got into ze leetle apartment of ze
Rue Cardinet to interrupt Debussy at 'is music. When Lilly 'ad finished
telling Mary ze story, ze surgeon came in to dress 'er wound and opened 'er
nightdress. Mary said zat in 'er life she 'ave never seen anything so beautiful as Lilly Debussy from ze waist up. Eet was just like a glorious marble
statue, too divine for words, she said. Debussy had always said to 'er, 'Mary,
zere eez nothing in ze world like Lilly's body.' I wish I could have seen ze
breasts." His gaze drifted longingly toward Charly's cleft again: freckled,
full, and enticing. Pierre reached for the wine bottle. "More wine?"

"Last call? Good. When does the subway close?"

"You can stay 'ere."

"No, thanks. Was it all impressionistic?"

"No." He held up his glass as though to inspect for cork, but more to
posture. "Eet's not so, but some pieces, eet's true zat Debussy disliked ze
term 'Impressionism,' particularly as applied to 'eez music, but 'ee was ze
father of that style, eet eez no doubt. And if Le Grande Frommage over zere
would wake up he must agree. Many European artists 'ave been influenced
by eet; many 'ave imitated eet, but nobody surpassed Debussy or Ravel, at

least in ze magic and enchantment wiz which eet was performed."

"I suppose, but nobody listens to them in the States, unless they happen to be in shampoo commercials."

"Can you be so sure? Besides, America is America; you're not known for your culture, only ze cheeseburgers and interstates."

"I only know what I like."

"Ha! 'Like!' What do you 'like?'" he chortled. "Ze question eez, what do you understand?" he said derisively. "'Ow would you know what you like if you are—'ow do you say—deprived—ignorant?"

"Deprived? You mean depraved?" she said, considering whether to set him up for a solid punch. "I am ignorant, and it's being demonstrated more every day. Who's going to listen to music without words for hours, much less in a hot theater, tied to your seat like tourist class on 'Hobo' airlines."

"Ze truth eez, you're not listening to classical music! Friend of my friend, eet's from ze Romantic period. Not zat you would know—you 'ave to 'ave an imagination, you 'ave to see ze play in your mind: fairies, nymphs, forests, animals. You must put ze characters, story, and music together. You must have ze romantic imagination. Eet's not all about Elvis, ze Jacksons, and Madonna. Anyway, classical music eez dead in ze US; your culture eez ze Internet. Zere will always be ze pretenders, but in ze end, when your gray 'eads die, you can say bon voyage to sophisticated music."

"Fairies? Nymphs? Have you ever smelled a cow-plop up close and fresh? The only nymphets I knew were tenth graders bangin' their brains out in the back seats of old Chevys. Bob Dylan sang in that ludicrous voice of his about what me and my kind knew pretty well—poverty and frustration. I used to jump around in my back bedroom, sing-shouting the lyrics to *Positively Fourth Street* and *Subterranean Homesick Blues* to my posters and the mosquitoes. Bob Dylan and I were, or so it seemed at the time, ticked off about the same things—American vanity and crewcut hypocrisy; and in love with the same things—anarchy and freedom. I never heard of Debussy, Diaghilev, and the rest. Hearing Dylan sing *Just Like a Woman* or *Blonde on Blonde* gave me those jangly goose bumps."

"Eez lyrics were cruel."

"Maybe, but they had conviction, I know now better what he meant."

"And what was ze truth?"

"The truth was, is, we're all longing for happiness."

"'Appiness? You don't like ze sex?" he smirked.

"I think it's time for me to be going."

"Was it something Ah said?"

"Not really, if you can learn to keep your hands to yourself. I've got to pick up my kid tomorrow morning at the airport, so I need some sleep."

"But you can sleep 'ere."

"Yeah, I heard you the first time." She gathered her things to leave. "Ciao."

"A bientôt," he said, nonchalantly stretching out on the couch while Charly stood, looking around for her sweater and purse.

"Who's going to take care of Monsieur Levasseur?" she asked over her shoulder.

"'Ee doesn't need ze care," Pierre said offhandedly.

She felt pain. "He does, after what happened to his wife and children," she said, looking at some photographs on the bookcase.

"'Eez wife and child," he corrected her. "'Eez wife and daughter died in ze accident. Did 'ee tell you about ze son?"

"Not really."

"Then eet eez not ze time; probably never eez ze time." He rolled over on the couch and plumped one of the pillows. "Fausto," he grunted. "Just one piece of ze advice: never touch Emma," he said, pointing over to the bookcase.

CHAPTER 5

══ THE ARRIVALS ══

The passengers began pouring through the gate just as Charly arrived. Within minutes she saw them: he was tall, tanned, and thin, wore a cowboy hat, plaid shirt, and blue jeans; Jodie had an armful of presents and that big grin of her father's. She ran up to Charly and grabbed her in a strong embrace.

Jodie was taller than her mother, athletic looking, with thick, dark eyebrows, long ponytail, a periwinkle scarf around her neck, and tiger-print cowboy boots on her feet. They talked excitedly for some moments and then Jodie introduced her new beau, Randy.

He was nice looking, better than Charly expected. His constant references to Charly as "Mother Brooks" were the only irritant from a man who was ten years younger than she and ten years older than her daughter. Charly hadn't seen Jodie since Christmas, but was astounded at how much she had matured; she was more sure and her eyes had aged—sex does that to a girl after she has come to know a man. And she didn't look pregnant. Charly breathed easier.

His name was Randy J. Cochrane, known as RJ to his friends. And, contrary to the manic enthusiasm of born-agains, he offered in that soft, range-hand drawl from those desultory days on the range, an apology: the drunkenness, fighting, and thievery were of a bygone era—a vow every mother would have hoped to hear from a young man intent on marrying her daughter, and whose ever-present Bible was carried in fingers tattooed H-A-T-E, with panthers clawing up each arm.

Later on, Jodie confirmed that he had even tried to dissuade her from the nipple piercing, but in the best feminist tradition understood her right to choose, and had met the test in challenging the scriptures. Not long after, however, she had had to remove the rings from her tender and swollen nipples, the consequence of a botched piercing job in Nogales. The tongue piercing was never brought up, but obvious when Jodie laughed. And that was one of her gifts that Randy preferred to keep, since fellatio was an ancient art not easily adorned.

They were both Evangelical Christians, Baptists who had been baptized down on the banks of the River of Life, Jodie only months ago casting out the thong-flashing Gomorra hussy she once was, and Randy having forsworn the whiskey-toting debauched cowboy over four years in the past.

These were the new soldiers of Christ, not in the sense spoken of more than sixty years ago by Neibuhr, who summarized the creed of an easygoing Christianity that had come to pass in America, one in which a God without wrath brought men without sin into a kingdom without judgment through the care of a Christ without a cross. Rather, they strode the path of Jesus as Martin Luther saw Him, the theology of the suffering Savior crowned violently with thorns, whipped within an inch of His life, and hung bleeding on the cross until dead. Christ demonstrated that, for mortal sins, there would literally be hell to pay.

Randy and Jodie had met at a summer Bible camp for teenagers, where Randy, after his conversion some four years now, was a counselor. It was a sanctuary for fundamentalist parents to send their children, a place where strict parental rules would be enforced and religious commitment expected. Jodie's father had signed her up for a three-summer investment, called Stairs to Christ, where first-year students were to learn the Word; second-year students the Life; and third-year students the Lord. Randy had established himself early on with Jodie by asking her, "Have you been to Calvary?" On that starry night, next to the lake, beneath fragrant pine boughs, she had come to the Lamb of God in his arms. They held hands across the table in the hotel lounge as they related their story for Mother Brooks, and when they kissed she felt ashamed.

The question on everyone's mind was, what were the sleeping arrangements?

"Are you married?" Charly asked, as mother and daughter stood in the hotel foyer of the ladies' room.

"Of course not, Mom, we are only pledged—you know, sort of engaged. She pulled up her necklace to display a ring featuring clasped hands. Randy gave me this as a token of our love. But we're pure of heart, read the Bible every day, and witness to our friends. It's just like being married," Jodie said gaily.

"Not 'just.'"

"You know what I mean."

"No, I don't. Tell me."

Jodie's look hardened. "Well, we ain't like you and Daddy. We're going to get married in style."

"Couldn't you just try living in sin for a while?"

Jodie gave her an icy stare.

"Are you pregnant?" Charly asked quietly.

"Randy's waiting. It's been a long flight and I want to go to my room. *Mother*."

"Does your father know?" Charly called after her, but Jodie had turned on her tiger-skin heels and was gone.

———

"Hello?"

Charly held the phone for a moment, trying to put together the words for Jean-Michel. "It's Grandma Brooks."

"Pardon me?" he said, startled.

"It's Grandma Brooks. I'm going to be a grandmother."

The phone was silent. Then, quietly, "Congratulations."

"Thanks. I don't know why I'm surprised. This little scene has been replayed a million or so times a year I suppose, in practically every country in the world. I guess I should be happy."

"You should."

"Why ain't I?"

"Charly, you're fighting an uphill battle. They are a couple."

"A couple of what?"

"Look," he said, "somebody once said of lovers that one is not half of two, rather two are halves of one."[30]

"Um-hm. Well, I'd just say it was Satan's work."

"Maybe you should look at the bright side: perhaps it is the heavenly Father's work," he had little talent for proffering religious solutions, "...as they say."

"Well, if that's so, at least by today's standards, He should be convicted of child abuse. Jesus!" She exclaimed. "I thought I was just about through tryin' to raise one child with that ham hock in Texas; now I have to start all over again."

"I'm sorry."

"Yeah, I appreciate that...."

"Have you got plans?" he said hesitatingly, fearing the answer.

"Well, we did have, but I don't know at the moment. Some feathers were ruffled. We were going to visit the Eiffel Tower, take a boat ride on the Seine—you know the gig. Want to come?" she said hopefully.

He started to backpedal, "I'm going over to the office to work on the manuscript for a while."

She was tired of his excuses. "You and that goddamn book; every time I want to do something, you're supposedly busy monkeying around with that fucking *manuscript*."

He avoided the bitching and confrontation. "Maybe we could meet later?"

"Like Christmas, right?"

"Oh, Charly, I'm not good at this stuff, you understand that."

"Um-hm, I know. I've got to handle these two 'halves' by myself. Thanks."

He tried to hold his ground; after all, it was her flesh and blood. "Bring them over to *Chrysalis* later."

"They don't drink, J.M. These kids are Bible readers, not just Bible owners. What do you want to talk about—'How I became a Christian at camp last summer'? Or the more thorny, 'Who killed Christ'? One is sixteen years old and the other an ex-cowhand; you can expect their conversation will be as dull as linoleum."

"Okay, we can all take Astérix for a walk and stop by Notre Dame," he offered lamely.

306

"The headquarters of papist ascendancy in France. They should enjoy that."

"Fine, then what the devil to you suggest?" he growled. "The revolutionaries turned Notre Dame into a saltpeter factory and wanted to use the stones to build bridges; they should like that. Maybe we can take them to Disney's *Hunchback of Notre Dame,* since Hugo is the one who saved it"

"Hardly. My future son-in-law, sworn enemy of the devil, has it all written down. He suggests, if I may read, '...the Sainte-Chapelle, located within the Palais de Justice complex on the Ile de la Cité.'"

"I know where it is," he said with irritation.

She continued, "It was erected by Louis IX, king of France, to house the Crown of Thorns and a fragment of the True Cross, precious relics of the Passion. Louis had purchased these in 1239 from the Byzantine emperor Baldwin II —"

"You are not serious," he broke in.

"Couldn't be more so."

He started to whine and complain again.

"Thanks, J.M.," she said. "We'll stop over later for some whine and jeez."

"Charly." He couldn't compete, she was a professional. "Listen, there is one other little problem."

"Problem? No more *problems.*"

"It is no big deal," he said. "I just received a fax from Voyages Classiques that a British woman is coming here with a bunch of farmers from Kansas in a week or so, and I have to host them a bit, just a lecture or two. She is trying out for a travel-guide position. Don't worry, no problem."

"Terrific," she said glumly. "Competition from Mary Popper...er, what's her name."

"Charly," he tried to be consoling, "not to worry. I'm in your corner. You don't have to be concerned about competition from some old Cockney lady in a bulky sweater who only knows about Paris from her travel brochures, and waddles when she walks."

"Sure," she said tiredly. "Okay, whatever. Why don't you come with us? The kids could use a real guide."

"Merde!" he whimpered, "I have got to finish — "

307

She cut him off, "Thanks J.M., for all the support. *You* are a goddamn prince."

He tried to recover, "Wait, hey, we're scheduled to do Le Belvédère Thursday morning."

She hung up without responding.

CHAPTER 6

═══ LE BELVÉDÈRE ═══

"We're finally here?" she groaned. The taxi, train, and walk had exacted a heavy toll. "Tourists do this on purpose?"

"Not many," Jean-Michel said. "You have to be a music lover, or a Ravel aficionado. On the other hand, there's probably a music teacher from Iowa or some other exotic place who brings her classes here."

"How far did we just go?"

"Took over an hour. Fifty kilometers outside the city; somewhat longer from Iowa, I imagine."

"Seemed longer."

"Than Iowa?"

"Iowa!" she scolded. "What the hell is all this about Iowa?"

"Don't know. Never been there," he said, placing his foot on the curb and reaching down to tie his shoelace. "Have you?" He farted.

"Jean-Michelly! Jesus, was that the cheese? Anyway, who cares! That's my point."

"Oh." One was never sure whether Jean-Michel, like an Indian in the forest, hid in innocence, ignorance, or perversity.

She surveyed the ornamental house on the hill. "It's not quite what I expected."

"You are not alone. It is commonplace," he said, gazing at the house. "Sort of vulgar in a way, miniature suburban villa with its primly 'capped' tower and its general mixture of the pretentious and the twee."

"Twee? Jesus." Her mood was dark.

"Twee. You'll see. You sound ... dare I ask, is it that time of the —"

"Can it!" she snapped, striding forward.

"Yes, my sweet," he mumbled, gratuitously falling in behind her. They climbed the hill and entered the little house through the street door with its small commemorative plaque, and stood in the vestibule of Maurice Ravel's pride and joy, waiting for the attendant. Jean-Michel looked about and spoke in hushed tones, "Ravel bought the house in 1920. Made some modifications, moved in a year later naming it 'Le Belvédère.' Reminds me of Hemingway. Have you been to Hemingway's house in Key West?"

"No."

"Well, while Hemingway made the counters in his house higher to fit his height, Ravel made them lower to meet his. He spent the rest of his life here in Montfort L'Amaury—a decade and a half—when he was not touring or undertaking engagements in the capital."

"Is this Bois de Boulogne?"

"No. Montfort L'Amaury. Why?"

"I told the kids they could meet us out here."

"I think they'll have a hard time; it's Ile-de-France."

"Probably not interested anyway. Randy has the military museum on his mind."

"Maybe I can show them around on Saturday."

"Oh, thanks, J.M., how kind," she said cynically. "You're a little late—they're going back Friday."

"I…" he gave up. "So soon?"

"Jodie's got stomach problems. I would say it's morning sickness. She's blaming it on the airlines, but just wants to go back to Texas; claims no one knows a word of English, and people are staring at Randy's Stetson."

"Sorry. Probably wouldn't like it anyway, it is almost the same as when Ravel went looking for a home, an intruder in a French village atmosphere, and this house, almost an enlarged doll's house, shows the fastidious taste of its owner, no?" She simply shrugged her shoulders.

"Let me know if I am boring you," he murmured.

"I have to pee."

"Pee, or—?"

"Pee! And soon, or I'll be using his garden."

"Garden? Ah, Paris exclusive!" he said mockingly, then mimicked a newscaster: "Today the ghosts of Maurice Ravel and mother Marie watched in horror as an American woman of low birth excreted a direct hit of hot pee on one of their exotic plants, a cherished miniature Japanese tree, causing irreparable damage." She sighed. He sighed—and left to find the attendant.

The urge became too great, and Charly, aware of Jean-Michel's addiction to distractions, headed off in search of a toilet, only to find one proclaiming, STAFF ONLY, and used it. Considering that she had almost been forced to use the garden, and curious, she wandered downstairs and out the back door, leaving Jean-Michel to his own devices. An old man sat on a bench facing the valley before them. She glanced with mistrust at his stubble-covered face, as it bent over the long, stained fingers through which he was rolling his cigarette. The garden was too small to avoid each other, and she decided to accommodate the situation. "Comfortable little place, isn't it?"

She was struck with pity at the mild, faded blue eyes, which looked up abruptly from the task and gazed vaguely into the hazy distance, while his slender fingers ceased their unsteady rolling and strands of tobacco fell back into the pouch wedged between his legs. He had a hearing aid clamped on one ear, and a ragged copy of *Finnegans Wake* sat beside him.

"I beg your pardon?" he said, in a heavy Irish brogue.

"I said it is a comfortable place, here," and she waved toward the garden.

He grunted and went back to his work. She took a few steps away to sniff some yellow flowers on a nearby bush. The old man looked like her uncle, Barnaby, who often took her on long walks. Her thoughts went back to Texas, where they were such an odd couple, short and tall, and neighbors would smirk: it's those two again. Barnaby usually wore his old high school football helmet, having a distinct fondness for its soft leather, warmth, and protection on their walks. They would often pay a visit to a small chapel along the way and, as the holy water font was above Charly's reach, the old man would dip his hand and then sprinkle the water briskly about Charly's clothes and on the floor of the vestibule. While he prayed, he knelt on his red handkerchief, helmet respectfully under his arm, and read, at times short of breath, from a thumb-blackened prayer book. Charly knelt at his side, respecting, though too young to share, his piety. She often wondered what her great uncle prayed for so seriously. Perhaps he prayed for the soul of his beloved wife or for the grace of a happy death, or perhaps he prayed that God might send him back a part of the fortune he had squandered in Houston.

The old man ceased his rolling, gave a final lick down its side, and lighted his cigarette with shaking hands. He took a drag, and spoke, "Are ya lookin' for a comfortable place?"

"Yes."

"This ain't one."

"Yeah, you're probably right." She had better things to do and turned to leave.

"American, right?"

"Right"

"What'd ya expect?" he said aggressively.

"I didn't expect anything. I don't know about Ravel, just thought I'd check out his house."

"He was a wee bastard."

"I found out that much," she said coldly.

"Did ya know," he turned and pointed with a twitching finger to the porch on the second level, "he committed suicide by jumping off the railing?"

"I thought he died of a brain tumor."

"Probably did—who knows?"

"I thought you said he committed suicide."

"I thought ya said ya knew nothin' of the man." He sat squinting up at her, pinching his cigarette tightly between stained forefinger and thumb. "Ya got any money?"

"I gotta go," and she turned back toward the door.

"Ya do that, Ms Brooks."

She stopped dead in her tracks and looked around at him. "How do you know who I am?" she demanded, instinctively reaching for her purse.

He smiled, yellow teeth framed by crusty lips, and pointed again toward the second level of the house. She turned to see Jean-Michel laughing and waving. He called down, "I see you've met Terence."

CHAPTER 7

═══ TERENCE ═══

Jean-Michel's friend, Terence, was an Irish musician, an alcoholic pianist fallen on hard times, who created a meager living by his journalistic efforts as a critic, some club stints — if he had medicine — and odd jobs around the Ravel museum. Jean-Michel brought some folding chairs out to the garden, and, setting them next to Terence's bench, lost no time putting him to work. Time was short, and Jean-Michel had paid him more than he was probably worth. They took their seats next to him and he began as if on cue.

"Ravel never did mature in the ordinary sense, ya know. He was no more grown up emotionally than he was physically; never even reached average height, except if ya consider any o' these Frogs average," and snickered. He leaned heavily against the arm of the bench, crossed his skinny legs, and held his cigarette off at an angle to avoid tobacco brands falling on his grubby suit. "He was always keepin' those fookin' cats around; anyway, all these psycho-biographical mumbo-jumbo types have a nasty whiff of arrogance about them — what is 'maturity' anyway?" he asked rhetorically, perhaps to ease his own failures. He spoke to no one in particular, finding more interest in picking lint off his suit or staring into the distance.

"Then what, was he gay or antisocial or…?" she asked.

"Antisocial? What the hell's that?" he said, squinting at her. "Ravel was hardly antisocial. He was a dandy for sure, and drank his share — not like me an' Jean-Michel here — but I'll grant ya he was an authentic personality." He chuckled.

"Dandy?" she asked.

"Dandy."

She got exasperated. "What's a 'dandy?'"

"Anybody who remembers Ravel knows he was a dandy his whole

313

life. Jesus!" He squinted at her against the sun. "Do you know Barbey d'Aurevilly?" Charly looked at Jean-Michel and shrugged her shoulders, accusing her mentor of negligence.

"Well, if you've a mind, miss, you might consider reading a book or two on the subject before you start makin' a livin' jostlin' tourists." And he flicked away his cigarette.

"Indulge me," she said sarcastically.

"Read a book," he grunted. "Try one that Ravel himself liked: *Du Dandysme et de George Brummel* was one of his favorites. You'll find the dandy's features described in Barbey's essay on Brummel: glacial wit, ya know; the appearance o' total self-control; sober and rigid elegance, and an ability to wound others with words and ignore his victims' discomfort." He looked malevolently at her. "I'm sure ya'd understand, miss."

"I understand well enough. The deficiencies of males are legend. So?"

"So, Ravel adopted the dandy behavior in his social circles, all of it inspired by British dandies like Brummel or Horace Walpole." He began fumbling for his tobacco pouch again.

"Tell her about Poe," Jean-Michel urged.

"Ah, Poe," he seemed to sniff air. "Well, Ravel drew some elements o' his persona—ya understand persona, don't ya, miss?" He smiled his crack-lipped, crusty smile. "His persona as a dandy from the works o' Edgar Allan Poe, at least from Baudelaire's point of view. Ya know Baudelaire, miss?" And he began to quote the poet in a singsong type of voice:

"Learn that you must love, with all your heart

The poor in body and spirit, the low, the lost...."[31]

Charly ran out of patience; that she was now in an audience of two to a rumpled old man in a tattered suit smelling of urine and sweat irritated her even more than the hot afternoon and insects. "Hey! Old man! Forget Baudelaire, he was an opium addict. If you can't keep your mind on your business, just say so, or we're outta here."

"You're probably right, miss, Sartre was wastin' his time writin' about Baudelaire,[32] just a pain in the neck to his family an' friends, o' course: money grubbin', sadomasochist, and all that." He continued fusing with his tobacco pouch till he had his papers and tobacco applied. "But little point in chidin' the ghost for his misdemeanors, wouldn't ya say?"

"So he enjoyed heaping misery on himself," she retorted.

Terence looked up wide-eyed and admonishing. "Then how could his addict's vision speak so persuasively to so many: to Mallarmé an' Verlaine, Rimbaud an' the others? If ya don't mind me askin'."

"I don't mind you askin. Let's see, maybe it's the pathetic role of the drunken, careless, sentimental boys of culture we're always reading about?"

"Oh...go find yourself some stupid boy," he mimicked with the poet's own words, "and give his lust your virgin heart to maul; ...livid with disgust, bring back to me your mutilated breasts.... Like Rousseau's Italian whore with no nipple." [33]

Charly winced.

He bent to rolling his cigarette. "Um-hm, 'pathetic role.' Oh, just askin', miss. I was thinkin' ya might have read *Les Fleurs du mal*." He sniggered. "Baudelaire, the greatest lyric poet o' the age." He looked up. "But, every well has its bottom."

"I am not here for your smarmy remarks or to swoon over addicts. Get on with your work, Terence," she warned. *How ugly people are,* she thought. *It's a pity they don't try to make up for it by being agreeable. Perhaps we could buy Terence a bottle and drop him off at Guy's apartment.*

Terence enjoyed provoking her and ignored the attack. He licked his lips. "Speakin' of a little drop, Jean-Michel, maybe ya could fix me a quick cup o' tea"—his signal for a whiskey.

"Let's see now, yeah, Sartre said that Baudelaire's myth o' the dandy conceals not homosexuality, but exhibitionism." He finished rolling his cigarette and lighted it, inhaled deeply, coughed, put his head back, and exhaled a narrow stream of smoke. "Ya like fags, miss?" Charly was ready to pounce, but he saw the signal and held up his hand. "Well, Wilde — Oscar, ya know — an' other gay writers were always talkin' about an androgynous dandy. Lemaître," he glanced at Jean-Michel, an urgent prod for his 'tea,' "Jules Lemaître, said, the dandy has something against nature, something androgynous with which he can endlessly seduce." He accented the word "seduce" and sought her eyes. She looked over at Jean-Michel through dark slits, felony in her eyes.

Reluctantly, Jean-Michel knew he had to get involved. "Most vexing side of Ravel's personal life, Charly, is his sexuality or lack of it, but not much to tell. The words in 'L'Indifferent' from *Shéhérazade* can be taken as, at least to me, an artist clearly interested in homosexuality, but even Ravel's close associates describe him as a man whose only known sexual encounters were with prostitutes."

"Male?" she asked.

"Female. Those who hold out for a 'closeted' gay Ravel will be disappointed: one might suppose that, with a minimum of discretion, a man of means could have a robust gay sex life at the time. As with Baudelaire, opiates were legal and widely used. But citing the subject of 'L'Indifferent,' Larner, one of Ravel's best biographers, paints a portrait of Ravel's erotic ideal as something akin to neither heterosexual nor homosexual, neither bisexual nor asexual, but an ambiguity so evenly balanced that the masculine and the feminine cancel each other out. We probably need a societal model of a 'normal' personality range that is more inclusive of natural variation — less Freud, more Jane Austen. In the end, though, it looks like, intentionally or not, he eluded our best efforts to explore his mind." Jean-Michel paused to see if Terence would pick up on the story.

Terence had returned to grooming his flannel trousers, oblivious to the various crescendos of body language and voices surrounding him, and was peering down at the microcosmic debris of his daily life, opaque to his companions. "Ya see, miss," he began, "to young Maurice, Poe was twice an influence, not just as a dandy, but also as a creative sort. He told his friends that Poe's essay, 'The Philosophy of Composition,' was the most important lesson he ever received about composin'. The idea was that every plot worthy of the name had to be elaborated to its dénouement before anything be attempted with a pen." Terence's belly ached for alcohol, and the urge to taunt Charly about dénouement was being cowed by an urgent thirst. Sweat gathered on his upper lip. "So ya see, this became Ravel's approach to composition, thinkin' everything out in his head before settin' pen to paper. I tried, o'course, a lot o' young composers did, but sweet mother of Jesus, it took concentration an' constant pressure, conscious, even unconscious, durin' the creative act. Ya heard o' *The Raven* right, miss?" She nodded warily, and Terence turned his head up to face her, squinting and wrinkling his nose. "Poe described his writin' o' *The Raven* step by step with the precision of a math problem. Ravel liked to tell his students, 'I do logarithms,' to arrive at compositional solutions. That was their genius, I suppose. Both Poe and Ravel thought their creations might go uncontrolled; the need for discipline in creativity obsessed both of 'em." Terence was beginning to feel dizzy. "Where's the *tea?!*" he grumbled. "Sweet mother of Christ!"

"Okay..." but Jean-Michel held back.

"I take it you don't like him," Charly said.

"Who? Jean-Michel?" Terence was becoming confused.

"Ravel!" she exclaimed.

He turned to give her a long, hard stare. "Listen, miss, I don't just 'like' the wee bastard; he is — was — one of the finest musicians on earth. I love what he was," he said and almost inaudibly, "an' the music." He looked up. "Jesus, Jean-Michel, do ya need some help, for Christ's sake?" he bellowed.

Charly and Jean-Michel looked at each other, and Jean-Michel stood up, putting his hand on Terence's shoulder, "Terence, I —" and was cut off by Terence's rambling.

"Fag? I suppose in a way he was, an' as I said, a dandy for sure, but even had some whores, they say. He never married. Wife would've eaten him alive, like Debussy's did. After '17, when his mother died, he had no one. Poor bastard was so lonely he had to concentrate all his affection on his villa here," and he patted the bench. "Good ol' Belvédère, good ol'...became mother, wife, an' child to him, the only physical expression of his entire life."[34] He turned and waved in the direction of the house. "Decorated it himself and liked nothin' better than to exhibit it to visitors.

"Ya see, he lived here with that solicitous old maid, Madame Reveleau, an' the fookin' Siamese cats. I don't understand it, ya know, he an' Debussy had a passion for those animals. Goddamn cat hair, you can still find some of it in the cracks of the floor if you look hard enough. They were with him continually, on his lap when he was relaxin', even on his table when he was workin'." He stopped for a moment as though he could see the maestro and his animals standing before him. "He was as devoted to them as if they were his children. Sure," again he wagged his head, "an' he told his friends their antics in his letters.

"He would romp an' play with 'em around the house, ya know, or try to make them understand him. Li'l shit spoke to them in cat language! Crazy wee bastard, he insisted that cats understood him, just as he understood them. Prob'ly died of a hairball to the brain … shit!" He took a drag of his cigarette, hand quivering near his lips, and stared off into the distance.

"Was he?" Charly asked.

"Was he what?"

"Crazy."

"You callin' him lazy, missy?"

"No, crazy," she all but shouted. "You…"

"Look here," and he pointed his tobacco-stained fingers clamped to his cigarette in her direction. "When he was jokin' around he'd give the impression of a tike who had never grown up. He had a lad's sense of fun: he'd suddenly interrupt a serious conversation by tossin' his head to one side and emittin' a bird cry; and listen to this." He reached over and clutched Charly's arm. "He would imitate a seasick Chinese by coverin' an orange with a napkin and then squeezin' it so it splashed all over the floor! Shit! Then he would pester his friends to play those goddamn adolescent games right here in this garden. Listen," Terence ran his coat sleeve across his mouth to mop up the spit. "Roland-Manuel said," then paused and squinted into the horizon while gathering up his thoughts. "Somethin' like, Ravel had more frankness than elegance; more courtesy than cordiality; and more devotion to friendship than indulgence in camaraderie." He stopped, then, eyes wide, coughed and swallowed hard. "An' more ingenuousness than anythin' else!'"[36] A little spittle flecked on his chin. He sat poised as if startled, then, "Jean-Michel and I'll have a wee break, could ya excuse us?"

Jean-Michel looked at Charly and back to Terence. "A short one Terence, Ms Brooks is on a tight schedule."

Terence was already off the bench. "Oh yeah, she's tight, all right, yeah." And on his way toward the house, light-footed for a man of his age.

Charly looked at Jean-Michel. "You take one drink and I'll slug you."

Jean-Michel, hooked on the dilemma, hesitated.

"Or I can just leave now," reaching for her purse.

Jean-Michel called after Terence, "Go on, I…" but Terence was already gone.

"Why in God's name are you hanging around with that old derelict?" she demanded.

318

"He's pretty much gone, I guess. He used to give me piano lessons. I feel sorry for him."

"So?"

"So?" He stared at her.

"So, you're an alcoholic too. Where does that leave me?"

There was a long silence. "You know I drink some."

"My father drank 'some.' He died of liver failure, a jaundiced old gutter tramp muttering about the marines."

"I've gotten help; I can quit whenever I want."

"I hope you can, Jean-Michel, I really do, because that old man's about where you're headed, bitter and alone, sharing swigs of wine next to some old drifter with a whistling hearing aid."

Terence shouted from the house, "Jean-Michel!"

"I've got to go. If he doesn't get a stiff drink, that is it for today."

"You got a flask?" she asked.

He gave her a hard look.

"Look, I feel bad for Terence," she said, "but he's already gone; you're just helping him get through the last days. You still have a life."

Jean-Michel said nothing, turned, and walked back toward the door. "Would you like some water?" he asked without looking.

"No, God damn you!" she yelled, her eyes brimming with tears. "I would like a *future!*"

———

"May I apologize, Miss Brooks?" Terence looked subdued as he came up to her. "Jean-Michel has pointed out my language is a wee bit colorful for your dainty ears."

"You're a toilet-mouth, Terence, and no Irish bullshit about the local color; it isn't colorful, it's boring. I thought you'd be able to come up with some real color, not homily anecdotes for a conversation." Charly's stern looked grabbed him by the ears, focused on his eyes, and didn't pull off until he blinked.

"Yeah, miss, I'll grant you've a point. Like I said, I apologize."

"Let me make another point: what makes you an expert on Ravel, anyway?"

Jean-Michel intervened, "He met some of Ravel's students back in the forties, when Terence was just a teenager looking for work playing the piano in the bars of New York, and he—"

"And I idolized him, memorized his music, followed his people around like a goddamn dog—sorry, miss." He sat down carefully on the end of his bench, crossed his legs again, and seemed to drift off.

"Terence?" Jean-Michel prompted him.

"Terence's eyes widened momentarily. "Yeah, I studied Ravel, Debussy, Satie, all of 'em, but, ya know," he looked at his fingers, his eyes dimmed, "I got old somehow, just got old; those fellas were unique, but in less time than it takes to kill a bottle there were a thousand musicians like me tryin' to imitate 'em. Then I got Parkinson's and had to take a little whiskey for medicinal purposes. Tough to accept, ya know. Acceptance is an aspiration, never got to be a solution. I just denied it, never had the stomach for confronting it." His eyes sought his shoes and he wagged his old bald head with its prickly white hair. "Fookin' disease."

Charly decided to plow ahead. "What was the controversy between Ravel and Debussy?"

The alcohol had soothed Terence; he seemed comfortable sitting there with his bony legs crossed, tattered socks slack around fish-belly-white ankles and ancient brown shoes bouncing at times to his conversation. "Controversy?" He seemed puzzled. "Well, not between the maestros. Anyone could see that Ravel's virility and wit were a world apart from Debussy's refinement." One could almost see the music dancing in his mind.

"You have to concede that Ravel had been influenced," Jean-Michel ventured.

"I don't have to concede shit!" Terence spat out, but waved his hand for Charly's forgiveness. "An imitator? Never!" He looked at Charly and pointed at Jean-Michel. "He's not teachin' you anything about music, is he?" Terence said, squinting angrily at Jean-Michel. "Don't listen to him. When the critics finished, Ravel wasn't discredited; he was famous, for Christ's sake! All that when you were still just a glint in your mama's eyes. Ravel's personality dominated the Paris musical scene. His music was demanded, and premieres of his works became events of first importance."

Terence just sat looking a his hands, slowly shaking his head.

"Look at it this way, Charly," Jean-Michel said. "If taste means decorum, boundary, measure, then Ravel's jeweled box holds jewels, but in my opinion, Debussy's jeweled box holds a heart."[35]

"He was in World War I, wasn't he?" she asked, tired of the talk of music.

"Oh, yeah," Terrence said animatedly. "With the outbreak of the war, Ravel tried to enlist in the army, but was rejected because of his, ya know, delicate constitution. He then made an effort — no more successful — to get into the air corps. Finally, they took him for the motor convoy. He served at the front. Must have been tough," he said, shaking his head. "Had a shattering effect on him both physically and emotionally."

"Is that what killed him?"

"Nah. In the fall of 1932 the poor bastard suffered an accident in a Paris taxi. His injury was minor, at least we thought, but within a few months he had bad symptoms, lost powers of coordination, ya see. The doctors disagreed in their diagnoses. For a time Ravel suffered terrible pain together with partial paralysis. In 1935 a trip to Spain and Morocco perked him up a bit, but back in Paris he got melancholia again, and the physical disability grew worse. The doctors finally decided on a brain operation in Paris in December 1937. Ravel never regained consciousness; he passed away quietly nine days later."

"Sad," she offered.

"Death's comin'," he said matter-of-factly.

"How did Debussy die?" she asked.

"Debussy? He died in March 1918 during the bombardment of Paris by Boche airships and long-distance guns during the last German offensive of World War I."

"I mean, what did he die from?

He glanced over at Jean-Michel. "Morbid, ain't she?" He pulled some tobacco strands from his lip. "He died of cancer of the rectum, miss. Not much they could do for him. This was a time when the military situation of France was considered desperate by many, ya see, and these circumstances did not permit his bein' paid the honor of a public funeral or even ceremonious graveside orations. The funeral procession had to make its way through deserted streets, as shells from the German guns ripped up the city."

"Where is he buried?"

"Cimetière de Passy. It's in the commercial district of the Right Bank, near the Champs-Elysées. It's a fine one—even warm up your little toes, miss."

Charly looked at Jean-Michel questioningly.

"It is the only cemetery in Paris with a heated waiting room, Charly. The place has become the aristocratic necropolis of Paris: Debussy, Manet, Berthe Morisot, Talleyrand, even Princess Leila, the daughter of the former shah of Iran, are all buried there," Jean-Michel said quietly.

"It's beautiful," Terence said wistfully. "Shady chestnut trees, and sits in the shadow of the Eiffel Tower." He looked off into the distance. "Nice this time of year." He turned to Jean-Michel, his eyes beseeching. "You know I'd love to be there, Jean-Michel; you could stop by and say hello."

Ravel's Death[36]

The reason for Maurice Ravel's death has always been a mystery. There was no question, however, that something neurological was wrong and its ill effects dragged on for months. During the waning weeks of 1937, however, Ravel's condition rapidly became worse. On 17 December he was admitted to a clinic on the rue Boileau in Paris. Within a few days the eminent brain surgeon Professor Clovis Vincent carried out a difficult and delicate operation. Unfortunately, he did not find the suspected tumor, and in fact found nothing overtly wrong. The cause of Ravel's physical distresses were never to be discovered.

At the time it appeared that he had come through the operation. He rallied strongly and there were hopes for the future, but those hopes were soon to be disappointed. He lapsed into a coma and remained in that condition for several days. It was clear there could be no further improvement; he would not, the doctors said, rally again.

On 28 December 1937 Maurice Ravel died peacefully, without regaining full consciousness. For him, the foremost French composer of his time, the final dance, the protracted dance macabre, one might say, was at last over. It was offered by his friends that he looked at the time of his death a little, wizened old man. Only two years past his sixtieth birthday, the elegant, fastidious dandy-like fellow of fashion, of youth, and prime years, the neat, taut figure of a man of the world, was gone; the Basque with the big, finely shaped head, the prominent nose, the hair that had turned from Mediterranean black to glistening silver at a comparatively young age—all that was gone too, shriveled to physical ruin by some unexplained malady.

Some had called him an "artificial man," a person who at times seemed to miss some essential piece of humanity that would make his life more transparent; that, however, was not to be. He was what he was, and died like the diminishing refrains of his beautiful Boléro.

≡ *VII* ≡

Coco Chanel

Fashion dies very young, so we must forgive it everything.

Jean Cocteau, French playwright

"Where should one use perfume?" a young woman asked.
"Wherever one wants to be kissed," I said.

Coco Chanel

CHAPTER I

$\equiv$ LA BELLE DAME SANS... $\equiv$

Somerset Maugham famously described the Côte d'Azur as "a sunny place for shady people." And, it could be added, the vacation haunt of artists in all shapes and sizes. Maugham had bought Villa Blanche in Menton, just up the road from Genoa; his neighbors were Picasso in Mougins, Graham Greene in Antibes, and Marc Chagall close by in Saint-Paul de Vence.

Not to be outdone, Cap d'Antibe had its Americans: Cole and Linda Porter, and the Hemingways, Fitzgeralds, and Murphys, who also scampered about the sand and lingered in the warm waters of the French Riviera. However, the most famous woman in France, Coco Chanel, had come to the seaside for a grander plan. She bought an elegant villa called La Pausa — just a few kilometers up the road from the bathers — at Roquebrune, a small village high on the hillside overlooking the Mediterranean and not far from Menton. It was a beautiful summer retreat, to which any number of exalted friends received invitations; as far as history records, however, despite neighborly distance to Cap d'Antibe, Menton, and Mougins, no suntan lotion ever changed hands.

As everyone knew, Coco was secretly being courted by the Duke of Westminster, and if things went well — a "surprise" pregnancy was not out of the question — she would become a member of the royal family.[1] The relationship, or more precisely, the companionship, lasted over ten years (with various beaus and beauties flowing about in the nooks and crannies of each), and may have had more to do with his prestige and social standing than any personal attraction on her part.

But the duke did have fine taste in clothes. If he indeed left some things to be desired, Coco became attracted to his clothing, and began raiding his wardrobe for tweeds, waistcoats, and cardigans. It didn't take long before

Coco was applying the principles of Saville Row couture to her own concepts of women's fashion. And it didn't stop there: on cruises along the Riviera on the duke's yacht, where boat trousers, caps, T-shirts, and striped pullovers were commonplace and considered inappropriate attire for women, she adopted all with ease.

Those were lighthearted times, and prominent guests were frequently in residence at Roquebrune. At one point even the Churchills came for a visit — more than a social visit, of course. A wily politician, Winston knew strategic considerations were in play, and sought to have his hand in the match.[2] Keeping him happy on some of those quiet afternoons strained even the most determined guests, so Coco would suggest piquet, the only two-person card game she knew. She worked creatively at losing, lest the entire household suffer Churchill's ill-tempered moods. Winston was fond of her:[3]

> The famous Coco turned up & I took a gt fancy to her — a most capable & agreeable woman — much the strongest personality Benny (Duke of Westminster) has yet been up against," Winston wrote home to his wife from Bendor's hunting lodge at Mimizan in 1927. "She hunted vigorously all day, motored to Paris after dinner & is today engaged in passing and improving dresses on endless streams of mannequins."

It turned out well that he and Coco got along, since it was this friendship that she, with her Nazi lover, later leveraged into a plot to end the Second World War.

Chanel was forty-six that summer of '29, energetic and prominent, but there would never be talk of children again. The duke, an acknowledged bon vivant and married twice before (but without heirs) avoided being too serious, and, like most interlopers standing in the shadow of royalty, Chanel understood the penalties of a demeaning, artificial position. The relationship died a natural death. She had almost married one of the richest men in Europe; when she didn't, her explanation was: "There have been several Duchesses of Westminster. There is only one Chanel."[4]

Chrysalis was dark, it was 2:00 a.m. and the Seine eddied and flowed quietly along her sides. In the stateroom, Jean-Michel sat, naked, in a large leather chair. He was lonesome, tired, and stoned—the best time to call friends.

The phone rang in Charly's apartment in New York. She was watching TV. "Hello?"

"*Bonne nuit....*" The phone went silent.

"Hello," she said hesitantly.

He dropped the phone and searched around his chair until he found it, with accompanying scratches and clunks. "Merde ... sweet, how are ... things?" he huffed.

"Hey, J.M.! Nice surprise. How is Paris's number one menace after dark?"

"What?" He breathed a tired sigh.

"What's happening?"

"Poking smot and stuck to the chair."[5]

"Oh, Jesus!" she groaned. "Naked too? I sure would hate to be the poor soul who inherits that piece of furniture."

"How are things?"

"You already said that. If you're going to call, you really should wait until you're sober, or straight. But less profoundly, better watch the ashes. I'm down and out and lookin' for work. J.M., you're up a little late, something wrong?"

"Hm?" He felt heavy and dizzy. "Any luck? You should come back. We all miss you...." His voice dropped off. "Miss you," he sighed. No woman, since his wife in playful moments, had endeared herself so quickly.

"What's going on? Who's 'we?' Were you hanging out with that rat pack you call friends? You sound a little peculiar...." She waited, the phone was quiet. She tried again. "Earth to J. M.?"

"What?" he mumbled.

"Geez, this is fun. How's the new travel guide doing? What's her name ... Weatherspoon? Voyages Classiques' girl wonder."

"Um-hm. She's all right," he said thickly. "It is *Wither*spoon; but she can't wear a mini-skirt."

"Now, there's a positive turn ... dimpled knees?"

329

"Nope, you could see her balls." He giggled. "A cross between Aphrodite and Jean Crawford."

"*Joan* Crawford, sweetheart. So, things are looking up. Has she pissed off anyone enough to get fired?"

"I wouldn't say that...she's getting coffee."

"What?!"

"Uh ..." there was a pause. "You know, she gets me coffee."

"If I thought you were balling her I would cut your *cojones* off with a butter knife."

He sobered up. "Not to fear, my dear, no need to speak of knives."

"So, got her trained already?"

"I don't think the tourists like me."

"Hard to believe. So, the million-dollar question: *Why*, dear? Afraid they'll vote you off the island?"

"Island?"

"You know, the survival shows, first one to eat a dog turd or bury his face in a bowl of tarantulas wins."

"Um-hm. They don't like me; no tarantulas, just turds."

"Don't worry, those goobers were already thinking about lunch or switching travel guides. Guess you really miss me."

He hadn't realized just how much, and with alcohol muddling his brain, it left him witless. "I do. I was lecturing on Royce."

"Who's Royce?"

He had lost his concentration, "Royce who...?"

"You just said, 'Royce!' You're drunk as a rat," she said with irritation.

"Yes, Joyce." He fought to suppress a burp. "I was lecturing on—" he gave a loud burp, "Joyce! So how is the job shurch going?"

"Jesus Christ, Jean-Michel...lecturing? In front of tourists?! Work? I'm a copywriter, writing slogans for cards...you better hope there's work enough for two."

"Such as?"

"God, things must be real slow over there; you sure you have time...and money?"

"Um-hm."

"Well, how about this one: 'If I were a better person, I would sing your

330

praises / but I am an irate, self-involved bitch.'"

"Colorful. Any others?"

"Okay, I've got a bunch. How's this for going the peace and friendship route: 'When life's problems and inscrutability begin bewildering / I long for the comforting hush of death.'"

"Inspired … wasting time in the travel industry … Nobel Prize in phraseology. Guess you're not coming back?"

"You know the old saying: 'Too short for basketball and too nervous to steal.' Got any ideas?"

"Maybe," he yawned. "Things that desperate?"

"Not really. But I don't have a sugar daddy, and they repossessed my Lexus."

"Like Thoreau said, you're rich in relation to what your needs are."

"Yeah, and he lived in a shack on a pond. The bus is fun, though; I only get hit on two or three times a day by derelicts or dykes. I could still break down and ask to mow Silverstein's lawn, but things are looking up. I thought of a neat way to nail that hawk-nosed little fucker and his fat-ankled wife."

"Mon Dieu! Seriously, are you coming back?"

"First *I need a job*, dear. Anyway, why do you ask? Inquiring minds want to know? Or just horny?"

CHAPTER 2

$=\!\!=\!\!=$ A GLASS OF WATER $=\!\!=\!\!=$
BETWEEN ASSOCIATES

In France there has always been something a bit iffy about water drinkers: "A man who drinks only water has something to hide," said Baudelaire. At French spas, where people drink or sit in the water, the more mundane could easily associate the stuff with punishment, since it looks and tastes as if the country's famous soccer team had soaked their socks in it. However, if in Paris times change slowly, fashions change quickly, and water, as everyone knows, is now a distinctly modish drink. At Colette, the urgently "in" Right Bank Waterbar has seen sales soar.[6] The menu features over fifty sparkling waters and thirty that are still. Sources range from Corsica to Martinique, but a favorite classic is San Pellegrino, which Leonardo da Vinci claimed had restored him to health and which now sells in midrange at six Euros a bottle[7] (Colette's waters are not sold by the glass).

Stop in for lunch or dinner at the better Paris restaurants, however, and the star is Chateldon, a light still water that has not only a clean taste but an unequaled pedigree: Louis XIV drank it, and the Sun King's symbol still decorates the label on a bottle that has been slimmed down for that healthier look. Many patrons like the brand's Multi V, which claims 100 percent of the daily requirements for vitamins A, C, and E, without those annoying flavors of fruit juice.[8]

Amid these salubrious libations, two men sat together sipping nature's humble essence, one in his mid-fifties, slim and composed; the other slightly younger, curly-headed, and uncomfortable. One drank Chateldon, gladly, the other San Pellegrino, grudgingly.

The Chateldon drinker, Jerôme Dumas, successful financier, Sorbonne don, and intimate friend of Jean-Michel's nephew, Guy, adjusted his chair, freeing himself from the table, and sat back to survey his new acquaintance. As was his habit when careful thinking was required, he smoked his favorite Turkish cigarettes — disdainful of house rules and china. Despite liberal leanings, he was a man of conservative tastes in haut couture, where even those apathetic to fashion would appreciate the meticulously tailored satin lining of his jacket, which coordinated with his mauve silk tie. He adjusted his vest, followed by a short sip of his Chateldon, as though preparing for a speech, and after a few civilities boldly offered the first gambit. "I know your mission, of course, but you should also know that Guy and I are profoundly in love," he said earnestly, "and what you have to say must respect that."

Jean-Michel, in rumpled linen suit, Hermès tie, and worn espadrilles, nodded, and reflected on his glass, tilting it slowly for the water to swirl, longing for a beer. He looked up. "I do, and appreciate your willingness to meet," he said, grimacing as he surveyed his surroundings. "However, it's not my intent to involve myself in your relationship with my nephew; nonetheless, these circumstances have come as a surprise, and as you can understand, Dumas, an unwelcome one to both his mother and myself."

"Then neither of you knew Guy well; it was my suggestion that he be truthful with his family."

Jean-Michel nodded. "I've tried to love Guy like a son since his father's death. Unfortunately, he has been avoiding us." Jean-Michel found it irritating to be discussing his nephew with Guy's pederast lover, a man old enough to be Guy's father.

Dumas studied Levasseur intently for a few seconds, and softened. "I know you also lost your wife and daughter. Guy told me of your tragedy."

"You mustn't trouble yourself, we haven't come to discuss my past," Jean-Michel said flatly.

Dumas stiffened. "Of course, Levasseur, your past is neither here nor there with me; I only meant to be considerate," and leaning forward stubbed out his cigarette. "I'm told you need a favor?"

The meeting was getting off to a bad start; Jean-Michel intentions were slipping like footing on a grassy slope. "I have an American friend, whom you've met, who needs a job. Our mutual acquaintance at IPCA told me that you have some connections in the publishing area, and my friend—"

"Charming woman," Dumas interjected.

"I'm glad you think so."

"She's also, shall we say, a homophobic person."

"I would call her honest, and unfortunately at times outspoken."

"A true American: all heart and something less than profound."

"Then you share Guy's opinions of Americans?" Jean-Michel asked cynically.

"I don't intend pretension. He is your nephew, Professor. He is my muse. The Guy I know is true French, high-strung and very profound. Unfortunately, he lacks sentimentality toward foreigners, particularly Americans. Guy and I share a great deal in this respect, despite my Algerian roots. All beside the point, it so happens that a close and dear friend of mine is going to produce a film of Coco Chanel's life.[9] The project is being financed by an American actress and already under way. Unfortunately, they need an associate editor here in Europe for the script, since their producer is grappling with the consequences of a rather nasty disease in Italy and needs assistance."

Spite overcame Jean-Michel's otherwise calm demeanor. "I assume for Guy's sake you're not HIV positive."

Dumas' face turned dark. "Permit me a cliché, Levasseur. I'm not in the habit of discussing my private life with strangers. Our acquaintance mentioned your directness; insensitivity is more the word, perhaps one of the reasons they terminated your appointment."

"Goodbye, Dumas." Jean-Michel got up to leave.

"You were here to ask a favor, I believe. Ask it. Or, if you wish, we can conclude our business now."

"I was only concerned with Guy's well-being," Jean-Michel said standing over him. "Perhaps you are not as concerned as his family for the respectability of this situation."

Dumas looked up at him with tired eyes and gestured toward the seat. "Sit down." Jean-Michel continued to stand, but Dumas beckoned him toward the chair. "Please, Professor." Jean-Michel relented and slid into the seat. "I'm not sure what type of respectability you are speaking of; however, I am sure respectability arguments reach far beyond the gay community. Certainly, we all must bear our foibles, even you, Professor. I would simply like to make a final comment for Guy's sake, then ... leave if you are determined to leave. May I?" Jean-Michel nodded his consent.

"Imagine, Professor, a religion one enters against one's parents' will and against one's own. Imagine a race of people made from every culture, that one joins at sixteen or sixty without changing one's hue or hairstyle, unless at the tanning or beauty salon. Imagine if you can a barren nation without descendants but with a long, misty generation of ancestors with a venerable history. Imagine an exclusive club that includes a Puerto Rican boy of sixteen wearing ankle-high black-and-white Converse basketball shoes and a soccer shirt sawed off to reveal a muscular stomach — and also includes a public relations executive of forty in his Blackwatch plaids and Bass Weejun tasseled loafers. If one is gay, Professor, one is always in a crucial relationship to his queerness, if you will.[10] This rather unique existence is the world of your nephew."

Jean-Michel sighed. "So, he is loved," he reflected, then added, "He's not easy to love. I suppose that's something," then shrugged, "and not to be abused."

"Perhaps we should talk of your friend. Do you think Ms Brooks could handle the job?" He peered at Jean-Michel with a hard, steady gaze.

One could go all his life without having this type of conversation, and Jean-Michel, despite being a man of nimble intellect, was inept at negotiating favors from his nephew's lover. "This is uncomfortable for me," he said. 'I don't know how well she would perform; it is true she isn't a script writer, but she has substantial experience as a professional editor."

As in chess, if the gambit falters, superior players must employ force from other parts of the board. "Also," Jean-Michel added earnestly, "I'm impressed with her affection for the theater and excellent contacts in New York. She's a very versatile and creative young woman."

"That can be determined," Dumas said briskly. "Creativity is overrated: God made the universe in a week and still took a day off. I was asking about her aversion to gay men." He made his move. Check. He had come prepared to win, taking Jean-Michel by surprise and throwing him again off balance.

"Ms Brooks isn't a bigot, if that's your meaning, but I ... I uh, I couldn't speak for her feelings about gay men."

"You are not spending enough time with her, Professor, at least enough to know her well. Perhaps you should have joined us at Giverny."

"It is a subject she didn't share; to her credit, I think. All I know is that she's interested in having a position in Paris."

"She would have to work in both Paris and New York. Salary and benefits would easily surpass her previous employment, and all her expenses of course."

Interesting, thought Jean-Michel. *Dumas is selling!* "That wouldn't be a problem," he said, perhaps too eagerly. "She already has an apartment in New York. As for a project involving Coco Chanel, most women would love the chance." He became more aggressive; the game had taken a positive turn and he sought an advantage. "She would be excellent for the job, but would your associate not have to review the situation?"

Now Dumas pressed his moves forward, deftly, with his own intensity. "Chanel?" he chuckled. "So most women would." He betrayed some nervousness and went back to his habit of sucking air between his two front teeth. "It's hardly science, pssst, and in this case the decision has been given to me." He minced and pressed his point. "But my interest is your nephew. Guy is not on the project; however, as you're aware, he is suffering terribly for the lack of a job. My judgment is that Ms Brooks can handle the editing position for the script. The condition for her employment, however, pssst, between us, is that you hire Guy as her assistant, with reasonable latitude, and that this arrangement between us is to remain strictly professional and confidential even from Guy—most assuredly from Guy. He doesn't know of my financial involvement in the film, and he is to have no knowledge of this meeting nor my relationship with the project, and no lapses of bigotry or she's through." Check. Dumas' gambit was revealed.

In an instant Jean-Michel knew what was in store. "I don't think, Dumas, that…" he began to stutter, "I mean how–how would I–how could they work toget—"

Dumas stood. "Those are the conditions, Levasseur." The trap slammed shut; he gathered his leather pocketbook from the table and prepared to leave. "You're a capable man, your woman and nephew need jobs; work it out. I'll take care of the bill," he said, tipping his hat. "Call me by Tuesday if we have an agreement." Check.

336

Jean-Michel's position untenable, he struggled to escape from the trap. "I'll have to call Ms Brooks and —"

Dumas broke in, "Please give Ms Brooks my regards. I'm sure she'll be happy with the assignment, considering her interest in…what was it, the theater?" He smiled. "Goodbye, Levasseur." Checkmate.

CHAPTER 3

═══ A JOB FOR CHARLY ═══

"You are *kidding!*" she shouted over the phone. "*Chanel!?* Jesus, I can *not* believe it! Whose crotch…uh, couch, do I have to mount?" She hesitated, restrained, "Don't kid me, okay? What's the bad news? It's for no pay, right? Maybe they just want me as an intern, job probably has the life span of a fruit fly."

"So, you are not sure?" Jean-Michel teased. "Certainly isn't all perfume and roses; you have to read, write, and edit scripts. Helping to produce a movie about Chanel is not what I call stirring, but it is a job. Are you interested?"

"Hm. You didn't have to submit to any major indignities, right? You know, like wearing what's-his-name's ponytail, collar, and sunglasses?" Then a burst of enthusiasm. "I'll take it!"

"Terrific. What about Jodie?"

"Working on her portfolio for art school."

"Um-hm. Sounds solid."

"And the Texas Ranger?"

"He's helping dye her hair at the moment. Can we talk about them some other time?"

"Right, sounds sticky. I don't suppose *you* have any experience in cosmetics?" he taunted. "You may have to interview."

"I thought this was all about film."

"Just checking. I mean, you have to have a genuine feel for the industry."

"You mean like my collection of scented pencil erasers?"

She was perhaps the only person who could leave him perplexed and momentarily speechless. "Uh…you know—more like the things you put on your body."

338

"Oh, those. I know enough to put highlighter in my cleavage and keep my eyelashes in the fridge."

"Good. Sounds like you might qualify. Where do you buy your cosmetics Ms...ah, the name's Brooks, correct?"

She decided to turn the cards on him. "Well, sir, like most women, I buy my skin care in the supermarket, along with the celery and the disinfectant."

"Not exactly Ivana Trump now, is it?"

"No, but I'm into perfume, you know, not so much hope in a jar."

"Tell me, Ms Brooks, how do you feel about cosmetics overall—you know, the bottom line, as you Americans say? We're looking for motivated employees."

"Now that you ask, most beauty products are a total waste of money, simply lies. Anita Roddick admitted as much when she said that women would be better off buying themselves a nice bottle of wine."

"Anita Roddick?" he asked.

"Founder of the Body Shop, a good place for Christmas shopping or those special occasions, if you're wondering."

"Okay, a bar of soap it is."

"On second thought, perhaps you should try Aedes de Venustas in New York."

"Toiletries?"

"Um-hm. 'Lucifer' is nice, if you're taking down names."

"Isn't that the one with the rope that you can wear in the shower?"

"No, sweetheart, it is a perfume, comes in a bottle— you know, an atomizer, no corks."

"Sounds like you have a firm grasp of the cosmetics industry."

"I do. It's easy," she said. "A good walk every morning, preferably with a friend like you, will do more for a woman than any amount of face creams. Peace of mind equals good skin."

"A little jog," he began.

"Whoa, I didn't say that, but running—as I dimly recall—was a form of reflection."

"And the fashion industry?"

"Truthfully?"

"Is there any other way?"

"Frankly, I find it hard to understand women who talk about being empowered by tailoring. Besides, Karl Marx would say it was an instrument of class oppression."

You win," he laughed. "Sounds like you are perfect for the job; just get back over here and start working. I am not sure how long it will last, but it will go a good ways toward getting you started in Paris. The pay is probably more than you made before. I have a number for you to call and get the essentials. He doesn't speak English well, but your French will do."

"I'm already on my way. Actually, when do I have to be there?

"Immediately."

"Boy, you *are* horny. But there's this little issue of money. Are you into second mortgages?"

"Okay, so it is a loan."

"And where do I stay? Paris's Barbizon Hotel for Women?"

"Astérix mentioned that he would like you here."

"Well, Klaus offered to let me use his place a while ago."

"Klaus? That skinny bicycle rider?"

She paused. "Yeah, the one with big feet."

"I didn't notice. Besides, what about Astérix?" he said petulantly. "You are needed here."

"Of course I am: man-care—dishes, clothes, and dog. I've seen your place; perhaps a nice youth hostel nearby?"

"I have to admit, I had reservations," he said, "you know, stockings and panties hanging about, and a forest of pink tubes and lotions littering the bathroom, but Astérix loves it when you walk him, and is even willing to put up with a leash."

"Well, as long as it's for free."

"I don't recall saying that it is free."

"Listen, you old monkey, consider Astérix walked every day—perhaps even a dance or two naked on your bed—for a plane ticket. Just, well, you know, puh-leeze hold that job."

"Such reverence for an older man, so tender, and for a little laundry, a mere dance or two with bouncing breasts, and a thong." He went for the close, "Okay, so it is agreed: you walk the dog, and I get a first mate, so to speak. There are a few particulars to go over when you get here, and you will be on your way."

"Particulars?" she said hesitantly. "Oh, I know, I have to wear the little black dress[11] to work, with the sunglasses and ponytail," she sighed.

"I don't think so. You know—staff, that sort of thing."

"Staff? Staff! You *are* kidding!" she chortled.

"Well, it's just an assistant; we'll talk about it when you get here."

"Holy cow. A job! An assistant! I can't tell you how much this means to me, Jean-Michel. One more day on the highway ramp holding a sign, WILLING TO WRITE FOR FOOD, and I'd…"

"Sorry to tear you away my love. I know the kind of company you cherish, but it is the only way I can get belly dancers in my stateroom."

"Can I wear pasties?"

"Can I video?"

"Digicam, sweetheart." There was a pause; neither knew quite how to end the conversation. "*A bientôt,* you're terrific," she said quietly.

"*A bientôt,* my love. E-mail me the flight number, et cetera. Safe trip." There were other things he needed to say, but couldn't. His longing for her company lacked the words, or at least those that would not scare her. An inspiration struck him: he'd send Chanel No. 5. A nice touch.

Chanel No. 5

Gabrielle loved the summers in Biarritz. During the summer of 1920 she met Grand Duke Dmitri Pavlovich, who was also on holiday, and it soon became obvious that they were very attracted to each other, even though he was eleven years younger than she was. Dmitri was a member of the Romanov family, and treated as a son by the tsar. Unfortunately, after the Revolution he was left with very little money. They lived together for a year, and in that year he collaborated with Chanel and her most successful product was created: the perfume Chanel No. 5.

Perfumes had previously been based on natural flower fragrances, which were very concentrated essences, but once in use they quickly evaporated and faded. Dmitri, a frequent guest at the Russian court, knew the product well. He also knew Ernest Beaux, a perfume chemist at Grasse, the headquarters of the industry, and introduced Gabrielle, who sought to create her own perfume. The idea was to be based, not on flower essences, but on eighty different ingredients, creating a more stable base and a distinctively unique product, which could also be used in smaller quantities. Gabrielle left the mixing of the ingredients to Ernest Beaux, but made the final decisions about the finished product herself, sampling it several times before deciding on the fragrance that she thought reflected the image she wanted to portray. Even the packaging was a totally new concept, moving away from the elaborate, frivolous designs of other manufacturers, to a sharp-cornered cube in which the perfume was visible through the glass bottle. The label was also devoid of ornament, in plain white, with the words "No. 5 Chanel" printed boldly in black.

Her product was an immediate success; though other manufacturers tried to produce copies, no one was able to capture it exactly, and Chanel No. 5, (the number of one of the samples sent to her) remained everyone's favorite. Parfums Chanel was founded in 1924, run by the Wertheimer brothers, Pierre and Paul, with Ernest Beaux as technical director.

At the end of 1921, Gabrielle and Dmitri parted company as friends. He married an American beauty, but he and Gabrielle remained close associates for many years. The villa at Garches was also sold and Gabrielle moved back to 29, Faubourg St. Honoré in Paris. Her theatrical friends were soon filling the apartment with their singing and dancing, much to the annoyance of the neighbors, but Gabrielle shrugged off their complaints. Picasso, Stravinsky, and Diaghilev were all to be found there, pursuing their particular interests.[12]

CHAPTER 4

═══ "MY FRIENDS, ═══
THERE ARE NO FRIENDS."

It could be said that Gabrielle Chanel—Coco to a few intimates and millions of other women—came from nothing. Eventually she became a symbol of emancipation and casual feminine allure, but when she became famous and seemingly everything was known about her—her income, love affairs, tastes, successes, and sorrows—she kept telling lies. When in old age she was confronted by a young woman who suggested she see a psychiatrist, Chanel looked slyly at her and said: "I, who never told the truth to my priest?" She even went to her grave as Gabrielle Chasnel because legally correcting the misspelled name on her birth certificate would reveal that she was born a bastard child in a poorhouse hospice on 19 August 1883 in the village of Saumur.

When Gabrielle was in her early teens, her mother died, and her father, who was a traveling wine peddler, left Gabrielle and her sister in a convent and disappeared forever. The convent was a challenging experience for six years, particularly for poor girls who were separated from the paying girls, wore a different uniform, and in general were looked down on. With unusual insight, a friend said much later that Coco was simply trying to put all the world's women into the uniform she wore back then, a black dress with white collar.[13]

She left the convent in her later teens and worked in a tailoring shop, with aspirations to be a music-hall performer. She tried singing for a while, and her nickname, "Coco," came from a song she sang in a local bistro about a little dog, although she later protested that it was a pet name her father had called her. Although small, the Auvernois town where Chanel tried to

343

launch her singing career did have some compensations, foremost among them for the young ladies of the village a fashionable and aristocratic cavalry regiment. One of its officers, Etienne Balsan, a sportsman and horse breeder, was attracted to young "Coco." At twenty-five she became his mistress, and was brought by Etienne to live in his chateau. Balsan's home was a retreat from his military duties and the source of considerable entertainment for his numerous hunting friends and their fashionable mistresses. Coco began to attract attention, not only for her bearing on a horse, and her saucy courage, but also for her captivating beauty.[14]

She made and wore very attractive hats, but the opposite of the huge decorated hats then in fashion. Her hats were small and chic. They were greatly admired by many women who asked to buy copies. So, in 1908, Chanel began selling the new-style hats from Balsan's ground-floor Paris apartment. She and Etienne were together when possible, but a man named Boy became her muse.

Arthur "Boy" Capel was a member of Balsan's inner circle, and the only one who worked for a living. Chanel became infatuated with him: she loved the way that he smelled — of leather, horses, forest, and saddle soap — and she liked his easygoing ways. He was handsome by all accounts, with his darkish skin, straight brown hair, and striking green eyes. While Etienne judged people according to the depth of their equestrian knowledge, Boy's passion was people, which attracted Chanel. He was interesting, and interested in society, a man so engaging that those around him found it easy to confide in his trust.[15]

As a businessman, Boy recognized a potential businesswoman in Chanel, and in 1910, helped to set up a small shop for her in Paris. The shop was located on a mezzanine at number 31, on the west side of Rue Cambon. She brought pretty things from the apartment to fix the place up, and hired a young woman as her assistant. Coco knew little about business — where could she have learned? The bank only allowed overdrafts on her business account because Boy had deposited securities to back her up. Chanel didn't know, of course, and felt humiliated when she found out. She threw her handbag in his face and resorted to tears. Sixty years later she would tell friends of the unobtrusive solicitude with which Boy had propped up her business venture. "I was convinced I was making money, that I was becoming rich."[16]

In order to act, to build, she needed a solid companion by her side, some-one she could lean on. Arthur Capel was that companion. Coco had always longed to break out of the subservient role in which frivolous officers and bla-sé sportsmen had cast her while living with Etienne, and they separated.

Boy was the one showing her affection, confidence, and esteem, and although he had had innumerable mistresses, he abandoned them all.[17]

Boy showed her a Paris where English lords and Russian grand dukes played. This was the famous time for Paris, and Coco was fascinated by high society. If the time with Etienne had schooled her about the habits and tastes of the wealthy, living with Boy had exposed her to social nuance, caste, and family scandals.

Of the men in Coco Chanel's legendary life, Boy Capel was the only one about whom she almost told the truth, the only one she truly liked to talk about. "We were made for each other," she would say late in life. She called him the one man she could never forget, and most agreed. She liked to tell of her own naiveté, timidity, and little revolts, to underline his ardent nature and strong personality and how women were attracted to him.[18]

She repaid Capel's investment, but still needed his love. Unfortunate-ly, this was denied her, as he was killed in a car accident on Christmas Eve 1919. She said later that this was the year she became famous and the year she lost everything. Capel had left Gabrielle £40,000 in his will, and, three months after his death, she moved from their apartment into a new villa at Garches. So began a new era in Chanel's life, full of painters, composers, and dancers. Misia Sert, a pianist of some renown and one of Chanel's most trusted companions, had a large circle of friends in the theatrical world, and it was she who introduced Gabrielle to this exciting environment.[19]

As her business grew, so did Chanel's social reputation and her person-al legend. Her success and her fortune were her entree and she manipu-lated them brilliantly. She now had a new lover: the Duke of Westminster, certainly influential and fabulously wealthy. The Paris of the "Roaring Twenties" was the city of the artist, writer, and thinker; the new women seized on the chic, the dash and glamour. Chanel, from her mansion on the Faubourg St. Honoré, played hostess to this new world, friends with Picasso, Stravinsky, Cocteau, Hemingway, and many others. Colette called her "a little black bull" for her energy and verve.

CHAPTER 5

===== A MUG FOR CHARLY =====

Jean-Michel had created a small but comfortable second bedroom for Charly on *Chrysalis* after her return to Paris, and a daily routine of sorts was established. *Chrysalis* on the Seine was to be home now, New York simply a receding memory refreshed periodically by CNN or the BBC's noteworthy items of finance, global warming, and the war on terrorism. All that was left to finish his project was to present Charly with her recently appointed administrative assistant, Guy, then phone him with the good news about the job — circumstances no less exhilarating than having your wisdom teeth ripped out by the roots.

Jean-Michel had decided to invite Charlie to an outing at the Maison Fournaise, near Chatou, where Auguste Renoir set his famous *Le Déjeuner des Canotiers*. It was an inspired location to break the news about Guy, before the anticipated explosion became too dangerous to contain. The locality was a wise choice for pleasing a woman because it was both public and beautiful, which discouraged scenes of anger and aggression. The restaurant was a Guinguettes, one of a small number of outdoor cabarets on the edge of Paris where the lower classes used to go on holidays because the wine, which some said was so sour it made goats dance, was exceedingly cheap.[20] Now it was usually crowded, noisy, and a bit pricey.

They walked in and were shown to their seats at a table covered by a checkered tablecloth with a small vase of flowers. They made themselves comfortable.

"Hey, this place is great," Charly offered, looking around. She leaned forward and said quietly, "Neat people, and the landscape is beautiful. How come we haven't been here before?"

"A little crowded on weekends," he said, and signaled the waiter.

"I'm not that hungry, maybe just a fruit salad," she murmured as she scanned the menu.

"I think I'm going to have a Steak Béarnaise," he said, paging through the selections. He murmured, "Guy likes steak."

She looked up. "Pardon me?"

He hesitated. "Uh, Guy likes steak," and pretended to scrutinize the menu.

"What's that got to do with the price of butter in Brazil?" she said suspiciously.

"Nothing, just mentioning that he likes steak."

"Who doesn't?"

"Well," he shrugged, "vegetarians."

"Vegetarians," she repeated and looked back at her menu.

"Real Madrid is playing tomorrow night, would you like to see the game?"

"Soccer?" She said absent-mindedly, continuing to read the menu. "Soccer? I hate soccer, most boring game in the world after bowling, but just after. You know that. Now take the Dallas Cowboys, they..." She became suspicious. "Why do you ask?"

"Well, if you didn't want to go, I thought I would ask Guy."

"What!" She looked up again, this time fiercely. "What's all this about Guy? You haven't mentioned his name in at least a month, you know, since... " She leveled her gaze at him as a multitude of spinning wheels in her brain began to accelerate. "Ever since I told you I hated that little prick."

He had to face the situation squarely or run like hell. He began to evade. "I wish you wouldn't use that word. Besides, he's really not so 'little' you know, he's athletic. We thought at one point he would become a professional figure skater."

"You don't say. A figure skater. How unusual. I don't suppose he's going to join us for ice skating this afternoon in some snug little rink with his boyfriend, or perhaps we could all go to Poilâne and snack on those yummy cupcakes?"

"Of course not," he grumped, "but if he was, what of it?"

"If my grandmother had wheels, she'd be a bus; what of it?"

He was sinking up to his knees in front of a green-eyed mountain lion.

"Well—"

"Well, what?" She goaded him. "What's going on? Do you have something that you would like to say, which includes my name and his in one sentence?"

"No. Charly. He's just a young man trying to make his way in the world," he said defensively.

She interrupted him icily, "Did you forget, Jean-Michel, that I hate that *little* snot—excuse me—I hate that snot. And, in case you don't recall, that snot hates me."

Fear seized him, and he got up. "I have to go to the men's room," he said, tossing his napkin defiantly on the table, and began to walk away. "All I was saying" he said over his shoulder, "is that he will probably be working with you on the Chanel project as your assistant," and then slid quickly between two tables filled with happy guests.

When Jean-Michel returned, the table was empty. He began to imagine where she would be waiting for him: hidden in the restaurant's lobby, or behind a bush, or in the parking lot. He had the car keys, so she couldn't get home. He felt apprehensive, like when the high school bully of his old alma mater was waiting after school to inflict pain and humiliation on him. He called the waiter over to the table.

"She left." The waiter grinned mischievously.

Jean-Michel was not inclined to discuss his situation with a stranger in front of strangers. "We have to leave, we're in a hurry."

"She's angry. Very angry," the waiter cautioned. Other guests were looking.

"Um-hm, I know."

The waiter's face brightened. "Maybe you should give her a present; we have some nice Renoir prints on T-shirts and mugs in the gift shop."

He dismissed the idea, but then reconsidered. *A mug might be nice*, he mused, although she was partial to T-shirts.

CHAPTER 6

$=$ SIRMIONE $=$

Fashion does not exist unless it goes down into the streets. The fashion that remains in the salons has no more significance than a costume ball.

Chanel

Plans for August had been organized, and the Chanel Project put on hold for a few weeks while its producer, Jürgen Huber, recuperated from a chronic illness in Italy. Nonetheless, Charly's contact at the project's Paris office had arranged for her to meet Huber in Italy and recover lost time. Rough drafts of the script needed to be revised, and the quicker the work done, the better. After the revisions, Charly would return to Paris with instructions for developing the new material. Guy's appointment, which he had accepted with the same élan as Charly, had also been put on hold until she returned. Charly was, after some explosive words with Jean-Michel in the restaurant parking lot—the Renoir mug notwithstanding—reconciled to the fact that this job, like all jobs, had a few downsides. She resolved not to quit until Guy's first day.

Huber was convalescing at a fashionable sanatorium in Sirmione, a small town at the southernmost point of Lago di Garda not far from Verona. After a short flight to Linate airport, train to Sirmione, and registration at the Corte Regina Hotel, Charly was—as well as one might expect—prepared to meet her new boss. The sanatorium, or *terme* as it is called in Italian, faced Lago de Garda and its crown of snow-covered mountains to the north. The terme was landscaped with large cypress and pine trees, the usual expanse of soft green lawns, oleander, and strategically placed park benches where patients and relatives made themselves comfortable. The building, a masterpiece of Mussolini Modern, square and imposing, and fronted by tasteless columns, sat like a squat octogenarian, truculent if not forbidding. It was not one of Sirmione's best edifices. The lobby floor was tiled with large, shiny, brown marble squares common to the region, surrounded by white plaster walls and rectangle pillars displaying institutional art of the local area. To move through the quiet hallways was to create a ricocheting sound of clicking heels and muffled voices, and to raise inquisitive eyes.

An attendant at the reception desk directed her to a secured wing of the building, then through a checkpoint manned by a laconic *vigilise,* and into a luxurious, richly carpeted hallway with Italian paintings and antique furniture, none of which could mask the smell of fresh laundry and antiseptic. She found the right location and knocked timidly on a heavy wooden door. There was that disagreeable feeling of catering to strangers, and she wished to leave, but after a few moments was met by a young man in slacks and short-sleeved shirt, who smiled and politely ushered her into the suite. He led her through a sparsely furnished living room dimly lit by shuttered windows, and finally out through French doors to a shady covered terrace and wrought-iron furniture cushioned in plush yellow pillows. Above, two brass fans hung on metal bars, their blades making lazy turns below the awning. The view of the lake from the terrace was partially obscured by a ceiling-high ragged hedge of fragrant basil through which small shafts of sunlight pierced the shade, making mottled spots on the floor and offering at least some sense of privacy with its pleasure. It was vacation time, and the distant sounds of bathers calling and laughing from the shore was bittersweet for Charly, recalling memories of parties and carefree days on Texas lakes.

"Please, seniora," he offered a comfortable chair, "Senior Huber arrivi, ee momento." Chagrined by his inept language, he reverted back to Italian. "Posso offrirle un aperitivo, signora?"[21] Italian, but she got the message.

"San Bittér, please." She smiled self-consciously.

Charly was nervous, despite a determined effort to create at least the veneer of confidence and professionalism. This man, after all, came from that class of the very rich who lived extremely well and experienced obsessions with issues no less important than helping to name the next president of the United States or having the right kind of Scandinavian leather in their private jets. To prepare herself she had read Plum Sykes' novel, *Bergdorf Blondes,* since it was about those women who wore three-carat diamond earrings with jeans to feel informal at their book clubs.[22] Above all she was curious; unfortunately, the project officer in Paris could add little information about the director, a wealthy and discerning type to be sure, and that Huber was recovering from an unexplained illness. It had seemed unprofessional to ask if he was handsome, sweet, and considerate — unmarried, that is. Then, with a perfunctory adieu, she had been given money and tickets for the trip.

She was not prepared, therefore, for the shock of seeing Huber. Peering toward the lake, Charly heard a noise and turned to look as he appeared at the French doors. He was dressed in a white terry-cloth robe, dark blue sandals, and black wraparound sunglasses. He was older, late fifties perhaps, tall — almost two meters — heavily built, a sportive physique long since gone to flab.

She instinctively held her breath. He looked threatening: a bald head that accommodated two large folds of flesh connecting the back of his neck to his scalp in that fashion preferred by prison inmates, bullies, and skinheads. He had snow-white skin and a fine sheen of white body hair, in brief, a giant albino. The contrast of his sunglasses on a sagging face, three-days' growth of prickly white beard, white arms, legs, and ugly feet in the toeless sanatorium slippers and thick robe made him look like a fearful, furry apparition. In sum, he exhibited most of the attributes Charly found instantly repulsive.

He saw the shock on her face. "Brooks," he said, addressing her without title, as though officer to enlisted. "Sorry to receive you so informally," he said, sweeping his hand along his robe, and then sat down across from her, "but I have just completed one of my treatments and their schedule was delayed." His English was thickly accented and guttural.

"Ah, and Bruno has gotten you a drink. San Bittér. It happens I prefer Crodinol, but the difference seems only in its color." He chuckled. "An appropriate start for a conversation on fashion." There was an awkward silence and he used the moment to wrap the robe tightly about his knees, as though somehow cold, then called over his shoulder, "Bruno! Arachidi!" And turned back. "As you can see, Brooks, I am not a healthy man. In fact, normally I would not have taken on this assignment, but it is for a friend to whom I owe a favor, and, well…" he shrugged.

Charly's mind raced for something useful to say, only to be beset by total inanity. "It's a beautiful place…and, oh, thank you for the boxes of Vuitton accessories you left in the room…I guess—I mean, there was no card." Bruno arived with the peanuts.

He nodded but took little notice and continued, "I have some recurring aggravations, which are periodically driven into remission here in Sirmione. Perhaps I'm getting older." He smiled, his lips forming a slanted pink line, and raised his glass in salute—meager efforts lacking personality, since his eyes remained masked behind his sunglasses and his teeth showed crooked and yellow against his white skin. "I have to move quickly and this damnable condition is slowing me up. As you are aware, I need help on the project. Therefore, your presence at this uncomfortable affair." He crossed his legs, reached down, and began absentmindedly fondling his toes, followed shortly by scooping peanuts from the bowl beside him with the same hand.

"I will do my best," she ventured.

"I can assure you, you will. Your references—for the most part—are acceptable." He paused. "Outspoken, I understand, but it seems there is a British woman casting aspersions." He leaned forward. "Are you having a catfight, Brooks?"

"No. I don't even know any British women." She wanted to interrogate him, but didn't dare.

"Good. Just some travel guide, and I don't like distractions. Your job depends on me, and if you make mistakes there is always someone in the wings, as they say. Enough. Let's talk about Chanel. I would like your opinions, not as an editor, but as a woman. Have you any feelings for her?" There would be no inching into unknown waters; he wanted her to dive.

"I don't—" she started, but his words rolled over hers again.

"For example, she was a very dramatic woman." He began to quote Chanel in thickly accented German, "'Fashion is not simply a matter of clothes. Fashion is in the air, borne upon the wind. One intuits it. It is in the sky and on the road.' What do you think?" He reached for his lighter and, without

352

offering or asking permission, lit a cigarette, exhaling gratefully. "Brooks?" He looked at his cigarette, "What do you think she meant?"

She hesitated, expecting him to interrupt again. "I don't know how good at this I can be. I read Axel Madsen's book and, of course, Charles-Roux's, but I've had only a little time to familiarize myself with her life."

He paused, disappointed. "Brooks, in the space of approximately one year I must bring this woman to the world through cinema with the help of some very wealthy and temperamental people. It has been tried before both on film and stage; neither did justice to its subject, and both—both, mind you—lost considerable money in the process. That won't happen this time. Coco Chanel, the heroine of this legend, must be an attractive, abrupt, vengeful, stubborn, lonely, and miserly megalomaniac femme fatale. She is mine to capture if I can. Now, Brooks, tell me in one hundred words or fewer whom I am looking for."

Charly saw her professional life flash before her eyes; this great snow-man was about to fry her.

"Brooks?" he said.

She hesitated…waited…nothing was coming…conjuring without success. Finally, like jumping from a fearful height into strange black water, she blurted, "You won't find her, she's all smoke and mirrors!"

Silence. He was intrigued, and took a drag on his cigarette. "Explain."

"Well, to try to explain the creativity of Coco Chanel might be easy for some, but for me the difficult part is to understand the paradoxes within the woman. I saw some of her interviews. She said that *she* was fashion, that she was style. Whatever she wore, or even how she cut her hair, was fashion because it was she who created it, and thousands of other women copied it." Charly had unconsciously been holding her breath and trying to speak at the same time. She wavered, her voice cracking, "You're looking for a paradox, someone who *is* fashion, not someone who fabricates it."

"*Ja, ja,* keep going," he urged.

"Judging from what I read, some would say it's fitting, no pun intended, that Chanel was often photographed holding a cigarette or standing in front of her famous Art Deco wall of mirrors…you know—all smoke and mirrors."

He nodded. "She sat at the top of the stairs in her studio and used the mirrors to see the reactions of her clientele."

"My view of Chanel's version of her life involved a multitude of lies, inventions, cover-ups, and revisions, so…" she hesitated again.

"So!?"

"So, she seemed to be all wool and silk, and yet somehow you're going to have to deal with that contradiction."

"Good! That was the failure of the first attempts. But why do you think she behaved that way?"

Charly took refuge in a sip of San Bittér, its clean, cold taste giving her strength. "Probably had to, but that takes a psychiatrist. Maybe it had something to do with her poverty and early failures."

"Like?"

"Well, like when she couldn't make it as a cabaret singer. Evidently, she was no Piaf." She felt more confident.

"What do you know of Piaf?"

"Practically nothing, I'm quoting from Madsen. Chanel couldn't dance, either, but I think that's where she took the name 'Coco,' right?"

He paused, resting back in his chair, cinched at the waist like a weisswurst,[23] and reached again for his toes with his free hand. He mused for a moment, ignoring her question. "Do you know what Napoleon said was one of his greatest failings?" She shook her head. "Judging people on first impressions and appearance." He smiled his crooked smiled. "Napoleon felt he had made that mistake with Talleyrand, his minister of state, whom he liked immensely at first. You know what he called Talleyrand later?"

Again she shook her head.

"Shit in silk stockings." He licked his lips and, judging from his sunglasses, was staring at her breasts. He took the peanut bowl and held it before her. "Peanuts?"

Charly, like so many Americans, abhorred conversational vacuums and sought to fill the silence with something, anything—but intuition said no.

Finally, he spoke. "I value two things in people above all, regardless of whether they are friends or employees or both: intelligence and loyalty. I'm betting you have the ability to demonstrate both. I need some help getting this film off the ground." His voice became seasoned with irritation. "There are a couple of people, however, who would love nothing more than to see me fall on my *hintern*."

"Hintern?"

"Ass, Brooks. It's German. Your job will be to do what I tell you to do, completely, quickly, and no mistakes; your other job is to keep Dumas' boyfriend from getting in my way. From what I've heard, that shouldn't give you any problems." He looked for a reaction. "Does it?"

"No," she said, noting that the man obviously had his contacts.

"Good. I'll meet you at the Caffè Grande Italia at 10:00 p.m. Don't do any foolish female things like come late. If you don't see me, ask for Mario. Have Alba and Lorenzo treated you well?"

"Alba?"

"The manager of one of our most comfortable *alberghi* in Sirmione."

"Our?"

"I am Sirmionese, Brooks, treated like a local, a villager. You are among family here unless you misbehave. "Do you need anything?" He heaved a heavy sigh without waiting for her to answer, stubbed out his cigarette in the ashtray, and rising, mumbled, "Tonight, Brooks." He lumbered away, disappearing ponderously through the French doors, like a great polar bear to his den.

CHAPTER 7

═══ CAFFÈ GRANDE ITALIA ═══

Stupidity and meanness, error, vice,
Inhabit and obsess us every one
As for remorse, we find it rather fun:
We nourish it, as beggars feed their lice.

Baudelaire

Located on a small peninsula at the southern shore of Lago di Garda, the ancient village of Sirmione, with the majestic Scaligero Castle at its entrance, stands as a permanent sentinel gazing across the lake, first toward the hills of Monte Baldo, covered by the ascending vineyards of Bardolino and Val-policella, then sweeping northward toward the great, snowcapped Alpine mountains glistening above the distant haze over the lake.

Graceful old ferryboats arriving intermittently from the north glide up to the dock, each with its proud name, like *Goethe,* or some other saint of culture, painted in large black letters along their gleaming white sides. They come to an expert stop, followed by clanking gangplanks, which announce to the passengers their arrival at the pier. Then, a smorgasbord of Europe-ans, waiting impatiently on the concrete pier to board, pass over the gang-plank quickly onto the ship, while the crew takes tickets and welcomes them aboard. Last calls are announced, and the gangplanks are rapidly recovered on deck to be safely stored. Finally, the ropes are cast off and the ferries begin to chug forward, their deep-green bow waves scattering the ducks and swans. The departing vacationers hurry to the rails for their last glimpse of friends and Sirmione's famous landmarks before the ferries take them out of sight. The ships' paddlewheels churn and accelerate, cruising off toward Desenzano, Salò, or other ports north.

Sirmione's Piazza Carducci features five cafes wedged among assorted pizza and gelato shops leading to the aged pier through which many of Lago di Garda's arriving tourists make their way into the quaint Italian village. Visitors wandering into the piazza are treated to cafés festooned with giant shady umbrellas, a multitude of small tables, and faux-rattan chairs serving colorfully dressed tourists sipping tall specialty drinks featuring stalks of fresh celery, or spooning fruit-laden sundaes with exotic names like "Macedonia de Fruita."

The Caffè Grande Italia is without question the oldest and most cherished of the lot. Maria Callas once drank and sang songs with Mario's father in the bar. Alfred Lord Tennyson's poem "Ave Atque Sirmione," composed as he rowed across the lake, is etched in marble on a wall across the square, while Ezra Pound lived in the Hotel Eden around the corner during the Second World War, and invited his friend, James Joyce, to join him from Trieste. Napoleon marched along Garda's shores, and a century later, Churchill painted its stately villas and castles. Goethe was seized by a crowd of suspicious Italians and almost hanged as a spy in Malcesine while drawing pictures of its castle. All of this and more, choreographed under the watchful eyes of the spirit of Catullo, the first of Italy's famous Romantic poets, who lived in ancient times on the northernmost part of the peninsula, wrote poems to his lost love, and whose bronze bust commands the public square.

Charly approached the bar at the appointed hour. It was filled with lounging tourists. Huber was sitting under the awning with a woman, her face ancient and wrinkled like an oriental grandmother's. She leaned on the table, her arm propping up a bony hand used to support her chin. She squinted as though from the sun, her gray hair hanging in waxy strings. She was dressed in an oversized sweater, the rolled-up sleeves revealing flaps of liver-spotted skin where muscles once flexed. Both she and Huber were talking with Mario, a balding, friendly man of easy demeanor and wit, the great-grandson of the founder and owner-manager of Caffè Grande Italia. Huber was dressed in a blue paisley shirt, casual tan pants, and a black baseball cap that proclaimed "Raptor" stitched across its front in block letters. Despite the night and the dim glow of the café lights, he wore his sunglasses.

The piazza's relaxed ambiance was cooled by a soft breeze off the lake. Two musicians, one older, who sported a ponytail and played an electric piano while he sang, and the other, a younger man who seemed happy to simply amuse himself stroking chords on an aging guitar, serenaded the crowd. The musicians were set up near the pier, on a small platform facing their noisy audience, as excited kids ran gaily about the piazza and made nuisances of themselves, jabbering for attention in Italian or German. Huber and the older woman were speaking in rapid Italian as Charly arrived; Huber didn't get up, but gestured toward his friend Louise. "Ms Brooks, meet the most knowledgeable artist in Milan. She is eighty-four, eccentric, reclusive, and imperious; known to break things, attack journalists, and totally intimidate women like you." He offered his twisted smile again, while Charly was left standing, not sure what to do.

Huber pulled an empty seat toward him and gestured for Charly to sit.

"Sit here, dear," commanded Louise, touching a chair across the table from Huber and nearer to her.

Charly's face flushed, irritated at being pushed around by strangers.

Huber was having fun. "Louise, here, has her daily copy of the *Corriere della Sera*, ironed every morning before she reads it."

"Yes, why not?" she said.

Removing his sunglasses for a brief moment, Huber looked at Charly and winked with a pink eye. "It's a little unusual."

"What kind of a crack is that?" Louise replied. "When it lies at the door in a place like Milan it's filled with germs." She looked at Charly, cigarette in one hand, holding her drink with the other. "I can tell you" she said, "it doesn't change the content."

Huber continued, "She reads while eating her breakfast. What do you think this Delphian woman eats?" Charlie shrugged her shoulders.

"Orange marmalade straight from the jar — no toast!" He seemed pleased with his modest audience of tourists doing their supposed best not to listen. "And tea. Green tea. Every morning. What do you think of that, Ms Brooks?" Charly remained silent — but now it was 'Ms' Brooks — waiting for the inevitable interruption. "Louise and I are old friends. She paints for a living. I've asked her for advice on this film; can't be just another biography of Chanel, it has to be about twenty-first-century fashion with its roots in

358

the twentieth. Chanel is the inspiration of modern fashion, and that's where it has to start. But marrying the two is the key.

Louise snorted. "He wants Cruise to play Boy Capel. Jesus! Can you believe that? Probably wants Madonna to play Coco!"

Huber laughed, took off his hat, revealing pale white skin and bristly hair, and handed it to Mario as he passed. "No. Demi. You know, Ms Brooks, Louise had ... uh, a 'crush,' I think you call it, on your friend Richard Nixon."

"The last real man in America since fifty years." Louise said defensively, tapping her cigarette ash on the floor with one hand and pushing her hair back with the other.

Charly had a distasteful image of two octogenarians going at it. "Yeah, too bad he's gone." she said.

"She's had any number of energetic lovers, even at seventy!" Huber exclaimed.

"What do you know about romance? Germans know nothing of love they haven't learned in a book or an alley. *Ich liebe dich!*"[24] Louise growled, leaning heavily on the German accents, "With language like that, how do they make love?" she said in disgust. "Jürgen tells me that you want to help him work on this cinema project. They call you Brooks, right?

"No. I prefer Charly to Brooks," she said, looking at Huber.

Louise took a sip of her drink, then asked, "Are you in love?"

Again Charly was off balance. Any number of answers came to mind, most of which started with *None of your fucking business.* "Why do you ask?" she said coldly.

"I want to know."

"Are *you*?" Charly said, holding her ground. "Frankly, I can't imagine anyone with a crush on Nixon."

"Of course I'm in love," Louise said. "I'm in love with everything. I'm old. There's going to be too much to miss, all too soon." Huber sat contented to observe with a sardonic grin.

Louise continued, "Americans have only one word for love. They love cheeseburgers like they love sex or love God. The Greeks have four words for love. They don't mix romantic love in with God or cheeseburgers."

"Thanks. What's your point?"

Louise glanced at Huber, then back. "Chanel was a lover of men and women, of fashion and of money. I want to know what you've been in love with. Are you a lesbian?"

"No. I love … a lot of things, the most important is my daughter."

"No men?" she said.

"Or animals?" Huber sniggered.

"I have other fish to fry," Charly said flatly.

Huber laughed. "Frying fish! She's going to ask you about Arthur Capel, Ms Brooks, not mackerel."

"No, I'm not," Louise said. "I'm going to ask her and see what she feels and thinks; it's not some goddamn Teutonic test." She looked at Charly. "Germans," she said and ignored him.

"Coco was twenty-seven when she fell in love with Arthur Capel, but everyone knew him as 'Boy' Capel. How old were you?"

"I got pregnant when I was very young, it didn't have anything to do with love."

"Lost your virginity in the back seat of a car to some farmer's son? Well, Boy Capel wouldn't have been your type. Boy was someone solid, someone who assumed Chanel had a mind, and asked what she thought. To him, she was a singular beauty." Louise removed a cigarette from her pack. "Oh, I remember seeing her when I was young, and haven't forgotten: slim, straight, and with an aristocratic head on a long, graceful neck, she looked like a Gainsborough duchess in profile." Louise was lost momentarily in her memories, then focused on her cigarette, which Huber reached over and lighted. "Full face, she had a full face," she said, and blew out a stream of smoke. "And those mocking raven eyes. Generous mouth, too, charming dimple, and knowing presence, she was an alluring street urchin to any who saw her. There were few in Milan, Paris, or London who could compare." She looked over at Jurgen. "Like Merca" she whispered, and he nodded agreement.

"Merca?" Charly asked.

"A friend who shared these tables with us until last year. She owned one of the finest villas on this peninsula, but, unfortunately, died a few months ago." Louise moved quickly toward a new subject. "What city would you begin the script in?" she asked.

"Why a city? I'm a Texan, impressed with Chanel's interest in horses," Charly said, seeking familiarity.

Louise smiled. "Romantic, I suppose, an open field near the Pyrenees, Coco and Boy racing their horses. See?" She looked over at Huber. "Women want romance, forget the goddamn Nazis."

"Were they a good match?" Charly asked, choosing to avoid the debate.

"Perfect. Boy had come to appreciate her acid charm, her spontaneity and sharp tongue, in their trips to the Pyrenees. Coco was lively, blunt, and clever, yet just beneath that deceivingly approachable manner there was by all descriptions something from a harsh past that was severe.

"You see, dear, she loved what was attractive and disliked what was merely pretty. Even at your age back then, she loved sophisticated men, not redneck boys. Her taste was nervy and she easily saw the hypocrisy in people. That she was Etienne's mistress somehow added to her stature in Boy's eyes.

"Etienne? He was the wealthy military officer who gave Coco an early start—" Charly began, only to be interrupted by Huber.

"As a mistress."

"Etienne was a lifelong friend and even gave her an amethyst ring, which she wore around her neck on a gold chain," Louise countered. "But Boy was the important one. Etienne was going to Argentina for an extended visit, which only served to entice Chanel into inviting Boy to attempt her as his conquest."

Louise continued, "What Gabrielle would discover in Boy was his irrepressible taste for fast living, a taste for elegance, success, and bold women. Everyone could see that they were meant for each other.

"Boy was a year older than Gabrielle, and had spent his adolescence in boarding schools. He spoke French fluently. Do you speak French?"

"Some."

"German?"

"No."

"Italian?"

"No."

"Do you have a big family?"

Charly shook her head. She was tired, but felt forced to be on guard.

"Neither did Chanel; Capel was her family." Charly was unable to hide her boredom, and Louise was having none of it. "Why are you here, dear?"

"To earn a living."

"Then you should begin working at it. Would you like another drink?"

"No. Sorry, it's been a long day."

"Would you like to go back to your hotel?"

Charly was dying to do exactly that, but not at the cost of her job; besides, she could outlast an eighty-year-old woman and a sick man any day of the week. "No, thanks. Maybe an Irish coffee would do the trick," and she turned to find Mario.

"Good," Louise replied. "What do you think Chanel felt being bedded by two men?"

"I learned early on that, for men, women are sex objects; for women, men are money objects. So she had two, like men dream about with women … but two men? More practical," Charly said matter-of-factly. "I assume the two men shared her?" She felt Jürgen watching her behind his sunglasses.

"Or she them," Louise said. "But not officially. On the other hand, regardless of what the two men's feelings were, it was not in character, from what's known of Coco's upbringing and her fear of being regarded as a kept woman, to imagine her sleeping in turn with Boy and Etienne until the two decided who should pick up the tab—and her. Boy put up the money for Coco to rent some commercial space in the street that would be associated with her name for the next eighty years, Rue Cambon." Louise was wistful. "I had my first studio there."

"There?" Charly prompted.

"In the first arrondissement, heart of the tradespeople's shops. It was home. We were poor, but the narrow street ran parallel to the Rue Royale and the Place Vendôme and all those elegant boutiques, and the Hotel Ritz, so we felt in some ways rich." Louise spoke the words lovingly, like speaking of her children.

"Near the Holiday Inn Express?" Charly ventured, trying to look knowledgeable.

"No, dear, near Voisin's, the gourmet's haunt; the Ritz bar, and at the Rue de Rivoli corner. It is across from Smith's English Tea Room."

"It is behind the Ritz Hotel, Brooks," Huber interjected. "You'd better get to know the hotel; we're going to be there often. The main entrance is at 12 Place Vendôme."

Louise cut in, "It has a back entrance on the Rue Cambon. Perhaps you should get to know it." Louise shifted in her chair. "The reason Boy helped Chanel get started on her own store was that her inactivity irritated him and he needed to find something for her to do. Certain women can't handle being idle, especially when they are intelligent, and Coco was intelligent. When she was through polishing her nails, the time between two and eight p.m. was a void."

"Sorry, but I'd like to try it."

"Don't you think women should work?"

"Of course. But with children, things get different: kids are tougher than the office; anyone who's tried to pile three or four into their car seats knows that."

Mario brought Charlie's drink and whispered for Huber to come over to a different table and meet a friend. Huber stood. "Excuse me ladies," he said, and left.

Louise looked up and waved a laconic hand to dismiss him. "I remember once, I had left my place to look for some cleaning rags. I stopped by her place, and there she was, her scissors hanging from a ribbon around her neck, working on a mannequin. Her four fingers held firmly together in spite of severe arthritis, she would feel the dress for defects." She shook her head in admiration. "Working directly on some model, she often picked the dress apart with the point of her scissors, complaining that it was unwearable. But that's not how her generation remembers her. She had a few more illusions to lose before work became her one object in life."

"How do you mean?" Charly asked.

"Well, I knew her when she was much older, disappearing from the world stage, but when she was young—twenties and thirties, she was loved. She was beautiful, and more important, she was unique. Slender, dark, bursting with vitality, supple beyond words, and filled with charm. And her shop? At the time, it was just a hobby, commissioned by Boy. I think her only reason for caring about it was that she didn't want to disappoint Boy, in whom she had placed all her hopes.

"That she ardently longed to marry him was beyond any doubt for those of us who knew her. You know, contentment, respectability, the good opinion of society; those, along with a nice fortune, were what this marriage would have brought her, but it was never even remotely in the cards.[25]

"Seems like a marriage to a handsome young millionaire would be worth a lot more than a dress shop," Charly said sarcastically.

Louise reached over and took her hand. "Forget the present, dear, and address the past: by the 1920s this woman was recognized in *Vogue* and *Harper's Bazaar* and in every major city in the world. Her clients were some of the best-dressed women, not of the year, but of the century: Princess Grace, Queen Fabiola, Marlene Dietrich, Ingrid Bergman, all the Rothschilds, and most of the Rockefellers. She was on a first-name basis with people too famous to need first names: Cocteau, Colette, Diaghilev, Dali, Picasso…Chanel! Yet, at the time of her death, the woman Picasso called, 'the most sensible in the world' had a Paris wardrobe consisting of only three outfits—three outfits, dear—and the broad-brimmed Breton hat that was her hallmark."[26]

Huber had returned. He stood over them, then sat down and broke in as if to assume authority, "You know, Brooks, if Chanel was queen of fashion, as Louise was saying, it wasn't because she just cut women's hair, combined silk and wool, put pearls on sweaters, changed waistlines, and all that. It was because there was nothing in her era that she missed."[27]

Sniggering, Louise arced her thumb like a hitchhiker at him. "He's quoting Jean Cocteau."

"I'm not!" he said defensively.

"You are, or trying, don't lie. Germans," she said again derisively.

Huber started to tap the table impatiently with his index finger. "Germans may not have the gift of fashion, but they can buy and sell old women who think they do," he hissed.

"How courageous," Charly shot back.

He turned his sunglasses on her. "What do you know of the fashion industry, Brooks? You're a textbook editor."

"She's a woman, for God's sake," Louise grumbled.

Here it comes, Charly thought. "Okay, I'm a textbook editor, from New York. What do you want to know?"

Louise stepped in. "You have those beautiful eyes in your head for more than flirting. What are women wearing?"

"I come from a different set of people than either of you is used to dealing with. I doubt that what I wear, or know about what others wear, would mean much to you."

"Let us judge that, dear," Louise said.

"All right," Charly said, and took a sip of her drink and put it down. "My women friends in New York would not be spending money on a dress that cost the same as a long-haul flight. They're professionals, used to managing money. But they're not dumb enough to think they can afford luxury."

"All our brands are luxury," Huber said harshly. "You have to know good quality."

"Like Firestone 500s? You going to chip off a hunk and test it?"

"Luxury is luxury," he retorted.

"Only if you believe that a luxury brand and luxury good are the same thing; only if you believe that a luxury is a luxury only if lots of people can't get it," Charly said. "And honestly, lots of people still can't get Vuitton, so it's probably the only luxury brand not in airports.

Charly was encouraged. "See, my friends are not, like most women, interested in a new look or something stunning to wear to work or a party or a wedding. The easy answer is a new outfit. You know: the silken wisp of a designer dress like you're probably used to, the sexy tailoring of a fancy name, or the eye-catching jacket. They take them home, hang them up carefully, and think their problems are solved. In my opinion, they're just beginning. No matter how big a blow they've inflicted on their platinum cards or how fancy the label, team it with last year's shoes, an ill-judged bag, and a dated hairstyle, and they might just as well have saved their money."[28]

"So you're saying it's just accessories," Huber interrupted.

"I'm saying that whereas manners maketh the man, accessories maketh the woman. It isn't new, of course. Fashion editors have been running "dressing it up and dressing it down" features for years. But these days my friends and I could be a lot better off spending more on a bag or shoes than a swanky jacket, so that's what's being sold in the city. They're not stupid in those great designer studios." She looked at Huber. "Are they?"

"So clothes don't count, Brooks?" he scoffed. "Would you like to remove yours?"

"I didn't say that. I'm just saying that, once you've gotten the grooming, the shoes, bags, and the rest sorted out, you can slip in the soup stock."

They both looked at her, puzzled.

"You know—a couple of trendy outfits like a Hitchcockian post-war ret-ro feel, where you need a little 1950s shaped skirt, maybe, and a nipped-in jacket, some substantial stuff that fits the new look this winter, something quality that you'd find for a hundred dollars at Goodwill down in Boca or Palm Beach."

"Goodwill!" he said, surprised, but Louise waved him back.

"Black?" Louise asked.

"Nah, too dowdy. These days black is boring, or at least that's the word on the street—my street, anyway. Grooming is going to be at least as impor-tant as accessories. Make very good friends with your hairdresser; think a soft-focused Mrs. Thatcher." Charly glanced at Louise's gray straggles. "A real honest-to-God hairdo would look great." Louise fingered her hair. "A wash and a set. Coiffed." Charly's voice trailed off. Then she looked at Lou-ise's tobacco-stained fingers, reached over, and took her hand. "Plus nails, of course. Manicured, and no vulgar talons or fancy paint jobs you see mod-eled on porno sites. Just some see-through stuff, say, pale or crimson if that's your style. You have," she swallowed hard, "nice hands."

Louise became intrigued. "Jewelry, there's got to be jewelry, dear."

"Well," Charly leaned over confidentially toward Louise, "I've got some friends in the business and they say buy shares in Swarovski now. Jewels this winter aren't the discreet bits of real jewelry of yesteryear. According to one of my friends, there's sparkle on everything—not just at the throat and in the ears, but on belts, shoes, bags, and clothes. They don't have to be real, of course," she looked over at Huber, "although that's not going to be an inhibitor in this company. Just make sure that they're big and glittery, not too restrained or, you know, 'arty.'"

Louise was getting into the mood. "You could think about wearing, say, a crimson cashmere twin set, with a jeweled brooch or—"

"Mist!"[29] Huber said, unable to take it any longer. "I'm going to the Spiag-gia Bar," he said petulantly.

"Do that," Louise said.

He labored to his feet and threw some bills on the table.

"What's this?" Louise demanded, fingering the money. "The tip? Mario's got two daughters to support!" He threw more Euros on the pile, and lum-bered off across the piazza in the direction of the beach.

"Have you known him long?" Charly asked.

"Long enough." She turned in her seat and called after Huber, "Tell Kiko and Michaeli to stop by after they close the shop. And get your hat!" He ignored her. She turned back and leaned toward Charly. "Have you ever heard of Charles V. Habsburg?"

Charly shook her head.

"He was one of the Holy Roman emperors. An intelligent man, spoke five languages. You know what he used to say?" Charly shook her head again. "I speak Spanish to God, Latin to my confessor, Italian to my mistress, French to my men, and German to my horse.'"

"He's your friend. You don't like Germans?"

"Oh, he's all right. No one around here dares to speak back to him except me. He lives in Paris at the Hôtel de Crillon. In case you don't know, it's near where the revolutionary guillotine relieved about 1,300 citizens of their heads." She took another drag on her cigarette and blew out a steady stream of smoke. "We have some history; he paid to set up a studio for me in Milan. But he's a sick man."

"Cancer?"

Louise laughed, a throaty cackle. "Cancer? Well, that's one possibility. He should be so lucky, at least they might cut it out. He's got nerve problems" she said, and puffed on her cigarette. "Serious nerve problems: his eyes, feet, and hands always have a burning sensation. He's taking treatment at the terme."

"Isn't there help?"

"Over-radiated, probably, during a new prostate treatment with some bad side effects. There's no real help, they just work at managing the pain."

"Why is he working?"

"He wants to ... has to, committed to one of his friends." She held up her hand. "It's not the money, and don't ask who. Jürgen is one of the last great film producers in Europe. He's a financial wizard," she wagged her head, "but he's surrounded by fags on this one. He needs some help."

"The fashion industry is run by gays; he's going to have his hands full," Charly ventured.

"Yes, he will, but he can handle them. You know, it angered Chanel that men ruled the fashion industry," Louise said. "And there was no question that homosexuals were the principal offenders in her view. She hated the pederast mentality that pervaded the industry, and didn't mind saying so. She said that when a woman is stupid she sees a homosexual as a pathetic person, funny to be with, you know, and not treacherous. If she's smart, however, she finds him to be someone who divines her, knows and listens to her, which is dangerous, of course.

"Makes sense to me. Women are gullible."

"Yes. All women, whether stupid or clever, adore compliments and since pederasts know how to couch praise, or have the gall, or the malice, to toss out their flattering adulation, women are their chosen victims."

"It's true," Charly said. "The perversity of it all is that women are so willing to believe them. Gays speak the same language, like nasty girls: caustic remarks out of hearing, and hypocrisy. I just don't understand why women keep falling for it."[30]

"It's easy," Louise sniggered. "Chanel said pederasts put garlands of compliments, necklaces of flowery flattery, around women's necks, with which they then strangle them. Then, of course, they take over. Their beautiful men friends, happy to be in control, no longer dress the women to please men, but to please the pederasts, and to shock other women, of course, because what the boys like is what is far-out, *outré*.[31] Their best models have to look like skinny boys."

Charly nodded in agreement.

Louise continued, "I think Chanel was struck by the number of young women she'd seen die under the influence of 'awful queers,' as she called them — death, drugs, ugliness, ruin, divorce, scandal, nothing was too much when it came to demolishing the competition and taking revenge on a woman." Louise put her hand on Charly's arm and sought her eyes. "Do you have a problem with that, dear?"

"Not me." Charly said. "You're not talking to a fan of the gay movement."

"Well, as I was saying, to triumph over women, they followed her like a shadow, everywhere, except in bed, of course. Homosexuals took what they could get in the industry; they become stage designers, hairdressers, interior decorators, and especially couturiers. Their dilemma was that they rushed into some peculiar form of lethal eccentricity, into their own artificial netherworld, so to speak, that forbids men and perverts women."

368

"Was there someone in particular she was against?"

"No, dear, when she said 'pederasts,' she meant the pederast mentality, which is even more widespread. Paris was full of them back then, probably still is. Homosexuals are the escorts of high society and the life of decadence. They are, she said, the ones who inspire hats no woman can wear, the ones who applaud unwearable dresses; they are the crafty, chatterbox commentators on stilt heels, and furniture upholstered with satin. They are, she said, the only men who love makeup and red nail polish, the backbiting and perceptive army, but they serve as links between the industry and womanhood; they are the ones today who make up the mood and the climate."[32]

Relieved at the ease with which Louise confided in her, Charly sought the confidence of her new acquaintance. "Obviously, Jürgen isn't gay, but he's a little threatening."

"Don't worry about him. But your assistant may prove a problem."

"I don't want him!" Charly exclaimed.

"My understanding is that he comes with the deal. Just keep him busy where he can posture and play with his boyfriends. You'll be fine."

"But Jürgen?"

"I told you, he's not a problem. He's generous and mostly toothless when it comes to young women. He's chasing a Polish waitress working at the beach bar." She took another drag from her cigarette, then stubbed it out. "How conventional are you with men?" Her eyes narrowed.

"Meaning?"

"Sex."

Charlie tried to pick up on the message from the old woman's face. "Broad topic. I told you I'm not a lesbian. What're you driving at?"

"If you haven't noticed, that old hulk of a man is going to do his best to get you down to the beach tonight. If you decide to go, I'm driving at the fact that he has unusual tastes."

"I'm never going to bed with that," and Charly wagged her thumb in the direction Huber had gone.

"I didn't say 'bed,' I said, 'beach.' There's a difference. This is Italy, dear; he doesn't expect sex the way you think, a little hand-job now and then like they all do. He, however, prefers a golden shower; that's why he likes beaches—less messy. Could be worth the investment if you like your job.

He's getting old and doesn't demand much; he gets sweeter once you've pissed on him."

"Speaking from experience?"

Louise looked at her like a disapproving grandmother. "We weren't always this dilapidated pair, dear. There were times when Maria Callas and Aristotle Onassis sat across from us, no different than this evening, at one of these very tables."

Charly was in no mood to relive the good old days. "What's golden sh—?"

"Are you really from New York?" Louise said dejectedly, the skin folding beneath her hazel eyes reflecting the light like transparent brown tallow, a tired candle whose flame would soon flicker out. Her mouth was drawn down like a sad clown's. "You know—golden shower…actually, he mostly likes the *spargel* sparkle." Waiting for Charly to grasp the point, she waved her hand around in the air. "You know—squat and, well, you can imagine the rest."

"Spargel sparkle? What are you talking about? I thought you were speaking euphemistically."

"No. Simply squat and piss in his face, dear." She leaned over and whispered, "German men seem to prefer the flavor of spargel…asparagus, to the English. Then he will suggest a nude swim in the lake to wash off. It is warm this time of year."

"Forget it!"

"I will. He won't. Particularly tonight. That's about all he really likes; he can only get it up then, and it is obvious he's taken a particular fondness for you."

"Thanks, but I don't plan on letting anything get up that far."

Irritated, Louise looked directly into Charly's eyes. "Listen, dear, he's going to try. As soon as he suggests going to the Lido Biondi[33] to see the mountains in the moonlight, then up to his apartment at the Villa Cortine Palace Hotel on the hill for a drink, you'll have a strategic decision to make."

"Jesus Christ, men! I thought he was interested in that Polish woman."

Louise shrugged her shoulders. "You're on duty tonight, and besides, it's not just men, dear. Coco enjoyed experimenting on her own with other women—there's enough precedent. We humans aren't some deified species, you

370

understand; we are miscarriages, half-portions, half animal.[34] All we can do is work so that those who come after us don't resemble us."

"That's not how I read it in the Bible."

"Read what you like, dear," and she drained the last of her scotch.

It was late, and Louise, not one to rush things, appeared bent on spending the evening. Charly was getting her second wind. "Obviously, you knew Chanel, or about her. I have no idea why Huber is interested in my help."

"He wants your editing experience, but most, I think, he likes the fact that you've got pretty breasts, chutzpah, and brains, or at least that's the word on the street—his street." Charly gave her an odd look. "Believe me, dear, he's definitely not without his sources," and she brushed her stringy hair behind her ear with her arthritic fingers. "By the way, he's Jürgen to me and his friends. Probably best you call him Mr. Huber, at least while you're getting paid. Jürgen's okay after you've come to some sort of understanding."

"I appreciate this job, and he gets a 'Mr.' until he proves otherwise. I can't imagine sex with him, much less discussing the finer points of asparagus. Can you say what Chanel was really like?" Charly asked, wishing to drop the subject.

"No, dear." Louise ate some potato chips, leaving crumbs on her lower lip and chin. "No one can. But I can give you some observations. Coco came by my studio a few times to shop my creations, but she was simply an older woman by then, drifting. In my opinion, Coco Chanel had no patience and too much talent. By her death in 1971, when she was eighty-seven, she was the twentieth century's single most important arbiter of fashion." She saw the skepticism in Charly's eyes. "There's no question, dear. Her innovations were basic to the wardrobes of generations of women: jersey suits and dresses, the draped turban, the chemise, pleated skirts, the jumper, turtleneck sweaters, the cardigan suit, the blazer, the little black dress, the sling pump, strapless dresses, the trench coat."

"I don't know if you've looked lately, but the hoi polloi aren't wearing suits, jumpers, and turbans."

"History, dear. Chanel was going to be part of a fashion revolution, not just in the radical simplicity of her style. but even in the materials she used to achieve it, and particularly the accessories she used. Jersey was a flexible silky material that clung to the body, a controversial choice for high fashion

371

back then. Just as controversial was the length of her hemline, which made a woman's ankles visible. With jersey, Chanel declared, I have liberated the body. At that time, she said 'You have to be light, quick, to run to catch a bus or a taxi, and in 1905 or 1910 you couldn't take two steps in the street.' Her understanding of the proper sort of relationship between a woman and fashion was unique to Chanel. She was completely modern in this respect.[35] She's why women dress they way they do today. There's fashion and there's fad. You're talking about the teenage girls who sample fads, like bare bellybuttons, tattoos, and nipple piercing." She wagged her head disgustedly. "Certainly will be far from cute when their stretch marks and flab take over."

"You can say that again."

"Pardon me?"

"I have a teenage daughter."

"Too bad. I never had children."

"Sorry."

"What's to be sorry about?" Louise said archly. "Neither did Coco. Strange how most parents regret the blessing."

"Don't you miss children?"

"Why? You can have as many as you want on any given day — their mothers are just dying to get rid of them for a few hours. You can even rent a few on weekends if you really need it."

"Well, at least you're practical."

"The reason I liked Coco so much was simply her practicality, and I'm not talking about kids. Chanel wore bell-bottom trousers in Venice, the better to climb in and out of gondolas, and started the pants revolution. Sometimes it was purely accidental: after singeing her hair, she cut it off completely, made an appearance at the Paris Opéra, and started the craze for bobbed hair. But always, dear, a Chanel idea commanded respect." She pulled another cigarette from the pack, lighted it, inhaled deeply and let out a long stream of smoke."

"Was it really true that Coco was a Nazi collaborator?"

"Nazi collaborator? It always gets around to that. Let me put it this way: in 1938, with the war coming on and the Italian designer, Schiaparelli, moving in on her trade, Chanel figured it was a smart time to retire. She was an anti-Semite, you know; that's why those rumors about Boy Capel being the illegitimate son of a Jewish father are ridiculous. Plus, she was homophobic—although she tried her hand at bisexuality, as I said. She responded to the war by shutting down her fashion business and hooking up with Hans Gunther von Dincklage, a wealthy tennis player turned Nazi officer thirteen years her junior—she was fifty-six—whose favors included permission to reside in her beloved Ritz Hotel. She was disgraced, but didn't seem to care. Jürgen knows the espionage stuff; he's the German, ask him about the collaboration. You know how he wants to start the film?" Louise began to muse.

Charly shook her head.

"He'll be talking to you about it, with Modellhut."

"Modellhut?"

"Operation Hat. It's the name given by the Nazi intelligence officers to Coco's idea of saving Europe for them, and, I suppose, to be its de facto queen."

Perplexed, Charly looked at Louise. "Saving Europe? With what? New uniforms?"

"Don't knock uniforms, dear. The Italian and French officers were more concerned about making fashion statements than attacking the enemy, which is not to say that the top Nazi and Allied officers didn't also have a yen for the best."

Charly shook her head. "I guess those were the days."

"Those *were* the days, my dear," Louise said. "Nothing now could match them."

"Mr. Huber wants to start the film with Operation Hat? Sounds like the musical *Springtime for Hitler.*[36] I think there'll be a lot of disappointed ladies who were planning on the Chanel romances—men *and* women."

"Well, he's going to do it, mark my words," Louise offered. "Although I agree, it sounds like a comedy."

"Then why?"

"It will get the men in the theater. He's a businessman, and they are the ones who will pay for it, anyway." She took a short sip of wine and wiped her lips with her fingers. "Jürgen could be right, it's where the money is. A film like that has all the excitement of a spy novel: sex, intrigue, and danger.

Thank God not a fashion show—you know, like Ginger Rogers and Fred Astaire waltzing around in tuxedo and chiffon."

"What do you think Huber will be interested in?"

"The good Nazis, power, money, and women, in that order, of course."

"Why do you keep saying the Nazis? Isn't that a little, you know, historical?"

"You mean hysterical?" Louise smiled.

"You know what I mean. Is this whole thing real?"

"Let me give you some advice, dear. Jürgen Huber is going to produce and direct a film about Coco Chanel that begins with Operation Modellhut. He may ask you your opinion of things—that's why he says he likes honesty—but unless you come up with something better, which he likes and will claim as his own in any case, you'd better be prepared to go with the flow. He wants to make money, a lot of money."

"I thought you liked Chanel and Boy on horses dashing toward the Pyrenees."

"I do. I'm a romantic. He doesn't, and he isn't."

"Modellhut?" Charly finished her drink. "Well, you never know."

Louise's cell phone went off. She fumbled around in her purse, pressed the button, and answered in rapid Italian. She nodded and held it toward Charly.

Charly saw the look. "Does he want me?"

"In a manner of speaking," Louise said dryly. "I told him we're just about finished."

CHAPTER 8

═══ MODELLHUT ═══

Louise turned in her chair, signaled for another glass of Scotch from Mario, who responded with a nod and continued serving other tables. She turned to Charly. "How much do you know of the Second World War?"

Charly made a face. "I saw 'Saving Private Ryan.'"

Louise got irritated. "You can never ask an American what books they've read; instead it's what movie they liked best. Americans are so energetic and yet so stupid."

Charly's shotgun came out: "So? Gritty peasants from around the world, what of it?"

"You never tire of being proud of it," Louise grumbled. "That and your insufferable manners."

Rapidly tiring of the whole thing, Charly was about to fire back, but Louise raised a hand to calm her. "Look, dear, I'll make this short, but it may come in handy, since I doubt you remember your history lessons: just let Huber buy you a drink and see what happens.

"Back in the middle of the Second World War, at a place called Casablanca in Morocco — and please don't start talking about Bogart and Bergman — Roosevelt and Churchill announced their decision that unconditional surrender would be exacted from Germany, and there would be no peace on any other terms. This came as a blow to both German and Allied pacifists who were intent on ending the war through negotiations and lessening the consequences for all involved. The German high command, on the other hand, though they wanted peace, secretly wanted to have a free hand to deal with the Red Army in the east, while disposing of Hitler, which would leave them in charge of Europe, England isolated, and a pacified Russia."

"Um-hm," Charly said. The later it got, the less chance she'd have to entertain Huber, so she feigned interest. "Logical enough, but Coco Chanel in all of this intrigue? You said she was shrewd and creative; I didn't hear anything about politically astute," she said skeptically. If she could stall long enough, she could just blame it all on jetlag, beg off, and head back to the hotel with a headache.

"Chanel had an instinctive intelligence, like an animal." Louise said. "She saw advantages and grabbed them. You see, dear, what all the partisans of a negotiated peace had in common with their brethren from different countries was a fervent desire to communicate, let's say, negotiate a peace — excluding Hitler — with the English authorities, and left no stone unturned in their effort to do so."

"Okay, but why Chanel?"

Louise nodded. "Look at it this way: here was Chanel in a conquered country, bound to its conquerors and yet on intimate terms with the person on whom the outcome of the war would largely depend."

"But there must have been others as good," Charly argued.

"Others? What others? Remember: Chanel had been wooed by one of England's richest men, the Duke of Westminster, and one of the royal family. She hosted Winston Churchill and his wife in her home, and was on a first-name basis with the political, social, and cultural leaders of France. And she had the perfect argument — peace."

"Not a bad argument, but it doesn't seem like what's his name, the German lover, was right up there with Himmler," Charly said sarcastically.

Louise drew back; at least the woman was listening. "Spatz — it means 'sparrow' — the German officer, von Dincklage, who held the keys to the Ritz Hotel, was her lover, but he had friends in high places. The relationship wasn't much, that's true, but Chanel needed a couple of favors. Spatz's boyhood friend, Rittmeister Momm,[37] was in Paris to supervise the French textile industry under German administration. Coco wanted her nephew, a prisoner in Germany, returned to Paris to run a small textile plant, for obvious reasons. She met Momm and was impressed with his knowledge of the industry and his connections in Berlin. So, one night over dinner, it's said, she laid out the line of reasoning for Momm that she had come to believe would save Europe from the Europeans and the Third Reich."

"And why the Germans couldn't do it themselves." Charly added.

"Exactly. The ineptness with which the Germans dealt with the English, of course. Her plan was simple: to persuade her friend Churchill to agree to the idea of Anglo-German talks that would be held in strictest secrecy. It was time, past time, she argued, to spare human lives and end the war. By holding out their hand to the Allies, specifically the English, for peace, the Germans would show their strength.

"Not a bad idea," Charly said.

"Rittmeister Momm — Chanel had taken to calling him Theodor — saw the possibilities, a credit to his intellect, and immediately took the message to Berlin. He found a friendly ear at AMT VI, the office of foreign intelligence, and its director Walter Schellenberg. The youngest SS leader, Schellenberg was a genius of sorts, with Hollywood good looks and polished speech, and who despite his youth was present at all the great moments of Nazism. Schellenberg found Momm's proposal exceptionally interesting, since he himself was actively engaged in making contacts in the western camp — with Himmler's knowledge, I might add.[38] German intelligence was working desperately to keep the Red Army at bay by advancing a permanent peace with the Allies, while seeking to halt the Soviet advance and seize the initiative on the Eastern front. If the Allies had thought about it, they should have let the Germans just take care of the Soviets, and the Cold War would never have happened — even your General Patton said so.

"Momm returned to Paris with a plan for Chanel to travel incognito, first to Madrid, where the Nazis were particularly favored over the Allies despite its being a neutral city, then contact the English Ambassador, Sir Samuel Hoare, and have him pass a message to Churchill that Gabrielle wanted to meet with him."

"Seems simple enough. Why didn't it happen? Or did it?"

"First, it wasn't that simple. Coco was going to provide a guarantee by using Vera, a close friend from the old days. Vera was married to an Italian officer. She was a bastard daughter of the British royal family and was particularly close to Churchill. Gabrielle wanted to lure Vera up to Paris under the belief that she need Vera's help in opening a new fashion shop, then bring her to Great Britain in order to help influence Churchill.

Unfortunately, Vera was living in Italy at the time, with her husband, who was hiding in the hills from the Germans. Due to a circumstance of very bad timing, Vera had been inadvertently arrested by the Gestapo in Rome. Schellenberg got her out of jail, of course, but the poor woman thought that the Germans were trying to kill her, so she was very suspicious of any German plan, particularly that of joining Coco in Paris in order to open her new dress shop."

"Yeah, I would guess you don't see many SS officers concerned about fashion boutiques."

"True, but it worked in their favor, since most of the Allied intelligence analysts would be perplexed and probably ignore the idea that the German High Command was so interested in both she and Coco that they would go out of their way to help the two."

"So, what did she do?"

"Well, given the choice between an Italian jail or trip to Paris and Gabrielle, Vera chose, as one might suspect, the latter, with the one condition that she be allowed to take her dog, a giant standard white poodle name Teage."

"This has to be the comedy part."

"It would be the best part of the film, just to see the Gestapo officers strenuously objecting, and then losing to the demands of a couple of defenseless women, one in Rome and one in Paris. I mean, the Gestapo officers were trying to make the whole thing as inconspicuous as possible," Louise laughed. "They had to ferry Vera and her bodyguards in cars and planes all the way to Paris without being seen, a well-known British woman and big white dog in an expensive car being driven by what appeared to be gangsters speaking bad Italian and clipped German, through a dangerous part of Italy. Must have been difficult.

"When Vera finally arrived from Rome, Gabrielle revealed that she had decided to open the shop in Madrid, a neutral country, rather than Paris, which Vera found all the more enticing."

"So, it worked?"

"Not exactly. Once in Madrid, Vera and Coco each had different agendas. Vera's idea was to barricade herself, so to speak, as a member of the royal family, in the British embassy of a neutral Spain until the end of the war. Coco's was to get to Churchill as soon as possible, and, if anything slowed up the situation, produce Vera. They both were hiding their agendas from each other, so, when they separately turned up at the British embassy in Madrid with rather weird stories involving the Gestapo and each other, the British intelligence people held them off. The British position was that Churchill was very ill and not available to see anyone. Some speculate that the true reason was that Churchill refused to be put in the position of entertaining proposals from the Gestapo for a peace offer that would cause the Allies significant political problems from the peace activists around the world."

"Actually, doesn't sound like a bad screenplay. What happened?"

"Vera stayed in Madrid until after the war, and eventually made her way back to Italy. Coco returned to Paris without ever seeing Churchill, and after the war—things being made a little uncomfortable for collaborators by some resistance members called "the Cleanup Committee"—left for Switzerland. The Gestapo put the peace idea on hold, since other aspects of the war were beginning to look bad for them. Meanwhile, Churchill remained steadfast in his demand for the Germans' unconditional surrender."

"Why wasn't Coco arrested when the Allies liberated Paris?"

"She was, for a couple of hours. Two young men from the Cleanup Committee were sent to arrest her, and actually took her from the Ritz Hotel, which must have been a little embarrassing. But she certainly gave them a good tongue-lashing, as you might suspect. She was released almost immediately; no one knows for sure why, but the word was that Churchill sent word at the highest levels that she was not to be harmed."

"What was it like?"

"What?"

"The liberation of Paris. It must have been unbelievable. Were you there?"

Louise smiled slightly. "Oh, my *carissima*, those indeed were the times. Nothing can compare. I was on my way to Paris from Milan, as a volunteer to help save what was left of the city's art. It was August the twenty-fifth when I arrived at La Gare du Sud. Everyone was in the streets, laughing, shouting, crying, embracing, and even plunging to the ground as gunshots continued to ring out the next day. De Gaulle had walked through what he called a sea of faces on the Champs-Elysées and joined the Te Deum at Notre-Dame."

"How many died defending the city?"

"Oh, who knows? All the accounts of that day were filled with contradictions. Who can make sense of mass delight? How many died in the streets, and whether it was a lone Paris fireman or six who hoisted the tricolor flag to the top of the Eiffel Tower for the first time in four years." She shrugged her shoulders. "In the days following, the GIs arrived with their candy and cigarettes, but the Day of Liberation was strictly a French affair, either because de Gaulle manipulated them, or the Allies knew that the Germans wouldn't put up much of a fight, preferring to save their strength for the Battle of the Rhine. In any case, most of the German officers were running away with their mistresses and their loot."

"Was it tough living in an occupied city?"

"We Milanese were used to being occupied, mostly by the French. But during the war I remember Simone de Beauvoir wrote, 'I calmed down and lived wholly in the present.'" Louise chuckled. "The present meant seeking heat in the Café de Flore and cooking up her infamous turnip sauerkraut soup."[39]

"I wonder if any of the old Parisians are still the same — you know, like the soul of what it was then," Charly said.

"The foreigners say Paris isn't what it used to be, of course, but the locals say *Paris sera toujours Paris*."

"Paris will always be Paris," Charly responded. "What happened to Chanel?"

"For the next fifteen years, she shuttled between Vichy and Switzerland, finally returning to reopen her Paris salon in 1954, but only to boost lagging perfume sales. Then, contrary to most expectations, she made a return to the fashion community, selling primarily to Americans, and produced some of her finest work.

"Coco wasn't a revolutionary in fashion in that regard. She sprang no surprises, only refinements on what was her classic look — you know, the short, straight, collarless jacket, the slightly flaring skirt and hems that never budged from knee length; but at her death, her fashion empire brought in more than 140 million dollars a year."[40]

"Amazing woman."

"She was. One of the first to really make it in business. By the time

Katharine Hepburn played her on Broadway in 1969, Chanel had achieved first-name recognition around the world and was simply Coco."

"You haven't said anything about the other designers. Shouldn't that be a consideration?"

"Surely, dear, but you're missing the point. French women, epitomized by Coco, Bardot, and Deneuve, are — or were — elegant, striking, chic. That is the mystery that women of all countries try to penetrate: how do the French succeed in capturing this indefinable chic? That's the magic."

"Um-hm, but—

"Listen, dear, fashion is a form of theater; French women are 'all entrance, effect, brilliance.' For example, the English have often been more inventive than the French; they provide excellent ideas for the young, but they seldom pursue their success into clothing for the middle-aged. It is only those who are willing to devote themselves to clothes with total dedication who can aspire to be stunning. It's easier to do in Paris than anywhere else in the world, certainly more than Milan, because more skilled craftsmen dedicated to the study of luxury have congregated in Paris over the past century than in any other city. You see, dear, it's the same sort of reason that makes Paris an intellectual capital: there are more people there stimulating each other to ever higher flights of fancy, or deeper explorations of, let's say, profundity."[41]

"But who is the leader of all that?" Charly asked.

"Well, there isn't a 'leader of all that.' French leadership in female elegance rests on the reputation of the twenty-three men and women who constitute the Chamber of Parisian Couture, who have won that reputation because they work in dream-like conditions. They dress, among them, only about two thousand of the world's richest women and most beautiful actresses. Some, for example, serve only seventy-five clients a year; it is very personal attention that they are after."

"We're just talking about tailoring, right? I guess I'm supposed to be impressed that some bimbo will pay $2,000 for a sweater, or some jock $10,000 for a watch. To paraphrase Raymond Chandler, if brains werer elastic, these folks wouldn't have enough to make suspenders for a parakeet."

Louise simply looked at this young woman of little or no account, and thinly smiled at her bourgeois manners.

CHAPTER 9

═══ SWEET DREAMS ═══

"So that's it? That's the film?" Charly stifled a yawn. "Great. I might not be able to make it over to the bar—you know, late and all. Did you say it was called the Beach Bar?"

Louise looked at her. "Spiaggia Bar. If you aren't at that bar in less than fifteen minutes, I would suggest you go back to your room, pack, and leave."

"Is he dangerous?" She caught Louise eyes. "Aren't there police here?"

"I already told you he's harmless, but he likes his games, and in this village the police are traffic supervisors, not carabinieri. You're a sophisticated woman. Go over to the bar. You've been dealt a good hand, play it!" she demanded.

"It's not my hand I'm worried about."

"Do your best to listen, dear: Jürgen has his mind made up and will expect you over there shortly to help in official and unofficial ways." Cocking her head sideways to avoid the cigarette smoke, Louise took on the profile of a gecko, one eye seemingly operating alone and targeting Charly as she spoke. "Just pretend that you're Chanel, he'll like that; shouldn't be hard for you to at least *act* like a great woman. It could be worth a lot." Louise leaned close. "I told you, there is a decision to make. Make it. Are you going over there or not?" she said impatiently.

Louise was trying hard—too hard for Charly's taste. The idea of a risky midnight stroll with an albino the likes of Bigfoot was more than she was prepared to make. "He's creepy, and I don't like the idea of walking on lonely beaches with a stranger who glows in the dark."

Louise became stern. "Let me remind you who this 'creepy' person is, dear: he's an integral part of the circle of investors who are major shareholders in one of the top luxury-goods conglomerates in the world, like—"

"Like?" Charly said sarcastically.

"Listen, my young friend, I suppose you are used to holding men hostage with those beautiful green eyes and pretty breasts of yours, but you are a very small chocolate in a very large box. These people deal daily with the likes of Christian Dior, Givenchy, Celine, Kenzo, Christian Lacroix, Dom Pérignon, and the Paris department store Le Bon Marché, among others. They can have any women they want. They are the first reality-based fashionistas, who pay as much attention to manufacturing costs as to designer trends. Plus, Jürgen and a special friend—"

"Special friend?"

"An investor, and a finance professor at the Sorbonne, or part-time something like that, why?"

"No reason."

Louise gave her a questioning look. "Does that have something to do with your assistant?" Charly shrugged. "Anyway, Jürgen and his investment partner have been helping them to acquire new companies at the rate of one a week: Bliss, Hard Candy, Fendi, and others. Few people you will ever meet can do more with any brand than he and his partners, who control more than 50 billion dollars in assets. And that 'creepy' man, as you call him, has amassed a personal fortune estimated at more than 2 billion dollars in the process. No other fashion brands are big enough to bid against them." Louise finished off the last of her mineral water and tried to suck the lemon, making her Adam's apple bounce as she swallowed. She turned as though looking for someone. "I wouldn't keep him waiting," she said over her shoulder.

"Any time I hear 'billion' and 'personal fortune' I know someone, somewhere, is getting ripped off. And Gucci?" Charly stalled for time.

"What about Gucci?" Louise said impatiently.

"You didn't mention them. I was just curious as to why."

Louise snickered. "Gucci's sales are lower than these people's profits. They conduct business amid a backdrop of gallons of perfume rather than racks of couture outfits, because fashion is a sinkhole. You don't make profits from the glitzy couture collections, no matter how many lunching ladies and OPEC princesses visit your atelier.

"Listen," Louise said, "forget Karl, Calvin, Ralph, and even Giorgio or

Miuccia. Bernard Arnault, this narrow-faced, thin-lipped, dimpled French-man they hang around with, is the most powerful person in fashion today. Like you said about the needs and tastes of your girlfriends, these men have built an empire on the premise that high fashion is a marketing tool for selling handbags, shoes, makeup, and bottles of *J'adore;* the gaudy, celebri-ty-driven Paris collections are just costly advertisements for their handbags and scents. No other group harnesses their collections so tightly to the task of moving mountains of leather and tubs of cosmetics as they do.[42]

"They hire edgy, critically acclaimed young designers who never made a centime of profit when they ran their own houses, but who excel at engag-ing, exciting, and infuriating the fashion press. Their ideas aren't meant to be worn, but the ideas descend down to *prêt-à-porter* and to everything in the line. And that's what they sell."

"The buzz that drives the biz, right?"

"Oh, oh." Louise shook her old head. "It's time, dear."

At that moment Jürgen came striding up to the table. "You're late, Brooks," he said in a harsh tone. He stood looming over her. "Are you com-ing?"

Charly's face became flushed. She pushed her chair back and stood up to face him. "No, *Huber*, I'm not." She stepped in close, right up to his face. "There's a classic quote from an American congressman, who once said of two rivals, they 'never open their mouths without subtracting from the sum of human knowledge.' That's my take on you and the high-fashion gnomes. You are all a pack of misogynists, rapacious and affected, preying on the insecurities of women and the wealthy, whose only wish is to hide them. You see the rest of us are just trying to find some comfortable clothes and shoes that look nice and aren't too expensive. You are high priests in a sham religion of which I want no part."

Louise looked up at her in amazement. Huber snorted. "You're fired, Brooks."

"*Gee.*" She didn't blink.

"And I wouldn't look for a job in the fashion industry if I were you."

"Really? No sweat. I ate before I met you." So saying, she drained her glass. Then, placing it carefully on the table, said to Louise, "I feel sor-ry for both of you that you're stuck creating a film in this charade of an industry. It's a joke, not because of what fashion is, but because of what these men are," and she jerked her thumb at Huber. "Chanel was right about the pederasts. And she was right about putting quality fashions for the consumer on the street. She was also a lot of other things, both good and bad, that I'm not sure are fit topics for a decent movie." She looked back at Huber. "I'm not going to get caught up in this fraud any more than I have to. I'm going back to my room now, piss in the toilet, get a good night's rest, have a wonderful breakfast, perhaps go for a swim, then head off to the airport and never see or think of you again." The café noise had dropped by a few decibels. Mario stood across the bar, staring at the two facing each other.

Then Jürgen began clapping his hands. "Admirable, Brooks. Fine speech. Enjoy your swim, and your piss too, and all the features of our little peninsula before you get back." Then he sat down and leaned back in his chair.

Charly looked at him skeptically.

"Sorry, Brooks, didn't you hear?" He created an animated quizzical look. "It's your," Jürgen chuckled, "*boyfriend,* Jean-Michel, I think they call him. He's not home. Seems he told some people about your little secret, which my friends are preparing to cache online. And don't bother calling, he won't be at the airport to meet you, he's in bed fucking that Witherspoon woman, your replacement at the travel agency. And," he grinned mischievously, "we enjoyed the photo diary from your recent, shall we say, honeymoon."

Charly became dizzy and nauseated. She had sat too long and drunk too much. The point was to walk away without staggering, and she headed across the piazza. She heard a voice call after her, but it was jumbled and lost in the noise of the crowd. She turned back to look, only to hear the word "Google" and see them laughing.

Chanel's Death

I am chided for my taste for publicity, as though God
Himself had no need of his church bells!

Georges Simenon

Certainly, at eighty-eight, her time had come. But on the only free day possible: Sunday. Because the rest of the week she was working, and to die at work in the infinite reflection of her mirrors would have looked theatrical. Bad theater. As Reverdy said, avoid anecdote.

She could not have been more discreet.

Coming back from her walk that January Sunday, in her bedroom at the Ritz, she did not intend to disturb anyone. She lay down fully dressed on her brass bedstead decorated with four big gilt balls. A single bed. A bed to sleep alone in or to die like Chanel…. Again, it would have been difficult for things to be otherwise. Her maid, Céline, to whom she confessed that she felt atrociously tired, could not get her to take off anything but her shoes. She would undress later, after dinner. All right.

Céline—whom she called Jeanne because she was one of those absolute masters who changed their servants' names if their real names didn't please them—Jeanne, then, left her to rest without leaving the room. Gabrielle always got her strength back on Sunday evenings, and on Monday she got up and went to work.

On her unpainted pine bedside table there were two objects: a cheap little religious image, a gold-painted St. Anthony of Padua standing on a sort of altar base, which was a souvenir of her first trip to Venice with Misia. To get better; and an icon that never left her side. A present from Stravinsky in 1925, after his long stay at Bel Respiro. The bedroom walls were hospital white. Gabrielle used to say that she loved that room for its simplicity: "A real room for sleeping in." Nothing on the walls, not one painting, not one drawing. "Ah no! None of that here. This was a bedroom, not a drawing room." In the next room stood a very ordinary little screen, which she called "My travels." On it she pinned the postcards her friends sent her. There were more of them lining the mirror of her dressing table under a strong light bulb. "Ah, no! No fuss! It's not a mirror for showing off. It's a mirror that throws a true image right back in your face."

Such was the décor of the room on Sunday, January 10, 1971, when Gabrielle was lying on her bed and a motionless figure sat in the room watching her from a distance. Alone, then, with a woman to help her entertain her last caller. She was going to die alone.

Suddenly Gabrielle cried out. "I can't breathe ... Jeanne!" Céline-Jeanne went to her. Gabrielle had seized a syringe she always kept within reach. But she no longer had the strength.... And the vial wouldn't break. She had time to say, "Ah, they're killing me.... They'll have killed me." (*Elles me tuent ... Elles m'auront tuée.*) But who? Who were these monstrous female "theys" who were killing her? Were they dresses, women? All together, they became the criminals. Her employees? Weren't they killing her too?

Vainly, Gabrielle tried to beat off the final insurrection. What did they want now? She had to take those shadows apart. She had to unsew them. But she no longer had strength to do it.

"So that's how you die," she said and closed her eyes. [43]

═ VIII ═

Charles de Gaulle, Arrogant Autocrat

I cannot think of anything more unpleasant and impossible than having this menacing and hostile man in our midst, always trying to make himself a reputation in France by claiming a position far above what France occupies, and making faces at the Allies who are doing the work.

Winston Churchill

CHAPTER 1

═══ FEET OF CLAY ═══

Americans (those old enough to remember him) hate Charles de Gaulle. We saved his country in WW II and he thanked us by forsaking NATO and trying to muscle the United States and Britain out of Europe. The story is told that when de Gaulle demanded that all American forces be withdrawn from France as part of the deadline he had set for the expulsion of Allied troops, President Johnson instructed then Secretary of State Dean Rusk to ask bitterly, 'Do you want us to move the American cemeteries out too?'[1]

Whether American, British, German, or even French, you have to get in line to hate de Gaulle. Biographers, seeking adjectives to describe the man, have come up with an impressive list. To cite only one by Charles Williams, de Gaulle was immensely able and conceited, brilliantly arrogant, infuriatingly obstinate, aloof, a nuisance, a scold, susceptible, sulky, prickly, suspicious, and remote. None other than Churchill's daughter-in-law, Mary Soames, told de Gaulle during a conference, "Mon Général, you should be very careful not to hate your friends more than your enemies." Balancing the paradox between the personage and the person, one could contrast a very cold, ruthless, and proud public man with de Gaulle's gentleness toward his daughter, Anne, afflicted with Down syndrome, which still leaves the scales weighted against him.[2]

Perhaps the troublesome part is acknowledging that de Gaulle, despite his irascible reputation, also personified the French character in his single-minded devotion to his country and in his skill and strength in its service. He was undaunted in alienating a goodly share of his electorate in pursuit of what he thought was right. If French anti-Americanism and de Gaulle's disdain for the United States anger its citizens, perhaps a modest self-examination would be in order. Americans, for example, find it patently easy—and wax pathetically ignorant—when equating French aloofness and her foreign policy with the demeanor of their French waiter. The twenty-first century has been ushered in by a rapidly maturing European Union, led by France and Germany, creating for the first time a real look at what could be the future United States of Europe, an immensely powerful economic and political competitor to America. Was de Gaulle in part responsible, or did he lead France into a series of international "grand design" ambitions that eventually crippled the future of his beloved France, leaving world leaders to question his sanity?

At the latest count, some 1500 books and articles have been written about de Gaulle, analyzing in scholarly detail almost every aspect of a long life. While there have been many biographies of de Gaulle, the prince of which is the three-volume work by Jean Lacouture, the finest English biography is *The Last Great Frenchman* by Charles Williams. No matter what conclusions these works draw on this extraordinary and contradictory personality, of this there is no dispute: he was unparalleled in his time; as Williams put it, he was in fact, the last great Frenchman.

―――

For all of his life, de Gaulle thought of France in a special way and attributed it more to his sentiment than reason. His emotional side imagined France like a princess in a fairy tale or the Madonna in frescoes, female figures dedicated to an illustrious and exceptional destiny. Instinctively, he felt that Providence had created her either for great successes or for consummate misfortunes. He could not envision mediocrity in French acts and deeds, and considered such events as an absurd anomaly, more the consequence of French citizenry than the genius of the land. France, he proclaimed, was not really France unless she stood in the front rank of world affairs, a leader at the highest levels of courage and character, on pain of mortal danger. In short, as he said, France could not be France without greatness.[3]

―――

His cell phone beeped. It was Charly.

"So." A pause. She waited until she had his undivided attention. "I hear you've been popping Ms Poppins."

"What?"

"You know. Sport fucking, I believe they call it. With Lady Wither-spoon. 'The *old* fat travel guide in the gray sweater,' as you characterized her. The one with tits the size of melons and hair the color of honey, who took my place."

Silence. He couldn't think of anything to say. *How could she have known?* His mind raced for a reply but none came, because he was guilty as charged.

"I guess that says it all. Thanks, J.M." She clicked off, and the line activated a busy signal.

CHAPTER 2

≡ THE AIRPORT ≡

Overhead speakers droned announcements in a tinny cadence, seeking wayward passengers for departing planes through the corridors of Charles de Gaulle Airport. Each arcane command prodded well-wishers and small groups of stragglers jostling coats and bags toward their gates for greetings or good-byes. At terminal C, among those awaiting arrivals, two rumpled-looking Frenchmen sat conversing quietly.

Jean-Michel stifled a yawn. "I didn't know you had a priest in the family."

"Yes, you did." The colonel looked at him sourly. "I told you before, he's not a priest, he's a brother. You know, my brother's a brother. He left France thirty-five years ago to join his monastery."

"Sorry. Monastery?"

The colonel turned in exasperation. "Haven't you been listening to anything I've said? Not just any monastery, it is a strict abbey of French Canadian Trappists in Manitoba."

Jean-Michel nodded his head. "Trappists, they're a tough lot."

The colonel took satisfaction. "The marines of religious life," he said stiffly.

"Is that what he said?"

"He hasn't communicated much, just a few letters every couple of years."

"No calls at Christmas?"

"They take vows of silence."

"Hm. Why is he coming home?"

"He has some business to attend to."

"Business? You said he hasn't been here in thirty-five years and can't talk."

"He's absolved of his vow of silence while he's here," de Monteaux said, looking away. "It is a long story."

Jean-Michel glanced at his watch. "Well, his plane's an hour late...."

De Monteaux turned sideways to Jean-Michel and sighed, "He's my brother, he's a beekeeping monk from a Trappist abbey in Canada, and he's coming back for a short visit, leave it at that."

"Ever thought about the priesthood?" Jean-Michel said.

"Me? Priesthood?" the colonel grunted. "The army was bad enough!"

"Maybe it runs in the family," Jean-Michel said, scanning the arrival screen. "You know—your brother, being a brother," he added sarcastically. "After all, it's not a bad life: Mass in the morning, organize some parish functions, golf in the afternoon, and evening dinner with some of the best families in the city."

"Mother of God!" The colonel exclaimed, putting his hands on his knees and looking sternly at Jean-Michel. "You're talking about priests. I told you, he's a brother; brothers don't offer Mass. The only thing the clergy might have in common with you is the dullness of their virtues!" He shook his head in amazement, wondering how anyone, particularly Jean-Michel, could mistake the two.

Used to the colonel's prickly parts, Jean-Michel settled back in his seat and wistfully surveyed the terminal. "I know about brothers; I was talking about serving at Mass, not offering it. Want something from the coffee bar?"

"No."

The time was beginning to drag, and de Monteaux, lost in his own thoughts, did little to help. Smoking forbidden, Jean-Michel fussed absent-mindedly with his watch. "I'm going for a magazine, would you like anything?"

"No...yes, get me anything on Giscard."

Jean-Michel had gotten up. "Giscard? The Académie Française[4] thing?"

"Of course."

"Has he been accepted?"

"That's what I'm trying to find out!" de Monteaux said exasperatedly.

"We need men like him," Jean-Michel declared.

"They're a bunch of arrogant old bastards! '*Immortels*,'" de Monteaux said snidely, "him and his goddamn constitution."

"So, it's over, rejected, you don't have to worry anymore."

"European *Union*," de Monteaux said disparagingly. "A constitution nobody has read, a flag nobody salutes, and an hymn nobody knows."

"Giscard tried his best," Jean-Michel ventured, turning to leave.

"Jesus, Mary, and Joseph!" the colonel howled, scaring those around him. "It was ten times longer than the US Constitution, and had 448 articles—441 more than the Americans. It amazes me how those old fools could be reading that pompous solemnity without laughing. Maybe now Europe's elite will learn the limits of their ability to impose their political fetishes on innocent Frenchmen!"[5]

The little groups of families around them began to watch; one or two moved away.

"*Maurice*," Jean-Michel said tiredly, trying not to notice the gathering audience, "do you *want* anything?" He was weary and depressed.

"No." De Monteaux could see on Jean-Michel's face, however, that he was distracted, his mind somewhere else. "Just call her up, God damn it, and get this thing over with. You can't think, you are terrible company, and you're pouting like a spoiled teenager."

"I need a walk."

"Just stick with the magazines."

"What?" Jean-Michel said quizzically.

"Avoid the bar," the colonel commanded.

He ambled away toward the newspaper stand. "Avoid the bar," he mimicked churlishly.

The colonel overheard him. "What?"

"A foolish consistency is the hobgoblin of little minds,"[6] Jean-Michel mumbled under his breath, leaving the old man grumbling amidst the collection of waiting families. What could he say—she hadn't answered any of his calls.

———

The reality of the airport welcome was different, of course, and de Monteaux disliked lying to his friend, but it would be best to put off the true meaning of Brother Merton's visit for a while. In any case, the colonel had hoped his younger brother would not come. Now that he had, all the familiar antagonisms would surface, unless he had changed. Thirty-five years ago, the colonel's words to his brother were 'Monks are a bunch of beggars. They go from door to door asking for whatever you'll give them. Where is the life in that?' But Lieutenant Paul de Monteaux left all that he knew and loved in France for a small Trappist monastery on the High Plateau in the Canadian Rockies. His reasons were secret and starkly simple: a botched assassination attempt by the army's OAS on Charles and Yvonne de Gaulle's lives.

Maurice knew Paul would come back when he heard the reports. The news was always a lot more interesting if your life depended on it. Paul had no choice; the French government had recently released additional and damning evidence, trumpeted by the press, of widespread use of torture and assassination of political opponents during the French occupation of Algeria. The origin of these revelations was an investigation by the French weekly magazine *Le Point* into the role of the French military's "special forces," including the OAS, during Algeria's war for independence in the late '50s. The recent riots surrounding Paris had seriously stirred the waters of French politics and brought up unpleasant debris from the muck of Algerian hostility. Eventually, Paul's complicity would be found and exposed. A French judge who was investigating the disappearance of French citizens in Algeria and Argentina during the last military regime interrogated a high-level French general about his knowledge of training in torture techniques given by his soldiers to the Algerian military. The general's testimony helped draw a complex picture of the French military's responsibility in teaching torture to their Algerian and Argentine colleagues. Details of the OAS activities in France were sure to be exposed and their leaders summoned.

France has never apologized for its conduct during the Algerian war, although recent surveys indicate that most French citizens would approve such a move. Nonetheless, keeping out foreigners had been a neuralgic issue of European politics since the '80s. The war, which lasted from 1954 to 1962, cost the lives of 30,000 French men and women and at least a half million Algerians. In the 1950s the French had more than a half million troops trying unsuccessfully to suppress the Algerian rebellion, a fact the Americans hadn't learned in Vietnam and Iraq. The army left more or less to its own

397

devices, torture and other atrocities became widespread.

A certain Lieutenant Colonel Roger Trinquier was reportedly the architect of brutal repression in Algiers and of the development of the concept of "modern war." Of that concept's basic tenets, one was the "secrecy doctrine," which was to cause havoc in the Algerian and, later, Argentine populations. An important premise of that doctrine was the need to hide the detention of political prisoners, as well as their deaths and the elimination of the bodies.

Many of those bodies were dumped in the sea, and several later washed ashore along the Mediterranean beaches. The use of military personnel, frequently dressed as civilians, looking for political opponents to interrogate and torture, was a technique implemented by the French in Indochina and Algeria; Colonel Maurice de Monteaux saw it employed in Indochina. Suspects were gathered up off the streets, driven to secret locations, then forced into helicopters and taken sufficiently high to intimidate them. Once out at sea, two of the suspects' own—promised safety if they carried out the executions—shoved their bound comrades toward the open door. The condemned men and women, promised safety if they talked, frantically clutched at their executioners, shrieking until their resolve cracked and, in garbled terror, they gushed information and pleaded for their lives. Through training by French military advisers, the concept was later exported to Argentina, where these and many other techniques led to the "disappearance" of almost 26,000 political prisoners in the 1970s, almost all of whom are still unaccounted for.

The origin and justification for such methods was the paranoid fear (if, depending on one's political perspective, one wished to characterize that fear as 'paranoid') of communism, best exemplified in a document written by General Jacques Massenu, one of the leading French officers in Algeria. In a note dated March 19, 1957, General Massenu exposed the subversive and revolutionary war orchestrated by international communism as impossible to fight with the classic combat procedures; on the contrary, it would be necessary to use clandestine and counterrevolutionary methods and actions, and it would also be necessary that these methods were accepted by Frenchmen's souls and consciences as needed and morally valid. It was, after all, a war.

If this seems somehow treacherous, most would be well advised to substitute the word "terrorism" for "communism," and they would understand the dynamics of French foreign policy put in play back then, as they are employed by the world's leading countries today.

In those days, the French army saw its mission very clearly. De Gaulle was abandoning them. Without explicitly saying so, General de Gaulle's obsequious policy toward the Soviets was laying a clear path for détente with the Russians, to thwart the growing influence of NATO, thereby assuring the French preeminence as the peacemaker in Europe. To French military leaders, however, the former hero was becoming a traitor to French democracy, the French people, and, most dangerously, the French army, which would be shut off from its traditional ally, the United States.

Was there a moral to be derived? Brother Merton, formerly known as Lieutenant Paul de Monteaux, an aggressive and decorated combat officer and former adjutant to a top-ranking French military officer in Algeria, was about to find out.

CHAPTER 3

═══ BROTHER MERTON'S RETURN ═══

Colonel de Monteaux recognized his brother instantly among the disembarking passengers: medium build, rangy, a high forehead, close-cropped gray hair, and a disarming smile, misleading by its innocence. He had the lively blue eyes of his mother—now strikingly so with age—and dressed in black, her favorite color. Paul looked smaller than his brother, which he was, but more because his suit was too large. It smelled strongly of mothballs, befitting the occupation of its owner. Both men shook hands, while Brother Merton attempted an awkward embrace, self-consciously given and similarly received. "You look tired, would you like coffee, or...?" the colonel offered.

"Tea." Paul's eyebrows shot up. "Sûreté men?" Odd words after these many years. Wide-eyed he waited expectantly.

"Not to my knowledge, but they're a secretive lot; probably one in our trunk."

Maurice took Paul's arm as they walked toward the bar. "You look well, Paul."

"Mother?" Paul asked, his eyebrows furrowed.

"No change, although she can't last much longer, she—"

There's a fat man waving at us," Paul warned anxiously.

"He's a friend—Jean-Michel."

"Was that wise?" Paul whispered urgently as Jean-Michel approached.

"Welcome home!" Jean-Michel said, joining the two men and offering Brother Merton a wide smile and handshake. Introductions took place and the men exchanged some halting pleasantries, punctuated by uncomfortable moments of silence.

"Brother Merton has been released from his vows of silence, for the trip," the colonel said. "He's not used to making conversation except with his order's own sign language." The colonel put his hand on his sibling's shoulder in a brotherly show of solidarity. "The Trappists express themselves as much with their faces and bodies as their voices."

Brother Merton smiled simply, displaying neither teeth nor kindness. Jean-Michel felt inhibited without recourse to his usual banter, and worse, felt like an intruder. "Well, it's late. Perhaps I'll just take a taxi back to the city. No sense taking you both out of your way."

"If you like," the colonel replied. "We can meet during the week." Brother Merton stood patiently, hands clasped at his waist, surveying the terminal, waiting for Jean-Michel to take his leave.

"Of course," Jean-Michel nodded, relieved of his obligation. Brother Merton's facial contortions and staccato speech presented themselves as borderline schizophrenic, which left Jean-Michel wary and uncomfortable. He shook hands and left for the exit, turning briefly to wave before disappearing among the travelers.

"He knows why I'm here?" Brother Merton asked, as they headed for a small concourse café, the only refuge for late travelers at the terminal.

"A little about the monastery. Under the circumstances, I felt his presence would be useful: he's over at the ICPA if for some reason a reporter might learn of your arrival.

"Influential?"

"He has contacts, but got axed at Saint de Just a while ago for a drinking problem and some other things."

"Can you trust him?"

"Can 'we' trust him? I've nursed him along; he's turned out to be useful, has some excellent research on the kings' tombs in Phnom Penh. He's had to pay his dues, but I'm afraid he might be slipping back," the colonel sighed.

Brother Merton frowned. "That could be a problem."

The colonel decided to change the subject. "Are you planning on staying at the villa or the apartment? Jean-Michel's living on my houseboat."

"Houseboat?"

"I kept it after some of the Romanian deliveries to Belgium a couple of years ago, but customs police searched it, so it's been noted. I thought I wrote you about it; turned out to be too damp anyway." Paul shook his head. Maurice caught his brother's eye. "And mother needs to see you ... soon."

Paul's hands rose to respond, only to drop again. "Of course. A room at the Bonaventure House has been arranged for me. I will see her tomorrow."

"Probably best." They walked into the bar. Brother Merton set down his small valise and ordered his tea.

"I'm thinking of selling the old place, you know;" the colonel said. "I believe the attorney wrote you last year. Mother is incompetent.

"Incontinent?"

"That too. There will be some paperwork. I am her guardian, of course. Not sure she will recognize you."

"Do what you like. Treat your son. I've no interest." He surveyed the bar, giving special attention to some explicit advertising featuring a full-breasted young woman.

"Thank you." Maurice hesitated. "Vivian is still here."

"Married?"

"Divorced. She's dying of cancer."

Paul turned, his face registering surprised pain. "May God have mercy. I'll pray for her."

"Will you see her?"

His hands jumped, then, his eyes wide, he stuttered, "I can not, can't. I cannot! Nothing could come of it."

"When are you leaving?"

"When the courts are finished with me."

"You might have more to fear from the press. Those bloodsuckers will never leave you alone."

"Bloodsuckers? Harsh. Journalism is the first draft of history. Besides, I'll have my say."

"Then you are determined to go through with it?"

"I can't run; we can't afford any compromises in the media, you know that. Besides, those 'judges' are not the only ones I fear."

"Then, who?" the colonel said, surprised.

"And if I drive out demons by Beelzebub, by whom do your people drive them out?" His voice was sterile and flat. "So then they will be your judges."

"Paul, you know I resent Christian parables."

Brother Merton's hands once again came up to sign and then down again. "Matthew's Gospel. It is by a Jew, about a Jew, for Jews," he said quietly. "We're both getting old, *are* old," his voice turned loud. "Matthew's Gospel is," then fell to a whisper, "I'm not going to jail, Maurice, no matter what, and you know that," he said urgently.

They stood searching each other's faces for an instant, for some trace of the past, a twitch or twinkle, a familiar sign, where memories could intersect. There was none. Paul finished his tea, carefully disposed of his tea bag, and made preparations to leave.

"I know, Paul. Don't worry, I've been working on it." His voice was commanding, an older brother in charge. "Let me at least drive you into the city, for God's sake!" Maurice said, his voice softening.

"I have catching up to do. I want to go home."

"Home? The city's changed, Paul." But the colonel nodded his understanding. "Of course."

"Go *home*," Paul repeated. "It's intimidating, you know, like a trip to the attic. I've been imagining this, and now so much time has been lost." His melancholia was bitter and sweet by turns. "But go home, patiently if possible, into the most beautiful city on earth." He reached down for his valise. "To see my memories." He stood and smiled slightly. "Thank you for coming. I will call you in the morning," he said, and patted his brother affectionately on the arm. They left the bar toward the terminal exit, a thin figure in a black baggy suit, a deception of frailty. Paul parted from the colonel and continued walking a few steps, then turned. "*Dominus vobiscum*, Maurice."

For an instant they shared the distant past of a Catholic blessing. "*Et cum spiritu tuo*, Paul."[7]

———

Paul de Monteaux, from one of France's best families, graduate of the École Speciale Militaire de Saint-Cyr, and an appointee to the Office of Algerian Affairs for the French Foreign Ministry in Algiers, was slated for success. Although not ideologically driven at the time, his family had high expectations of his commitment, like his brother's, to a sterling and valiant military career. It was only natural that he volunteered for the French Naval Intelligence service, an elite group of French officers whose loyalty and courage were unquestioned. He passed all tests at the highest level and was selected from many capable candidates for his intuition, youthful charm, rapacious intellect, and nerve.

Unfortunately, by fate's fickle finger, Captain Paul de Monteaux's career had effectively ended with de Gaulle's decision to grant independence to Algeria, forever sealing France's fate as a defunct colonial power—a decision de Monteaux and thousands upon thousands of patriotic Frenchmen abhorred.

CHAPTER 4

≡ THE GHOST FROM ALGIERS ≡

Jean-Michel heard light steps in the hall, like those of a child approaching. The steps halted and a pallid, expressionless face appeared at his half-open door. "Professor Levasseur?"

Jean-Michel turned from his monitor, looked over his glasses, and, nodding, gestured to a seat near his desk and waited. Brother Merton pushed open the door, then tried to close it, but it didn't close properly; he gave it a hard shove, closing it firmly. "*Il faut qu'une porte soit ouverte ou fermée,*"[8] he grunted, addressing the door, then walked silently, as if in Vespers, across the office's worn Persian rug, and sat down stiffly, deferentially. He embodied contrasts: pale complexion and silver hair, but black suit; hesitancy in his manner, belied by total composure; the appearance of frailty, yet formidable inner strength; a minor Trappist beekeeper from the hinterlands, but ecclesiastical veteran, a man, one supposed, as capable of wrestling devils as cavorting with saints. One trained to keep secrets and even kill.

Paul glanced curiously about. The office had the appropriate aesthetic accoutrements of a chancellor's office, based on the heavily ornate gold-and-boiserie Louis Quinze furniture, and ostentatious, he thought, for the likes of a simple professor. The décor was a mixture of old and new, with a medium-sized plasma screen at one end, but including the necessary elements of marble, gilt, statuary, and garden vistas, a suitable subject for the likes of a Walter Gaye painting or Edith Wharton book.

The building itself was nineteenth century, and the room, sufficient in size to house the sensibilities of a senior corporate executive, was made even more spacious by its high ceilings and an old rococo marble fireplace. One antiqued orange-colored wall, holding walnut bookcases and braced by windows overlooking a shady green courtyard, was filled with a large number of books, current and early tomes providing the backdrop. There were four or five paintings from what appeared to be the Renaissance period, including a Vermeer, which despite its value, hung casually with the others located about the room. Bric-a-brac of anthropological interest, framed photos of military nature, and a bust of Rousseau peering steadfastly from his perch on a marble pillar overlooking the great Dorian wooden desk, which commanded the center of the room and was littered with reports and pipe paraphernalia—it all spoke of discordance, an office that couldn't place itself in history. Finally, the entirety was presided over by a well used, if not abused, large red leather office chair, which, when rotated a full three hundred sixty degrees, took its occupant to all the essentials of his work: computer, desk, phone, reference materials, and ancient hotplate supporting a calcium-crusted glass coffeepot.

"Thank you for seeing me," Brother Merton said, making no effort to shake hands. Rather, he leaned forward to touch a Moslem scimitar and scabbard mounted on a wooden stand next to the table. "Your office is a museum," he said, his experience in offices over these many decades having been limited exclusively to the austere.

"Not mine, really. I just have, as the Americans say, 'squatter's rights' for a while; it belongs to your brother, of course." Jean-Michel glanced about the room.

"This is Maurice's office?" Paul said with surprise.

"Founders' families have certain rights at the institute, so Maurice kindly offered to let me use it," he said, positioning his chair to better face Merton. "I guess he didn't tell you. I keep a few things here, and we both share an interest in archeology."

Paul pointed to the sidewall. "The Vermeer?"

"His, one of the few showing Delft itself."

"Is it wise to leave it hanging about?"

"Well, the institute has its security, and I guess your brother is satisfied."

Brother Merton got up and walked over to the painting. "I recognize it; it used to have a special place in our home." He scrutinized it carefully, looked behind it to see if it was wired, which it was, then walked back to his chair. He pointed to a diploma on the wall. "Jesuits?"

"Um-hm, mine. Expensive, too," Jean-Michel chuckled. "The cost of a minor painting. St. Peter's University."

Paul's face was expressionless. "I have always been impressed by Jesuit casuistry."

Jean-Michel nodded, "I hope in the positive sense," and waited.

"My brother said you might have some connections."

"Maurice exaggerates, one of his more endearing faults, I suppose. But I do have some well-placed friends with a taste for politics and scotch. Would you like some coffee?"

"No, thank you." A brief smile crept across Paul's face, an animated expression motivated by a pleasant memory. Then, suddenly, it vanished, blank, waiting. He held a briefcase in his lap. An embarrassing silence ensued.

"It must feel good to be back." Jean-Michel had turned from his coffee preparation to face his guest.

"I've dreamed of it often," Paul said sadly.

"Most French could never live elsewhere. Your brother, for example."

"Well, Maurice and I…" his voice trailed off.

Seeing that Paul was ill at ease, Jean-Michel changed the subject. "You've been here a few days, have you had the opportunity to see Wilson's interpretation of La Fontaine's *Les Fables*? It is playing at the Comédie Française. I have an American friend who loves the theater and thought it was superb."

"I haven't, but everyone enjoys his allegories. I read in *Le Figaro* this morning that it was well accepted. I also read about that actress…" he paused to search his memory.

"Fersen. Christine Fersen," Jean-Michel replied.

"Yes, Fersen. Introduces the animals and presides over the finale when the animals choose not to become humans, and does a commendable job."

"Chalk one up for the animals," Jean-Michel laughed.

"Despite their allegories about perverted human behavior. Do you have a favorite?" Paul asked, his face registering no pretense of humor or curiosity.

"I do. The Crow and Fox."

"Are you a wily fox, Professor, who can get someone to drop his cheese?"

Jean-Michel went on guard. "Perhaps." He scrutinized the slim figure in black before him. "I'd like to think so."

Paul continued without following his gambit. "It seems a paradox that an American director is finding acceptance in the shrine of French literary classicism."

"Um-hm. Well, he's no ordinary American. I believe he made his name as an avant-garde director in France, not the United States, about the time you must have left, three or so decades ago, I suspect. Perhaps he's the one who could carry your message to court," Jean-Michel said lightheartedly.

"I wouldn't want to degrade the power of theater by preaching from the proscenium."

"True, but the messages of playwrights aren't to be taken lightly," Jean-Michel replied.

"I believe, Professor, that it is important for artists not to confuse art with activism. Art has power, of course, but it is a mistake to think that people who watch your play will be organizing themselves in the lobby afterward."

"You know, your brother is something of a paradox for me," Jean-Michel said, pouring himself a cup of hot coffee. He held up the pot for Paul, who shook his head. "But we have a special relationship. I wonder if you could—"

"I'm sure you know him better than I," Paul broke in. "It's been so long, and we were never close, despite being brothers; a number of years separated us. But paradox? I'm here because of a paradox," he said coldly, ignoring Jean-Michel's comment. "I need your help, did Maurice tell you?" His hands moved to speak in anticipation, then lowered quickly to rest on his briefcase. Honest communication was often best understood through body language, as most psychologists believed, not misspoken words. Those who took the oath of silence could read the dilation of pupils, blush on cheeks, and pursing of lips as readily as others read the *Times*.

"Not really. He only told me that you needed a reliable attorney, that you are involved with the recent military scandals, and that a human-rights organization is after you."

"Yes, reliable. That's it…reliable!" Paul's face brightened and as quickly darkened. "It seems the statutes of limitations do not extend to the bravery of citizens, only the supposed violations of human rights and dignity."

"The Algerians?"

Paul sniggered. "Hardly. It was Frenchmen and women who fought to preserve what was ours and paid the ultimate price." He peered intently at

408

Jean-Michel, and without waiting for a response, frowned and said, "My private life is not going to be private much longer." His hands, white and slender, dipped into his briefcase. "I have received a letter from my prefect ordering me to report to the French authorities immediately. I have been instructed to retain an attorney or the order will provide one — unfortunately, a cheap one. I need a skilled advocate. Can you help me?"

"I can make some suggestions for counsel, but wouldn't your brother be better at this sort of thing?"

"He prefers that you handle it."

Jean-Michel was secretly pleased that he was being so closely relied on for such a weighty family matter. "Perhaps you could tell me which political party I should be courting; the political situation is changing, working-class France is the National Front's new heartland. The Right could be —"

"Gaullists."

Jean-Michel quit stirring his coffee. "Gaullists? The ones who are looking to bring you and your comrades to, uh . . . justice?"

Brother Merton's eyelids fluttered. "If . . . if the attorney is ethical he will see the challenge: with the public watching, I will be defended by a member of the opposition. He hesitated. "Of course, there is a duty in keeping one's mouth shut, but that can serve as a cover for cowardice. And then there is the duty of bearing witness." He looked small, gaunt, and forsaken in the overstuffed chair. As an afterthought, he added, "It is the best way to deal with a government known more for its pride than for its fortitude."

"Hm. Risky, but imaginative," Jean-Michel mused, thinking that at least Merton's self-pity was apt to be sincere. "Nonetheless, anyone who serves you will be under considerable pressure from his peers to throw you to the wolves. Perhaps, speaking of wolves, you can rely on La Fontaine."

"La Fontaine's talent was to create satires in verses that rarely run more than thirty lines, Professor; I doubt that will happen in court. Besides, the wolf demonstrated to the lamb, I believe, that might makes right. What you speak of was de Gaulle's doing. His weakness," Paul said flatly.

Jean-Michel bent forward and lighted his pipe, the propylene lighter shooting yellowish flames into the bowl. Smoke furling about his head, he leaned back in his chair. "Weakness?"

"The act, the rising. You must forgive me," Paul held up his hand for patience. "I am just getting used to the idea of spontaneously speaking again. The act of rising to a position of high political power demands a willingness to put ambition before humanity. He was a very ambitious man who feared weakness; it didn't mesh with his monstrous ego. It's elementary wisdom to fear weakness, of course, physical or psychological, and particularly one's own. I speak from experience, but it's true for all of us, including de Gaulle."

Jean-Michel hesitated. "You're referring to?"

"Fear."

"I understand that. What are you saying de Gaulle feared?"

"The hatred of France." Paul's face hardened. "Do you understand, Professor, that I hated de Gaulle, my comrades also despised him, and that the army itself wished him dead? He didn't fear his own death, he feared the enmity of France, France like a stern Madonna."

Jean-Michel again leaned forward on his desk. "Brother Merton, I don't hate de Gaulle and I seriously doubt 'the army' did. I credit him with a great deal of courage and tenacity, much of which was used to preserve the French government and its people in traumatic circumstances."

"Professor, you are an educated man, but you think like a hedgehog who knows one big thing."

"And I suppose you think like a fox, who knows many small things."

"So we've both read Berlin." Brother Merton looked aggrieved and tired. "Perhaps we should, if you agree to, discuss my case." A political argument with a naïve French intellectual, he knew, would serve no good end.

"I agree," Jean-Michel said, "and I apologize. I realize you have come for help. I understand something else, however: you were witness to very important events in French history. I have not been, and, with your indulgence, would like to hear what you have seen."

Brother Merton paused to reflect on his situation. "I think French, Professor. I am, one might say, inhabited by France. I am, however, also in a true fight for my life," he said slowly. "I must stay … yet, it is my sanity, you know; a monastery is one thing, a prison something else." He sighed and acquiesced. "All right, perhaps mine is a story you haven't heard. History books usually don't promote truth. I've had considerable time to think about these things, and," his hands went up to sign and down again, "with few distractions. Of course it is difficult now to think of these events and de Gaulle without prejudice."

"Um-hm." Jean-Michel nodded his head in understanding, casually holding his pipe to the corner of his mouth.

"De Gaulle feared the French people, since he saw himself as their loyal servant, but a servant nonetheless. In de Gaulle's mind he was two separate people: 'I' and 'de Gaulle.' If 'de Gaulle' demanded a particular course of action, 'I' could not possibly refuse to follow it," his eyebrows shot up in exclamation, "whatever the immediate cost. The alternative was to abandon the mission, which the general felt was his by destiny." The subtitles playing across Brother Merton's forehead as he spoke were created by years of penance and were easy enough to read. "By 1957 he was approaching a demented old man, *arrondi*, soft and myopic. Originally, we had no interest in having him back, but the colonies were at stake and he was once again in a position to reach for power, with our help. I think the English have a phrase for it, grabbing the tiger by the tail. He no doubt wanted to relive his great moments as the liberator of Paris as in '44, strutting down the Champs-Elysées like a peacock. In '57 he reached for power and couldn't let go of the tiger, or, once exposed, he'd be eaten by his own myopic perception of de Gaulle as France. The French people would see him for what he was. His dilemma was that he saw himself as having no choice but to hold on—what else could a self-appointed savior do? It was quickly becoming apparent, however, that he no longer had the strength or wit to lead."

"Do you remember what Brecht said? 'Unlucky the country that needs heroes.'"

"Truly," Paul replied. "We had no interest in having him back."

"We?"

"Any French patriot. Sartre, for example, denounced those Frenchmen who supported de Gaulle as 'frogs who demand a king.'"

"Sartre hated de Gaulle, didn't he?"

"Certainly," Paul said. "Sartre was the leading intellectual of France, but procommunist, not pro-Soviet like De Gaulle.

"You put a bomb in Sartre's apartment."

"Two. Neither worked. But it certainly wasn't my doing, there were others with different ideas. Probably did de Gaulle a favor. At least the

411

government had ordered the suppression of the Manifeste des 140." Paul snickered. "You know it was suggested to the general that since Sartre was the publisher, that he be jailed upon his return from a trip to Algiers. That's when de Gaulle declared: '*On n'arrête pas Voltaire*.'⁹ But Sartre wasn't the only one—de Gaulle had a host of powerful enemies."

"Like?"

"Valéry Giscard, who forced him from the presidency in 1969."

"I know. I was a young man, but aware of that. I'll never understand why de Gaulle didn't just arrest Sartre and be done with it.

"Sartre was an intellectual communist; de Gaulle simply courted the Russians, who happened to be communists. We French have always feared invasions from the north; and for his own enduring grandeur, of course, which, as I said, he saw as France itself." Paul hesitated, then asked shyly, "Do you know any of Giscard's men? Do you think they could be of help?"

"I have a friend who knows Druon," Jean-Michel said, gnawing on the end of his pipe while he thought. "But of course Druon dislikes Giscard. He's a very staunch Gaullist. Unfortunately, very elderly."

"What's he got against Giscard?"

"Other than shoving de Gaulle aside? It is typical of our intellectuals, I suppose," Jean-Michel sighed. "Believe it or not, it is the Académie Française lexicographers' committee. It is a very exclusive old-boy's club, you know—but you've been gone a while—green uniform and two-pointed hat; they're all over seventy and have been working for sixty years on a new French dictionary. They're up to the letter 'R,' I believe. Anyway, Druon, as you well know, a French Resistance fighter who has been an academy member for thirty-seven years, was against him. He criticized Giscard in the conservative French newspaper *Le Figaro* a month or so ago; no doubt you missed it in Manitoba. He said that when Giscard gave lunches at the Elysée Palace, he didn't allow anyone to sit in front of him, and ate his meals staring at an empty place, like the king at Versailles. Plus, he was upset with Giscard's longwinded preamble to the European Constitution, which failed, of course."¹⁰

"Well, notwithstanding Druon, Gaullism is finally sucking its last breath."

"I'm surprised to hear you say that. In any case," Jean-Michel considered,

"I seriously doubt you want anyone of Druon's stature meddling in your case."

"Meddling? Professor, please, even though these old men are on their last legs, they at least have character. Your recent national elections turned out to be a joke between two pretenders who have succeeded in leading the country to become the sick man of Europe, with an old conservative bigot and an old political hack like Chirac jousting for power. France has not only lost its influence, but we are no longer even an interesting gadfly on the world's stage, just an ineffectual crank. Someone should do some serious 'meddling.'"

"I disagree," Jean-Michel said firmly. "French strengths are exceptional: productivity, infrastructure, and investment performance."

"Professor, *Professor*. Even in remote Manitoba we get the news. In a country like France, roiled by rising crime, nearly continuous demonstrations and strike-related violence, poverty, and the largely failed integration of an Arab immigrant population of five or six million that is ready to explode, you're speaking of an impending train wreck. Add this outbreak of still-unresolved anti-Semitic crimes, and you have a potential voting pattern that is neither credible nor an intellectual curiosity. Pathetically, France has become this exotic little country that few if any take seriously."

"You've been gone a long time, Brother Merton. Perhaps you've forgotten what it means to be French," Jean-Michel said coldly.

"No!" Paul retorted, jutting out his chin. "I have given the greater part of my life, *'parce qu'on aimait la France, nous'!*"[11] It is this passion for France that keeps the army loyal despite the liberals, academicians, and immigrants who try to destroy her. These ghettos of Arabs, Africans, and Jews fighting among themselves are a festering sore on France. I remember reading about the French-Algerian football match in 2001, when young French Muslims ceremoniously burnt the French flag and booed the "Marseillaise." They should be rounded up and deported back to their accursed deserts and beloved camels. Where is the leadership of this country? What has happened to the republican values at the very core of what it really means to be French, Professor?!" he snapped.

"Perhaps you should run for office—you chronicle her failures well enough!"

"Perhaps," Paul said darkly, staring directly at him. "All this bodes ill for

Europe, because other countries share France's situation."

Jean-Michel was getting exasperated. "What's so bad about uniting Europe!"

"The question is: exactly how do you mean that? Do you want a Jacobin Brussels — secretive and regal in its authority? That was Jacques Delors in the full flowering of the French vision of Europe, Professor. Today's Europe will have to be Girondin,[12] sharing power, arriving step by step at improvements. The grandeur of France, unfortunately, is dead."

"I disagree." Jean-Michel poked his finger against the table, "At least de Gaulle was right to insist on the persistence of a national identity that no constitutional treaty will ever eradicate. A united Europe will never be built without France or against France!"

"Professor, you are witnessing a new Europe of twenty-five that at minimum will require the delicate balance sought by Talleyrand. That purported constitution was just an incoherent jumble of policies for an incoherent jumble of vastly different nations! There is no question in my mind that loyal French must have the courage to abandon the de Gaulle-type rhetoric of grandeur, status, and national independence so that they can commit themselves to shared European sovereignty. Of course, the French intellectuals would never admit to anything being their own fault; they hate the Germans and have nothing but contempt for the Americans. But it is easily enough seen, even across an ocean, that the French now live with a unique mixture of arrogance and self-hatred. They wish to lead a Europe from which they are effectively insulated."

"They?" Jean-Michel squinted malevolently at him; Brother Merton's obvious dislike for the contemporary affairs of France was becoming tiresome. "You and your friends certainly had your play."

"We had the courage to lead, Professor, and paid heavily for it," he retorted hotly. "This generation of French exemplify unparalleled vanity linked to the memory of the Revolution, Napoleonic depredations, and colonial empires. Now, on the brink of national collapse, they're uncomfortable and itching from their own lack of confidence in themselves.

"French elections used to mean something. After the war, they presented a clear choice between those who believed in capitalism and those who wanted to end it. But in the past decade the differences between political parties have become squashed together in a neo-liberal middle. Even seen from Canada it is obvious that Western Europe has become post-political. Rather than argue about politics, it seems modern Europeans spend their time wondering who'll win the soccer championship and worrying whether to spend the long summer vacation in Indonesia or Thailand."

"You exaggerate, Brother Merton."

"Thankfully, it's your problem, Professor. But the French people are basically ungovernable. Even Benjamin Franklin realized long ago that the key to French policy was pride — a proud people who enjoyed flattery and fealty. Something recent American administrations have only begun to appreciate. The French demonstrate a willingness to embrace anachronisms that point France back toward the Stalinist or Vichyist solutions it has historically rejected. This republic is through; since it seems that democracy is rapidly escaping their grasp, perhaps the army is the best choice of leadership."

Jean-Michel looked at him in disbelief. "You're speaking of the French army? The army, which was defeated in two world wars and Indochina? The army that brought immense amounts of shame for their actions in Algeria. The army that even the Americans refused to employ in any serious crisis? That army?"

Brother Merton eyed him haughtily. "Those defeats were inspired by political defeatism. We were cursed with inept governments in Paris, no less than Napoleon's Grande Armée. The French people lost faith in their leadership: de Gaulle and virtually no other is the source of France's decline. His failures powered our determination not to lose Algeria."

"I believe the army was charged with brutality in Algeria, not determination," Jean-Michel said, a hard edge to his voice.

Merton stared back at him, making up his mind about discussing matters of the present or the past. He spoke quietly, his voice dropping off in resignation as he reached down to close his briefcase. "The root of the problem, Professor, is that Gaullism itself is responsible for destroying France's relationship with America, the most powerful nation on earth."

"Meaning France has no role to play?!" Jean-Michel blurted.

"Of course it hasn't. The Gaullist claim that France should occupy a place of reverence in the community of nations is ridiculous."

"I disagree."

"Why should French views matter any more than those of, say, Italy, whose population and economy are nearly the same size?"

Jean-Michel snorted. "Brother Merton, please. France is like Great Britain in economy and power; it is a member of the Security Council."

There was a knock on the door: Jean-Michel's secretary. "Professor Levasseur, sorry to interrupt, there is an important caller on the line. Would you like to take it?" He paused a moment. "Uh, no, get his number and I'll call back."

"It is not a 'he,' she replied, and struggled to shut the door.

"You were saying?"

"If France threatens to undermine American interests with its Security Council veto, the Americans would call our bluff, pointing out that such behavior merely weakens the institution that is the prime source of France's undeserved prestige. Even the secretary general is calling for a major reorganization of the council."

"But—"

"Despite all the bluster, Professor, France has not used its veto power unilaterally since 1976. The only thing France and the neo-Gaullists can't possibly abide is being ignored."

Merton worried about his original intent of his visit. "I don't think this is the right time for this discussion. Perhaps you don't have time," he said flatly, wishing to change the subject back to finding a competent attorney.

"If you lack the stomach for defending France, Brother Merton, perhaps there will be no contest in court: the French people usually pity their clergy; of course, a little whining will be expected."

Lieutenant Paul de Monteaux, French Naval Intelligence officer, Office of Algerian Affairs, secret member of the OAS, shed his monk's image and leaped to his feet. His face became first red, then stern, and he assumed the disciplined, dedicated French officer he once was—a hardened veteran who had in the past helped to torture and kill political opponents of France, practiced at drowning his victims with teaspoons of water poured down their nostrils.

"Watch your *mouth*, Professor. It can get you into serious trouble," he commanded. "I have little respect for academicians. Good riddance." He reached for his valise.

"Wait, please! I have some whiskey, if you would like." Jean-Michel reached into his desk drawer, trying to recover.

Paul gave Jean-Michel a condescending look. "No. Thank you," he said, and turned to leave.

"Monastery doesn't allow it?" Jean-Michel tried to joke. "Please, Brother Merton, I aplogize for offending you."

Paul looked at him, his eyes narrowed. "You lack sensitivity, Professor, a fault most of you academics seem to share. No whiskey." He sat down.

"Just takes the edge off a long day," Jean-Michel said, pouring a shot into his coffee.

"It's liquor, Professor—it takes the 'edge off' everything."

Forgive me, Brother Merton, my comments were uncalled-for. I appreciate you are here." He tried to undo his earlier rancorous words. "Do you think terrorism got its start in Algeria in the Spring of '45? By all accounts it was a menacing situation, it seems to me that the roots of Middle East turmoil and even the War on Terrorism today can be attributed to the birth of Arab hostilities to the West back then." Both men felt awkward.

"It happened long before '45. Those ills came from Versailles," Paul said, massaging his hands as though washing them.

"Do you mean the rise of Hitler?"

"No. That's a fallacy, which the French seem to love. When war came in 1939, it was a result of twenty years of decisions taken or not taken, not of arrangements made at the Hall of Mirrors in 1919."

"But, Brother Merton, I think most people would agree that the Treaty of Versailles was responsible for the new world war that followed, that Clemenceau wanted his pound of flesh, since a militaristic Germany had invaded his homeland twice in his lifetime." Jean-Michel stated pedantically. "It certainly seems logical that we are suffering its consequences."

"Professor, the traditional view that those onerous war reparations drove the German economy to collapse and brought Hitler and the Nazis to power in 1933 is wrong. The problem with you academicians is that you spend too much time reading each other's books."

"And the reparations?" Jean-Michel challenged, tapping the stem of his pipe on the desk.

"The reparations, if you ever bothered to check, and almost *everyone* hasn't, demanded of Germany were less than those paid by France after its defeat in the 1870 Franco-Prussian war. Furthermore, Germany paid only one-third of what it owed in compensation for its occupation and destruction of Belgium and northern France."

"Then how do you account for the German attack?"

"It's simple: the real problem was that Germany didn't feel defeated; they didn't think they lost the war, Professor. Use your logic. They had never seen foreign troops on German soil. After World War I the German army marched back in good order to Berlin. German industry was intact. Germany still was the biggest European country west of the Soviet Union. It never really disarmed, and it was strong enough, less than a decade later, to conquer most of Europe. Could a militarily prostrate, economically destroyed country piled high with reparations bring most of Europe to its knees in less than two decades, Professor?"

Jean-Michel saw his arguments easily handled by an adversary who obviously read—a lot. "So why didn't the Western powers continue the First World War and take it into Germany?" He asked.

"Trench warfare. France and Britain were exhausted by prolonged trench warfare that had cost them millions of lives, and they had an even more political reason for signing the armistice in 1918: they felt that, if the war went on, the Americans would be that much more powerful, and they didn't want the Americans to be the dominant partner.

"You see, Professor Levasseur, most people seem to forget that the peace conference, which continued for three more years, has to be seen in the broader context of the extraordinary reorganization of European borders that followed the demise of the Austro-Hungarian and Ottoman empires. In the Middle East, too, new nations were created—Iraq, Syria and Jordan, among them—while the idea of a Jewish state was born. Versailles and subsequent agreements were meant to temper ethnic minorities, not inflame them."

Jean-Michel nodded agreement. "Those decisions made in such an offhand way that you think they aren't going to matter that much, matter an awful lot fifty years down the road, it seems."

"It is true. Some of the most intractable problems of the modern world have roots in decisions made right after the end of the Great War: the Balkan wars in the 1890s, for example; the crisis in Iraq from a little casual mapmaking in Franco-British rivalries; the Kurds' self-determination; disputes between the Greeks and Turks; and the seemingly endless struggle between Arabs and Jews over land that each thought had been promised to them.

"We could have colonized the Magreb[13] and built a French future for Northern Africa. Instead, thanks to de Gaulle, we abandon the Arabs to their radicals and caves." Paul again took a deep drag on his cigarette, a vice deferred, twice enjoyed. "What would the world be like today if France were still managing her colonies in North Africa and the Middle East. Above all, peace and progress! You know as well as I that the new leaders of the Muslim population emerged — not the least of them Nasser and his disciples, including Saddam Hussein — with a determination to achieve independence and Arab unity. The only concern of American and European leadership was to block the Soviets, not help the Arabs. The charade was obvious; Arab leaders were preaching revolution even then.

Jean-Michel sat forward again as if to confront Paul, but reconsidered. "Were you part of the FNF?"

Paul looked at him, sizing him up. "That's a very serious question."

"One you will have to answer in court, I presume."

Paul hesitated. "The FNF was a bunch of hotheaded French settlers in Algeria. I was a member of the OAS," he said proudly.

"Then there is no question why you had to leave France."

"None, Professor. I would have been imprisoned for life, or shot. But the world should know that Charles de Gaulle and his lackeys were about to send an invasion force into France from Algeria, under the code name 'Operation Resurrection.'[14] After he had left power in the '50s, like a pouting little boy with his ball, he wanted a coup d'état for his own return to power in the late '50s without the benefit of democratic elections — no less despicable than Hitler's Nazi Party and their political rise to power. Professor, it's getting late and we still need to work out an agreement. I would like to make a private phone call; I will need to step into the hall," Paul said, and left.

CHAPTER 5

═══ THE JACKAL ═══

When Brother Merton returned, Jean-Michel tried to relieve the tension. He offered tea by holding up a bag, but Paul refused with a wave of his hand. Jean-Michel started in again. "It must have been difficult in the monastery—you know..." he hesitated, "no sex."

"The monastery? Sex?" Paul grimaced. "No, not really. As Saint Augustine described, these temptations can be mastered, if necessary, by oneself." He looked at Jean-Michel, trying to judge whether to share with him any anecdotes from the cloister or his private life. He disliked academicians in general and the liberal cliques they formed, but in this case Jean-Michel would of necessity have to play on his team. "But fine food," he shook his head hopelessly and laughed a little for the first time, "was a serious temptation. Like the world's great courtesans, it was a luxury we could ill afford, spiritually or physically, in our dining hall. This turned out to be my worst cross to bear, for I had not realized how accustomed I had become to the texture, flavor, and quality of French food. But, you know, Professor," he said shyly, "I usually do the listening."

Jean-Michel waved him on. "Please. Politics in our case seems to have become rather thin soup."

"Well," Paul groped for the right words, "while one could rely on masturbation to quiet the urges of concupiscence every few weeks, the thought of food visited my imagination almost every day at the monastery. Now that I'm back in Paris, I realize one must learn again how to appreciate the art of cuisine, and its temptations. Believe me when I say that our consecrated table back in Manitoba was very Spartan." He looked over at Jean-Michel's portly physique. "If I may say so, I see you've been able to satisfy yours."

Jean-Michel grinned. "I have. I do love the food, but there was a special epiphany for my palate, that makes my mouth water still. Indeed, Brother Merton, it was almost sexual, like sex with a naive country maiden. It involved a simple slice of the creamy, blue-flecked cow's milk cheese called Fourme d'Ambert—perhaps you are familiar with it?" Paul shook his head. "It happened in my late teens at my grandmother's home near Lyon. While I was reading and absentmindedly eating a slice of Fourme d'Ambert as part of a late afternoon snack, I took a bite of cheese, a sip of red Côtes du Ventoux, and suddenly my mouth filled with an amazing, wintry sensation of fresh black truffles.[15]

"It was the earthiness of the blue cheese combined with the essence of the wine that triggered the sensation, I'm sure, and I didn't want it to disappear, like the stirring climax of lovemaking in the arms of a robust, fragrant young girl. Unfortunately, it was gone. I tried for a second morsel of cheese and a sip of wine, which were pleasurable, but not greater than the sum of the parts." He paused to relive his memories, then looked at Paul. "And you?"

Paul hesitated. He was there on business, uncomfortable being asked to share intimacies with a stranger. "Well, I...," but was captured by his own fantasies and became animated. "Late in the afternoon, just before dinner and while we brothers rested in our little rooms, I would often begin to create my special dinner. It would start with the appetizer, and such uncommon flavors as Manzanilla fino sherry—with its hints of hazelnuts and iodine—paired with soft and elegant fresh anchovy filets marinated in olive oil, the bones deep-fried to a brilliant crispness, and then a touch of the salty, silken Spanish ham called Jamón Ibérico Bellota."

Jean-Michel took the pipe from his mouth, leaned forward to savor the taste, and waited impatiently for the rest of the feast. "A tangle," as Paul continued, "of the bay squid (chipirons) stuffed with red pepper and smoky pork lomo, and squid tentacles fried and lightly stained with their ink." He stared into the distance as though visualizing his table. "There would be a cool, white Savigny les Beaunes, of course, from Domaine J. Boillot, with its earthy hints of the woods, served with a deep-fried beurreck of pastry-wrapped scallops in a cream of wild mushrooms, showered with lightly toasted almonds." Jean-Michel had begun to salivate and had to swallow. Paul halted his description to philosophize. "You not only had to pair the food and wine, of course," he cautioned, "but also to pause and reflect—to stop and pay attention to our endeavors at the table, and how mother nature had blessed us."[16]

"Finally," he raised his hands to sculpt the image, "a masterpiece of creamy risotto laced with scallops, lemon zest, and ginger from the Balearic Islands. So complex in execution, mind you, but simple for our religious palates to understand," he murmured. "Finished off with a warm puddle of creamy polenta combined with white truffles from Italy, a dream of smooth textures, intense fragrances, rounded out by a cool Corton Charlemagne from Domaine Bonneau du Martray, rich with truffle and woodsy essences of its own. At that point he was lost in his dreams, and the conversation, like that of a witness to a holy apparition, drifted off into sighs and, finally, silence. His new friend across the table, absorbed in his story, offered a moment of silence, but followed with polite applause.

Paul smiled. "Thank you. So you understand that food is not of the genus of sex, but somehow a powerful cousin."

Jean-Michel felt closer to this rather strange man, yet wary of his complexities. "It is ironic, you know, relating a tale of army complicity in a coup d'état against the legally constituted government of France, ostensibly led by your own General de Gaulle," Jean-Michel said. "Yet you tried to kill him."

"Maurice told me, Professor, that you were from Lyon; the men and women of Lyon have a great tradition of liberty. Lyon was the center of resistance in World War II. So you, more than most, should understand that de Gaulle was a traitor to us and to his country."

"Traitor? His photograph is on the wall of almost every home in France, including Lyon."

"So was Hitler's in Germany, and still would be had he won," Brother Merton replied. "We thought de Gaulle was with us, but he simply used the army as a tool for his own ends."

"Wasn't that evident from the first, Brother Merton? No one ever accused Charles de Gaulle of being naïve. Did you think he would serve as a hostage to the army?"

"You remember Prime Minister Coty, correct?" Jean-Michel nodded his head. "Well, on the evening of April 29, Coty issued a statement saying that he had agreed to de Gaulle's conditions under which he, Coty, could turn over control: full power to de Gaulle, as prime minister, to form a new government and a new constitution, no parliamentary interference for six months. Not many people know, Professor, that a second telegram went to Algiers along the following lines: 'President of the Republic receiving Great Charles; operation postponed.' De Gaulle was obviously working to take over the country then, and his plans for Operation Resurrection's paratroopers were again put on standby in Algiers. We were under the impression that this historical event was being done as a partnership. Despite de Gaulle's persuasive qualities with the political leadership, he never won over François Mitterrand, and admittedly the vote was going to be so close and the atmosphere so tense that the generals had reactivated Resurrection. When the vote was taken, the general won and Operation Resurrection was finally called off."

"It is hard to believe." Jean-Michel shook his head.

"Not so hard," Brother Merton allowed. "De Gaulle's next task, of course, was to assert his government's authority in Algiers. We knew it was certainly not going to be easy. Our generals were firmly of the view that it was they who had brought de Gaulle to power in France, and that they had done so in order that Algeria might be incorporated into France and the rebels dispatched. De Gaulle had done nothing to dispel that view while conducting his negotiations with Coty; indeed, he had not hesitated to invoke the threat of Operation Resurrection, a threat that was a powerful card in his hand.

"But, you see, having obtained power by whatever means, the general, as before in 1944, was not one to recognize debts to those who had put him there. A small delegation of generals led by Salan immediately flew to Paris to protest, but de Gaulle hardly bothered to listen. To make his point, and at his most frigid, de Gaulle was surprised, he said, that General Salan had not thought it proper to wear his uniform on his first visit to his new prime minister. Can you imagine that? The haughty bastard." Now it was Jean-Michel's turn to look askance at the good Brother Merton. Jean-Michel was not comfortable hearing a clergyman swear; he had never, despite his Catholic education, heard even one curse word. "We had been outmaneuvered, but back then, not quite sure how."

"Looking back now," he continued, "the position was quite simple. In August 1944 de Gaulle had refused to allow the Resistance a political role, and effectively dissolved it. Can you imagine the gall? No resister, dead or alive, was mentioned by de Gaulle in his August 25 speech at the Hôtel de Ville where, fearful of a communist takeover by Colonel Rol,[17] he declared that the broken city had risen to free itself, sparked by *la France éternelle*. It took over a week of 300 dead martyrs! Throughout his career, de Gaulle's only greatness was his useful gift for denial; he was a one-man show, Professor."

"And you?" Jean-Michel asked cynically. "What about the army?"

"This time we, the army in Algiers, were playing the role of the Resistance. Whatever our responsibility for having brought de Gaulle to power, we were not going to be allowed to set up or maintain any political power structure that might rival the government. There was only one government, and that was his. The general, as so often, had seen matters much more clearly than either his supposed allies, like us, or his opponents."

"Including the army," Jean-Michel said pointedly.

"I said that. He duped us all. On the morning of June 4, de Gaulle arrived, as promised, in Algiers. He landed at Maison Blanche airport, from where he had taken off just after D-Day in June 1944 to assume control of the liberation of Paris. He was driven by our military escort to the Government House, and as he came out on the balcony, the huge crowd below erupted. 'Then, in a speech of a few minutes,' which he wrote in his memoirs later, 'I tossed them the words, seemingly spontaneous but in reality carefully calculated ... I have understood you,' and he went on to speak of 'renewal and brotherhood.'

"The ambiguity was masterful." Paul shook his head in admiration. "The cheers that followed that one sentence lasted several minutes. Of course, what they thought they were cheering had nothing to do with de Gaulle's real intentions, but his purpose had been achieved, and he proceeded to speak of the 'magnificent work of understanding and pacification,' secure in the knowledge that he had gained the sympathy of the crowd without committing himself to anything. It was in his eyes only a political holding operation, but it had served its purpose.

"The people in charge seemed to be unaware of the simple political fact that there were only a million Europeans to nine million Moslems, but it was obvious to De Gaulle that 'we cannot keep Algeria.' The 'Ultras,' the white settler families who made their life there, were openly hostile, the junior officers in the army were uncertain, and probably most significant of all, the poster portraits of him, put up only a week or two earlier, were now being rapidly torn down.

"History has it that a sniper, backed by the white settlers and the army, was stationed in a window of an apartment block just opposite the balcony of the Gouvernement-Général in Algiers."

Jean-Michel looked at Brother Merton. "You were probably in the crowd."

"No, I was at headquarters, but by then it was obvious to our leadership in Algeria that de Gaulle's ultimate intention was to betray them."

"Do you know why he didn't shoot?" Jean-Michel said.

"He?"

"Some called him 'the Jackal.'"

"No." Paul hesitated. "But I have heard about the Jackal—if he or she existed. Just one of those great perversions of fate that history will probably never reveal."

"I'd rather believe the story that the sniper was swayed by de Gaulle's words," Jean-Michel said.

"Believe what pleases you," Paul said. "We'll never know. But think of it this way, Professor: had the sniper obeyed instructions, there would, of course, have been mourning at the murder of a prime minister, considered a heroic personality, no less than JFK's after his assassination five years later. Nonetheless, the events of May 1958 would have had a different sequel. Perhaps the military would have taken over, at least for a while, but even," he took out his cigarettes and lit another in mid-sentence, obvious satisfaction in his face, "under the shock of the incident, the Fourth Republic might have pulled itself together and produced a leader worthy of the name. And the general's passing would have been regretted, but nothing more."

Jean-Michel had picked up his pipe, an unconscious bond with his visitor, and massaged it with his thumb. "If, on the other hand, Brother Merton, a similar sniper had completed his work on inauguration day, 8 January 1959, the obituaries would have carried a quite different message. They would have covered de Gaulle's war record without question, but they would have also proclaimed his short period as prime minister, a time when the new government, his government, accomplished an astonishing outburst of activity in France. And," he signaled by tapping his pudgy finger on his desk, "by no means the least impressive feature, the amount of sheer intellectual and physical effort that the sixty-seven-year-old general put into his job, including the preparation of France for partnership in the Common Market."

"Ah," Paul complained, "little sweets that satisfy for a while; you, a history professor, are ignoring the historical consequences. What would your students think?" In return he pointed his fingers, like scissors clutching the cigarette, at Jean-Michel in admonishment. "Don't you remember the Berlin Crisis in '58? Again the Americans came to aid Europeans. Khrushchev's attempts to establish control over Berlin were stopped by American determination, American nuclear weapons, and NATO, the very NATO that, including Germany, kept de Gaulle's enthusiasm quite cool, resulting in NATO's expulsion from France. He even wanted the Americans to give him a finger on the nuclear weapons when France had none."

"France could have handled the responsibility," Jean-Michel said proudly.

"Perhaps France could have. But the precedent would have been established and given other NATO members like Greece and Turkey opportunities to demand equal nuclear weapons partnerships for their own nefarious uses. So, we have the dubious spectacle of our nearsighted and gawky peacock strutting about, voicing, from behind the skirts of the USA and Britain, hollow threats at the Soviets — the very group of communists, I might add, that he was also trying to court to the disadvantage of his allies. All of this over Berlin. And where did France obtain her piece of the city? Great battles dearly won? No, it was given to her, thanks to Churchill's efforts, while de Gaulle's major contribution to the military effort was keeping practically the entire French army tied down in Algeria and French Indochina. And you would balance all of this against his penchant to work hard? Please, Professor," he said patronizingly. "Work is for tractors; that old man had lost his nerve and his judgment and, like Napoleon, did more to threaten the future of Europe than practically any other."

"It is a complicated issue," Jean-Michel offered, giving ground to a determined adversary, and decided to get away from the difficult issues. "I never envisioned modems in monasteries."

Paul smiled, raised his hands, and then put them down again. "We're not on Mars, Professor. I have a very nice laptop computer and broadband with which I do a reasonable business in worldwide honey sales. Needless to say, we have few distractions, and the Internet is basically free." Paul paused. "Do you mind of I make use of your toilet, professor?"

Jean-Michel waved him to the door. "Around the corner, on your right."

When Paul returned he asked for a cup of tea.

Jean-Michel went about getting some water for the tea, left the room, and returned, putting the pot on the hotplate. "I was most concerned about your experience in Algeria."

"Algeria? It was messy, nasty, and dangerous. You could say it had all the characteristics that politicians most fear: no obviously popular solution; passions were intense; violence had become commonplace; and positions were so entrenched that there was no identifiable room to maneuver. De Gaulle, of course, had no choice; quite apart from the drain on France's resources, both material and human, it was to be the test of survival for de Gaulle's Fifth Republic.[18] Ironic...."

"How do you mean?"

"Algeria had been the Fifth Republic's midwife — and could just as easily have turned into its executioner."

"Could the army have done any better?" Jean-Michel asked.

"We'll never know, will we? I would say the Middle East is an abject failure of European politics. There is no such thing as a European foreign policy, let alone the capacity to carry one out. Instead, our old instincts and affinities have resurfaced. Germany supported Croatia's bid for independence even as Croats massacred Serbs, while Britain and France provided diplomatic backing to the Serbs as they killed Croats. EU governments bickered among themselves as pathetic lines of stricken refugees snaked back and forth across the Balkans. In the end it was the Americans at Dayton, Ohio, in 1995, who managed to bang Yugoslav heads together to stop at least that phase of the civil war."[19]

427

CHAPTER 6

═══ "THE CAT" ═══

"Were you there, at "Barricades Week?" Jean-Michel asked.

"No, just outside Algiers. With our tanks. If General Challe had ordered the tanks against Ortiz, I believe France would have entered civil war. He left Algiers on 28 January to avoid being kidnapped, I think."

"I remember it well," Jean-Michel said. "De Gaulle went on television at 8 p.m. on 29 January. I think we all realized that the Fifth Republic, his own creation, was on the brink of disintegration, and that the speech he had to make was to be the most important of his whole long life. Did you see it?"

"No, I was ordered to liaise with the tank commanders; as I recall I slept under a tank."

"My father and I were gathered with others in a café in Lyon. De Gaulle did not look well to me, but it was black-and-white TV," Jean-Michel said. "He seemed tired, had not been sleeping, I suppose, but he had his brigadier general's uniform on, that was obvious enough. When he spoke, I remember that his voice was determined, each point emphasized by a raised finger in what was otherwise a clenched fist. You know," his eyes became wide, "it wasn't simply the head of state speaking; it was General de Gaulle. Basically, he refused to waver from his decision of September: 'The Algerians shall have free choice of their destiny,' he pledged. He firmly ordered the army not to associate itself with insurgence in any manner whatsoever, and to re-establish law and order. I would have thought you'd have been on the receiving end of that order." Jean-Michel mused.

"There was chaos," Paul shrugged.

"Finally, he spoke to us, to France, and as he did so his voice softened; it was something I will remember all my life. '*Eh bien, mon cher et vieux pays, nous voici donc ensemble, encore une fois, face à une lourde épreuve.'* ('Well, my dear and old country, here we are together, once again, facing a harsh test.') There could be no concessions to those who, he said 'dream of being usurpers.' If there were, France would become a 'poor broken plaything adrift on a sea of chance.' For me, he was speaking straight from the heart. Everyone in the café cheered; the emotion of the moment made me cry. It was de Gaulle at his very best, and, as you know, the response from the French people was electric: thousands of messages of support were received at the Elysée, and within fifteen minutes, I am told, most of your army units in Algeria had declared their loyalty."

Paul shook his head knowingly. "There was a thunderstorm in Algiers that night and the insurgents had to listen to the broadcast in a crashing downpour. It seemed, as even de Gaulle himself wrote, 'symbolic.' It was for me as well.

"How so?"

"Our army—by then largely conscript—was getting bored and irritated when it wasn't frightened."

"How many troops were there?"

"Hard to tell. Around 400,000 would be my guess."

"The FLN?"

"The FLN had survived and had started to reassert its strength under a new leader, Houari Boumédienne. Politically, the anti-war movement in France was gaining ground. An anti-war manifesto was issued by a group of 121 intellectuals, including Jean-Paul Sartre, Simone de Beauvoir, and even Simone Signoret; it was followed by demonstrations on the Paris streets.

"I know they were gunning for de Gaulle. My father called him 'the cat.'"

"Cat?" Paul asked.

"Nine lives."

"A few weeks before Christmas that year, de Gaulle came back to Algeria. Do you know how many assassination attempts were made on him during his two-day visit?"

Jean-Michel shook his head.

"Four! There was universally hostility toward him by the white community."

"Why did they hate him so much?" Jean-Michel asked, his face wrinkled in question.

"Various reasons. At times he was their savior."

"We all know what happens to 'saviors.'"

"The day he left there was a great Moslem demonstration, FLN flags appeared everywhere, and the cry was 'Vive de Gaulle.' In the end it was his decision to announce a referendum to decide whether or not independence should be granted to Algeria once peace had been restored. He never returned to Algeria. That's when we knew it was time to take action against him."

"The OAS?"

"A camaraderie of patriots, Algérie Française, and special units of the army."

"Excuse me, you were exploding terrorist bombs almost at random in Paris."

"It was for the good of the nation."

"Ah, where have I heard that before? Means justifying ends."

"It takes courage."

"Camus said, 'It is better to be wrong by killing no one than to be right with mass graves....'"

"Ah, Camus. He was no doubt making quotes for the press. We tried to create a government that would have saved France."

"*From* whom and *for* whom? You're talking about the attempted putsch in April?"

"We simply announced that Algeria and the Sahara were under the army's direct control."

"Simply!" Jean-Michel was startled. "In Lyon we heard talk of your paratroopers from Algeria landing on the mainland and surrounding Paris. France was on the verge of panic. Even the British were frightened, and a cabinet meeting was held to assess the possibility of sending British troops to help de Gaulle in the event of an invasion from Algeria. Napoleon had already done it once from Elba. That's history, Brother Merton!"

"I do remember that broadcast; it showed how desperate he really was: '*Françaises, Français, aidez-moi!*' It made most of us laugh."

"It seems ironic that you choose the brotherhood of Christ to hide."

"I resent that," Paul said harshly.

"Brother Merton, you above all knew of the murderous campaigns of the FLN in Algeria and the OAS in France — innocent deaths."

"How many more deaths, Professor, had we allowed this farce to continue? The FLN were terrorists of the first order; they did a good job of killing even their rival Algerian factions. Their leader was a communist and terrorist. We were concerned about the withdrawal of French troops and leaving behind the innocent Algérie Française."

"Are you so sure?"

"Look what we have now. And if we hadn't left Indochina? The Americans left because of their liberal bleeding hearts marching around the White House with coffins and candles. All those hippies, and the European Left, those courageous Dutch who never seem to spill any blood, and French intellectuals who came to the parks on sunny afternoons, where are they now?"

"I don't follow—"

"Of course you don't. Have you heard of 'the killing fields' of Cambodia, Professor? Would almost two million Cambodians and Vietnamese still be alive if France and America had the political will to stay and fight the communists? This righteousness of you intellectuals almost makes me want to vomit even today. Where were the hippies, those beautiful demonstrators with body paint and flowers? In Paris and New York and all the other places where the TV cameras were out in force looking for sound bites, that's where, not in the muck of Vietnam's deltas, like Maurice, I'll tell you. They are afraid to even mention to their children that they were sunshine patriots back then, who contributed nothing to the situation except cowardice. Who are the heroes? The soldiers and pilots who died and are forgotten, that's who, Professor."

"And how many innocent people did all you patriots kill?"

Paul's face was flushed with anger. "You bastards demonstrated and then went back to your comfortable classrooms — fussed over by fawning coeds — and debates that cost you nothing except the freedom of Southeast Asia, while you masturbated your intellectual lives away, vicariously watching the real leaders of the world deal with its problems. The world is turning into a shit-hole now because the willpower of that bombastic old man and others like him couldn't take the heat in Africa! How many white settlers had to run for France in order to escape death at the hands of those ragheads who are now burning our cities? How many left their homes?" he demanded.

Jean-Michel kept silent.

"I'll tell you, at least 300,000. And for what?! Where were you, Professor, on the night of 22 August 1962? No doubt caressing a glass of wine in some cozy little bar. Do you know where I was? I was with an OAS commando group set up under Colonel Jean-Marie Bastien-Thiry to rid France of that pompous fool." He stood up with the energy of the moment and began to pace. "We saw General de Gaulle's convoy, he and his wife and son-in-law, leave across the Seine on their way out of Paris. We had set up a barricade at the crossroads of Petit-Clamart to intercept that old dragon and be done with him. There were twelve of us, armed with automatic weapons and four cars. At 20:08 p.m. I saw the general's car and its one escort approaching; Bastien-Thiry gave the signal to open fire. De Gaulle's driver, Marroux, sped past us, right into our second barricade. We got in fourteen shots that hit the car directly—tires, gear-box, windshield—but the devil was with him and they made it through." Paul was looking across years of time.

"So that was you," Jean-Michel said quietly. "I remember reading it in the paper."

Paul brightened. "It was magnificent."

"De Gaulle shrugged the whole thing off," Jean-Michel said. "The newspapers said he told Pompidou that you 'shot like pigs.'"

"How dare you!" Paul shouted, his arms trembling at his side.

Jean-Michel held up his hands before his chest and waved surrender. "Despite everything, you *did* stick to your guns, I'll say that," then shrugged, "even if the lot of you couldn't shoot straight."

CHAPTER 7

═══ A SPECIFIC DECEIT ═══

Paul had reached the limits of his patience. "Professor, these debates serve no purpose. My mission is to find a very competent lawyer who will keep me from jail. And my time is short." He walked back over to the Vermeer and touched the painting. "It is beautiful." He turned to face Jean-Michel. "Do you know of any attorneys who are collectors?"

"Possibly."

"It would provide great incentive."

"It's very valuable."

"All the better. In the end it is just a painting."

"Don't you think Maurice would object?"

"He doesn't own it. The true owners are either senile or dead and buried in Indochina. It has been a de Monteaux family secret for years. Does that surprise you?"

"In a manner of speaking. Hard to believe that Maurice has ever stolen anything." Nonetheless, memories of all the information about famous tombs that he had supplied the colonel began flicking across Jean-Michel's mind.

"'Anything?' You'd be surprised. The more accurate question might be 'from whom?' But I won't go into that. When it is appropriate, after the trial, I will retire from the Trappists. I have a few good years left, Professor, and I am not going to spend them in some dank prison filled with pederasts while this gaudy little trinket hangs on the wall. I want you to investigate secretly, who are the best — understand me, Professor — and locate one of the finest attorneys in France, a Gaullist attorney, a collector, who represents a distinguished law firm. Let me know in a few days who qualifies. Then we will make an offer. The attorney may have the painting appraised by a reputable dealer. Then, you will arrange the best deal you can with the firm, applying part of its value against the attorney's fees for my trial. Put the rest in a Swiss bank. I will send you the bank's address and contact in Zurich. There will be considerable money left; the attorney will disburse it to me when necessary, and collect a modest yearly retainer for himself and the firm. What is it the Mafiosi say? 'A deal they can't refuse.'"

Jean-Michel sat up, stunned. "What the devil are you talking about?" he demanded. "*We* make an offer!?"

"The 'devil,' I suppose. Are you a rich man, Professor? Of course not. You can't even afford your own office. Nor, by all appearances, am I. But then, you never applied yourself to the pursuit of money. With luck and determination, this painting will make you free of financial worries and, of course, me free of prison, plus, shall we say, an addition to my discretionary assets."

Jean-Michel hesitated. "I didn't expect this; perhaps you should be seeing a psychiatrist, not a lawyer."

Paul stiffened. "Hear me, Professor, this Vermeer will not hang here uselessly, to be admired by some graduate students who probably wouldn't know or care whether it was an original or a calendar. It belongs to my family and I need it."

"And your brother?"

"I'm not concerned. He stole it himself, and doesn't require its assets in any case. He has many more collectibles than a few Vermeers," he said offhandedly. He took a moment to light a cigarette. "Does he come here often?" Paul asked, exhaling, now looking a bit more formidable than a humble brother.

"No. No one comes here without your brother's permission," Jean-Michel said defiantly.

"Then you need not make a point of telling him. If eventually he comes by and asks where it is, tell him I borrowed it. Let's just say it belongs to the Museum of the Missing."[20]

"I've heard of that supposed place, a blot on the character of our heritage."

"Save the drama for those who listen to such whining. I'm sure Maurice will understand. Your commission shall be our little secret."

"It's hardly ethical, and..." Jean-Michel hesitated. "You trust me? A stranger?"

"Professor, from what I understand, you are impoverished financially and your future looks questionable.

"Did you think Maurice simply pulled you out of the gutter to emulate the Good Samaritan? Believe me, Professor, you are not the only one. He has cultivated relationships with academicians worldwide for a variety of reasons, one, and most important, the diminishing fortunes of the de Monteaux family. And now, you and your otherwise unknown associates are a reliable source for building his little empire in rare collectibles from pilfered tombs. For some, mere pennies, others a free dinner, perhaps," Paul looked around the room, "or a nice office. Thankfully, you all are among the most naive people on earth."

He looked back at Jean-Michel with hard, glistening eyes. "Did you think that I just sold honey and went to Vespers? Don't you know that the Middle Easterners are the most voracious honey eaters on this planet, *and* the most rapacious collectors? Hasn't it dawned on you that these wealthy men tire of their art? Did you, of all people, think their taste for collecting was limited to beautiful women and expensive cars? Why did you think Maurice had an interest in dungeons and tombs and, for that matter, Vietnam? Who do you think coordinates these black markets in stolen objects, Joey Two-fingers, the midnight grave robber? Ninety percent of all stolen art is gone forever, Professor, it is a fact. And, may I add, grave robbing is having a banner year, particularly for collectors in the Middle East and Asia who have preferences for Western creations, living...or dead." He snickered. "Muslims, you know...."

Jean-Michel sat bewildered.

Would you permit me a small quote from your friend Sartre?" Paul said calmly.

Jean-Michel stared at him, still disbelieving, but nodded.

"Moral problems, Professor, according to Sartre's *Ethics,* are specifically human, supposing choice and will, hence totally irrelevant to animals or gods. Since, as he said, one can seize the world only through a technique, a culture, or a condition, in other words only through what humans create, man finds anew everywhere his project, only his project. Thus human reality is moral only insofar as it is without God; or put another way, Professor, without the world, in which people determine themselves by choosing their concrete projects, there can be no values. His conclusion, as I'm sure you must know, is that through all his enterprises, man seeks neither to go beyond himself nor to conserve himself, but to establish himself. At the end of each such enterprise, he finds himself as he was: gratuitous to his very bones. He always seeks to be relevant, and never is, never can be. You and I, Professor, are about to embark on our project gratuitously and seeking relevance among ourselves. Nothing else matters." He shook his head. "Relevance... whatever that is."

Jean-Michel gathered his wits and, rising, leaned over his desk toward his antagonist. "I recall, Brother Merton, reading a review of *Macbeth* in which the reviewer wrote that everyone who sees *Macbeth* sees a different play. The point was, if you tell me what you think of *Macbeth*, that tells me more about you than about *Macbeth*. So, if there is someone who cannot feel passionate about preserving our shared global legacy, that tells me something about the person.[21] Are you and your brother proud of pillaging the past and looting countries of their heritage in some strange belief that it is *justified*—by Sartre, for God's sake?!"

Paul returned to his chair, seemingly humbled and subdued. He stubbed out his cigarette in the ashtray, and, picking up his briefcase, walked to the door. He reached for the doorknob and then turned, a thin smile on his face. "Who are the legitimate custodians of human achievement, Professor? Those rich rabble and their minions who run the museums and auction houses of the world for their own titillation and crowing rights? They pander to the rich and ignorant and are corrupt to their very core. My brother and I and our little team are simply competitors in a business where pillaging is rampant and an accepted form of commerce."

"Sorry, Merton, but you are rationalizing. Antiquities and historical sites should be policed, there is no question of that. Citizens should be taught the value and importance of local archeological remains."

Brother Merton became agitated. "Policed?" He looked at Jean-Michel menacingly. "You should know, Professor, you wouldn't live long after crossing me or Maurice, friend or not, inebriated or not. Bad accidents happen, and you should be mindful of your loose habits." He lingered as if in thought, then continued, "Think of it this way, Professor, I…" He changed his mind. "Rather, look at it from Sartre's point of view, since you seem to admire him so much. He told us in our search for self-knowledge and self-identity, I believe, that we must use what others say and think about us. Fair enough. However, the whole lesson is that there is no such thing as moral isolation or irresponsibility. Since others judge us by our acts, a genuine commitment, so to speak, and not by our gestures, which are a comedy, of course, we are not only defined by others, but we define ourselves by what we do. I wish to be defined by what I do, that is the "morality" that means something—in this case wealth and power. It has nothing to do with what is some kind of religiosity. Ours is nothing more than a kind of deliberately induced ethical anarchy, for which, if you do as I say, you will be compensated handsomely." He laughed hollowly. "Don't worry, Professor, it is a traditional intimacy among the French as we all know, which, if I may say so, is a comfortable deceit. Choose well and you will be one of us. And if not…," he left leaving the door open behind him.

CHAPTER 8

══ A COUPLE OF DRINKS ══
WITH SKINHEADS

"Mam'selle Buooks?"

"*Brooks*...yes."

"Uh, Mam'selle Buooks?"

"Yes."

"Alors, Mam'selle Buooks, a Colonel de Monteaux asked that I telephone. He is at the American Hospital. It saddens me to say that your friend, Monsieur Levasseur, has a, uh, a creases."

"Creases?"

"Mam'selle Buooks? Here is, uh, here—" the phone was abruptly taken out of the orderly's hand.

"Charly? It's Maurice," he said dourly.

"What's happened?" she asked, afraid to hear.

"It's Jean-Michel. He was attacked by skinheads."

"Oh, God," she moaned.

The colonel's voice ran thick with frustration, "You know how he is, he can't keep his mouth shut. Evidently he got tangled up with three or four neo-Nazis in a bar, over some extremist politician from the National Front, and was beaten quite badly. They've been rounded up by the police and carted off to jail, but Jean-Michel received a nasty beating and a hard kick to his head. The doctors are worried about a concussion and the use of his left eye. We are in the emergency room at the American Hospital[22]—you must come right away."

"Oh, Jesus. You know we haven't been getting along. We broke up. Are you sure he wants me there?"

438

"Charly, he loves you, you know that. Please, despite any problems you're having, get over here as fast as you can."

She hated hospitals—people got sick in them. Strangers in white outfits smelling of bleach poked and prodded you, while visitors you never cared for arrived to present inferior chocolates and silver balloons.

"He's going to be all right?"

"Come quickly. I don't know."

CHAPTER 9

═══ THE AMERICAN HOSPITAL ═══

By the time Charly arrived at the hospital, Jean-Michel was sitting in a wheelchair, a large bandage around his head, his nose swollen, and a thick, pink-stained padding over his left eye. His shirt was torn, and large splotches of blood had spattered down the front. Except for the swelling and purple stitches on his face, he looked almost happy.

"I got 'em, Charly," he grunted as she walked up. "They couldn't keep up, the lamebrains, couldn't even quote the Aryan pledge! I humiliated them. It was great," he said excitedly. "If only you and Maurice could have been there!" he exclaimed, then moaned and held the spot over his bandaged eye.

The nurse took charge. "Professor Levasseur, we have given you some medicine to keep you alert, but if you don't stay calm we'll sedate you into next week.

He ignored her. "They have wounded and humiliated France enough, those cretins."

"Jean-Michel, keep quiet," the colonel growled. "Besides killing yourself, you're going to make yourself a fool in front of these," he looked around disparagingly, "people."

"What people? You mean these little brown nurses and orderlies looking after me?" he snapped back.

"Relax," the colonel demanded.

"I feel stronger than I have ever been, don't tell me to relax!" And he carefully felt the metal shield being taped over his swollen nose by an intern.

"Sweetheart?" Charly said softly.

"Yes?"

"Great nose."

He smiled. "And it's sooo big," she exclaimed.

Charly sat on a small examination stool and tried to ascend from depths of what she had feared to be the very worst. She had had no intention of ever seeing him again, and now this. Despite moving out of *Chrysalis,* she felt at home with the two men beside her.

Jean-Michel looked toward her with his one good eye: "Charly, I'm sorry. Please forgive me. I've tried to tell you, but you just wouldn't listen. That woman was nothing to me except…" His head sagged.

She sighed. "Except a good sports fuck, no doubt more talented than mine." She went back over to the colonel, who stood next to a gurney exhibiting a blood-spattered white sheet. He was speaking to the doctor.

———————

Jean-Michel was in a hazy fog. He remembered that a moment of testing had come only hours ago, when all of his past posturing, foibles, and failures were made bearable by his courage to confront a real and imminent danger. If only, he had thought, maybe for just some minutes in front of a small group of people in a bar, it had made a difference, a situation in which every man and woman must choose to do what's right.

Charly watched him, pitying him in his wheelchair as his head kept sagging. She saw the moment for what it was: the brief adventure of an ordinary man who in his battle for self-esteem had risen to his very best and had been rewarded with his own red badge of courage, for what it was worth, for all to see.

"Jean-Michel, sweetheart, the doctor wants you to stay awake. The medicine is going to kick in pretty soon and you'll feel better. Are you okay?"

He looked up. "Charly, I feel great!" he croaked. "A little sore, but I saw light out of my left eye coming in and, oh," he squeezed his fists tightly. "Charly, it was so glorious to lash those pathetic mutants with all my might. If only…" His head hurt, and he began to sink into unconsciousness again, getting lost in his own playback.

She walked over and put her arm around him. "I know, sweetheart, but calling a bunch of skinheads pathetic mutants would be considered an insult." He smiled. "It's not funny, you know," she admonished. "It's on a par with making disparaging remarks about somebody's poor taste in curtains…" She couldn't finish. He tried to retort, but barely moved his lips, wavering in and out of consciousness, his chin sunk on his chest, his hands squeezing into fists over and over again.

She sighed, reached for his hand, and grasped it, whispering to no one in particular, "People are sensitive, honey. You know you have to be careful, never know what they might do. I'm sorry I was angry with you. British tart didn't know who she was dealing with when she tangled with a Texan over the Lion of Lyon."

He nodded, relieved that it was over. But this was his moment, a moment he would never forget and would tell later in great detail to all along the bar whose battles were never joined. He drifted away, imagining himself the center of a morality play in which he would share with his friends the struggle and excitement of winning over evil. He had voluntarily left their humble ranks, he would boast, and when called upon to wrestle with the enemy at the price of death, had strapped on armor, mounted his horse, and gloriously prevailed. He would look at the eager faces around him and paint the scene of battle, skinheads everywhere, but he had stepped forward onto the field and trod victoriously among the fallen. He had made his choice, for it is in the yearning of all men that their destinies lead to the honor rolls of village greens. There would be no medals, of course, and his friends, in their common wisdom, would simply sigh and shake their heads. He would smile. He should have just walked away, they'd say. But the truth is, he stood his ground in a pathetic little bar. It was his virtue that was his strength, that stood up against evil. A strength few have, to combat ignorance and violence, when others would have found their excuses to turn and run from certain danger. He couldn't expect his comrades to hoist him on their shoulders, fat men are not prone to illusions of grandeur, but —

"Jean-Michel," Charlie was gently shaking him. "Wake up. They've given you some strong drugs. The doctor says you gotta stay awake, honey."

He felt overwhelmingly sleepy, but tried to nod his head that he understood.

"Do you feel okay?" Charly was bending over him, clutching his shoulder. Again, she shook him softly. "Jean-Michel?"

442

He awoke again to see Charly standing over him. He sat looking up with his one good eye. "What month is it?"

"Month? It's August."

"Did you marry Pierre?"

She stared at him. "Doctor!" she yelled across the room. "He's *hallucinating!*"

Charles de Gaulle's Death[23]

Frenchmen, Frenchwomen; General de Gaulle is dead; France is a widow.

Georges Pompidou

Charles de Gaulle died on 9 November 1970. The long life that had begun in the middle of the night at his grandparents' home in Lille had ended nearly eighty years later, in his own home at Colombey-les Deux-Eglises. De Gaulle died at approximately 7:25 p.m. Death, when it came, was quick. In the early evening, just after supper, he was sitting quietly in his favorite chair in the library, having just closed the shutters against the cold of night, when he suffered a rupture of the lower aorta, which led to massive bleeding into the abdominal cavity and consequent intense pain in the spinal area. The loss of blood to the brain, together with what must have been acute pain, sent him into unconsciousness almost instantly, and by the time the doctor arrived, having left another patient's bedside to attend to the general, it was too late for anything to be done.

The funeral preparations, at his own wish, were as simple as his house. His coffin was transported from La Boisserie to the parish church of Our Lady of the Assumption in the middle of the village by an armored car. His family, some old friends, and the villagers attended the simple ceremony. The body was buried in a plain grave in Colombey churchyard. There was on the same day as the modest funeral in Colombey a solemn Requiem Mass in the Cathedral of Notre-Dame in Paris, celebrated by the Cardinal Archbishop of Paris in great splendor and style.

De Gaulle had said, "I declare that I refuse in advance any distinction, promotion, dignity, citation, or decoration, whether French or foreign. If any whatsoever were conferred upon me, it would be in violation of my last wishes." It is obvious the man was used to giving orders. Nevertheless, the Council of the City of Paris decided that the Place de l'Etoile, where the Arc de Triomphe stands today, should be renamed the Place Charles de Gaulle.

═ IX ═

Jean-Paul Sartre

"My first real love affair, a few years later, was with
a woman, an actress who used to kid me, but without
any harshness, about my ugliness.
'So how come you love me?' I asked her.
'You talk good,' she replied.
'What if I were uglier still?' I insisted.
'Then you'd have to talk all night,' she responded."

Jean-Paul Sartre

═══ JEAN-PAUL'S STORY ═══

On a summer's day at a park in Milan where great oaks spread canopies of leafy shade, a teenager in rebellious plumage appears on a macadam path, wiggling to his Walkman. He ambles along, moaning to his muse, baggy pants flopping rhythmically about worn sneakers. Passing strollers look back as he passes and shake their head in disgust — kids and their scatological rap, they snicker. His long black vest hangs open, revealing pasty white skin and nipples pierced by pins. Adorned as others his age and sect, he sports a topiary of sparse facial hair, tattooed vines encircling skinny biceps, and cheap rings adorning dirty fingers.

He notices a frail old man reading a book on a park bench. He stops, stares, and walks over to face him. The man looks up, contemptuous, but surely frightened of the lanky spike-haired kid, and shrinks back. The kid bends over, nose ring to old nose, his eyes crazed, face contorted, mouth in a satanic grin. Carefully, he removes the man's hat and lays it next to him on the bench. Like a rabbit before a viper the man is frozen. The youngster, his eyes wide and dancing, removes his earphones, carefully puts them on the elderly citizen, and stands back. The man recoils, body stiff, arthritic fingers trembling about his book in fear. The kid points to his ear, grinning. The man lifts his hands and clasps the headphones to his ears, expecting a stream of screaming, cursing, cacophonous rap, but he hears only the deep sonorous tones of a poet's voice. Bewildered, he listens. Now, incredulously, aware of the mellifluous cadence of soothing words from a Shakespearean sonnet, he looks up at the kid, amused. No words, just a glance between generations, like echoes from the moon. Then the kid lifts the earphones from the old man's head, places them back on his own, and with a wink continues on his way.

The kid's name was Fausto Fattorini. Not his real name, but he enjoyed the vowels rolling over his tongue. Through an odd turn of events, he died, or at least disappeared with no trace, not long after this incident, early in the third millennium. There was no mythology of the beautiful loser, or romantic self-destruction and existential cool, although, if one hung around him, he, like Rimbaud, did have an air of vulnerability that made people care about him even as he took advantage of them. He left a notebook, a diary of sorts, the only evidence of his short life that his family cherished.

The notebook begins with what his family assumed was his end. Inserted in small, cramped letters at the top of the first of many well-worn and greasy pages was printed the word "Emma," and farther down, where once the photo of a golden-haired little girl had been taped to the page, a smiley-face sticker stared back. Directly below her name he left a short sentence, a postscript: "Hey, Emma, today I died." Most likely he had postdated his brief inscription to the next day, an act not unheard of, and reminiscent of a young soldier's letter to his wife the night before he was to fight and die in battle. How Fausto knew that, during an otherwise peaceful day, in the grimy industrial section of Milan, he would never see the sunset is, or was, a mystery; or, for the more skeptical, a certain condition of statistical probability and possibly a lie.

A "runaway" was discounted by the Italian police, since everything Fausto needed and held dear was as he had left it, scattered about in his seedy hotel room, including diary, wallet, and French passport. On the other hand, it was said by some of the family that he could have been speaking metaphorically. Certainly, the period of his boyish existence was coming to an end, that his persona of rebellion was finished, and possibly he was attempting to be reborn. Or, perhaps more likely, hatred for his father had finally consumed his young life. For those who looked to the obvious, the last entry in "Emma," dated a few days after her birthday, said it all: "Blue Sky." He was put on Interpol's missing persons alert.

A careful observer would have seen other signs early on in the life of a boy on the skids. An alcoholic father and prissy mother, parents who preferred to talk about their children rather than to them, had created the classic dysfunctional family. Fausto was French-American and a citizen of Paris, but he had rejected both societies and chosen to become Italian. Or more precisely, he chose in his early teens to experience an Italian metamorphosis, since he wished to escape all that he was, and became a boy who leaned toward the Northern League, had a taste for gelato, and idolized Italy's most famous cyclist.

Fausto was easily conversant in English and French, with a smattering of Spanish for good measure, but his abilities in Italian, despite common Latin roots, were limited. His efforts to improve relied on a discarded book, practically new, entitled *Italian for Filipinos*. He was only marginally successful. He listened closely to Italian TV quiz shows and similar glitzy productions featuring sparsely attired, big-breasted women. This, besides its titillation, had the effect of making his pronunciation resemble that of a quiz-show host or an Italian disc jockey, with all their dramatic inflections. His aspirations as a holistic masseur, and his bizarre looks, combined with the nature of his speech, led acquaintances to believe he was retarded. Why Italy was anybody's guess, but not everyone who entered a cloister had the qualities to become a saint.

Some years ago, at a local lake near Paris, the day of May 8 changed his young life forever. It was on that fateful day, after a faculty picnic, as his father, mother, and younger sister drove back home, and he stayed at the lake with his best friend, Nizan, that tragedy overtook the young family.

Oblivious of forthcoming events, Fausto had spent his afternoon windsurfing, carefree and fanatical. He and Nizan challenged each other to the limits of the sport, never giving way to any object on the water except startled swimmers, while racing desperately to their destination. Late in the afternoon, Fausto had left the grassy shores of the lake, headed, with Nizan, for the opposite side. There was only time to wave a distracted goodbye to his parents, with tickles and a hug for his little sister Emma.

The circumstances for the tragedy were easily seen. Fausto's father, a self-absorbed professor bent on success in life through pedantry, pandering, and dabbling at golf like so many French professionals of his ilk, had been repeating his rapacious excesses at the picnic table. Therefore, when it came time to drive home, Jean-Michele was, in those durable traditions of gluttony, stuffed and drunk. Since his wife, Arlene, the former Georgia homecoming queen, sneakered and lacking in *petits soins*—including depilation—was similarly employed, hints of caution were brushed aside. Those more circumspect picnickers who understood the dangers urged the couple to wait a while and have some coffee before leaving.

Arlene, tired and cranky, but attempting the modicum of decorum so essential in French society—to the extent that peroxide hair, bulging plaid Bermudas, and dimpled knees allowed—refused the kindly advice. Embarrassed and chagrined by her bumbling husband as he conducted a putting demonstration, bent over precariously in his favorite stance, exhibiting bulbous cheeks and teetering above the imaginary golf ball for all to see, she was determined to leave. Attempting to sweeten their departure, lest any of the staff take offense, she offered an apology: "We gotta get home to feed the ducks."

So, not far outside of Paris, on a busy highway heading west toward the setting sun, Professor Jean-Michel Levasseur, his wife, Arlene, and sweet little Emma, snug in their old platinum-colored Peugeot, returning home from a faculty outing of a local friendship society (as the newspaper poignantly described the event), hit a bridge abutment at 60 miles per hour, killing wife and daughter instantly in an explosive mix of screeching tires, gasoline, and kinetic energy. Miraculously, the perpetrator of events was thrown into a ditch filled with water, mud, and trash, which cushioned the impact of his landing. Not long after, the driver was helicoptered away from his close brush with oblivion to a nearby hospital's trauma unit. He was released with bruises and abrasions some sixteen hours later, his stiff, blubbery body intact. Soon, as with the tragedy of Lady Di and her lover, plastic flowers were left roughly tied to a utility pole to mark the spot.

God works in not-too-strange ways, the neighbors whispered among themselves, witnessing the family in their bereavement. Most in the neighborhood knew that nothing good would come of the couple, for those two had pierced many a night with their drunken brawling and name-calling, which echoed from their apartment. But the absence of poor little Emma, with golden hair, angelic looks, and sunny disposition, saddened all, leaving those along her quiet street to shake their heads in painful resignation.

Fausto's real name was Jean-Paul, son of Jean-Michel and Arlene Levasseur, and older brother of Emma. The accident caused the death of two and the birth of one, since Jean-Paul was reborn as a clinically psychotic teen. He could not accept the death of his sister, and vehemently rejected the existence of his father. More precisely, he chose, in the fashion of Shakespeare, to become an actor—comfortable with living and telling lies, and understanding better than most that all the world's a stage.

Not long after the tragedy and the burial of mother and daughter, father and son moved from the old family apartment into a small two-bedroom flat in a northeast section of Paris called Tremblay-en-France. These suburbs and their projects were home to a large segment of Paris' Arab population, including a large number of Algerians whose poverty defined the quality of their lives. Fausto felt at home with his new teen friends, dropouts and rebels, and quickly learned their street language, a hectic, Arabic-accented *"verlan,"* or salty French slang that sounded like gang rap. He joined a gang and took a certain pride that everyone in Paris talked about the violence in the projects, and by association, him. Nonetheless, it was humiliating in its own way, so the gangs learned to gesture and posture, to boast and bitch, in a neighborhood where the rich played at being poor and the poor at being rich.

Jean-Paul spent two years in the projects, formative years, as they say, a time when his quirky grins turned into an adolescent's insolent laugh, and the awakening of his sexuality expressed itself by searching online personals, pornography sites, and late-night viewings of Aqua Teen Hungerforce. He did his utmost to avoid his father, who was grappling with a succession of obstinate sieges of alcoholism. Fausto watched from the mute corners of the flat while Jean-Michel would get drunk, scribble nonsensical prose as he sprawled across the dinning room table, then, rising unsteadily, stagger about the apartment in the dead of night, shouting quotes from Flaubert, Proust, and Baudelaire. He would stand before the television set, bragging to the talk-show host of his trysts with a young Egyptian woman in the neighborhood who reminded him, he said—in Flaubert's words—of Kuchuc and her cunt like rolled velvet,[1] which made him feel like a tiger.

The two lingering remnants of the family existed together like pieces of the same tattered cloth, precariously held whole in the swirl of events by little more than the seams of necessity.

CHAPTER 2

═══ FAUSTO MEETS THE AMISH ═══

Relief eventually came to both tormented souls in the person of a caring colonel. A few years after the death of his mother and little sister, Fausto left France for the United States in late August to participate in an international exchange program conducted by a local business club for high schoolers at Lancaster, Pennsylvania. He had recently turned eighteen, but the family's sense of security came from his aging grandmother, who was living in New Jersey. Despite Fausto's acknowledged tendencies to the wild side, his father thought the experience of a year abroad would be good for him. A briefer version, for those who knew the situation, was that their greatest wish was distance from each other. For Professor Levasseur it was an opportunity to have a sullen, disruptive, out-of-control teenager out of the apartment; for Fausto it was an opportunity to divest himself of everything his father stood for, from his narcissistic diction, rich food, and paternalistic French know-it-all attitude, to his drunken flatulence. For both antagonists what distinguished grinding hatred from simple anger was its sustained nature. Fausto's psychiatrist had struggled to break the link, but with little success; as many know, however, distance makes the heart grow fonder.

In truth, Fausto had already been on the run from the people who conceived him. It seems overly generous to call them "parents," since it was a role they neither desired nor understood. "More wine anyone?" was his father's way of changing the topic, while his mother went for refreshments. But his sister, Emma, despite her youth, was his soul mate: innocent, precocious, beautiful, and dedicated to her brother in a mutually loving bond far exceeding that with their parents. A fickle fate, the embodiment of existential perversity, had taken Fausto's joyful, golden-haired playmate forever,

452

and substituted a fat, distracted, adult male of no apparent talents except drinking, eating, and reading. Fausto knew there would never be "peace of mind." Time would not heal these wounds. Revenge on the only surviving member of his immediate family danced before his eyes in such seductively gory attacks as to leave him, during periods of heavy stress, psychologically crippled and a victim of epileptic seizures. His days of carefree youth, windsurfing, and even driving, were over.

———

Predictably, Fausto no sooner set foot into his new American high school than he fell head-over-heels in love, as teenagers often do, with Verna Eldermann, a young woman from an Old Order Amish community. Fausto had an impetuousness that attracted some and frightened others, but Verna was smitten, as they say. A veteran of name swapping in his own right—his new American moniker among his peers being "Cheese," since he always smiled, appropriately or not—he went about convincing Verna to change hers, at least informally, to Esquive or L'Esquive, since among her limited talents one stood out: the ability to avoid responsibility. Fausto had convinced her that the mellifluous name meant "exquisite."

It was a fortuitous time for Fausto, since he had met Esquive during her *rumspringa*—"running around period" in Pennsylvania Dutch. The Anabaptist faith practiced by the Amish includes the belief that only adults who have made a conscious choice to join the church should be baptized. In her strict sect, the result was rumspringa. When children in Amish families turn sixteen, they are free to experience the world. For some this could mean listening to rock music or driving cars; for others, like Esquive, it meant getting drunk or high and meeting boys. Fausto's insolent attitude, delivered with sneering smiles to superiors and peers alike, in any venue from classroom to gym, fell enticingly far afield of Amish humility. Wolfishly, he seized on Esquive's innocent admiration, an awestruck lamb. After a brief courtship of posturing and various teenage rituals, they ran off together to his den. She consumed him just as passionately as his lust for her snow-white body and ample breasts crowned with raspberry-shaped nipples allowed. Once wrapped like pythons in urgent, naked squirming, their copulation succeeded in frequent sweaty climaxes and, inadvertently, conception. This once and future son, in the years to come, was to be called Emanuel.

Given that the concept of "existence" had intersected his life at such harsh and unremitting angles, Fausto, while browsing books that his father kept readily at hand, had become attracted to existentialism by its very name. The idea that people actually studied the circumstances of one's existence gave birth to fantasies, stirring his imaginings of a reunion with Emma on some distant plane denied lesser souls. In his search for information, he found an immediate kinship with the absurdities of Camus' death in a car accident in Provence, and even Baudelaire's hatred of humankind. He read, with difficulty, their intellectual paths.

But Jean-Paul-Charles-Aymard Sartre, to cite his full name, was another matter.[2] He may well be best known as a philosopher, but his contributions as a playwright were substantial, and for Fausto the preferred medium of the messenger. Sartre had few rivals for the title of most important French dramatist of the second half of the 20th century.[3] His talents were recognized in every French classroom, and Fausto was an eager student. On the other hand, Sartre was hardly a pragmatic approach to teenage mental health for a kid who, like many kids, hid in a prolonged adolescence of sports leagues, sexual fantasies, and video games.

Nonetheless, there was a kinship. What was true of Sartre, was, Fausto believed, also true for him, and created what he saw as some significant similarities and common bonds. For example, both he and Sartre had lost parents at an early age; each had delusions of grandeur and struggled in school. Additionally, it had been revealed in Fausto's philosophy class that, on Sartre's report card his teacher had written, "Never gives the right answer on his first try. Must learn to think more," a trait that, considering Fausto's fondness for drama-club roles, bonded him even closer to his hero, who it is known began to think more.

Life, Fausto believed, was indisputably "absurd" and painfully so, which in his case had left him bereft of females in his house and enduring an alcoholic father. Existentialism, despite its esoteric labyrinthine ways, could, he judged, offer the means by which he might gather up the pieces of his life and draw Emma into his own existence, to assuage a longing for her that, when aroused, sometimes occasioned prurient desires. He tried to speak with Emma, but it was difficult to know whether it was her conscience or his own that was answering. He struggled with many books, cast most aside, but periodically discovered Sartre's reassuring revelations, which he would pen in his diary. One of his favorites, "Freedom is not what you do gratuitously. It is what you do with what has been done to you," seemed written just for him. And freedom, as old patriots said, wasn't free.

Esquive worked assiduously at dealing with Fausto's own brand of existentialism, but, finding both him and it difficult to comprehend, began drifting to other boys. One new beau from Salisbury, Maryland, who, in those seminal moments while unzipping his fly, revealed himself to be a nut-case, prattling about "the Revealed Earth Order," moved her to begin the long journey back home. When she asked, for example, the nature of this new order, he described a society run by modern-day radicals who, with evil and ingenious methods, aimed, he assured her, "to turn us into slaves." The new social order would, he said, use satellites to melt all the electronic chips on recent-model cars, and enslave white people, and—even worse —subject us all to the Law of the Sea.

CHAPTER 3

═══ BEANNIE DOYLE ═══

For Fausto, life in an American high school was unhappy until a friend called Beannie came along. Fausto had become a searching, often bitter, if not suicidal, aspiring existentialist contemptuous of his own cultures, seeking only the brotherhood of nihilists like Sartre, and avoiding his American contemporaries.

Beannie Doyle was Fausto's best friend in America. Old enough to be Fausto's father and then some, Beannie owned a small gas station, appropriately named "Doyle's Diner," near the interstate, outside Lancaster, Pennsylvania. The diner section had long since closed, replaced by a food service of sorts featuring refrigerated cases stocked with numerous cans of beer and soft drinks, multiple shelves of cookies, candy, and chips, plus one of those stainless steel roller contraptions that mercilessly grilled hot dogs for the 'Big Bun,' and a special table for microwavable burritos with fresh condiments.

The gas station had been recently renovated in a bright yellow plastic motif that glowed into the evening and through the night like a seductive lamp for wayward teenagers. Doyle dealt in various automotive supplies, sex magazines, and, as neighborhood kids knew, privately grown marijuana rivaling the mellow and psychedelic properties of Thai stick, surreptitiously for sale behind the counter. For the boys it was sold for hard cash; for particularly voluptuous young girls, however, it was their panties. After a little banter to plumb the limits of their delinquent natures and a brief family background check—daughters, and for that matter sons, of police or town officials were summarily excluded—Beannie would ask the girl to go to the ladies room and take off her panties, put them in one of his plastic Have-a-Nice-Day sacks, and bring it back in exchange for a small bag of grass packaged in kind. A digital photo of Beannie with the sexy ingénue was always an appreciated gesture on her part, and usually resulted in extra grass: "Sort of a baker's dozen," he joked. He had little to worry about from the police, since a close relative was strategically employed by the force. In any event, no one told, and few pubescent girls, of a more advanced calling, were going to quibble over inexpensive and used underwear for a bag of prime weed. They learned early on to wear only their most profane panties for the appointed day. Fausto, in Esquive's absence, enjoyed the overt degradation of it all, and volunteered to take the photos, encouraging the girls' participation in his carefully nurtured Pennsylvania Dutch dialect accented in French, which never ceased to charm.

Several months after arriving in America, Fausto had been caught lying naked on his bedroom balcony at his sponsor's house, after late-night toking on some two-hit shit, staring, trance-like, beyond the stars. His sponsoring mother, though not particularly shocked by her discovery, since she had suspected as much within days of his arrival, had told Fausto in no uncertain terms—that is, without cursing, being a god-fearing family—to leave for the sake of her son and fourteen-year-old daughter. Nonetheless, it was decided by the international program's administrator to allow Fausto to complete his education, and with the reluctant acquiescence of the high school's psychologist, Fausto's program was allowed to continue. His father, having moved from the family apartment to a houseboat, eagerly contributed money from a generous friend for a small flat and a stipend to meet Fausto's daily needs, thus avoiding his return. Fausto, absolved of the subterfuge and posturing around his adopted family, was given a new, adult-free existence—his first—and a very small place of his own, the envy of any eighteen-year-old in America.

Early in his acquaintance with Beannie, Fausto made one of those mistakes that had a silver lining: During one of his trips to Doyle's, before he had officially met Beannie, Fausto had run short of money and resorted to shoplifting a few necessities in order to recoup some budgetary overruns, but he was caught red-handed by Beannie and sternly lectured. Beannie saw at once that the insolence and bravado was an emotional carapace across the foreign kid's brow, keeping all databanks secure against attacks on his self-esteem. Since on that fateful evening it was closing time, Beannie decided to take Fausto to his mobile home, where he sat Fausto down in an old stuffed chair under the awning outside, overlooking fallow cornfields, and decided they should come to terms. They talked and talked into the wee hours, a surprising and pleasing event unknown in Fausto's previous experience. He had suffered through some of those inescapable moments when a male teacher befriended him for questionable purposes, or when his father, routinely swilling port, lectured him in reverential tones, of not-so-veiled admonishment, on the profiles of France's finest young graduates at École des Hautes Études en Sciences Sociales.

Fausto envied Beannie's powerfully positive outlook on life, which Beannie considered, as he said, the ultimate consumer item. Beannie was big and had the animal-quick knack of charm and energy produced by a brawny power source whose glow, it was said, turned people into moths. Fausto saw in Beannie everything a son could love in a father: broad shoulders, hairy arms, strong chin, large nose, and bald head with pale rusty curls piling out over his ears. Beannie was instantaneous, as if he'd gained a microsecond in everything he did, down to rolling a joint with his big, deft fingers. Real fathers could smoke dope with their sons.

A '60s hippie, Beannie was a chronicler of the great events of those good old days. He never tired of talking about Neal Cassady, a man Jack Kerouac turned into a legend as Dean Moriarty in *On the Road*. Cassady later showed up at a place owned by a wild man named Ken Kesey, to drive his bus, named "Further," nonstop across the country, speed-rapping all the way.[4] Cassady, to Kesey, was the noble savage, freedom incarnate, and Kesey to Doyle the same. Enthralled by the stories, Fausto dreamed of being on the road himself, doing his best to assume the characteristics and language of a '60s hippie, "peace, man" and "fuckin' far out" among his favorites. The basic ground rules were to expunge all that was in his father's image, particularly his manner of sophistry and pedagogical French habits.

Sometimes, while Beannie and Fausto sat in those dilapidated stuffed chairs under the decaying striped awning of the Frontier Finder mobile home, exploring life or talking about the topic of the day, routine thoughts would hit Beannie as if they were revelations. "Hey!" he'd say, as if he'd just discovered relativity, "let's feed the cows!" Fausto would jump from his chair, whoop, and holler, "Fuckin' far aus!" in his new dialect. Beannie would pull on his pointy-topped, ear-flapped Swedish knit cap, grab Fausto by the arm, and both would rush out to hump hay bales from his old ford pickup to his sixteen cows in the pasture behind the trailer. At other, more reflective times, they would take a twenty-second journey out to some celestial outpost and back, with sniffs of nitrous oxide from the industrial-sized tank Beannie kept hidden under 'Bertha,' the name he'd given his ramshackle home.[5]

Fausto found in Beannie the only true medium through which he could talk about Emma without slipping over the edge. When he felt the edge come near he would prompt Beannie into reminiscing about his younger days, driving cross-country or poking fun at one of life's great commitments: "All I know is," Beannie would say in that deep baritone, "for my next wedding I'll be wearing a hairy, flesh-toned ensemble, because I'll be buck naked, with a toe tag, lying on slab."

"Because…?" Fausto would lead him.

"Because I would have killed myself!" he'd roar and take a swig of his beer.

Over the kitchen sink, Beannie kept a photograph of himself in drag all dressed up for Halloween. "It's the first time," he'd say, "I've been inside something feminine that didn't nag me to take out the garbage."

Beannie loved to talk about the old days.

"Oh, Kesey?" Beannie would chuckle, like he'd never told the story before. "Well, Kesey, you know, Fausto, was one of the last of the barbaric-yawp men in the tradition of Ginsberg and Whitman, sounding their voices over American rooftops, trumpeting their rue, saluting every leaf of grass.[6] He was one of our last frontiersmen."

"Frontiersmen?"

"Yeah. You know—Ginsberg heading into the wilderness of himself. Sort of like you'd go lookin' for Emma."

"Yeah. Is he dead?"

"Who, Ginsberg? Yep."

"Miss 'em?"

"Sure. I'm gettin' old, kid. Ain't many real ones left. When they died of cancer, drugs, and who knows what else, the energy of America dropped by a volt or two, I can tell you that.[7] Kesey was a great guy, but he ain't ever comin' back."

Fausto looked at him questioningly.

"Look, kid, you know what I've been sayin'. Stick with the real ones; you got to drop this stuff with Sartre. He was an ugly little wall-eyed scribbler hooked on communism."

Fausto gave him a hurt look. "Sartre created existentialism," he said defensively.

"I know you like him and all, but you're idolizin' a weird guy who talked a good game, procured students for sex, and experimented with mescaline."

"We do drugs," Fausto retorted defiantly.

"Sure, kid, but we're not scared as hell that we're bein' chased by lobsters.[8] You've got infinite possibilities, you're smart as a whip, and disrespectful as a lifer, and you got Kesey written all over you; but people like Sartre ain't goin' to help you find your sister. She's gone, kid." He shook his head sadly. "You gotta bury Emma."

Shortly after that night, Fausto was reported missing from high school.

CHAPTER 4

══ A STEAMY NIGHT IN PARIS ══

Back in Paris, several weeks after Fausto was reported missing, Jean-Michel and his woman friend, Charlene Brooks, were looking for a bar to escape the heat.

It was unusually hot that week, forcing the locals whose homes and offices lacked air conditioning to seek shelter in expensive bars or cinemas, or the adventurous to go wading in fountains. Jean-Michel knew a number of breezy, if not cool, bars. They decided to take refuge on the verandah of an Indian café near Sacré Coeur overlooking the city. They sat down and glanced at the menu, then looked around. There was a small breeze, the food smelled spicy but tempting, and the crowd was sedate.

"I always wanted to go to Minnesota," he mused, using his handkerchief to wipe his forehead.

"Minnesota!" Charly was startled. "Why, for heaven's sake?"

"Bound to be cooler than here, and beautiful, or at least that's what I heard. You know," he said longingly, "beautiful lakes. I read that it is supposed to be one of the most livable states."

"Most livable? For what species?" she said.

"Hm?"

"I said, 'For what species?' I spent time there," she said, "and it's the kind of place you begin your day with an ice scraper on the mirror."

"Car?"

"Bathroom."

"Oh," he snorted. "I heard it was cold. An American Siberia, but—"

The waiter arrived and they ordered.

"My cousin's best friend lived there," she mused. "Missed a turn on a ski trail near Vail and hit a tree. He died and was buried with his skies.

461

Buried!" she said incredulously. "All that great stuff: parka, mittens, the whole works."

"Goggles too?" He had a vision of the corpse with goggles. "Sounds like a nice place for Fausto to cool off."

"Have they found out anything more?" she said solicitously.

"Well, they tracked him to an old hotel we used to stay at in Milan; after that to Corfu, I think, and then the trail went cold. Probably left for Africa—hanging out with his loser friends in Marrakech."

She was offended by parents who abused the image of their children, suspecting the abuse ran deeper than just their image. "I don't understand your animosity toward your own son," she said. "I thought you went to see him in Greece—"

"Please," he interrupted. "It's not an endearing topic. I would just as soon we talked about something else."

"So. We can," she said coolly. He had obviously lied about his intentions earlier in the summer, probably to engender pity. Nonetheless, she was disappointed, since talking about family relationships was far more interesting than getting tied up in one of his diatribes about the world's troubles or France's faltering soccer team. She tried another favorite subject. "But at some point you and I are going to have to get real about this bizarre relationship—"

He held up his hand to quiet her. "Sshh, not here."

She leaned in toward him. "Bizarre, *Professor*! This very weird relationship of ours."

"Weird?" He gave her the look, which provided a good opportunity to make her point. She could never quite determine why he gave her that perplexed stare, as though she had just suggested a blowjob in public. Or, perhaps it was just a common fault among stunned academics unaccustomed to challenges.

"Listen," she said sternly. "Besides your dalliance with that female British ogre, the age thing, and some very questionable foibles concerning your sex games—"

He raised a hand for her to desist. "I know," he said earnestly. "But those were professional sex videos," he said under his breath.

"Professional?"

462

"'Advanced Techniques for Intermediate Learners,' it said so right on the box."

"And you want me to buy into this once tragic life of yours that happens to include these recent revelations about your son—which you know, J.M., you've kept fairly well hidden—and other questionable career misfortunes?"

He was ill at ease in these personal show-and-tells, such that he had to finagle the conversation around to something else to avoid feeling harassed and becoming angry. They were a couple now, skipping quickly over the earlier sexual follies, and had moved on to friendship in which enduring each other's faults presented daily challenges. He'd been married before, and needed no lessons in relationships; bridegrooms were to spend the rest of their lives grooming their brides. Over half failed. He had tested the exalted claims made on behalf of "friendship," principal among them the claim that "our friends" afforded us a chance to express our deepest selves, that the conversations we had with them were privileged get-togethers in which to say what we really thought, and, by extension and with no mythical allusion, be who we really were—an image often betrayed.[9] He believed such claims to be poppycock.

Jean-Michel's situation had evolved over the years and was not significantly different from that of Roquentin, a dejected researcher in Sartre's novel, *Nausea*. Roquentin, who lived in an area similar to Jean-Michel's, becomes starkly conscious of the fact that inanimate objects and situations remained absolutely indifferent to his existence. When he imagined himself dead, gone from where he might be sitting at the moment, his surroundings showed themselves resistant to whatever significance his consciousness might perceive in them. Home, favorite furniture, loyal dog, disgruntled wife, and other objects would be, within days of his passing, scabbed over like a rapidly healing wound, an existence of disappearing ripples. This indifference of "things in themselves" had the effect of highlighting his insignificance. Hence the nausea referred to in the title of Sartre's book. All that Jean-Michel encountered in his everyday life these days was suffused with a pervasive, disagreeable taste of himself, which he compulsively offered each day for others to sample, then, ashamed of its paucity, retreated to his own revolving regrets.

Jean-Michel hid in his books and manuscripts, finding far more comfort among their pages than among meddlesome acquaintances or being cross-examined for his failures by a female intimate. Conversations, particularly with women, allowed little room to revise his comments, which ill suited his tendency not to know what he was trying to say until he had had at least one go at saying it. Writing, on the other hand, accommodated, as it was largely made up of rewriting, during which original thoughts, often bare and inarticulate strands, were, like his lectures, enriched, nuanced, and woven into his vision of life over time.

A woman could spend hours discussing these damn things. Men had neither the patience to answer—correctly by female standards—nor the agility to thwart them. "I assume you've heard the phrase many parents find useful concerning their teenagers, he offered: "We love them, we just don't like them."

"Yeah. I just don't like it."

"Wait till you meet Fausto, which, the colonel or Pierre probably told you, is not his real name; but the grander question is whether he's uniquely disturbed or is simply an example of the whole damn generation." There would be little use—except to perpetuate the Q and A period—in telling her about a note, rambling though it was, found in Fausto's hotel room, stating his son's intention to kill his father.

"I want to meet him. He's just a kid, and kids are a little weird, it's part of their nature. Jodie used to call herself 'Saturn' and claim extrasensory powers. If this is a new 'lost generation,' maybe it's not all that bad: Fausto probably taught you all you know about computers, ever think of that?" she said.

"They're all lost. Jodie obviously didn't realize that 'Saturn' ate his young, and with that rap shit banging in their earphones all day it's easy to see why," he replied. "But it's more *Lord of the Flies* than anything cooked up by Baudelaire or Hemingway. The movies, music, dress, and behavior seem to be leaning just as much toward a culture of cretins as anything else, a generation seeking fulfillment in bare midriffs, shaved heads, and GameBoys."

"Come on, it is not all that bad, Jean-Michel. Every generation has their thing; my friends and I did the same."

Listen to that! he thought. *This little homily coming from one who still perceives herself as an accepted—albeit maturing—member of the youth culture.*

464

And patronizingly confident of their habits despite her not-so-recent transition to an alumnae of youthful used-to-be's, with their sprouting wrinkles, sagging breasts, and belly pouches. It irritated him, the very smugness of it. He hesitated, caught in choices, barely able to resist the urge to point it out.

"Well?" she said impatiently.

He gazed at her. *Who in the hell does she think she is?*

"Well?" she repeated irritably.

"Well, what?" He took a sip of his beer. The whole thing tired him. He wanted out.

These moods of his scared Charly. Was this what it would be like with someone you're supposed to love and share life's sparkling moments with? A grump? Someone fifteen years older, who saw his wife and daughter burned to a crisp and can't stand his son? Who can't get through the day without a series of stiff drinks? Forget the tender moments and romance, the man will never get past his past. Men proclaimed the distinction between relationship and sex. So be it. Besides, it was likely there would be few 'firsts' left for her to share, just a host of 'used-to-do's' and embellished stories she was rapidly tiring of, delivered at his habitual bars to friends who had heard most of them before and couldn't wait to tell their own musty yuks.

So what about her future? The security of marriage? He was determined to avoid it. Her thoughts wandered to a newspaper article in which a young French woman had married a dead man. The woman had carried a bouquet of yellow roses and gleefully ducked rice after the ceremony in Nice. About forty people later attended her reception at a local restaurant where the champagne bottles bore custom labels with the newlyweds' names. The only thing missing was the groom. In France it was possible, so the article claimed, to marry the dearly departed thanks to a law that turned the vow "until death do us part" on its head.[10]

Still lost in thought, she was staring off into the distance when he spoke. "Are you still with us? No interest in the plight of our adolescents?"

"Lighten up," she said sarcastically. "They'll rejoin the herd when they have to get a job."

"I *know* that," he said irritably. "The vulgar are always with us, but it doesn't go away just because they get a job, it just goes subliminal. Look," he gestured, pudgy fingers wrapped about his cold pipe, "today's casual coarseness

465

suggests that it is part of a larger phenomenon, and this damnable incivility of theirs is the worst part."

"Incivility is normal, J.M., at least with New Yorkers and every other waiter in Paris. It always has been," she said defensively.

"No!" he whined, tapping the gnawed mouthpiece of his pipe on the table. "Damn it, the whole confounded world lacks a conscience." He disliked being negative, since she reminded him of it so often, but that's the way it was. The world seemed destined to implode, and she was trying to paint it like just another generation of Beatles and the Bomb on the mend. And here she was, just biding her time for another marriage discussion, one of those golden opportunities for a life of sparring with her every night as they sat down to dinner, on some issue of note, which she eventually turned banal. It was the ideal formula for predictable sex, a short vignette on her nipple-less tit and his creeping ulcer. "Never mind," he said. "Anyway, we're being hit with an epidemic of rudeness. People here act as badly as the *arrivistes* in Balzac tales. Worse, actually. At least Balzac's characters were oblivious of manners, not hostile to them. Today's generation are both." He stuck his pipe back in his pocket.

"Maybe." She reached to finish off his French fries, pressing the last onto the plate like a squeegee to scrape up the salt and grease. "What are you saying? That it's because of—"

He shrugged his shoulders. "That's not good for you," he said, pointing at the fries.

"Yeah, I'm doing it for you. They're just creatures of the e-culture," she said.

He didn't respond, simply kept twisting his glass on its coaster, staring into it, cloaked in thought. She habitually irritated him, helping herself to his plate, mumbling some deferential "Do you mind?" and taking whatever portions they then shared, or rather, she preferred, without a moment's thought. She was relying, he felt, on the special privileges of women who take the offerings of men of manners—like held doors, the last piece of chocolate, and lifeboats on the *Titanic*—as their birthright, while they made no social or redeeming gestures in return; similar to his deceased wife, who never learned to cook, clean, or shop, but expected solicitous behavior nonetheless. It was one of his favorite peeves, but had he mentioned it, Charly would have responded that it was just recompense for enduring screaming kids, centuries of abuse and discrimination, or some lack of chivalry lost to history. Since the tradition had little chance of being changed, least of all by him, it was easier to swallow than daring a challenge, and he unconsciously resorted to humming a few bars of Nancy Sinatra's "These Boots Are Made for Walkin'."

"Have you given any more thought to getting married?" she asked.

To him it was like suggesting a new game of relationship rugby. He frowned. "You know, too constraining, and I don't want kids," he said ruefully. "Bad investments." Women could make it snow, like a shaman of the north, each guilty flake piling silently and heavily on his shoulders till the center came crashing down around them and they stood incredulous. Surprise, surprise! She remained quiet watching the snow accumulate. Then he brightened, as if struck by the joys of honeymooning in Niagara Falls. "You know, we have something in France called *pacte civil de solidarité*. Very popular now, gives many of the same legal rights as married people, but not," he said reassuringly, "you know, like being committed together forever."

"Sort of like 'rent-a-wife?'" she said coldly. "You just want a maid who's happy giving a blowjob after doing the bathroom."

"Not true!" he protested. "I was thinking more of a cohabiting relationship; they're recognized all over the world. Even the Na," he said, a keen reader of *National Geographic*.

"Na?"

"Chinese. The Na completely shun marriage. We will probably all be like the Na in the future," he said confidently.

"Probably," she sighed. "But the decline of marriage doesn't have to spell catastrophe. You used to say you liked kids."

"I love kids," or as far as he was concerned, the idea of kids. "It's just this fading difference between children and adults. These arrested-development fifteen-year-olds." He felt more comfortable lecturing. "Their rapacity turns appetites into belligerence when someone gets in their way. The technological sensations today are just distractions to facilitate their self-absorption—you know, with their damn cell phones, electronic games, and pocket computers."

"Sorry," she said, "but I think a lot of people, even kids, are more considerate than ever before." She saw he was back on a roll, but enjoyed tripping up his half-baked theories. As far as Charly was concerned, lovers and friends were still supposed to satisfy each other's needs, yet agreeing to any of his silly theories and imagined injuries was tedious. The marriage idea was probably a bad one. Living together caused people to come up with a hundred ways to put each other down, a continual battle of superegos and ids, waged until one or the other surrendered or the relationship expired, which was the norm. She looked at him. Always waxing eloquent. *Once a professor, always a professor,* she thought. And to her complete exasperation, the waiter had brought him another beer. "Because they immoderately value efficiency and crave immediacy," he was saying, "they are impervious to the idea that manners should moderate social life. In my opinion manners are important."

"Of course they are. So what?"

"How are they supposed to know how to behave? Molière's *Misanthrope* is probably as strange to these snotty know-it-alls as Mongolia.

"Um-hm. Let me give you a hint, Maestro: Molière is a little strange to *everyone.*" It was getting late, and she looked distractedly at the customers clustered about their tables in the dim light under the trees. The smell of Indian food was nauseating her. The self-improvement she longed for in Paris was simply turning into a form of acquisitiveness: get a new language, new life, new body, new recipe, and new man. Perhaps it was time to go home, to the old gym, the old job, and the old fiancée.

Jean-Michel didn't notice, or perhaps care, now that he was relieved of struggling with his regrets. "Take the new movies, for example, long and ridiculous." He talked without engaging her. She was caught between trying to signal her boredom while maintaining eye contact without instigating an argument, listening vaguely to communicate some imprecise middle ground that safely guarded the moment while she ignored him. He took another sip of his beer, a process that always annoyed her, since, like most alcoholics, he drank copious amounts of beer, but always seemed to sip them until you weren't looking. She was looking in another direction. "Am I boring you?" he said finally, to validate her presence in some small way.

"Apparently." She stared at him coldly. "J.M., it's late, and you've said nothing about Fausto except lecture on the deficiencies of the world's youth," she said impatiently.

His lips curled into a cruel smile; "Oh. Who, Fausto?" he sneered, "Fausto, my son?" And leaned across the table toward her. "Jean-Paul, my son, that tattooed, foul-mouthed, ingrate; that boy who's fathered a bastard son—my grandson—coming due shortly to an illiterate girl in an Amish family somewhere in Pennsylvania? That fine young addict who is creating séances with his sister and faked his death so we could lament his passing? That son?" He sneered, then said flatly, "Was there something in particular you wanted to know?"

"Don't you miss him?" she said softly.

"No. Anything else?" he said harshly.

She was fed up with his sweat, beer, and potbelly. "Yeah," and she got to her feet. "If I was your wife I'd put rat poison in your ratatouille."

"And if I were your husband I'd eat it!" he snarled.

She looked at him painfully, grabbed her purse, and left. He didn't even bother looking after her.

CHAPTER 5

=== THE CORFU CLINIC ===

The clinic at Corfu was poorly equipped, like so many institutions of Greek social services, but its location on the magnificent coast of the glistening Adriatic more than made up for its quality of care and creature comforts. Unfortunately, the attitude of the Greek population toward the Americans and British worked contrary to Fausto's need for work and companionship. Hopes of sun and fun on a Greek island were not to be realized. He had been apprehensive since arriving, the proverbial stranger in a strange land. The local boys' chiding and condescension for American culture and its foreign policies mostly fell on deaf ears, since, being French educated, Fausto had neither the interest nor the combativeness to defend either American or French political machinations, as one could not succeed with the one without validating the other.

The romance and adventure of Greece was quickly dissipated by the harsh circumstances of making a living in a country where he didn't hold a visa, know the ropes, or speak the language. Things went badly. When Fausto was found, comatose from a drug overdose in an alley behind the restaurant where he had worked washing dishes, he was taken to a hospital in Dassia. He carried an American passport. Greek police contacted Interpol and determined that he had dual citizenship, French and American, and he was taken off the missing persons list in Italy. His family was notified; the good news was received with great relief and not a little ambivalence and discussion about his future. His aunt flew to Corfu from Lyon to provide for his care. Jean-Michel, heavily committed to his institute projects, including training assignments for his client from Voyages Classiques, could not, in view of his professional obligations, spare the time or, more accurately, interest. Fausto was to be left in the care of his doctor at the clinic in Corfu.

470

Fausto's doctor, Theodore Hephaistos, was an ex-priest from the Ortho-
dox Church in Thessalonica who had resigned his calling because of grave
doubts of faith. After medical school he spent two years training as a resident
physician in psychiatry at a medical facility in Marseilles. He had recently returned to Greece, and was assigned to the clinic. Short, with a slight
build, he had tight black hair, soft brown eyes, and an easy manner usually
delivered with a smile. One of his first privately funded patients was Jean-
Paul Levasseur. Theodore deferred to Jean-Paul's alias, Fausto, and since
the two were the only residents at the institute who spoke fluent French,
their relationship began favorably.

Theodore's office was clean and sparse, a small stand of books next to his
desk, the usual photograph of wife and children, and a picture-perfect view
of the Aegean from his window. It was unusual in only one respect—skulls.
One wall was made of shelves that displayed a hundred skulls of all shapes
and sizes. He was an expert in phrenology, a hobby. As the sun rose and
set on the windows in his office, the indentations, foramens, and jaws of
his collection responded accordingly: grim, sinister, complacent, or happy.
He mused on their former residents: perhaps cruel sailors, beautiful wom-
en, and innocent children. At one point he had thought to have his own
skull crafted by a forensic sculptor and have it placed among the others.
His wife objected.

The first few sessions with Fausto had gone as expected: evasiveness, pro-
fanity, some bravado, cynical rejoinders, and obfuscation. Fausto's past was
not to be revealed easily, his drug taking, sexual fantasies, and anger remained
well hidden. But Theodore's patience and his youth were enough to bridge
the generation gap. His knowledge of contemporary music, a certain kinship with Fausto's infatuation with Sartre, and a unique interest in making
feta cheese, served with the island's delectable black olives—which Fausto
eagerly consumed in large quantities—facilitated their relationship.

A few month's into Fausto's treatment, his prognosis was improving, and,
to the relief of his family, he was allowed to participate in a halfway-house
program. He was placed in a small apartment and given a job working as a

furniture mover. Every Tuesday and Thursday afternoon, however, he was expected back at the clinic to spend consultation time with Theodore. Fausto actually began to enjoy these sessions and look forward to them, since his circle of acquaintances was small by any measure; but he engrossed Theodore in bizarre interpretations of existentialism, which Theodore felt were causing recidivist tendencies in Fausto's struggle with patricide. Theodore tried instead to work toward resolving Fausto's fantasies and angst about Emma and assuaging his tormented feelings and possible past sexual involvement with his sister. Fausto would quote Sartre and Camus frequently and dramatically, but had little insight into their philosophy.

Two personalities struggled for supremacy inside Fausto: Number one was the more immediately present person, young and brash, whose needs sought to prevail or at least survive over everyday circumstances, that provided the basis through which Fausto's social existence was determined. Number two, however, was a much more difficult figure, an older, transcendental persona who sought to wrest a position in an obtuse metaphysical world, a subconscious that crawled and darted like an iguana among the camouflage of shrubs and rocks, easily discernible but not easily caught.

At times, however, when loneliness began to chew on his self-confidence, and the hostility of his environment fused with the futility of his predicament, a new, more sinister creature appeared from the deepest wells of Fausto's subconscious. Hiding above his bed after midnight, it emerged to cling to the ceiling in the form of a large black spider covered in glistening jewels, crouching in the blackest corner of his room. It moved slowly and menacingly in some atavistic way above him. Fausto scrambled to escape, but lay paralyzed in fear, twisted in the covers of his bed, until his breath and control were lost in fits of panic and silent screams, leaving his bed reeking of sweat and urine. This creature inhabiting Fausto's mind was, as his doctor knew, a predator, a stealthy killer that put its victims at great risk for their sanity.

―――――――

"Fausto, your aunt has provided a budget, which you are not meeting. Are you spending any of the money on drugs?" Theodore asked. Fausto shook his head, but then lapsed into excuse after excuse and quoted non sequiturs from Sartre.

Theodore had become exasperated with such quotes. Fausto understood little of the philosopher's views, which obscured his thinking. Theodore, had therefore decided to prepare a little skit for Fausto. "Have you heard of Zeus?" Theodore put Fausto in a chair and placed another across from him.

"Sort of," Fausto replied. He popped an olive in his mouth, rolled it around on his tongue, pushed it off to shear its flesh, and spat the seed into his hand, to be flipped into the wastebasket, followed by a gratuitous burp.

"Well, Zeus was the king of kings, god of gods, the last living and youngest child of Saturn, but unfortunately he made one terrible blunder: he created man free." Fausto released a petulant puff of breath and gazed at the skulls. Theodore ignored him. "He was talking with Orestes. Orestes had killed his mother, Clytaemnestra, and ... actually, never mind, forgot about that."

Fausto immediately reacted. "He killed his own mother?"

"Well, I don't want to get into that right now," Theodore said, and handed Fausto a small white card with typed words on it.

"What's this?"

"We're going to perform a small dialog from a Greek tragedy today."

"Cool."

"Yes, it is. Anyway, in the *Odyssey* ... you haven't read the *Odyssey*, have you?" Fausto shook his head. "Okay, this fellow Orestes was talking to Zeus and said, "You are God and I am free; each of us is alone, and our anguish is akin.""

"Akin?"

"Similar. Zeus, you see, wants to stop Orestes from opening the eyes of his countrymen, people like you and me, and what does he say?" Theodore leaned over and pointed to the first sentence on Fausto's card. "You can be Zeus, here" and he handed the cards to Fausto. "Read it."

Fausto felt uncomfortable, but being Zeus was gratifying, so he fell in with the act and read slowly: 'Poor people! Your gift to them will be a sad one, one of loneliness and shame. You will tear from their eyes the veils I had laid on them, and they will see their lives as they are, foul and futile, a barren boon." Fausto understood the words, but not necessarily the message.

Then Theodore read the part of Orestes: "Why, since it is their lot, should I deny them the despair I have in me?"

"Then Zeus responds," Theodore prompted. Fausto, who was getting into the act, so to speak, said forcefully: "What will they make of it?"

Then Theodore again as Orestes said forcefully, "What they choose. They're free; and human life begins on the far side of despair."

"Fausto, do you see what I am trying to say?" asked Theodore.

"No."

"Do you know the meaning of despair?" Theodore asked.

Fausto smiled. "Better than you, I'd wager."

"Why do you say that?"

Fausto giggled. "Why do I say that?"

"Yes."

"You're the doctor, you tell me; isn't that what you get paid for?"

"Are you being smart with me?"

He sniggered. "Naw. You know me, Doc."

"Why don't you use correct French when we talk instead of that damnable slang?"

"I like it. It sounds —"

"It sounds," Theodore broke in, "like a thieving Algerian selling chestnuts to tourists in Marseille." When Fausto resorted to his word games and frequent American insolence, Theodore regretted ever getting into this line of work in the first place and, like a true Greek, did little to hide his irritation. "There are some other doctors available, Fausto, and I can guarantee you won't like them."

"Hey, Doc, don't get angry on me, I don't like the angries," Fausto demanded, turning sullen.

"Perhaps that's enough for today," Theodore said, putting his eyeglasses away in their case.

"You're married, Doc, right?" Fausto said. He hadn't moved. "Goin' home to your missus and kids?"

Theodore was already on his feet and walking to his desk from the little coffee table where they held their conversations. "Right."

"What makes you think they'll be there when you get home?"

"Oh, they will be."

"You mean you hope they will be." Fausto stressed *hope*, but his voice cracked.

"Yes Fausto, I hope they will be." Theodore had turned back to face Fausto, and leaned against the back of his office chair, sensing something was up.

"I don't hope anything," Fausto said. "I'm alone, just like what's his name, Orestes." He had removed one of his horsehair bracelets, played with it, then held it up and looked through it at Theodore. "That's despair."

"Fausto, you can hope what you will. Lots of things are possible, you are simply in a realm of probability. You have a future, if you want it." He paused. "Don't you?"

"Well, you see, Doc, those things I can't change, I ain't interested in. Maybe there's no God, or only some sort of great game that's just a joke we don't know about that's gonna make the world come to me and makes a joke of choosing. Isn't that the way it is? My friend, Beannie, says that's why human beings invented drugs. You act with hope, Doc. I act without hope. You think you can change things. I don't."

"So," Theodore sighed, "no illusions. Life is devoid of meaning, and that life isn't worth living."

"Yeah, kinda."

"Isn't that pretty uncomfortable?"

"Yeah."

"Fausto, you're not alone, you know. Everyone, or almost everyone, desperately demands meaning and clarity from the world around them, but finds themselves up against a universe that is irrational and meaningless," he paused to gather his thoughts. "Like your mother and sister's death." Fausto had moved to Theodore's large leather chair and sank down between its arms, chin on chest, playing with his bracelet and not looking up. Theodore continued, "You see, Fausto, in the face of this basic need that goes unanswered for the human spirit, the stance to assume—just like in any sport, even like windsurfing—is one of technique, strength, and defiance. Have you heard of Sisyphus?"

"No," he mumbled, and looked away. "Maybe."

"Not many have, but there's a lesson there. According to Homer, Sisyphus was the wisest and most prudent of mortals." He lobbed a paper clip at Fausto to get his attention. "On the other hand, some people say he was just a highway robber. Anyway, the gods were jealous and sent Mercury to catch him. As punishment, they made him push a heavy round rock up a mountain, and just when he got it to the top, it would roll back down, and he would have to start all over again."

"You're talking about Camus, right?" At least Fausto was listening.

"Right, *The Myth of Sisyphus*. You see, Fausto, Sisyphus was the absurd hero as much through his passions as through his torture. He scorned the gods, but his hatred of death and passion for life won him that difficult penalty in which his whole being was exerted toward accomplishing nothing. That's the price that must be paid for our passions on this earth. They mean nothing; earth is a small ball in an extremely large vacuum. But, Fausto, for a brief time his purpose was achieved. After the rock rolls down the hill, and Sisyphus walks back down to start over again, that's the hour of consciousness, you see. That's when he's stronger than the gods' punishment and his rock. He can see the sky, hear the animals, taste the wine from his canteen, eat his bread, and—who knows, maybe he sits on an old fallen tree and thinks about the mystery he's locked in but can do nothing about, and then dies. But he is there, he exists, struggling against gravity, and he is dealing with it, day in and day out, and in that there is some majesty in this strange universe, because he exists.

"Look at me, Fausto." Theodore's voice became earnest. "Despite that hopelessness, Camus argues that it is this very defiance and revolt in the face of a world without meaning that enables man to live life as fully and passionately as possible. Those hours going down the mountain after the rock keeps rolling down, those hours are what we have to use. Don't you see, Fausto, it is what you have to use, it is what makes existence possible."

"Doesn't God care?" Fausto said in a little voice, "while we're pushing the rock around, all the time pushing?"

"That's a good question. Some Christians think that mankind did something to upset God and that's why we got thrown out of Paradise —that's original sin. The answer is, we don't know if God cares or not. If you believe like the faithful, He does. Have you heard of Goethe in school?" Fausto nodded. "Goethe wrote a poem about how he saw God. Want to hear it?"

"All of it?"

"It's short, but there is a situation sort of like yours, where Goethe is talking to Zeus." Theodore quoted part of Goethe's *Prometheus*.

> *While yet a child*
> *And ignorant of life,*
> *I turned my wandering gaze*
> *Up tow'rd the sun, as if with him*
> *There were an ear to hear my wailings,*
> *A heart, like mine,*
> *To feel compassion for distress.*
> *I honor thee! And why?*
> *Hast thou e'er lighten'd the sorrows*
> *Of the heavy laden?*
> *Hast thou e'er dried up the tears*
> *Of the anguish-stricken?*
> *Was I not fashion'ed to be a man*
> *By omnipotent Time,*
> *And by eternal Fate,*
> *Masters of me and thee?*
> *Didst thou e'er fancy*
> *That life I should learn to hate,*
> *And fly to deserts,*
> *Because not all*
> *My blossoming dreams grew ripe?*
> *Here sit I, forming mortals*
> *After my image;*
> *A race resembling me,*
> *To suffer, to weep,*
> *To enjoy, to be glad,*
> *And thee to scorn,*
> *As I!*

Fausto remained looking out the window. "Goethe didn't believe in
God?" Then he looked up to challenge Theodore. "And you don't believe
in God?"

"I'm sorry, Fausto, I don't know. Look at it this way: you have a little pocketknife, haven't you?"

Fausto nodded his head. "It's Swiss, my sister gave it to me."

"Nice. Well, it was originally made by an artisan who had a conception of it for making them so you could have one. He paid attention to the preexisting technique of production, sort of like a formula. He knew he needed a design, metal, a way to make a blade, and some plastic and stuff like that. So the knife is at the same time an article producible in a certain way, and one that serves a definite purpose. Obviously, no one is going to produce a knife and not know what it's for, right?" Fausto nodded again. "Let's just say of the knife, then, that its essence, the sum of the formula and the qualities that made its production and its definition possible, precedes its existence. The presence of such-and-such a knife is therefore determined before our eyes. Here, then, we are viewing the world from a technical perspective, and we can say that planning precedes existence, right?"

"Um-hm."

"Well, when we think of God as a creator, we are thinking of him as a super sort of tech guy. We assume that if he wants something, he creates knowing precisely what he is creating. Therefore, Fausto, the conception of man in the mind of God is comparable to that of your knife in the mind of a guy who's good at making knives: God makes man according to a procedure and a conception, exactly like the guy who manufactures a pocketknife like yours, following a definition and a formula. So each individual man is the realization of that certain conception, that definition, that dwells in the divine understanding—like the knife, but the knife can only do certain things, and nothing more than it was created for. So, essence is prior to existence, see? Important men like Diderot, Voltaire, and even Kant, said that man possesses a "human nature," which is that conception of human being and is found in every man, woman, and child, for that matter in every thing, which means that each man is a particular example of a universal conception, the conception of man, someone just like you, or your landlady, or your sister."

"So, if God made us, maybe he should be ashamed of himself," Fausto countered.

"Well, you know Fausto, there's a lot to what you say, but maybe it is man's

478

doing, not God's. Your father got drunk and had an accident, and it killed your mother and dear little sister. But it was not God's doing. God made the knife, but he didn't use it." Theodore pondered the moment, trying to avoid involving his personal life, but decided, against professional ethics, to do so. "I was going to be a priest some years ago, but I lost my faith. I thought, if people are being bad all over the world, maybe God didn't have anything to do with their essence. So now I'm what you'd call a follower of atheistic existentialism, which says that if God does not exist, there is a least one being—there could be many others, of course, like your cat or dog—whose existence comes before its essence. For example, you and I are beings that existed before any definition of us came about."

"Yeah, but I still don't understand. What do you mean that I existed before my essence?" Fausto asked.

"What I mean is that man, you, for example, first of all exist. Your forefathers go back through thousands and thousands of generations to the original slime of the earth. They progressed up through, among other creatures, monkeys, of which you are a prime example."

Fausto laughed and made monkey sounds.

"You see, you're a man-monkey, born, and then you encounter yourself." Fausto looked at him strangely, but Theodore continued, "Like when you first come to know that you exist, then rise up in the world and define, that is, do things that make you what you are afterward. You can see man is nothing to begin with, right? Just a baby who if not taken care of dies. You will do what you're told and not be anything until later, and then you will be what you make of yourself. Therefore, there is no human nature, because there is no God to have a conception of it. Man simply is; you and I simply are, or became, from our great-great-grandfathers, the monkeys, and they themselves protoplasm from the sea. But, not that we simply are what we conceive ourselves to be—the world's best windsurfer for example, or me the finest cheese maker—but we only are what we *will* ourselves to be, what we make ourselves to be. Wishing what we should be and being what we should be is the difference between talking the talk and walking the walk. So, you see, you are nothing else but that which you make of yourself. That's the first principle of existentialism"

"Nope," Fausto said easily.

"Nope? What do you mean, 'Nope?'"

"I believe in human nature."

"Human nature?"

Fausto searched for words. "It's, sort of, well, like you said, God made me!"

"I didn't say that. You said 'God ought to be ashamed of himself.'"

"Yeah," he hesitated.

"You see, Fausto, the first effect of existentialism is that it puts every person in possession of him or herself as he or she really is, and places the entire responsibility for our existence squarely upon our own shoulders, not God's. And when we say that man is responsible for himself, we don't mean that he is responsible only for himself, but that he is responsible for all men."

Fausto looked puzzled. "Can we talk about it some more?"

"Sure. Next week."

In 1964 Jean-Paul Sartre refused the Nobel Prize for literature on the grounds that such honors could interfere with a writer's responsibilities to his readers.

CHAPTER 6

═══ THE DIARY ═══

In a small halfway house for juvenile addicts on the outskirts of Corfu, Fausto, on his doctor's advice, made preparations to write in his new diary. His room, a little cubicle painted tan, three meters square, held a small green metal desk, plus a chair made of two square green leatherette cushions on an aluminum frame, one for the seat and one for the back.

Desks are revealing, both for what they have and don't have. They display one's priorities and status in stark terms. Messy, orderly, sparse, crowded, rich, or poor. There was little to be proud of on this desk: an open package of cigarettes, sex and soccer magazines, ashtray and plastic lighter, cheap lamp previously abused, notebook, ballpoint pen, and an opened package of biscuits. Fausto wanted a cell phone to wear on his belt, but couldn't afford one. There were no photographs. The entire atmosphere reeked of cigarette smoke, which, hampered in its search for exits, gave a feeling of confinement and dissolution, relieved only by a smallish window overlooking the bay, offering a view of small boats tied to a dock.

In his most dedicated American lingo, a circumstance he believed his little sister would like and, being an angel, would understand, Fausto began to write each day, sometimes for minutes, other times longer, all that he remembered from his father's chiding, Beannie's philosophy, Sara's homilies, Sartre's quotes, and a plethora of blue-colored slang learned from his classmates in America, he composed his first letter to Emma in slightly over a year.

Thursday Oct 23

Hey Emma,

I'm in Corfu! Two or three months now. I left the angries behind. And the old times. Today, I'm startin' again. I have a new notebook, they told me I ought to get one, one you would have bought...its cover is blue with little goats on it and white windmills. I put your picture in this one too. I forgot to tell you, after you died I gave your CD player to Margo. She says she really misses you. I left Esquive, the girl I told you about in the States. I tried to talk with her like we used to with Margo, but she wouldn't. She's got one in the oven...that's what Beannie always says, you know, pregnant...me a father! Nope, not me. She's cryin' and her sister was always callin'. The professor gave her the number here. She keeps callin'. Always ringin' down the hall. Then Esquive gets on. Fausto, she says, what about the baby? Always whinin' about the baby. Well, what about the goddamn baby? She wanted it, and threatenin' me with fuckin' lawyers. Baby's better in Pennsylvania, specially with the professor around.

I left my best friend Beannie there too. When I'm anky, you know, I miss Esquive sometimes, but she won't leave me alone, and Beannie...it helps to write their names, I'm a lonesome son of a bitch. I just got outta there. Beannie's busy with his gas station and Esquive with her girlfriends and the baby in her belly, which Beannie says is real big now. I flew to Milano last summer and dumped all the stuff in a room at our old hotel near the Duomo. Remember? Seventh floor, we could see the top of Duomo and Castle Fortze and watch the guy and his girl doin' it on the roof garden? I was gonna jump from that window. All seven floors. Probably woulda landed right on a car. But I couldn't do it. So I took the train to Venice and hopped on a ferry called Blue Sky for Corfu. Know what my room number was? Piraeus. It's a lifeboat! I slept under it next to the railing! Me and some gypsy kids. We ate potatoes, lots of potatoes and bread.

I got into some trouble in Corfu and they eventually called the professor. He was too busy to come. Aunt Jeanette came. So

482

I'm in and out of a halfway house. I got a job at a truck company movin' furniture for rich Germans. I can't speak much Greek, but I know more German than the Greeks so I'm getting' by … you know how I am, not good to let people know you speak anything. Yesterday me and a kid with a bunch of rings in his ears were helping the driver move some stuff for an old German guy. We were sittin' in the sun, lookin' at the sea from his patio, takin' a Coke and enjoyin' the moment, when my boss Nick said — "Well I suppose we oughta get back to work."

The old guy who owned the house said — "Yeah, but you know I just turned 60 a while ago and now when it comes to getting back to work, I just say, well fuck it, in its own good time. I mean, getting things done and keeping other people happy."

You know what the kid with the rings in his ears said? — "Yeah, I know what you mean, I felt that way when I was seven!"

HA, HA.

I miss you Emma, but when I do I can still hear Mom's voice, me sittin' on the toilet and her screamin' at you in the kitchen, the professor screamin' at her, but I don't hear the words exact, like it's someone goin' deaf, no paper, then I just wiped my ass on the inside of her stupid pink robe. Yep, ol' Mom, she slammed me good.…

Friday, Oct 24

I found a bird's nest today. Funny how ugly the baby birds are and then they grow up beautiful. Not like us. Little kids are beautiful and they grow up to be ugly. This morning I'm here and death is right beside me. A hole in the ground, a cardboard box, a dead bird. My boss said to get rid of it. Told me it was only a bird, and I asked him if he could make a bird?[11]

Emma, it is neat here. I swim and you can see fish goin' right by your legs. Your feet are on sandy bottom and soft green weed. A lot better'n ol' stony lake. You wake one mornin' now and it's autumn and notice that the feelin' of everything has changed, the sky shines pearl-like, and the sun rises like a ball of blood — really!

The peaks of the Albanian hills are snowy just like you could see the Alps from our balcony at aunt Jeanette's in Figino. Nizan said he'd write a postcard from Como. I wish he would write. The sea is near my apartment...apartment-needs-work, that's what I call it, "apartment-needs-work." Ha, Ha! The water below here has lead color and sluggish and the olive leaves are gray like the ol' Peugeot. Fires smokin' in the villages, and the breath of Maria—my landlady and her dirty dog, she farts and he stinks—is sort of white in the air when she passes—dog's name is carrot, it's Greek—on her way to the village. She fixes me an egg sandwich every mornin' when I come. All day she sits crouched on a curb downtown sellin' baskets to tourists, singin' in her small sort-of tired witch's voice, while the kids yell and dogs bark around her. She's always makin' baskets while she's talkin' to her friends. This old store across where she sits has apple pie. I love it, the crust is as thick as my little finger. The waiters keep it in a glass case and swear at me. I can't get at it. Maria watches the girls sellin' postcards and stuff. She is wrinkled and has violet eyes and spits in a nasty way in their direction before takin' up her little song—which she says is about two fishes swimmin' in the sea. She says now is the time to break logs for the fireplace she and her husband built themselves, and smell cypress wood smoke. So I'm breakin' wood for my sandwiches. It smells like tar or varnish. Ugh! But I guess winter's comin'. Nizan owes me. Is Nizan dead, Nizan's head is dead, can you see us?

The professor is time of waste and then to the turd of time he'll die at my taste, so here comes #2 and he's got pie, no pie, bye.

CHAPTER 7

$\equiv$ GOOD OL' DAD $\equiv$

De Monteaux brought in two aperitifs from his kitchen, sat down, and placed one before Charly. He lifted his glass in salute, she picked up hers, and they clinked glasses. "As I was saying, young Nizan was Fausto's best friend. Jean-Michel didn't like him much—rude and outspoken, apparently. The way I understand it, the boy took some antibiotics one night for a cold or something, and the next thing you know he is having a full grand mal. They operated and he's recovered to an extent. Fausto was in the States at the time, and Nizan didn't write for months. It is their common bond now, since Fausto started having attacks after Emma was killed. Anyway, when they finally found Fausto in Greece, he had to be put in a clinic in Corfu: too many drugs, too much ouzo, who knows?"

"Wait. You said, 'Emma was killed.' I thought it was an accident."

"Well, if it was an 'accident,' Jean-Michel caused it. Fausto has threatened to kill him for it."

"Why in heaven's name would he want to do that!" she exclaimed incredulously, "It was an accident; drunks cause accidents every day all over the world."

"A lot of people don't see it that way, and a sixteen-year-old who has grown up with alcoholic parents probably finds it hard to distinguish sober ones, so maybe he thought Jean-Michel did it on purpose."

"On purpose? Why?"

"Fausto saw his parents at their worst. No doubt he created some images that convinced him that his father was determined to kill his mother."

"Oh, Jesus," she sighed.

"Charly, there is more to this than meets the eye, as you say."

The colonel shifted his position and became visibly uncomfortable in his

485

chair. "I don't feel good about this, you know. These are very private matters in the Levasseur family."

"I need to know, Colonel. You can appreciate that we've been together for some time …I think he wants to get married, and I …you know." She looked down at her drink.

"And you don't."

"That's not it, really. It's just that I'm young and have a commitment to my daughter, and her …I don't know if I can simply sign on to a relationship that resembles the Leaning Tower of Pisa."

"Oh, I…" he hesitated. "Charly, it's just so…" he looked for a way out. "I don't know." He was laboring with his conscience.

"Colonel, I'm going back to the States shortly, and I'm not coming back unless I know what I'm coming back to. You have to understand that."

"How well do you know Jean-Michel?" he said quietly.

She caught his eyes. "It's been intimate. He's a kind and intelligent man. I'm not looking for a partner that's much else. He's also things that are unpleasant, and in a way, I have no idea what's going on."

"Did he ever mention Bianca?" he said.

"No," she sighed again.

He groaned. "I suppose if he had, he would have wanted you to know. If not…"

Charly reached for her purse. "I respect your confidence, Colonel, honestly, and I understand why you wouldn't want to break yours with Jean-Michel. I guess we should leave it at that." She made ready to go.

He put his hand on her arm. "Please, sit for a moment or so longer. I can only reveal some things that I hope allow you to understand Jean-Michel and his unfortunate past a little better.

"Bianca, a black woman from Jamaica, I think, was a student of his wife's.

Charly shook her head in dismay. "Oh, jeez."

"His wife was tutoring her," the colonel continued. "Jean-Michel and Bianca had something going on, and some mulatto from the Caribbean was involved, a man from Jean-Michel's school days. A Vietnam veteran. Drugs were involved, and eventually the three were caught and arrested. Fausto was interviewed by the police."

"That's about enough for me," she said.

"Charlie, look at it this way: we all do things we shouldn't, but when you think about it, it was just two former college buddies and a pretty young woman who had some pot and got caught, sharing nothing more sinister than that."

"And Fausto? I don't suppose he thought it was so innocent." She began to gather her things.

"True. His statement to the police was that he and his sister had seen the three together in a nasty way and were disgusted by what they saw. He said some threatening things around the neighborhood. Everyone wrote it off, since Fausto was deranged."

"And Jean-Michel's wife?"

"She was going to divorce him. She wanted to go back to the States anyway. It wasn't long after that that the accident happened."

She shook her head dejectedly. "So Fausto ran away, and now Interpol is looking for him?"

"He was simply a missing person, which is not enough to get the police truly involved. Anyway, it seems, as I said, he's turned up in Greece."

"Yeah, I heard," she said.

"Well, he left…swearing to make his father pay."

***

Sartre's Death

It seemed Sartre's health was never the same after his second heart attack. On 20 March 1980, he was hospitalized for what was diagnosed as edema of the lungs. His bedsores had begun to develop infections, and his bladder was functioning badly. When he got out of bed he supported himself with a mobile stand from which a small plastic bag of urine hung for all to see. No longer adequately supplied with blood, his kidneys could not eliminate urea, and he was too feeble for an operation to save one of them.

When friends came to see him, Sartre, after asking for a glass of water, assured his companions that the next time they had a drink it would be whiskey at his place. But no later than the next day he asked de Beauvoir how they would pay for the funeral. The following day, he took her by the hand and told her: "I love you very much, my dear Beaver." When she came on Monday, April 14, he murmured a few words without opening his eyes, and when he pursed his lips to be kissed, she kissed both his mouth and his cheek. By the evening he was in a coma, and did not recover consciousness, though it was about twenty-four hours before he died.

His closest friends stayed overnight with the body, but when de Beauvoir, asking to be left alone with it, tried to lie down next to him under the sheet, a nurse warned her that the gangrene was dangerous. She lay down on top of the sheet and slept — or thought she slept — for a while. At five in the morning, male nurses covered the body and took it away.

Wanting to see the body again, de Beauvoir went the following day to the lecture theater of the hospital, a large, cold room with a tiled floor, and the double coffin was brought in. Inside it Sartre was dressed in the clothes he had worn for going to an opera: a maroon corduroy suit, a light shirt, a tie with an abstract pattern on it. The spectacles were missing, the hair carefully combed, the well-shaven face made up.

On Saturday, April 19, he (his ashes) was buried. From the hospital, which is in the middle of the 14th arrondissement, to the cemetery in Montparnasse, the hearse had to travel through narrow streets that were more than usually congested. Traffic was halted as the procession, moving slowly thorough the streets, doubled in size and went on growing till about 50,000 people were following the coffin. There was no ceremony, no speech. De Beauvoir did not get out of the hearse until the coffin had been lowered into the grave. After asking for a chair, she sat at the edge of the open grave for at least ten minutes, surrounded by the vast mass of people. All around her, camera shutters never stopped clicking. Sartre could not have pictured anything like this when at the age of twenty he had written the one-act comedy *J'aurai un bel enterrement (I'll Have a Nice Funeral)*.[12]

The drama of Sartre's life is as paradoxical as his thoughts. For all the fame he gained in life, he remained a man of simple tastes, a man committed to a principle worth dying for, a man capable of empathizing with the oppressed of the world. When interviewed five years before his death on how he would like people to remember him, Sartre replied that he would like them to remember *Nausea*, one or two plays: *No Exit* and *The Devil and the Good Lord;* and then his two philosophical works, particularly the second one, *Critique of Dialectical Reason.* Then with an afterthought, his essay on Genet, *Saint Genet,* which he had written quite a long time ago. If these were remembered, that, he felt, would be quite an achievement, and would ask for no more. As a man, if a certain Jean-Paul Sartre was remembered, he would, he said, like people to remember the milieu or the historical situation in which he lived, the general characteristics of this milieu, how he lived in it, in terms of all the aspirations, which he tried to gather up within himself. That, he said, was how he would like to be remembered.[13]

$$=== X ===$$

Cousteau

We are living in an interminable succession of absurdities imposed by the myopic logic of short-term thinking: the population big bang, the North–South divorce, the climatic changes of all sorts, the elimination of thousands of species, the new dictatorship of materialism. All these evils must be cured urgently, and the only medicine is a recourse to Utopia. In a remarkable speech at the Ateneo Veneto on April 6, 1990, Federico Mayor, Director General of UNESCO, said: "Since the Renaissance, one has often ascertained that today's utopias are the realities of tomorrow.... Utopia is the necessity to get over and break the barriers of the established order."

Jacques Cousteau
United Nations Conference on
Environment and Development,
June 1992, Rio de Janeiro, Brazil

$\equiv$ JOHN-MICHEL'S "BEST" FRIEND $\equiv$

Hemingway, like Cousteau, loved the sea and a good beach, of course. He wrote as much in *The Sun Also Rises*. He was talking about San Sebastian, that most cosmopolitan of cities by the bay. When hot, he said, there was a certain early-morning quality to the place; that the trees seemed as though their leaves were never quite dry, and the streets felt as though they had just been sprinkled. And it is true, at least in summer. On the other hand, he didn't mention the ocean breeze off the Bay of Biscay, which is fundamental to the climate of the city. Plus, for my taste, he used that 'early-morning' sketch too many times in his book.

Like Hemingway's main character, Jake, I also left Paris because of a Jew. But he was a she, and her name wasn't Cohn. She did, however, want me to go to Spain and meet her in Pamplona for San Fermin, just like the book. But, my plans to write a speech honoring Jacques-Yves Cousteau for an American oceanographic institute took me no farther than the Hotel de Londres y de Inglaterra in San Sebastian, only an hour away. It was a challenge, since Cousteau wasn't a particular interest of mine and had no connection with the area that I could discern, while Hemingway was a regular. Besides, my friend Carole was a fan of Hemingway, not Cousteau, and swore that I looked just like the old codger.

She wasn't particularly pretty, nor did she have that Rue du Faubourg Montmartre chic that Ernest preferred; still, she had a cocky panache that I favored in women. Not to mention marvelous pointy breasts mounted on a teen body that she displayed bra-less with a coyness, jiggle, and verve that, like powerful magnets, drew every eye. But, as with Hemingway's heroine, Brett or Lady Ashley, she was chasing a Spaniard—as I had suspected—who was young and handsome in his way, with a long black ponytail.

I'm bald, but secure in the knowledge that tails were conceived by nature to cover things otherwise embarrassing. Nonetheless, in my youth I had vainly fought thinning hair, even tried dyeing it. I found it tough to keep it trimmed, though, much less freshly painted. Unfortunately, hair sort of defines who we are, the hat we can't take off.[1] Despite the Spaniard's hair and its statement about where he was at, what his needs were, and whom he was trying to please, my pate was mute.

Her lean little man didn't fight the bulls, but he had this thing about running with them at San Fermin like Hemingway and his comrades, all dressed up with the rest in their white outfits and red bandannas. I'll say this about Cousteau: I don't think he ever ran with the bulls. Smart man, although swimming with sharks would have given most people pause. The whole bull business smacked of idiocy, since honest citizens got gored and killed doing such things. She wanted to be chased by her Spaniard, he wanted to be chased by the bulls, and I wanted to be free of the whole foolish mess. She was half my age and, like Hemingway's Jake, I couldn't get it up. Sadly, nothing as poignant as a war wound, where there was a certain role to play. Mine, like the good senator's and 20 million others, was simply a dysfunction relieved with a little blue pill, which was expensive, the cost of two erections equaling a substantial meal at the Brasserie Mari Galent in the Hotel de Londres. The pills, as spam reminded me daily, were cheaper on the Net of course, but tricky on international deliveries and chancy due to scams. My priorities had changed with age, but I probably should have followed Hemingway's seminal advice about not exhausting the supply.[2] Therefore, taking only modest turns at sexual encounters, I leaned toward the corpulent and orally erotic, favoring red meat and wine, rich desserts, and, periodically, the gout.

Cousteau wasn't much of a writer. I guess that's why I wasn't attracted to him. He was a film man at heart, always looking outward, never in. So I didn't have much to go on for the speech, which was the point of this whole endeavor. Matter of fact, I didn't like the way Hemingway wrote, either, never did: too dry and simple, purportedly his way of searching for that clean, pure sentence, I suppose. Both authors left something to be desired.

Ernest sounded to me like the semester-abroad students I passed every day hanging out by McDonald's in San Sebastian's Parte Vieja, writing in their diaries, trying to snare ideal words like those in never-to-be-forgotten Hemingwayesque poignant moments in which his sparse writing covered swimming at the beach in the best traditions of a fifth grader reciting her show-and-tell essay from last summer's lake visit: I waded out. The water was cold. I swam out to the raft. A boy and girl were at the other end. She laughed.

Well, you get the idea, all black and white, no color. Appropriate for his time, perhaps. His boxing partner, Ezra Pound, was advocating the cause of *le mot juste*, which the French writers, particularly Flaubert, practiced: the principles of directness, precision, and economy. Hemingway was dutifully influenced by Pound in any number of ways, and certainly his distrust of the adjective, but still a pity that in describing a beach scene with an ingénue, there was not even one vignette about pert suntanned breasts, that when rolling on her back her nipples would..., etc. But what can you say about a man who took his comb to the beach? So, if you were mesmerized by that style, you'll love all 218 pages, ending the book with a wet noodle of a line by Jake to Brett while promising that it was "pretty to think so." It's hard to imagine an old sea dog like Cousteau ever reaching for that kind of fluff.

I don't mean to carry on, but "pretty"? Hemingway has his main character, with a name like "Jake," who starts out the book talking about boxing and later catalogs the fine points of bullfighting, segueing into a line that finishes the book like—well, like Liberace. That's a line Maureen Dowd would love to prove her point about emasculated males, "metrosexuals," as she calls them, the new term for straight men who are feminized and into "manscaping," with a taste for facials and home design. Even the back cover of the book sounds infinitely more exciting than anything Hemingway dreamt up: "When the couple drift to Spain to the dazzle of the fiesta and the heady atmosphere of the bullfight, their affair is strained by new passions, new jealousies, and Jake must learn that he will never possess the woman he loves."

The critics must have been suckers too: Hemingway, they said, had capture the atmosphere by reticence and breathed life into his characters by pages left unsaid. (I'll say). It was American, they proclaimed (no denying that), and was literature. (So is the *Communist Manifesto*.) I wonder if the person ever put aside his or her dissertation on genius long enough to read Stevenson's *Treasure Island* or volunteer to crew aboard the *Calypso*?

As I said, I don't like the way he writes, and long ago received the bad grades in American Lit class at St. Bonaventure to show for it. You could say that's the reason I ended up in San Sebastian this week. Couldn't get into med. school with average grades back then, so the money thing was gone. (Please note: Average US doctor's gross income in year 2000: $245,190, Medical Economics Web site; average professor's salary, $64,700, Department of Labor. Result? A lot less rashes and considerably more ignorance. Sour grapes? Yeah, you could say that.)

I opted for a master's in technical journalism at St. Peters, followed by a Ph.D. in order to avoid the nine-to-five jive. Couldn't stand the smell of hospitals anyway. The literature prof was gay, which I was not quick to grasp, and read to us from the textbook for fifty minutes each class as his form of instruction. The jocks loved it, since it presumed no preparation, but bored me to death while being forced to squirm in molded plywood seats. Being naive, I never quite figured out what was wrong with him, although it's obvious now why he was in love with Hemingway, who was still alive back then, full of whiskey and swagger. The prof was short and skinny with thick glasses, queer in the true sense of the word, and had an unusually bad complexion. He was married, or so he said; therefore, from my seat, he must have been okay; somebody—undoubtedly desperate—loved him. Besides, it was a Catholic university. What would the good fathers have said?

Anyway, this Jewess of mine is in Pamplona, drinking with the jolly San Ferminers, cheering her swarthy bull runner for his daily five-minute tryst with danger—longer if someone gets gored by a reckless bull—listening raptly with the others to his stories while she ministered to his gashes and aches, just like Brett, did for "the Kid" Romero, the bullfighter in Hemingway's book. Brett was waiting for her bullfighter back then, impatient, no doubt, to test the bedsprings in their hotel room across from the bar Iruña to prove their love. Don't get me wrong: I'm not motivated by jealousy, nor worried, since her friend can't afford more than a weekend, in any case. Loading cigarette machines around Barcelona doesn't pay well, and therefore he insists on my lovely partner paying her half, which sits poorly with aging JAPs,[3] ponytail or no. So, when their money runs out, she'll be back here with her bouncing tits and curly hair, to caress and fool me into believing I am something worth possessing. She doesn't, of course, but there are few young women who'll put up with the looks and likes of a sixty-year-old man willingly. So she's earning her money, although she thinks I'm fifty-eight and is perplexed by the unruly hairs nestled in my ears. She always wins her point by positing the reverse situation: would I, when I was thirty-five, be with a fifty-eight-year-old woman? Probably not. Then again, taking into consideration the legal escapades embraced by my ex-wife at the time, with some small vision of the future my sexual priorities might have changed to a good-looking stud enjoying a modest family allowance, who always carried the bags and had the aspirations of a sous-chef.

I get to walk her dog, a Border collie that has more sense than both of us. When Carole is gone like this, getting her sex and living free, I have a modest rendezvous with what the old-timers called Five-Finger Mary, and Catholic priests called sins of impurity. But the collie — a female — growls and petulantly paces the apartment when I'm in the midst of my fantasies. Eventually, she seeks refuge, at least for her head, behind a large leather chair in the living room, where she sighs and groans until things are over. Granted, it's not a pretty sight. If there is an afterlife wherein all beings communicate with perfect recollection, I am going to have to face that dog in what will undoubtedly be a very unpleasant moment for both of us.

But I digress.

All of this is beside the point. I am now in San Sebastian at an oceanographic conference as a speechwriter (they call me "Doctor") and consultant to an obtuse group of people — older in most ways, but not actively drooling — who, like Captain Cousteau, have a mission to save the planet. The conference is at the Hotel de Londres y de Inglaterra, and this year they are honoring his memory. The festivities will begin tomorrow at the Plaza Jacques Cousteau, where crowds will gather in a commodious square that could easily fit eight or so automobiles parked side by side and fronts the entrance to the city aquarium.

This region of Spain, Euskadi to its native Basque people, is not far from the oil spill caused by the breakup of the ship *Prestige* a few years back, which pollutes Spanish waters and many of its beaches to this day. So, there will be your predictable demonstrations, probably small but earnest, against just about everything. Certainly the major petroleum companies will get their share, and McDonald's too, of course, for encouraging the industrialization of methane by their flatulent cows. All of this guarantees good media coverage, but a dearth of fast food for the demonstrators and those about town, not to speak of higher gasoline prices. Any rioters with half a brain should demand that McDonald's stay open for the rioters' evening meals under their protection — for 80 percent off. The oil companies having nothing practical to offer, except perhaps the world's chemical industry will all point to the billions spent on repairing the environment they helped destroy, continue referring to themselves benignly as energy companies of the future, and blah, blah, blah, sneak out the proverbial side door with all questions being directed to one of their institutes, which have somehow been oblivious of the environmental destruction fueled by their products these many years.[4]

Unfortunately, we have all had a major part to play in this moral arithmetic. And, as Eldridge Cleaver (*Soul on Ice*) of decades past said, if you're not part of the solution, you're part of the problem.[5] Too bad he was only speaking of race.

Conversely, I am honoring my interest in the Tour de France, which starts soon in Paris, allowing me to follow the race much closer than in the States. Great fun, of course, and important fans galore, like Robin Williams, who last year was wearing a T-shirt bearing Cousteau's image. Since the image on the shirt was faded, a reporter supposedly asked him, "Robin, are you wearing a Jerry Garcia T-shirt?" Williams replied: "Are you off your medication? It's a Cousteau T-shirt. He's Jerry Garcia underwater."

This year it goes through Bayonne — home of the famous bayonet — and I get to dine on French cuisine just across the border from San Sebastian, while pondering the marriage of sword and gun. And lastly, to meet my old chum, Jean-Michel Levasseur, from graduate school days in Newark, who is in trouble.

CHAPTER 2

═══ JEAN-MICHEL AND ME ═══

Jean-Michel is in trouble.

And when wasn't he? He wouldn't agree, but he fit the Yeats version of Swift's internal world: "in ceaseless conflict with itself, unsatisfied, unappeased, unreconciled ... rather than settled into untroubled patterns of tranquillity and unchanging order."

Proof? He always drank, so he was always fat, phlegmatic, a failure with women, and shirked work. He was neither good-looking nor healthy of appearance in those days, leaving people who looked closely to surmise that he cut his own hair with nail scissors. He was badly and untidily dressed, except for his taste in pastel Hermès ties, which in the old days he considered a signature of that known to be irrepressibly French. The more pedestrian view, taken by the locals, was that his ties were to help obscure the notion that he never ironed his shirts. Socially, he had a tendency to embroider anecdotes, a sardonic humor, and a way of insincerely flattering people after a couple of drinks, which gave him some amusement when he saw that they were taken in by the blather.

Don't get me wrong: he had his good points. He played the piano well, or at least the music he liked, so he was a hit at the parties, and had a preference for impressionist compositions, particularly Ravel's *Pavane pour une Infante Défunte*, which I later learned had a sad and prophetic association to his own daughter. He was intelligent and kept in his room a lot of school prizes for scholarship, exhibited in the usual way. But few ever saw his room, except shoddy prostitutes and truly lonesome women who happened to take his cab. He spent a lot of time in his cab, a master of tête-à-tête par excellence with his customers; but his teeth suffered because of all the Milky Way and Snickers dinners he had had. If he didn't know you socially, he would lean heavily on a series of weak clichés and excuse himself. Among friends, however, or at least acquaintances in the local bars, he proved a riveting conversationalist. Unfortunately, the entertaining talk usually degraded drink by drink until he chronicled happier times with a bleary levity that bored. But it wasn't for me to fault him; back in the old days his taxi rides to campus were gratis. We were awarded our Ph.D.s the same year, got drunk on graduation day, and skipped the talk and walk.

The cops finally stopped him one night on a rain-slick highway and ended his career as an inebriated taxi driver and aspiring up-and-comer in the Newark transportation system. He complained privately that he thought he had a drinking problem, when truth be told he had an addictive-genes problem. He had wanted to go back to France in any case, and spoke longingly in the local bars of the easy life, which he portrayed in delightful colors to ease our daily doses of Newark's drab nightlife. His grand vision was to wander through Cognac's green countryside, take a hike on the Compostela trail,[6] rest his feet in the blue Antenne River, and get plastered on Jean Martell's Cognac Cordon Bleu under France's oldest live oak. He liked the symbolism. The oak was planted, he said, at the birth of François I, in 1494, Cognac country's one and only king of France,[7] who also could lay claim to having bought the Mona Lisa from Leonardo da Vinci; he came to power just about the time that distillation of eau de vie was catching on and the world was becoming unflat.[8]

I shared his vision, but preferred Armagnac. It has always been overshadowed by cognac, sort of a hick cousin, J.M. liked to say. I favored the bohemian nature of Armagnac. From brand to brand, my taste showed jagged differences in its personalities, from butterscotch to rich orange, as opposed to cognac's smooth consistency. According to the locals, the colombard and folle blanche grapes make the difference in Armagnac, since both brandies distill the ugni blanc. I see it differently: Armagnac's intensity is greater, as in the difference between Jean-Michel and myself.

CHAPTER 3

═══ LONELINESS ═══

Jean-Michel called to confirm that he was coming to San Sebastian, that he would meet his lady friend, arriving with some college kids in her care, and, while sending them off on a tour, the three of us would quite literally have a happy hour at the Brasserie of the Hotel Londres. There was an attempt at lightheartedness in his voice, and he assured me that drafting the Cousteau speech would be a breeze.

Nonetheless, while advising me about a teaching job at the University of Innsbruck, it was easy to tell he was depressed. He had a son lost in space, buried a wife and daughter, father gone, mother in poor health, and poor old Astérix, his most loyal companion, like many of his breed, suffering with lymphoma. His sister was his only refuge, and she had her own problems and family. Finally, he felt that his new love was tiring of him. With no new prospects on the horizon, and his last-chance job crumbling like drying sand, he sounded like a suicide case. A lonely soul, like a solitary albatross gliding far out on an overcast green sea, with nowhere to land.

What do you say to someone like that: Quit whining and pull your oar, we are all in the same boat? You should thank God that you are not sick, starving, or demented like the rest? That you are not doing hard time in some cell, dodging tsunamis or pushing up daisies in Rwanda? That with his great gifts there was a world to be won: Africans and Arctic icepacks to be saved? Find another woman, get a new apartment, buy a big-screen TV? Serve other people, volunteer at the hospice for people who really need help — probably like he will shortly — or take that once-in-a-lifetime trip? Fall on his knees and accept Christ, let Him do the planning? Ask any friend, and they will tell you that every day is the first day of the rest of your life? Jean-Michel was beyond being fooled by any of those illusions.

Nonetheless, he had touched a sore spot: my loneliness. A longing for the past of family and friends now deceased that back then presumed a certain future, with your parents' generation up in front of you, saluting your successes, while still taking life's hits, people you could love and still feel sorry for and have a reason to help. Sort of like being a young medic on the battlefield of life, supremely confident of yourself and your place, proudly ministering to the older ones struggling on the front lines, soon to be dead. A pride that comes from being close enough to the edge, which impresses your peers with stories from the front, but not so close as to know you are next.

But that was then, this is now, in the present, with no place to go except the edge; with those dear siblings and durable friends—and some not so durable—of your own generation (there is really no other) somewhere out there in life's vicinity, battling for relevance, going down one by one: heart attacks, cancer, and auto accidents, screaming, "Medic!" I dreamt my way to their bedsides. But it was predictable and unalterable; the screams when you go over the edge will be in fear, or if you are fortunate, a groaning relief that it is finally over, or "Boy, that was fun!" Life, as any fool knows, is just a state of mind. For me there will be a forgiving God if I am met at the Pearly Gates by my dogs, or if not, by the aborted fetuses of elapsed love from distant mistresses.

Jean-Michel was being marginalized by society. He wasn't looking for pity, he said, hated pity in fact; just some reasonable answer about his future, while harboring a veiled hate for that superlative cosmic creator to whom so many prostrated themselves and who dreamed all this sick crap up.

My take on it was that in heaven, at the Almighty's magnificent court, with all of the universe present, it seemed that mankind—the whole past, present, and future of us as one organism, standing there with that dumb look on our collective face—had somehow pissed off the heavenly host. God of the quick temper, who then smacked us with His magic wand, banishing us to earth, and created...well, let's put it this way: a merciless, frothy-mouthed savage in his native land (most upscale boardrooms), in whom we will feel terribly ashamed and fervently hope that the blood of some more humble and noble creature flows in our veins.

Our sentence, or penance if you will, was an appropriate amount of suffering on earth until we had enough; that is, until mankind itself committed suicide (coming soon to a theater near you) and we all headed home to heaven, limping, tattered, and worn like a defeated army, leaving earth considerably the worse for wear. Home with the knowledge that, as billions of interlocking individuals wailing for redemption, we each mattered about as much to the Almighty as a hair follicle on the ass of humanity.

Jean-Michel asked what I thought.

It was easy, I said. Don't feel bad. That's life. You do what anyone does at a bad movie: get up and walk out. Just step in front of a fast car. So you've lost a little of life's spare change. He wasn't satisfied, needed more, he said.

"Okay," I offered, "you are a sniveling, contemptible piece of shit. Why don't you just get out and join the whole fucking pack of life's sleepwalkers?"

At that he laughed—Jesus, did he ever laugh, like a tiger roaring in the jungle. Delighted. What did I really think? He would drink himself to death. Take it from an expert, one who has licked the bitter breast of oblivion.

CHAPTER 4

══ OLD HAT: ══

THE SIXTH MAJOR EXTINCTION EVENT

Jim and his partner were late.

'Jim' was Jean-Michel's nickname in the States, since Americans had little patience to mouth all of those vowels in Jean-Michel, so it was shortened to J.M. and finally just 'Jim.' We needed to get down to work. He could be relied upon to help, as I recalled, for a free dinner, if he didn't get totally tanked in the meantime. But that remained to be seen. I had called him and during a rather lengthy discussion, told him of my plight and asked him to lend a hand. Unfortunately, the premise I was given by the oceanographic institute for the Cousteau speech was that the public had to try harder, a point he ignored. His point was that when the public's sacrifice part comes up, like making our teens forego their Mustangs, the crowd would moo and shift uncomfortably in their seats, fearful of facing their children, and whining about all the other guys. I couldn't get him on message; he kept repeating that the audience tomorrow would think the solution is before us, and nod their heads when we mention being threatened by pollution and scarcity for the thousandth time; that is, old hat. Then they will make an impressive agenda for Earth Day[9] next year, and go about doing what they were doing before, only with a Save-the-Earth pin on their collar. Therefore, since the ecological implosion was already well underway, our job would be to simply release the august deliberations of the so-called experts to the press and adjourn for lunch, followed by a quick tour of the Basque countryside, preferably to a bodega in a rented Mercedes cabriolet, sample the wines, and talk about the old days.

His final argument about global warming and the irony of a new ice age was classic J.M.: "Okay, so we are at the tipping point, that's at least agreed.

504

Does that mean that two or three hundred years from now, when all the northern and southern hemispheric societies have migrated to the equator, our great-grandchildren will all look and act like Mexicans, Moroccans, or porpoises? And if so, what of it?"

Since the beginning of mankind, our societies could be divided into two categories: those who ran at the first sound of danger, and those who waited until they could feel its breath … and the consequences. The lifestyle of those good folks I mentioned before, living well in Connecticut and other such places, who are paying my bills, certainly hear the sound of danger and know something must be done (the state committed to having 20 percent clean energy by 2010 and 100 percent by 2050).[10] Unfortunately, as one old crone pointed out, it is our lifestyle (despite our trash compactors), created by our social and political leadership, or more precisely the lack of it. Instead of running for help, not knowing quite where to run, everybody else will simply shrug and point his or her finger at the wealthy or at least well-off enjoying their excesses, the most destructive of which is pollution from carbon. The leadership of America, from the Congress to the Executive, embodied by dufus number one and his Texas gang, claims, after *thirty years* since the first energy crisis, that America is addicted to petroleum (Exxon claimed the largest corporate profits in the world in 2005), and we must find alternative sources of energy. Duh!

Who knows when it all started? I don't think it was with Cousteau; I suppose Rachel Carlson would get the most votes for her book *Silent Spring* back in '62. But, for me it began in the '80s. That was when our society took a collective decision that it was prepared to sacrifice Rousseau's social provision for individual affluence, and interdependence for personal autonomy, or as one writer[11] put it, to reframe greed and selfishness as "attitude."

Attitude, as in Wordsworth's "getting and spending," epitomized by our gated communities and rolling rockets. Surely, we are not bad people.

505

We have, however, learned to reach for nature by mowing our lush green lawns on Saturday morning, raise fragrant roses, and fondle puppies, with the same unfortunate naive and blasé proportions as burning billions of gallons of gasoline, dispersing untold tons of fertilizers, and feckless euthanizing of abandoned pets. The tension between these impulses characterizes what Roger Rosenblatt once portrayed as strenuously running to keep up with our heady commercial present and our future in cyberspace, while being called back, at the drop of rose petals, to a life that connects us with all life. The trouble, of course, is that nature—usually pretty good in her own right at dislodging those species she doesn't particularly like—exhibits some serious changes in this tug of war.

The supremacy of the human being, on the other hand, no matter how ignorant, perverse, or corrupt he or she may be, somehow supersedes the rights of nature by our inherent "respect for *human* life." That is, God gave us permission. His Bible says we have "dominion over all," thereby letting loose a host of injustices, from the exhaustion of natural resources, to the pain-inflicting confinements and mutilations of animals by the $125-billion-a-year livestock industry. (Of course we Americans are not the only ones: did you happen to catch the bit on CNN showing the Chinese meat market with its great net bags packed tight with terrified cats? Yum.)

———————

Actually, if you think about it, nature really doesn't care. Nature, as Rosenblatt points out, does not seek a relationship with humanity. Difficult as that is for most of us to swallow—being nature's premier egoists—our dear *mother* nature could care less if we lived or died. One might surmise that the natural world exists to test our capacity to care or to preserve us, but even that little fancy, he says, is manmade. Nature, headless and heartless, of course, takes its own path, and we are left to do with it what we will. We are, he said, animals after all, among whom it is accepted that the greater eat the lesser, and all of our ideals of equality and justice are only witness to acts of casual carnage.[12]

Jean-Michel, as I recall, didn't agree, and when pressed would go about quoting Oscar Wilde. So, despite being a fatalist, he was also a Utopian, not a pessimist like me, who saw quite clearly that everything and everybody on this earth was in serious trouble.

Anyone who reads a newspaper, watches TV, or sits in a café and listens to the banality of what people have to say, knows we are headed for one hell of a crash. It is true there has always been violence in the news, no different, one might venture, from the nineteenth century, when the efficiency of killing depended on dry days and bouncing cannonballs. As we all recognize, however, the cannonballs have been improved, and some borrowed by the terrorists. And even nature has been rebelling: 14,802 French dead from the heat wave during the summer of 2003. We are being shaken from our sleep by the uncomfortable shift in our natural range of expectations; the paradox whereby global warming leads to cooling and the kick-starting of another "Little Ice Age."

Unfortunately, like all of our other good intentions, communicated into our living rooms each night by the singular acts of self-sacrifice and heroism of some—for example, the Nobel Peace Prize winner, Wangari Maathai and her trees—our species is rapidly approaching hell, buoyed along by selfish, corrupt, and ignorant governments that, when distracted from their pilfering and squabbling, find it unpopular to say no to their electorates' own rapacious misbehaviors (this is less a reference to the pillaging of natural resources by Third World dictators than to the tax rebates for owners of SUVs in the United States).

It is as if citizens of the Global Village are milling about in the cabin of a gigantic 747—first class, business, and economy—pretending that the plane could never go down. We are all watching the overhead videos, playing seriously with our laptops, snacking, sipping, and snoring, confident of our future, but, epistemologically speaking, going nowhere; while in the cockpit, our politicians, like Moe, Larry, and Curly, are fighting for the pilot's seat, up to their asses in shenanigans, mindless of the gauges.

How nice it would be to awaken from this trip and land in the sweetness of a progressive world. And who doesn't prefer an optimistic future? But, by all indications, ours will not be a soft landing, or a distant one. In the overall scheme of things, that is, since time began until our grandchildren begin to take over, the Last Generation (being the last and therefore capitalized) should probably spiral down and impact in something less than seventy-five years, when the petroleum, drinking water, and air conditioning, among other strategic materials, are gone. We all know the scene, like in apocalyptic movies, in which the Statue of Liberty is buried up to her neck in rubble, ice, or billions of used cars. How do we know this? We don't. But, like the gauges in our cars, it is useful to note when spaceship earth's fuel is low and the engine is overheating.

This was the sort of philosophy espoused by comedian and writer George Carlin, otherwise known as the Prince of Outrage, whose comments describe the way many of us feel about this behavior: we really don't have a stake in this adventure now — the adventure of our species on this planet, since there is no changing the way it is headed, is over, so all we can do is watch it as entertainment, kind of like a hurricane party.[13]

─────────

*It took us 125 years to use the first trillion barrels of oil.
We'll use the next trillion in thirty.*

Chevron Advertisement[14]

And then it's all gone, including the chemical industry, which could be a trifle more painful than carpooling.

Scientists have identified five extinction events in Earth's history, coming as glaciers, meteors, or volcanoes.[15] But the current killer is still the planet's two-legged prime tenant and all his fuel-gulping, air-polluting, habitat-destroying, climate-changing ways. We are earth's "sixth major extinction event." Even Cousteau's last interviews were warnings not to let this happen, and anyone who assigns the attributes of a Chicken Little to such a seasoned intellect and explorer does so at their peril.[16]

Look at Easter Island, he said. Once, it was home to a thriving culture that produced those enormous stone statues that continue to inspire awe. It was also home to dozens of species of trees, which fashioned and protected an ecosystem fertile enough to sustain as many as 35,000 people. Today, it is a pathetic empty outcropping of volcanic rock. So, what happened? Was a rare plant disease the culprit? No. Like Dr. Seuss' Lorax, the Easter Islanders chopped their trees down, one by one, until they were all gone. Conclusion? Those trees were felled by rational actors (well, human beings), people who must have suspected that the destruction of this essential resource would result in the devastation of their civilization. Our lesson, according to Jared Diamond (*Collapse*), is that societies, as often as not, aren't massacred, they commit suicide by slitting their wrists, and then, over the period of many decades, stand by compliantly and watch themselves bleed to death.[17]

Too harsh and depressing? A bit of self-righteous moralizing? Hey, ours is a tradition of superlatives. We always win in the movies. We know how to sacrifice — remember WW II — don't we? I mean, how many of us wouldn't jump into the water to save a whale in peril? When one got lost going up the Thames a while ago, people applauded on the riverbank when the barge carrying the whale made its way back out to sea. Great media event; I think they called him Westminster Whale. Too bad he died. The perversity of it all is that, while the media will cover a trapped whale or a tragic plane crash, it seems incapable of covering the harbingers of a catastrophe that will, quite literally, alter the fundamentals of life on this planet.

Garrison Keillor, as good a guy as guys go, says that when summertime comes we forget about our lofty moral values, such as saving energy, and are forced to take the short view; that is, turn on the air conditioning and burn up precious nonrenewable resources for our own comfort and pleasure, even if it does mean that glaciers shrink and the Arctic tern is threatened. Who would disagree with Garrison? It is a simple need: all we want is some cool air to blow on us as we sip a cool drink. Everyone knows those damn environmentalists are a gloomy bunch, fascinated, he says, by visions of tribulation, armageddon, and the last judgment.[18]

Unfortunately, there is little question that Mr. Keillor speaks for most Americans. We are the 7 percent of the world's population who consume over a quarter of the world's petroleum, and rely heavily on the golden rule: those with the gold, rule.

This rather tired but dreadful news portrayed so eloquently by Cousteau at the Rio Environmental Conference in 1992, which has been played over and over to us since, has brought barely a shrug from a majority of the world's population. Rather, the media feeds us riveting TV images of morbid beheadings and suicide bombings by Muslim fanatics, screaming Palestinians, and radical Jews, with their ever-present parades of coffins and raised fists; Africa fratricides; and fundamentalist Christians spouting political mischief, all addressing mankind's pernicious fascination with itself in the name of God, borders, or money, while overlooking the ecological chaos mounting on the horizon like ominous clouds.

So, Garrison notwithstanding, what should we do?

That challenge could be the speech theme I was looking for—funny how creativity just boils up. We all know that Americans, having that can-do spirit, will have to roll up their sleeves and get to work. We have to be creative, that's for sure: new slogans and logos with some stirring music—some things are a given. It has to be media oriented, since nothing gets done unless it is entertaining. Therefore, I would humbly suggest beginning the recovery of our natural world in the virtual world by human sacrifice, that is sacrificing our entertainment celebrities, specifically young divas, which we have learned from our distant forefathers does wonders for nature. I would like to say our virgin divas, since we all appreciate virgins, but that is an oxymoron. We should create a new TV series (ironically, the "survival" shows are passé) that has themes for programming the sacrifices of these yummy sex objects, which mass media organizations, for example, seem to appreciate (the yummy sex-object part). These special events (with stunning trailers of the superstar divas online promoting various and sundry must-haves) would be named to grab the attention of our society's tastes for sacrifice. Thus, the *Cultural Sacrifice* would take place by throwing some famous blonde sex-bomb off the Eiffel Tower, warbling the Marseillaise while dressed as Charles de Gaulle in drag, to the accompaniment of the now famous Shit Eating Toadstools from Hell band playing noisily at the bottom. Or, the *Save Our Oceans Sacrifice,* dropping some petite blonde sex-bomb in a skimpy mermaid outfit, to the soundtrack from "Jaws," into a shark-filled pool from 10,000 feet up, with laser-guided accuracy, from a stealth bomber (fitted with catalytic converters and neo-conservative bumper stickers proclaiming FREE TIBET). Or, the *Spiritual Sacrifice* by one of the famous ballet troops of the world, throwing some little blonde sex-bomb into a volcano, accompanied by the world's largest organ (the musical instrument) and corps of cheering mullahs in Gucci robes. Or, the more modern,

Sport Utility Vehicle Sacrifice, driving some blonde sex-bomb dressed as a yuppie into a concrete wall at 100 miles an hour in a brand-new pearl-colored, pony-leather-interior, eleven-miles-per-gallon SUV, a tall cup of decaffeinated cinnamon-curd coffee laced with Botox glued to her hand.

Really, the themes, as well as the bare-belly-tattooed, firm-titted, warbling little sex-bomb victims are endless, and certainly stirring for the large majority of the developed countries' young populations seeking relevance (the Third World would have to be left, as usual, to its own devices for moral ascendancy). With the TV ratings going through the roof, and great opportunities in the residuals market, advertising revenues would pay for the remaining 40 percent of the rainforests to be sprayed with epoxy by low-flying C-130s and preserved for the world's—or at least America's (after all, rank has its privileges)—children of the future. Animals, fish, flowers, and rainbows come next.

So. The environment...nah, shit, that won't work.

Nggzzzzzzzzzz ....

Hey! Anybody awake out there? Hello ...?

CHAPTER 5

═══ HUMANS ═══

Antoine de Saint Exupéry once said that there was nothing dramatic in the world, nothing pathetic, except in human relations. So, writing a speech for the president of the oceanographic society to open the festivities honoring Cousteau tomorrow is going to be tough. Tough only because it is hard for me not to be pessimistic, if not somewhat cynical, and nobody, including yours truly, likes a cynic. The institute will, of course, ask our state's senior senator to read the president's speech — my speech — into the *Congressional Record* under the name of our astute leader, so assuming I like and want my job, and I do (I think), discretion reigns.

What's new? We all have issues like that, but certainly nothing for the speech. Our stirring words, written over and over again about our plight and duty, are so pathetic when compared with the nobility of earth's other species, like lions and tigers, polar bears, and butterflies,so many of which we have diminished into virtual extinction, that such appeals can only serve to embarrass.

I had been going through some stuff on my desk that I took off the Internet for ideas. If you're an optimist, here's what one of your guys said: the life of Captain Cousteau reminds us that "we may all rise to our full stature as human beings (what, pray tell, is that?), and stand straight and proud of our humanity (yes, I believe he is from California, but I forget which celestial ministry), and of the legacy we leave to the next generation (which — short of disaster — is?). But we cannot reach this stature by complacency, indifference, or blind obedience to authority or dogma (that is, everybody from republicans to Jesuits beware). We must think for ourselves, and believe as Captain Cousteau did (I really believe he had Captain Nemo in mind, but got confused), that a better future is not only necessary, but possible — if we are willing to work for it."[19] Yes, he really wrote that, probably stuck in traffic on the Santa Monica Freeway. When I spoke with Jean-Michel, his term for it was poppycock, drivel, and pap, of course, to be consumed by those most happily distracted by the good things in life, those accustomed to first-class literally and figuratively, the ones, according to Jean-Michel, who need most to believe that something constructive is being done to avoid Armageddon (ergo their attendance at gala fundraising dinners and cryogenic seminars), since they have so much to lose, including their pampered and droll little lives. These folks don't behave well under stress (many of us saw *Titanic*), and having been tricked by their wealth into believing that money was the answer, are earnestly searching for security through increasing the size of their houses, breasts, and cars, while pretending to be: normal.

In other words, most of us are deceived into thinking the problem is something it isn't. The problem isn't ecological decline — it is less complicated than that — — it is that we are too human to do anything about it. And we all know what that means, since it resides in the very core of human nature: selfishness. Which is not to say that good things aren't being done. Some truly splendid things are being done: Earth Day, wildlife preserves, hybrid cars, hydrogen highways, Boy Scouts and Girl Scouts cleaning up the beaches, and energy-efficient homes, for example, which the media portrays as progress. But there is a balance to be had, which anyone can see, watching the mindless rapacity of our consumption, isn't working — like applying Grandma's trusty hand cream on a full-blown case of melanoma.

We humans do not attack the environment with malice, of course, except those demented or greedy few; however, we would prefer its inevitable decline, flowing like a poisoned river into our future generations, to the inconveniences of sacrificing in the here and now, until it is too late — and as far as the great majority of us are concerned, it's never too late. Unfortunately, the huge advertisement budgets of the American automotive industry (perhaps the biggest sinners in the ecological decline), for example, work energetically to convince us that substantial technical progress is being made. If one looks beyond the hype of speeding convertibles over endless grassy plains, however, the US Department of Transportation reports (as of 2004) *passenger vehicles*[20] have increased efficiency by an astounding 9.5 miles per gallon over twenty-six years (that is, since consumers began caring), and that the average fuel consumption in Europe is 47 percent better than in the United States. That's progress? Goooo Congress. Thanks GM. Nice job, guys. Keep up the good advertising...the public's right there with you.

Separate out the bête noire of the green brigade, the SUVs, and the statistics are actually going in reverse (yes, I heard about the Lexus RX400h, and that's great at 37.2 mpg in town on the battery—if you have $60,000 to spend on an automobile). Like BP says, "It's a start." Okay, but what's taken them so long? The first severe energy crisis was in 1974, brought to us by the same friends as the guys responsible for the destruction of the World Trade Center.

If we leave the aspirations of our society to the action and communication of corporations, destruction of our environment is sure to follow, since capitalism, functioning as a "free" market, meets the "demands" of its public, which as we all know is lacking in the sacrifice department. And as Pogo said so many years ago: "We have met the enemy and he is us."

Thereafter, however, as things begin to get real nasty (9.3 billion people by 2050), we will be left to our religious incantations, begging God's intercession to alleviate our suffering, and bleating our woes to a prostrate and embarrassed planet, for the punishments that we so richly deserve. The weakest will simply roll over and die, while the strong, adept at stepping on others, will hold the keys to the new world's igloos. That's very hard to write about from the motivational point of view. On the other hand, it must be equally tough to be standing on the corner, swept along by the crowd, with a sign that says "The End is Near!" when you know it is.

Soon enough, the question on everyone's mind will switch from political elections, terrorists, wrinkles, weight, and the wives of prominent figures, to exactly when will we wreck the system? Then the questions will be not, "What can we do about it?"...being too late, but rather—like the bunker mentality—"What are the kindest ways to kill our children?"

Concerning the Cousteau speech, pessimism—despite its veracity—as I said, won't sell, since it sounds disagreeable, if not somehow defeatist, over a nice lunch. I could try the Hemingway technique, "by pages left unsaid...," but that makes for a short and somehow empty message. Jean-Michel likes the smarmy stuff: Cousteau breaking seventeen windows at his high school and being expelled, or taking his very first swim, which was in a Vermont lake. Jim was fond of little vignettes like that. "Stick with the stuff of giggles and family," he would say, "nothing serious." But there's not enough meat on those bones to draw any clear conclusions concerning the proposition on the total destruction of civilization as we know it. My position is that the critical mass of intelligent people is far too small to control the growth of social ignorance and technical bliss; therefore, such points are generally avoided in polite conversation, since references to the end of humanity usually leave a bad impression.

Let's see: you could try to hit the audience from the blind side, like, sport diving might never have existed had a certain set of headlights not failed one night in 1935, causing a French naval midshipman to crash his father's sports car into a hairpin mountain bend. That would get their attention, or at least those heavily invested in sports marts, but most would conclude that the presentation was about Pirelli Tires and safety on slippery roads, while drifting off to thoughts about lunch and a nap.

I was getting desperate; I needed an angle. An acquaintance at the bar had suggested the beginning of diving might be segued into Cousteau and oceanography, which, though a tad trite, had an interesting angle for the speech, since there was good human interest in it. The suggestion had something, of course, since it was supposedly what I was paid to write about. The story goes that after Cousteau graduated from the French Naval Academy at Brest in Brittany, and was well on his way to becoming a naval pilot, his main interests, like most young cadets', were planes, cars, and girls. An invitation to a friend's wedding in the Vosges mountains was a good excuse to borrow his father's Salmson sports car. The peppy car made fun of the hairpin bends, and Cousteau made good time despite the darkness—until his headlights reportedly failed. He slammed on the brakes but it was too late; the car flew off the edge of the mountain. Years later, Cousteau recalled the crash: "It was about two in the morning and as I lay in the wreckage, I thought I was going to die. I was losing blood and there were twelve bones broken in my body." Both arms were broken, his left arm in five places, and he was paralyzed on one side. The surgeons wanted to amputate the arm at once, but Cousteau refused. Nonetheless, his dream of being a navy pilot was over. On his recovery, he was reassigned as a lieutenant at the Toulon naval base, where he was assigned to gunnery. He found himself working with another lieutenant, Philippe Tailliez, who suggested that Cousteau's right arm, still slightly twisted, would benefit from plenty of swimming. The two swam every day and soon found that another man was swimming from the same beach — Frederic Dumas. "Didi" Dumas swam to spear fish, and he soon taught Tailliez and Cousteau to do the same. Cousteau was twenty-six when he took his first look underwater, under the guidance of Didi, off the beach at Le Mourillon, now a suburb of Toulon. His life, he said, was changed forever.[21]

Great story, but not one to tell an audience, most of whom have never used scuba[22] gear. And more important, the audience will be getting hot and hungry, so the speech shouldn't be long, or upsetting, or folks will be heading for the exits.

I could try sensationalizing things a bit, by going the media route. After all, sex sells. Perhaps I could focus on Cousteau's personal life, pick up on the adulterous affair with the Air France flight attendant, for example, and his two illegitimate children by her while having fathered two sons by his wife, Simone, who found out about his double life three days before she died. But, according to relatives, Cousteau's quest for fame was his fatal flaw. He was, they said, a producer and filmmaker, not a scientist, so above all, perhaps, he was a great PR man: the Calypso, red knit caps, cute sea lions (two of which died in captivity), and all great entertainment, most likely containing fake undersea footage of shark attacks and the like. Or maybe even throw in a Cousteau contemporary such as Charles Lindbergh. Hm. Both the Europeans and Americans would like that, since it was still fresh in the newspapers. Could test one's tolerance for moral turpitude, however. Lindbergh was no doubt a titan in many ways, but the Associated Press[23] and German news magazine *Focus* had recently reported[24] that, during the same years of Cousteau's fame, Lindbergh was involved with a Ms Brigitte Hesshaimer, a Munich hat maker, by whom he had three illegitimate children;

but he supposedly also had affairs with her older sister, Marietta, and his personal secretary, Valeska, that produced two children each. He used a post office box in Connecticut to get letters from Hesshaimer, and wrote to her at her home in Germany, signing only with his first initial.

This strategy would be problematic, though, since focusing on two national heroes, one French and one American, both sticklers for family values, but each having fathered illegitimate children — and in Lindbergh's case with two German sisters and a secretary out of wedlock — could incense tomorrow's audience to grumbling and untoward gestures of discontent.

The fact that both famous men led secret lives of restless travel and lengthy absences from their wives was not unusual. Nor was the fact that both men, our enduring symbols of adventure and courage, were entwined by the Nazi regime. Cousteau's beloved brother was a journalist and Nazi collaborator, while Lindbergh served as a pre-war Nazi fan. This is simply to say that almost anything for anybody was possible. But then again, this was not the theme by which our institute's president could expect freshly minted invitations from a conservative White House.

I was dry. Maybe not writer's block, more like writer's contempt for my present state of affairs, but definitely things were not going according to plan — a plan being constructed mostly from my superbly crafted procrastination and ambivalence. I had only myself to blame. The speech should have been done by now; Jean-Michel and his lady friend were due an hour ago, yet the sun was setting on Bahia de la Choncha, and I was snuggled into a soft couch at the Hotel Londres bar, staring alternately at the screen of my laptop, still without a first line for tomorrow, and the fading light with a head emptier than a chips bowl.

CHAPTER 6

═══ A TICKET TO PARIS ═══

It had all started out so promising. About three years ago, after my Caribbean adventure, followed by the requisite clinic visit, I migrated back to France, assuming the pretensions of the proverbial American in Paris, doing research on yet another golden, but acclaimed, book to be. I enjoyed making like the idolized expat (to my chagrined, but pliable and financially solicitous aunt), sauntering along the boulevards, lounging at cafes while listening to Brazil 66 on expensive earphones, and ostentatiously reading *Le Monde* in front of admiring tourists. If they seemed ignorant of my presence at the café, I would call out to supposed friends in English and snarl at the waiters in French, then bask in the patrons' stares and whispers. Usually, some timid souls would visit my table to test my nationality, then ask naive questions about the French, which I answered by way of great insight.

I had tried to make contact with Jean-Michel at that time, and we even met twice briefly, but he was in rehabilitation and made no effort to renew our old friendship. I felt then, not without some experience, that, like an animal facing death, he sought to be alone and would eventually crawl off under the boughs of some private place to experience the final act of life. So, I was surprised to receive his call for a rendezvous in San Sebastian.

It happened like this: Less than a year ago I left my so-called home in Paris to take an assignment in Mystic, Connecticut, as a technical correspondent on an environmental research project at the local oceanographic institute. It paid well, but turned out to be acutely boring; however, a recent phone call to my answering machine in SoNo, South Norwalk, was an unexpected gift from heaven. It was the institute's staff director, offering to send me to Spain, all expenses paid, if I would put together a speech for the institute's president on the anniversary of Jacque Cousteau's death in San Sebastian. It seems the original writer, a consultant, had lost his thumb in a sailing accident, thereby crimping his style at cocktail parties with the membership.

The staff director was a good-Joe, semi-retired, and a competent sailor, who interceded at opportune times, like a kindly uncle, for my better interests. He knew that, as an American expatriate living abroad, I had a special insight ("You can fool all of the people some of the time") into Cousteau's work, a man who had given so much to both sides of the Atlantic and who had treasured his American experience. In short, would I like the assignment?

Did I want to go? he asked. Oh boy, did I! I wanted to jump up and thrust a punch in the air. How could I not? What could go wrong? Cousteau, about whom I knew little, was a man who was regularly voted France's most loved figure in opinion polls, and whose goal in life seemed to be that of teaching the world to save itself. JFK had presented him with the National Geographic Society's Gold Medal on his seventy-fifth birthday, and he was presented with America's highest civilian honor, the Medal of Freedom, by President Reagan. Naturally, I waited almost two hours before returning the call, so I could not be accused of appearing too anxious; plus, I dithered around, negotiating over business versus tourist class on Air France in order to certify my professional credentials.

Timing was everything, since in a week I had to be at the Reveil Matin, in the Paris suburb of Montgeron, not later than the evening of July 4, one or two days before the environmental conference in San Sebastian, in order to attend the beginning of the Tour de France. All of which is to say, I would have done the whole San Sebastian thing for a tourist-class round-trip ticket to Paris from JFK. How shameless we all are when, like prostitutes, we sell ourselves for so much when we amount to so little. Yeah, right, spread 'em, baby. Who else in America was going to see the Tour de France?! All for free! Unfortunately, like so many things in life, the devil himself seemed to creep into the details.

The confusing aspect in all of this was that my aforementioned girlfriend, Carole, had been determined, as I said, to go to San Fermin in Pamplona to see the bulls run and, considering my resemblance to the famous author, get into the Hemingway spirit. Her take on that scene, among other diversions, being heavy drinking, carousing, and me winning a Hemingway look-alike contest, included the chance of her friends in New York seeing our photograph in one of the great international newspapers, which would be, as she averred, thrilling.

I, on the other hand, had been determined to fly to Paris to check on my apartment and its renters, see the beginning of the Tour de France, then go to San Sebastian for the institute function. My employers were determined and confident of having me in San Sebastian, stroking our membership's egos, while writing a uniquely creative speech that would guarantee their president yet another year in office and at least a few prestigious invitations. The icing on the cake, so to speak, turned out to be my ill-timed if not misguided phone call to my old college friend, Jean-Michel, suggesting that we get together in Paris, an invitation he graciously declined, but, seeing the coincidence, eagerly suggested meeting in San Sebastian, where his new lady friend, a Charlene somebody or other, was leading a group of students from a small college in Switzerland on an academic travel.

The Chinese have that saying we are all taught to appreciate: "May you live in interesting times." So be it. My bags were packed and I was on my way.

CHAPTER 7

═══ CHARLENE ═══

I had not seen Jean-Michel in over a year, but he actually looked great when they arrived at the bar. Why? Among other incidentals like weight, fashion, and complexion, he had a genuine fox on his arm, although her heart supposedly wasn't in it. In short, he looked like money.

There were times in the past that Jean-Michel could have passed for Bibendum — the Michelin Man, as most Americans know him — replete with curly red hair and a bushy mustache to match the all-purpose tires he carried on his midriff. Surprisingly, he had slimmed down somewhat, and the blush on his face had migrated primarily from crimson nose to pink cheeks, giving him a more honest look. He had taken on what appeared to be the accoutrements of a dandy: traded in his ties for bow ties, tattered broadcloths for colorful new shirts, a green silk suit handmade in Asia, no doubt, and small, oblong, rather stylish tortoise-shell glasses straddling his nose. I suspected a sham, and I expected to see him in espadrilles, but he wore leather loafers with tassels. I was even tempted to believe that somewhere in the foyer he had inconspicuously hung a purple fedora.

They had come into the bar through the glass door behind me. He had approached stealthily and asked in perfect Castilian Spanish — deferentially, as if one of the waiters — would I like another drink? My first reaction, without looking up, was no, since my past career at inebriate behavior had now relegated me these last years to drinking diet cokes. (I had learned, where Jean-Michel had not, the wisdom of repugnance.) The bartender in the Brassiere, being a friend, served them as though they were modeled on the Big Swig, but when Jean-Michel touched my shoulder and the hugs were finished and the laughing began, I signed on for another half liter stuffed with limes. My mood had changed for the better; I was now in the company of a very pretty woman for entertainment, and an intelligent friend who could help lift me out of my speech dilemma.

I felt Charlene, or Charly as he called her, immediately sizing me up, then scanning the bar. I don't think women do that unless they have a good reason. Hers was protective, I suppose; that is, was I Jim's genuine friend? Or suspicion: what did I have in mind for her? I don't mind saying that, despite my years and predilections for fine dinners versus sex, I envisioned her clothes off in seconds, constructing erotic fantasies as I went, while she surveyed her surroundings. She wore heavy eye makeup and obviously wasn't into gardening. Jean-Michel caught on and leaned over. "I told her about you," he murmured.

"So?"

"So it seems you have all the appeal of wet pajamas."

This could have otherwise been painful, except, and not incidentally, Ms Charlene Brooks was a woman I had bedded, as I recall, during a rather tedious night at a book faire in Boston not more than a year or so earlier. Her hair was longer and styled differently then, plus lighter makeup, but it was her, all right. Such things don't frequently happen, akin to coincidences like the existence of an ice dealer named I.C. Shivers, but we have all chanced upon acquaintances in faraway places.

"Wet pajamas" indeed. No doubt she was checking out the lounge, to see which exit was the closest.

This was going to be fun, or hell, for somebody. The ball was in her court; I would just sit back and see what the evening would bring. One thing sure, this was not going to be some tetchy little sales rep gushing over a modestly successful textbook author (yes, I had one modest triumph). Back then she stood out in the crowd: raven-haired and green-eyed, like a skittish colleen in Gucci spectacles and plaid, trying to look educated; one of those rare occasions when a fellow actually finds an intelligent lay worth taking to dinner and keeping until breakfast. We had gone to my room where, sans panties, she had ridden me across the bed like a bouncing cowboy, driving me forward into a juicy crescendo that exploded into a frantic embrace such as I hadn't enjoyed since a high school tryst with an eager cheerleader howling for more.

Yet here we were, less than two years later, making comfortable on the blue velvet couches facing the panoramic windows overlooking Concha Bay, and exchanging the usual banter that new acquaintances often do—while pretending to be strangers. Eventually, the conversation turned to dinner, then good restaurants of the Basque country, of which there were none.

The Basque, whose taste buds were excited by rice cooked in squid ink, a plate of plain peppers, lamb cheeks, and various internal organs, had the worst kitchen in Europe, by my estimation, and therefore, the population resorted in desperation to decorative hors d'oeuvres that relied heavily on eggs, fish, and mayonnaise, called pintxos in Basque. Jean-Michel paid deference to the Basque for their famous sour cider, which he nevertheless disliked, and a peculiar-tasting dessert made of goat curd, similar to seventeen-day-old milk in the fridge, which would have kept all dessert-loving Americans skinny as rails. Gratefully, with nary a word mentioned about McDonald's, we continued on to the weather, where I was from—which caused Charlene's sultry gaze to lock momentarily on mine, giving me a very stirring sexual twinge—and finally the usual blather about French discrimination against Americans in Paris, orchestrated by Ms. Brooks herself.

It annoyed me, but of course it was true; it was Paris, for Christ's sake. I had been explaining the Michelin tradition and Derek Brown, its director, to Charlene, when Jean-Michel, with a sigh, decided to order another drink and rather than wait for the waiter, excused himself to the bar.

"How come the final arbiter of good food in France is an Englishman?" Charlene wondered innocently, as he left. I gave Derek Brown's standard answer to the question, something along the lines that you don't have to be German to appreciate Beethoven.[25] Then I played my cards, "nor an American to appreciate a memorable acquaintance. Haven't we met less formally somewhere before? I believe you left before I got your card."

She took a sip of her daiquiri and then held her glass in front of delectable red lips, which had left their print on her glass. She raised one eyebrow skeptically and smiled slightly, "I'm not sure, it was dark." I remembered that look. Christ, she simply oozed sex and smelled of Fendi. A small wisp of black hair rested carelessly over smoldering green eyes. She brushed it back, looked around, then a seductive glance at me, which seized every synapse.

"Perhaps it was someone else," I suggested.

"Perhaps," she smiled again and leaned forward to put her drink on the coffee table, revealing a curvaceous cleft sprinkled with freckles, bordered by the loose neckline of a white silk blouse. My eyes locked on. She knew it; women always know it, they have every move perfected. She wore a beautifully engraved gold locket that beckoned from the crevice between her breasts. It would be the second thing I demanded to see after disrobing her and making love once again to that black-haired pudendum, moist and fragrant.

"You're a long way from home," I said.

"Really? I heard you could swim out a few hundred yards and just turn left," she said, and gave a fleeting look at my left hand, useless in any water.

"Might take you a while, and probably end up in Cuba," I said. "Are you coming or going?"

"I don't mean to be evasive, but neither."

"So, you like it here?"

"It's okay, you know. No breakfasts."

"Just scramble some eggs."

"I'm talking about America. You can get eggs in Egypt." She assumed a deep southern accent: "Hi, honey, want some fresh juice and coffee … how 'bout some grits with your eggs … links or patties … a side of pancakes?" Then smiled. "It's all about the culture, not the eggs."

She was good. "True. So what are you doing here?"

"Earning a paycheck. At the moment I'm a tour guide for a bunch of kids at an American college in Lugano."

"Sounds like fun."

"Sort of like herding cats."

"So, you've joined academia?"

"Beats a nail technician in Nogales."

I felt like I was trading one-liners with Jay. "How's your Spanish?"

She shrugged. "Border-town Chicana." She seemed determined to wait until Jim returned.

"Jean-Michel?" I inquired.

"Your old friend?"

"Um-hm. Just wondering how long you and he have known each other."

She smiled at me and then looked toward the bar. "He's an intelligent man."

"When he isn't drinking."

"You don't like him?"

"Of course I do, he's a congenial fellow and wears his erudition lightly. On the other hand, I don't think you two go together."

"Listen, uh, Tinsel, he's a friend of mine. I respect friendship."

"It lacks a certain permanence, don't you think?"

"Friendship?"

"Friendship. You could say I've known you longer than he has, and I would guess as intimately."

She avoided the gambit. "Why does Jean-Michel call you Tinsel?"

"My parents made it up, because I always loved Americans' Christmas. I was born in the Caribbean—you know, voodoo and santeria—but we moved to Miami and then Newark when I went to college. Christmas was exciting with its snow, and music, which I played year-round, and, of course, fir trees covered with tinsel and lights, so my parents' first choice was obvious: Jabreen."

She giggled. "So, you like Christmas traditions?"

"We didn't have traditions. Large families of color have blurs."

She giggled again, a good sign. "Are your Christmas decorations still up?"

"Decorations?"

"Yeah—you know, pine-scented candles and reindeer on the mantel."

"Not exactly. I only listen to the music. Been pretty busy. Newspapers to be read, mail to be opened, pizzas to be ordered, naps to be taken...it's all pretty hectic, as you can see. I long for the laid-back days of the Caribbean."

"Yeah, I know what you mean, it's like white after Labor Day. Where in the Carib*bean*?"

"You makin' fun of my accent?"

"No, I like it. I like the French way you pronounce my name."

"Char*lene*? We all talk like that in Martinque. The Caribbean is the Caribbean, *mahn*, we're just simple island people. Have you been to the islands?"

"Once. St. Maartin. I wouldn't label the locals as 'simple.'"

"Just an expression. Lecherous waiters and attendants hitting on white men's girlfriends is more like it. Taxi drivers with leopard-skin dashboards, driving like fiends and overcharging. I don't miss it much. I'm an American," I said. "See, Tinsel," and demonstrated its dangling character with the fingers of my right hand. "Tinsel Adams."

"Jean-Michel told me you're an author."

"I write, but can't make a living at it. Just a textbook, as you may remember, and some articles. Probably the same ratio of out-of-work actors to movie stars. My byline is Tinseladams. Most people can't pronounce it, and end up with something like Tinsela Dams. They think I'm a Dutch journalist. For the most part I'm a professor of English literature, when there's a job to be had. I did some research in the Caribbean. Do you like it here?"

"In Europe? Not really." She seemed sad, and the conversation was becoming strained. She couldn't make up her mind whether to take up my gambit and talk about old times or not. Men enjoy talking about sex as a prelude to sex; women talk about sex as a prelude to relationship. "Sort of like the movie about getting lost in translation. I'm in between—you're an American, so you know: one foot on the dock and one in the boat. I'm making a living, and have friends, but I'm bored, miss the States, and my, uh," she hesitated, "family."

"Um-hm." I let it drop—not smart to delve too quickly.

"Where do you live?" she asked.

"Like I said, it all started with a poor boy in the Caribbean selling mangoes to tourists. Now, it depends. Didn't we talk about this, you know, before?"

She shrugged again, "It was dark, remember? I meant now."

"Yeah," I said. She was, I hoped, getting high. "Well, I'm on a job now, but I live in Lauderdale mostly, in a comfortable old motel run by a family of immigrant Poles.

She was about to reply when Jean-Michel returned. "I brought you a Jean Martell. Sorry, no Armagnac."

"Kind of you, but remember, I'm on colas."

"I guess I could sip it," Charlene said, reaching for it. "Tinsel looks like Hemingway, don't you think, Jean-Michel?"

He shook his head. "If he just had a turtleneck, he'd look like a bald turtle with whiskers and a noteworthy tan."

His face was becoming flushed. He looked hot and sweaty, and, judging from his determined attack on the hors d'oeuvres, seemed in no mood to stop his grazing. I didn't want to lose him just yet. It was time to move to the real purpose of the evening. "I'm writing a speech for our oceanographic institute and would appreciate some ideas — you know, global warming, rising seas, and all that, they're crucial issues," I said pedantically.

I could see they had no interest. Charlene started in, "Isn't it a little late? Maybe we could go outside for a bit to get some fresh air and then give it a go."

I agreed and we left the bar and wandered outside to the beach walk. It was getting late, the air was humid, and the stars covered the heavens. Suddenly, in the south, a large meteorite entered the atmosphere. "Look," I said excitedly, "there's a shooting star." But they had both missed it.

"What did you wish for?" Charlene asked coquettishly.

"I thought it's bad luck to tell," I purred.

"Considering you," Jean-Michel said, putting his arm over my shoulder, "it's in bad taste."

We walked, wandering around, then stopped at a café, took a table, and ordered espressos all around. Jean-Michel decided to add some Irish Whisky to his, and rocked benignly in his chair. He assumed that shit-eating grin that didn't take an AA member long to see the evening was over. Provocation usually came next, but I was out of there in any event, since my goals had changed. I was determined to set Jean-Michel up with a bottle and then head off with Charlene for my room at the hotel, just like the old days, or in Charlene's case, to be more precise, day. It was easy; he loved Cracklin' Rosie more than women. And women don't like that. Certainly, Charlene was all that I remembered: cocky, sexy, and having left me without a return engagement. I wanted a revenge fuck, which are some of the most satisfying, except for the inevitable abrasions.

The next morning I surfed the Net until I found an appropriate item for the speech, downloaded it, cleaned it up, and had the printed document delivered to the president's hotel room. The speech took approximately the same time as Lincoln's Gettysburg Address, so I met the basic requirements for a good oration. I'm sure he would have liked something more, but hey, he wasn't Lincoln. I was bored with the institute anyway, and figured they would have dropped me sooner or later. I decided that the vacant faculty position Jean-Michel mentioned for a guest professor's job in the University of Innsbruck's literature department this October was worth a shot. I had found Charlene in the Brasserie bar, sipping orange juice and nibbling on a brioche, intently reading a handwritten letter.

"Family?" I asked. "You don't see many of those anymore."

"Nope," she said without looking up, then folded the letter and put it in a book lying on the table.

"Where's Jim?"

"Taking a nap." She looked up and smiled. "Would you watch my stuff while I go to the ladies' room?"

Moments later she returned, sat down, and looked around for the waiter. "Want another juice?"

"Not really. Charlene, don't know whether I mentioned this, but I'm looking to take a job teaching English literature at the University of Innsbruck in October."

She scrutinized my face. "Yeah, I heard Jean-Michel talk about it."

"Beautiful place, Innsbruck." I said urging her on.

She nodded her head. "So I've heard."

"Would you like to see it?"

CHAPTER 8

═══ OFF TO THE RIVIERA ═══

Surprisingly, Charlene was interested, so I decided to ask her along. If the Innsbruck job materialized, I'd need a warm companion with some work credentials, and if it didn't, her income was better than none, and I could work on my manuscript. Actually, I didn't think she would leave Jean-Michel, but alcoholics were rarely fun, and of her prejudices, those I could pick up — gays, Jews, and gelded horses — she never mentioned persons of color. She was distant, this is true, but focused, and said she could put the students on the plane right on schedule, as it happened, and e-mail the school that she wasn't coming back. And Jean-Michel? Well, that's life in the big city. If he wanted to drink, that was his choice. Neither she nor I saw any future in their relationship and decided to leave him to the elements.

We talked about life, Europe, and home, while making plans to leave for the French Riviera in the morning. In those moments we became a couple, bonding, like duplicitous thieves, planning the heist of a friend's trust: leaning close, inhaling each other's pheromones with titillation and, if I do say so, damn little remorse. Jean-Michel was upstairs sleeping it off once again — too bad that losers always seem to lose.

The take-home was, there would be hell to pay when he awoke.

═══

Eventually, Jean-Michel showed up at the bar. The three of us, like the previous evening, were once again in the Brassiere, seated on our velour couches, only this time sipping cappuccinos among hotel guests — those bland souls whose penance it was in life to listen to other people's business — which added a stilted if not surrealistic affect to our conversation. Mostly, I am unguarded in this respect, but some things are best shared in private if possible. After the usual small talk, including why yours truly wasn't at that very moment attending the Cousteau conference (I explained I'd had the speech placed under the door of the president's room earlier in the morning, with a short note advising him of my resignation), I mentioned that we, that is Charlene and I, were going to head south toward the Côte d'Azur the next day. Other than a sporadic twitch in his left eye, Jim seemed to betray no emotion and asked where "we" were going. Nice to be considered a couple; that certainly broke the ice.

He was angry and instantly bitter. You could smell it, like an aggressive dog that gets the scent of adrenaline and sweat from an intruder, then, lowering its head, snarls and bares its teeth. But I knew he wouldn't say so. It seems people will own up to the deadliest of sins, reveal disquieting medical conditions, and prattle on about their sex lives, but they will never, ever, confess to being bitter.[26] That, of course, was good. Nonetheless, it had always puzzled me why people found bitterness so repugnant. After my battles in academia, which were almost exclusively lost, there were frequent reasons to be bitter. Originally, it had felt good to rage, which predictably frightened friends and lovers, so I spent some time attending workshops and learned to carefully craft steps for letting go of the desire for revenge. The theory was obvious. I readily accepted the conclusion that bitterness was not a good idea and that career-wise, if you were bitter, you were finished, ergo I didn't subscribe to the behavior and wondered why anyone else would. At this moment Jean-Michel was doing well to control his. On the other hand, he was speechless for one of the few times in his life.

So, the situation was tense. I was cool, Charlene stolid, looking out the window at the passersby and beach. The situation, being somewhat unique, left me searching for the tone of voice and selection of words that could best be used to address a jilted lover and soothe the trauma. I envisioned my lines: "Well, Jim, Charlene and I thought we would do the Condé Nast thing and trip the light fandango along the French Riviera." (Here I would fondly look over at Charlene.) "Then I plan on fucking the little missus, here, silly (patting her paternally on the thigh), and blowing what money we have left on tasty French cuisine at snug coastal restaurants overlooking the sea. Finally, we'll be settling into a modest pension outside Cannes until accepting the Innsbruck job you told me about and I applied for this morning. (I would lean back into the couch, cross my legs, and, with an earnest look, ask the big question.) And what will be your plans, Jim — you know, after you have a go at the suicide thing?'

I offered words to that effect, whereupon Jean-Michel, sitting forward on the couch, looked down at his fingernails and simply wagged his head. Finally, he glanced over at Charly disdainfully, then across to me, gathered himself up and, standing, smiled down at both of us, all curly red hair and green suit. His mouth turned into a memorable rictus of disgust and his eyes grew dark. "Next year on Nebo," he said, looking severely at me, began to hum his favorite tribute to Nancy Dawson,[27] and, turning away, offered a loud fart while proceeding out the door. That was the last time I would see him, or at least I thought so.

───────

It was definitely time for a walk, so Charlene and I left the bar to buy the train tickets for the morning, with hopes that Jean-Michel would not be lurking about. Charlene, uneasy, reviewed the possibilities of him coming after us with a gun as his final salute to our connivery, but I wasn't worried: every time Jean-Michel had a crisis he routinely took a few drinks to boost his courage and then, incapable of starting on his quest, would have a few more and collapse onto the bar or any other flat surface in sight.

"Suppose he's waiting for us? I don't want to be shot," she said.

"He's French. The French shoot the way they drive: you hit some, you miss some."

"How can you be so blasé about it?"

"It's funny in a way. After so many years, you know someone. Trust me."

"Next year on Nebo?' What's that supposed to mean?" she asked.

"Mount Nebo. Where Moses was shown the promised land."

"Egypt?"

"Jordan. Where he's buried, according to legend. It was an inside joke between us back in graduate school."

"Are you going to meet him there?"

Interesting question. We had agreed that if either of us died, the other would take the urn to Mount Nebo on Pentecost Sunday and let fly the ashes. Being an eternal optimist, I assumed that we had plenty of time to kill before I would ever have to decide. Besides, I was focused on leasing a comfortable little apartment at Juan Les Pins on the Côte d'Azur, since both Charlene and I — well, one of us — needed some sun; then, if all went well, on to the University of Innsbruck guest professorship.

And Carole, you may ask? Another good question. Maybe I would put her in touch with Jean-Michel. He was a tit man at heart, and she had a weakness for Jimmie's Specials.[28]

We checked out of the hotel the following morning, no Jean-Michel in sight, no threatening notes or unsettling calls, and took a taxi to the station. I picked up a newspaper at the magazine stand while Charlene bought some snacks, bottled water, and reading material.

We boarded the train and located our cabin. The journalists at the conference must have liked the speech, because they printed it in the *Tribune* along with all the other gala stuff. Charlene found the article and read it as we chugged our way toward the French border and down to the Riviera, me with a pocketful of cash, my severance pay still to come, and a genuine fox of Hellenic proportions. Then she came to the text of the speech, which, being short, was included in the article. It read like this:

Honored guests,

Jacques Cousteau was from the sea. He made his living from it as an award-winning filmmaker, sailor explorer, inventor, ardent environmentalist, astute businessman, and best-selling author. We all knew him by his red cap, pipe, and gaunt silhouette, and if de Gaulle was considered by many to be France's last great Frenchman, Cousteau was arguably its most popular. For legions of scuba divers — and an army of armchair explorers — Cousteau literally took us beneath the waves and opened our eyes to the world below our oceans.

But Jacques Cousteau also knew something else, which he spoke of just before he died. It was a warning, a danger that our forefathers saw coming three centuries ago and I encourage you to consider today. First, I offer you a quote from Charles Lamb in the eighteenth century:[29]

"Can we ring the bells backward? Can we unlearn the arts that pretend to civilize, and then burn the world? There is a march of science; but who shall beat the drums for its retreat?"

Indeed, who shall? Lamb's warning and our own Jacques Cousteau's metaphor using Easter Island as Planet Earth is one we cannot ignore. Imagine our Captain Planet, seeing the ecological and technological storm approaching on the horizon, urgently ringing the bell on deck to arouse us, the crew, to action.

This morning as I stand before you, the most profound danger to world peace in the coming years will stem not from the irrational acts of states or individuals, but from the legitimate demands of the world's dispossessed. Of these poor and disenfranchised people, the majority live a marginal existence in equatorial climates. Global warming, not of their making but originating with the wealthy few, will affect their fragile ecologies most. Their situation will be desperate and manifestly unjust.

It cannot be expected, therefore, that in all cases they will be satisfied to await the beneficence of the rich. If then we allow the devastating power of modern weaponry to spread through this combustible human landscape, we invite a conflagration that can engulf both rich and poor. The only hope for the future lies in cooperative global action, legitimized by democracy. It is time to turn our backs on the unilateral quest for security, in which we seek to shelter behind our walls. Instead, we must persist in the search for united action to counter both global warming and a weaponized world. These twin goals will form vital components of stability as we move toward the wider degree of social justice — and spoken of by the first environmentalist, Jean-Jacques Rousseau — that alone gives hope for peace.

Some of the needed legal agreements are already at hand, such as the Convention on Climate Change, the Kyoto Accords, Strategic Arms Reduction Treaties, and the Comprehensive Test Ban Treaty. As concerned citizens, we should urge all governments

to attain these goals that constitute steps on the way to replacement of war and waste by law. To survive in the world we have
transformed, we must learn to think in a new way, seeking a new
Utopia. As never before, the future of each depends on the good
of all. I would like to leave you with a recent quote from a high
official at the United Nations on the state of our oceans.

So-called dead zones, oxygen-starved areas of the world's oceans
that are devoid of fish, top the list of emerging environmental
challenges, the *United Nations Environmental Program* warned
in its global overview (2004). The spreading zones have doubled
over the last decade and pose as big a threat to fish stocks as over-
fishing. 'Human kind is engaged in a gigantic, global experiment
as a result of inefficient and often overuse of fertilizers, the dis-
charge of untreated sewage, and the ever-rising emissions from
vehicles and factories. Unless *urgent action* is taken to tackle the
sources of the problem, it is likely to escalate rapidly.'"

Klaus Toepfer, United Nations Environmental Program [30]

As you can see before me, ladies and gentlemen, there is a table
where we solicit your signatures to be presented at the United
Nations to the leaders of all the countries of the world. Now, if
you would all come forward....

Charlene thought it was brilliant, of course, and, judging from the tone of
the newspaper article, so did the institute's president, who was probably
looking for me at this very moment to shake my hand and say goodbye, as
he must have been doing with all the dignitaries in the crowd who were lining up to sign their names. Truth be told, they were happy with the results
and thankful for having avoided a prolonged speech in the sun. A three-
minute oration and hundreds of people—well, at least eighty—signing
their names fulfilled my obligations to the letter, so she and he were both
correct. It was brilliant in its way, since I was relieved of doing anything
intellectual or inspired. It was simply resourceful. I even had time to have
breakfast, read a little Baudelaire, watch the demonstrators, and dash off an

application letter to the University of Innsbruck instead of fretting about how well the speech might be received. No one could really criticize the speech, since most of it had been created by the Nobel Peace Prize Centennial Symposium in Oslo, Norway, on December 7, 2001.[31] I had simply downloaded their superb statement and reworked their ideas a bit. I doubted anyone would know that, certainly not the president, who limited his education to immersing himself in the society pages and yacht ads in his local newspaper. But no one can argue that it didn't bear repeating over and over again; no one can doubt that. I just helped to spread the word, while our association's president took the glory. Probably wouldn't be found out in any case, since people are mostly busy with the fashion section, stock market, and soccer scores, and even if it came to light that the president was a plagiarist, he would simply blame me, his speechwriter, who subsequently had quit or—as I am sure they would swear—was fired.

I'll also admit that it was Cousteau's "Bill of Rights for Future Generations," signed by millions of people throughout the world, that inspired me. The First Article of this document stated, "Future generations have a right to an uncontaminated and undamaged Earth and to its enjoyment as the ground of human history, of culture, and of the social bonds that make each generation and individual a member of one human family." So, signing things sometimes helped people commit themselves.

Unfortunately, a nasty little bias has crept in with the growth of our society, which promotes rights but ignores our obligations—you know, rights *and* obligations. Though it is true that our streets, water, and air are sometimes cleaner, there has been pathetically little effort to create a sound "thou shalt and *shalt not*" for our ecological future. We will eventually pay heavily for that little omission.

CHAPTER 9

══ KUFSTEIN ══

18 Fischer Gries Strasse
Kufstein, Austria.
October 20, Notes to myself…

Last winter, summer was very far away. Now, autumn has returned — melancholy, cold, and damp, still with little to do. Nothing is romantic about this mixture of nature's olive drab, dripping. Rain dribbles down my window. Below, leafy trees along the riverbanks obscure the muddy flow, and then a train whistles, passing over the River Inn, north to Munich or south toward the Brenner Pass, Bolzano, and Italy. My small collection of Christmas CDs, usually the best antidote for the blahs of any season, is only a brief respite from this migraine of homesickness. Even a good dose of Fleetwood Mac has gone stale. This is not Tinsel's town. Charlene left last February, on Valentine's Day, ironically. Some blather and tears about romance and a lack of compassion for her nipple-less breast.

Alone is no place to be.

Just go, the inner voice demands, just buckle-up and head out of here, homeward bound for the sunny streets of Miami with my own culture and kin. But when the bravado's over, my longing to leave is all that's left. It is impossible, of course, things being what they are: money has become a serious issue, and those snug rustic apartments above the garages of Coconut Grove are at a premium, even for gays.

My semesters at Innsbruck came and went, and through those dull, wet months, my chums from the university, seated about heavy wooden tables bracing dimly lit corners of Kufstein's Goldener Löwe[32] sought, along with dear Rosie, our waitress, to bolster my flagging spirits. They

536

offered—between modest sips of lager chased by countless drags on cigarettes—that the charm-less fate of America seems pretty much like what
I knew; that which the poet W. H. Auden once described as the state of
most poets' output: good ideas, badly executed.

We Americans, they say, are wealthy, work-obsessed, one-dimensional
people gobbling down small hurried pleasures in cholesterol-laden chunks,
while contemplating the ambivalent Dow or another war of liberation. They
compare the charm of Europe's great cities with our own banal testaments
of urban sprawl. Without the perspicacity of knowing, they suggest that
charm, as Camus observed in *The Fall,* can offer us a way of getting the
answer "yes" without having asked any obvious question.[33] I truly like that
from Camus. On the other hand, we're not sure what he meant either. Hein-
rich Heine wrote, after a fashion, that several bottles of poetry are required
to see beyond your desk and bed—plainly less obtuse. My friends' advice
comes from the sagacity of Tyrolian farmers: bloom where you're potted.
But I was root-bound.

Then something quite unusual happened.

CHAPTER 10

$=\!\!=$ THE MANUSCRIPT $=\!\!=$

A year or so ago there was a pounding on my apartment door one night. When I opened it, admittedly with some hesitation, a punk teenager grinning in a disagreeable manner delivered the pages of a voluminous manuscript in a soiled cardboard box. I asked who he was, and he said his name was Fausto, which meant nothing to me, and that we had met only once when he was much younger. I asked him in, but he declined with a wave of his hand. Then I asked after his father, who, he said, was living somewhere in Spain. He stood for a moment and just looked at me in a rather wild-eyed way, and for a moment I was alarmed. Then he turned, mumbled something in Italian, and bounded down the stairs into the dark.

It was an unpleasant experience.

In the box was an envelope containing a hand-scrawled note from Jean-Michel, messy even for him, with some rather cynical references to Charlene, and asking me to clean up and publish the manuscript, plus an illegible reference in Latin to Nebo and his son. The manuscript was enclosed in a binder of sorts that I remembered well from our days at St. Peters, since it was a macabre affair made of smooth, golden human skin, a trophy of sorts from a nineteenth-century robber who had bound his memoirs in his own hide and left the volume to one of his victims. Jean-Michel was very proud of that find, and it was unusual he would give it up to simply send it to me as a binding for his manuscript. I was tempted to throw it out—a disgusting piece of work—but not uncommon in centuries past. Plus, there was always that tantalizing question of its value.

And there was a certain annoyance to all this, since he was the master of his own destruction, and not, incidentally, way back when, Jim had described my manuscript in less than glowing terms. That its characters were nothing but clichés: the weirdly passive hero, the peculiar yet redemptive heroine, bumbling villains, and replete with fractured narrative, unreliable soliloquies, and oblique reflections. Other than that, Mrs. Lincoln…I had simply dismissed his critique as the jealous musing of an acute drunk.

Unfortunately, he was, as usual, right, but I hadn't the ability or perhaps willingness to see it at the time. Of course, he was younger than I—to bloom takes time.

Having little interest in Jim's manuscript, I left it to gather dust. But it was always there, in the corner of my eye, lying inert and hostile on my desk, his proverbial son, a fat white brick of a child, insidiously demanding attention, chiding at my glances, reminding me that—like he used to say of my dissertation—it may never be finished; or finished, read.

On the contrary, however, his material was quite unusual—ghoulish even, but interesting. I had hidden it from Charlene, who had been out the night of its arrival, and I retrieved it only after she had left me. No sense in complicating one's life. But boredom had its way, and lacking other distractions I read it. In his characters he had written some extraordinary disclosures that had been reflected in his life, beyond what I had imagined he was capable of. It was a story of a militant band of wealthy people, aficionado art collectors bent on saving antiquity's finest artifacts—including famous corpses and their possessions—for themselves and from earth's ignorant rabble. A sophisticated gang that practiced deception, deceit, and theft to further their interest, with little or no compunction for ravaging countries of their cultural heritage, which admittedly, almost none of their inhabitants understood or appreciated, except for the museums' air conditioning and cheap cafeterias.

His directions to me centered more on deliberately obscuring what he felt might be apparent references to people and issues that he believed were potentially dangerous to the manuscript's well-being, if not its author. This was surprising to me, and probably exaggerated on his part, since he had never impressed me as anything but a drunken taxi driver turned professor, with a similar coterie of acquaintances. In the end, his book was all fiction as far as I was concerned, except for some out-of-place quotes that I knew came from Diderot's *L'Encyclopédie,* and I saw little profit in following his instructions.

After some cursory revisions and rewriting, I mailed the package to my agent. Surprisingly, she too was impressed, and, following the appropriate editing, we hunted for a publisher until it was finally sold. It seemed all too easy, but Jim had been thorough enough to provide for commissions on any profits. There would be not money to speak of, since sixty percent of new books never make any.

Thankfully, those struggles were soon to be over as far as I was concerned. I was more fortunate; that is, no longer on the street.

Chance had provided me the rationale for a beneficent God, as it sometimes happens with my people. We islanders have learned to nurse our fate as we have nursed the white people's aged parents, walking arm in arm with their rickety gait of sickness and wheelchairs.

Eventually, death seeps in through the covers, and alone in the house, we are left to rummage through the drawers and closets of our employers' lives before their relatives come to claim the booty. Some jewelry, a silver setting or candlestick holders perhaps, a few rare coins, cigar boxes filled with old twenty-dollar bills, that sort of thing. It usually wasn't much, and took a talent for surmising what might be missed, but my aunt could easily discover the hiding places and parse the carat of a diamond without the aid of a loupe.

Through this magnificent old woman, I was offered a superb opportunity by fate not more than a few days after the release of Levasseur's book. It came in the form of a letter from my dear old aunt's attorney in Miami, stating that she had passed away from old age at an assisted-living center. It was time, since nature has it that the men seem to die in minutes or hours, while the women hang on for weeks or months, the price, perhaps, of their enduring strength. She had the character of wood: the resilience of oak, the color and complexion of monkey pod. Even so, I would miss her checks, soft cheeks, and little hand-scrawled notes, smelling of her island's nutmeg, to her favorite nephew.

The attorney had advised there was a will, a copy of which was enclosed, that provided I receive title and deed to her summer home, a place called Calella de Palafrugell. I had been there once, many years ago, when my aunt was a favored nanny to a wealthy family. It was a town on the eastern coast of Spain, a hundred or so miles northeast of Barcelona, as comfortable and beautiful as its mellifluous name implied. The sole survivor of the family—that blessed and most kind man—had left her their summer home, for possibly more than just nanny duties. Following his death, she had for many years traveled to the house each summer, escaping the heat and hurricanes of Florida, until age became a challenge and the house fell into neglect. All the same, it was on the Costa Brava in Spain, and just a few kilometers down the coast from Cadaqués[34] where my new spiritual neighbors, Salvador Dali and his wife, Gala, had lived for most of their lives, thriving by their wind-swept harbor, sheltered in their unique studio of a home.

Of course I was thrilled. The house, named Camino Real, was neither large nor ostentatious, quite common in fact, but sat looking over one of the most rugged and magnificent coastlines on the Mediterranean, and I owned it. I must tell you, dear reader, that I slept easy that night, one of the first in a very, very long time, since, as everyone knows, the softest pillows, warmest covers, and most sensuous dreams were woven from the fabric of comforting riches. I was off to Spain and I was happy. Giddy happy.

Cousteau's Death

In the July 7, 1997 issue of *US News & World Report*, a journalist wrote that it was curiosity that first drove Jacques-Yves Cousteau underwater. Thanks in part to that intense pleasure with what he found, and his invention of the Aqua-Lung (and its demand regulator, scuba), the rest of the world was kept glued to their television sets for more than forty years, watching "The Undersea World of Jacques Cousteau" until he died of heart failure outside of Paris at the age of eighty-seven. He was buried at Saint-André-de-Cubzac Cemetery, Saint-André-de-Cubzac, France.

JYC, or "Zheek" to his friends, is the last of the creative minds of France to be covered in this book, and brings the evolution of thought from Rousseau, who, by celebrating the supremacy of the individual, established the new democratic paradigm by opening the doors of freedom for mankind. Jacques Cousteau helped to continue this tradition into the twenty-first century by being one of the first to call for preservation of man's habitat by his adventures in *Calypso,* around the world, on and under the sea. We have learned that our gift of "freedom" politically and ecologically be perverse, unless we recognize our responsibilities.

Perhaps it is possible for those whose imaginations can run and skip with the whims of fantasy, that Jacques Cousteau, reincarnated, is somewhere in the ocean swimming to his heart's delight, perchance as an orca. If so, his legacy could not have been better represented than by the whale turned diplomat, Keiko (starring in "Free Willy" in 1993), for whom Cousteau's son, Jean-Michel Cousteau (Ocean Futures Society), had nothing but praise. Keiko himself died of pneumonia on December 13, 2003, and was buried in a small ceremony along the shoreline of Taknes Bay, Norway.

Jean-Michel Cousteau spoke on Keiko's passing in a column on the Ocean Futures Society website. Reflecting on the success that was Keiko's, Jean-Michel's vision saw Keiko swimming through the gates of his enclosure to freedom, meeting other wild whales, feeding himself, taking his own path through the northern seas where he was born, and exercising the freedom of choice that so many had worked so hard to restore to him.[35]

I believe Jean-Michel's father, Jacques Cousteau would have echoed his son's wishes by proclaiming the same freedom and goals for every being on earth. But he would not be proud of our behavior.

The End

═ Notes ═

Introduction

1. J. H. Newman. *Apologia Pro Vita Sua.* Penguin Group, 1995, p.13
2. W. H. Lewis, *The Splendid Century: Life in the France of Louis XIV,* A Doubleday Anchor Book, 1953.
3. Ibid.
4. Priscilla P. Ferguson, *Paris as Revolution.* University of California Press, 1994.
5. Simon Schama, *Citizens: A Chronicle of the French Revolution,* Knopf, 1990.
6. John Leonard, "Brilliant Together in Paris," book review, http://past.thenation.com/issue/970728/0728leon.htm.
7. Ibid.
8. Milan Kundera, *The Art of the Novel,* Grove Press, Inc., 1986, 2000, pp. 3, 4. Kundera also wrote *The Incredible Lightness of Being.*
9. James Joyce, *A Portrait of the Artist as a Young Man,* Penguin Books, Ltd. (originally published 1916 by B. W. Huebsch), p. 253.

Book I

(None)

Book II

1. Georg Holmsten, *Voltaire,* Rowohlt Taschenbuch Verlag GMbH, 1971, p. 152, 1290-ISBN 3499501732.

   See also Jean Orieux, *Das Leben des Voltaire,* 1994, vol. 2, pp. 382–84. No one was the wiser for approximately fifty years when the sarcophagus was checked and the remains were gone.

2. There have been a number of arguments concerning the contents of the two graves, which led to a highly unusual ceremony in December 1897. A committee consisting of politicians and historians went down into the underground church,

and opened Voltaire and Rousseau's coffins in order to find out whether they did indeed still contain the remains of the two men. (The question obviously existed.) The report states that the tombs themselves were in no way imitations. Valérie-Noëlle Jouffre, *The Panthéon,* Caisse nationale des monuments historiques et des sites, Éditions Ouest-France. There is something disingenuous about this statement since (1) it does not mention anything about the contents, i.e., bodies or ashes, of the tombs and their condition; and (2) the statement is made next to a painting attributed to De Machy (1791), which clearly shows the body of Voltaire (his head wrapped in a linen turban, bare chest, and wrapped again from the waist down) being brought to the Panthéon on a gurney-like affair, surrounded by mourners, the subscript of which says: "Voltaire's Ashes being brought to the Panthéon." In any case it is suggested by a number of researchers that the body was not that of Voltaire in the first place, but a substitute corpse. Today, the coffins themselves appear (cracked areas on the corners of the sarcophagi) or indicate they may be made of plaster of Paris or some such material. When asked by the author if the bodies were missing, the guide's response was evasive: "I've heard that story," she said, and continued on her tour.

3. Suzanne Clover Lindsay, "Mummies and Tombs: Turenne, Napoleon, and Death Ritual," *The Art Bulletin,* September 2000, www.collegeart.org/artbulletin/.

4. Ibid.

5. The "Institute of Philosophy and Cultural Antiquity" (IPCA) is fictitious.

6. Lemaître, Jules, J-J Rousseau, London, 1910, p. 361.

7. Maurice Cranston, *Jean-Jacques Rousseau: The Early Life,* University of Chicago Press, 1982. Rousseau was not French, but born "a citizen of Geneva" on June 28, 1712 in a patrician townhouse located at No. 40 of today's Grand Rue, which climbs steeply up the hill from the left bank of the Rhône toward the Hôtel de Ville (town hall) and the ancient 12th-century Cathedral of Saint-Pierre.

8. Pause for Thought, "Why a peace-loving nation is seen as a threat," *Financial Times,* Oct. 20/21, 2001, p. 26.

9. David Brooks, "The Hookie Awards," *The New York Times,* December 25, 2004. p. A21.

10. Thomas L. Friedman, "It Takes a Village to Stop Suicide Bombings," *South Florida Sun-Sentinel,* May 19, 2005, p. 15A.

11. Benjamin Barber, *Jihad vs. McWorld: How Globalization and Tribalism are Reshaping the World,* Ballantine Books, 1995, p. 23.

12. Peter Aspden, "Menace of the Dream Machine," *Financial Times*, May 7/8, 2005, p. W6.

13. Adrian Turpin, "Morality Tales out of Africa," *Financial Times* (Weekend page W3), August 21–22, 2004.

14. Rousseau had to urinate frequently and probably at times uncontrollably. He took to wearing long robes to hide the fact.

15. Will and Ariel Durant, *The Story of Civilization*, vol. 10, NY: Simon and Schuster, 1967, p. 3.

16. Le Procope: Reported to be the oldest operating restaurant in the world (established 1686), 13 Rue de l'Ancienne-Comedie, Paris, France 75006. Tel: (1) 43 26 99 20 Metro: Odeon.

17. www.procope.com.

18. *My Struggle*, Adolph Hitler.

19. Denis Diderot: French philosopher, and man of letters, the chief editor of the L'Encyclopédie, one of the principal literary monuments of the Age of Enlightenment. The work took twenty-six years of Diderot's life. In seventeen volumes of text and eleven of illustrations, it presented the achievements of human learning in a single work. Besides offering a summary of information on all theoretical knowledge, it also challenged the authority of the Catholic Church.

20. George F. Will, "The Oddness of Everything," *Newsweek*, May 23, 2005.

21. Alain de Botton, *How Proust Can Change Your Life: Not a Novel*, Pantheon Books, Random House, 1997, p. 50.

22. Ibid.

23. Cranston II, 65.

24. Ibid.

25. Translation: "a little fire."

26. Unnamed individuals who spied on Rousseau and Thérèse from their house across the way.

27. Maurice Cranston, Jean-Jacques Rousseau, University of Chicago Press, 1982.

Book III

1. Cited in J. Christopher Herold, ed. and trans., *The Mind of Napoleon* (New York, 1955), p.67.

2. Dominique de Villepin: *Les Cents-Jours ou L'Esprit de Sacrifice, Le Cri De La Gargouille, Eloge des Voleurs de Feu, Un Autre Monde.*

3. Vincent Cronin, *Napoleon*, HarperCollins Publishers, 1971 (preface).

4. Philip J. Haythornthwaite, et al (anthology), *Napoleon: The Final Verdict.* Arms and Armour Press, 1996, p. 243.

5. The memoirs that appeared under Bourrienne's name, and for which he was well paid, were hardly more than a travesty of Napoleon's life conjured up for Louis XVIII's reading public, the tone of them set by a bitter personal enemy, whose mind was already becoming deranged. The most perverse falsehood in Bourrienne's memoirs is the statement that Napoleon had no friends and cared nothing for friendship. The truth is different: Napoleon went to great pains to hush up the scandal of Bourrienne's embezzlements, and it was precisely out of loyalty to a boyhood friend that he did not publicly disgrace Bourrienne. Cronin. Op. cit. pp. 442–43.

6. Ibid.

7. Ibid.

8. Ibid.

9. According to this theory, Montholon was possibly secretly employed by the British government, or even the Bourbon family, to finally dispose of Napoleon by administering small but regular quantities of arsenic to him at St. Helena.

10. The world has experienced many great generals whose brilliant displays of military leadership changed the course of history. There have been only four Great Captains, men whose combination of inspiring leadership and consummate tactical and strategic skill rank them significantly ahead of all others: Alexander, Hannibal, Genghis Khan and Napoleon." James R. Arnold, "Napoleon and His Men," *Napoleon the Final Verdict,* Op cit. p. 213.

11. Translation: "until then"

12. L'Avili, 27 rue du Roi de Sicile, 4e, Mo Hôtel de Ville, Tel: 01 48 87 90 20, open daily. Distinguished by an ideal corner location with a small but charming terrace, this justly reputed restaurant serves authentic Corsican dishes with pride and flair. http://parisvoice.com.

13. Translation: "false friends."

14. Napoleon's birthplace.

15. We are taking editorial liberties here…Universite de Corte is a recognized university.

16. Charcuterie: considered by some to be the finest sausage in the world, has been made for centuries by the Corsicans. The main ingredient is pork. Usually raised in the wild at high altitudes, the pigs feast on wild chestnuts, acorns, and a sweet jungle of plants like myrtle, lavender, rosemary, and thyme. The special diet is said to give the meat a flavor of nuts, sugar, and herbs unique to Corsica. The animals are kept away from both the olive trees and beechnut, which would make their flesh oily. Castration of males and neutering of females helps produce a better quality of pork. Traditional farmers slaughter pigs only in the winter (preferably when the moon is full). Elaine Sciolino, "1,000-year-old ways defended in Corsica" *International Herald Tribune*, July 11, 2003, p. 11

17. Translation: "Front Pour la Liberation Nationale Corse."

18. An aperitif made from aniseed.

19. Guentte.

20. Some would argue the opposite. James R. Arnold, *Napoleon: The Final Verdict*, op. cit., p. 243. While First Consul, Napoleon took a keen interest in the redrafting of France's legal code, personally attending no fewer than fifty-seven of 109 meetings devoted to the Civil Code. A participant recalls that these meetings reviewed every aspect of administration, finance, and law, and that Napoleon made significant contributions to the discussions.

21. *Concordat*: At the beginning of the consulate, the religious institutions of France were in a state of hopeless confusion. These documents show the general character of the reorganization effected by Napoleon. (See: NapoleonSeries.Org) Document A is the compact between France and the Papacy, which still controls the position of the Roman Catholic Church in France. The two dates ascribed to it represent those of its signature by the French and papal envoys and of its promulgation in France. Document B was purely a French legislative act; the consent of the Pope was neither asked nor given. Document D did for the two recognized Protestant sects what the other documents did for the Roman Catholic Church. In 1808 a similar arrangement was made for the Jews.

22. Translation: Italian–"boy."

23. Ibid., pp. 89–90.

24. See: Josephine Beauharnais at Malmaison: www.napoleonguide.com. Josephine Beauharnais, wife of Alexandre, mother of Eugene and Hortense (later the wife of Louis Bonaparte). Josephine married Napoleon Bonaparte in a state ceremony, was later crowned empress, divorced, and died of pneumonia. Described by Napoleon as the "torment, happiness, hope and soul of my life."

25. Sandra Gulland, author of historical novels, www.pbs.org/empires/napoleon. Josephine had great charisma, long eyelashes, and big eyes. She wasn't a beauty, according to many, but she was really striking…. She had a very elegant and indolent walk that was enchanting. And she had a beautiful voice, a really sexy voice, very low and musical. She just seemed to enchant people.

26. Ibid., p. 105..

27. Margaret Laing, *Josephine and Napoleon,* Mason and Charter, 1974, pp. 55–6.

28. Cronin, op. cit.

29. Cronin, Ibid., p. 402.

30. Emil Ludwig, *Napoleon,* Horace Liveright, Inc., 1926, p. 88.

31. Cronin, op. cit., p. 131.

32. Ibid.

33. Ibid.

34. Erica Goode, "Oh La La! Sex in US Rivals the Best in Paris," *International Herald Tribune,* May 31, 2001, p. 1.

35. Cronin, op. cit.

36. "Napoleon ruled his Empire to the sound of war. It seemed that, for the Empire's duration, he was locked in a life-or-death war with England, or with one or more of England's allies. So, while he was encouraging the movement toward self-government—excluding his own reign—he retained the basic structure of royalty. The most important titles he entrusted to his brothers and sisters. Napoleon was no lover of past royal methods, but he was extremely fond of his brothers, always seeking to build them up, and believed, for the most part, that they would make good rulers. He counted on their loyalty, while the blood link with him as Emperor would epitomize the spiritual unity he wished to establish among the countries of the Empire. Nevertheless, they lacked Napoleon's ability. Buonaparte made his brothers kings in their own

right, but expected them to obey orders. He once complained, 'From the way they talk, one would think that I had mismanaged our father's inheritance'." (Markham, op. cit., p. 144).

37. Ibid.

38. Ibid., p. 151.

39. "Napoleon: An Intimate Portrait," www.National Geographic.com.

40. Cronin, op. cit., p. 307.

41. Ibid.

42. Ibid., p. 202.

43. Peter G. Tsouras, "Napoleon and his Words," *Napoleon: The Final Verdict*, Arms and Armour Press, 1996.

44. Cronin, op. cit., pp. 370–71.

45. Ibid., pp. 438–9.

46. Will and Ariel Durant, *The Age of Napoleon,* Simon and Schuster, New York, 1975, pp. 775, 776.

47. Tim Hicks. "St. Helena: Controversy to the End." *Napoleon: The Final Verdict,* Arms and Armour Press, 1996, pp. 202, 203

48. Catherine Field, op. cit., p. 7.

Book IV

1. Translation: "Shit! I hate this horrible traffic!"

2. Translation: "Star."

3. Liberally translated: "Up yours, you bastard!"

4. Clan of Richard "the Lionhearted."

5. Annie Dillard, *The Writing Life*, HarperPerennial, 1989, pp. 11–12.

6. Jean-Benoît Nadeau and Julie Barlow, *Sixty Million Frenchmen Can't Be Wrong,* Sourcebooks, Inc., 2003, p. 24.

7. Robyn Crennan, Remsenberg, New York, Christmas 2004.

8. A fictitious organization.

9. Translation: *"Inner Voices."*

10. Graham Robb, *Victor Hugo: A Biography*, W.W. Norton, 1998.

11. Lee Dembart, "Back to Old Habits," *International Herald Tribune*, May 14, 2001, p. 15.

12. Edmund White, *Marcel Proust*, Viking Press (Penguin Lives), 1999.

13. When Oscar Wilde was released from prison on May 19, 1897, he was a broken man in many ways. Wilde left England and died in sad circumstances in Paris on November 30, 1900. His remains were buried in the insignificant Bagneaux Cemetery. There must, however, have been plans to transfer the body from the start, since Wilde was buried in quicklime. This was done to transfer the corpse to bone, so moving it to another location would be a 'clean' affair. But, when the day finally came, according to the reports, the gravediggers were shocked by the sinister sight of Wilde: his body was preserved very well, and supposedly his hair and beard had grown even longer. The quicklime had only served to preserve the body, instead of skeletonizing it. Wilde's remains were moved to Père Lechaise on July 19, 1909. http://www.xs4all.nl/~androom/dead/story003.htm.

14. *The Hunchback of Notre Dame.*

15. Milton Hindus, *The Proustian Vision*, Southern Illinois University Press, Feffer & Simons, Inc., p. 10.

16. John Weightman, "Molière Imaginaire," a book review, *The New York Review of Books*, Volume XLVIII, No. 8, p. 41.

17. France's famous Viking-like cartoon character, which may soon be representing McDonald's, and in a film in which Gerard Depardieu plays Astérix.

18. *Les Mislabels*, III 6, 1.

19. *Baudelaire: Selected Poems*, translation and selection J. M. Dent, The Orion Publishing Group, 1999, p. 3.

20. Graham Robb, op. cit., p. 220.

21. Quoted by Graham Robb in *Balzac* but also Traveller's Literary Companion, p. 263.

22. Ibid.

23. Charles Dickens visited France often and developed an affection for the country and its culture. He felt increasingly at home there, becoming proficient in the language and taking great pleasure in the huge success of his books with French readers. He wined and dined in the top Parisian literary circles, and met, among others, Hugo, Lamartine, Sand, and the historian Jules Michelet.

24. Ibid.

25. (*'Quand je ne serai plus...'* Dernière Gerbe.)

26. Graham Robb, op. cit., p. 530.

27. Ibid.

Book V

1. The original Café Riche no longer exists, but at the time the friends could have gathered there.

2. Sophie Fourny-Dargère, *Monet,* Konecky and Konecky, 1992. Sophie Fourny-Dargère is the curator of the Monet Museum in Giverny.

3. Annual unjuried exhibition of the Société des Artistes Indépendants. Organized as a second Salon des Refusés, it was established in response to the rigid traditionalism of the official government-sponsored Salon.

4. Theodore Zeldin, *The French,* Pantheon Books, 1982.

5. Ibid.

6. http://wwar.com/masters/movements/symbolism.html, Emile Bernard: Symbolist painter. Symbolist painting emphasized fantasy and imagination in the depiction of objects. The artists of the movement often used metaphors and symbols to suggest occult themes. Influenced by Romanticism, the movement strove to depict the symbols of ideas. The Symbolists' aim was to portray mysterious and ambiguous interpretations of emotions and ideas by using symbols. Some artists borrowed their imagery from Symbolist writings, often containing grotesque and fantastical imagery such as severed heads, monsters, and spirits.

7. Translation: "The Drunken Boat."

8. In the 1950s and '60s, the Puces de Saint-Ouen was a market place to buy cheap but good and old furniture. This is not the case anymore, but it is still a very interesting place to visit since there are over 2000 shops. The choice is large: old furniture, old art pieces, clothes, shoes, timepieces, military pieces, etc.

9. www.constable.net/arthistory/.

10. Modern Art: From Fauvism to Abstract Expressionism (Vol. 8). *The Book of Art,* Ed. David Sylvester, Grolier, 1965, p 9.

11. Alain De Botton, op. cit., p. 137.

12. Edmund White, "Sexual Culture," L. H. Peterson, et al., *The Norton Reader*, Norton, 9th Ed., p. 291.

13. Ibid.

14. Ludovic Hunter-Tiney, "Lunch with the FT Todd Solondz, 'I think the satire is very loving'" *Financial Times*, May 7/8, 2005, p. W3.

15. Maureen Dowd, *International Herald Tribune*.

Book VI

1. Montmartre. Hill of martyrs, where Saint Denis had his head chopped off. It is also the place of artists, beatniks, avant-garde writers, and drifters.

2. Close to the Port Saint Denis, Rue Saint-Denis has always maintained a disreputable standing, as the area hosts 80 percent of Paris's prostitutes. Uniquely enough, it used to be the road taken by the kings of France to Notre Dame for their coronations, as well as their route north for burial in the St. Denis Basilica.

3. Crazy Horse. "Something of a stage art, leading erotic visions, sardonic humor and inventive conceits." An ad in the *International Herald Tribune*, www.lecrazyhorseparis.com.

4. Anthony Weller, "Les Girls," *Travelers' Tales Guides: Paris*, Travelers' Tales, Inc., 1997. p. 132.

5. Ibid., Alain Bernardin, the man whom the fictional character is patterned after, died in 1994. Bernardin was fascinated by the America of the cowboy saloons and myth of the Far West. He wanted to distance himself from the "Left Bank" spirit so prevalent in the post-war period, associated with St-Germain des Prés. See: www.lecrazyhorseparis.com.

6. Ibid., p. 134.

7. Ibid.

8. Hélène Jourdan-Morhange, *Ravel et nous*. Most people don't know what the Boléro is. The majority of Americans who have seen the beach scene between Bo Derek and Dudley Moore think it's simply the background music to the movie "10," if indeed anyone under forty has even seen the movie. Europeans who would know see it as a generic Spanish dance in ¾ time introduced in the late 18th Century. Calling Ravel's Boléro simply dance music, however, would be like calling Tchaikovsky's Nutcracker Suite the "two-step." It is Ravel's greatest success, a monumental exercise in instrumentation and sonority,

but he himself was heard to agree with the critics who called it simply "circus music."

9. (Published in *Psychiatric Bulletin*), see Culture*kiosque* Publications Ltd. 1996–99 (online at: klassik*net*).

10. Ibid., p. 135.

11. Fostle, D. W., "The Audio Interview: Marc Aubort," *Audio*, Sept. 1994, p. 26.

12. Shakespeare and Company: 37 rue de la Bûcherie. A unique bookstore and private library situated across the river from Notre Dame in the 5th arrondissement of Paris. Go online to www.thinkparis.com.

   Shakespeare and Company opened in November 1919 on Rue Dupuytren, a humble nondescript bookshop on a tiny cobblestone alley, followed in July 1921 by a more spacious and easier to find store at 12 rue de l'Odéon practically across the street from Café Voltaire. The cafe has since given way to the Benjamin Franklin Library. The French knew little of American literature beyond Walt Whitman and Mark Twain, but within two years Shakespeare and Company's founder, Sylvia Beach, would become an acknowledged literary spokeswoman by publishing Joyce's *Ulysses*. Within six years she had become the best-known American woman in Paris. Shakespeare and Company was closed down during the war; Sylvia was arrested by the Nazis and confined with others at various hotels. On a more heroic note, Hemingway 'liberated' the rue de l'Odéon, on Saturday, 26 August 1944, the day after the German surrender of Paris. It's a fitting conclusion to a wonderful saga of that old store, arriving as he did in the street with four BBC cars full of men. In fact the story of his visit forms the dramatic conclusion of Sylvia's memoirs in 1959. "I flew downstairs," she recalls, "we met with a crash; he picked me up and swung me around and kissed me while people on the street and in the windows cheered." Then he took his men to the roof to check for snipers. Although encouraged by many friends to reopen the shop, Sylvia refused. She was tired, she said, and at fifty-eight years of age afraid of taking risks.

13. Elsie de Wolfe, eventually Lady Mendl, *House in Good Taste*, (1911), is sometimes credited with being the first interior decorator, though certainly most aristocrats of the time put their decoration in the hands of their architects, who saw to the decoration along with the building.

14. A putrid-smelling beer-based vache (cow cheese) rolled in red pepper dust.

15. Translation: "Pavane (a courtly dance) for a Dead Princess." Ravel would get

angry over the maudlin interpretation of this work and insist that he was trying to describe the death of the music more than the death of the child.

16. Translation: "Shut up!"

17. *French Toast*, op. cit.

18. Translation: "Yes, of course."

19. *French Toast*, op. cit.

20. Translation: "Hand-kiss."

21. Definition: "That light little kiss that just brushes the cheek."

22. Ibid.

23. *French Toast*, op. cit.

24. Stéphane Mallarmé, the French poet and essayist who was the leading figure
of the 19th-century Symbolist Movement. According to some, the period in
which he lived could easily be called the Mallarmé century, since he influenced
music, the visual arts, dance, theater—all of modern thought.

25. Erik Satie, eccentric French impressionist composer and musician. Close friend
of Claude Debussy; and during WWI also befriended Cocteau, Diaghilev, and
Pablo Picasso. An eccentric and humorist, he was not well accepted by the general public of his time, it seemed, despite efforts of Debussy and Ravel to promote his works.

26. Le Placard d'Erik Satie, the world's smallest museum, in the "cupboard" where
he lived, and which reveals how he made music in a chaotic life.

27. http://www.jazclass.aust.com/satie.htm.

28. Born in Saint-Germain-en-Laye, easy town to reach from Paris: 30 minutes/23
km. A royal retreat, now a wealthy bourgeois suburb. Musée des Antiquités
Nationales; Louis XIV was born in the chateau.

29. Claude Debussy, *Bibliothéque Nationale Rés. Vmf .ms. 53*. In 1899, Debussy
married Rosalie Texier, a dressmaker. He left her in 1904 for Emma Bardac,
an amateur singer and the wife of a Parisian banker. He moved into an apartment with Emma in the Avenue du Bois de Boulogne, where he spent the rest
of his life. Debussy married Bardac in 1908, following the birth in 1905 of his
one daughter, Claude-Emma, the "Chou-chou" to whom the Children's Corner Suite (1906–08) was dedicated.

30. E. E. Cummings.

31. Charles Baudelaire, *Flowers of Evil,* David R. Godine, Publisher, Inc. 1983.

Verses do not rhyme in translations, whereas almost all of Baudelaire's poetry rhymed.

32. In 1947, Jean-Paul Sartre published a short, beautifully written study of the 19th-century poet. The project was to analyze Baudelaire's character in the light of existentialism, without recourse to the fashionable Freudian psychology of his day. Robin Buss, *Financial Times*, February 7–8, 2004, W-4, book review, *Baudelaire in Chains: A Portrait of the Artist as a Drug Addict*, by Frank Hilton.

33. Ibid., p. 128.

34. Burnett James, *Ravel,* Midas Books, 1987, p. 136–7.

35. Ned Rorem, "Notes on Ravel," *Commentary*, Vol. 59, May 1975.

36. Burnett James, *Ravel,* Midas Books, 1987, p. 136–7.

Book VII

1. Chanel worked hard to keep her personal life hidden, but those that cared usually knew the situation. Nonetheless, the thought of investigative reporting that would include interviewing her two brothers (Alphonse, who worked behind a *tabac* counter, and Lucien in a shoe stall in the Clermont-Ferrand area), filled her with dread. Tales of her childhood were not going to be released by relatives for public consumption, so she paid her brothers handsomely to stay out of sight.

   Chanel: A Woman of Her Own. Axel Madsen. Henry Holt and Company, New York, 1990.

2. Ibid. The Duke eventually married Lady Emilia Ponsonby in 1930. It was London's wedding of the year and Winston Churchill was the best man. Chanel spent that summer in the South of France with her grand-niece, Gabriella Labruin, whom she always considered to be her own child.

3. Ibid.

4. Chanel denied ever saying this, but others protested it was true.

5. Translation: "Smoking Pot", From Michael and Shannon.

6. Mary Blume, "Designer Water, Flooding the Hip Scene," *International Herald Tribune,* July 22–23, 2000, p. 20. (The French drink 125 liters each a year and spend more than 14 billion francs to do so.)

7. That is $3.55 for a 50-centiliter (17 ounce) bottle or approximately $14/gallon.

8. Ibid.

9. Katherine Hepburn played the part of Chanel in a Broadway musical about her life entitled: *Coco.* It was by most accounts a failure. According to the critics, Lerner's story was simple to the point of disappearance and his dialogue only occasionally witty. *The New York Times* critic, however, said the evening was about a new phenomenon named Katherine Hepburn. Her voice the *New York Post's* Clive Barnes said was, "a neat mixture of faith, love, and laryngitis, unforgettable, unbelievable, and delightful."

10. Edmund White, "Sexual Culture" from *The Burning Library* by Edmund White. Alfred A. Knopf, 1994, pg. 289

11. The "little black dress" displayed in *Vogue* in 1926 was a classic Chanel style. It was done in black crepe de chine and tight fitting on the hips, with no collar and long, straight sleeves.

12. Gwendoline Hirst, "Chanel," www.ba-education.demon.co.uk

13. http://www.designerhistory.com/historyoffashion/chanel.html see also: website: www.chanel.com

14. Ibid.

15. Ibid.

16. Op cit. Madsen, p. 57.

17. Edmonde Charles-Roux, *Chanel,* The Harvill Press, 1995 (first published in France 1974 as *L'Irrégulière* by Grasset, Paris), p. 117.

18. Ibid.

19. Ibid.

20. Mary Blume, "Dance Hall Daze: Lore and Lure of Guinguettes," *International Herald Tribune,* September 5, 2003, p. 20. As two enthnologists, Kali Argyriadis and Sara Le Menestrel, point out in the book *Vivre la Guinguette* (Presses Universitaires de France), nostalgia is an immensely strong current in France to "rediscover the innocence of olden days." Bauby has created an organization called Culture Guinguette, and there is now a guinguette museum at Nogent-sur-Marne.

21. Translation: "May I offer you an aperitif, madam?"

22. Susie Boyt, "Strange Creatures in NY," *International Herald Tribune*, April 24–25, 2004.

23. Translation: "White sausage."

24. Translation: "I love you." A circumstance from Carlo Paina's creative mind (Milan).

25. Op. cit., Charles-Roux, p. 121.

26. Ibid.

27. http://www.time.com/time/time100/artists/profile/chanel,

28. Lucia van der Post, "Every Inch a Lady," *Financial Times, How to Spend It*, August 2004,

29. Translation: German "Shit."

30. Madsen, op. cit., p. 222.

31. Ibid.

32. Ibid., p. 223.

33. Translation: "Blond beach." Spoken of by the Italians to signify the German bathers who gather topless at the beach.

34. Gerassi, op. cit., p. 163.

35. http://www.designerhistory.com/historyofashion/chanel.html.

36. Fictitious play dreamed up by the two characters in *The Directors* to rob the insurance company.

37. Cavalry Captain.

38. The head of the Reich Central Security Office and responsible at all times for the Führer's safety.

39. Mary Blume, "60 years of memory: Paris of myth, Paris of reality" *International Herald Tribune*, August 25, 2004, p. 7.

40. http://www.time.com/time/time100/artists/profile/chanel.

41. Theodore Zeldin, *The French*, Pantheon Books (Random House), 1982, p. 306.

42. Karl Taro Greenfeld, "Battle Deluxe," *Time*, May 8, 2000, p. 60.

43. Edmonde Charles-Roux, *Chanel*, The Harvill Press, 1995 (first published in France in 1974 as *L'Irrégulière* by Grasset, Paris) pp. 372–3.

Book VIII

1. Charles Williams, *The Last Great Frenchman,* John Wiley & Sons, Inc., 1993, p. 154.

2. Ibid.

3. Charles de Gaulle, *War Memoirs,* Weidenfeld and Nicolson, London, 1955, 1959, and 1960, p. 1.

4. Craig S. Smith. "Giscard joins ranks of Gallic 'immortels'" *International Herald Tribune,* December 12, 2003, p. 4. The academy, founded in 1635 by King Louis XIII's chief minister, Cardinal de Richelieu, is the official guardian of the French language and now spends much of its time weeding out persistent Anglicisms and coming up with Frenchified alternatives to newly imported words: *courriel,* to replace e-mail, is one of the academy's latest selections.

5. George F. Will, "The European project is foundering – as it should," (Washington Post) *St. Petersburg Times,* May 29, 2005, p. 3.

6. Ralph Waldo Emerson.

7. Translation from Latin: "God be with you." And the response: "And the Holy Spirit with you." (Thank you, Carlo)

8. Translation: "A door must be open or shut." Alfred de Musset.

9. Translation: "One doesn't arrest Voltaire."

10. Smith, op. cit.

11. Translation: "Because we loved France!"

12. Denis MacShane, *"Une entente (pas très) cordiale,"* *Financial Times,* February 28–29, 2004, p. W5.

13. Magreb: land of the setting sun. Western North Africa.

14. Charles Williams, op cit. p. 372. Operation Resurrection: Charles de Gaulle came to power in 1958 with the support of the French army. The army was engaged in Algeria because of the uprisings created by Arab nationalists who, like many in the emerging Arab states, sought independence from their European masters. De Gaulle had three problems: 1. the FLN. which composed the rebel faction; 2. the army itself. which had pretensions of political aspirations in its top ranks and. with the strong exception of some of its most senior officers, had strong Pétainist roots; and 3. the white settler families who hated him and whom he despised. This trident of special interests ran counter to his strategy

for returning to the presidency in Paris. He knew he would need the powerful forces of the army located, as in chess, on a clear diagonal from Algeria. A great deal rode in the balance, since, if his political aspirations were thwarted, he was prepared to initiate a coup d'état in the very home of European democracy. He saw himself as a national arbiter, to calm the incendiary situation in Algiers and at home, essential for managing the government. The high command of the army in Algeria had committed itself to de Gaulle, whom they saw as one of their own, the general who ran the Free French movement, for the last of the war years, from its shores. But, there was one essential condition: the army would entertain no political moves that would turn over Algeria to its native sons. Algeria and the French colonies of Africa were to remain French. Not unlike Napoleon's strategy, the army was determined to dictate policy to the republic. And then as now, the sitting government in Paris, weak and disorganized, was no match for him. The students were in the streets, the economy was in peril, and colonial wars had all but drained the present government. By late spring of 1958, Western leaders watched a politically progressive and economically developed, permanent member of the United Nations Security Council succumb to a political putsch.

15. Patricia Wells, "Alain Senderens and the triumph of the wines." *International Herald Tribune*. November 22, 2002, p. 6.

16. Ibid.

17. Resistance groups were under the leadership of Henri Tanguy, know today as Colonel Rol-Tanguy, a Spanish Civil War veteran and Communist. Mary Blume, "60 Years of Memory: Paris of Myth, Paris of Reality," *International Herald Tribune*, August 25, 2004, page 7.

18. Charles Williams, op. cit., p. 399.

19. Judy Dempsey, "Follow My Leaders," Financial Times, July 12–13, p. W9.

20. Edward Dolnick, "The Unlovely Truth about Those Who Steal Beauty," *International Herald Tribune*, August 25, 2004, p. 9. This imaginary museum, whose collection would consist of stolen paintings and drawings, would match the Louvre. Its treasures included 551 Picassos, 43 Van Goghs, 174 Rembrandts, and 209 Renoirs. Vermeer would be there ("The Concert"), and Caravaggio, Van Eyck, and Cézanne.

21. Paul Sullivan, "Hunting for Stolen Relics in Fog of War," *Financial Times*, November 27–28, 2004, p. W3.

22. The early 20th century found many Americans, including students, tourists, and residents, in France. During the summer months, their number reached 100,000 in Paris alone. In 1904 Dr. Magnin and Harry Antony van Bergen, an American friend, created an association whose name reveals an ambitious project: "Society for the Foundation of the United States Hospital in Paris." Its goal, to offer American expatriates access to care provided by physicians trained in the United States. In 1909 Henry White, Ambassador of the United States to France, and Gaston Doumergue, Minister of Public Education and future president of the French Republic, inaugurated the new, twenty-four-bed hospital. In 1913, the United States Congress, by a special act, granted the American Hospital of Paris federal status.

23. Charles Williams, op. cit., pp. 5, 6.

Book IX

1. Gustave Flaubert, *Flaubert in Egypt*, (trans. Francis Steegmuller, 1972), Academy Chicago Press.

2. Sartre's mother, Anne Marie Schweitzer, was the daughter of Charles Schweitzer and cousin of the famous medical missionary Albert Schweitzer.

3. www.sartre.org.

4. Henry Allen, *International Herald Tribune*, November 16, 2001.

5. Ibid.

6. Ibid.

7. Ibid.

8. Jim Holt, "Exit, Pursued by a Lobster," http://slate.msn.com/id/2088648/.

9. Alain de Bottom, *How Proust Can Change Your Life : Not a Novel*, Random House, 1997, p. 113.

10. Craig S. Smith, "In France, Some Brides Wear Black," *International Herald Tribune*, February 18, 2004, p.1. The law dated back to December 1959 when southern France's Malpasset Dam burst, inundating the town of Fréjus and claiming hundreds of lives. When former President Charles de Gaulle visited the town a week later, a young woman named Irène pleaded with him to allow her to follow through on her marriage plans even though her fiancé had drowned. "I promise, Mademoiselle, to think of you," de Gaulle was reported

to have replied. Later that month, the National Assembly drafted a law to permit the young woman to marry her deceased fiancé.

11. François Camoin, Untitled, *Crazyhorse*, July 2003.

12. Ronald Hayman, *Sartre*, first published by Simon and Schuster, First Carroll & Graf edition 1992, copyright 1987, p. 473–75

13. Ibid.

Book X

1. Ralph de La Cruz, "Dyeing for a New Look Because I was in Gray Area," *Fort Lauderdale Sun Sentinel*, December 14, 2003, p. 4D.

2. Hemingway's opinion on ejaculation: A man needs to limit his ejaculations while young, so as to have a supply of them in his old age.

3. JAPS: "Jewish American Princesses."

4. See: www.willyoujoinus.com, a Chevron web site that includes a letter from its Chairman & CEO David J. O'Reilly.

5. Eldridge Cleaver, *Soul On Ice*, Dell Publishing (Random House), 1968.

6. The Original Pilgrims' Way to Santiago de Compostela and the tomb of the Apostle St. James. The French Route is the most famous and well-traveled; however, it is the Original Route, followed by King Alfonso II, which is the most scenic, and the one that the pilgrims Nicholas, Sadie, Connor, Zoe, Camille, and Valeri should take.

7. Few will remember him except to point out that he was the one to purchase the Mona Lisa for France.

8. Kyle Jarrard, "A Walk in Cognac Country," *International Herald Tribune*, February 6, 2004.

9. Earth Day, April 22, was created by Senator Gaylord Nelson in 1970. The grandfather, so to speak, of all that grew out of the event: the Environmental Protection Act, the Clean Air Act, the Clean Water Act, and the Safe Drinking Water Act, he was a great champion of conservation policies, including legislation to preserve the 2,100-mile Appalachian Trail.

10. Periscope, "Power in Advertising," *Newsweek*, July 25, 2005, p. 16.

11. David Honigmann, "Friends reunited," *Financial Times*, September 11–12, 2004, p. W4.

12. Roger Rosenblatt, "All the Days of the Earth," *Time,* April–May 2000.

13. Warren St. John, "Building Humor Around the Taboo," *International Herald Tribune*, December 15, 2004, p. 11.

14. Op. cit., Periscope.

15. The last and most famous extinction was the Cretaceous-Tertiary event about 63 million years ago that killed all of the dinosaurs and allowed the rise of mammals. It is thought to have been caused by an asteroid hitting Earth. The causes of the other extinctions are not well understood. Paul Martin, a zoologist and geochemist at the University of Arizona in Tucson, is convinced that we are in the middle of the sixth extinction event, which began about 50,000 years ago with the onslaught of human beings.

16. There is an argument by Bjorn Lomborg, author of *The Skeptical Environmentalist*, in which he argues that in the past fifty years humankind has experienced unprecedented improvement in almost every welfare indicator. Jason Cowley, *Scanorama*, October 2004, pp. 27–29.

17. Malcolm Gladwell, "The Vanishing" (book review: *Collapse*, Jared Diamond), *The New Yorker*, January 3, 2005, pp. 70–71.

18. Garrison Keillor, "When it's Too Hot for Moral Arithmetic," *The Times*, July 13, 2005, p. 13A.

19. 2002 by Nuclear Age Peace Foundation. Reproduction encouraged. The source requests acknowledgment that this information was provided by the foundation. "Captain Cousteau's Legacy: Rising to Our Full Stature As Human Beings" by David Krieger.

20. CAFE: Corporate Average Fuel Economy.

21. Kendall McDonald, "Cousteau the Sea King," *Diver,* August, 1997.

22. Self Contained Underwater Breathing Apparatus.

23. Reported in *The Times*, June 4, 2005, p. 4a. Rudolf Schroeck, *The Double Life of Charles A. Lindbergh*, published by Heyne, Velag, a division of Random House. The book describes a longtime secret relationship between Lindbergh and Brigitte Hesshaimer.

24. According to Lindbergh's putative daughter, Astrid Bouteuil.

25. Paul Betts, "The Tourists' Bible Looks to Evolve," *Financial Times*, July 12, 2002, p. 11.

26. Sathnam Sanghera, "When Life Turns Sour, *Financial Times Weekend*, June 19–20, 2004, p. W10

27. "Nancy Dawson," the tune to which, by tradition, the daily issue of grog was distributed in the British Navy. It was a popular song among seamen during the 18th century and may perhaps have become associated with the daily grog issues, as one of the effects of the spirit upon many men was to encourage them to burst into song. *The Oxford Companion to Ships & The Sea*, Oxford University Press, Peter Kemp, editor, 1976, p. 571.

28. Jimmie's Special: A drink with an aphrodisiac impact, from which women would supposedly undress themselves in public. This recipe is for two drinks. Add to your cocktail mixer: 1 small glass Cognac and ½ small glass each, Pernod, Amer-Picon, Mandarin, and Cherry liqueur. Shake well. The cocktail is drunk pure or with soda.

Note: James Charters was a former boxer from Liverpool. He was supposedly the best bartender in Montparnasse. An entire generation of Americans knew him as Jimmie the bartender. Interesting to know is Jimmie's analysis of the drinking habits of the artists: according to him, painters and photographers are the heaviest and noisiest drinkers; sculptors are the most melancholic, and writers prefer white wine above all. His "Aphrodisiaka" is his most popular drink for obvious reasons (Rodriguez-Hunter, p. 112).

29. Born in London in 1775, and despite his period of insanity studied at Christ's Hospital where he formed a lifelong friendship with Samuel Taylor Coleridge and a group of young writers who also favored political reform, including Percy Shelley and Lord Byron.

30. Note: On the day that the *International Herald Tribune* reported Klaus Toepfer's announcement concerning the rapid and careless destruction of our oceans, published on the second page of the *International Herald Tribune*, March 30, 2004, the first page covered such epic events as: Pressure Mounts on Presidential Aide; French Prime Minister in Balance After Vote; Terrorists Blamed; Irish Smokers; Jailed Russian Tycoon; NATO; a Farewell to a Movie Star; and a watch ad. The IHT should, however, at least be lauded for the second page.

31. Nobel Peace Prize Centennial Symposium (100th anniversary of the Nobel laureates statement and signed by 100 Nobel laureates). OTVNewswire.

32. Translation: "Golden Lion (Bar).

33. Michael Blumenthal, "Life in the Charm Lane," *Time*, March 12, 2001, p. 26.

34. The home and studio of Dali were actually located just outside Cadaqués in a small place called Portlligat.

35. See Humane Society of United States website. Those sentiments were echoed by David Phillips, executive director of the Free Willy-Keiko Foundation (which oversaw Keiko's freedom campaign), who believed it was the most spectacular effort ever launched on behalf of an animal. Keiko lived for nearly three years at the Oregon Coast Aquarium. No matter where Keiko lived, he seemed to touch people.